CALIFORNIA REAL ESTATE

PRACTICE

FIFTH EDITION

WILLIAM H. PIVAR
LOWELL ANDERSON
DANIEL S. OTTO

Dearborn™
Real Estate Education

This publication is designed to provide accurate and authoritative information in regard to the subject matter covered. It is sold with the understanding that the publisher is not engaged in rendering legal, accounting, or other professional service. If legal advice or other expert assistance is required, the services of a competent professional person should be sought.

President: Roy Lipner
Publisher: Evan Butterfield
Managing Editor, Print Products: Louise Benzer
Development Editor: Christopher Oler
Production Coordinator: Daniel Frey
Typesetter: Daniel Henrick and Janet Schroeder
Qualilty Assurance Editor: David Shaw
Creative Director: Lucy Jenkins

Published by Dearborn™ Real Estate Education
a division of Dearborn Financial Publishing, Inc.®
30 South Wacker Drive
Chicago, IL 60606-1719
312-836-4400
http://www.dearbornRE.com

Printed in the United States of America.

05 06 10 9 8 7 6 5

Library of Congress Cataloging–in–Publication Data

Pivar, William H.
    California real estate practice / William Pivar, Lowell Anderson,
Daniel Otto.—5th ed.
      p. cm.
    Includes index.
    ISBN 0—7931—8017—1
    1. Real estate business—Law and legislation—California. 2. Vendors
and purchasers—California. I. Anderson, Lowell. II. Otto, Daniel. III.
Title.
    KFC446.R3A93 2003
    346.79404'37—dc22
CIP   2003018444

CONTENTS

PREFACE

Real estate practice is the practical application of real estate knowledge to meet the needs of buyers, sellers, lessors, and lessees. As a course, it teaches what to do for success in meeting these needs.

Real Estate Practice is not a repetition of Real Estate Principles, a required course for real estate applicants before they can take their real estate salesperson's examination. However, it does cover the practical application of much of what you learned in Real Estate Principles.

Because of the importance of real estate practice, the California Department of Real Estate has mandated that one of the two additional courses, required to be taken by new real estate salespersons within 18 months of being licensed, must be Real Estate Practice. Real Estate Practice is also one of the required courses for applicants for the real estate broker's examination.

ACKNOWLEDGMENTS

The authors wish to express their thanks to those educators and specialists who contributed their time and expertise to this edition of *California Real Estate Practice:* Bud Zeller, GRI, CRS, RIM, *sierraproperties.com;* Professor Donna Grogan, El Camino College; Joe M. Newton, Bakersfield College; and Ignacio Gonzalez, Mendocino Community College.

In addition, we wish to acknowledge the invaluable assistance given to us in previous editions from the following professionals and educators: Janet Wright, Placer Title Company; Ronald Dean Schultz, Diablo Valley College; Evelyn W. Winkel, Esq., Rancho Santiago College; Joyce Emory, Real Estate Advisory Council; Keith H. Kerr, City College of San Francisco; Pamela Pedago-Lowe, RE/MAX South County; Charles E. Krackeler, CRS, GRI, College of San Mateo; Nancy E. Weagley, Saddleback College; and Judith Meadows.

CHAPTER ONE

GETTING STARTED IN REAL ESTATE

■ KEY TERMS

assistant	independent contractor	100 percent commission
California Association of	inventory	office
REALTORS®	mentor program	Realtist
caravans	multiple-listing service	stratified marketplace
completed staff work	must-buy buyer	will-buy buyer
daily planning	must-sell seller	will-sell seller
e-mail	National Association of	workers' compensation
employee	REALTORS®	insurance
goal setting	office procedures manual	

■ LEARNING OBJECTIVES

This chapter explains what it means to be a real estate professional. You will learn about the unique nature of the real estate marketplace and the many alternatives available to you within the real estate profession. You also learn the importance of understanding the broker/salesperson relationship and how to prepare yourself to choose a broker affiliation based on your specific needs.

You learn about the importance of a positive attitude, the training opportunities open to you, setting goals, and the knowledge you must gain for success. This knowledge includes learning the available inventory, understanding office procedures, basic computer literacy, and an understanding of taxes as they relate to real estate sales. You will also be introduced to the tools that can aid you in achieving your goals.

■ WHAT IT MEANS TO BE A REAL ESTATE PROFESSIONAL

It has been said that without the first real estate salesperson, human beings would still be living in caves. While possibly overstated, the real estate profession has played a significant role in improving the living conditions and lifestyles of our citizens.

Although we deal with a product—real estate, namely the land and that which transfers with it—the human factor of identifying and fulfilling the needs of others is the dominant emphasis of the real estate profession. You reach success in the real estate profession by first successfully meeting the needs of others. Real estate is, therefore, more a *people* than a *property* profession. Your understanding of people and their motivations will determine your future as a real estate professional. You might consider taking an interest aptitude test to see if you have the *people interests* that fit a career in real estate.

This is a profession that you can be properly proud of because in its practice you guide buyers in making the largest purchase of their lives and one that will become a significant part of their lives: their homes. You guide sellers in selling what has likely become more than just real estate, but a place of memories, their homes. For the buyer as well as the seller, home purchases are important in both emotion and dollars.

■ REAL ESTATE AND THE ECONOMY

The real estate industry, which includes both the production as well as the distribution of real estate, is truly the engine of both the California and U.S. economy.

More jobs have been created in the real estate and related supply and construction industries than from any other source. Additionally, industries such as furniture and appliances require a steady flow of product, real estate, for their economic well being.

Real estate salespeople work at the end of the production and marketing pipeline keeping our products moving. If we were unable to effectively market products, the entire process would slow, resulting in increased unemployment, which would have a recessionary effect on our entire economy.

■ TRENDS IN REAL ESTATE BROKERAGE

The real estate profession has been undergoing significant change in the past few years. This change has included

- better trained and technology oriented salespeople who regard real estate as a profession;

- buyers and sellers showing greater interest in professional designations, education, and experience of agents;

- the merger of firms that has resulted in multioffice firms offering economics of scale in that the overhead percentage per sales dollar can be reduced. (There will still be a place for small offices specializing in a geographic area or type of property);

- the growth of the team concept where real estate salespeople form partnerships within a firm;

- the greater use of the Internet by homebuyers as well as a marketing tool;

- increased use of personal digital assistants (PDAs) by salespeople;

- increased use of licensed and unlicensed professional assistants by real estate salespeople;

- the ability to better meet buyer needs with a broader range of loan products;

- the growth in one-stop shopping where real estate firms are able to offer affiliated services; and

- the increased importance of marketing to both seniors and singles.

■ THE REAL ESTATE MARKETPLACE

The real estate marketplace, where you will be aiding buyers and sellers, is generally regarded as an imperfect marketplace. Prices asked for similar properties vary, and the selling price generally is less than the asking price. Values generally are set by buyers, not by sellers. It is the price a buyer will pay and not the price a seller desires that ultimately determines value. Some of the reasons that make real estate sales so different from sales of other commodities include

Real estate is not homogeneous.

- *product differentiation*—Every property is different. No two locations are exactly the same. There are usually differences in square feet, interior design, architectural style, landscaping, decorating, age, maintenance, and other amenities. Because of these differences, it is impossible to determine value scientifically. An appraiser tries to evaluate these differences but only estimates what the sale price should be.

- *emotion*—Emotion plays a significant part in a purchase decision. Often a buyer doesn't know why but wants just one particular property after having turned down similar offerings. This emotional desire can play a significant role in determining what a buyer will pay.

■ *buyer and seller knowledge*—A number of buyers and sellers in the marketplace have imperfect or erroneous knowledge of prices paid for similar property. Because of this imperfect knowledge, there are sellers who sell at what we regard as a below-market price and sellers who price their property so high that buyer show no interest in it. Similarly, imperfect knowledge can result in a buyer paying more than what might be regarded as a reasonable price. The growth of buyer brokerage where a sole agent represents a buyer has reduced the likelihood of a buyer overpaying.

The growth of Internet use has resulted in both buyers and sellers checking real estate sites, and that has resulted in educating buyers and sellers to their local real estate market conditions.

■ *uneducated and unprofessional agents*—While not common, an agent who is unfamiliar with a particular area or type of property will at times suggest a selling price that is not supported by market conditions. In addition, some unethical agents may suggest selling prices that are too high solely to obtain a listing. Instead of competing based on a professional approach, they appeal to an owner's greed. Similarly, a buyer's agent who is ignorant of market conditions could recommend a buyer offer that is not in the buyer's best interests.

■ *will-sell versus must-sell owners and will-buy versus must-buy buyers*—Buyer and seller motivation play a significant role in what is asked for a property by an owner, what is offered by a buyer, and what the owner will accept. Unmotivated sellers, that is, **will-sell sellers** (those who don't need to sell but who will sell if the price is right), frequently place property on the market at an above-market price. Sellers who are motivated to sell will be more realistic in their pricing. When a seller is highly motivated or desperate, a **must-sell seller,** the price asked could be less than the sale prices of similarly desirable property. The degree of seller motivation also will affect the likelihood of a below-list-price offer being accepted. **Will-buy buyers** are buyers who don't really have to buy. Investors and speculators are included in this group. Will-buy buyers generally look for motivated must-sell sellers. In other words, they're often bargain hunters. **Must-buy buyers** generally look for property that meets their specific needs. While even must-buy buyers like bargains, they are more likely to pay a reasonable price. When a buyer needs a particular property or has developed a strong emotional desire to own a particular property, a price above market value is likely if the seller is a will-sell rather than a must-sell seller.

■ *terms*—Because of the dollar value of the purchase, real estate sales tend to be very sensitive to interest rates. Higher interest rates can depress the marketplace, whereas lower rates tend to stimulate the market. If a seller is willing to finance a buyer at a below-market rate of interest, the seller might be able to obtain a premium price for his or her property.

The real estate marketplace is also a **stratified marketplace**—stratified based on price range. As an example, there could be a sellers' market in homes priced under $150,000 with many more buyers than sellers. At the same time, there could be a glut of homes priced between $300,000 and $500,000, with few buyers.

The real estate professional helps to bring a measure of order to what could otherwise be a chaotic marketplace. A broker's inventory gives both buyers and sellers comparables and enables the agent to educate them in the realities of the current marketplace. Membership in a **multiple-listing service** (MLS) expands the inventory of comparables to provide information on a much broader scale. This information includes more than offering prices, it includes actual sale prices and special sale conditions.

> The real estate market is stratified based on price.

By serving as a marketing center or clearinghouse for both knowledge and properties, real estate brokers can analyze buyer needs and resources to match buyers with properties and guide them through to culminations of sales.

◼ AN OVERVIEW OF GENERAL BROKERAGE

The majority of real estate licensees are engaged in representing either buyers or sellers or both buyers and sellers in the sale of residential property. The reason is fairly obvious—most properties that are sold are improved residential properties, and most of these are single-family dwelling units.

Real estate salespeople find owners willing to sell their properties or buyers desiring to buy property and secure agency agreements (listings). They then seek buyers for their property listings or property for their buyer-agency listings. Real estate brokers and salespeople are able to expand their activities beyond their own listings because of a unique system of cooperation that exists among brokers.

Brokers who are members of an MLS make their sale listings available for other agents to sell. Therefore, any member of an MLS can show and sell a listing of any other member. By having access to this huge market inventory, an agent can locate a property that best meets the needs and is within the resources of a prospective buyer. Cooperation is the cornerstone of modern real estate brokerage.

There are other areas of activity besides the listing and selling of residential property. These areas of real estate activity include

- *mobile-home sales*—While the industry prefers the name *manufactured home*, most people still refer to these homes, which are transported to the site on their own chassis, as *mobile homes*. Mobile homes differ from other types of housing in that the homes are normally located on leased sites (mobile home parks). Real estate licensees can list and sell mobile homes in rental spaces as well as with the land. Real estate licensees cannot sell new mobile homes without land. These new mobile homes can be sold only through dealers licensed by the Department of Housing and Community Development. Mobile homes fill a significant need for lower-cost housing as well as a lifestyle need in retirement housing. Many salespeople specialize in mobile-home sales—some, in particular mobile home parks.

■ *residential income property (multifamily residential units)*—Brokers as well as salespersons often choose this specialty, although agents who handle primarily single-family home sales often are involved with this type of income property also.

■ *commercial property*—Brokers and salespersons may choose this as a specialty; furthermore, many agents may further specialize by type of property. As an example, some agents handle only minimalls; others may specialize in office buildings, retail stores, or warehouses.

■ *industrial property*—Factory and warehouse specialists make relatively few sales, but the dollar volume tends to be high. Within this field, there are subspecialties such as research and development facilities.

■ *business opportunities*—Businesses are listed and sold with or without real estate. It is a specialized field, and very few residential sales agents ever get involved in a business opportunity sale. Some specialists handle only particular types of businesses, such as taverns, restaurants, or motels.

■ *land and farm brokerage*—Generally, these specialists cover large geographic areas. Knowledge of farming is an important attribute for these agents. In California, many agents specialize in selling acreage parcels to investors and/or developers.

■ *lot sales*—Many agents specialize in listing and selling lots for investment purposes as well as to provide builders with a supply of real estate. General real estate brokerage offices also handle the sale of lots as well as sales of land parcels of all sizes.

■ *auction sales*—Auctions are now being used to sell all types of real property. In England and Australia, auctions play a greater role in real estate brokerage activity than in the United States. The importance of auction sales in the United States is likely to increase in the future. There are a number of firms that deal only in auction sales.

■ *loan brokerage*—Loan brokers generally find investors for trust deeds and property owners who desire to borrow on their property. They bring these lenders and borrowers together for a fee.

■ *mortgage loan activities*—Real estate licensees may act as lenders or agents in making and arranging loans. These activities differ greatly from normal brokerage in that greater administrative skills are needed. However, both sales and mortgage activities require a strong desire to meet the needs of others. Mortgage loan activities that require a real estate license are discussed in Chapter 12.

■ *salaried assistants*—Many licensed agents have chosen to work for other agents as salaried assistants. They like the security of a regular paycheck as well as the chance to use organizational skills.

Assistants allow an agent to better utilize his or her time by handling tasks that can be delegated.

Some agents use virtual assistants for the Internet. They update Internet information, send additional data to responses, answer e-mail requests and provide names and information to their employing agent. The National Association of REALTORS® developed a virtual assistants training program for military spouses.

- *property management*—As in other specialties, there are subspecialties, based on the type of property. Property management is covered in detail in Chapter 15.

- *leasing agent*—Leasing agents are not necessarily property managers. They generally charge a fee based on the gross receipts of the lease entered into. There are subspecialties such as industrial leasing and commercial leasing.

- *appraisal*—Although a separate license is required, a great many appraisers started out in real estate sales.

■ BROKER/SALESPERSON RELATIONSHIPS

The real estate broker is almost always an **independent contractor**. According to the *Real Estate Reference Book*, "An independent contractor is one who, in rendering services, exercises an independent employment or occupation and is responsible to the employer only as to the results of his or her work." Very simply, this means that an independent contractor is not under the direction and control of the employer regarding the manner in which work is carried out. The independent contractor is responsible to the employer only for the results. For example, the real estate broker is responsible for results to his or her principal (employer) who could be a buyer, seller, lessor, or lessee.

Every real estate broker is required to have a written contract with his or her salespeople. Most contracts identify the working relationship of the salesperson as that of an independent contractor (Figure 1.1). Despite these agreements, salespersons are actually **employees** of the broker and not independent contractors because Section 10177(h) of the Business and Professions Code requires that brokers supervise their salespeople, and exercise of supervision in the performance of work precludes an independent contractor relationship. Formerly the broker was required to review contracts prepared by salespersons within five days. This has been replaced by a policy of "reasonable supervision."

Brokers and salespersons contract as independent contractors because of requirements of the Internal Revenue Service. The IRS will treat the real estate salesperson as an independent contractor if the following three criteria are met:

1. The salesperson is licensed as a real estate agent.
2. Reimbursement to the salesperson is based solely on sales, not on hours worked.
3. There is a written contract that states that the salesperson shall be treated as an independent contractor for tax purposes.

FIGURE 1.1

Independent Contractor Agreement

CALIFORNIA
ASSOCIATION
OF REALTORS®

INDEPENDENT CONTRACTOR AGREEMENT
(Between Broker and Associate-Licensee)

This Agreement, dated _____ is made between _____
_____ ("Broker") and
_____ ("Associate-Licensee").
In consideration of the covenants and representations contained in this Agreement, Broker and Associate-Licensee agree as follows:

1. **BROKER:** Broker represents that Broker is duly licensed as a real estate broker by the State of California, ☐ doing business as _____
    _____ (firm name), ☐ a sole proprietorship, ☐ a partnership, ☐ a corporation.
    Broker is a member of the _____ .
    Association(s) of REALTORS ®, and a subscriber to the _____ multiple
    listing service(s). Broker shall keep Broker's license current during the term of this Agreement.

2. **ASSOCIATE-LICENSEE:** Associate-Licensee represents that, (a) he/she is duly licensed by the State of California as a ☐ real estate broker,
    ☐ real estate salesperson, and (b) he/she has not used any other names within the past five years, except _____
    _____ . Associate-Licensee shall keep his/her license current during
    the term of this Agreement, including satisfying all applicable continuing education and provisional license requirements.

3. **INDEPENDENT CONTRACTOR RELATIONSHIP:**
    A. Broker and Associate-Licensee intend that, to the maximum extent permissible by law: **(i)** This Agreement does not constitute an employment
       agreement by either party; **(ii)** Broker and Associate-Licensee are independent contracting parties with respect to all services rendered under this
       Agreement; **(iii)** This Agreement shall not be construed as a partnership.
    B. Broker shall not: **(i)** restrict Associate-Licensee's activities to particular geographical areas or, **(ii)** dictate Associate-Licensee's activities with regard
       to hours, leads, open houses, opportunity or floor time, production, prospects, sales meetings, schedule, inventory, time off, vacation, or similar
       activities, except to the extent required by law.
    C. Associate-Licensee shall not be required to accept an assignment by Broker to service any particular current or prospective listing or parties.
    D. Except as required by law: **(i)** Associate-Licensee retains sole and absolute discretion and judgment in the methods, techniques, and procedures
       to be used in soliciting and obtaining listings, sales, exchanges, leases, rentals, or other transactions, and in carrying out Associate-Licensee's
       selling and soliciting activities, **(ii)** Associate-Licensee is under the control of Broker as to the results of Associate-Licensee's work only, and not
       as to the means by which those results are accomplished, **(iii)** Associate-Licensee has no authority to bind Broker by any promise or
       representation and **(iv)** Broker shall not be liable for any obligation or liability incurred by Associate-Licensee.
    E. Associate-Licensee's only remuneration shall be the compensation specified in paragraph 8.
    F. Associate-Licensee shall not be treated as an employee with respect to services performed as a real estate agent, for state and federal tax
       purposes.
    G. The fact that the Broker may carry worker compensation insurance for Broker's own benefit and for the mutual benefit of Broker and licensees
       associated with Broker, including Associate-Licensee, shall not create an inference of employment.

4. **LICENSED ACTIVITY:** All listings of property, and all agreements, acts or actions for performance of licensed acts, which are taken or performed in
    connection with this Agreement, shall be taken and performed in the name of Broker. Associate-Licensee agrees to and does hereby contribute all
    right and title to such listings to Broker for the benefit and use of Broker, Associate-Licensee, and other licensees associated with Broker. Broker
    shall make available to Associate-Licensee, equally with other licensees associated with Broker, all current listings in Broker's office, except any listing
    which Broker may choose to place in the exclusive servicing of Associate-Licensee or one or more other specific licensees associated with Broker.
    Associate-Licensee shall provide and pay for all professional licenses, supplies, services, and other items required in connection with Associate-
    Licensee's activities under this Agreement, or any listing or transaction, without reimbursement from Broker except as required by law. Associate-
    Licensee shall work diligently and with his/her best efforts: **(a)** To sell, exchange, lease, or rent properties listed with Broker or other cooperating
    Brokers; **(b)** To solicit additional listings, clients, and customers; and **(c)** To otherwise promote the business of serving the public in real estate
    transactions to the end that Broker and Associate-Licensee may derive the greatest benefit possible, in accordance with law. Associate-Licensee
    shall not commit any unlawful act under federal, state or local law or regulation while conducting licensed activity. Associate-Licensee shall at all
    times be familiar, and comply, with all applicable federal, state and local laws, including, but not limited to, anti-discrimination laws and restrictions
    against the giving or accepting a fee, or other thing of value, for the referral of business to title companies, escrow companies, home inspection
    companies, pest control companies and other settlement service providers pursuant to the California Business and Professions Code and the Real
    Estate Settlement Procedures Acts (RESPA). Broker shall make available for Associate-Licensee's use, along with other licensees associated with
    Broker, the facilities of the real estate office operated by Broker at _____
    _____ and the facilities of any other office
    locations made available by Broker pursuant to this Agreement.

        Broker and Associate-Licensee acknowledge receipt of copy of this page, which constitutes Page 1 of _____ Pages.
        Broker's Initials (_____) (_____)   Associate-Licensee's Initials (_____) (_____)

THIS FORM HAS BEEN APPROVED BY THE CALIFORNIA ASSOCIATION OF REALTORS® (C.A.R.). NO REPRESENTATION IS MADE AS TO THE LEGAL VALIDITY OR
ADEQUACY OF ANY PROVISION IN ANY SPECIFIC TRANSACTION. A REAL ESTATE BROKER IS THE PERSON QUALIFIED TO ADVISE ON REAL ESTATE
TRANSACTIONS. IF YOU DESIRE LEGAL OR TAX ADVICE, CONSULT AN APPROPRIATE PROFESSIONAL.

R|I Published and Distributed by:
E|N REAL ESTATE BUSINESS SERVICES, INC.   **REVISED 10/98**
B|C a subsidiary of the *CALIFORNIA ASSOCIATION OF REALTORS®*
S| 525 South Virgil Avenue, Los Angeles, California 90020

┌─ OFFICE USE ONLY ─┐
Reviewed by Broker
or Designee _____
Date _____
└──────────────────┘

EQUAL HOUSING
OPPORTUNITY

PRINT DATE

INDEPENDENT CONTRACTOR AGREEMENT (ICA-11 PAGE 1 OF 3)

FIGURE 1.1

Independent Contractor Agreement (continued)

5. **PROPRIETARY INFORMATION AND FILES:** **(a)** All files and documents pertaining to listings, leads and transactions are the property of Broker and shall be delivered to Broker by Associate-Licensee immediately upon request or termination of their relationship under this Agreement. **(b)** Associate Licensee acknowledges that Broker's method of conducting business is a protected trade secret. **(c)** Associate-Licensee shall not use to his/her own advantage, or the advantage of any other person, business, or entity, except as specifically agreed in writing, either during Associate-Licensee's association with Broker, or thereafter, any information gained for or from the business, or files of Broker.

6. **SUPERVISION:** Associate-Licensee, within 24 hours (or ☐ _____) after preparing, signing, or receiving same, shall submit to Broker, or Broker's designated licensee: **(a)** All documents which may have a material effect upon the rights and duties of principals in a transaction, **(b)** Any documents or other items connected with a transaction pursuant to this Agreement in the possession of or available to Associate-Licensee and, **(c)** All documents associated with any real estate transaction in which Associate-Licensee is a principal.

7. **TRUST FUNDS:** All trust funds shall be handled in compliance with the Business and Professions Code, and other applicable laws.

8. **COMPENSATION:**

    A. **TO BROKER:** Compensation shall be charged to parties who enter into listing or other agreements for services requiring a real estate license:
       ☐ as shown in "Exhibit A" attached, which is incorporated as a part of this Agreement by reference, or
       ☐ as follows: _____
       _____
       Any deviation which is not approved in writing in advance by Broker, shall be (1) deducted from Associate-Licensee's compensation, if lower than the amount or rate approved above; and, (2) subject to Broker approval, if higher than the amount approved above. Any permanent change in commission schedule shall be disseminated by Broker to Associate-Licensee.

    B. **TO ASSOCIATE-LICENSEE:** Associate-Licensee shall receive a share of compensation actually collected by Broker, on listings or other agreements for services requiring a real estate license, which are solicited and obtained by Associate-Licensee, and on transactions of which Associate-Licensee's activities are the procuring cause, as follows:
       ☐ as shown in "Exhibit B" attached, which is incorporated as a part of this Agreement by reference, or
       ☐ other: _____
       _____

    C. **PARTNERS, TEAMS, AND AGREEMENTS WITH OTHER ASSOCIATE-LICENSEES IN OFFICE:** If Associate-Licensee and one or more other Associate-Licensees affiliated with Broker participate on the same side (either listing or selling) of a transaction, the commission allocated to their combined activities shall be divided by Broker and paid to them according to their written agreement. Broker shall have the right to withhold total compensation if there is a dispute between associate-licensees, or if there is no written agreement, or if no written agreement has been provided to Broker.

    D. **EXPENSES AND OFFSETS:** If Broker elects to advance funds to pay expenses or liabilities of Associate-Licensee, or for an advance payment of, or draw upon, future compensation, Broker may deduct the full amount advanced from compensation payable to Associate-Licensee on any transaction without notice. If Associate-Licensee's compensation is subject to a lien, garnishment or other restriction on payment, Broker shall charge Associate-Licensee a fee for complying with such restriction.

    E. **PAYMENT:** **(1)** All compensation collected by Broker and due to Associate-Licensee shall be paid to Associate-Licensee, after deduction of expenses and offsets, immediately or as soon thereafter as practicable, except as otherwise provided in this Agreement, or a separate written agreement between Broker and Associate-Licensee. **(2)** Compensation shall not to be paid to Associate-Licensee until both the transaction and file are complete. **(3)** Broker is under no obligation to pursue collection of compensation from any person or entity responsible for payment. Associate-Licensee does not have the independent right to pursue collection of compensation for activities which require a real estate license which were done in the name of Broker. **(4)** Expenses which are incurred in the attempt to collect compensation shall be paid by Broker and Associate-Licensee in the same proportion as set forth for the division of compensation (paragraph 8(B)). **(5)** If there is a known or pending claim against Broker or Associate-Licensee on transactions for which Associate-Licensee has not yet been paid, Broker may withhold from compensation due Associate-Licensee on that transaction amounts for which Associate-Licensee could be responsible under paragraph 14, until such claim is resolved. **(6)** Associate-Licensee shall not be entitled to any advance payment from Broker upon future compensation.

    F. **UPON OR AFTER TERMINATION:** If this Agreement is terminated while Associate-Licensee has listings or pending transactions that require further work normally rendered by Associate-Licensee, Broker shall make arrangements with another associate-licensee to perform the required work, or Broker shall perform the work him/herself. The licensee performing the work shall be reasonably compensated for completing work on those listings or transactions, and such reasonable compensation shall be deducted from Associate-Licensee's share of compensation. Except for such offset, Associate-Licensee shall receive the compensation due as specified above.

9. **TERMINATION OF RELATIONSHIP:** Broker or Associate-Licensee may terminate their relationship under this Agreement at any time, with or without cause. After termination, Associate-Licensee shall not solicit **(a)** prospective or existing clients or customers based upon company-generated leads obtained during the time Associate-Licensee was affiliated with Broker, or **(b)** any principal with existing contractual obligations to Broker, or **(c)** any principal with a contractual transactional obligation for which Broker is entitled to be compensated. Even after termination, this Agreement shall govern all disputes and claims between Broker and Associate-Licensee connected with their relationship under this Agreement, including obligations and liabilities arising from existing and completed listings, transactions, and services.

Broker and Associate-Licensee acknowledge receipt of copy of this page, which constitutes Page 2 of _____ Pages.
Broker's Initials (_____) (_____)   Associate-Licensee's Initials (_____) (_____)

REVISED 10/98

Page 2 of ___ Pages.

┌─ OFFICE USE ONLY ─┐
Reviewed by Broker
or Designee _____
Date _____
└──────────────────┘

EQUAL HOUSING OPPORTUNITY

PRINT DATE

INDEPENDENT CONTRACTOR AGREEMENT (ICA-11 PAGE 2 OF 3)

FIGURE 1.1

Independent Contractor Agreement (continued)

10. **DISPUTE RESOLUTION:**
    A. **Mediation:** Mediation is recommended as a method of resolving disputes arising out of this Agreement between Broker and Associate-Licensee.
    B. **Arbitration:** All disputes or claims between Associate-Licensee and other licensee(s) associated with Broker, or between Associate-Licensee and Broker, arising from or connected in any way with this Agreement, which cannot be adjusted between the parties involved, shall be submitted to the Association of REALTORS® of which all such disputing parties are members for arbitration pursuant to the provisions of its Bylaws, as may be amended from time to time, which are incorporated as a part of this Agreement by reference. If the Bylaws of the Association do not cover arbitration of the dispute, or if the Association declines jurisdiction over the dispute, then arbitration shall be pursuant to the rules of California law. The Federal Arbitration Act, Title 9, U.S. Code, Section 1, et seq., shall govern this Agreement.

11. **AUTOMOBILE:** Associate-Licensee shall maintain automobile insurance coverage for liability and property damage in the following amounts $_____ /$_____. Broker shall be named as an additional insured party on Associate-Licensee's policies. A copy of the endorsement showing Broker as an additional insured shall be provided to Broker.

12. **PERSONAL ASSISTANTS:** Associate-Licensee may make use of a personal assistant, provided the following requirements are satisfied. Associate-Licensee shall have a written agreement with the personal assistant which establishes the terms and responsibilities of the parties to the employment agreement, including, but not limited to, compensation, supervision and compliance with applicable law. The agreement shall be subject to Broker's review and approval. Unless otherwise agreed, if the personal assistant has a real estate license, that license must be provided to the Broker. Both Associate-Licensee and personal assistant must sign any agreement that Broker has established for such purposes.

13. **OFFICE POLICY MANUAL:** If Broker's office policy manual, now or as modified in the future, conflicts with or differs from the terms of this Agreement, the terms of the office policy manual shall govern the relationship between Broker and Associate-Licensee.

14. **INDEMNITY AND HOLD HARMLESS:** Associate-Licensee agrees to indemnify, defend and hold Broker harmless from all claims, disputes, litigation, judgments, awards, costs and attorney's fees, arising from any action taken or omitted by Associate-Licensee, or others working through, or on behalf of Associate-Licensee in connection with services rendered. Any such claims or costs payable pursuant to this Agreement, are due as follows:
    ☐ Paid in full by Associate-Licensee, who hereby agrees to indemnify and hold harmless Broker for all such sums, or
    ☐ In the same ratio as the compensation split as it existed at the time the compensation was earned by Associate-Licensee
    ☐ Other: _____
    _____
    _____
    Payment from Associate-Licensee is due at the time Broker makes such payment and can be offset from any compensation due Associate-Licensee as above. Broker retains the authority to settle claims or disputes, whether or not Associate-Licensee consents to such settlement.

15. **ADDITIONAL PROVISIONS:** _____
    _____

16. **DEFINITIONS:** As used in this Agreement, the following terms have the meanings indicated:
    (A) "Listing" means an agreement with a property owner or other party to locate a buyer, exchange party, lessee, or other party to a transaction involving real property, a mobile home, or other property or transaction which may be brokered by a real estate licensee, or an agreement with a party to locate or negotiate for any such property or transaction.
    (B) "Compensation means compensation for acts requiring a real estate license, regardless of whether calculated as a percentage of transaction price, flat fee, hourly rate, or in any other manner.
    (C) "Transaction" means a sale, exchange, lease, or rental of real property, a business opportunity, or a manufactured home, which may lawfully be brokered by a real estate licensee.

17. **ATTORNEY FEES:** In any action, proceeding, or arbitration between Broker and Associate-Licensee arising from or related to this Agreement, the prevailing Broker or Associate-Licensee shall be entitled to reasonable attorney fees and costs.

18. **ENTIRE AGREEMENT; MODIFICATION:** All prior agreements between the parties concerning their relationship as Broker and Associate-Licensee are incorporated in this Agreement, which constitutes the entire contract. Its terms are intended by the parties as a final and complete expression of their agreement with respect to its subject matter, and may not be contradicted by evidence of any prior agreement or contemporaneous oral agreement. This Agreement may not be amended, modified, altered, or changed except by a further agreement in writing executed by Broker and Associate-Licensee.

Broker:

_____
(Brokerage firm name)

By _____
Its Broker/Office manager (circle one)

_____
(Print name)

_____
(Address)

_____
(City, State, Zip)

_____
(Telephone)   (Fax)

Associate-Licensee:

_____
(Signature)

_____
(Print name)

_____
(Address)

_____
(City, State, Zip)

_____
(Telephone)   (Fax)

This form is available for use by the entire real estate industry. It is not intended to identify the user as a REALTOR®. REALTOR® is a registered collective membership mark which may be used only by members of the NATIONAL ASSOCIATION OF REALTORS® who subscribe to its Code of Ethics.

PRINT DATE

REVISED 10/98

Page 3 of ___ Pages.

┌─ OFFICE USE ONLY ─┐
Reviewed by Broker
or Designee _____
Date _____
└──────────────────┘

EQUAL HOUSING
OPPORTUNITY

INDEPENDENT CONTRACTOR AGREEMENT (ICA-11 PAGE 3 OF 3)

FIGURE 1.2

Employee or Independent Contractor? IRS Considerations

FACTORS INDICATING CONTROL	EMPLOYEE	INDEPENDENT CONTRACTOR
Is the worker required to comply with employer instructions about when, where, and how work is to be performed?	Yes	No
Is the worker required to undergo training?	Yes	No
Does the worker hire, supervise, and pay others to perform work for which he or she is responsible?	No	Yes
Must the worker's job be performed during certain set hours?	Yes	No
Must the worker devote full time to the job?	Yes	No
Must the work be performed on the employer's property?	Yes	No
Must tasks be performed in a certain order set by the employer?	Yes	No
Is the individual required to submit regular written or oral reports to the employer?	Yes	No
Is payment by the hour, week, or month?	Yes	No
Is payment in a lump sum?	No	Yes
Are the worker's business and travel expenses paid by the employer?	Yes	No
Does the employer furnish the tools and materials required for the job?	Yes	No
Does the worker rent his or her own office or working space?	No	Yes
Will the worker realize a profit or loss as a result of his or her services?	No	Yes
Does the individual work for more than one firm at a time?	No	Yes
Does the worker make his or her services available to the general public?	No	Yes
Does the employer have the right to fire the worker?	Yes	No
Does the worker have the right to quit the job at any time, whether or not a particular task is complete?	Yes	No

Note: These factors are only possible indicators of a worker's status. Each case must be determined on its own facts, based on all the information.

If the above criteria are met, brokers are not required to contribute to their salespersons' Social Security accounts (a savings to the broker of approximately 7½ percent of a salesperson's earnings), nor are brokers required to withhold income taxes from salespersons' earnings. Salespersons, of course, must file their own estimated tax returns and pay the full Social Security contribution of 15 percent.

If the broker exercises too great of control over a salesperson, the salesperson might be considered an employee by the IRS, despite the contract to the contrary. Figure 1.2 will help you to understand the factors indicating control.

While the broker is an independent contractor, a salesperson is considered by the Department of Real Estate to be an employee of his or her broker.

Despite the IRS treatment of a real estate salesperson as an independent contractor, the broker is responsible for wrongful acts (torts) of his or her salespeople within the course and scope of employment. Because of this potential liability, many brokers require that their salespeople carry high limits of automobile liability insurance and that brokers be named as insured under the policies. If a salesperson has access to the funds of others, such as a property manager who collects rents and deposits, brokers might obtain fidelity bonds to protect themselves from a salesperson's embezzlement. Many offices also carry errors and omissions insurance policies that offer liability protection for acts of brokers and agents.

Brokers should carry **workers' compensation insurance** for salespersons who are considered for this purpose to be employees. Brokers need not carry unemployment insurance coverage because commission salespeople are not eligible for unemployment insurance benefits. Also, because salespeople are paid solely by commission, minimum wage laws do not protect them.

■ SALESPERSON/SALESPERSON CONTRACTS

Real estate salespeople often team up with one or more other salespeople to form a partnership or selling team. These partnerships are usually organized under written agreements for a specified time period that provide for renewal by agreement. They call for a splitting of the combined earnings of the group. Advantages of such arrangements are

- being better able to meet needs of buyers and sellers because of greater likelihood of availability of a team member,

- having someone to help in an area where help is needed,

- positively motivating members because all members share in each other's successes,

- providing more even income flow to members because there is a greater likelihood of income being earned every month,

- better utilization of time, and

- better utilization of paid assistants.

A partnership choice should not be taken lightly. You should choose not only a person or persons you like but those who are similarly dedicated. You want partners you can rely on.

■ CHOOSING A BROKER

At one time, the majority of real estate offices seemed to be running a numbers game. They would take in every real estate licensee willing to come to work for them. Most firms have come to realize that such a practice can be counterproductive in that it can waste both time and money. Today most offices are interested in agents they believe will fit in with their office and either have experience or the drive to learn what is necessary for success. Brokers realize that who they hire can effect their bottom line—profit. Direct and indirect costs in hiring an agent who fails to produce can be in the thousands of dollars.

Expect to be asked direct questions about your past work history, what you expect from being a real estate agent, and what you are willing to give to the job as far as effort and dedication.

Your job interview is really a two-way interview with the broker trying to do what is best for the brokerage firm while you are seeking the firm that will best meet your personal goals.

Your choice of broker could have a significant effect on your success or failure as a real estate professional. Don't jump to accept the first "come to work for me" offer. It might result in wasting a great deal of what otherwise could be productive time. More importantly, an initial experience of feeling like a square peg in a round hole could lead you to abandon what would otherwise be a rewarding career.

Before you even think about talking to brokers, you should understand why fewer than 50 percent of new real estate licensees are still actively engaged in real estate one year after starting work. More disheartening is the fact that fewer than 25 percent of new licensees are earning what we regard as a "good living" after one year. Your initial choice of a broker will reduce your likelihood of becoming a "failure statistic."

A contributing reason for such a high rate of failure is lack of training in what to do to be successful. While some successful agents have come into an office absolutely green, observed what successful agents were doing, and then did it themselves, these agents are the exceptions. In some offices, a new licensee is assigned a desk, is provided with rudimentary information about using the computer, and (perhaps) receives a 30-minute briefing. The new agent might be given a rather boring task, such as telephone solicitations. Even then, the new licensee likely begins without knowing anything about how to achieve telephone success. New licensees are often left to sit at their desks, to observe what is going on around them, and to emulate what they consider to be successful tactics. This learning-by-osmosis approach is far more likely to result in failure than success.

Many offices have weekly sales meetings with craft improvement sessions. Some offices use a **mentor program** in which the new hire assists a successful salesperson for several months. This approach can be very good if the mentor is knowledgeable. The idea of a mentor seems to be disappearing because successful agents are reducing the time they spend in their offices. Many agents today have home offices and even mobile offices in their cars.

Most large offices have a formal training program. Some are excellent, providing motivation as well as the skills necessary for success. Some offices have training directors who not only conduct training sessions but also work closely with agents to improve their performance. Some offices have extensive CD, video, and audio training libraries as well as excellent books to augment their training programs and to help develop the skills of success.

Your first few months in real estate are critical because if you can't see success in the near future, you are likely to drop by the wayside and be added to the failure statistics. You need a broker who will provide you with the training you need for success. When you talk to brokers, find out details about their training programs, what the office does about continuing skill improvement, what the office has in the way of a library and training aids. Ask to talk to a recent licensee who works in the office. Ask pointed questions about the training and broker assistance. You should be actively interviewing the prospective broker rather than being a passive listener.

Find out about the broker's present employees. How long have they been with the office? If everyone seems to be a relative newcomer, it could indicate a serious problem. Find out about the earnings of the full-time salespersons. This is very important because working around successful people can serve as a great personal motivator. If you are working in the midst of a group of marginal producers, their attitudes, likely negative, could make it difficult for you to maintain the positive approach required for your success.

You will likely give your greatest consideration to a broker involved in residential sales because most sales are residential. Commercial or industrial sales might offer huge commissions, but the deals that come together are few and often far apart. As a new licensee, you are unlikely to develop the skills needed to succeed in commercial/industrial selling before financial pressures drive you toward a salaried position.

Keep in mind that the sales skills learned in residential sales can be transferred to other areas of real estate. After you have developed these skills, a number of alternatives will be open to you.

Many real estate boards and associations offer training opportunities. The largest broker organization is the **National Association of Realtors**® (NAR). The **California Association of Realtors**® (CAR) is the state organization of NAR. There also are other organizations, for example, the National Association of Real Estate Brokers, which uses the designation **Realtist**. Many Realtists are also Realtors®.

Some of these organizations offer regularly scheduled training sessions; others sponsor special training programs. Many board and association offices have libraries that contain excellent training material, and some have bookstores where training material and supplies can be purchased. The training publications along with ideas you gain from your local real estate board or association can materially affect your future.

If you have already achieved success in real estate, the initial training offered by a broker would not be a major consideration in working for that broker, although other support services and commission arrangements could be very important.

Some offices offer a sliding commission scale under which the salesperson keeps a greater portion of the commission dollars as his or her commissions increase. The purpose of this type of arrangement is to motivate salespeople to achieve greater success as well as to retain top producers.

Health insurance coverage with a broker-paid portion (often related to performance) has proven to be an excellent salesperson retention tool for some brokers.

There are a number of **100 percent commission offices.** In these offices, the salesperson pays a flat desk fee or a desk fee plus a transaction fee to the broker and then keeps all the commission earned. Generally, the brokers in 100 percent offices provide little help to the salespeople. The salesperson pays for his or her own support services. This type of arrangement should not be chosen by a new licensee, although it can offer benefits for experienced real estate professionals who generate much of their own business. If you are just embarking on a real estate career, don't worry about commission splits: 100 percent of nothing is nothing. Generally, the higher the split, the fewer services provided by the broker to the agent. As a new hire, you want all the help you can get. Figure 1.3 is a worksheet for selecting a broker's office that allows the agent to compare three different brokers.

> The salesperson pays the broker in a 100 percent commission office.

How to Choose Where to Work
A new licensee is wise to go to work for an office

- that offers a training program as good as or better than those offered by other area brokers.

- that offers assistance when you need it. An office that has a designated person in charge of your training is a definite plus.

- with a good library of books, audiotapes, CDs, and videos available for your use.

- that is primarily devoted to the sale of and/or lease in the real estate specialty area you desire to work in.

- where salespeople have good morale, reflected in their periods of employment.

- that has a significant proportion of successful agents.

- that is comfortable *for you*. You must feel comfortable with the broker, your coworkers, and the operation of the office. If you are uncomfortable, your chances of success are going to be materially diminished.

FIGURE 1.3

Checklist for Selecting a Broker's Office

Brokers' Names

1. _____
2. _____
3. _____

Benefits provided by the broker	Broker 1	Broker 2	Broker 3
1. New-agent training program			
2. Ongoing training program			
3. Use of a mentor system			
4. Computer training			
5. Quality phone systems (voice-mail, call forwarding, etc.)			
6. Fax machine availability			
7. E-mail address			
8. Office Web site (grade on a 1 to 10 scale)			
9. Multiple-listing service (MLS)			
10. Success of current sales staff			
11. Forms and stationery availability			
12. Open-house signs and flags			
13. Desk fees and MLS board fees			
14. Advertising support			
15. Amount of floor time required and/or offered			
16. Organized farm for new agents			
17. Weekly meeting and caravans			
18. 800 number availability			
19. Broker's interest in you			
20. Can you work with management?			
21. Estimated start-up costs			
22. Supports part-time agents			

Reprinted with permission, California Association of REALTORS®. Endorsement not implied.

■ SUCCESS AND YOUR ATTITUDE

If you expect failure, you will not be disappointed. Your belief in your inadequacies will be reflected in your actions and will become a self-fulfilling prophecy. Lack of positive motivation is a significant factor in the failure a great many agents experience.

For success, you need a positive mind-set. You must believe that you will grasp success. Without this belief, you are unlikely to put forth the level of effort that your success demands.

We know that simply moving an agent's desk can change an agent's production. Having successful coworkers around you can serve to give you ideas as well as motivate you to achieve your own success. Unfortunately, the opposite is also true. Having people around you who are unsuccessful or who have a negative attitude can affect your attitude. If they are failures, your chances of failure will be increased. If you associate with successful people, you will likely be associating with people who have a positive attitude. A positive attitude can be infectious, just as the negative attitude of friends and associates can lead you to failure. A negative attitude will lead to a "they aren't really buyers" prejudgment that can make the difference between marginal results and great success.

No one will stand over you in real estate to watch your every move and prod you on. Others can reinforce your resolve to succeed, but the real motivation for success is internal. You must want to succeed so much that you will continue to strive despite setbacks or the negative attitudes of others.

By completing the Success Questionnaire, Figure 1.4, you will gain an understanding of where you are now as well as areas where improvement is needed.

Certainly, motivational seminars, tapes, and books help, but these are short-term motivational aids. Long-term success is based on internal motivation to expend the extra effort to learn, to plan, and to practice for your success.

Use the success of others as a guide to show yourself what can be done. In the same vein, don't become complacent because you are doing better than others. In real estate, don't feel that you are in competition with any other agent. Your only competitor should be yourself. Strive to "be all that you can be."

We are seeing a change in the way that many successful salespersons do business. Many have significantly reduced the number of hours they spend in the broker's office. With personal digital assistants, cell phones, voice mail, **e-mail,** and fax machines, the majority of their office time has become home-based or car-based. With reduced direct contact with brokers and coworkers, self-motivation becomes essential for success.

■ PROFESSIONAL DESIGNATIONS

The National Association of REALTORS® as well as numerous other real estate organizations offers a myriad of professional designations. Some designations relate to general brokerage while others are specific to specialized areas of activity. To earn these designations requires a course of study and, in some cases, examinations. Achieving these designations opens up many opportunities because many are regarded highly by others. A designation frequently sought is the Graduate, REALTOR® Institute (GRI). Achieving designations such as the GRI will increase your confidence as well as your sense of self-worth.

FIGURE 1.4

Success Questionnaire

1. **Are you enthusiastic about your work?**
   Study the unusually successful people you know and you will find them imbued with an enthusiasm for their work that is contagious. Not only are they excited about what they are doing, but they also get you excited. Remember the maxim: "Enthusiasm is like a contagious disease. It must be caught and not taught."

2. **How do you overcome objections?**
   Numerous spoken questions and written questions are being fired at you every day. Do you answer them without hesitation, drawing on your reservoir of knowledge? Do you do so to the satisfaction of the client or prospect? Or is there sometimes a hesitation followed by a garbled description that leaves the client as much in the dark as he or she was before?

3. **Are you self-confident?**
   Knowledge gives confidence. A thorough knowledge of both the property in question and the exact advantages that the customer will receive develops this quality of confidence in you, which shows itself in your personality. If the client or customer has confidence in you and your company, a sale may result naturally. The main factor that determines whether customers will have confidence in your product or service is whether they have confidence in you. Your knowledge gives you assurance, a prime factor in assuring others.

4. **Do you have the courage of your convictions?**
   Many times, we cease to be courageous in the face of opposition. It is a sad commentary, but we live in an era when rapid change breeds fear. Conquer fear! Banish worry, because, as someone once said, worry is the interest you pay on trouble before you get it. Keep your fears to yourself, and share your courage with others. Remember, fear is only in the mind.

5. **Are your actions and speech positive?**
   A number of years ago there was a popular song with the words "Accentuate the positive, eliminate the negative." You need to think and act positively.

   Those who think *negatively* say, "Business is poor; unemployment rates are more than 9 percent. That means 9 percent of the people cannot be considered potential prospects."

   Those who think *positively* say, "Business is great, with only 9 percent unemployment. That means 91 percent of the people are potential prospects." However, being positive does not imply that it gives us the right to be dishonest. But we can state facts positively without being dishonest.

6. **Are you persistent?**
   Customers admire a salesperson who has developed persistence. No one has respect for a quitter, a person who readily takes no for an answer. If only 1-in-20 presentations results in a sale, your attitude should be: "Thanks for the no. I'm now closer to the yes." (You should of course be considering as a goal to reduce 1-in-20 to 1-in-19.)

7. **Are you a problem solver?**
   Be a problem solver, not a problem. Problem solvers are people helpers. The basic principles of problem solving are

   ■ despite any problem, you can persevere, think, and reach a solution.·

   ■ relentless pressure, persistence, and determination.

   ■ acting as if the problem can be solved. Use the power of positive thinking.

   ■ remember, you do not sell properties; you sell solutions to people's problems.

   ■ understanding completed staff work. The idea of **completed staff work** is that you should never present your broker with a problem unless you also present your broker with the possible courses of action to take—your recommendations as to a specific action and why.

8. **Are you willing to fail?**
   Perhaps this should be phrased as "willing to try, regardless of the chance of failure." Success cannot be achieved without failure. An old story is a good example of this concept: Robert Bruce, King of Scotland, had just been defeated for the eleventh time by his enemies, the English. He was dejectedly resting by a tree, ready to give up, when he saw a spider persistently trying to spin a web from one limb to another. After eleven times, in which the spider failed to reach its goal, it finally succeeded on the twelfth try. Inspired by this incident, Bruce went forth against his enemy for the twelfth time. This time he was victorious, defeating the English at Bannockburn, winning independence for Scotland. To be a successful salesperson, you must be willing to try and perhaps to fail in order to succeed in the end.

■ CONTINUING TRAINING

Training is not a one-time program. As a real estate professional, you should constantly be working on improving your skill as well as increasing your knowledge. The most successful agents are constantly striving for improvement, and this striving continues throughout their careers.

Seek out available training sessions and group-sponsored seminars applicable to your work. *California Real Estate Magazine*, the magazine of the California Association of REALTORS®; *Real Estate Today*, the magazine published by the National Association of REALTORS®; and REALTOR® *News*, the biweekly newspaper of the National Association of REALTORS® are examples of excellent publications with articles that will help you succeed. Many offices have back issues of these publications in their libraries.

When a new idea or approach is proposed during office training sessions, take notes and try to use that idea or approach as soon as possible. Keep in mind that listening may give you ideas, although a demonstration is even better because it *shows* the applicability of ideas; however, using the ideas yourself makes them yours. By using them they become part of your personal "sales software," to be retained in your memory bank and taken out when the situation warrants their use.

Besides office training sessions, you may have a training supervisor who will critique your efforts. Pay attention. Take criticism as an opportunity for improvement, not an indication of failure.

Ask questions of the more successful salespeople in your office. Generally, they will share ideas gladly. Consider building a special relationship with a successful agent in your office. In doing so, you will be developing your own mentor. Having someone supportive of you who possesses both knowledge and experience can be of great help to you during your first few months in real estate. This is especially important in offices where the broker or office manager has limited time to work with you.

You will find that there are more good ideas for prospecting, listing, and selling than one person could possibly use. By *trying* various approaches, you will find ideas you feel comfortable with. If you have an approach with which you are comfortable, you will work that approach with greater enthusiasm and heighten the likelihood of its leading to your success.

Check the course offerings of your local colleges and business schools. Besides specific real estate courses, consider more general business courses in salesmanship, marketing, advertising, and so forth. The knowledge gained in many general courses will have direct application to real estate activities. A number of courses also are offered by correspondence. While some correspondence courses are quite good, they do not provide the insights of an instructor or the give and take of a classroom environment. There is a great deal more to learning than just what is "in the book."

Real estate licensees are required to take continuing education courses for license renewal. Many of these courses will provide you with knowledge directly applicable to your work. Even if you are not required to take a course, you should evaluate what the course can do for you. As an example, every agent should consider taking one of the many continuing education courses offered in how to use a financial calculator.

The Internet can be a great learning tool. Two of the many Web sites you should consider visiting are: *www.relibrary.com/* and *www.agentnews.com/*.

Many excellent commercial seminars are available to licensees. Besides providing new ideas and approaches, these seminars are motivational in nature. In making decisions about which courses and seminars to attend, ask your broker and/or successful salespersons you know who have attended the courses for their evaluations of the programs.

For a rating of real estate seminar provider's check the Web site: *www.JohnTReed.com/rateseminars.html*. While these ratings are the personal evaluations of John Reed, a real estate author, Mr. Reed receives input from attendees of these seminars.

Self-Training

In your training, you should realize that the quicker you acquire the basic skills needed for success, the greater the likelihood that you will remain in the real estate profession. The simple economics of trying to survive a lengthy training period of months without any income forces many agents to leave real estate when they might otherwise have realized great success. Stated simply, the quicker you learn your survival skills, the more likely you are to survive and succeed.

Therefore, it is important to use every bit of available time toward this goal of self-improvement. As a new licensee, you cannot afford the luxury of relaxing in front of the television after an eight-hour day.

Check your office library as well as city libraries for real estate training books, tapes, even videos. Study them, take notes, and then verbalize (role-play) the approaches presented (more about this later). Chances are a number of people in your office have trainer material from various seminar presenters. Borrow it; some of the private presenter material is excellent.

Learn the inventory in your market area. Learn about schools, recreation facilities, cultural opportunities, etc. Only with product knowledge will you be able to successfully match prospective buyers to properties meeting their needs.

As a word of caution, keep in mind that some of the poorest producers may have excellent resource material available. Even the best material is worthless if it isn't used.

Role-Playing

To communicate effectively with buyers and sellers, you must be able to take your ideas and verbalize them in an effective manner. By the use of role-playing you can train yourself to handle telephone inquiries; make listing, showing, and selling presentations; learn to effectively qualify buyers; and learn to overcome both buyer and seller objections. Role-playing can help you overcome the fear that grips many agents when it comes time to ask an owner or buyer to sign a contract. Role-playing can give you the self-confidence to close (obtain signatures on the contract) in a natural and effective manner.

Role-playing is acting as the person you wish to be.

Role-playing is a mind game. It is also basic acting. In role-playing, you imagine yourself in a situation. Imagine unexpected objections of all sorts, then decide on the best way to handle them. (The training material we discussed will provide you with many ideas.) Verbalize your responses before a mirror. Watch your expressions.

Always remember that you are playing the part of a knowledgeable professional. You should constantly strive for improvement. The beauty of role-playing is that you can do it mentally, even when others are present. You can use otherwise nonproductive driving time for role-playing exercises. By role-playing, you will gain confidence and will become at ease in dealing with people. An excellent training approach is to role-play with another person with whom you can exchange characters. This really is a team-teaching exercise. Having a third party observer will increase the effectiveness of this technique as it will help to keep you focused.

By taping presentations, you will hear how you sound. You might feel you need better enunciation or the need to speak with greater confidence. Annoying verbal habits become evident, such as verbalizing your pauses with "ahhh" or repetition of a phrase such as "You know." If you realize you have problems, you can work to overcome them.

After you make any type of presentation, ask yourself afterward, "Could I have handled the situation better?" By thinking about what you *should* have said, you are actually preparing yourself for future encounters with similar situations. You can thus benefit by failures as well as successes.

Role-playing will improve your communication skills, and as your skills improve, so will your confidence. You will thus overcome fear, a significant factor in the failure of many salespeople. If you fear failure, you are likely to betray your fear by appearing nervous. A prospective buyer or seller is not likely to become convinced to buy or list property by an agent who appears to lack confidence. As you progress, you will become the person whom you were portraying in your role-playing; a confident, knowledgeable, and caring person interested in fulfilling the needs of others.

Planning

Planning is the process of plotting your course of action to reach specified goals and objectives. It is a blueprint of what you intend to accomplish. Add a timetable and you also have a tool to evaluate your performance. Planning is never a waste of time. The insignificant cannot be trimmed until the significant is singled out.

The less time you have to spare, the more important it is to plan your day carefully. Do not forget the oft-repeated statement that 20 percent of your effort will produce 80 percent of your results.

Adopt your own system of planning, but be sure to plan. Any system that does away with time-wasters and puts the focus on planning will increase productivity. Self-discipline is the key. If you have it, you will have great success with time management and the other aspects of your life.

Sometimes it may seem that no matter how hard you apply yourself and how efficiently you allocate your time, you have more work to do and more people to see than you can handle satisfactorily. Time management is part of the solution. A good time-management system rounds out your plan and helps you improve your efficiency and income. As you refine your techniques of self-management, you may expect a release from the pressure of time as your first dividend.

Goal Setting

Can you imagine yourself in a race without a finish line? That is what it is like to work without goals. You can travel a great distance but get nowhere.

Goal setting is a tool for making intelligent decisions. Use the following seven principles to help you set your goals effectively:

1. Goals in real estate selling should be exact rather than abstract. For example:

   - *Abstract:* I will do my best to improve my sales techniques during this week.
   - *Exact:* I will obtain at least one listing and make at least three sales presentations during this week.

2. Goals should be in a time frame. Set short-term, intermediate-term, and long-term goals. (The short-term, intermediate-term, and long-term goals listed below are representative only. Goals will vary based on your area of specialization and your geographic area, as well as your individual needs). For example:

Short-Term (less than one year):

   - This week I will pass out 50 calling cards.
   - Today I will call on three owners who are advertising their property for sale.
   - I will obtain a minimum of three listings this month.
   - This week I will enroll in a college-level course in property management.

Intermediate-Term (one to five years):

   - I will complete the required eight broker courses within two years.
   - I will obtain the GRI designation within four years.

Goal Setting (continued)

Long-Term (more than five years):

■ I will open my own real estate office within eight years.
Your short-term and intermediate-term goals should flow toward meeting your long-term goals.

3. Goals should be put into writing

■ It is easier to determine your priorities when your goals are written.

■ Written goals are easier to examine and revise.
Translating goals onto paper makes them appear more manageable and helps licensees overcome selling fears.

4. Tell someone, such as your spouse or a trusted friend, of your goals. Telling another person will serve as motivation to continue striving for your goals.

5. Goals should be reasonably attainable. If your goals are not attainable, you are likely to become discouraged and disappointed.

6. Goals should be adopted only after careful and considerable thought. Think about what you really want and why. Reaching goals can take hard work, so you probably will devote time and energy only to those you are really committed to.

7. Goals should not be cast in stone. If interests change, your long-term and intermediate-term goals should change accordingly. If you are no longer motivated to reach a goal, your likelihood of accomplishing that goal will be significantly lessened.

By evaluating yourself, you will discover that wishes can become reality if you have a plan that leads toward their fruition.

The paradox of time is that there is never enough, but we have all there is. A time-management authority who conducted a poll of managers found that 90 percent said they needed more time to get their jobs done right.

Unsuccessful real estate licensees often waste 40 percent to 50 percent of every workday. Just think of your first hour on the job: Are you guilty of the behavior one time-management expert witnessed? Do you do nothing more than participate in "opening exercises": have a cup of coffee, socialize, read the paper? Little gets done, and the trouble is that sets a pattern for the day. There's an old proverb that reads as follows: "As the first hour goes, so goes the day."

Time management can make the whole day more productive, allowing you to produce more, get better results, and probably get more rewards as well.

Remember, time is capital. Know what it is worth.

$$\frac{\text{Desired annual earnings}}{1{,}952 \text{ working hours a year}}$$

The figure of 1,952 is based on 244 working days x 8 hours per day.

■ **EXAMPLE:**   Salesperson Goodolboy makes $100,000 per year, his hourly wage is approximately $51 per hour ($100,000 ÷ 1,952 hours) = Dollar value of one hour.

Allowing for other activities and unavoidable delays, you will be fortunate to have one-fourth that time (488 hours a year) actually to spend with clients or customers. Thus, the dollar value of your time is even greater than the equation above indicates. To start thinking about how to get the maximum return on your time, ask yourself, "How can I raise the

- number of calls per week?"
- number of interviews per call?"
- number of presentations given per interview?"
- number of closes per presentation?"
- number of new prospects per week?"
- number of repeat sales?"
- dollar value of selling time?"

> **Note:** You must comply with the federal do-not-call registry for all solicitation calls. See margin note on page 120.

Your **daily planning** is the foundation of your goal setting. Your planning for each day should include steps leading to your short-term, intermediate-term, and long-term goals.

Before you start daily planning, analyze how you spent your time yesterday and how it was spent so far today. How productive was that 20-minute discussion on how the Dodgers will do this year? Besides identifying the time-wasters, ask yourself, "Were my efforts devoted more to probabilities rather than mere possibilities?"

Some agents like to divide their activities into A, B, C, and D categories:

> Simply increasing *A Time* will increase productivity.

A Time   Time spent making listing presentations and showing property for sale. This is time spent that can lead directly to a commission.

B Time   Time spent in prospecting for buyers and sellers and in preparing for showings.

C Time   Caravaning, studying inventory, and doing necessary tasks and paperwork in support of A Time and B Time activities.

D Time   Time spent for personal and nonwork-related activities.

This simple rating of time presents a basic truth. If you can double your *A Time*, you will double your income, even without any improvement in your skills. When coupled with skill improvement, you can readily see how incomes can soar. Some successful agents hire assistants to take care of a great deal of their *B Time* and *C Time* activities. You can see why a productive salesperson would want to do this.

With the above understandings, you are ready for your daily plan. There are quite a few real estate daily planners available. Figure 1.5 shows a simple daily planner. By carrying your professional planner with you, you can set appointments several days in advance when necessary.

We recommend you use an electronic planner. A personal digital assistant (PDA) provides planning ability as well as provides much of the information needed to fulfill the tasks in your daily plan.

Just having a planner isn't enough—you must use it. Keep in mind that every activity on your daily plan will not be accomplished. Your schedule will change because of unplanned opportunities. Grab an *A Time* opportunity whenever it comes your way.

At the end of each day, evaluate what you have accomplished. If a task was not accomplished but is still relevant, set it forward to the next day; if not, delete it. If a task is unpleasant but must be done, set it for the beginning of a day. After it is accomplished, you will have a sense of relief rather than worrying about it all day.

Assistants

Some new licensees will work as salaried **assistants** to successful sales agents to gain the experience and confidence necessary for success in sales.

While assistants do not make much economic sense for new agents (who must learn before they can train others to help them), they can handle a great deal of a successful agent's *B Time*, *C Time*, and *D Time* activities, thus allowing for greater *A Time* work. Hundreds of agents in Southern California engage paid full-time assistants, and one agent we know has a personal staff of four full-time aides.

■ ADDITIONAL PREPARATION

Additional preparation will be required to prepare for your career.

Learning the Inventory

When you go to work for an office, you will want to learn about the office **inventory** as soon as possible. This means you must visit office listings. Call ahead if a listing is inhabited. Don't take too much time with each owner, or you will have a long-term job just visiting inventory. In the case of large offices with hundreds of listings, personal visits to each listing would not be possible. As a suggestion, use your office Web site to review listings and then visit those listings that are in the area, price range, and of the type you feel you would like to concentrate on. You may wish to take Polaroid photographs of features of the property, if they are not covered by your office Web site or property flyers. Until

FIGURE 1.5

Daily Planning Sheet

Source: Loonday, Jim, List for Success (Chicago: Real Estate Education Company®, 1986), P. 10.

you understand the inventory, you will be unable to field telephone inquiries or to properly prepare for a showing.

Another benefit of visiting office inventory is that it will give you a sense of area value based on listing prices. You should be able to judge within a relatively short period of time if a listing is priced competitively. Check out homes listed by other offices within the geographic area or specialization area if you have decided to specialize in a particular market segment. In smaller communities, you might be able to see everything that is available, but in larger markets, you will have to be selective and choose homes for which you feel you might have interested buyers.

Of course, you should go on office and board **caravans** of new listings. Avoid visiting properties where you feel the likelihood of your having a buyer is slight. Try to avoid wasting time.

Abraham Lincoln said, "A lawyer's time is his stock in trade." It holds true for real estate agents as well as lawyers.

Office Procedure

If your office has an **office procedures manual,** study it. As soon as possible, learn what is expected of you. Know your office meeting and/or training schedules, and enter them in your daily planner for the month ahead. Find out what the procedure is for depositing checks and cash. You must know what to do when you take a listing or an offer to purchase. Every office is run a little differently from every other office, so be certain you understand what is expected of you.

Understand the forms used by your office so that you will be able to complete them and explain them to others without hesitation.

As a personal training exercise, complete a listing for a property you know of, and then complete an offer to purchase for that property. Have them reviewed by another agent.

Find out how to use the fax machine, voice mail, and other features of your office communications systems. What are the procedures for long-distance calls and overnight express services? Understand the systems your office provides and how to use them.

Computer Literacy

In today's sales environment, you must have computer knowledge. At a minimum you should be able to

- have an e-mail address and know how to send and access e-mail;
- search for available properties from MLS data based on specific criteria (for example: 4-bedroom houses in a particular area priced under $200,000);

■ obtain a printout of houses sold within an area showing features and sale price;

■ be familiar with your office Web site and its links;

■ know and access additional Web sites covering your market area;

■ use word-processing software to produce personalized sales letters, as well as other correspondence;

■ use office software to produce an attractive property brief (one-page description) for a listing; and

■ obtain comparables (listing and sale prices of similar properties).

Tax Knowledge   You must understand real property taxation and special benefits available. You should also have knowledge of the income tax benefits of home ownership, as well as the tax treatment for investment and income property, including trading. (See Chapter 14.)

Sales Equipment   You must be equipped to be a successful real estate salesperson. You should consider the following:

A *personal digital assistant (PDAs)*—Consider a PDA, such as a Palm Pilot, with perhaps the following features:

■ daily planning;

■ store addresses and telephone numbers;

■ contact management for return calls, action, etc.;

■ make to-do lists;

■ take notes;

■ write memos;

■ do calculations;

■ universal connector for add-ons, such as portable keyboard, modems, and more;

■ retrieve and send e-mails;

■ download from the Internet;

■ access Web sites;

■ transfer data to and from desktop computers;

■ appointment reminder with alarms; and

■ enter business-related expenses for tax purposes.

(For more information on PDA, check *www.howstuffworks.com/pda.htm.*)

Business cards—These should include your e-mail address as well as your cellular telephone number. If you are fluent in another language or languages and you are targeting persons who speak that language, then your business card should indicate your language fluency.

Cellphones—Cellular telephones, once considered a luxury that only a few agents carried, have become a necessity. A cellular telephone allows you to change appointments, schedule homes to show, and give flexibility to salespersons. Phone numbers should be programmed into your cellphone for quick calls, such as your office or escrow offices. You will probably want telephone features such as caller ID, call waiting, call transfer, and digital answering.

Your car—Your car should be kept clean at all times. Avoid smoking in your car because many people are offended by the smell of tobacco. You might want to use an air freshener. If you are going to purchase a car, consider a full-size four-door model for ease in entering and exiting. This is of particular value when dealing with older prospective buyers. To test for comfort, sit in the rear seat of the vehicle before you decide to purchase.

In the car—Carry the following items in the trunk, glove box, or under the seat:

1. A plastic bag with extra forms and pens
2. A flashlight
3. A For Sale sign and stake
4. Basic tools (hammer, screwdriver, pliers, assorted nails, screws, nuts, and bolts)
5. A spare telephone directory
6. A reverse directory that lists occupants by street address
7. A 50-foot tape measure (and/or an electronic measuring device)
8. An amortization schedule (in case your PDA and pocket calculation fail)
9. A small tape recorder to record your thoughts or ideas
10. A supply of business cards
11. A pocket calculator if your PDA does not have calculation ability (preferably a financial calculator)
12. Maps showing school districts, recreational areas, etc. (use colored marking pens)
13. Maps for Natural Hazards Disclosure (as applicable):

    - Special flood hazard areas (designated by Federal Emergency Management Agency);
    - Area of potential flooding (areas subject to inundation if a dam fails);
    - Very high fire hazards severity zone;

■ Designated wildland area (state responsibility area with substantial fire risks);

■ Earthquake Fault Zone;

■ Seismic Hazard Zone (areas subject to severe shaking, landslides or soil liquefaction);

The county recorder's office, county assessor, and local planning agency will have a posted notice as to the location of maps.

14. A digital camera

15. Portable Fax Machine (If your work reveals the advantage of being able to send and receive fax messages from your cellphone, you should consider a portable fax machine)

If your office does not have an 800 number and your buyers come primarily from outside your local calling area, you might consider your own 800 number. An 800 number is available for as low as $5 per month with long-distance charges in the 10¢ per minute range. Many independent providers offer these services.

Computer

As you gain experience and knowledge, you will find that you will be spending more time away from your office. Your office will become more of a place to meet clients than a work station. Your own computer to access your office computers and/or MLS services will become a necessity. Your home office should also include a printer, scanner, and copier, now available as 3-in-1 machines. You will need them. Having a home office will reduce wasted time and also allow you to utilize spare time at home.

You

You want to dress as a professional within your area would dress. Your clothes reflect the image you want to convey, that of a person who feels competent in his or her role.

Avoid far-out fashions; conservative is best. Avoid overly flashy or expensive jewelry. You don't want to divert attention from what you are saying. Use cologne or aftershave lotion sparingly. If people can smell you coming, chances are you overdid it.

Learn to smile. Smile while you are on the telephone and when you talk to people. An upbeat person can make others feel good and can set an upbeat mood for a sale.

Take care of yourself. Your body is the only one you have. Watch your diet, get adequate sleep, and exercise on a regular basis. A healthy body will be reflected in your energy and productivity.

■ SUMMARY

Real estate professionals deal in the fulfillment of needs. The product that fulfills these needs is real estate.

Real estate activity can be an important engine for economic growth because more people are employed in real estate and construction-related jobs than in any other industry.

Real estate is changing with new technology as well as with better educated and trained professionals.

Real estate professionals work in an imperfect marketplace. The reasons for this imperfection include product differentiation, emotions, imperfect buyer and seller knowledge, uneducated and unprofessional agents, buyer and seller motivation, and the differing terms of the sale. The real estate professional brings a degree of order to this marketplace.

The majority of real estate agents are engaged in listing and selling single-family residences residences. Other areas of activity or specialization include

- mobile-home sales,
- residential income property,
- commercial property,
- industrial property,
- business opportunities,
- land and farm brokerage,
- lot sales,
- auction sales,
- loan brokerage,
- land development,
- property management,
- leasing, and
- appraisal.

The real estate salesperson is considered an employee of the broker, for most purposes, but usually is contractually designated as an independent contractor.

If the salesperson meets the IRS criteria as an independent contractor, withholding tax is not deducted from the salesperson's commission checks. Also, the employer need not contribute to the salesperson's Social Security.

Choosing a broker is an extremely important decision. A new licensee should be particularly interested in the aid and training provided by the broker. Brokers want to hire salespersons who will succeed, and salespersons want a broker who can meet their needs.

Your attitude can be a significant factor in your success. A negative attitude will be reflected in your production.

Working for a REALTOR® and/or Realtist will give you the advantage of a broad educational program as well as publications. Keep in mind that training is a career-long activity and is an integral part of your career as a real estate professional. You must equip yourself with the basic tools of the real estate profession and know how to use them. Besides office training and Board of REALTORS® sessions, engage in self-training. This includes reading books and periodicals, using available tapes and videos, and, most important, role-playing to prepare yourself to handle any conceivable situation.

Establish goals for yourself. These should include short-term as well as intermediate-term and long-term goals. You need a plan to meet these goals. Your planning will reduce wasted time and lead to realization of your goals. The basic building block of your planning is a daily plan.

One of your first steps toward success in a new office is learning your inventory. You must learn office procedures, acquire basic computer literacy, and have basic knowledge of property and income taxes as they relate to real estate sales activities. You must also acquire some basic tools so you can perform as a real estate professional.

Of course, you want to personally convey the image of a professional in your dress and manner. Take care of yourself because health is related to productivity.

■ CLASS DISCUSSION TOPICS

1. Describe your local market area and evaluate it. Is your local market stratified? How? If you were to choose an area of specialization, what would it be? (Consider both geographic area and activity.) Justify your choice.

2. Describe the training programs provided by local offices.

3. What are your long-term goals? What, if any, short-term goals would help in meeting these long-term goals?

4. What training material is available for your use within your office?

5. What training material is available through your Board of REALTORS® library?

6. Prepare a daily plan in advance. How was your time actually spent on that day? Discuss deviations from the plan and the reasons for the deviations. Were they justified?

7. Evaluate your average day. What percentage of your time is spent in Category A *Time* activities? Category B *Time* activities? Category C *Time* activities? Category D *Time* activities?

8. What could you do now to increase the percentage of your time spent on Category A *Time* activities?

9. Check John Reed's Web site for a real estate seminar presenter you are familiar with (*www.JohnTReed.com/rateseminars.html*). Do you agree with Mr. Reed's assessment? Why?

10. Do you know of any real estate firms in your area that have merged? If so, what benefits do you feel the merger has led to?

11. For class discussion, bring to class one current events article dealing with some aspect of real estate practice.

■ CHAPTER 1 QUIZ

1. The real estate marketplace could best be described as being
   a. homogeneous.
   b. stratified.
   c. perfect.
   d. uninfluenced by emotion.

2. The majority of real estate agents are primarily engaged in which area of activity?
   a. Residential property
   b. Raw land and lots
   c. Commercial property
   d. Development

3. The IRS will treat real estate salespersons as independent contractors if three criteria are met. Which of the following is NOT one of the criteria?
   a. The salesperson's reimbursement is solely based on sales, not hours worked.
   b. The salesperson represents himself or herself as an independent contractor when dealing with third parties.
   c. There is a written contract that states that the salesperson shall be treated as an independent contractor for tax purposes.
   d. The salesperson is licensed as a real estate agent.

4. A broker ordinarily would be liable to salespersons for
   a. unemployment compensation.
   b. workers' compensation.
   c. Social Security contributions.
   d. none of the above.

5. In choosing a broker, a new licensee should be least interested in an office that
   a. has a high percentage of successful salespeople.
   b. has a good library of books, tapes, and videos for training.
   c. offers 100 percent commission.
   d. is a member of a local multiple-listing service.

6. The best way to learn is to
   a. listen to what others say.
   b. read instructional material.
   c. watch what others are doing.
   d. use the ideas you observe or read about.

7. Which of the following is true of role-playing?
   a. Role-playing situations are limited only by our own imagination.
   b. Role-playing can be verbalized or nonverbalized.
   c. Role-playing exercises can involve more than one person.
   d. All of the above.

8. Which of the following is an exact goal?
   a. I will work harder next week.
   b. I will improve my listing presentation.
   c. I will make ten calls tomorrow on "for sale by owner" ads.
   d. I will learn by observing successful agents.

9. All of the following will aid you in goal achievement except that goals should be
   a. attainable.
   b. based on what you really want.
   c. kept to yourself because they are personal.
   d. exact so that you can measure their attainment.

10. By proper daily planning you should endeavor to
   a. reduce *D Time* activities.
   b. increase *A Time* activities.
   c. place more emphasis on probabilities than on possibilities.
   d. accomplish all of the above.

CHAPTER

2

ETHICS, FAIR HOUSING, AND TRUST FUNDS

■ KEY TERMS

Americans with Disabilities Act	Commingling	REALTORS® Code of Ethics
blockbusting	diversity training	redlining
Civil Rights Act of 1866	ethics	Rumford Act
Civil Rights Act of 1870	Fair Employment and Housing Act	sexual harassment
Civil Rights Act of 1964	familial status	steering
Civil Rights Act of 1968	Golden Rule	trust funds
	law	Unruh Act

■ LEARNING OBJECTIVES

The purpose of including the material and discussion cases on ethics is to provide you with a basis for evaluating your daily actions, not just in terms of legality and effectiveness but also in terms of "Is it right?" You will learn to evaluate your actions as well as the actions of others from an ethical point of view. While you will never reach a point of perfection, you must nevertheless strive to do what is right for others. In doing so, you will help yourself.

You will also gain an understanding of the various laws dealing with fair housing and your obligations under those laws. These laws relate to ethics because they set forth an ethical approach to dealing with others.

■ WHAT IS ETHICS?

The word **ethics** comes from the Greek *ethikos*, meaning *moral*, and *ethos*, meaning *character*. Ethics is a moral standard for life, and the test for that standard is quite simple. It is the **Golden Rule**: "Do unto others as you would have them do unto you." To evaluate conduct to determine if it is ethical, simply ask yourself, "If the roles were reversed, would I consider the conduct I am contemplating to be proper?"

An Arizona real estate broker, Irv Also, has defined ethics in six words: "Don't hurt anyone" and if you hurt someone, "Make it right." These six words are really the essence of the Golden Rule.

| The best test of ethics is the Golden Rule. |

You should do right not because of a fear of punishment or exposure but because the reward is the conduct itself. George Bernard Shaw stated, "You cannot believe in honor until you have achieved it." Similarly, you cannot truly understand why you should be a moral person until you become such a person.

The fact that everyone is doing an unethical act does not make it right. Neither does the fact that if you didn't do it someone else would.

Ethics and the Law

Ethics has nothing to do with legality or illegality. **Laws** set minimum standards for what a society regards as acceptable behavior. Violation of the law is an illegal act for which the state has set penalties. Laws can change; what is illegal today could be legal tomorrow, and what is legal today could be illegal tomorrow. Similarly, a legal act could be unethical, and an illegal act could be ethical. As an example, not many years ago a number of states regarded marriage between members of different races as a violation of the law. While such a mixed marriage was considered illegal, it would not violate ethical standards.

| Ethics goes beyond the law. |

Ethics deals in what is right, not in minimum standards. While laws change to accommodate current attitudes, ethics remains constant. If conduct is wrong, based on the application of the Golden Rule, it remains wrong, even though others may engage in such conduct.

Ethics tends to precede the law. As an example, in the early 1980s, we had a rash of home purchases with loans being assumed and the sellers carrying the balance of the purchase price using a second trust deed. These no-down-payment purchasers would then rent the homes and pocket the rent receipts, but they did not make payments on either the first or the second trust deed, a practice called *rent skimming*.

Some purchasers were able to delay foreclosure for more than a year. While not at the time a specific violation of the law, when the Golden Rule was applied, this conduct was reprehensible and, of course, unethical. Statutes were later enacted that made rent skimming illegal.

Gray Ethical Areas

Ethics is not an exact science. What is ethical or unethical is not always clear. Our sense of right and wrong is based upon our past experiences.

If in your heart you believe an action is proper, then it is ethical to you. However, if you have to ask someone if an action is legal, then you clearly feel there is something wrong in the action.

If you would not want others to know what you have done, then it is also clear that you feel the action is tainted.

If you feel you have to justify an action with a defense such as, "If I didn't do it, someone else would," it is clear that you know the action is wrong.

Shakespeare said it best over 400 years ago: "To thine own self be true, and it must follow, as the night the day, thou canst be false to any man."

Ethics and Motive

Your motive for an action could determine if the action is ethical or unethical.

As an example, assume that you are on a caravan visiting new listings when you notice several building code violations in one of the properties and you notify the county authorities of the violations. If you did so because you felt the violations presented a real danger to present occupants and any future buyers, then your action would have to be viewed as ethical. If, however, safety was not a concern, but you reported the violations solely because of a personal animosity toward the listing agent and you hoped it might ruin his day, then your action would clearly be viewed as unethical because you were intentionally trying to hurt another without any redeeming reason.

Ethics and Your Career

Ethics is not incompatible with good business practices. Successfully meeting the needs of buyers and sellers will reinforce your self-esteem and will serve as a motivator for further success. Over the long haul, an ethical professional will be rewarded with a loyal clientele and a steady stream of referrals. Most successful real estate salespersons obtain the greater portion of their business from referrals from people with whom they have worked in the past. If you want long-term success, you must earn the trust of others. From a pragmatic viewpoint, good ethics is good business.

Do not fall into the trap of measuring your success by dollars earned rather than by how you have successfully helped others. If you measure success solely in dollars, it becomes easy to take a pragmatic approach to real estate. You can lead yourself to believe that because the end—dollars—is important, the means to reach that end are of less importance. You could find yourself acting in a self-serving manner, placing your own interests above the best interests of those you are serving. In short, it can be easy to become an unethical real estate salesperson or broker. Unfortunately, some real estate agents take a pragmatic approach based on "What will it do for me now?" A great many real estate license revocations have been the result of this "now attitude."

■ CODES OF ETHICS

REALTORS®

A number of professional organizations have Codes of Ethics. The REALTORS® Code of Ethics is based on the Golden Rule and is an excellent guide to ethical behavior. The word REALTOR® denotes a member of the National Association of REALTORS® (NAR). But even if you are not a member of the NAR, you should read this code and use it as a guide in your relations with others.

Realtists

At one time, African Americans were excluded from just about every professional business group. In 1947, a group of African American brokers founded the National Association of Real Estate Brokers and adopted the word *Realtist* to designate their members.

The National Association of Real Estate Brokers, like the NAR, is constantly striving to increase the professionalism of the real estate industry.

California Code of Ethics

In 1979, former Real Estate Commissioner David Fox expressed a need for a California Code of Ethics. This code was known as the *Commissioner's Code of Ethics*. Because it was a repetition of conduct made illegal by other sections of the law, it has now been deleted from the administrative code. While illegal conduct is generally unethical, the code failed to carry ethics beyond the law. Legality or illegality of an act does not make it ethical or unethical.

The Real Estate Commissioner has issued suggestions for professional conduct in sale, lease, and exchange transactions and suggestions for professional conduct when negotiating or arranging loans secured by real property or sale of a promissory note secured by real property. These have been included as Figure 2.1.

■ FAIR HOUSING AND ANTIDISCRIMINATION LEGISLATION

Fair housing legislation and practices involve almost every activity in real estate. The federal and state governments have passed legislation in the areas of fair housing and antidiscriminatory practices. Material regarding housing discrimination also appears in the Real Estate Commissioner's Rules and Regulations and in the Business and Professions Code.

FIGURE 2.1

Suggestions for Professional Conduct

The Real Estate Commissioner has issued Suggestions for Professional Conduct in Sale, Lease, and Exchange Transactions and Suggestions for Professional Conduct When Negotiating or Arranging Loans Secured by Real Property or Sale of a Promissory Note Secured by Real Property.

The purpose of the Suggestions is to encourage real estate licensees to maintain a high level of ethics and professionalism in their business practices when performing acts for which a real estate license is required.

The Suggestions are not intended as statements of duties imposed by law nor as grounds for disciplinary action by the Department of Real Estate, but as suggestions for elevating the professionalism of real estate licensees.

As part of the effort to promote ethical business practices of real estate licensees, the Real Estate Commissioner has issued the following Suggestions for Professional Conduct:

(a) *Suggestions for Professional Conduct in Sale, Lease, and Exchange Transactions.* In order to maintain a high level of ethics and professionalism in their business practices, real estate licensees are encouraged to adhere to the following suggestions in conducting their business activities:

  (1) Aspire to give a high level of competent, ethical, and quality service to buyers and sellers in real estate transactions.

  (2) Stay in close communication with clients or customers to ensure that questions are promptly answered and all significant events or problems in a transaction are conveyed in a timely manner.

  (3) Cooperate with the California Department of Real Estate's enforcement of, and report to that Department evident violations of, the Real Estate Law.

  (4) Use care in the preparation of any advertisement to present an accurate picture or message to the reader, viewer, or listener.

  (5) Submit all written offers in a prompt and timely manner.

  (6) Keep oneself informed and current on factors affecting the real estate market in which the licensee operates as an agent.

  (7) Make a full, open, and sincere effort to cooperate with other licensees, unless the principal has instructed the licensee to the contrary.

  (8) Attempt to settle disputes with other licensees through mediation or arbitration.

  (9) Advertise or claim to be an expert in an area of specialization in real estate brokerage activity, e.g., appraisal, property management, industrial siting, mortgage loan, etc., only if the licensee has had special training, preparation, or experience in such areas.

  (10) Strive to provide equal opportunity for quality housing and a high level of service to all persons regardless of race, color, sex, religion, ancestry, physical handicap, marital status, or national origin.

  (11) Base opinions of value, whether for the purpose of advertising or promoting real estate brokerage business, upon documented objective data.

  (12) Make every attempt to comply with these Suggestions for Professional Conduct and the Code of Ethics of any organized real estate industry group of which the licensee is a member.

(b) *Suggestions for Professional Conduct When Negotiating or Arranging Loans Secured by Real Property or Sale of a Promissory Note Secured by Real Property.* In order to maintain a high level of ethics and professionalism in their business practices when performing acts within the meaning of subdivision (d) and (e) of Section 10131 and Sections 10131.1 and 10131.2 of the Business and Professions Code, real estate licensees are encouraged to adhere to the following suggestions, in addition to any applicable provisions of subdivision (a), in conducting their business activities:

  (1) Aspire to give a high level of competent, ethical, and quality service to borrowers and lenders in loan transactions secured by real estate.

  (2) Stay in close communication with borrowers and lenders to ensure that reasonable questions are promptly answered and all significant events or problems in a loan transaction are conveyed in a timely manner.

  (3) Keep oneself informed and current on factors affecting the real estate loan market in which the licensee acts as an agent.

  (4) Advertise or claim to be an expert in an area of specialization in real estate mortgage loan transactions only if the licensee has had special training, preparation, or experience in such area.

  (5) Strive to provide equal opportunity for quality mortgage loan services and a high level of service to all borrowers or lenders regardless of race, color, sex, religion, ancestry, physical handicap, marital status, or national origin.

FIGURE 2.1

Suggestions for Professional Conduct (continued)

(6) Base opinions of value in a loan transaction, whether for the purpose of advertising or promoting real estate mortgage loan brokerage business, on documented objective data.

(7) Respond to reasonable inquiries of a principal as to the status or extent of efforts to negotiate the sale of an existing loan.

(8) Respond to reasonable inquiries of a borrower regarding the net proceeds available from a loan arranged by the licensee.

(9) Make every attempt to comply with the standards of professional conduct and the code of ethics of any organized mortgage loan industry group of which the licensee is a member.

The conduct suggestions set forth in subsections (a) and (b) are not intended as statements of duties imposed by law nor as grounds for disciplinary action by the Department of Real Estate, but as guidelines for elevating the professionalism of real estate licensees.

Federal Laws

Real estate brokers and salespersons should heed these laws in every stage of the real estate process. An understanding of the history of antidiscrimination laws will help you understand the need for this legislation.

Although the Declaration of Independence originally contained language condemning slavery, that language was removed shortly before the document was signed to ensure the consensus of all the states. However, the Declaration of Independence did retain the following statement: "We hold these truths to be self-evident, that all men are created equal, that they are endowed by their Creator with certain Unalienable Rights, that among these are Life, Liberty, and the pursuit of Happiness."

There was also a later attempt to outlaw slavery when the U.S. Constitution was written. Because of strong opposition, wording that would outlaw slavery was not included based on "practical" considerations.

While there was strong antislavery sentiment in the northern states, by the mid-1800s the South's economy had become dependent on slave labor. The invention of the cotton gin and the Industrial Revolution had made cotton-growing very lucrative. In 1820, the Missouri Compromise allowed Missouri to enter the Union without restrictions as to slavery, while Maine would enter as a free state. The western territories were to be free.

In 1857, the U.S. Supreme Court issued the Dred Scott decision that basically was an order to the federal government to keep out of the slavery issue because this was a matter for the states. The court held that only a state could exclude slavery and that Congress had exceeded its authority by prohibiting slavery in the territories. The Missouri Compromise was thus held unconstitutional.

Declaration of Independence is Not Law

While inspiring, the Declaration of Independence is not law. Had it been law, there likely would not have been the necessity for most of the federal and state antidiscrimination laws. When an attempt was made to include antislavery language in the Constitution, the attempt failed. In fact, the Constitution provided that a slave should be considered as being only three-fifths of a person in determining the Congressional representation of a state.

The court also made clear that "Negroes" were not entitled to rights as U.S. citizens and had "no rights which any white man was bound to respect." The court pointed out that slaves were property and that the U.S. Constitution guaranteed property rights.

The Dred Scott decision was received with anger in the North. It led to sectionalism that divided the nation and was a prime cause of the Civil War.

Thirteenth Amendment.   The Thirteenth Amendment to the Constitution abolished slavery, but it did not specifically address the rights of former slaves.

The Civil Rights Act of 1866 had no exceptions.

The Civil Rights Act of 1866.   The **Civil Rights Act of 1866** was intended to provide equal treatment for former slaves. It states: ". . . all citizens of the United States shall have the same rights in every state or territory as is enjoyed by white citizens thereof to inherit, purchase, lease, sell, hold, and convey real and personal property."

While this act was broad in its protection, it applied only to race. There were no exceptions to the act, which could be enforced by any individual who was discriminated against. Remedies included injunction and compensatory and punitive damages.

The Fourteenth Amendment.   The Fourteenth Amendment to the Constitution was passed after the Civil Rights Act of 1866. Supporters of the amendment pointed out that it would protect the rights granted in the 1866 act by providing protection in the U.S. Constitution. This would prevent a later Congress or court from taking away these rights.

The Fourteenth Amendment states: "All persons born or naturalized in the United States, and subject to the jurisdiction thereof, are citizens of the United States and of the State wherein they reside. No State shall make or enforce any law which shall abridge the privileges or immunities of citizens of the United States; nor shall any State deprive any person of life, liberty, or property, without due process of law; nor deny any person within its jurisdiction the equal protection of the laws."

Obviously, the Fourteenth Amendment did not limit itself to race. A reasonable interpretation of the above would be that the Fourteenth Amendment offered comprehensive civil rights protection.

Civil Rights Act of 1870.   Some attorneys were of the opinion that because the Fourteenth Amendment was passed after the Civil Rights Act of 1866, that act had been effectively replaced and was no longer law. So to protect against later courts taking away the remedies granted by the 1866 act, a statement was tacked on to a voting rights act in 1870 (**Civil Rights Act of 1870**) that stated: ". . . and be it further enacted that the act to protect all persons in the United States in their civil rights and furnish the means of their vindication, passed April nine, eighteen hundred and sixty-six, is hereby re-enacted."

Thus, the Civil Rights Act of 1866 was passed twice to make certain it would withstand possible future challenges in the courts. However, the act was effectively gutted by court decisions that limited the enforcement to government property. The act, as well as the Fourteenth Amendment, was ineffective in providing equal rights for approximately one hundred years.

Executive Order 11063.   On November 21, 1962, President John F. Kennedy issued an order that prohibited discrimination in housing wherever federal funds were involved. The order affected property sales involving FHA and VA loans, as well as other government-subsidized programs. It stated: ". . . the executive branch of the government, in faithfully executing the laws of the United States which authorize federal financial assistance, directly or indirectly for the provision, rehabilitation, and operation of housing and related facilities, is charged with an obligation and duty to assume that the laws are fairly administered and that benefits there under are made available to all Americans without regard to their race, color, creed, or national origin."

Civil Rights Act of 1964.   The **Civil Rights Act of 1964** made the 1962 executive order into law and is considered among the first of the modern civil rights acts. While it prohibited discrimination in all federally assisted programs, prior and later acts are far more comprehensive.

Jones v. Mayer upheld the Civil Rights Act of 1866.

Jones v. Mayer. In the same year that the Civil Rights Act of 1968 was passed (below), the Supreme Court held in *Jones v. Mayer* that the Civil Rights Act of 1866 applied to private property and could be enforced by the party discriminated against. The court based its decision on the Thirteenth Amendment.

Civil Rights Act of 1968.   The **Civil Rights Act of 1968** prohibited discrimination in housing based on national origin, race, religion, and color. (Sexual discrimination was added in 1974.) The act prohibits

- discrimination by brokers toward clients and customers;

- refusal to show, rent, or sell through the false representation that a property is not available;

- discrimination as to access to multiple-listing services;

- discriminatory sales or loan terms;

- **steering**, the act of directing people of different races, religions, etc., away from or toward particular areas;

- **blockbusting,** the process of inducing panic selling by representing that prices will drop or crime will increase because of the possible entrance of minority group members to the area;

- **redlining,** the refusal to loan within an area;

- retaliatory acts against persons making fair-housing complaints and intimidation to discourage complaints; and

- discriminatory advertising, which is prohibited even when related to activities exempt from the act.

Steering is directing based on group, *blockbusting* is inducing panic selling, and *redlining* is refusal to loan in designated areas.

There has been a great deal of concern as to what advertising might be considered discriminatory. Advertising that a property is close to a particular house of worship or a place that has a racial connotation (such as "Martin Luther King Hospital") has been held to be discriminatory, as have ads that indicate a preference for a particular race or marital status or ads that indicate a member of a protected category is not welcome.

Advertising Terms Acceptable by HUD

HUD has indicated that use of the following terms and phrases are not discriminatory: master bedroom, rare find, desirable neighborhood, kosher meals available, apartment complex with chapel, Santa Claus, Easter Bunny, St. Valentine's Day, Merry Christmas, Happy Easter, mother-in-law suite, bachelor apartment, great view, fourth-floor walkup, walk-in closets, jogging trails, walk to bus stop, nonsmoking, sober, two-bedroom, family room, no bicycles allowed, and quiet streets.

There is still a great deal of confusion as to what HUD will consider discriminatory advertising. Several groups have published lists of terms that are acceptable, that are to be used with caution, or that are to be regarded as discriminatory. However, clearance through one of these lists does not mean that HUD will not regard the language as discriminatory. One problem is that words have different connotations within different groups, as well as regional differences. The authors have evaluated numerous lists. We particularly like the "Fair Housing Advertising Word and Phrase List" developed by the Miami Valley Fair Housing Center, Inc., Dayton, Ohio (*www.mvfairhousing.com*).

There are some exemptions to the Civil Rights Act of 1968. Understand that the following exemptions apply to the Civil Rights Act of 1968, but they are not exemptions under the Civil Rights Act of 1866:

■ Religious groups, which can discriminate in providing nonprofit housing, provided that the religion is open to all, regardless of race, sex, color, or national origin;

■ Private clubs, which can discriminate or give preference to members when selling or leasing housing for noncommercial purposes;

■ Owners of single-family homes, who can discriminate when selling or renting without an agent, provided that they do not own more than three such homes and are not in the business of renting; and

■ Owners of one to four residential units who occupy a unit can discriminate, provided an agent is not used in renting.

The *1988 Fair Housing Amendments Act* extended protection in regard to familial status and the handicapped.

1988 Fair Housing Amendments Act.   This important law extended federal protection against housing discrimination to include **familial status** and handicapped persons. It also strengthened the enforcement mechanisms and gave HUD greater enforcement power.

The real estate agent should also be aware that adult-only designations are no longer possible, although there are exceptions to this rule. Housing units where 80 percent of the units are occupied by at least one person aged 55 years or older are subject to exemption.

Even if an apartment complex has a family section, designation of an area as all-adult still is prohibited. Steering prospective tenants toward a particular area in an apartment complex and away from another area also violates the act.

Apartments can have rules for children's use of facilities when there is a nondiscriminatory reason for the difference in rules. The Civil Rights Act of 1968 does not prohibit owners from setting maximum occupancy of units as long as the rule is enforced without discrimination. (It is likely that unreasonably limited occupancy rules would be unenforceable as it would discriminate against families with children.)

Discrimination against the handicapped is prohibited. *Handicapped* refers to both mentally and physically handicapped persons. AIDS is considered a handicap under the act, so landlords and sellers cannot discriminate against a person with AIDS or HIV infection. The law specifically prohibits discrimination against guide dogs and support animals. Landlords cannot require additional security deposits because of these animals.

Property managers should be aware that the handicapped must be allowed to alter their units as well as common areas if such alterations are necessary for reasonable use and enjoyment of the premises. The property manager cannot increase the security deposit because of these alterations. However, the landlord *can* require that the tenant agree to put the premises back as they originally were if an able-bodied person would not wish the alterations to remain.

FIGURE 2.2

Equal Housing Opportunity Poster

U.S. Department of Housing and Urban Development

EQUAL HOUSING
OPPORTUNITY

We Do Business in Accordance With the Federal Fair Housing Law

(The Fair Housing Amendments Act of 1988)

It is Illegal to Discriminate Against Any Person Because of Race, Color, Religion, Sex, Handicap, Familial Status, or National Origin

---

- ■ In the sale or rental of housing or residential lots
- ■ In advertising the sale or rental of housing
- ■ In the financing of housing

- ■ In the provision of real estate brokerage services
- ■ In the appraisal of housing
- ■ Blockbusting is also illegal

Anyone who feels he or she has been discriminated against may file a complaint of housing discrimination:
   1-800-669-9777 (Toll Free)
   1-800-927-9275 (TDD)

**U.S. Department of Housing and
Urban Development
Assistant Secretary for Fair Housing and
Equal Opportunity
Washington, D.C. 20410**

Previous editions are obsolete

form HUD-928.1A(8-93)

Brokers should prominently display the Equal Housing Opportunity poster (Figure 2.2) in all rental offices. Failure of the broker to post this poster in his or her place of business can shift the burden of proof to the broker to prove that an act was nondiscriminatory under federal law, should a complaint be made.

FIGURE 2.3

Reasonable Modifications to Public Facilities or Services

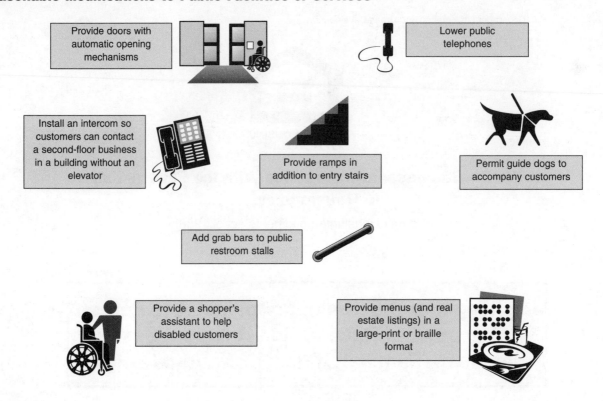

Provide doors with automatic opening mechanisms

Lower public telephones

Install an intercom so customers can contact a second-floor business in a building without an elevator

Provide ramps in addition to entry stairs

Permit guide dogs to accompany customers

Add grab bars to public restroom stalls

Provide a shopper's assistant to help disabled customers

Provide menus (and real estate listings) in a large-print or braille format

Americans with Disabilities Act. The Americans with Disabilities Act (ADA) prohibits discrimination that would deny the equal enjoyment of goods, services, facilities, and accommodations in any existing place of public accommodation, based on an individual's physical or mental disabilities. A "place of public accommodation" applies to stores, offices, and other nonresidential, commercial facilities open to the public.

Owners and operators of such establishments (including property management firms) must make the facilities accessible to the extent readily achievable. (See Figure 2.3.) "Readily achievable" is defined as *easily accomplished without a great deal of expense.* This would be based on the cost of compliance related to property values and on the financial abilities of the person(s) involved. New construction must be readily accessible unless it is structurally impractical.

The ADA also applies to employment discrimination. Employers having 15 or more employees must alter their workplaces to provide reasonable accommodations for handicapped employees unless it creates an undue hardship on the business.

Compliance for a real estate office might consist of designating parking spaces for the handicapped, ramping curbs, adding railings on steps, lowering counters, creating wider aisles between desks, etc.

The act provides for civil penalties of $50,000 for the first discriminatory act and $100,000 for each subsequent violation, including compensatory damages and attorneys' fees.

California Fair Housing Laws

California has several fair housing laws as well as administrative regulations dealing with discrimination. A single act could be a violation of more than one state and/or federal law or regulation.

> The Unruh Act applies to business discrimination.

Unruh Act.   The **Unruh Act** prohibits discrimination in all business establishments. The Unruh Act applies to real estate brokers, salespersons, and anyone managing an apartment building or other business establishment.

The fine for noncompliance with this act includes personal damages plus $250. The act has been expanded to apply to age discrimination in rental apartments and condominium properties. Housing developed and designed for the special needs of senior citizens is exempt from this act.

Rumford Fair Housing Act.   The **Fair Employment and Housing Act**, also known as the Rumford Act (Government Code Sections 12900 et seq.), prohibits discrimination in supplying housing accommodations on the basis of sex, color, race, religion, marital status, ancestry, or national origin. Anyone selling, renting, leasing, or financing housing must comply with the Rumford Act.

AT HOME WITH DIVERSITY

In today's market, the average real estate agent no longer reflects the typical buyer. In recognition of our rapidly changing national demographics, the National Association of REALTORS® and the U. S. Department of Housing and Urban Development created the "At Home With Diversity" program to expand home ownership opportunities for more Americans by training real estate professionals to actively and aggressively seek out potential home buyers from all racial and cultural backgrounds. Licensees who take this **diversity training** program, sponsored by NAR, will

■ learn how attending diverse cultural and community events can expand their client base,

■ find out how simple multicultural etiquette can lead to success with new clients and customers, and

■ develop sound diversity strategies to incorporate into their overall business plan.

An individual violating any part of this act may be reported to the Fair Employment Practices Commission within 60 days of the occurrence. The Rumford Act predated the Civil Rights Act of 1968. Rumford Act violations are also violations of the federal act.

The California Business and Professions Code

The California Business and Professions Code govern real estate licensees' behavior, in addition to federal and state fair housing laws. The code provides detailed antidiscrimination material, including a definition of the term *discrimination* as used within the code, and sections detailing behavioral guidelines for licensees and grounds for disciplinary action in cases of noncompliance.

Section 125.6: Disciplinary Provisions for Discriminatory Acts

Under Section 125.6, every person who holds a license under the provisions of the code is subject to disciplinary action if he or she refuses to perform the licensed activity or makes any discrimination or restriction in the performance of the licensed activity because of an applicant's race, color, sex, religion, ancestry, physical handicap, or national origin.

Section 10177(l): Further Grounds for Disciplinary Action

Discrimination occurs if a licensee "solicited or induced the sale, lease, or the listing for sale or lease, of residential property on the ground, wholly or in part, of loss of value, increase in crime, or decline of the quality of the schools, due to the presence or prospective entry into the neighborhood of a person or persons of another race, color, religion, ancestry, or national origin."

Section 2780: Discriminatory Conduct

Prohibited discriminatory conduct by real estate licensees based on race, color, sex, religion, physical handicap or national origin includes

a. refusing to negotiate for the sale, rental or financing;
b. refusing or failing to show, rent, sell, or finance;
c. discriminating against any person in the sale or purchase, collection of payments, performance of services;
d. discriminating in the conditions or privileges/of sale rental or financing;
e. discriminating in processing applications, referrals, assigning licenses;
f. representing real property as not available for inspection;
g. processing an application more slowly;
h. making any effort to encourage discrimination;
i. refusing to assist another licensee;
j. making an effort to obstruct, retard, or discourage a purchase;
k. expressing or implying a limitation, preference, or discrimination;
l. coercing, intimidating, threatening, or interfering;
m. soliciting restrictively;
n. maintaining restrictive waiting lists;
o. seeking to discourage or prevent transactions;
p. representing alleged community opposition;
q. representing desirability of particular properties;
r. refusing to accept listings;

s. agreeing not to show property;

t. advertising in a manner that indicates discrimination;

u. using wording that indicates preferential treatment;

v. advertising selectively;

w. maintaining selective pricing, rent, cleaning, or security deposits;

x. financing in a discriminatory manner;

y. discriminating in pricing;

z. discriminating in services;

aa. discriminating against owners, occupants, guests;

ab. making an effort to encourage discrimination;

ac. implementing discriminatory rule in multiple listings and other services; and

ad. assisting one who intends to discriminate

Section 2781: Panic Selling

Section 2781 prohibits discriminatory conduct that creates fear or alarm to induce sale or lease because of the entry into an area of persons of another race, color, sex, religion, ancestry, or national origin.

Section 2782: Duty To Supervise

A broker shall take reasonable steps to be familiar with, and to familiarize his or her salespersons with, the federal and state laws pertaining to prohibition of discriminatory process.

The Holden Act (Housing Financial Discrimination Act of 1977). The Holden Act prohibits financial institutions from engaging in discriminatory loan activities or practices. Activities covered under this act include awarding building, improvement, purchase, or refinancing loans using the criteria of race, color, national origin, ancestry, sex, religion, or marital status. Discrimination based on the ethnic composition of the area surrounding a property (*redlining*) is also illegal.

■ COMMISIONER'S RULES AND REGULATIONS

Article 10 of the Real Estate Commissioner's Rules and Regulations concerns the discriminatory activities of real estate licensees. Regulations 2780, 2781, and 2782, contained within Article 10 (summarized above), list unacceptable discriminatory practices by licensees. Regulation 2780 indicates that discriminatory conduct by real estate licensees is a basis for disciplinary action by the Commissioner.

Licensees must be color-blind in their relations with owners as well as prospective buyers and tenants. Anything less is a violation of the law as well as just "bad business."

■ SEXUAL HARASSMENT

In today's workplace, you must be cognizant of what could be regarded by others as being **sexual harassment.** Charges of sexual harassment could result in legal expenses and significant damage awards or settlement costs. Sexual harassment can be defined by *how your actions are viewed by others*, not necessarily by your intent.

Besides the costs involved, a claim of sexual harassment can adversely affect your working relationship with others. This would include coworkers, and agents in other offices, as well as buyers and sellers.

> Jokes, remarks, and touching might be regarded by others as sexual harassment.

Always conduct yourself in a businesslike manner. The only needs of others that you try to fulfill must be those relating to real estate.

In general, observe the following:

- Avoid sexually oriented jokes and anecdotes. Don't use "cute" double-meaning terms. Never discuss your love life or that of others in the workplace.

- Avoid patting, hugging, and touching others. What you might regard as a sign of "friendship" might be regarded differently by others.

- Allow others space. While in some cultures it is acceptable to talk to others with your face just inches from the other person, many people regard this closeness as intimidating and/or sexual harassment.

- Avoid romantic overtures or entanglements in the workplace.

- Avoid asking a coworker for a date. If repeated on numerous occasions, it could be regarded as harassment. If a romantic relationship gets started in the workplace, a difficult working relationship will normally be the result should it end.

If a buyer or seller seems to be inviting sexual advances, ignore the signals. You could be wrong, and if you are, you could find yourself facing a charge of sexual harassment.

■ TRUST FUNDS

When a broker receives funds for a transaction, the broker must, within three days of receipt of the funds, do one of the following:

1. Give the funds to the principal.

2. Deposit the funds directly into escrow.

3. Place the funds in the broker's trust account.

Holding the funds without authorization would be **commingling,** a violation of the real estate law. (The broker can hold a check uncashed at the direction of the buyer before acceptance of an offer and at the direction of the seller after acceptance.)

It is important that **trust funds** be handled properly. Improprieties regarding trust funds are the number one reason for disciplinary action against real estate licensees. Some general rules for trust funds include the following:

- Accounts must be balanced daily and reconciled with bank records monthly.

- Accounts must be demand deposits (noninterest bearing that can be withdrawn without notice) with the exception that accounts may be kept in an interest-bearing account with a federally insured lender at the direction of the owner of the funds. The broker may not benefit as to interest earned.

- A broker may keep no more than $200 of broker funds in the trust account.

- Earned commissions must be withdrawn from the account within 30 days.

- Columnar records must be kept (double entry) with separate records for each beneficiary and transaction.

- The account must be open for inspection by the Department of Real Estate.

- Records must be kept for three years.

CASE EXAMPLES

The following case examples are included to help you understand how ethics applies to you and to help you recognize your responsibilities regarding fair housing.

Case Example 1

Broker McIntosh realized that Henry Higgins was extremely naive about financial matters. While McIntosh almost always charged a 6 percent commission for similar residential property, when she filled out the listing for Higgins's home, she wrote "11 percent" in the commission block. She did, however, explain to Higgins that her fee was 11 percent and provided Higgins an estimate of what he would receive based on a sale at the list price, which was realistically set. Analyze McIntosh's actions from an ethical perspective.

Analysis 1

Legally, McIntosh did nothing wrong. Commissions are negotiable and she simply negotiated to her advantage.

Ethically, there are some problems. McIntosh charged almost twice her customary fee for the service, not because of problems the property presented but because she thought she could. This action certainly would not pass the test of the Golden Rule. How do you suppose McIntosh would feel if she found that a mechanic charged her an exorbitant fee for a simple adjustment to her vehicle because she was naive about mechanical matters?

A more interesting ethical question arises regarding other owners who have listed similar property with McIntosh for 6 percent commission. With an 11 percent listing, other salespeople as well as McIntosh will likely give priority to the Higgins listing, which could work to the detriment of the other owners. They would, in effect, have a second-tier listing in terms of sales effort. Therefore, applying the Golden Rule from the perspective of other owners also indicates that the 11 percent commission is unethical.

There could be circumstances, however, in which a higher-than-normal commission is justified. These could include property that requires greater sales effort as well as situations in which a quick sale is essential to protect the owner's interests, for example, a pending foreclosure.

Case Example 2

Tom Huang wanted to buy a lot in Sunrise Estates. While there were several dozen vacant lots in the subdivision, none currently had For Sale signs. Tom contacted Omni Realty and met with Salesperson Upton. Upton told Tom that if a lot could be purchased in Sunrise Estates, she would find it.

By use of tax records, Upton contacted owners of the vacant lots and asked them if they wanted to sell their lots. Owner Pike was receptive to the idea of a sale and indicated he would sell if he could net $25,000. Upton knew the lots were worth between $35,000 and $45,000, so she purchased it for $25,000. She then contacted Tom Huang and told him about the lot and that she was now the owner. Huang was delighted and agreed to buy the lot for $42,500. Upton never revealed the transaction to her broker. What ethical problems are raised by this case?

Analysis 2

Tom Huang could reasonably assume that Upton was working on his behalf when she agreed to locate a lot for him. Instead, Upton acted on her own behalf; she purchased a lot for herself and offered it to Huang at a higher price as a principal.

While Huang may have been comfortable with Upton's purchase and may not have objected to the price, what started as a clear buyer's agency relationship was unilaterally changed by Upton to her own benefit. Tom Huang paid more for the lot than he should have, had Upton been properly serving him. Upton had no duty to disclose to Pike that she felt the price was too low or that she had a buyer whom she believed would pay more money. Upton was not Pike's agent.

Although Huang had contacted Upton through Omni Realty, she turned what was originally contemplated as a brokerage situation into her own purchase and sale for profit. She in fact deprived her broker of a commission by her self-serving actions. Application of the Golden Rule would indicate unethical conduct on the part of Upton.

Case Example 3

Broker Zwerik was a member of a listing service. While Zwerik almost always submitted his listings to the service, whenever he took a high-value listing that was also highly salable, he would recommend to the owner that for the owner's protection it would be best that Zwerik Realty be the only firm allowed to show the property. He would then cross out the listing authorization to cooperate with other agents and to give the listing to a listing service. He had the owner initial these modifications.

When other agents called Zwerik about his signs or ads on the property, Zwerik would tell them that the owner had specified in writing that only his firm would be allowed to show the property and that the listing information should not be given to any other agent. Was Zwerik's conduct proper?

Analysis 3

Broker Zwerik wants to be able to sell other office listings and wants other offices to help in the sale of most of his listings. But when he takes a listing that offers a substantial commission and is exceptionally desirable, the spirit of cooperation ends. The reason he persuades owners that he alone be allowed to show the property is based solely on the value and salability of the listing, not on the owner's best interests. Apply the Golden Rule: Would Zwerik want other brokers to withhold their better listings from him and give him only properties less likely to be sold? The answer is obvious. Broker Zwerik is guilty of unethical conduct.

In addition, keeping a listing off a listing service reduces the likelihood of a sale. Even for a highly salable listing, it is unethical because it is not in the best interest of Zwerik's client. Zwerik clearly misrepresented the reason to exclude other agents.

Case Example 4

Mr. and Mrs. Jones and their two small children call at your office inquiring about a three-bedroom condominium that you have advertised. The unit is in a six-unit complex and is four years old. While you had intended to show the prospective buyers other units as well, it's love at first sight and they want to buy the unit advertised. You know that Tom Sinn lives in the unit next to the unit that is for sale. Sinn's well-publicized child molestation conviction was recently set aside by a higher court that ruled the photos taken from Sinn's home were illegally obtained and should not have been allowed admissible as evidence. What should you do?

Analysis 4

To fail to inform Mr. And Mrs. Jones about their next door neighbor could subject their children to danger. Application of the Golden Rule would require disclosure even though disclosure is not required by law. The answer would be in the gray area if the prospective buyers had no children because visitors are a possibility.

There is another problem as to the agent's duty to the owners. The owners must be told if you will be disclosing information as to the neighbor and why. Since disclosure will materially affect the chances of a sale or sale price, you should consider offering the owners the opportunity to cancel the listing.

Case Example 5

Salesperson Garcia was contacted by a representative of an organization for the developmentally disabled. The representative was looking for a group home with at least five bedrooms on a large lot. Checking the multiple listings, Garcia discovered that three homes were currently available that met the location, price, and size criteria of the organization. One of these homes was on the same block as the home of Garcia's broker, Douglas LaRue. Garcia contacted LaRue, who told her to show the other two homes to her prospect but not the home on his block because he thought he had a buyer for it.

What ethical issues are raised by this case?

Analysis 5

Garcia should have treated the prospective buyer as any other buyer. By contacting her broker before she showed the properties, Garcia was, in effect, saying, "What do I do if they want to live near you?" She was assuming that these citizens should be treated differently from other buyers, for example, a large family looking for a large house. Garcia's conduct does not pass the test of the Golden Rule.

If broker La Rue did not want the house shown because he felt that it could take away a sale he was going to make, then La Rue is not treating Garcia fairly. The Golden Rule would seem to dictate that until sold, everyone should have an equal opportunity to sell it. There is also an ethical problem as to the owner in that La Rue is withholding a potential buyer from the property. It is the owner's best interests that the property be available to all prospective buyers.

If Broker La Rue directed the home on his block not be shown because he believed that presence of developmentally disabled citizens would be a detriment to his neighborhood, it would clearly be unethical because he is willing to locate them close to someone else and to profit on the sale. This certainly would not pass the test of the Golden Rule.

LaRue and Garcia were likely in violation of the 1988 Amendment to the Civil Rights Act of 1968 in discriminating against the disabled by refusing to tell the organization about an available home.

Case Example 6

Henrietta Jackson, a single African American woman, inquired about an apartment with a For Rent sign. The manager showed her a vacant 3-bedroom, 2½ bath unit. The manager told her the rent was $1,450 per month. She was told to think it over, and if she decided that she wanted the apartment she should contact the manager, who would give her a rental application.

Gomer Clyde, a single white male, inquired about apartments one hour after Henrietta Jackson left. He was shown the three-bedroom apartment, which he was told was the only current vacancy. He was informed that in four days a studio apartment would be available at $500 per month and a 1-bedroom apartment would be available in about 40 days for $750 per month. The manager took Clyde back to her office, where she showed him diagrams of the floor plans of the two additional apartments.

She asked Clyde which of the three apartments best met his needs. When Clyde indicated that he liked the studio apartment best, the manager handed him an application and said, "Fill out this application now and give me a deposit check for $100. I will call you tomorrow to let you know if your application has been approved." Is there a problem with the actions of the manager?

Analysis 6

It appears that the apartment manager violated the Unruh Act (discrimination by a business), the Rumford Act, probably the Civil Rights Act of 1866, certainly the Civil Rights Act of 1968, and the Commissioner's Regulations.

The two prospective renters were treated differently. Whether the discrimination was because she was a single woman or because she was African American, Jackson was discriminated against. It was illegal as well as unethical.

While Jackson was not denied a rental, she was not told about upcoming vacancies that would better meet her needs. This information was volunteered to Clyde, a single white male.

Jackson was told to think about the unit and contact the manager about a rental application if she was interested. The manager not only did not try to sell her on the units, but the manager's conduct was likely to discourage a rental application. On the other hand, the manager used good sales techniques to get Clyde to submit an application and pay his deposit on the first visit.

While the discrimination in this case is certainly more subtle than discrimination encountered by African Americans and single women in the past, nevertheless, disparate treatment is discrimination.

Case Example 7

A country home had been the scene of a horrible crime that had drawn national attention. The home had been boarded up for a number of years, but the present owner has just finished decorating the home and has placed it on the market through your firm. Your broker tells all the agents, "The law does not require disclosure of a death from any cause after three years," implying that the crime need not be mentioned to prospective buyers.

You show the house to a family that is moving to the area due to a job transfer. They have three small children, and they love the huge yard and bright and cheery rooms. Because of the very reasonable list price, they want to put in an offer right away. What do you do?

Analysis 7

This is an example of "when in doubt—disclose." While California law does not mandate a disclosure after three years, place yourself in the shoes of the buyers. Consider how it would affect your peace of mind as well as that of your children (if any) when you learned the past history of the house. The application of the Golden Rule clearly indicates that while nondisclosure is legal, in this case it also could be unethical.

The owner should have been informed at the time of listing that your office would disclose the crime to any prospective buyers before an offer was taken.

The broker's action seemed to encourage nondisclosure by relying on the letter of the law. In this case such action appears unethical.

Case Example 8

Henry Shibata of Shibata Realty managed a small commercial building in a stable neighborhood of middle-class homes. The building had been vacant for more than six months, and the owner was concerned about the loss of income.

Shibata received a deposit and a lease from Ms. Corcoran, who wished to lease the building for ten years. The rent specified was higher than the rent being asked for the property. Shibata knew that Corcoran was one of the largest owner/operators of adult bookstores in the region. The lease provision regarding use read, "Any legal purpose." An adult bookstore was not in violation of the current zoning codes, although there were no such stores within a three-mile radius of the property. What should Shibata do?

Analysis 8

Shibata must inform the owner about the lease and about the proposed tenant. He can point out that the presence of an adult bookstore might create a great deal of animosity toward the owner as well as have a possible negative effect on area property values.

If Shibata believes the lease would be detrimental to the community and the owner wants to accept it, an ethical approach would be to ask to be relieved from the management contract.

However, if he believes that even though the presence of the business would hurt the area, First Amendment rights of free speech should be paramount and Corcoran should not be stifled, then handling the lease would be ethical conduct.

Case Example 9

Salesperson Chan kept a tape recorder on the front seat of his car. He used the tape recorder to record ideas and information on properties. Each night he would go through the recorded comments and enter items in his daily planner, write letters, or make notations on listings if appropriate.

When reviewing his notes, Chan realized that he must have inadvertently turned his recorder on when he left the car to make a telephone call while showing listings to prospects that day. The conversation indicated that his prospective buyers were excited about a property and that unless they found something they liked better that day, they would submit an offer of $185,000 on the house. If the owner countered, they would accept the counteroffer because they were willing to pay up to the list price of $210,000. The prospects had made a $185,000 offer, and Chan was scheduled to meet with the owners to present the offer the following morning. The offer made it clear that Chan was the sole agent of the seller. What should Chan do?

Analysis 9

As soon as he realized that the conversation was not his, Chan should have stopped listening and erased that portion of the tape. Continuing to listen to what was clearly a private conversation has to be considered unethical. The question is, however, what does Chan do now?

Regardless of the type of agency involved, Chan should contact the prospective buyers and tell them about the tape. He could also tell the buyers that his discovery of their intentions was tantamount to having received the information in confidence. Therefore, he would not reveal it to the sellers because to do so would breach that confidence. Chan also could tell the buyers that if they were uncomfortable with this, they could revoke their offer any time prior to acceptance.

Chan should tell the sellers that he inadvertently recorded a private conversation of the buyers relating to the offer. Because he was, in effect, eavesdropping in listening to the recording, he could not reveal any part of the conversation.

If the information had come to Chan from another source, such as a remark by a friend of the buyers, then Chan would have a duty to disclose the information to the owners.

Case Example 10

Broker Esposito has his office in the small town where he lives. The local high school recently was destroyed by fire. Because the structure was supposed to be "fireproof," the school board had no insurance on the structure. The students are now being bused to five other community high schools. The bus rides for the students range from 40 minutes to almost two hours each way.

A special bond election is coming up for a citizens' vote to provide funds for a new high school. The additional tax burden on the largely low-income and middle-income residents will be significant. Esposito has talked to several retirees who have indicated that they will have to sell their homes and move elsewhere if the bond passes.

The local real estate association has asked for a vote to assess members a special fee to fight against the bond issue because it feels the issue will depress local property values, cause people to move to nearby lower-taxed communities, and increase residential and commercial vacancies.

Esposito voted to assess members and to fight the bond issue. Were his actions ethical?

Analysis 10

This case is unusual because a vote either way could be ethical or unethical, based on the reasons for the vote.

If Esposito's vote were based on the fact that a bond issue would personally hurt his business, although he believed it was necessary for the long-term growth of the community, then his vote would be ethically wrong.

If he voted for the assessment because he felt that the damage to retirees and the community as a whole outweighed having a community high school and the long bus rides, then such a vote would be ethically correct.

Similarly, if Esposito had opposed the assessment, the ethics of his opposition would be based on his reasons. As an example, if Esposito believed the bond issue would be bad for the community and create hardships far beyond the benefits but favored a bond because he had nine children in school, then his decision would be self-serving, and voting against the assessment could be unethical.

Esposito could also have ethically voted against an assessment or bond position based on the belief that the real estate association should not be involved in local political decisions.

Case Example 11

J. LaMont, a mortgage broker, has 14 licensees working at his firm. Most of the loans arranged by LaMont are with a particular institutional lender. The lender currently requires that the borrower pay one point to obtain the quoted rate. LaMont is allowed to keep any overage that he is able to obtain. LaMont splits the overage equally with his salespeople. To determine how he could maximize income, LaMont analyzed loans arranged over the past six months. He discovered that points charged for loans averaged out as follows:

■ Loans over $200,000 = 1.1 points

■ Loans for $125,000 to $200,000 = 1.35 points

■ Loans under $125,000 = 1.64 points

He also discovered that points paid by borrowers varied by race. LaMont's results indicated the following:

■ Caucasians = 1.17 points

■ Mexican Americans = 1.62 points

■ African Americans = 1.73 points

Do these results indicate any ethical problems?

Analysis 11

From the facts it appears that LaMont's staff is targeting minorities and less affluent borrowers for disparate treatment. They appear to be taking advantage of these borrowers by quoting and/or insisting on more points than others are paying. Apparently, LaMont's employees are taking the position that, "We will get what the market will bear."

A person applying for a loan would ordinarily believe that the terms quoted are the same for everyone and are not based on race or other factors. The fact that this is not a level playing field does not pass the test of the Golden Rule. Obtaining a loan should not be like buying a used car. Buyers of used cars know that everything is negotiable. Most borrowers wrongfully believe that they are required to pay what is quoted.

While the agents' intent may not have been to discriminate, that is the result.

Case Example 12

Broker Thall owns Thall Mortgage Company. About 20 percent of his loans failed to close because of appraisals that were significantly below the purchase prices. The broker for Big Realty Company, which gave Thall Mortgage Company about one-half of its business by their referrals, told Thall that the appraiser would have to do better or he would find a more cooperative mortgage company.

Broker Thall told its appraiser, Adam Fine, that appraisals had to more realistically reflect the marketplace. There were too many appraisals below the purchase prices. Adam Fine told Broker Thall that what a single buyer was willing to pay did not change the fair market value. He indicated that he had data to strongly support all of his valuations and had followed the Uniform Standards of Professional Appraisal Practice (USPAP).

Broker Thall stopped using Adam Fine and now uses Willard Fast for the appraisals. For the last 132 appraisals over a two-year period, not a single one has come in under the contract purchase price. What if any are the problems in this case?

Analysis 12

The broker for Big Realty acted unethically in trying to induce Broker Thall to act in an unethical and illegal manner. Big Realty also disregarded the interests of their buyers. (If there was a buyer agency or dual agency, they would have breached that agency to the buyer.)

In trying to influence Adam Fine, Broker Thall was encouraging appraisals related to contract prices not necessarily fair market value.

This could be a fraud on both the borrower and the lender who would be led to believe that the appraisal fairly reflected fair market value. If the lender was federally insured, it would be a federal crime as well as unethical behavior. Foreclosures could result in lender losses because of inflated appraisals and loans.

Willard Fast apparently understood the game that was being played and had agreed to do what was expected of him instead of following the Uniform Standards of Professional Appraisal Practice (USPAP).

■ SUMMARY

Ethics differs from the law because the law sets minimum standards of acceptable conduct, whereas ethics deals in what is right. The test for determining if an action is ethical is the Golden Rule.

The National Association of REALTORS® and the National Association of Real Estate Brokers have developed ethical codes to promote professionalism in the real estate industry.

Federal Fair Housing legislation began with the Civil Rights Act of 1866, which applied to racial discrimination. The Civil Rights Act of 1870 reiterated the 1866 act. The Civil Rights Act of 1964 elevated a 1962 executive order into law. The act prohibited housing discrimination when there was any government assistance or involvement. The Civil Rights Act of 1968 expanded discriminatory protection to include national origin, color, and religion, as well as race. By amendment the act has been extended to sex, physical handicaps, and familial status. The act specifically prohibits steering (that is, directing persons to housing based on race), blockbusting (obtaining listings or sales based on the fear of loss in value because minority group members are entering the area), and redlining (refusing to loan within a certain area).

The Americans with Disabilities Act requires that owners and operators of places of public accommodations make the premises accessible to the extent readily achievable.

Diversity training programs aid licensees in understanding the customs and culture of other peoples, as well as the motivations in their decision making process. The National Association of REALTORS® has developed a diversity training program.

The Unruh Act is a California act that prohibits discrimination by a business establishment. The Rumford Act is considered to be California's Fair Housing Act. The Holden Act prohibits financial institutions from engaging in discriminatory practices, and the California Business and Professions Code and the Real Estate Commissioner's Rules and Regulations provides details regarding discriminatory practices of California real estate licensees.

Trust funds must be protected and kept separate from broker funds. Records must be kept for each beneficiary and transaction.

■ CLASS DISCUSSION TOPICS

1. Without giving names, discuss any ethical problems you have observed in the real estate industry.

2. You have just brought in a cash deposit for which your broker gave you a receipt. Later, you find a duplicate deposit slip on the floor for that exact amount for deposit into a personal account of your broker. What should you do?

3. Salesman Rutkowski was showing a couple a home in a beautiful subdivision. Rutkowski took a route to the property that added three miles to the trip in order to avoid driving through a racially mixed housing area that contained many structures in need of repair. Discuss the ethics of Rutkowski's actions.

4. Broker Shimato was handling the grand opening of Big Town Estates. To emphasize the desirability of the property, Shimato sent out a press release indicating that 71 of the 400 homes to be built were sold before the grand opening. At the grand opening the model of the subdivision showed sold flags on a large number of sites. Actually, Shimato had only three advance sales. Analyze Shimato's actions from an ethical standpoint.

5. Salesperson Sven Petersen took a listing for $289,500, although his competitive market analysis indicated a sale price between $195,000 and $210,000. Sven's broker, Olaf Petersen, told Sven to "start working on the owner to reduce the price." He told Sven, "It isn't a good listing now, but it will be one in a few months. Anyway, any listing is better than no listing." Discuss ethical problems raised by this case, if any.

6. In Britain, the National Association of Estate Agents (a real estate professional organization) considers contacting bereaved relatives of a deceased person to obtain sales inventory to be an unethical practice. Do you agree? Why?

7. Billie Bob Smith built a model home for his new subdivision. His newspaper ads showed an artist's rendering that made the home appear much larger than it was. In small letters the ad stated "Not To Scale."

   The price printed next to the drawing was $89,500. The small asterisk at the bottom of the page said "Plus Lot." The model itself, which had a sign

FIGURE 2.4

Top Ten Enforcement Violations

The following is a list of the top ten violations of the Real Estate Law that are filed by the Department against real estate licensees. All references refer to Sections of the California Business and Professions Code and the Regulations of the Real Estate Commissioner

(1) Trust Fund Record Keeping

Section 10145 – General statute governing the handling of trust funds.

Regulation 2831 – Maintaining columnar records for trust funds received.

Regulation 2831-a – Maintaining separate records for each beneficiary.

Regulation 2831.2 – Performing monthly reconciliation of trust fund accounts.

Regulation 2834 – Allowing unlicensed and unbonded signatories on a trust account.

(2) Trust Fund Shortages

Section 10145 – General statute governing the handling of trust funds.

Regulation 2832 – Trust fund handling.

Regulation 2832.1 – Trust fund shortages.

(3) Section 10176 (e) – Commingling of the broker's property with the money or property of others which is being held by the broker.

(4) Section 10177 (d) – Willful disregard or violation of the real estate law.

(5) Section 10177 (h) – As a real estate broker, failed to exercise reasonable supervision over the activities of salespersons, or as the officer of a corporation failed to exercise reasonable supervision over the activities conducted by the corporation for which a real estate license is required.

(6) Section 10127 – Unlawful employment or payment to an unlicensed individual or to a real estate salesperson who is not employed by the broker.

(7) Section 10176 (a) – Making a substantial misrepresentation in a transaction for which a real license is required.

(8) Section 10176 (i) – Conduct which constitutes fraud or dishonest dealing in a transaction for which a real estate license is required.

(9) Section 10177 (j) – Conduct which constitutes fraud or dishonest dealing in a transaction while not acting in the capacity of a real estate licensee.

(10) Section 10130 – Unlicensed activity.

The above-referenced violations are the most frequently sited by the Department for conduct engaged in while acting in the capacity of a real estate licensee, or while engaged in a real estate transaction as a principal. In addition to these violations, individuals are very often either denied licenses or disciplined by the Department for violation of Section 10176 (a), failing to disclose a criminal conviction on an application for licensure, and being convicted of a substantially related criminal offense Section 10177 (b).

"From $89,500," included upgraded carpets, tile, cabinetry, landscaping, patio, etc. If a prospect wanted a home just like the model, the price would be $118,450 plus a lot starting at $55,000. Discuss the ethical problems, if any, of Smith's advertising and model home.

8. You are presenting an offer to owners represented by another agent. The offer requires that the owner carry back a second trust deed for $20,000. The other agent tells the owner that the buyer has "ace-high credit, and he has an excellent employment history." You are the selling agent, and you know from prequalifying the buyer that he has had prior credit problems owing to a lengthy period of unemployment; however, he has been working steadily for the past two years and is now up to date on all payments. What should you do?

9. While on caravan viewing new listings, you see another agent from your office, who is also a close friend, slip a small Hummel figurine into her purse. What should you do?

10. Figure 2.4 is a list of the ten most common real estate licensee violations. Which of these reasons are clearly unethical and which could be ethical?

11. Give an example of a broker violation. Using Figure 2.4, what code section was violated?

12. Bring to class one current-events article dealing with some aspect of real estate practice for class discussion.

■ CHAPTER 2 QUIZ

1. Which of the following best describes ethics?
    a. Doing what is legal
    b. Doing what best meets your personal needs
    c. Doing what is right because it is right
    d. Caveat emptor

2. Ethics' relationship to law is that
    a. if an act is illegal it is also unethical.
    b. ethics tends to precede the law.
    c. ethics and the law both set minimum standards for behavior.
    d. what is ethical is legal.

3. Which of the following words would be considered nondiscriminatory in an advertisement for a rental?
    a. Christian family
    b. Prefer working married couple
    c. Just two blocks to St. Michael's
    d. None of the above

4. A broker who had a disabled employee widened the doorway to the restroom to accommodate a wheelchair. This work was performed to comply with the
    a. Unruh Act.
    b. American with Disabilities Act.
    c. Rumford Act.
    d. Fair Housing Amendment Act of 1988.

5. The Civil Rights Act of 1866 specifically covers what type of discrimination?
    a. Sex   c. Marital status
    b. Age   d. Race

6. A broker showed African American prospective buyers homes in African American and racially mixed neighborhoods. He would show African American prospects homes in predominantly Caucasian areas only if the prospects specifically requested to see homes in those areas. The broker's action would be described as
    a. illegal.   c. steering.
    b. unethical.   d. All of the above

7. A broker refused to show a young Hispanic family of five a condominium about which they had inquired. The broker's action would be proper if
    a. the broker considered the unit too small for the family.
    b. there were no other children in the development.
    c. the development has an exemption because all occupants are 55 years of age or older.
    d. 70 percent of the units are occupied by elderly.

8. A landlord can properly refuse to accept an applicant because the applicant
   a. has a guide dog and the apartment is on the fourth floor.
   b. is a single but obviously pregnant woman.
   c. appears to be gay and the landlord is afraid of catching AIDS.
   d. None of the above.

9. The state act that specifically prohibits discrimination in business establishments is the
   a. Unruh Act.
   b. Rumford Act.
   c. Holden Act.
   d. Civil Rights Act of 1968.

10. Which of the following actions dealing in trust funds would be a violation of the law?
    a. Giving trust funds received to a principal
    b. Depsitory trust funds directly into escrow
    c. Placing trust funds in a trust account
    d. Placing trust funds in the personal care of a bonded employee

CHAPTER THREE

3

MANDATORY DISCLOSURES

■ KEY TERMS

agency disclosure
Agent's Inspection
  Disclosure
AIDS disclosure
buyer's agent
common interest
  subdivision
dual agency
earthquake safety
  disclosure
Easton v. Strassburger
Elder Abuse Law
environmental hazards
  disclosure

fiduciary responsibility
fire hazard areas
flood hazard areas
good faith estimate
hazardous waste
  disclosure
home inspection notice
Megan's Law
Mello-Roos Bonds
military ordnance
  location
public report
Real Estate Transfer
  Disclosure Statement

red flag
rescission rights
seller's agent
seller financing
  addendum and
  disclosure
Sick Building Syndrome
smoke detector disclosure
stigmatized property
toxic mold
water heater bracing

■ LEARNING OBJECTIVES

Disclosure is one of the most misunderstood areas in real estate today. Parties often feel that agents have failed to adequately disclose all facts pertaining to a transaction. There are many lawsuits that allege failure to disclose detrimental facts or inadequate disclosures. In this chapter you learn of agent and lender disclosure requirements under the law as well as owner disclosure obligations. A thorough knowledge of these obligations will aid you not only in meeting the needs of buyers and sellers in real estate transactions but also in retaining the goodwill of the parties and in protecting yourself from personal liability.

■ UNDERSTANDING DISCLOSURES

Real estate agents used to say the three main factors in real estate were "location, location, and location." Today they are "disclosure, disclosure, and disclosure." Although the concept of caveat emptor, or "let the buyer beware," has been around for centuries, the past decade or so has seen California legislators, courts, and the Department of Real Estate (DRE) pushing enactment of disclosure laws. Although many agents think these laws are new, in reality real estate law has always stressed full disclosure. However, in the past some agents did not understand what full disclosure meant or when it was necessary to disclose certain circumstances. As a result, buyers and sellers began to take agents to court for nondisclosure. Such court cases became so numerous in certain areas that California legislators and the DRE worked to enact laws and regulations to force agents to disclose certain items. These new laws and regulations have led to increased paperwork for real estate transactions, so agents must be familiar with all aspects of disclosure to complete transactions properly.

The disclosure laws discussed in this chapter primarily involve one- to four-unit residential real property. Also, the information given here is general in nature. In situations involving specific facts, consult your attorney concerning your specific case. To help avoid future disputes and litigation, always disclose the issue in question.

> A *material fact* is any fact that, if disclosed, would affect the decision of an entity in completing the transaction.

Full disclosure means disclosing, or giving notice of, all material facts in a transaction. A *material fact* is any fact that, if disclosed, would affect the decision of an entity (person or persons) in completing (to buy, to sell, etc.) a transaction. Many facets of a property might need to be disclosed to a prospective seller, buyer, or borrower to complete a transaction legally and to secure the financing necessary to purchase the property. The disclosure laws impose obligations not only on real estate licensees but also on the principals to the transaction as well. This is why the agent must consider all of the material facts.

Full disclosure will

- protect the principals (buyers and sellers),

- establish and build trust and confidence between the licensee and principals, and

- satisfy the law.

The agent not only must disclose the information but also must make certain that the principal understands the information and the importance of the information disclosed. Disclosures should be in writing to protect all parties involved.

Certain disclosures are "mandated." A *mandated disclosure* is an item of information required by law to be conveyed from one entity involved in a real estate transaction to another entity in the same transaction. *Information* means some type of material data, facts, news or figures. The phrase *required by law* means some obligation imposed by a legal authority such as the DRE, the state legislature, or a court. *Convey* means to present from one entity (person or persons) to another entity. Thus, a mandated disclosure is simply a material fact obligated by law to be disclosed.

While the latest California Association of REALTORS® forms for listing, purchasing, and leasing property provide for most mandatory disclosures, outdated forms as well as forms produced for national use can result in a failure to properly disclose. You are not excused from disclosure because a form you used did not include or reference the disclosure.

Disclosure obligations in residential real estate sales of one- to four-unit properties are many and varied. Some are mandatory for real estate agents, some for sellers, some for both licensees and principals. At times every agent is in doubt about exactly what to disclose. The general rule is "When in doubt on a particular issue, always disclose."

■ FIDUCIARY RESPONSIBILITY AND DISCLOSURES

When a real estate broker acts as an agent of only the seller or only the buyer, this is called a *single agency*. The dual agency may be utilized only if the buyer and seller are both aware of the situation and approve of the arrangements. Although this type of agency is in common use, many attorneys look on this arrangement as a conflict of interest, "ripe for lawsuits." Real estate agents often carry errors and omissions insurance to help protect against this problem. If the agent represents both the buyer and the seller without the approval of both, he or she is guilty of a divided or dual agency and is in violation of the real estate law (Business and Professions Code 10176(d)).

An agent's **fiduciary responsibility** to his or her principal is one of trust. The agent must be loyal to his or her principal, placing the principal's interests above

Fiduciary duty is one of good faith and trust.

those of the agent. An agent's actions, therefore, cannot be inconsistent with the principal's interests. The agent cannot act in a self-serving manner to the detriment of his or her principal. As an example, assume a buyer's agent in seeking property for a buyer discovered a property meeting the buyer's needs that was bargain priced. If the broker purchased the property to resell at a profit, the broker would be competing with the principal. This would be a breach of fiduciary duty.

In dual agency situations, caution must be exercised so that aiding one principal is not detrimental to the other principal.

The agent's duties to the principal include obedience. The agent must obey the principal's lawful directions. The agent also has a duty of skill and diligence and must diligently exercise his or her skills in the performance of agency duties.

The agent's duty of trust prohibits the agent from revealing confidential information about the principal to others without the consent of the principal. As an example, if a seller's agent revealed to a prospective buyer without the principal's permission that the principal was in serious financial straits, the agent's action would be a violation of the duty of trust. This information could seriously reduce the principal's bargaining ability. It could also encourage an offer at a lower price than was originally intended. Similarly, a buyer's agent could not inform a seller that the buyer had a particular need for the seller's property or that the buyer considered the seller's asking price extremely low.

The fiduciary duty of the agent includes full disclosure of material facts discovered by the agent that the principal would reasonably want to know in making decisions. Full disclosure would likely include the duty to warn a principal of any known dangers, such as possible problems relating to an offer, lease, or option. It also includes a duty to fully and honestly convey information concerning value and market conditions. Again, if there is any doubt as to the material nature of information, disclose.

Duty to Other Party (Nonagency)

Even though you do not represent a buyer or seller in an agency capacity, you still have disclosure duties. For example, you must disclose to the buyer any detrimental information you know concerning a property that might affect its value or desirability to the buyer.

If you realize a buyer is mistaken about a property, you have a duty to let the buyer know the facts. Suppose, for example, that a buyer indicates he wants a site for an automobile repair facility. If you know that the current zoning precludes this use, you have a duty to inform the buyer about the zoning restriction.

If you have knowledge of a problem concerning the property prior to an offer, your disclosure must be prior to the purchase offer. Your duty of disclosure, however, extends beyond the offer and acceptance of the offer. As an example, if you discover a serious structural problem after acceptance of an offer, you have a duty to inform the buyer, as well as the owner, of the problem.

The listing agent has a duty to conduct a diligent visual property inspection.

For one- to four-unit residential property, you have an actual duty to conduct a reasonably diligent visual inspection of the property. (See Agent Inspection Disclosure later in this chapter.) While the law does not require a visual inspection for other than one- to four-unit residential properties, you still have a duty to disclose known detrimental information to the buyer.

Facilitators and Designated Agents

Though not allowed in California, real estate brokers in some states are allowed to work as facilitators or intermediaries. These are third parties who are not agents of either the buyer or the seller; instead they assist the buyer and seller in the transference of real property ownership. They do, however, have a duty to treat all parties fairly and must disclose known defects in a property.

A number of states allow a broker to designate one salesperson as a principal's sole agent. When the listing broker is also the selling broker, the selling salesperson would then be the buyer's sole agent. An advantage of the designated agent concept lies in the fact that it is used to avoid problems often associated with conflicting duties of dual agency. Both buyer and seller have separate agency representation. Again, this agency relationship has not been adopted in California.

■ AGENCY DISCLOSURE

Civil Code Sections 2373-2382, dealing with agency relationships in real estate transactions involving one- to four-unit residential properties, became law on January 1, 1988. Any licensee in a transaction involving residential real property of one unit to four units must disclose his or her agency.

To understand the **agency disclosure**, brokers and salespersons must understand the term *agency*. An agent is one who represents another, called the *principal*, in dealings with a third person(s). Such a representation is called *agency*. The agency disclosure form defines agency as "a person acting under provisions of this title in a real property transaction, [including] a person who is licensed as a real estate broker under Chapter 3 (commencing with Section 10130) of Part 1 of Division 4 of the Business & Professions Code, and under whose license a listing is executed or an offer to purchase is obtained."

The word *agent* is synonymous with *employing broker*. Though it is common in the real estate industry for salespersons to call themselves *real estate agents*, it is important to understand that there is only one agent in a company, the real estate broker, and all agency comes under that person. The law now uses the term *associate licensee*, defined as "a person who is licensed as a real estate salesperson or broker who is either licensed under a broker or has entered into a written contract with a broker to act as the broker's agent and to function under the broker's supervision." There is but one broker per company, and all associate licensees (salespersons) are subagents of that broker.

Brokers and salespersons also must understand the various ways the word *agent* can be used in a real estate transaction. The licensee who lists the seller's home is called the *listing agent*. The licensee who brings the buyer into the transaction is called the *selling agent*. An agent who represents the seller is called the **seller's agent**, and the agent who represents the buyer is called the **buyer's agent**.

When an agent represents a buyer *or* a seller, it is considered a single agency. When an agent represents both buyer *and* seller, it is known as a **dual agency**.

Many brokerage offices have elected single agency. *Single agency* means that they will represent the buyer or seller but not both. Their reason is that they feel duties to both principals in a transaction can create the appearance of a conflict of interest. This can result in lawsuits because of the perception of the parties. Single agency, representing one party to the transaction, reduces the likelihood of misunderstandings.

While the listing agent for a property could be either a seller's sole agent or a dual agent, the selling agent could be a buyer's agent (representing the buyer alone), a seller's agent (representing the seller alone), or a dual agent (representing both buyer and seller). (See Figure 3.1.)

Even in a large company with multiple offices, there still is only one broker. For example, Bigtime Real Estate Company has an office in Los Angeles and another in San Francisco. If the agent from the Los Angeles office lists a property for sale and the agent from the San Francisco office brings in a buyer, whom does each agent represent or owe a fiduciary responsibility to? Does the listing agent exclusively represent the seller and the selling agent exclusively represent the buyer? The agents are under the same employing broker (agency), so either both agents represent the seller or both agents represent both the seller *and* the buyer (dual agency). **Note:** An agent (broker), however, is supposed to get the best and most honest deal for his or her principal. In a dual agency situation the agent is compelled to obtain the highest price and best terms for the seller and also the lowest price and best terms for the buyer. In court it is often hard to convince the jury that a dual agent has accomplished that. This is why full disclosure is extremely important.

Franchise offices are usually independently owned, with a different broker for each independently owned office. Thus, different agents from different offices may not be under the same agency (the same broker). Because the listing associate licensee is from a different office (different agency), the licensee can exclusively represent the seller, and the selling licensee can create an exclusive agency with the buyer. However, under the new law of disclosing agency, all types of agency must be disclosed.

FIGURE 3.1

Agency Relationship

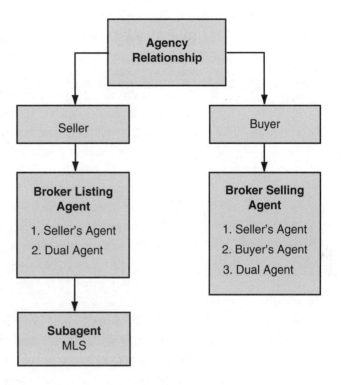

Any associate licensee who acts on behalf of others in selling, buying, exchanging, or leasing real estate creates agency for his or her broker (the agent).

An agent can receive a commission from a seller but still be the buyer's agent. Agency has nothing to do with who pays the commission. Buyer's agents frequently receive their compensation from the sellers.

Agency relationships can be either implied or express. Formalities are not necessarily required to create an agency relationship; the licensee can create an implied agency with a buyer or seller simply through the words used when talking to prospective clients. For example, a court might determine that an implied agency is created when a licensee says to a buyer on the phone, "I have time today to look for property for your specific needs, to help you solve your housing problems." Agency can also be created by an express contract, called a *listing* agreement. (See Chapter 6.)

Remember, once this agency relationship is created, the licensee has a fiduciary relationship with his or her principal. A fiduciary incurs the highest obligations under the law.

The Disclosure Process

The three-step process of disclosing agency can be remembered by using the acronym DEC.

Step 1: Disclose.   This step will be in writing. Using a prescribed disclosure form (Figure 3.2), the licensee must educate his or her principal about the three different types of agents—seller's agent, buyer's agent, and dual agent—and how they operate. After this full disclosure, it is necessary to obtain the principal's signature. In dealing with consumers (buyers) the broker should educate the buyer about agency relationships as soon as possible, provide the potential buyer with the disclosure regarding agency relationships and obtain the buyer's signature.

> The three steps of the disclosure process are Disclose, Elect, and Confirm.

Step 2: Elect.   In this step the agent and principal decide which type of agency will be used. Because circumstances can change with each transaction, it is imperative that the principal and the agent thoroughly understand the implications of the agency roles they agree on and elect. Nothing has to be signed in this step, but care must be taken that both principal and agent enjoy full understanding (disclosure) of the agency elected.

Step 3: Confirm.   The confirmation of the type of agency elected in Step 2 must be in writing. (See Figure 3.2.) The agent and the principal(s) must sign the confirmation statement. Sometimes this confirmation is included as part of the purchase contract (also known as a *deposit receipt*), but it is also available as a separate document. If dual agency is elected, the agent must disclose that fact to both the buyer and the seller because a dual agent needs the consent of both. Because the broker is the agent, it is the broker's responsibility to make certain that proper disclosures have been made.

The selling agent should confirm the agency with the buyer, even if the buyer is not to be represented by an agent.

Timing of Disclosure

When should an agent disclose agency? The Department of Real Estate mandates "as soon as possible," and most offices have a policy manual that addresses the requirement of prompt disclosure. The three steps in the process may be taken at different times. Below are some general ideas on when to disclose, when to elect, and when to confirm.

Listing Agents Not Selling Their Own Listings.   In these cases agents should provide the disclosure to the seller before entering into the listing agreement, elect as soon as is practical, and confirm the agency prior to or coincident with the seller's acceptance of the purchase contract.

Listing Agents Selling Their Own Listings.   In this case the agent should disclose (that he or she is either the seller's exclusive agent or a dual agent of both seller and buyer), elect, and confirm to the seller and buyer as in the preceding transaction.

FIGURE 3.2

Disclosure Regarding Real Estate Agency Relationships

CALIFORNIA
ASSOCIATION
OF REALTORS®

DISCLOSURE REGARDING
REAL ESTATE AGENCY RELATIONSHIPS
(As required by the Civil Code)
(C.A.R. Form AD-11, Revised 10/01)

When you enter into a discussion with a real estate agent regarding a real estate transaction, you should from the outset understand what type of agency relationship or representation you wish to have with the agent in the transaction.

SELLER'S AGENT

A Seller's agent under a listing agreement with the Seller acts as the agent for the Seller only. A Seller's agent or a subagent of that agent has the following affirmative obligations:
To the Seller:
   A Fiduciary duty of utmost care, integrity, honesty, and loyalty in dealings with the Seller.
To the Buyer and the Seller:
   (a) Diligent exercise of reasonable skill and care in performance of the agent's duties.
   (b) A duty of honest and fair dealing and good faith.
   (c) A duty to disclose all facts known to the agent materially affecting the value or desirability of the property that are not known to, or within the diligent attention and observation of, the parties.

An agent is not obligated to reveal to either party any confidential information obtained from the other party that does not involve the affirmative duties set forth above.

BUYER'S AGENT

A selling agent can, with a Buyer's consent, agree to act as agent for the Buyer only. In these situations, the agent is not the Seller's agent, even if by agreement the agent may receive compensation for services rendered, either in full or in part from the Seller. An agent acting only for a Buyer has the following affirmative obligations:
To the Buyer:
   A fiduciary duty of utmost care, integrity, honesty, and loyalty in dealings with the Buyer.
To the Buyer and the Seller:
   (a) Diligent exercise of reasonable skill and care in performance of the agent's duties.
   (b) A duty of honest and fair dealing and good faith.
   (c) A duty to disclose all facts known to the agent materially affecting the value or desirability of the property that are not known to, or within the diligent attention and observation of, the parties.

An agent is not obligated to reveal to either party any confidential information obtained from the other party that does not involve the affirmative duties set forth above.

AGENT REPRESENTING BOTH SELLER AND BUYER

A real estate agent, either acting directly or through one or more associate licensees, can legally be the agent of both the Seller and the Buyer in a transaction, but only with the knowledge and consent of both the Seller and the Buyer.

In a dual agency situation, the agent has the following affirmative obligations to both the Seller and the Buyer:
   (a) A fiduciary duty of utmost care, integrity, honesty and loyalty in the dealings with either the Seller or the Buyer.
   (b) Other duties to the Seller and the Buyer as stated above in their respective sections.

In representing both Seller and Buyer, the agent may not, without the express permission of the respective party, disclose to the other party that the Seller will accept a price less than the listing price or that the Buyer will pay a price greater than the price offered.

The above duties of the agent in a real estate transaction do not relieve a Seller or Buyer from the responsibility to protect his or her own interests. You should carefully read all agreements to assure that they adequately express your understanding of the transaction. A real estate agent is a person qualified to advise about real estate. If legal or tax advice is desired, consult a competent professional.

Throughout your real property transaction you may receive more than one disclosure form, depending upon the number of agents assisting in the transaction. The law requires each agent with whom you have more than a casual relationship to present you with this disclosure form. You should read its contents each time it is presented to you, considering the relationship between you and the real estate agent in your specific transaction.

This disclosure form includes the provisions of Sections 2079.13 to 2079.24, inclusive, of the Civil Code set forth on the reverse hereof. Read it carefully.

I/WE ACKNOWLEDGE RECEIPT OF A COPY OF THIS DISCLOSURE.

BUYER/SELLER _____ Date _____ Time _____ AM/PM

BUYER/SELLER _____ Date _____ Time _____ AM/PM

AGENT _____ By _____ Date _____
         (Please Print)   (Associate-Licensee or Broker Signature)

THIS FORM SHALL BE PROVIDED AND ACKNOWLEDGED AS FOLLOWS (Civil Code §2079.14):
•When the listing brokerage company also represents the Buyer, the Listing Agent shall give one AD-11 form to the Seller and one to the Buyer.
•When Buyer and Seller are represented by different brokerage companies, then the Listing Agent shall give one AD-11 form to the Seller and the Buyer's Agent shall give one AD-11 form to the Buyer and one AD-11 form to the Seller.

SEE REVERSE SIDE FOR FURTHER INFORMATION

R E B S Published and Distributed by:
I N C   REAL ESTATE BUSINESS SERVICES, INC.
         a subsidiary of the CALIFORNIA ASSOCIATION OF REALTORS®
         525 South Virgil Avenue, Los Angeles, California 90020

Reviewed by _____
Broker or Designee _____ Date _____

EQUAL HOUSING
OPPORTUNITY

AD-11 REVISED 10/01 (PAGE 1 OF 1)   Print Date

DISCLOSURE REGARDING REAL ESTATE AGENCY RELATIONSHIPS (AD-11 PAGE 1 OF 1)

Reprinted with permission, California Association of REALTORS®. Endorsement not implied.

Selling Agents Working with a Buyer.   Selling agents who are not listing agents always should disclose as soon as is practical and prior to a buyer's making an offer. As above, they should also elect as soon as is practical and confirm prior to or coincident with a buyer's and a seller's execution of the purchase contract.

Selling Agents Working with a Seller.   Selling agents who are not listing agents should remember to disclose to sellers as soon as is practical. They should elect as soon as is practical and confirm prior to or coincident with a buyer's and a seller's execution of the deposit receipt.

The chart in Figure 3.3 sums up the important information on disclosure that will be found in many offices' policy manuals. Agency Disclosure and Confirmation forms are available on separate sheets or in a combined form (AD-11/AC-6).

■ REAL ESTATE TRANSFER DISCLOSURE

Under current law (California Civil Code Sections 1.102-1.102.14) the purchaser of residential real property (including residential stock cooperative housing) of four units or less is entitled to a **Real Estate Transfer Disclosure Statement** (TDS) from the seller. The term *transfer* refers to sale, exchange, real property sales contract (installment land sales contract), option, lease option, and so forth. Since January 1, 1987, any seller, whether represented by an agent or not, has been required to give to the buyer a written disclosure statement of the condition of the property. The disclosure statement must identify (1) items in the home and whether these items are operational (part A); (2) significant defects of the home, if any (part B); and (3) all information regarding improvements and alterations as well as concerns with neighbors and the neighborhood (part C).

A copy of the form must be delivered to the buyer. If only one agent is involved, that agent must deliver it to the buyer. If two agents are involved, it is the responsibility of the selling agent (the agent who obtained the offer) to deliver it to the buyer. If the seller has not filled out the disclosure statement, the buyer should be notified in writing of the buyer's right to receive such a statement.

Right of Termination

The disclosure statement should be delivered as soon as practical and before the execution of the offer to purchase. If the statement is not delivered before the execution, the buyer has the right to cancel the offer within three days after delivery. To cancel the offer, the buyer must write a notice of termination and deliver it to the seller or seller's agent. The two-page transfer disclosure form is shown in Figure 3.4.

■ AGENT'S INSPECTION DISCLOSURE

Whenever an agent takes a listing on one- to four-unit residential properties, he or she should fill out a Real Estate Transfer Disclosure Statement. Even if the seller is exempt from the transfer disclosure statement requirements—for example,

FIGURE 3.3

Summary of How To Comply with the Agency Legislation for Listing

FOR LISTING AGENTS

WHAT?	WHO?	WHEN?	HOW?
DISCLOSE	Provide disclosure form to seller.	Prior to entering into the listing agreement.	Retain signed copy of disclosure form for your file.
ELECT	Tell seller whether you are seller's agent or dual agent.	As Soon As Practical (ASAP)	Orally or in writing.
CONFIRM	Confirm with seller whether you are seller's agent or dual agent.	Prior to coincident with seller's execution of deposit receipt.	In the deposit receipt or another writing by seller and listing agent.

* Listing agent's relationship with the buyer is discussed below.

FOR AGENTS SELLING THEIR OWN LISTINGS

WHAT?	WHO?	WHEN?	HOW?
DISCLOSE	Provide disclosure form to buyer.	ASAP before buyer executes offer.	Retain signed copy of disclosure form for your file.
ELECT	Tell buyer and seller whether you are seller's agent or dual agent.	ASAP.	Orally or in writing.
CONFIRM	Confirm with buyer and seller whether you are seller's agent or dual agent.	Prior to or coincident with buyer's and seller's execution of deposit receipt.	In the deposit receipt or another writing by buyer, seller and listing agent.

FOR SELLING AGENTS

WHAT?	WHO?	WHEN?	HOW?
DISCLOSE	Provide disclosure form to buyer.	ASAP before buyer executes offer (i.e., after more than a casual, transitory or preliminary inquiry).	Retain signed copy of disclosure form for your file. (1) Obtain signed copy directly from seller or through listing agent or (2) Provide by certified mail to seller.
ELECT	Tell buyer and seller whether you are seller's agent, buyer's agent or dual agent.	ASAP.	Orally or in writing.
CONFIRM	Confirm with buyer and seller whether you are seller's agent, buyer's agent or dual agent.	Prior to or coincident with buyer's and seller's execution of deposit receipt.	In the deposit receipt or another writing by buyer, seller and listing agent.

if the property is being sold to a co-owner—the agent is responsible for conducting an investigation and inspection independent of the seller and for filling out a transfer disclosure statement. The agent uses the same disclosure statement as that in Figure 3.4. Section III of that disclosure statement, the **Agent's Inspection Disclosure**, is to be completed if the seller is represented by a listing agent.

On May 31, 1984, the California State Supreme Court refused to hear the *Easton v. Strassburger* ([1984] 152 Ca.3d 90) case, making the decision of the appellate court case law in California. Under *Easton* a real estate agent was deemed responsible not only for what was known or accessible only to the agent or his or her

FIGURE 3.4

Real Estate Transfer Disclosure Statement

<table>
<tr><td>

CALIFORNIA ASSOCIATION OF REALTORS®

</td><td>

REAL ESTATE TRANSFER DISCLOSURE STATEMENT
(CALFORNIA CIVIL CODE 1102, ET SEQ)
(C.A.R. Form TDS, Revised 10/01)

</td></tr>
</table>

THIS DISCLOSURE STATEMENT CONCERNS THE REAL PROPERTY SITUATED IN THE CITY OF _____
_____, COUNTY OF _____, STATE OF CALIFORNIA,
DESCRIBED AS _____.
THIS STATEMENT IS A DISCLOSURE OF THE CONDITION OF THE ABOVE DESCRIBED PROPERTY IN COMPLIANCE
WITH SECTION 1102 OF THE CIVIL CODE AS OF (date) _____. IT IS NOT A WARRANTY OF ANY
KIND BY THE SELLER(S) OR ANY AGENT(S) REPRESENTING ANY PRINCIPAL(S) IN THIS TRANSACTION, AND IS
NOT A SUBSTITUTE FOR ANY INSPECTIONS OR WARRANTIES THE PRINCIPAL(S) MAY WISH TO OBTAIN.

I. COORDINATION WITH OTHER DISCLOSURE FORMS

This Real Estate Transfer Disclosure Statement is made pursuant to Section 1102 of the Civil Code. Other statutes
require disclosures, depending upon the details of the particular real estate transaction (for example: special study
zone and purchase-money liens on residential property).

Substituted Disclosures: The following disclosures have or will be made in connection with this real estate transfer,
and are intended to satisfy the disclosure obligations on this form, where the subject matter is the same:

☐ Inspection reports completed pursuant to the contract of sale or receipt for deposit.

☐ Additional inspection reports or disclosures: _____
_____

II. SELLER'S INFORMATION

The Seller discloses the following information with the knowledge that even though this is not a warranty, prospective
Buyers may rely on this information in deciding whether and on what terms to purchase the subject property. Seller
hereby authorizes any agent(s) representing any principal(s) in this transaction to provide a copy of this statement to
any person or entity in connection with any actual or anticipated sale of the property.

THE FOLLOWING ARE REPRESENTATIONS MADE BY THE SELLER(S) AND ARE NOT THE
REPRESENTATIONS OF THE AGENT(S), IF ANY. THIS INFORMATION IS A DISCLOSURE AND IS NOT
INTENDED TO BE PART OF ANY CONTRACT BETWEEN THE BUYER AND SELLER.

Seller ☐ is ☐ is not occupying the property.

A. The subject property has the items checked below (read across)

☐ Range	☐ Oven	☐ Microwave
☐ Dishwasher	☐ Trash Compactor	☐ Garbage Disposal
☐ Washer/Dryer Hookups		☐ Rain Gutters
☐ Burglar Alarms	☐ Smoke Detector(s)	☐ Fire Alarm
☐ T.V. Antenna	☐ Satellite Dish	☐ Intercom
☐ Central Heating	☐ Central Air Conditioning	☐ Evaporator Cooler(s)
☐ Wall/Window Air Conditioning	☐ Sprinklers	☐ Public Sewer System
☐ Septic Tank	☐ Sump Pump	☐ Water Softener
☐ Patio/Decking	☐ Built-in Barbecue	☐ Gazebo
☐ Sauna		
☐ Hot Tub ☐ Locking Safety Cover*	☐ Pool ☐ Child Resistant Barrier*	☐ Spa ☐ Locking Safety Cover*
☐ Security Gate(s)	☐ Automatic Garage Door Opener(s)*	☐ Number Remote Controls _____
Garage: ☐ Attached	☐ Not Attached	☐ Carport
Pool/Spa Heater: ☐ Gas	☐ Solar	☐ Electric
Water Heater: ☐ Gas	☐ Water Heater Anchored, Braced, or Strapped*	☐ Private Utility or
Water Supply: ☐ City	☐ Well	Other _____
Gas Supply: ☐ Utility	☐ Bottled	
☐ Window Screens	☐ Window Security Bars ☐ Quick Release Mechanism on Bedroom Windows*	

Exhaust Fan(s) in _____ 220 Volt Wiring in _____ Fireplace(s) in _____
☐ Gas Starter _____ ☐ Roof(s): Type: _____ Age: _____ (approx.)
☐ Other: _____
Are there, to the best of your (Seller's) knowledge, any of the above that are not in operating condition? ☐ Yes ☐ No. If yes, then
describe. (Attach additional sheets if necessary): _____
_____

(*see footnote on page 2)

Buyer and Seller acknowledge receipt of a copy of this page.
Buyer's Initials (_____)(_____)
Seller's Initials (_____)(_____)

EQUAL HOUSING OPPORTUNITY

TDS-11 REVISED 10/01 (PAGE 1 OF 3) Print Date

Reviewed by _____
Broker or Designee _____ Date _____

REAL ESTATE TRANSFER DISCLOSURE STATEMENT (TDS-11 PAGE 1 OF 3)

FIGURE 3.4

Real Estate Transfer Disclosure Statement (continued)

Property Address: _____   Date: _____

B. Are you (Seller) aware of any significant defects/malfunctions in any of the following? ☐ Yes ☐ No. If yes, check appropriate space(s) below.

☐ Interior Walls ☐ Ceilings ☐ Floors ☐ Exterior Walls ☐ Insulation ☐ Roof(s ☐ Windows ☐ Doors ☐ Foundation ☐ Slab(s)
☐ Driveways ☐ Sidewalks ☐ Walls/Fences ☐ Electrical Systems ☐ Plumbing/Sewers/Septics ☐ Other Structural Components
(Describe:_____
_____)

If any of the above is checked, explain. (Attach additional sheets if necessary):_____
_____
_____

*This garage door opener or child resistant pool barrier may not be in compliance with the safety standards relating to automatic reversing devices as set forth in Chapter 12.5 (commencing with Section 19890) of Part 3 of Division 13 of, or with the pool safety standards of Article 2.5 (commencing with Section 115920) of Chapter 5 of Part 10 of Division 104 of, the Health and Safety Code. The water heater may not be anchored, braced, or strapped in accordance with Section 19211 of the Health and Safety Code. Window security bars may not have quick release mechanisms in compliance with the 1995 Edition of the California Building Standards Code.

C. Are you (Seller) aware of any of the following:
1. Substances, materials, or products which may be an environmental hazard such as, but not limited to, asbestos, formaldehyde, radon gas, lead-based paint, mold, fuel or chemical storage tanks, and contaminated soil or water on the subject property....☐ Yes ☐ No
2. Features of the property shared in common with adjoining landowners, such as walls, fences, and driveways, whose use or responsibility for maintenance may have an effect on the subject property ....☐ Yes ☐ No
3. Any encroachments, easements or similar matters that may affect your interest in the subject property ....☐ Yes ☐ No
4. Room additions, structural modifications, or other alterations or repairs made without necessary permits...........☐ Yes ☐ No
5. Room additions, structural modifications, or other alterations or repairs not in compliance with building codes ......☐ Yes ☐ No
6. Fill (compacted or otherwise) on the property or any portion thereof..☐ Yes ☐ No
7. Any settling from any cause, or slippage, sliding, or other soil problems...☐ Yes ☐ No
8. Flooding, drainage or grading problems...☐ Yes ☐ No
9. Major damage to the property or any of the structures from fire, earthquake, floods, or landslides.................☐ Yes ☐ No
10. Any zoning violations, nonconforming uses, violations of "setback" requirements ....☐ Yes ☐ No
11. Neighborhood noise problems or other nuisances ....☐ Yes ☐ No
12. CC&R's or other deed restrictions or obligations ....☐ Yes ☐ No
13. Homeowners' Association which has any authority over the subject property ....☐ Yes ☐ No
14. Any "common area" (facilities such as pools, tennis courts, walkways, or other areas co-owned in undivided interest with others)...☐ Yes ☐ No
15. Any notices of abatement or citations against the property ....☐ Yes ☐ No
16. Any lawsuits by or against the seller threatening to or affecting this real property, including any lawsuits alleging a defect or deficiency in this real property or "common areas" (facilities such as pools, tennis courts, walkways, or other areas, co-owned in undivided interest with others) ....☐ Yes ☐ No

If the answer to any of these is yes, explain. (Attach additional sheets if necessary): _____
_____
_____

Seller certifies that the Information herein is true and correct to the best of the Seller's knowledge as of the date signed by the Seller.

Seller_____   Date _____

Seller_____   Date _____

TDS-11 REVISED 10/01 (PAGE 2 OF 3)   Print Date

Buyer and Seller acknowledge receipt of a copy of this page.
Buyer's Initials (_____)(_____)
Seller's Initials (_____)(_____)

Reviewed by
Broker or Designee _____ Date _____

EQUAL HOUSING OPPORTUNITY

REAL ESTATE TRANSFER DISCLOSURE STATEMENT (TDS-11 PAGE 2 OF 3)

FIGURE **3.4**

Real Estate Transfer Disclosure Statement (continued)

Property Address: _____   Date: _____

III. AGENT'S INSPECTION DISCLOSURE
(To be completed only if the Seller is represented by an agent in this transaction.)

THE UNDERSIGNED, BASED ON THE ABOVE INQUIRY OF THE SELLER(S) AS TO THE CONDITION OF THE PROPERTY AND BASED ON A REASONABLY COMPETENT AND DILIGENT VISUAL INSPECTION OF THE ACCESSIBLE AREAS OF THE PROPERTY IN CONJUNCTION WITH THAT INQUIRY, STATES THE FOLLOWING:

☐ Agent notes no items for disclosure.

☐ Agent notes the following items: _____

_____
_____
_____

Agent (Broker Representing Seller) _____ By _____ Date _____
   (Please Print)   (Associate-License or Broker Signature)

IV. AGENT'S INSPECTION DISCLOSURE
(To be completed only if the agent who has obtained the offer is other than the agent above.)

THE UNDERSIGNED, BASED ON A REASONABLY COMPETENT AND DILIGENT VISUAL INSPECTION OF THE ACCESSIBLE AREAS OF THE PROPERTY, STATES THE FOLLOWING:

☐ Agent notes no items for disclosure.

☐ Agent notes the following items: _____

_____
_____

Agent (Broker Obtaining the Offer) _____ By _____ Date _____
   (Please Print)   (Associate-License or Broker Signature)

V. BUYER(S) AND SELLER(S) MAY WISH TO OBTAIN PROFESSIONAL ADVICE AND/OR INSPECTIONS OF THE PROPERTY AND TO PROVIDE FOR APPROPRIATE PROVISIONS IN A CONTRACT BETWEEN BUYER AND SELLER(S) WITH RESPECT TO ANY ADVICE/INSPECTIONS/DEFECTS.

I/WE ACKNOWLEDGE RECEIPT OF A COPY OF THIS STATEMENT.

Seller _____ Date _____   Buyer _____ Date _____

Seller _____ Date _____   Buyer _____ Date _____

Agent (Broker Representing Seller) _____ By _____ Date _____
                                                    (Associate-License or Broker Signature)

Agent (Broker Obtaining the Offer) _____ By _____ Date _____
                                                    (Associate-License or Broker Signature)

SECTION 1102.3 OF THE CIVIL CODE PROVIDES A BUYER WITH THE RIGHT TO RESCIND A PURCHASE CONTRACT FOR AT LEAST THREE DAYS AFTER THE DELIVERY OF THIS DISCLOSURE IF DELIVERY OCCURS AFTER THE SIGNING OF AN OFFER TO PURCHASE. IF YOU WISH TO RESCIND THE CONTRACT, YOU MUST ACT WITHIN THE PRESCRIBED PERIOD.

A REAL ESTATE BROKER IS QUALIFIED TO ADVISE ON REAL ESTATE. IF YOU DESIRE LEGAL ADVICE, CONSULT YOUR ATTORNEY.

TDS-11 REVISED 10/01 (PAGE 3 OF 3)   Print Date

REAL ESTATE TRANSFER DISCLOSURE STATEMENT (TDS-11 PAGE 3 OF 3)

principal but also for what the agent "should have known," following a reasonably competent and diligent inspection. This court case has been codified in the Civil Code, beginning with Section 2079, and became effective January 1, 1986. It requires that all real estate agents conduct a competent and diligent visual inspection of all accessible property areas in a real estate sale involving one- to four-unit residential properties and disclose to the prospective buyer all material facts affecting the value or desirability of the property. There are no exceptions to or exemptions from this law. If an agent does not comply with this code section, the statute of limitations for bringing suit is two years.

> **Seller Disclosure Exemptions**
> Exempted from disclosure are transfers
> ■ requiring public report,
> ■ pursuant to court order,
> ■ by foreclosure,
> ■ by a fiduciary,
> ■ from one co-owner to one or more co-owners,
> ■ between spouses or to a direct blood relative,
> ■ between spouses in connection with a dissolution,
> ■ by the state controller,
> ■ as a result of failure to pay property taxes, and
> ■ to or from any government entity (including exchanges).

A difficulty with this section of code is that it does not tell the agent what to inspect or how. The following suggestions may help the agent find physical problems and fundamental defects in the home. The major factors contributing to defects in homes are structural failure, material deterioration, water damage, and insect infestation. When one of these factors is found in a home, some or all of the other factors often are present.

■ **EXAMPLE:** While inspecting a home, Broker Nono finds cracks in the walls and foundation (structural failure). He realizes that these cracks could allow water to penetrate (water damage) and insects to penetrate (insect infestation), which could cause additional structural failure.

Structural Failure

Structural failure can be caused by environmental extremes, poor design, material deterioration, water, or insects. When inspecting for structural failure, agents should look for

- cracks in structural walls, beams, and columns (outside and inside), particularly foundations, or in corners of walls and around doors and windows (large V-shaped cracks may indicate settlement, upheaval, or lateral movement of soil; minor cracking is normal);

- severe bulging in floors or structural walls;

- floors that slope;

- excessive deflection of girders and joists evidenced by a caved-in and creaky floor;

- doors that fail to close or that have been trimmed to close;

- a roof ridgeline that is not straight; and

- instability in any structural member.

Material Deterioration

Material deterioration can be produced by substandard material or construction procedures. A moist environment can produce damp rot (a decaying fungus), one of the most severe types of material damage. Principal items to look for when inspecting for material deterioration include

- decay or warping of wood members (porches are a prime candidate);

- rotting, cracking, or warping—check around doors and windows especially; and

- erosion of concrete, masonry units, or mortar.

Water Problems

Water problems can be caused by faulty plumbing, a rising ground water level, seepage, improper drainage, or condensation from inadequate ventilation. Water is a common enemy of a house. Principal items to look for when inspecting for water problems include

- water stains on ceilings that may be coming from leaky plumbing or a leaky roof;

- mold, mildew, and rust—be particularly alert for black mold;

- loose or warped wood members;

- rotted wood;

- cracked, chipped, or curled tile;

- premature interior paint deterioration—check for peeling and flaking; and

- roof defects.

Toxic Mold

Sellers of one- to four-unit residential property must disclose in the Real Estate Transfer Disclosure Statement if the owner is aware of mold on the premises.

The presence of *toxic mold* can have serious health effects. It is caused by damp conditions. Solving mold conditions can require walls being torn open. In some cases, buildings have been razed because the cost to cure the problem was too great. If a house has a dampness problem, you should recommend to a buyer that the home inspector test for mold.

Insect Infestation

Carpenter ants and subterranean termites are the most damaging of all insects. Both attack wooden structures internally and leave few visible signs of infestation on the surface, making their presence virtually impossible to detect. Undetected and therefore untreated insect infestation could make the home structurally unsound over time. The following are some insect signs to look for:

- Carpenter ants: wood shavings near wood members.
- Termites: earth and wood droppings, which look like sawdust and mud tubes leading from ground to wood or marks where mud tubes were removed.

There are too many possible defects to mention here, but agents have developed inspection techniques to detect some of the more common problems. For example, defective wood framing can be detected after a few years by unlevel floors and windowsills. If an uncarpeted floor looks uneven, a simple test is to place a marble at several places on the floor; rolling marbles may indicate a problem. Resawn doors or doorjambs reworked because they were no longer perpendicular to the floor signify a structural defect. Sticking doors and windows can indicate green lumber, sloppy workmanship, foundation settling or imperfect framing. Ceiling stains generally indicate a past or current roof problem. A **red flag** is anything that indicates that there may be a problem. Any red-flag information should be conveyed to the purchaser with a warning that it could indicate a problem. Remember, agents' legal responsibility extends only to a visual inspection of reasonably accessible areas.

> A *red flag* is a visual sign or indication of a defect.

Many agents today use the following three techniques to help protect them in the area of inspection disclosure.

> Real estate agents are required only to visually inspect the property.

1. Have the buyer pay for a home inspection, whereby a professional inspector examines the property, verifies defects on the transfer disclosure statement, and points out any defects that are not on the statement.

2. Have the seller pay for a home protection plan that will pay for repair of items named in the plan during the first year of ownership or over a specified extended period.

3. Have the seller supply the buyer with a Pest Control Inspection report.

Even if any one or all of these techniques are used, the agent is still responsible for inspecting the home and retains liability for any undisclosed defects that the agent knew about or should have discovered with a reasonably diligent inspection.

In addition to physical problems of the property itself, the agent must disclose anything else that might affect the buyer's decision to buy the property. These factors range from the property's being in a flood zone or on or near an earthquake fault to the presence of a nearby nuclear power plant. The agent needs to learn as much as possible about the house and the area around it.

■ DISCLOSURE OF DEATH OR AIDS

While an agent need not disclose a natural death on the property, he or she should disclose other deaths that have occurred within the prior three years. After three years, however, such disclosures need not be made. **AIDS disclosure** is unnecessary. An agent does not have to disclose that a former owner or resident ever had AIDS or died of AIDS.

Stigmatized Property

Stigmatized property is property that may be perceived to be undesirable for other than physical or environmental reasons.

Stigmatized property is property that may be perceived to be undesirable for other than physical or environmental reasons. Besides murder or suicide, a house could be stigmatized by the fact that molestations occurred there in the home, that the property has a reputation of being haunted, that satanic rituals had taken place there, or that the property has the reputation of being unlucky because of calamities that befell prior residents.

Because we don't know what a court will say should have been disclosed, as well as because disclosure is the right thing to do, if a fact or reputation could conceivably affect a buyer's decision, disclose it.

Licensed Care Facilities

Opinion 95-907 of the California Attorney General makes it clear that a real estate agent need not disclose the location of a licensed care facility that serves six or fewer people. (A larger facility close to a property being sold would likely require disclosure.)

■ NATURAL HAZARDS DISCLOSURE

Earthquake Safety

As of January 1, 1993, the state law requires that when selling one- to four-unit residential property built prior to January 1, 1960, you must disclose whether the dwelling has earthquake weaknesses. The California Seismic Safety Commission has published a booklet called *The Homeowner's Guide to Earthquake Safety* to help buyers, sellers, and real estate agents recognize some of the weaknesses in houses that affect earthquake safety.

For all houses sold in California, an **earthquake safety disclosure** statement must be filled out and signed by the buyer and seller. This disclosure statement is called the "Residential Earthquake Hazards Report" (Figure 3.5). The agent should prepare to answer the following seven questions, which are answered in the booklet on the pages noted:

1. What is a braced water heater? (page 6)
   A braced water heater is one that has metal strips to attach it to the wall.

2. Is the house bolted to the foundation? (page 7)
   If the house has a crawl space, you should be able to see the tops of the anchor bolts every four to six feet along the sill plate.

3. What is a cripple wall? (pages 8 and 9)
   A cripple wall is a short wood wall on top of the foundation that creates a crawl space.

FIGURE 3.5

Residential Earthquake Hazards Report

RESIDENTIAL EARTHQUAKE HAZARDS REPORT

Refer to Section 8897 *et seq.*, California Government Code

Name	Assessor's Parcel No.
Street Address	Year Built
City and County	Zip Code

Answer these questions to the best of your knowledge. If you do not have actual knowledge as to whether the weakness exists or not, answer "Don't Know." If your house does not have the feature, answer "Doesn't Apply." The page numbers in the right-hand column indicate where in this guide you can find information on each of these features.

		Yes	No	Doesn't Apply	Don't Know	See Page
1.	Is the water heater braced, strapped, or anchored to resist falling during an earthquake?	☐	☐	☐	☐	6
2.	Is the house anchored or bolted to the foundation?	☐	☐	☐	☐	7
3.	If the house has cripple walls:					
	° Are the exterior cripple walls braced?	☐	☐	☐	☐	8
	° If the exterior foundation consists of unconnected concrete piers and posts, have they been strengthened?	☐	☐	☐	☐	9
4.	If the exterior foundation, or part of it, is made of unreinforced masonry, has it been strengthened?	☐	☐	☐	☐	10
5.	If the house is built on a hillside, answer the following:					
	° Are the exterior tall foundation walls braced?	☐	☐	☐	☐	11
	° Were the tall posts or columns either built to resist earthquakes or have they been strengthened?	☐	☐	☐	☐	11
6.	If the exterior walls of the house, or part of them, are made of unreinforced masonry, have they been strengthened?	☐	☐	☐	☐	12
7.	If the house has a living area over the garage, was the wall around the garage door opening either built to resist earthquakes or has it been strengthened?	☐	☐	☐	☐	13

If any of the questions are answered "No," the house is likely to have an earthquake weakness. Questions answered "Don't Know" may indicate a need for further evaluation. If you corrected one or more of these weaknesses, describe the work on a separate page.

As Seller of the property described herein, I have answered the questions above to the best of my knowledge in an effort to fully disclose any potential earthquake weaknesses it may have.

EXECUTED BY

_____   _____   _____
(Seller)   (Seller)   Date

I acknowledge receipt of this form, completed and signed by the Seller. I understand that if the Seller has answered "No" to one or more questions, or if Seller has indicated a lack of knowledge, there may be one or more earthquake weaknesses in this house.

_____   _____   _____
(Buyer)   (Buyer)   Date

This earthquake disclosure is made in addition to the standard real estate transfer disclosure statement also required by law.

Keep your copy of this form for future reference.

FIGURE 3.6

Earthquake Safety Client Card

TO WHOM IT MAY CONCERN:

I have received a copy of "The Homeowner's Guide to Earthquake Safety".

Date: _____ (Signature) _____

Time: _____ (Printed Name) _____

Date: _____ (Signature) _____

Time: _____ (Printed Name) _____

---

4. Is the foundation made of unreinforced masonry? (page 10)
   Most brick and stone foundations are unreinforced. For concrete block, check the blocks on the top of the foundation. If they are hollow, the foundation probably is not reinforced. (Generally, steel rods are embedded in grout in the cells if the foundation is reinforced.)

5. If the house is on a hillside, two questions need to be answered: (1) Are the exterior tall foundation walls braced? (2) Were the tall posts or columns either built to resist earthquakes or have they been strengthened? (page 11)

   If wall studs are without plywood sheathing, diagonal wood bracing, or steel bracing, the wall is not braced. Consult an engineer to determine if posts or unbraced walls need strengthening.

6. Are the exterior walls strengthened? (page 12)
   If the house was built before 1940, walls are most likely not reinforced. You can check the house plans, which are probably on file with the building department. Otherwise, it could be difficult to determine if walls are reinforced. There are professional testing services that can determine the presence of steel in the walls.

7. If the house has a living area over the garage, was the wall around the garage door strengthened or built to resist earthquakes? (page 13)

   Check if there are braces or plywood panels around the garage-door opening. If the garage-door opening is in line with the rest of the house, additional bracing is probably not needed.

If these questions cannot readily be answered by a cursory inspection, the services of professional inspector or engineer may be required.

Commercial Property Earthquake Hazards

Sellers or sellers' agents must give buyers a copy of the *Commercial Property Owner's Guide to Earthquake Safety* for sales or exchanges of any real property built of precast concrete or reinforced/unreinforced masonry with wood frame floors or roofs built before January 1, 1975, unless such property falls within an exemption category.

Natural Hazard Disclosure Statement

The Natural Hazards Disclosure Statement sets forth the following additional natural hazard disclosures that must be made on a statutory form:

■ *Special flood hazard areas*—**Flood hazard areas** are indicated on maps published by the Federal Emergency Management Agency (FEMA). The seller's agent must disclose this to the buyer if the agent has knowledge that the property is in such a zone or if a list of areas has been posted in the County Recorder's Office, County Assessor's Office, and County Planning Agency.

■ *Areas of potential flooding*—These areas are subject to possible flooding as shown on a dam failure map. Disclosure must be made if the seller or seller's agent has knowledge of the designation or a list of properties, including seller's property, has been posted at the County Recorders Office, County Assessors Office, and County Planning Agency. (**Note:** If an owner has received federal flood disaster assistance, then the seller must notify the purchaser of the requirement to obtain and maintain flood insurance.)

■ *Very high fire hazard zones*—The state has imposed in these **fire hazard areas** fire protection requirements that subject owners to property maintenance requirements.

■ *State fire responsibility areas*—These are areas where the state not only sets protection requirements but also has primary fire-fighting responsibility. This disclosure must be made if the seller or seller's agent has actual knowledge of this designation or the local agency has a map that includes the seller's property that has been posted at County Recorders Office, Assessor's Office, and Planning Agency.

■ *Wildland area that may contain substantial fire risks and hazards*—Unless the Department of Forestry enters into a cooperative contract, the state is not responsible for fire protection services within wildland areas. The seller must make this disclosure if the seller or seller's agent has knowledge that the property is in a designated area or if maps showing the property to be in such an area is posted at the office of the Country Recorder, County Assessor, and County Planning Agency.

■ *Earthquake fault zone as indicated on maps.*

■ *Seismic hazard zone*—An earthquake in such a zone could result in strong shaking, soil liquification, or landslides. The seller or seller's agent must disclose to the buyer that the property is in such a zone if the seller or seller's agent has actual knowledge that the property is in such a zone or maps showing the property is in such a zone have been posted at the offices of the County Recorder, County Assessor, and County Planning Agency. **Note:** If upon looking at a map a reasonable person cannot tell with certainty if a property is within a designated area, then the Natural Hazards Disclosure Statement should be marked "Yes."

The statutory form Natural Hazard Disclosure Statement must be used and is included as Figure 3.7.

■ ENVIRONMENTAL HAZARDS DISCLOSURE

California legislation mandates **environmental hazards disclosure** (AB 983) to inform homeowners and prospective homeowners about environmental hazards located on and affecting residential property. The seller seldom knows if there are any environmental hazards. Thus, a statement that the seller is unaware of environmental hazards is not a guarantee that the property is free of such hazards. It is in the seller's and future buyer's interest to know what hazards are common, where they might be found, and how they might be alleviated.

California's Environmental Hazards Booklet

The Real Estate Transfer Disclosure Statement specifies environmental hazards. By providing the booklet *Environmental Hazards: A Guide for Homeowners, Buyers, Landlords, and Tenants* neither the seller or the seller's agent need furnish the buyer any more information concerning hazards unless the seller or agent have actual knowledge of environmental hazards concerning the property.

Hazardous Substances Released

Health and Safety Code Section 25359.7(a) requires **hazardous waste disclosure**. Owners of *nonresidential* property must give prior notice to buyers or lessees if they know of the release of hazardous substances on the property or if they have reasonable cause to believe hazardous substances exist on or beneath the property.

Tenants are required to notify landlords (both *residential* and *nonresidential*) of hazardous substances that they know have been released or believe to exist on or beneath the property. Failure to disclose constitutes a default under the lease.

Lead-Based Paint

The seller or lessor of residential property built prior to 1978 must deliver to prospective buyer or tenant the booklet prepared by the Federal Environmental Protection Agency entitled *Protect Your Family from Lead In Your Home*.

Providing the California booklet entitled *Environmental Hazards: A Guide for Homeowners, Buyers, Landlords, and Tenants* meets the federal requirement.

Owners must disclose to their agents as well as prospective buyers and tenants the presence of known lead-based-paint hazards. Any available records or reports as to lead-based paint must be provided.

FIGURE 3.7

Natural Hazards Disclosure Statement

CALIFORNIA
ASSOCIATION
OF REALTORS®

NATURAL HAZARD DISCLOSURE STATEMENT

This statement applies to the following property: _____

The transferor and his or her agent(s) disclose the following information with the knowledge that even though this is not a warranty, prospective transferees may rely on this information in deciding whether and on what terms to purchase the subject property. Transferor hereby authorizes any agent(s) representing any principal(s) in this action to provide a copy of this statement to any person or entity in connection with any actual or anticipated sale of the property.

The following are representations made by the transferor and his or her agent(s) based on their knowledge and maps drawn by the state and federal governments. This information is a disclosure and is not intended to be part of any contract between the transferee and transferor.

THIS REAL PROPERTY LIES WITHIN THE FOLLOWING HAZARDOUS AREA(S): (Check the answer which applies.)

A SPECIAL FLOOD HAZARD AREA (Any type Zone "A" or "V") designated by the Federal Emergency Management Agency.

Yes _____   No _____   Do not know and information not available from local jurisdiction _____

AN AREA OF POTENTIAL FLOODING shown on a dam failure inundation map pursuant to Section 8589.5 of the Government Code.

Yes _____   No _____   Do not know and information not available from local jurisdiction _____

A VERY HIGH FIRE HAZARD SEVERITY ZONE pursuant to Section 51178 or 51179 of the Government Code. The owner of this property is subject to the maintenance requirements of Section 51182 of the Government Code.

Yes _____   No _____

A WILDLAND AREA THAT MAY CONTAIN SUBSTANTIAL FOREST FIRE RISKS AND HAZARDS pursuant to Section 4125 of the Public Resources Code. The owner of this property is subject to the maintenance requirements of Section 4291 of the Public Resources Code. Additionally, it is not the state's responsibility to provide fire protection services to any building or structure located within the wildlands unless the Department of Forestry and Fire Protection has entered into a cooperative agreement with a local agency for those purposes pursuant to Section 4142 of the Public Resources Code.

Yes _____   No _____

AN EARTHQUAKE FAULT ZONE pursuant to Section 2622 of the Public Resources Code.

Yes _____   No _____

A SEISMIC HAZARD ZONE pursuant to Section 2696 of the Public Resources Code.

Yes (Landslide Zone)   _____
Yes (Liquefaction Zone) _____   No _____   Map not yet released by state _____

THESE HAZARDS MAY LIMIT YOUR ABILITY TO DEVELOP THE REAL PROPERTY, TO OBTAIN INSURANCE, OR TO RECEIVE ASSISTANCE AFTER A DISASTER.

THE MAPS ON WHICH THESE DISCLOSURES ARE BASED ESTIMATE WHERE NATURAL HAZARDS EXIST. THEY ARE NOT DEFINITIVE INDICATORS OF WHETHER OR NOT A PROPERTY WILL BE AFFECTED BY A NATURAL DISASTER. TRANSFEREE(S) AND TRANSFEROR(S) MAY WISH TO OBTAIN PROFESSIONAL ADVICE REGARDING THOSE HAZARDS AND OTHER HAZARDS THAT MAY AFFECT THE PROPERTY.

The information in this box is not part of the statutory form.

☐ (if checked) The representations made in this form are based upon information provided by an independent third-party report provided as a substituted disclosure pursuant to California Civil Code §1102.4. Neither the seller nor the seller's agent (1) has independently verified the information contained in this form and the report or (2) is personally aware of any errors or inaccuracies in the information contained on this form.

Transferor represents that the information herein is true and correct to the best of the transferor's knowledge as of the date signed by the transferor.

Signature of Transferor _____ Date _____

Agent represents that the information herein is true and correct to the best of the agent's knowledge as of the date signed by the agent.

Signature of Agent _____ Date _____

Signature of Agent _____ Date _____

Transferee represents that he or she has read and understands this document.

Signature of Transferee _____ Date _____

THIS FORM HAS BEEN APPROVED BY THE CALIFORNIA ASSOCIATION OF REALTORS® (C.A.R.). NO REPRESENTATION IS MADE AS TO THE LEGAL VALIDITY OR ADEQUACY OF ANY PROVISION IN ANY SPECIFIC TRANSACTION. A REAL ESTATE BROKER IS THE PERSON QUALIFIED TO ADVISE ON REAL ESTATE TRANSACTIONS. IF YOU DESIRE LEGAL OR TAX ADVICE, CONSULT AN APPROPRIATE PROFESSIONAL.

This form is available for use by the entire real estate industry. It is not intended to identify the user as a REALTOR®. REALTOR® is a registered collective membership mark which may be used only by members of the NATIONAL ASSOCIATION OF REALTORS® who subscribe to its Code of Ethics.

The copyright laws of the United States (Title 17 U.S. Code) forbid the unauthorized reproduction of this form, or any portion thereof, by photocopy machine or any other means, including facsimile or computerized formats. Copyright © 1998-1999, CALIFORNIA ASSOCIATION OF REALTORS®, INC. ALL RIGHTS RESERVED.

R I
E N Published and Distributed by:
B C REAL ESTATE BUSINESS SERVICES, INC.
S   *a subsidiary of the CALIFORNIA ASSOCIATION OF REALTORS®*
     525 South Virgil Avenue, Los Angeles, California 90020

PRINT DATE

Page ___ of ___ Pages.
REVISED 10/99

┌ OFFICE USE ONLY ┐
Reviewed by Broker
or Designee _____
Date _____

EQUAL HOUSING
OPPORTUNITY

FORM NHD-11

Landlords who receive any federal subsidies or have federally related loans, when confronted with deteriorating paint in a pre-1978 housing unit, must alert tenants to the possible health dangers and use government-certified workers and special containment practices to minimize risk of public exposure.

(**Note:** The above could place a significant financial burden on an owner, and this burden is not limited to one- to four-unit residential properties.)

Military Ordnance Location

If a transferor has knowledge that a property is within one mile of a former **military ordnance location** (military training ground) that may contain explosives, the transferor must disclose in writing that these former federal or state locations may contain potentially explosive ammunition. (The buyer has a statutory right of rescission.)

Water Contamination

Well water has been seriously contaminated in many areas of California by industrial, agricultural, farming, and military operations. Many wells have been capped. Besides arsenic from mining, there are countless insecticides and chemicals of all types that were not known to be harmful when discharged.

Perchlorate, the primary ingredient of solid rocket fuel is believed to be particularly dangerous to health. It alters hormonal balances (thyroid) and impedes metabolism and brain development. The EPA has urged the Pentagon to conduct widespread testing, but the Defense Department has resisted.

If an agent knows of problems in a water supply or a house has it's own well in an area where water contamination has been found, then the broker has a duty to provide the information he or she has to a prospective buyer.

Sick Building Syndrome

Many modern commercial buildings have sealed windows and receive fresh air through their ventilation systems. Some of these buildings have developed what is known as **sick building syndrome** (SBS). Common tenant complaints include headaches; eye, nose, and throat irritations; dry cough; dry or itchy skin; dizziness; nausea; difficulty in concentrating; fatigue; and sensitivity to odors. The problems relate to time spent in the building, and most sufferers report relief soon after leaving the building.

SBS problems may be located in the entire building or just in one area. A problem with SBS is that a specific cause is not known, although it appears to be related to inadequate ventilation. Corrective action has been to increase ventilation and to clean the ventilation system.

If an agent knows that a property has a reputation as a sick building, the agent should reveal this fact. Failure to do so could expose the agent to significant liability. However, specific SBS disclosure is not mandated by law.

Environmental Hazards Booklet

The Department of Real Estate and the Department of Health Services have prepared a booklet for homeowners and buyers. This booklet is distributed by the California Association of REALTORS® for use by real estate agents to fully disclose environmental hazard issues to prospective buyers. The booklet contains approximately 50 pages to be read by buyers, who should sign a form signifying that they have received the booklet. Inside the back cover is a tearout sheet (Figure 3.8), to be signed by the buyer(s) and retained in the broker's files.

Under the mandated disclosure of environmental hazards, it is important for brokers to have copies of these tear-outs in their files. Sales agents should make their own photocopies to keep in their personal escrow files.

The booklet is divided into six sections and two appendixes.
The sections are as follows:

1. Asbestos
2. Formaldehyde
3. Lead
4. Radon
5. Hazardous Waste
6. Household Hazardous Wastes

The appendixes contain the following:

1. A List of Federal and State Agencies
2. A Glossary of Terms

All agents should obtain copies of this book and familiarize themselves with the six basic topics. You will be asked questions by your buyers and sellers, and every buyer must be given a copy of the booklet and sign for it (Figure 3.8).

■ SUBDIVISION DISCLOSURE

There are a number of disclosures that relate to subdivisions.

Public Report

The purpose of the California Subdivided Lands Law is to protect purchasers in new subdivisions from fraud. A disclosure known as a **public report** must be provided to purchasers, who must sign that they have received and accepted the report before they are bound to complete the purchase. The California Real Estate Commissioner must approve the public report, which simply discloses information on the project such as location, size of the offering, identity of the subdivider, the interest to be conveyed, provisions for handling deposits, purchase money, taxes, and assessments. Also included are use restrictions, unusual costs that a buyer will have to bear at time of purchase, hazards, adverse environmental findings, special permits required, utility availability, and so forth. A public report is good up to five years from date of issuance.

FIGURE 3.8

FIGURE 3.8

Environmental Hazards Client Card

TO WHOM IT MAY CONCERN:

I have received a copy of "Environmental Hazards: A Guide for Homeowners and Buyers" from the Broker(s) in this transaction.

Date: _____   (Signature) _____

Time: _____   (Printed Name) _____

Date: _____   (Signature) _____

Time: _____   (Printed Name) _____

The Real Estate Commissioner may issue a preliminary public report, that is good for one year or until the public report is issued, whichever occurs first. A subdivider can accept a deposit with a reservation if there is a preliminary public report, but the purchaser is not obligated until signing that he or she accepts the public report.

A Conditional Public Report, that allows the subdivider to enter into a binding contract can be issued, but the escrow cannot be closed until issuance of the public report.

■ The Conditional Public Report period cannot exceed six months and may be renewed for one six-month period. If the public report is not issued within this period or if the purchaser is not satisfied with the final public report because of material changes, the purchaser is entitled to the full refund of any deposit.

■ COMMON INTEREST SUBDIVISION

A **common interest subdivision** is a subdivision in which owners own or lease a separate lot or unit together with an undivided interest in the common areas of the project. These common areas usually are governed by a homeowners' association (HOA).

In the sale of a common interest subdivision, along with the public report the purchaser must be given a brochure entitled *Common Interest Development General Information*. In addition, and prior to transfer of title, owners of condominiums, community apartment projects, cooperatives, and planned unit developments must provide purchasers with a copy of the covenants, conditions, and restrictions; bylaws; and articles of incorporation, plus an owners' association financial statement, including the current assessments, late charges, plans on change in assessments, and any delinquent assessments and costs. (A homeowners' association must furnish the owner a copy of the latest version of documents within ten days of request by the owner. A reasonable fee for doing this may be charged.)

If there is an age restriction, a statement must be included that it is only enforceable to the extent permitted by law (citing applicable law).

If the association plans to sue or has commenced an action against the developer for damages, the construction defects must be listed. If a settlement has been reached regarding construction defects, the defects must be described that are to be corrected, and an estimate of when the work will be completed as well as status of other defects must be provided to the buyer.

> For common interest subdivisions, buyers must be provided information about restrictions and the homeowner's association (HOA).

Condominium Conversion Notice

When a developer intends to convert an apartment to individual ownership the developer must notify current and prospective tenants of the intent, the public hearings and the right to purchase their unit.

Interstate Land Sales Full Disclosure Act

This federal act requires disclosures for interstate sale of unimproved lots for subdivisions of 25 or more parcels. The act, which was enacted to prevent fraud, requires disclosures as to title, location, facilities, utilities availability and charges, soil conditions, etc.

■ MELLO-ROOS BOND DISCLOSURE

Mello-Roos Bonds are municipal-type bonds issued to fund streets, sewers, and so forth for a new development. The bonds shift the expenses from the developer to each homebuyer.

A broker must disclose to a buyer that a project is subject to a Mello-Roos levy for a sale or lease for more than five years. Failure to give notice prior to signing the sales contract (or lease) gives the buyer or tenant a three-day right of rescission after receipt of the notice.

■ FINANCING DISCLOSURE

There are a number of broker as well as lender disclosures relating to financing.

Seller Financing Disclosure

Financial disclosure involving seller carryback financing of one- to four-unit residential properties was one of the first mandated disclosures. In the 1970s the term *creative financing* became very popular, and in most cases it meant the seller was to carry back (accept a note for part of the purchase price secured by a wraparound or junior mortgage, deed of trust, or contract for deed) a second or third trust deed on the property just sold. Although much of this creative financing was an honest attempt to sell the seller's property and provide a win-win situation for both the buyer and the seller, some agents were not prudent in their judgment. If the seller had to foreclose on the buyer, the payments on the home often were so high that the seller could not handle the foreclosure and would lose the equity in the note he or she was carrying.

Unethical or unsophisticated agents and buyers developed *walk-away financing* in the late 1970s and early 1980s. An unethical purchaser would convince the seller and his or her agent to let the purchaser buy the property with a low down payment and then borrow on the property and let the buyer pull cash out. The buyer would make no payments on the property and would let the seller and lenders reclaim the overencumbered property. Of course, the seller would be on the "short end of the stick."

This kind of financing and the complaints stemming from the victims helped enact Civil Code Sections 2956-2967, which became law on July 1, 1983. These statutes require disclosure of seller carryback financing on residential property of one to four units in the **seller financing addendum and disclosure**. (See Figure 3.9.) The disclosure must be made to both the buyer and the seller, and the units do not have to be owner-occupied for the statute to govern.

> If there is seller financing, the seller financing addendum and disclosure is required.

In mandating full disclosure, the California legislature began by defining seller financing and attempted to make the definition all-inclusive. The seller "extends credit" (carries back) whenever the buyer is given the right to defer payment of the purchase price, as long as a written agreement provides either for a finance charge or for payments to be made in more than four installments (whether principal and interest or interest only), not including the down payment. This definition includes notes, trust deeds, mortgages, land contracts, installment contracts, leases with the option to purchase, security documents, and any other name that might be given to financing agreements. We will use the term *note* to mean any of the above types of financing, the term *seller* to mean a seller who is carrying back a note, and the term *buyer* to mean the one giving the note.

Because any seller financing must be disclosed, it is important to know who has to disclose the financing. The disclosure requirements are imposed on the arranger of credit, often a real estate licensee or an attorney who is a party to the transaction. Where more than one arranger of credit exists, the arranger who obtains the purchase offer (the selling broker, the broker who arranges the sale) must make the disclosures unless some other person is designated in writing by the parties. Therefore, licensees should remember that even if another person or agent in the transaction volunteers to disclose the financing, unless that vow is in writing, the selling agent is ultimately responsible for any failure to disclose properly.

FIGURE 3.9

Seller Financing Addendum and Disclosure

CALIFORNIA ASSOCIATION OF REALTORS®

SELLER FINANCING ADDENDUM AND DISCLOSURE
(California Civil Code §§2956-2967)
(C.A.R. Form SFA, Revised 10/02)

This is an addendum to the ☐ Residential Purchase Agreement, ☐ Counter Offer, or ☐ Other _____
_____, ("Agreement"), dated _____,
On property known as _____ ("Property"),
between _____ ("Buyer"),
and _____ ("Seller").
Seller agrees to extend credit to Buyer as follows:
1. **PRINCIPAL; INTEREST; PAYMENT; MATURITY TERMS:** ☐ Principal amount $ _____, interest at _____%
    per annum, payable at approximately $ _____ per ☐ month, ☐ year, or ☐ other _____,
    remaining principal balance due in _____ years.
2. **LOAN APPLICATION; CREDIT REPORT:** Within **5 (or ☐ _____) Days** After Acceptance: **(a)** Buyer shall provide Seller a completed
    loan application on a form acceptable to Seller (such as a FNMA/FHLMC Uniform Residential Loan Application for residential one to four
    unit properties); and **(b)** Buyer authorizes Seller and/or Agent to obtain, at Buyer's expense, a copy of Buyer's credit report. Buyer shall
    provide any supporting documentation reasonably requested by Seller. Seller may cancel this Agreement in writing if Buyer fails to
    provide such documents within that time, or if Seller disapproves any above item within **5 (or ☐ _____) Days** After receipt of each item.
3. **CREDIT DOCUMENTS:** This extension of credit by Seller will be evidenced by: ☐ Note and deed of trust; ☐ All-inclusive
    note and deed of trust; ☐ Installment land sale contract; ☐ Lease/option (when parties intend transfer of equitable title);
    OR ☐ Other (specify) _____
**THE FOLLOWING TERMS APPLY ONLY IF CHECKED. SELLER IS ADVISED TO READ ALL TERMS, EVEN THOSE NOT
CHECKED, TO UNDERSTAND WHAT IS OR IS NOT INCLUDED, AND, IF NOT INCLUDED, THE CONSEQUENCES THEREOF.**
4. ☐ **LATE CHARGE:** If any payment is not made within _____ **Days** After it is due, a late charge of either $ _____,
    or _____% of the installment due, may be charged to Buyer. **NOTE:** On single family residences that Buyer intends to occupy,
    California Civil Code §2954.4(a) limits the late charge to no more than 6% of the total installment payment due and requires a
    grace period of no less than 10 days.
5. ☐ **BALLOON PAYMENT:** The extension of credit will provide for a balloon payment, in the amount of $ _____,
    plus any accrued interest, which is due on _____ (date).
6. ☐ **PREPAYMENT:** If all or part of this extension of credit is paid early, Seller may charge a prepayment penalty as follows (if
    applicable): _____. Caution: California Civil Code
    §2954.9 contains limitations on prepayment penalties for residential one-to-four unit properties.
7. ☐ **DUE ON SALE:** If any interest in the Property is sold or otherwise transferred, Seller has the option to require immediate
    payment of the entire unpaid principal balance, plus any accrued interest.
8.* ☐ **REQUEST FOR COPY OF NOTICE OF DEFAULT:** A request for a copy of Notice of Default as defined in California Civil
    Code §2924b will be recorded. **If Not,** Seller is advised to consider recording a Request for Notice of Default.
9.* ☐ **REQUEST FOR NOTICE OF DELINQUENCY:** A request for Notice of Delinquency, as defined in California Civil Code §2924e,
    to be signed and paid for by Buyer, will be made to senior lienholders. **If not,** Seller is advised to consider making a Request for
    Notice of Delinquency. Seller is advised to check with senior lienholders to verify whether they will honor this request.
10.* ☐ **TAX SERVICE:**
    A. If property taxes on the Property become delinquent, tax service will be arranged to report to Seller. **If not,** Seller is
    advised to consider retaining a tax service, or to otherwise determine that property taxes are paid.
    B. ☐ Buyer, ☐ Seller, shall be responsible for the initial and continued retention of, and payment for, such tax service.
11. ☐ **TITLE INSURANCE:** Title insurance coverage will be provided to **both** Seller and Buyer, insuring their respective interests
    in the Property. **If not,** Buyer and Seller are advised to consider securing such title insurance coverage.
12. ☐ **HAZARD INSURANCE:**
    A. The parties' escrow holder or insurance carrier will be directed to include a loss payee endorsement, adding Seller to
    the Property insurance policy. **If not,** Seller is advised to secure such an endorsement, or acquire a separate
    insurance policy.
    B. Property insurance **does not** include earthquake or flood insurance coverage, unless checked:
    ☐ Earthquake insurance will be obtained; ☐ Flood insurance will be obtained.
13. ☐ **PROCEEDS TO BUYER:** Buyer will receive cash proceeds at the close of the sale transaction. The amount received will be
    approximately $ _____, from _____ (indicate source of
    proceeds). Buyer represents that the purpose of such disbursement is as follows: _____.
14. ☐ **NEGATIVE AMORTIZATION; DEFERRED INTEREST:** Negative amortization results when Buyer's periodic payments are
    less than the amount of interest earned on the obligation. Deferred interest also results when the obligation does not
    require periodic payments for a period of time. In either case, interest is not payable as it accrues. This accrued interest
    will have to be paid by Buyer at a later time, and may result in Buyer owing more on the obligation than at its origination.
    The credit being extended to Buyer by Seller will provide for negative amortization or deferred interest as indicated below.
    (Check A, B, or C. CHECK ONE ONLY.)
    ☐ **A.** All negative amortization or deferred interest shall be added to the principal _____
    (e.g., annually, monthly, etc.), and thereafter shall bear interest at the rate specified in the credit documents (compound interest);
    OR ☐ **B.** All deferred interest shall be due and payable, along with principal, at maturity;
    OR ☐ **C.** Other _____

*(For Paragraphs 8-10) In order to receive timely and continued notification, Seller is advised to record appropriate notices and/or to
notify appropriate parties of any change in Seller's address.

SFA REVISED 10/02 (PAGE 1 OF 3) Print Date

Buyer's Initials (_____)(_____)
Seller's Initials (_____)(_____)

Reviewed by _____ Date _____

EQUAL HOUSING OPPORTUNITY

SELLER FINANCING ADDENDUM AND DISCLOSURE (SFA PAGE 1 OF 3)

FIGURE 3.9

Seller Financing Addendum and Disclosure (continued)

Property Address: _____   Date: _____

15. ☐ **ALL-INCLUSIVE DEED OF TRUST; INSTALLMENT LAND SALE CONTRACT:** This transaction involves the use of an all-inclusive (or wraparound) deed of trust or an installment land sale contract. That deed of trust or contract shall provide as follows:
  A. In the event of an acceleration of any senior encumbrance, the responsibility for payment, or for legal defense is: _____
  _____ ; OR ☐ **Is not** specified in the credit or security documents.
  B. In the event of the prepayment of a senior encumbrance, the responsibilities and rights of Buyer and Seller regarding refinancing, prepayment penalties, and any prepayment discounts are: _____ ;
  OR ☐ **Are not** specified in the documents evidencing credit.
  C. Buyer will make periodic payments to _____ (Seller, collection agent, or any neutral third party), who will be responsible for disbursing payments to the payee(s) on the senior encumbrance(s) and to Seller. **NOTE:** The Parties are advised to designate a neutral third party for these purposes.
16. ☐ **TAX IDENTIFICATION NUMBERS:** Buyer and Seller shall each provide to each other their Social Security Numbers or Taxpayer Identification Numbers.
17. ☐ **OTHER CREDIT TERMS** _____
  _____
18. ☐ **RECORDING:** The documents evidencing credit (paragraph 3) will be recorded with the county recorder where the Property is located. **If not**, Buyer and Seller are advised that their respective interests in the Property may be jeopardized by intervening liens, judgments, encumbrances, or subsequent transfers.
19. ☐ **JUNIOR FINANCING:** There will be additional financing, secured by the Property, junior to this Seller financing. Explain:
  _____
20. **SENIOR LOANS AND ENCUMBRANCES:** The following information is provided on loans and/or encumbrances that will be **senior** to Seller financing. **NOTE:** The following are estimates, unless otherwise marked with an asterisk (*). If checked: ☐ A separate sheet with information on additional senior loans/encumbrances is attached

		1st	2nd
A.	Original Balance	$ _____	$ _____
B.	Current Balance	$ _____	$ _____
C.	Periodic Payment (e.g. $100/month):	$ _____	$ _____ / _____
	Including Impounds of:		$ _____ / _____
D.	Interest Rate (per annum)	_____ %	_____ %
E.	Fixed or Variable Rate:	_____	_____
	If Variable Rate: Lifetime Cap (Ceiling)	_____	_____
	Indicator (Underlying Index)	_____	_____
	Margins	_____	_____
F.	Maturity Date	_____	_____
G.	Amount of Balloon Payment	$ _____	$ _____
H.	Date Balloon Payment Due	_____	_____
I.	Potential for Negative Amortization? (Yes, No, or Unknown)	_____	_____
J.	Due on Sale? (Yes, No, or Unknown)	_____	_____
K.	Pre-payment penalty? (Yes, No, or Unknown)	_____	_____
L.	Are payments current? (Yes, No, or Unknown)	_____	_____

21. **BUYER'S CREDITWORTHINESS:** (CHECK EITHER A OR B. Do not check both.) In addition to the loan application, credit report and other information requested under paragraph 2:
  A. ☐ No other disclosure concerning Buyer's creditworthiness has been made to Seller;
  OR B. ☐ The following representations concerning Buyer's creditworthiness are made by Buyer(s) to Seller:

Borrower _____	Co-Borrower _____
1. Occupation _____	1. Occupation _____
2. Employer _____	2. Employer _____
3. Length of Employment _____	3. Length of Employment _____
4. Monthly Gross Income _____	4. Monthly Gross Income _____
5. Other _____	5. Other _____

22. **ADDED, DELETED OR SUBSTITUTED BUYERS:** The addition, deletion or substitution of any person or entity under this Agreement or to title prior to close of escrow shall require Seller's written consent. Seller may grant or withhold consent in Seller's sole discretion. Any additional or substituted person or entity shall, if requested by Seller, submit to Seller the same documentation as required for the original named Buyer. Seller and/or Brokers may obtain a credit report, at Buyer's expense, on any such person or entity.

Buyer's Initials (_____)(_____)
Seller's Initials (_____)(_____)

Reviewed by _____ Date _____

EQUAL HOUSING OPPORTUNITY

SELLER FINANCING ADDENDUM AND DISCLOSURE (SFA PAGE 2 OF 3)

FIGURE 3.9

Seller Financing Addendum and Disclosure (continued)

Property Address: _____ Date: _____

23. CAUTION:

    A. If the Seller financing requires a balloon payment, Seller shall give Buyer written notice, according to the terms of Civil Code §2966, at least 90 and not more than 150 days before the balloon payment is due if the transaction is for the purchase of a dwelling for not more than four families.

    B. If **any** obligation secured by the Property calls for a balloon payment, Seller and Buyer are aware that refinancing of the balloon payment at maturity may be difficult or impossible, depending on conditions in the conventional mortgage marketplace at that time. There are no assurances that new financing or a loan extension will be available when the balloon prepayment, or any prepayment, is due.

    C. If **any** of the existing or proposed loans or extensions of credit would require refinancing as a result of a lack of full amortization, such refinancing might be difficult or impossible in the conventional mortgage marketplace.

    D. In the event of default by Buyer: (1) Seller may have to reinstate and/or make monthly payments on any and all senior encumbrances (including real property taxes) in order to protect Seller's secured interest; (2) Seller's rights are generally limited to foreclosure on the Property, pursuant to California Code of Civil Procedure §580b; and (3) the Property may lack sufficient equity to protect Seller's interests if the Property decreases in value.

If this three-page Addendum and Disclosure is used in a transaction for the purchase of a dwelling for not more than four families, it shall be prepared by an Arranger of Credit as defined in California Civil Code §2957(a). (The Arranger of Credit is usually the agent who obtained the offer.)

Arranger of Credit - (Print Firm Name) _____ By _____ Date _____

Address _____ City _____ State _____ Zip _____

Phone _____ Fax _____

> BUYER AND SELLER ACKNOWLEDGE AND AGREE THAT BROKERS: (A) WILL NOT PROVIDE LEGAL OR TAX ADVICE; (B) WILL NOT PROVIDE OTHER ADVICE OR INFORMATION THAT EXCEEDS THE KNOWLEDGE, EDUCATION AND EXPERIENCE REQUIRED TO OBTAIN A REAL ESTATE LICENSE; OR (C) HAVE NOT AND WILL NOT VERIFY ANY INFORMATION PROVIDED BY EITHER BUYER OR SELLER. BUYER AND SELLER AGREE THAT THEY WILL SEEK LEGAL, TAX AND OTHER DESIRED ASSISTANCE FROM APPROPRIATE PROFESSIONALS. BUYER AND SELLER ACKNOWLEDGE THAT THE INFORMATION EACH HAS PROVIDED TO THE ARRANGER OF CREDIT FOR INCLUSION IN THIS DISCLOSURE FORM IS ACCURATE. BUYER AND SELLER FURTHER ACKNOWLEDGE THAT EACH HAS RECEIVED A COMPLETED COPY OF THIS DISCLOSURE FORM.

Buyer _____ Date _____
        (signature)

Address _____ City _____ State _____ Zip _____

Phone _____ Fax _____ E-mail _____

Buyer _____ Date _____
        (signature)

Address _____ City _____ State _____ Zip _____

Phone _____ Fax _____ E-mail _____

Seller _____ Date _____
        (signature)

Address _____ City _____ State _____ Zip _____

Phone _____ Fax _____ E-mail _____

Seller _____ Date _____
        (signature)

Address _____ City _____ State _____ Zip _____

Phone _____ Fax _____ E-mail _____

THIS FORM HAS BEEN APPROVED BY THE CALIFORNIA ASSOCIATION OF REALTORS® (C.A.R.). NO REPRESENTATION IS MADE AS TO THE LEGAL VALIDITY OR ADEQUACY OF ANY PROVISION IN ANY SPECIFIC TRANSACTION. A REAL ESTATE BROKER IS THE PERSON QUALIFIED TO ADVISE ON REAL ESTATE TRANSACTIONS. IF YOU DESIRE LEGAL OR TAX ADVICE, CONSULT AN APPROPRIATE PROFESSIONAL.

This form is available for use by the entire real estate industry. It is not intended to identify the user as a REALTOR®. REALTOR® is a registered collective membership mark which may be used only by members of the NATIONAL ASSOCIATION OF REALTORS® who subscribe to its Code of Ethics.

SURE TRAC
The System for Success™

Published by the
California Association of REALTORS®

Reviewed by _____ Date _____

SFA REVISED 10/02 (PAGE 3 OF 3)

SELLER FINANCING ADDENDUM AND DISCLOSURE (SFA PAGE 3 OF 3)

Timing of any disclosure is extremely important. The financial disclosure must be made before execution of any note. Any notes signed prior to disclosure must be contingent on the buyer's approval before they are executed. The seller, buyer, and credit arranger must sign the disclosure statements. Copies must be given to both the buyer and seller, and a copy must be retained in the arranger's office for three years.

Many items and facts must be disclosed, including these major items:

- The terms of the note, such as original loan amount, interest rate, and term (number of payments)

- All other liens on the property: the original loan amount, current balance, interest rate and any provisions for variations in the interest rate, term, balloon payments, maturity date, and whether any payments are currently in default

- That the note, if not fully amortized, will have to be refinanced at maturity and that this might be difficult or impossible to accomplish in the conventional marketplace (If balloon payments are called for, the seller [holder of the note] must notify [send or deliver to] the buyer not less than 60 days or more than 150 days before the due date of the note. The notice must specify to whom payment is due, the due date, and the exact amount due [or a good-faith estimate], including the unpaid balance, interest, and other allowable charges.)

- That loans have or will have negative amortization, or that deferred interest ARMs (adjustable rate mortgages) could have negative amortization, and this fact must be clearly disclosed and its potential effects explained (*negative amortization* means that the monthly payments are less than the monthly interest on the loan, with the result that the borrower ends up owing more than the original loan amount)

- Who is liable for the payoff of the underlying loan in an all-inclusive trust deed (AITD) if the lender accelerates the loan

- The buyer's creditworthiness (credit report, job verification, etc.)

- "A Request for Notice of Default," filed and recorded for the seller, to help protect the seller in case any senior loans are foreclosed

- That a title insurance policy will be obtained and be furnished to both buyer and seller

- That a tax service has been arranged to notify the seller of whether property taxes have been paid on the property and who will be responsible for the continued service and compensation of the tax service, and that arrangements have been made to notify the seller if the casualty insurance payments are being paid

- That the deed of trust securing the note will be recorded, thus avoiding the problems of not recording the trust deed

■ The amount, source of funds, and purpose of the funds when the buyer is to receive cash from the proceeds of the transaction

Remember that the items above represent only a condensed version of the financing disclosure law. How disclosure must be made on the forms is shown in Figure 3.9, which meets the requirements set forth in the Civil Code.

Adjustable-Rate Loan Disclosure

Lenders offering an adjustable-rate residential mortgage must provide prospective borrowers the most recent copy of the Federal Reserve publication, *Consumer Handbook on Adjustable-Rate Mortgages*.

Blanket Encumbrance Disclosure

If there is an underlying blanket encumbrance that affects more than one parcel, the buyer's funds should be protected unless the unit can be released from the blanket encumbrance. The borrower must be made aware of and sign a notice that his or her interests could be lost if the holder of the blanket encumbrance forecloses, even though the borrower is current on his or her obligations.

Mortgage Loan Disclosure Statement

When a real estate broker solicits or negotiates nonfederally related loans on behalf of lenders or borrowers, the broker must deliver a mortgage loan disclosure statement (MLDS) to the borrower within three business days of receiving the borrowers written loan application.

Lender/Purchaser Disclosure

This disclosure applies to private party lenders and pension plans that make or purchase loans through a broker. The broker must provide a disclosure statement as to loan terms, loan status as well as information about the property securing the loan and other encumbrances.

Borrower's Right to Copy of Appraisal

If the borrower paid for the appraisal, a lender must notify the borrower that the borrower can request and receive a copy of the appraisal report.

Real Estate Settlement Procedures Act

The federal Real Estate Settlement and Procedure Act (RESPA) applies to one to four-unit residential properties. Within three days of the loan application for a federally related loan, the lender must furnish the buyer a **good faith estimate** of all closing costs as well as an information booklet prepared by the Department of Housing and Urban Development (HUD). Federally related loans include loans made by federally regulated lenders, lenders having federally insured deposits, loans that will be federally insured or guaranteed and loans that are to be resold to Fannie Mae or Freddie Mac.

One day prior to settlement, the borrower has a right to review the Uniform Settlement Statement, which must be given to the borrower on or before settlement.

RESPA allows a controlled business arrangement where a broker has a financial interest in a service provider. However, the relationship of the broker and the service provider must be fully disclosed, and the buyer must be free to utilize other service providers such as escrow services and loan brokerage services.

Lender Compensation Disclosure

A broker must reveal to all parties to a transaction if the broker is to receive any compensation from a lender before the transaction closes escrow. **Note:** California law prohibits a broker from receiving referral fees from service providers.

Notice of Transfer of Loan Servicing

For loans secured by one to four-unit residential properties the borrower must be notified when the loan servicing function (collection) is transferred.

Truth-In-Lending Act (Regulation Z)

This federal consumer protection act requires advertising disclosure of finance charges. Interest expressed as an Annual Percentage Rate (APR) and terms of credit if trigger terms are used in the advertisement (see Chapter 8). Before a borrower is obligated to complete designated loans there must be full credit disclosure.

Notice of Adverse Action (Equal Credit Opportunity Act)

When a creditor denies a loan applicant the creditor must provide a statement of reason for denial or the applicant's right to obtain such a statement. Generally, this must be provided within 30 days of loan application.

Housing Financial Discrimination Act (Holden Act) Disclosure

At time of the loan application, borrowers must be notified of the prohibition against lender discriminatory practices and their rights under the law.

Elder Abuse Disclosure

California's *Elder Abuse Law* requires that escrow holders, realty agents, and others report elder financial abuse, fraud, or undue influence. The county public guardian is authorized to take control of the elder's assets to prevent abuse. If an agent feels that an elderly person is being financially abused, reporting the abuse is mandatory.

■ OTHER DISCLOSURES

Megan's Law

Megan's Law provides for registration of sex offenders and public availability of knowledge regarding the location of these offenders. Now, every sales contract or lease of one to four-unit residential properties must include a notice informing buyers or lessees of the public availability of this information.

Structural Pest Control Inspection and Certification Reports

While the law does not require a structural pest control inspection, if required by contract or lender, a copy must be delivered to the buyer.

Energy Conservation Retrofit and Thermal Insulation Disclosures

Some communities require energy retrofitting as a condition of sale. The seller or agent should disclose the requirements of local statutes.

New home sellers must disclose in their sales contracts the type, thickness, and R value of the insulation.

Sale Price

Within one month of close of escrow for sale of real property through a broker, the broker must inform the buyer and seller, in writing, the sale price. **Note:** The Escrow Closing Statement is compliant with this requirement.

Foreign Investment Real Property Tax Act

The buyer must be informed about the IRS withholding requirement of 10 percent of the gross sales price when the seller is a foreign person. (See Chapter 14 for exemptions.)

Buyer State Tax Withholding

The buyer must be informed about the requirement to withhold $3\frac{1}{3}$ percent of the total sale price paid as state income tax. (See Chapter 14 for details about this requirement and its exemptions.)

Notice Regarding Advisability of Title Insurance

If no title insurance is to be issued through an escrow, the buyer must receive a separate notice about the advisability of obtaining title insurance. (See Civil Code Section 1057.6.)

Importance of Home Inspection Notice

For the sale of one to four-unit residential properties (including mobile homes) involving FHA financing or HUD owned property, the borrower must sign a **home inspection notice** entitled "The Importance of a Home Inspection."

Smoke Detector Notice

A buyer of a single-family home must receive a **smoke detector disclosure** written statement indicating that the property is in compliance with current California law regarding the presence of smoke detectors.

Window Security Bars

A seller must disclose on the Real Estate Transfer Disclosure Statement, the presence of window security bars and any safety release mechanism on the bars.

Water Heater Bracing

Sellers of real property must certify to prospective purchasers that the **water heater bracing** has been properly installed.

Commissions

A notice must be given to the party paying any real estate commission that commissions are negotiable.

■ RIGHT OF RESCISSION

For detailed California disclosure requirements, check the Department of Real Estate Web site: *www.dre.ca.gove/ disclosures.htm.*

There are statutory **rescission rights** for a number of transactions. The buyer (or borrower) must be informed of his or her rights. Failure to disclose rights of rescission extends this right.

Truth-in-Lending Act—When a loan (home equity loan) for consumer credit is secured by a borrower's residence, a rescission right exists until midnight of the third business day following the completion of the loan.

Interstate Land Sales Full Disclosure Act—This federal act calls for a disclosure statement, known as a *property report*, for subdivisions of 25 or more unimproved residential properties of less than five acres each that are sold in interstate commerce. Besides the required disclosures to the purchasers, the purchasers have a seven-day right of rescission.

Time-Share—Because of abusive sales tactics of many time-share developers, purchasers of time-shares now have a rescission right of three days after signing the contract.

Undivided Interest Subdivision—An undivided interest subdivision is one where the owners are tenants in common with the other owners but don't have an exclusive possessory interest in a particular unit or space. An example is a campground where owners have a right to use a space if available. Purchasers in undivided interest subdivisions have a three-day right of rescission following the day the agreement is signed.

Home Equity Sales—Because of fraud and unfair dealings by home equity purchasers, a homeowner has a rescission right when selling his or her equity interest in a residence in foreclosure. There is a right to cancel any contract with an equity purchaser until midnight of the fifth business day following the sales agreement or until 8 A.M. on the day of the sale, whichever occurs first.

Mello-Roos Disclosure—Failure to disclose the fact that a property is in a Mello-Roos district would allow the transferee a three-day to five-day right of rescission.

■ CALIFORNIA ASSOCIATION OF REALTORS® DISCLOSURE CHART

To aid members in understanding the numerous disclosure obligations that real estate professionals should be aware of, the California Association of REALTORS® has prepared a California Real Estate Law Disclosure Chart (Figure 3.10). In Chapter 10, you will find that the purchase contract includes many of the required disclosures.

FIGURE 3.10

California Real Estate Law Disclosure Chart

CALIFORNIA ASSOCIATION OF REALTORS®

California Real Estate Law
Disclosure Chart₁

Member Legal Services
January 22, 2002 (Revised)

Tel 213.739.8282
Fax 213.480.7724
www.car.org

SUBJECT	DISCLOSURE TRIGGER	DISCLOSURE REQUIREMENT (Brief Summary) FORM	C.A.R. INFORMATION SOURCE LAW CITATION
Agent's Real Property Inspection	Sale² of all residential real property of 1-4 units (No exemptions except for never-occupied properties where a public report is required or properties exempted from a public report pursuant to Business & Professions Code § 11010.4)	A real estate licensee must conduct a reasonably competent and diligent visual inspection of the property; this inspection duty does not include areas which are reasonably and normally inaccessible, off the site, or public records or permits concerning the title or use of the property; this inspection duty includes only the unit for sale and not the common areas of a condo or other common interest development. There is no requirement that the inspection report be in writing; however, it is recommended that all licensees put it in writing.	Q&A, "Complying With The Real Estate Transfer Disclosure Statement Law And The Broker's Duty To Inspect Residential Real Property."
	Also applies to Manufactured Homes (as defined in H&S § 18007, which includes personal property Mobilehomes)	C.A.R. Form TDS-11(or for mobilehomes and manufactured housing, C.A.R. Form MHTDS-11) may be used. If the seller is exempt from the TDS, then C.A.R. Form AID-11 may be used by the agent.	Cal. Civ. Code §§ 2079 – 2079.6

1

FIGURE 3.10

California Real Estate Law Disclosure Chart (continued)

SUBJECT	DISCLOSURE TRIGGER	DISCLOSURE REQUIREMENT (Brief Summary) FORM	C.A.R. INFORMATION SOURCE LAW CITATION
Commercial or Industrial Zone Location 2	Transfer[3] or exchange of residential real property of 1-4 units.	The seller of real property subject to the TDS law must disclose "actual knowledge" that the property is affected by or zoned to allow an industrial use of property (manufacturing, commercial, or airport use) as soon as possible before transfer of title. C.A.R. Form TDS-11 may be used.	Cal. Civ. Code § 1102.17; Cal. Code Civ. Proc. § 731a
Death and/or AIDS 3	Sale, lease, or rental of <u>all</u> real property.	The transferor/agent has no liability for not disclosing the fact of any death which occurred more than 3 years prior to the date the transferee offers to buy, lease, or rent the property. Any death which has occurred within a 3-year period should be disclosed if deemed to be "material." Affliction with AIDS or death from AIDS, no matter when it occurred, need not be voluntarily disclosed. However, neither a seller nor seller's agent may make an intentional misrepresentation in response to a direct question concerning deaths on the property.	Q&A, "Disclosure of Aids and Death: The Legislative Solution." Cal. Civ. Code § 1710.2.
"Drug Lab" – Illegal Controlled Substances Contamination 4	Transfer[4] or exchange of residential real property of 1-4 units and lease of <u>any</u> residential dwelling unit. Same exemptions as for the Transfer Disclosure Statement.	In the event that toxic contamination by an illegal controlled substance has occurred on a property and upon receipt of a notice from the Dept. of Toxic Substances Control (DTSC) or other agency—or if the seller has actual knowledge of the toxic contamination—the seller must disclose this information to the buyer by checking item II.C.1 of the TDS form and attaching the DTSC notice, there is one. In the case of rental property, the landlord must give a prospective tenant written notice of the toxic contamination. Providing the tenant with a copy of the DTSC notice will suffice if there is such a notice. C.A.R. Form TDS-11 may be used.	Cal. Civ. Code §§ 1102.18, 1940.7.5
Earthquake Fault Zones[5] 5	Sale of <u>all</u> real property which does contain or will eventually contain a structure for human occupany and which is located in an earthquake fault zone (special studies zone) as indicated on maps created by the California Division of Mines and Geology.[6] Also applies to Manufactured Homes (as defined in H&S § 18007, which includes personal property Mobilehomes)	The seller's <u>agent</u> or the seller without an agent must disclose to the buyer the fact that the property is in an earthquake fault zone (special studies zone), if maps are available at the county assessor's, county recorder's, or county planning commission office, or if the seller or seller's agent has actual knowledge that the property is in the zone. If the map is not of sufficient accuracy or scale to determine whether the property is in the zone, then either the agent indicates "yes" that the property is in the zone or the agent may write "no" that the property is <u>not</u> in this zone, but then a report prepared by an expert verifying that fact must be attached to the form NHD-11. If a TDS is required in the transaction, either C.A.R. Form NHD-11, "Natural Hazard Disclosure Statement," or an updated Local Option disclosure form must be used to make this disclosure.	Q&A, "Earthquake and Flood Hazard Disclosures." Q&A, "Natural Hazard Disclosure Statement." Cal. Pub. Res. Code §§ 2621 <u>et seq.</u>; Cal. Civ. Code § 1103

FIGURE 3.10

California Real Estate Law Disclosure Chart (continued)

3

SUBJECT	DISCLOSURE TRIGGER	DISCLOSURE REQUIREMENT (Brief Summary) FORM	C.A.R. INFORMATION SOURCE LAW CITATION
Earthquake Hazards – Homeowner's Guide 6	Mandatory delivery: Transfer of residential real property of 1-4 units, manufactured homes, and mobilehomes, of conventional light frame construction, and built prior to January 1, 1960, if not exempt (almost same exemptions as for the Transfer Disclosure Statement[7]). Additional exemption if the buyer agrees, in writing, to demolish the property within one year from date of transfer. Voluntary delivery: Transfer[8] of any real property.	Mandatory delivery: The licensee must give the transferor the booklet "The Homeowner's Guide to Earthquake Safety"[9] and the transferor must give this booklet to the transferee. Known structural deficiencies must be disclosed by the transferor to the transferee and the form in the booklet entitled "Residential Earthquake Hazards Report" may be used to make this disclosure. Voluntary delivery: If the Guide is delivered to the transferee, then the transferor or broker is not required to provide additional information concerning general earthquake hazards. Known earthquake hazards must be disclosed whether delivery is mandatory or voluntary.	Q&A, "Earthquake and Flood Hazard Disclosures." Cal. Bus. & Prof. Code § 10149; Cal. Gov't Code §§ 8897.1, 8897.2, 8897.5. Cal. Civ. Code § 2079.8.
Earthquake Hazards – Commercial Guide 7	Mandatory delivery: Sale, transfer, or exchange of any real property or manufactured home or mobilehome if built of precast concrete or reinforced/unreinforced masonry with wood frame floors or roofs and built before January 1, 1975, located within a county or city, if not exempt. Same exemptions as for Homeowner's Guide. Voluntary delivery: Transfer[10] of any real property.	Mandatory delivery: The transferor/transferor's agent must give the transferee a copy of "The Commercial Property Owner's Guide to Earthquake Safety."[11] Voluntary delivery: If the Guide is delivered to the transferee, then the transferor or broker is not required to provide additional information concerning general earthquake hazards. Known earthquake hazards must be disclosed whether delivery is mandatory or voluntary.	Q&A, "Earthquake and Flood Hazard Disclosures." Cal. Bus. & Prof. Code § 10147, Cal. Gov't Code §§ 8875.6, 8875.9, 8893.2, 8893.3. Cal. Civ. Code § 2079.9.

California Real Estate Law Disclosure Chart (continued)

▼ Legal Q&A		January 22, 2002

4

SUBJECT	DISCLOSURE TRIGGER	DISCLOSURE REQUIREMENT (Brief Summary) FORM	C.A.R. INFORMATION SOURCE LAW CITATION
Flood Hazard Areas (federal law) 8	Sale or lease of all improved real estate or mobilehomes located in flood hazard areas as indicated on maps published by the Federal Emergency Management Agency.[12]	The seller/lessor should disclose to buyer/lessee the fact that the property is located in such an area.[13] C.A.R. Form TDS-11 may be used (or for mobilehomes and manufactured housing, C.A.R. Form MHTDS-11).	Q&A, "Earthquake and Flood Hazard Disclosures." 42 U.S.C. §§ 4001 et seq., § 4104a.
"Special Flood Hazard Area" (state law) 9	Sale of real property located in Zone "A" or " V" as designated by FEMA and if the seller or the seller's agent has actual knowledge or a list has been compiled by parcel and the notice posted at a local county recorder, assessor and planning agency. Also applies to Manufactured Homes (as defined in H&S § 18007, which includes personal property Mobilehomes)	The seller's agent or the seller without an agent must disclose to the buyer if the property is in this Special Flood Hazard Area, if a parcel list has been prepared by the county and a notice identifying the location of the list is available at the county assessor's, county recorder's or county planning commission office, or if the seller or seller's agent has actual knowledge that the property is in an area. If a TDS is required in the transaction, either C.A.R. Form NHD-11, "Natural Hazard Disclosure Statement" or an updated Local Option disclosure form must be used to make this disclosure.	Q&A, "Natural Hazard Disclosure Statement." Cal. Civ. Code § 1103, Cal. Gov't Code § 8589.3
"Area of Potential Flooding" (in the event of dam or reservoir failure) (state law) 10	Sale of all real property if the seller or the seller's agent has actual knowledge or a list has been compiled by parcel and the notice posted at a local county recorder, assessor and planning agency. Also applies to Manufactured Homes (as defined in H&S § 18007, which includes personal property Mobilehomes)	The seller's agent or the seller without an agent must disclose to the buyer if the property is in this Area of Potential Flooding as designated on an inundation map, if a parcel list has been prepared by the county and a notice identifying the location of the list is available at the county assessor's, county recorder's or county planning commission office, or if the seller or seller's agent has actual knowledge that the property is in an area. If a TDS is required in the transaction, either C.A.R. Form NHD-11, "Natural Hazard Disclosure Statement" or an updated Local Option disclosure form must be used to make this disclosure.	Q&A, "Natural Hazard Disclosure Statement." Cal. Gov't Code §§ 8589.4, 8589.5; Cal. Civ. Code § 1103

FIGURE 3.10

California Real Estate Law Disclosure Chart (continued)

▼ Legal Q&A			January 22, 2002

5

SUBJECT	DISCLOSURE TRIGGER	DISCLOSURE REQUIREMENT (Brief Summary) FORM	C.A.R. INFORMATION SOURCE LAW CITATION
Flood Disaster Insurance (federal law) (Applicable for any flood disaster[14] declared after September 23, 1994) 11	Any transfer[15] of personal (e.g., mobilehomes), residential, or commercial property where the owner received federal flood disaster assistance conditioned on the owner subsequently obtaining and maintaining flood insurance.	The transferor must notify the transferee in writing on a document "evidencing the transfer of ownership of the property" about the requirement to obtain and maintain flood insurance in accordance with applicable Federal law. [Currently, there are no regulations detailing this requirement.] Failure to notify the transferee means that in the event the transferee fails to maintain the required flood insurance and the property is damaged by a flood disaster requiring Federal disaster relief, the transferor will be required to reimburse the Federal government. The law is unclear as to what document(s) should contain this notice. C.A.R. Forms RPA-14 and NHD-11 may be acceptable, but technically are not documents which "evidence the transfer of ownership." Clearly, a grant deed is such a document.	Legal Brief, "Federal Flood Insurance Disclosure." 42 U.S.C. § 5154a.
Home Energy Ratings 12	Transfer[16] or exchange of all real property. Also applies to Manufactured Homes (as defined in H&S § 18007, which includes personal property Mobilehomes)	If a home energy ratings booklet to be developed by the State of California is delivered to the transferee, then a seller or broker is not required to provide additional information concerning the existence of a statewide home energy rating program. NEITHER THIS PROGRAM NOR THE BOOKLET IS AVAILABLE AT THIS TIME.	Cal. Civ. Code § 2079.10; Cal. Pub. Res. Code §§ 25402.9, 25942.
Home Environmental Hazards 13	Transfer[17] or exchange of all real property. Also applies to Manufactured Homes (as defined in H&S § 18007, which includes personal property Mobilehomes)	If a consumer information booklet[18] is delivered to the transferee, then a seller or broker is not required to provide additional information concerning common environmental hazards. Although highly recommended, delivery is voluntary. However, known hazards on the property must be disclosed to the transferee.	Q&A, "Due Diligence and Disclosure of Environmental Hazards in Real Estate Transactions." Q&A, "Information Resources for Environmental Hazards." Cal. Civ. Code § 2079.7.
Home Inspection Notice (FHA/HUD) 14	Sale of residential real property of 1-4 units, including mobilehomes on a permanent foundation, which involve FHA loans or HUD-owned properties.	For all properties regardless of when they were built, the borrower must sign the notice entitled, "The Importance of a Home Inspection." C.A.R. Form HID-11 may be used for this purpose.	Q&A, "FHA Lead-Based Paint Disclosure Form and New FHA Inspection Disclosure Form," Legal Brief, "FHA Inspection Disclosure Form. " HUD Mortgagee Letter 96-10.

FIGURE 3.10

California Real Estate Law Disclosure Chart (continued)

SUBJECT	DISCLOSURE TRIGGER	DISCLOSURE REQUIREMENT (Brief Summary) FORM	C.A.R. INFORMATION SOURCE LAW CITATION
Lead Hazard Pamphlet 15	Sale or lease of <u>all</u> residential property, <u>built before 1978</u>, except as indicated below. Mobilehomes are also subject to this law. <u>Exemptions:</u> · foreclosure or trustee's sale transfer (REO properties and deed in lieu of foreclosure are NOT exempt!) · zero-bedroom dwelling (loft, efficiency unit, dorm, or studio) · short-term rental (100 or fewer days) · housing for elderly or handicapped (unless children live there) · rental housing certified free of lead paint	The seller/lessor must provide the buyer/lessee with a lead hazard information pamphlet, disclose the presence of any known lead-based paint and provide a statement signed by the buyer that the buyer has read the warning statement, has received the pamphlet, and has a 10-day opportunity to inspect before becoming obligated under the contract. The purchaser (not lessee) is permitted a 10-day period to conduct an inspection unless the parties mutually agree upon a different time period. The agent, on behalf of the seller/lessor, must ensure compliance with the requirements of this law. C.A.R. pamphlet, "Protect Your Family From Lead in Your Home," and C.A.R. form FLD-11 satisfy these requirements (except for sales of HUD properties—HUD forms required). The C.A.R. revised home environmental hazards booklet may be used in lieu of the pamphlet mentioned above.	Q&A, "Federal Lead-Based Paint Hazards Disclosure." Residential Lead-Based Paint Hazard Reduction Act of 1992, 42 U.S.C.S. § 4852d.
Megan's Law Disclosure 16	Sale[19] or lease/rental of all residential real property of 1-4 units (No exemptions except for never-occupied properties where a public report is required or properties exempted from a public report pursuant to Business & Professions Code § 11010.4)	Every lease or rental agreement and every sales contract is required to include a statutorily-defined notice regarding the existence of public access to database information regarding sex offenders. The following C.A.R. forms contain this statutory notice: LR-14, LR-14-S, RIPA-14, RPA-14	Q&A, "Megan's Law: Notifying the Public About Registered Sex Offenders." Cal. Civ. Code § 2079.10a
Mello-Roos District or Any Other Bond Assessment 17	Transfer[20] or exchange of residential real property of 1-4 units subject to a continuing lien securing the levy of special taxes pursuant to the Mello-Roos Community Facilities Act. Same exemptions as for the Transfer Disclosure Statement except that new subdivisions are not exempt.	The transferor must make a good faith effort to obtain a disclosure notice concerning the special tax or assessment from each local agency that levies a special tax or assessment and deliver the notice(s) to the prospective transferee. The disclosure notice also provides a 3 or 5-day right of rescission to the transferee. There is no affirmative duty by an agent to discover a special tax or district or assessment not actually known to the agent.	Q&A, "Mello-Roos District Disclosure Requirements." Cal. Civ. Code § 1102.6b; Cal. Gov't Code Sections §§ 53340.2, 53341.5, 53754.

FIGURE 3.10

California Real Estate Law Disclosure Chart (continued)

7

SUBJECT	DISCLOSURE TRIGGER	DISCLOSURE REQUIREMENT (Brief Summary) FORM	C.A.R. INFORMATION SOURCE LAW CITATION
Military Ordnance Location 18	Transfer[21] or exchange of residential real property of 1-4 units and lease of any residential dwelling unit. Same exemptions as for the Transfer Disclosure Statement.	Disclosure is required when the transferor/lessor has actual knowledge that a former military ordnance location (military training grounds which may contain explosives) is within one mile of the property. The transferor/lessor must disclose in writing to the transferee/lessee, that these former federal or state military ordnance locations may contain potentially explosive munitions. The transferee has a 3 or 5-day right of rescission. C.A.R. Form TDS-11 may be used.	Cal. Civ. Code §§ 1102.15, 1940.7.
Mold (Toxic) (no new disclosure duties upon transfer until after the DHS establishes guidelines) 19	Sale, lease, rental, or other transfer of any commercial, industrial or residential property	There are no current disclosure requirements until after the Dept. of Health Services (DHS) develops permissible exposure limits for molds and a consumer booklet. The TDS has been modified to include the word "mold" in paragraph II.C.1. As always, any transferor must disclose actual knowledge of toxic mold on the property.	Q&A, "Mold and Its Impact on Real Estate Transactions." Legal Update (November 19, 2001) Cal. Health & Safety Code §§ 26100 et seq., §§ 26140, 26141, 26147, 26148
Seismic Hazard Zones 20	Sale of all real property which does contain or will eventually contain a structure for human habitation and which is located in a seismic hazard zone as indicated on maps created by the California Division of Mines and Geology. Also applies to Manufactured Homes (as defined in H&S § 18007, which includes personal property Mobilehomes)	The seller's agent or the seller without an agent must disclose to the buyer the fact that the property is in a seismic hazard zone if maps are available at the county assessor's, county recorder's, or county planning commission office, or if the seller or seller's agent has actual knowledge that the property is in the zone. If the map is not of sufficient accuracy or scale to determine whether the property is in the zone, then either the agent indicates "yes" that the property is in the zone or the agent may write "no" that the property is not in this zone, but then a report prepared by an expert verifying that fact must be attached to the form NHD-11. If a TDS is required in the transaction, either C.A.R. Form NHD-11, "Natural Hazard Disclosure Statement" or an updated Local Option disclosure form must be used to make this disclosure.	Q&A, "Earthquake and Flood Hazard Disclosures," Legal Brief, "Seismic Hazard Zone Maps," Q&A, "Natural Hazard Disclosure Statement." Cal. Pub. Res. Code § 2690 et seq., § 2694; Cal. Civ. Code § 1103

FIGURE 3.10

California Real Estate Law Disclosure Chart (continued)

8

SUBJECT	DISCLOSURE TRIGGER	DISCLOSURE REQUIREMENT (Brief Summary) FORM	C.A.R. INFORMATION SOURCE LAW CITATION
Smoke Detector Compliance 21	All existing dwelling units must have a smoke detector centrally located outside each sleeping area (bedroom or group of bedrooms). In addition, new construction (with a permit after August 14, 1992) must have a hard-wired smoke detector in each bedroom. Any additions, modifications, or repairs (after August 14, 1992) exceeding $1,000 for which a permit is required will also trigger the requirement of a smoke detector in each bedroom. (These may be battery operated.)	The seller of a <u>single family home</u> must provide the buyer with a written statement indicating that the property is in compliance with current California law. Same exemptions from compliance and disclosure as for the Transfer Disclosure Statement but only for single family homes and factory-built housing, not other types of dwellings. Transfers to or from any governmental entity, and transfers by a beneficiary or mortgagee after foreclosure sale or trustee's sale or transfers by deed in lieu of foreclosure, which are exempt under the TDS law, are <u>not</u> exempt from this law. LOCAL LAW MAY BE MORE RESTRICTIVE! Check with the local City or County Department of Building and Safety. C.A.R. Form SDS-11 may be used.	C.A.R. Memorandum, "Important Smoke Detector Update." Cal. Health & Safety Code §§ 13113.7, 13113.8, 18029.6.
State Responsibility Areas (Fire Hazard Areas) 22	Sale of <u>any</u> real property located in a designated state responsibility area (generally a "wildland area") where the state not local or federal govt. has the primary financial responsibility for fire prevention. The California Department of Forestry provides maps to the county assessor of each affected county.[22] Also applies to Manufactured Homes (as defined in H&S § 18007, which includes personal property Mobilehomes)	The seller must disclose to the buyer the fact that the property is located in this zone, the risk of fire, state-imposed additional duties such as maintaining fire breaks, and the fact that the state may not provide fire protection services. The disclosure must be made if maps are available at the county assessor's, county recorder's or county planning commission office, or if the seller has actual knowledge that the property is in the zone. If the map is not of sufficient accuracy or scale to determine whether the property is in this Area, then either the agent indicates "yes" that the property is in this Area or the agent may write "no" that the property is <u>not</u> in this Area, but then a report prepared by an expert verifying that fact must be attached to the form NHD-11. If a TDS is required in the transaction, either C.A.R. Form NHD-11, "Natural Hazard Disclosure Statement" or an updated Local Option disclosure form must be used to make this disclosure.	Q&A, "Natural Hazard Disclosure Statement." Cal. Pub. Res. Code §§ 4125, 4136; Cal. Civ. Code § 1103
"Very High Fire Hazard Severity Zone" 23	Sale of any real property. Also applies to Manufactured Homes (as defined in H&S § 18007, which includes personal property Mobilehomes)	The seller must disclose the fact that the property is located within this zone and whether it is subject to the requirements of Gov't Code Section 51182 (e.g., clear brush, maintain fire breaks). The disclosure must be made if maps are available at the county assessor's, county recorder's or county planning commission office, or if the seller has actual knowledge that the property is in the zone. If the map is not of sufficient accuracy or scale to determine whether the property is in this zone, then either the agent indicates "yes" that the property is in this zone or the agent may write "no" that the property is <u>not</u> in this zone, but then a report prepared by an expert verifying that fact must be attached to the form NHD-11. If a TDS is required in the transaction, either C.A.R. Form NHD-11, "Natural Hazard Disclosure Statement" or an updated Local Option disclosure form must be used to make this disclosure.	Q&A, "Natural Hazard Disclosure Statement." Cal. Gov't Code §§ 51178, 51183.5; Cal. Civ. Code § 1103

FIGURE 3.10

California Real Estate Law Disclosure Chart (continued)

	Legal Q&A		January 22, 2002

9

SUBJECT	DISCLOSURE TRIGGER	DISCLOSURE REQUIREMENT (Brief Summary) FORM	C.A.R. INFORMATION SOURCE LAW CITATION
Subdivided Lands Law 24	Sale, leasing, or financing of new developments (condos, PUDs) or conversions consisting of 5 or more lots, parcels, or interests. However, a transfer of a single property to 5 or more unrelated people (unless exempt) may also trigger this law. There are exemptions too numerous to discuss in this chart.	The owner, subdivider, or agent, prior to the execution of the purchase contract or lease, must give the buyer/lessee a copy of the final public report (FPR), preliminary public report (PPR), or the conditional public report (CPR) issued by the DRE. No offers may be solicited until the DRE has issued one of these three reports. If the DRE has issued a CPR or PPR, then offers may be solicited, but close of escrow is contingent upon issuance of the FPR. Contracts entered into pursuant to a PPR may be rescinded by either party; contracts entered into pursuant to a CPR are contingent upon satisfaction of certain specified conditions.	Q&A, "Subdivided Lands Law," Q&A, "Subdivision Applicability Chart." Cal. Bus. & Prof. Code § 11018.1. Cal. Bus. & Prof. Code § 11018.12; Cal. Code Regs., tit. 10, § 2795. See generally, Cal. Bus. & Prof. Code §§ 11000 et seq.; Cal. Code Regs., tit. 10, §§ 2790 et seq.
Subdivision Map Act 25	Any division of real property into 2 or more lots or parcels for the purpose of sale, lease, or financing. There are exemptions too numerous to discuss in this chart.	The owner/subdivider must record either a tentative and final map, or a parcel map (depending on the type of subdivision). Escrow on the transfer cannot close until the appropriate map has been recorded.	Q&A, "Subdivision Applicability Chart." Cal. Gov't Code §§ 66426, 66428. See generally, Cal. Gov't Code §§ 66410 et seq.
Water Heater Bracing 26	All properties with water heaters. Legislative intent suggests this law applies only to residential properties, but the language of the statute does not limit the requirement to residential properties.	All owners of new or replacement water heaters and all owners of existing residential water heaters must brace, anchor or strap water heaters to resist falling or horizontal displacement due to earthquake motion. The seller of real property must certify in writing to a prospective purchaser that he has complied with this section and applicable local code requirements. This certification may be done in existing transactional documents, including but not limited to, the Homeowner's Guide to Earthquake Safety, a real estate purchase contract, a transfer disclosure statement, or a local option disclosure of compliance. C.A.R. Form WHS-11 may be used.	Q&A, "Water Heater Bracing and Disclosure Requirements." Cal. Health & Safety Code § 19211.

The information contained herein is believed accurate as of January 22, 2002. It is intended to provide general answers to general questions and is not intended as a substitute for individual legal advice. Advice in specific situations may differ depending upon a wide variety of factors. Therefore, readers with specific legal questions should seek the advice of an attorney.

ENDNOTES

[1] This chart is current as of January 22, 2002 and all laws are currently effective unless otherwise noted. Although this chart summarizes disclosure requirements in the transfer of real property, agents should be aware that the seller/transferor, as well as the agent, is required to disclose all known information affecting the property which may be deemed "material." In addition, it is imperative to check local disclosure requirements. Local law may be more stringent than state law in certain areas or there may be additional disclosures required.

[2] This provision also applies to leases with an option to purchase, ground leases of land improved with 1-4 residential units, and real property installment sales contracts. Cal. Civ. Code § 2079.1.

[3] "Transfer" for the purposes of this law means transfer by sale, lease with option to purchase, purchase option, ground lease coupled with improvements, installment land sale contract, or transfer of a residential stock cooperative. Cal. Civ. Code § 1102.

[4] Same as number 3 above.

FIGURE **3.10**

California Real Estate Law Disclosure Chart (continued)

 Legal Q&A   January 22, 2002

10

[5] These zones were formerly called, "Special Studies Zones." Some maps may still refer to the old name.

[6] The maps may be purchased from BPS Reprographics by calling (415) 512-6550 with the names of the required maps. Special Publication 42 indicates the names of the maps of the Earthquake Fault Zones. This publication is available from the California Division of Mines and Geology by calling (916) 445-5716.

[7] Transfers which can be made without a public report pursuant to Section 11010.4 of the Business and Professions Code are exempt from a TDS but not from the Homeowner's Guide.

[8] "Transfer" for purposes of this law means transfer by sale, lease with option to purchase, purchase option, ground lease coupled with improvements, or installment land sale contract.

[9] This Guide is available from CAR and/or local Boards/Associations.

[10] Same as number 7 above.

[11] This Guide is available from CAR and/or local Boards/Associations.

[12] The maps may be purchased from FEMA by calling (800) 358-9616

[13]. Federal law actually imposes the duty on a federal lender to notify the purchaser/lessee, in writing, "or obtain satisfactory assurances that the seller or lessor has notified the purchaser or lessee," of special flood hazards in advance of the signing of the purchase agreement. In any event, this information _may_ be deemed a material fact and, thus, should probably be disclosed by the seller/lessor.

[14] "Flood disaster area" means an area so designated by the U.S. Secretary of Agriculture or an area the President has declared to be a disaster or emergency as a result of flood conditions.

[15] Same as number 3 above.

[16] Same as number 7 above.

[17] Same as number 7 above.

[18] The consumer information booklet entitled "Environmental Hazards, A Guide for Homeowners and Buyers" is available from C.A.R. and/or local Boards/Associations.

[19] This provision also applies to leases with an option to purchase, ground leases of land improved with 1-4 residential units, and real property installment sales contracts. Cal. Civ. Code § 2079.1.

[20] Same as number 3 above.

[21] Same as number 3 above.

[22] The Department of Forestry's telephone number is (916) 653-5121.

■ SUMMARY

The purpose of the disclosure requirements in real estate practice is fairness. Parties deserve to have the facts before they make decisions. These facts include detrimental facts known by the agent that the buyer or seller would likely consider in decision making. The duty of disclosure is inherent in an agency. The fiduciary duty of the agent requires full disclosure.

To avoid misunderstandings, agents must explain the various agency options to both buyer and seller. The agent makes his or her selection and the parties confirm the selection.

The seller has disclosure duties to the buyer. For one to four-unit residential property, the seller must complete a Real Estate Transfer Disclosure Statement. The agent must also provide the results of his or her visual inspection to the owner.

An agent need not disclose a natural death on the premises or a death from any cause after three years. An agent also need not disclose that a former resident was afflicted with or died of AIDS, even if within the three-year period. Stigmatized property should be disclosed if a buyer would reasonably want to know about it.

When there is seller financing, a seller financing addendum and disclosure is required. Buyers must be warned of any dangers.

For one to four-unit residential property built prior to January 1, 1960, the agent must disclose whether the dwelling has earthquake weaknesses. This is accomplished with a Residential Earthquake Hazards Report. For commercial property of specified construction, the seller or seller's agent must give the buyer a copy of the *Commercial Property Owner's Guide to Earthquake Safety*.

Other required natural hazard disclosures are special flood hazard area, area of potential flooding, very high fire hazard severity zone, wildlife area that may contain substantial forest fire risks and hazards, earthquake fault zone, and seismic hazard zone. These disclosures are made in the statutory form, Natural Hazard Disclosure Statement.

Homeowners must be informed about environmental hazards on or affecting their property. The broker must provide a booklet to buyers on environmental hazards. Buyers and lessees also must be informed about hazardous substances released on or believed to be present on a property. Tenants must inform landlords if they release hazardous substances on the property.

For one- to four- residential property built prior to 1978, purchasers must be given a *Protect Your Family from Lead in Your Home* booklet. Giving the buyers the California booklet *Environmental Hazards: A Guide for Homeowners, Buyers, and Tenants*, also satisfies the Federal requirement.

Prospective purchasers must be notified if a property is within one mile of a former military ordnance site where explosives might be located.

Subdivision disclosures include the public report and common interest information. Notices must also be provided to tenants of their rights when apartments are converted to common interest developments.

The Interstate Land Sales Act is a disclosure act governing sales of unimproved lots in interstate commerce. Its purpose is to prevent fraud.

When a project is subject to a Mello-Roos bond, the purchaser must be informed.

Financing Disclosures include the following:

- Seller Financing Disclosure
- Adjustable-Rate Loan Disclosure
- Blanket Encumbrance Disclosure
- Mortgage Loan Disclosure Statement
- Lender/Purchaser Disclosure
- Borrower's Right to Copy of Appraisal
- Real Estate Settlement Act Disclosure
- Lender Compensation Disclosure
- Notice of Transfer of Loan Servicing
- Truth-In-Lending Act Disclosure
- Notice of Adverse Action Disclosure
- Housing Financial Discrimination Act Disclosure

Other disclosures include the following:

- Megan's Law Disclosure information as to sex offenders
- Structural Pest Control Inspection and Certification Reports
- Energy Conservation Retrofit and Thermal Insulation Disclosures
- Sale Price
- Foreign Investment In Real Property Act required withholding
- Buyer State Tax withholding information

■ Notice regarding advisability of title insurance

■ The importance of home inspection notice

■ Smoke detector notice

■ Water heater bracing certification

There are statutory rights of rescission after a number of notifications.

■ CLASS DISCUSSION TOPICS

1. A property you have for sale is about two blocks from a park frequented by homeless people and prostitutes. So as not to offend prospective buyers, you avoid this area by a roundabout drive. Have you acted in a proper manner?

2. A buyer offers to trade 50 emeralds for a home you have listed. What, if any, are your obligations?

3. What environmental hazards would be likely to be present in your community?

4. Are there agents in your area who operate solely as buyers' agents? What are the advantages to a buyer in dealing with such an agent?

5. You receive what appears to be a fair offer from a prospective buyer. However, you know the buyer has sued sellers after purchasing several other properties. What do you tell your seller?

6. Evaluate your own home for possible environmental hazards.

7. Complete a Real Estate Transfer Disclosure Statement as if you were the seller of the property where you presently live.

8. Bring to class one current-events article dealing with some aspect of real estate practice for class discussion.

■ CHAPTER 3 QUIZ

1. Which of the following is true regarding an agent's duty in a real estate transaction?
   a. An agent has a fiduciary duty to his or her principal.
   b. An agent must disclose any known detrimental information to a buyer, even when the agent represents the seller.
   c. Any material facts the agent becomes aware of must be disclosed to his or her principal.
   d. All of the above are true.

2. Which of the following is true regarding agency disclosure?
   a. An agent need not provide a seller of a 20-unit residential apartment complex with an agency disclosure.
   b. The listing agent cannot elect to be only a buyer's agent.
   c. Both a and b are true.
   d. Both a and b are false.

3. Which of the following is true regarding agency disclosure?
   a. The confirmation of agency must be in writing.
   b. The three steps of the disclosure process are disclose, elect, confirm.
   c. The selling agent must confirm the agency prior to the buyer's making an offer.
   d. All of the above

4. Which of the following sellers must provide a Real Estate Transfer Disclosure?
   a. The seller of a lot
   b. The seller of a four-unit apartment building
   c. The seller of a 16-unit apartment building
   d. All of the above

5. Under *Easton*, an agent's duty of inspection and disclosure covers
   a. all types of property.
   b. accessible and inaccessible areas.
   c. a visual inspection only.
   d. none of the above.

6. Which of the following is true about earthquake safety disclosure?
   a. It applies to one to four residential units.
   b. It applies only to homes built prior to 1930.
   c. The buyer can waive his or her right to a hazards report.
   d. Delivery of a copy of *The Homeowner's Guide to Earthquake Safety* is evidenced by an affidavit from the agent.

7. A buyer signs that he or she has received a booklet relating to
   a. environmental hazards.
   b. floods, tornados, and earthquakes.
   c. foreclosure rights.
   d. rescission rights.

8. A special study zone is an area that is in danger of what type(s) of calamity?
    a. Floods
    b. Earthquakes
    c. Pollution
    d. Fire danger

9. The purpose of the Subdivided Lands Law is to
    a. prohibit premature subdivisions.
    b. set minimum physical standards.
    c. protect purchasers from fraud.
    d. allow for a uniform growth pattern.

10. A right of rescission is provided by law for purchase agreements involving all except
    a. one to four-unit residential properties.
    b. time-shares.
    c. undivided interest subdivisions.
    d. both b and c.

PROSPECTING

Note: See margin note on page 120 as to do-not-call registry limitations on telephone solicitations.

■ KEY TERMS

bird dogs	endless chain farming	prospecting
centers of influence	geographic farms	real estate owned
contact management system	networking	telephone canvassing
door-to-door canvassing	niche marketing	
	nongeographic farms	

■ LEARNING OBJECTIVES

In this chapter you learn the importance of prospecting as a source of inventory as well as to locate prospective buyers. You will gain knowledge about a great many prospecting areas that will help you recognize opportunities.

You learn about systematically farming an area (geographic farm), a type of property, or an ethnic group (nongeographic farm) to produce a steady source of buyers and sellers. You also learn the importance of developing a prospecting plan.

■ WHAT IS PROSPECTING?

> *Prospecting* is locating potential buyers and sellers.

Prospecting is the process of locating owners who are interested in selling property and prospective buyers who are interested in purchasing property.

Without prospecting you would have much less inventory and fewer buyers. Real estate professionals know that even when buyers and sellers seek them out, it is usually the result of prior prospecting or successfully helping someone they know.

Successful real estate agents understand that prospecting is an important element in their success. It is a continuing process of being aware of what is happening around them, organizing their efforts, being persistent, and developing problem-solving and time-management skills. Not only must licensees constantly prospect, they must have the proper attitude toward prospecting. A professional attitude includes considering prospecting a challenge and being positive and enthusiastic in speech and action. The authors recommend the SSS system: See the people, Serve the people, Sell the people.

Develop the Proper Attitude

Prospecting is any method of exposure to people who can buy or sell real estate; hence, it is a major challenge to every licensee. The following questions will help you evaluate your own attitude toward prospecting:

- *Do you consider prospecting a major challenge?* Successful real estate selling entails countless hours and considerable expenditure of energy to keep up with a highly competitive market. Your attitude is the key to your success.

- *Do you recognize the urgency to maintain a constant supply of new prospects?* It is absolutely necessary to provide yourself with a constant supply of customers. Prospects may be found most anywhere; they are all around you.

- *Do you have a well-organized system to use in prospecting?* Because of many prospect sources available and the necessity of assigning priorities to these sources, advance planning is essential. To get the best results from your prospecting, an effective and well-organized prospecting system is essential.

- *Are you afraid of rejection?* Prospecting is searching for the one among many who needs your services. Therefore, you will encounter rejection more often than success. Fear of being rejected is one of the contributing factors to failure of new licensees.

Many successful agents use licensed assistants to aid them in prospecting. When an assistant locates prospective buyers or sellers, the agent then takes over. This frees the agent for *A-Time* activities (Chapter 1).

■ METHODS OF PROSPECTING

The successful salesperson is always prospecting. A good prospector knows and accepts that different groups of people not only have varying interests and motivations but also have substantially different political, social, philosophical, and economic views. Prospecting is less a matter of getting listings and sales than it is a matter of developing sources for listings and sales. A licensee's ability to do this is limited only by his or her imagination and commitment.

The prospecting method that will produce the best results varies according to the agent and the situation. The broker or salesperson should choose a method or methods based on

- the type of property involved;

- the period of time planned for;

- the types of prospects;

- neighborhood and property characteristics, including the properties themselves (number of bedrooms and baths, etc.), income characteristics of the neighborhood (income, family, and social interests), changes taking place (such as a changeover from single-family to multiple-family dwellings), special advantages of the location (schools, shopping centers, recreation areas, and so forth), and special interests and groups to which the agent belongs.

After taking these factors into consideration, licensees also should review their own sales skills and personality and choose a method that emphasizes their strengths and minimizes their weaknesses. The following material covers just a few of the methods for prospecting.

Door-to-Door Canvassing

While shunned by some real estate agents, **door-to-door canvassing** can be an excellent way to cover a geographic area. Successful canvassers know the number of people they must contact to obtain one good lead. They set goals of a particular number of contacts to achieve the number of leads they desire. They treat a rejection as one contact closer to another lead.

The best times to canvass are obviously when residents are home. With the large percentage of two-income families, early evening or Saturday mornings are effective times. In retirement areas, daytime canvassing between 9 A.M. and 11 A.M. and between 2 P.M. and 4 P.M. could be effective. Do not canvass door-to-door after dark.

Canvassing an area having many retirees can be particularly beneficial because many people welcome someone to talk to and a great deal of information can be gained as to needs of neighbors.

When you canvass door-to-door, step back from the door after you ring the bell so you won't appear menacing. Don't carry a briefcase because this also can be menacing. A notepad or a clipboard is far less intimidating. Smile when you talk, and keep in mind that you must get the homeowners attention within the first 20 seconds. In some areas, more doors will be opened to women than to men. Women are generally considered less dangerous.

By use of a reverse directory (photocopy the applicable pages), you can address homeowners by name. An excellent four-step approach is as follows:

1. Introduce yourself and give your broker affiliation.

2. Explain why you are at their front door. An excellent approach is to ask if they can help find a home for a particular family (more about this later). People often like to help specific persons but have little interest in people in general. Never use a fictitious family. Simply describe one of the persons you are working with to find a home.

3. Ask if they know of anyone in the area who is planning to move or has had a change in his or her family circumstances that might cause the person to contemplate a move. Also ask owners about their own specific plans. Ask owners if they or any of their neighbors might have any real estate purchase or sale plans for a home, second home, or investment property.

4. Thank the owner, leave your card, and jot down responses for future reference.

After a home has been sold by you or your office, a door-to-door canvass of the neighborhood can be especially effective. Consider the following approach, replacing the words in brackets with words that fit your situation.

Good morning [Mrs. Smith]. I am [Jane Thomas] from [Uptown Realty]. We have just sold the [Kowalski] home at [211 Elm down the block; the house with the large pine tree in the front yard]. The new owners are [Mr. and Mrs. Collins. He is an engineer, and she teaches first grade at Sunnyside School. They have one daughter, Mary Ann, who is nine years old]. I hope you will welcome them to your neighborhood.

As you undoubtedly realize, you live in a desirable area. In advertising the [Kowalski] home we were contacted by a number of families whose needs we were unable to meet. Right now, I am looking for a home for a very fine family [He is an accountant who is being transferred to our area from Ohio. They have two sons, ages three and six.] I need help in finding them a home. Do you know anyone who is planning to move? Has anyone in the area recently had a change in family size because of marriage, divorce, birth or death, or has anyone recently retired?

Note: You first showed competence by a sale, gave them information about a new neighbor and are now asking them for help for a particular family.

Besides canvassing for listings, you can canvass for buyers. By working an area around a new listing, you can approach owners with information about the listing and ask their help in choosing their new neighbors. Most people like their neighborhood and will tell you if they have any friends or acquaintances who might be considering relocating.

In some areas agents like to canvass in teams, with each agent taking every other house. Team canvassing can help keep agents motivated to continue at what can be a hard task. A team approach also gives a canvasser a feeling of greater security.

Note: In some communities, door-to-door canvassing is not allowed or might require a permit.

Telephone Canvassing

Despite challenges, national do-not-call legislation has gone into effect. Solicitation calls to parties who have registered on the do-not-call registry could subject the caller to a fine of up to $11,000 for each such call. The law applies to both intrastate and interstate solicitations. An exception applies to calls where there has been a prior business relationship.

While the National Association of REALTORS® is awaiting clarification from the Federal Trade Commission as to calls from expired listings, FSBOs, open house visitors, referrals, etc., unless the FTC indicates otherwise, the do-not-call registry should be honored.

Because of safety concerns as well as area restrictions on canvassing, in some areas **telephone canvassing** can be effectively used to make owner contact. The greatest advantage of telephone canvassing over door-to-door canvassing, however, is speed. You can cover territory faster by telephone than by knocking on doors. On the negative side, people will hang up far more quickly than they will slam a door in your face.

Telephone solicitations turn most people off. You must have a positive twist to your call to overcome immediate rejection. The twist we recommend is to help a particular person.

By use of a reverse directory you can canvass by area and still address the person by name. You will find that a carefully written script will improve your success rate. You can use an approach similar to that discussed under door-to-door canvassing.

Sample Telephone Script

[Mrs. Smith], my name is [Debra Collins]. I am an agent with [Sunrise Realty]. I am calling you for a particular purpose. I am looking for a home for a [young family. The husband, Jim, is an engineer with Latex Products, and his wife, Pamela, is a case worker with the county. They have two daughters, Cynthia, age 6, and Melanie, age 9].

They are looking for a home in your neighborhood. [They would like to be within walking distance of Glendale school.] They like your particular neighborhood because of the [Grant Park Recreational Center].

Are you or any of your neighbors considering selling a home?

Have any of your neighbors had a change in family size because of marriage, divorce, birth, graduation, or death?

Are you or any of your neighbors considering buying a home, a second home, or an investment property?

Do-not-call lists are available from the Federal Trade Commission by zip code and up to five zip codes will be provided free of charge. Each additional zip code requires a $25 fee. It is necessary to check the updates on the registry at least every 90 days. For greater details, visit the Web site *www.ftc.gov/donotcall*

If an owner indicates he or she is considering selling, your reaction should be

> I can stop by and look at your home at [7 P.M.] tonight, or would [8 P.M.] be more convenient for you?

If the call does not result in a lead:

> [Mrs. Smith], I want to thank you for your time. If you think of anyone who might wish to sell a home, please call me. Again, I am [Debra Collins] from [Sunrise Realty].

If the call does give you a lead, be sure you first have permission to use the referrer's name, and then call the prospect. Use a script similar to the following:

> [Mrs. Jones], I am [Debra Collins with Sunrise Realty].
>
> [Mrs. Smith], who lives [just a few doors down from you on Bellwood Avenue], suggested that I contact you. I am looking for a home for a [young family of four who want very much to live in your neighborhood].
>
> [Mrs. Smith] indicated that she thought you might be considering moving. I realize that such a decision should not be made hastily.
>
> Before you make any decision you should know the value of your property. I would like to prepare a competitive market analysis for you that will show you what you could expect to receive for your home, should you decide to sell. I can prepare such an analysis without any cost or obligation on your part.
>
> [Mrs. Jones], would you be offended if I stopped by to see your home? I can come over at [7 P.M.], or would [8 P.M.] be more convenient for you and your husband?

By making buyers appear as an attractive family unit, you will create an interest in helping them. Always use a real buyer you are working with. Never fabricate buyers. If you get an appointment, chances are the owner has been seriously considering selling.

One of the authors obtained three listings and a sale because he was looking for a home for an out-of-the-area family with two small daughters. The prospective buyer was being transferred to the area, and the couple wanted a home within walking distance of a particular church. By contacting the church secretary, the broker obtained a membership list with telephone numbers. Most of the calls to members were received in a very positive manner because they wished to help in locating a home for a potential new church member.

The words, "Would you be offended?" works well because very few people will state that they would be offended if you stopped by to see their home.

Direct-Mail Canvassing

Canvassing by direct mail is most effective when agents carefully plan their mailing pieces. To be effective, a mailing must get attention and result in action.

FIGURE 4.1

Sample Mailing

> **How Much Money Is Locked Up in Your Home?**
>
> Because of high demand in [*Orchard Ridge*], your home has experienced exceptional appreciation. If you wish to explore the possibility of taking advantage of the market opportunities, we can supply you with a supported estimate of your home's present market value without any cost or obligation on your part. I will be calling you in about a week to determine if you are interested in knowing what you could receive from a sale of your home.
>
> Yours truly,
>
> _____

Some general rules for direct-mail canvassing are

- use a number-10 plain envelope. Don't use a window envelope.

- don't use a mailing label. Type or, preferably, hand address the envelope.

- use first-class stamps (preferably commemorative stamps). If your letter looks like junk mail, it will likely be treated in that manner.

- don't try to indicate your letter is something it is not, such as by trying to give it the appearance of a government letter.

- if you get the reader's attention in the first few lines, the letter will be read in its entirety.

- if your letter indicates that you will be calling the recipient, the effectiveness of your letter will be magnified significantly. Owners will have to think about their response to your call.

- never send out a mass mailing without test marketing the mailing piece. By keeping track of responses to different mailing pieces, you can eliminate ineffective mailings.

- don't cold canvass by sending out fax messages. Besides creating ill will towards your firm, it violates federal law and is punishable by a significant fine.

Figure 4.1 and Figure 4.2 are examples of mailings taken from *Power Real Estate Letters*, William H. Pivar and Corinne E. Pivar, Dearborn Real Estate Education, Chicago, 1997.®

FIGURE 4.2

Sample Mailing

Listing Solicitation—Out-of-Town Owner

[Date]

_____

_____

_____

Dear _____:

As you undoubtedly know, owning property that is far away from you can be a real hassle.

Right now, we are experiencing an exceptional market. I believe we can sell your [*three-bedroom home*] in [*Midvale Heights*] at an attractive price.

I will be calling you in the next few days to ascertain your interests in selling the property.

Yours truly,

_____

■ EXPIRED LISTINGS

Never contact owners before their listing has expired. When contacting the owners, you want to find out immediately if they have relisted the property with their agent or another agent. If they have, wish them well and end the discussion.

When a listing contract expires, it means the listing office was unsuccessful in procuring a buyer for a property during the contract period. Owners will likely sign a new listing contract with their agent if they are satisfied with the efforts of that agent. If not, the owners may try to sell their property without an agent. But, in most cases, they will list their property with another office. If you can convince owners that you know why their property didn't sell and show them a plan likely to lead to success, you have a good chance at the listings.

> If you can show why a property failed to sell and how you can succeed, you have an opportunity to list the property.

The reason a property failed to sell could be related to an agent who failed to market it properly. More likely, however, it relates to the price asked and/or the appearance of the property. Very simply, a home must be competitive in the marketplace to sell. When there are many sellers and few buyers, being competitive is not enough. A home must appear and be priced in such a manner that it stands out above the competition as a "best buy."

An advantage of working expired listings is that owners generally now have more realistic expectations than they had when their property was originally listed for sale.

■ NEWSPAPER LEADS

Newspapers can provide a number of sources of buyers and sellers. When checking newspapers for leads, don't forget that there are other papers besides the large daily papers. There are "shoppers", throwaway papers, usually devoted entirely to ads; there are papers for groups such as mobile-home owners; and there are a wide variety of ethnic and foreign language papers. All of these papers contain leads.

For Sale by Owner (FSBO)

A major reason owners try to sell without an agent is that they feel they are saving a commission. Another reason could be related to a prior unpleasant experience with another agent. The owners must be shown that working with an agent is in their best interests.

A simple way to get to talk to a For Sale By Owner (FSBO) is to telephone and tell the owner about one of the buyers you are working with and then state, "If I had an offer from this buyer, would you want to see it?"

Because few people would not want to see an offer, the answer likely will be in the affirmative. Of course, this gives you the opportunity to view the home and talk face-to-face with the owners.

A front-door approach for an FSBO could be "I hope you don't mind, I took a photograph of your home. You can have it [hand it to the owner]. Perhaps you would like to use it in a newspaper ad." By giving the owners something, you obligate them to give you a few minutes of their time. You could then continue with "If I had an offer on your home, would you want to see it?"

Another telephone approach is "Would you be offended if I stopped by to see your home." Most owners will answer in the negative, because, again, to say otherwise would be implying that they are offended. You can then follow up with "Would four o'clock this afternoon be all right or would you prefer five?" The choice you give is not *if* you will be coming but *when*.

An excellent approach to owners who are advertising their own homes is to offer a For-Sale-by-Owner kit to them. You would begin with a telephone call on a For-Sale-by-Owner ad or sign:

> [Mr. Chan], I am [Gary Frank from Canyon Realty]. Have you been able to sell your home yet? Perhaps I can help you sell it yourself. Our office has put together a For-Sale-by-Owner kit that contains a For Sale sign, contracts, loan applications, required disclosures, instructions for open houses, and a lot more information. We provide these kits absolutely free as a goodwill gesture. Of course, we hope that if you decide later you want professional assistance, you will consider [Canyon Realty]. I would like to deliver one of these free kits and show you how to use the forms. Will you [and your wife] be home at seven tonight, or would eight be more convenient?

Your kit should be everything you discussed and more. Put warning labels on sheets that talk about subordination clauses, contingencies, owner points, etc.

When you meet with the owners, give them the For Sale signs and ask to sit down to go over the forms. Suggest the kitchen table because it is a nonthreatening environment and allows for a physical closeness. Go over the forms, explaining the clauses, importance of disclosures, etc. By the time you finish your presentation, the owners will probably be wondering if a sale without an agent is really as simple as they had imagined.

> Ask the owner how the price was arrived at.

Next, ask, "May I inquire what you're asking for your home? How did you arrive at that price?"

The owners' price likely is based on a single sale or what they would like to get for the property. Continue with "It would be presumptuous of me to tell you if the price is high or low, but our firm can prepare a competitive market analysis from our computer data. I would like to do a competitive market analysis on your home. This is, of course, provided at no charge."

Chances are the owners will accept your offer. They have already received valuable material, and you have likely sold yourself as a professional. Your appointment to present the market analysis should be on the next day.

After you present the market data analysis, ask the owners if you could just take a few minutes to express why you feel they should consider having an agent. After giving them all this valuable material, the owners will feel obligated to answer in the affirmative. You can then go into a listing presentation. (See Chapter 5 and Chapter 6.)

A variation of the above approach is to offer the owners the use of Open House signs and banners.

Rental Ads

When a single-family or a mobile home is advertised for rent, it may be a case of an owner who really wants to sell but who needs income for payments. If the owners indicate they will give a tenant an option to purchase, you know they want to sell. Telephone numbers outside the area are more likely than local numbers to signify owners highly motivated to sell.

Whenever you receive a rental inquiry at your office or through canvassing, don't dismiss the prospect because you don't have any rentals. Prospective renters can frequently be turned into buyers with just a few questions: "Have you considered buying?" "Why not?"

If you can show prospective renters how they can be buyers, you gain a lead for your existing listings and you increase the likelihood of closing a sale. If a prospective renter was formerly an owner, chances are he or she is not going to be happy as a renter.

Trades

People advertising willingness to trade usually want to sell. By explaining delayed exchanges (see Chapter 14), you can show owners how they can sell and still have their trade. Keep in mind that some people advertising trades may be dealers.

Marriage and Engagement Announcements

By checking addresses in your telephone books, you may be able to determine if the bride and/or groom lives with parents. When either lives with a single parent, a sale might mean a parent living alone. It could be not only a lead for a listing but also a sale lead for a smaller home or condominium.

When the bride and groom are older, they could be living in their own homes or condominiums. Such a situation could mean one or two separate sales and the purchase of a larger home. Even if neither bride nor groom owns his or her own residence, they are still purchase prospects worth talking to.

Birth Announcements

From the address of the parents you can determine if they live in an apartment, a condominium, or a mobile home. Many parents prefer a single-family home with its own yard. Birth announcements could be leads to listings of condominiums or mobile homes and/or to sales of single-family homes.

Legal Notices

Notices of legal action can be an excellent source of leads for motivated buyers and sellers. Rather than checking through county records, consider subscribing to a legal notice newspaper in your county.

> Legal notices indicate problems, and Problems = Opportunities.

Foreclosure. When a notice of default is recorded, it indicates an owner is in trouble. Often the only help is a speedy sale. Keep in mind that just because a property is in foreclosure does not mean it is a good listing opportunity. Prior to listing, obtain a property profile from a title company. (A *property profile* is a computer printout showing the owner of the property and the liens against the property. It is a free service that title companies provide to the real estate profession.) The liens against the property could exceed the property value.

Probate. Heirs who inherit property often would prefer cash. In other cases the property must be sold to pay debts of the estate or to carry out the wishes of the deceased. Contact the executor or administrator of the estate for a listing.

Divorce. The largest asset of most families is their home. Because California is a community property state, divorce often means that a home must be sold so the assets can be divided.

Bankruptcy.   In California, owners in bankruptcy may be able to keep their homes because of their homestead exemption. However, many people in bankruptcy seek a new start and often wish to relocate. A sale listing may therefore be possible.

Death Notices.   Although death of a spouse frequently means a sale, it can be difficult to solicit a listing after a death. We recommend that no approach be made for at least two weeks after a death and then the approach should be to help a particular family seeking a home.

Evictions.   An eviction means an owner with a problem. When owners of income property don't have problems, they are not likely to be highly motivated to sell. When owners have problems, motivation to sell increases in relation to the seriousness of the problems. Eviction notices are a good source of motivated sellers.

Building Permits.   An individual who takes out a building permit could still own another home. Because of the length of the building period, that individual might intend to place his or her other home on the market later. Building permits calls might produce excellent listings.

Code Violations.   Notices of code violations and/or fines indicate an owner with a problem property. Owners who don't want to deal with these problems can be motivated sellers.

Tax Delinquencies.   Owners delinquent in taxes could have financial problems. The solution to their problem could be a sale. These notices can be an excellent listing source.

When owners have legal problems or personal or family problems, the best approach is to ask the owner's help in meeting the needs of another. Any indication that your contact is because they are in serious difficulty would likely result in a defensive and negative reaction.

■ OTHER PROSPECTING METHODS YOU CAN USE

Advertising

Besides using it as a selling tool, advertising can be used to obtain listings.

Roy Brooks was a legendary estate agent in England. He gained celebrity status because of his unusual and very effective ads. He found that an advertisement for property to sell that was like everyone else's ads made his ad just one among many. He realized that ads for listings had to stand out from the others. To do this, he advertised for particular prospective buyers. One of the ads Roy Brooks used is:

| Make your ad stand out. | WE HAVE A RATHER REPULSIVE OLD MAN who, with his child-wife, are looking for an elegant town res. pref. Belgravia, Chelsea, or S. Ken. Price not important but must be realistic as he has, at least, his head screwed on the right way. Usual scale of commission required. ROY BROOKS. |

Note: Before you use an ad such as this, get permission from the "repulsive old man and his child-wife."

Look for Problems

As you drive around, look for problem properties: property in need of repair, overgrown landscaping, property obviously vacant, and properties that have had rental, and signs up for a long time. Also watch for For-Sale-by-Owner signs.

Visible problems usually mean the need for a change in ownership, a problem you, as a real estate professional, are prepared to solve. You can locate the owners of these properties by checking with the county tax assessor's office or a title company.

Internet Site

An Internet site can be referenced on all of your cards, ads, and letters. Such a site could show your success in an area as well as any value changes in the area. One way to show success is a "success list" of properties sold. The site also could show advantages of low interest rates, indicating that the time to sell or buy couldn't be better.

The design of an Internet site is not the place for economy. While there are self-help books for designing your own site and designers who advertise that they will prepare your site for $200 or less, site preparation is *not* the place for *bare bones* economy. View sites of others and strive for a site designer who will better your competition.

Some brokers have home pages on their sites where a viewer can click "find a home" or "What does (Jones Realty) have to offer." The latter sells your firm's competence and integrity.

The "find a home" portion of your site can result in calls from "half sold" buyers you didn't know existed who visited your firm on an Internet site or sites.

A single property can be presented on numerous separate Internet sites. As an example, a home located in the Coachella Valley could be presented on *www.Realtors.com* and/or other national sites. It could also be on an area site such as *www.homesinpalmsprings.com*. In addition, if the broker belongs to a relocation service and/or a franchise, property could be presented on additional sites. It is not unusual for a brokerage firm to have their offerings on from three to six Internet sites including their own firm's site.

By checking competitor's Internet presentations of their listings, you will see a significant variance. Some properties indicate "picture not available" while others not only have an attractive exterior photo but allow the viewer to click on to additional photos and to a detailed property description.

A visitor to your Internet site might not be interested in your offerings and go elsewhere. You want to know who that visitor was and what his or her interests are. You can get this information with a nonthreatening offer of help. Offering to provide e-mails of new listings before they are even advertised is a great *hook* because most buyers are interested in a *first chance*, especially in an active market. The visitor would then fill in price parameters, must have and would like features, and finally their name and e-mail address.

You can also prospect for both buyers and sellers by using mailings or ads offering to supply owners with details of sales (by e-mail), so that they can understand area values. They would register on your Internet site giving details of a home that they want comparables for. The e-mails they would receive would include photos and details, as well as sale prices of similar home sales. Because you are providing an owner with information of interest, a personal contact should result in a positive response.

Just as classified ads, discussed in Chapter 8, are in competition with other classified ads, your internet property presentations are in competition with many others. Therefore, it is important that you incorporate what you will learn in Chapter 8 into your Internet site.

Check Interested Parties

Property Neighbors.   When you have a listing of land or income property, contact adjoining property owners as well as owners of similar property in the area. Neighbors are a source of both buyers and sellers.

For residential property, the approach to neighbors could be "Would you like to help choose your new neighbor?" When neighbors have an interest in an outcome, they can be an effective source of prospects.

Investors and Speculators.   When an investment property is sold, find out who the buyer is. The same holds true for lots and fixer-uppers. Contact these buyers to find out if they have further interests in purchasing property and what their interests are. It isn't hard to find the active players in a market. Many of these buyers will welcome an additional pair of eyes, ears, and legs working for them. Keep in mind that these people can be prospects for both listing and selling.

Lenders.   Check with local lenders about their **real estate owned** (REOs). Find out how to get a key to show the property, as well as if and what commission will be paid.

Besides local lenders, contact the Department of Housing and Urban Development (HUD) and the Federal Deposit Insurance Corporation (FDIC), as well as the Federal Housing Administration (FHA) and Department of Veterans Affairs (DVA) for foreclosure lists. Many agents specialize in selling lender-owned property.

Chambers of Commerce. Check with your local chamber of commerce. Ask to be notified of inquiries made by people planning to relocate to your area. If you can reach them first by a phone call, you will be in a preferred position as a possible selling agent.

Open Houses. Open houses can be a good source of both buyer and seller leads. Many people who stop at an open house can't be buyers until they sell their present homes. Some agents will hold open houses on homes listed by other agents within their firm if the property has an attractive exterior (curb appeal) and is on a high traffic street. (Open houses are covered in detail in Chapter 7.)

The *endless chain* method is the process of using prospects to recommend other prospects ad infinitum.

Endless Chain. The basis of the **endless-chain,** or referral, method of prospecting is to ask every prospect to recommend other prospects. The use of an endless chain can result in an amazing number of referral prospects. For example, if you secure the names of two prospects from every person you interview, you would get two names from your first prospect; these two should yield four; these four should provide eight; and so on. This can continue, eventually resulting in thousands who are at least potential clients, people whose needs have not yet been determined.

Your Friends. One of the first things you should do on entering the real estate business is to make a list of all the acquaintances and friends you have made over the years. Your list should contain a minimum of 100 names. Send these people an announcement that you are in the real estate business, and indicate how proud you are that your work may give you an opportunity to help them in the future. It is a good idea to follow the announcement with a telephone call.

Another community resource that should not be overlooked is the people with whom you do non-real estate business. You have to buy food, clothing, gas, personal services and so on. Tell the people who sell things or services to you that you are in the real estate business. These people come in contact with other people every day, and from time to time they hear of someone who is thinking of listing and selling a home or buying a new home. Such communication is commonly called **networking.**

Be sure to send announcements to the professional people who serve you and who over the years have had your faith and confidence—your doctor, dentist, attorney, and any other professional people you deal with. Because you do business with them, it is likely that they will be willing to do business with you.

Your Sellers.   A sale normally is part of a chain reaction. Sellers of property generally become buyers of other properties, and those sellers, in turn, buy again.

Even before a property is sold, find out the intention of the owners. If they will be buyers within the area, you want to be the agent who will sell to them. If they are leaving the area, consider that a referral fee could be possible from an agent in their new community.

Your Buyers.   Most people are glad they purchased their homes. If you sold houses to some of these satisfied buyers, you can turn this positive feeling buyers have about their purchases to your benefit. Whenever you get a listing in the area, contact former buyers by phone or e-mail to see if they have friends who might be interested.

You can also use the approach of asking them to help another: "I could use your help. I'm trying to find a home for [a retired couple] who wish to live in your area because [they want to be close to their grandchildren]. Do you know anyone in the area who might consider selling or anyone who has had a change in family size because of marriage, divorce, birth, or graduation?"

Your Neighbors.   Another broker's sign on a neighbor's home shows that you have failed to make your neighbors realize that you are a real estate professional who is available to meet their needs. When you enter the real estate profession, consider a mailing to your neighbors. Figure 4.3 is a broker letter to neighbors of a new sales associate.

Take a walk around your neighborhood with your child or your dog to give you an opportunity to talk to neighbors. Let them know you are in real estate and where you live. Hand out business cards. By asking questions you can find leads. In most neighborhoods, there are a few people who seem to know everything that is happening. These people should be developed as your extra pairs of eyes and ears.

In condominium complexes and mobile-home parks, spend time around the recreational facilities. You will seldom have any trouble finding someone to talk to. By knowing what to ask you can quickly discover what is happening in the area.

Centers of Influence

Another successful prospecting method is to cultivate the friendship of influential persons in the community or territory. These **centers of influence** can help you obtain prospects by referring people who can use your services. In addition, these influential people can make appointments for you as well as give information and urge their acquaintances to buy from you.

FIGURE 4.3

FIGURE 4.3

New Associate Announcement Letter

Broker Letter to Neighbors of New Salesperson

[Date]

_____
_____
_____

Dear _____:

[*Judith Reilly*], your neighbor who lives at [*111 Midvale Lane*], has recently joined our firm as [*a sales associate*] [*an associate broker*]. [*Judith*] has been your neighbor for [*four*] years. [*She*] and [*her husband*] have [*two children, Lisa, age nine, and Jeffrey, age seven, both of whom attend Midvale School. Judith is a graduate of Ohio State and previously worked in marketing*]. [*She*] has just completed our training program and will be specializing in [*residential sales*] in [*Orchard Ridge*]. If you or any of your friends have any real estate needs, we hope you will contact [*Judith*]. I have enclosed one of her new cards.

Sincerely,

_____

Source: *Power Real Estate Letters*

The objective of cultivating relationships with centers of influence is to establish genuine friendship, whenever possible. Also important is their help in your search for new contacts. Let your centers of influence know the results of their efforts. This will come naturally if the friendship is genuine, and it will encourage the person to keep helping you.

Some agents refer to these helpers as **bird dogs.** This term is not derogatory. It merely indicates that they point the way. Keep in mind that help wont come to you unless you ask for it.

Centers of influence are people who are influential in your community.

You must explain what you are looking for, such as a friend or acquaintance who has had a change in family size. Having several dozen extra pairs of eyes and ears working for you can provide a great many leads. The best bird dogs are people who help you because they like you and want to see you succeed. However, for continued effort on your behalf, these helpers must feel they are appreciated. Your appreciation can be verbal; better yet, take them to dinner or give a small personal gift to show your appreciation.

Good Centers of Influence

■ Prominent club members
■ Friends
■ Relatives
■ Attorneys
■ Doctors
■ Ministers, priests, rabbis
■ Bankers
■ Public officials
■ Teachers
■ Bartenders
■ Health club employees
■ Business executives
■ People with whom you share a mutual interest, such as a hobby or recreational activity

Community Service

Closely akin to the center-of-influence method is prospecting through local community service groups. Making contacts by participating in community activities not only can bring in more business but also can give you personal satisfaction from working for the benefit of others.

Community service organizations recommended for involvement include

■ churches and other houses of worship;

■ the PTA;

■ educational groups;

■ college associations;

■ chambers of commerce;

■ civic organizations;

■ service groups;

■ boys' and girls' clubs;

■ Boy Scouts and Girl Scouts;

■ recreational clubs (ski, travel, biking, boating, etc.);

■ YMCA and YWCA; and

■ political organizations.

Community activities can also provide

- opportunities to counsel fellow members in such areas as investments, property management, and commercial realty;
- constant exposure to referral sources;
- constant exposure to other property owners;
- personal development, by learning and growing through participation; and
- development of a more professional image as a real estate licensee.

Your peers will have greater respect for a colleague who participates in community activities. The key is to get involved with people and help fulfill their needs. In seeking contacts through community service groups, however, beware of over-commitment. It is important to develop the ability to say no gracefully. Over-committing yourself can upset your timetable and also may jeopardize your health. Follow these guidelines:

- Work in only one or two organizations at one time. Strive for quality, not quantity.
- Anticipate time-consuming assignments before becoming involved.
- Do not play personalities for an advantage.
- Do not play politics.

To stay aware of what is going on, participate where possible in carefully selected committees. Membership on the following committees has proved to be most helpful to licensees:

- Greeting Committee
- Membership Committee
- Social or Party Committee
- "Sunshine" (visit the sick, etc.) Committee

Be cautious in using membership as a prospecting technique, because it is easy to turn off fellow members by being overaggressive. Obtain help from others but do not abuse them. When you first join a club or association, keep a low profile. It is advisable to do something for the organization before you ask members for referrals.

Fundraising for a worthwhile charity is an excellent way to meet people. While there may be a negative reaction to having to open their wallets, you will have shown that you are a person with a positive community interest.

■ KEEP A PROSPECT FILE

A well-organized salesperson keeps a prospect information file. The file should contain as much information as you can gather on each prospect. some personal digital assistants (PDA) come with an excellent prospect management system. A database contact management program for a laptop computer should handle prospective contacts, clients, and customers. These programs will produce letters and create tickler files (files that let you know when to call or write). Some of these programs are inexpensive and will only do the basics, whereas the pricier programs will do almost everything. This tool preserves the information in a systematic way and helps you set up future appointments. Many of these programs can be seen at real estate professional conventions. They are also advertised in professional magazines. Often manufacturers will supply a free sample disk so you can view the capabilities available for you. These programs are money-makers because they save time and make certain that contacts and possible customers or clients don't fall between the cracks and become forgotten.

Build a Referral List

Agents must bring some sort of order to their prospect lists to avoid getting stuck with a briefcase full of names and little else. To build a list and successfully use referrals, the licensee should follow these guidelines:

- Develop a systematic plan. This includes studying prospects as you talk to them. Ask for leads as soon after contact as feasible, and ask the prospects how you may improve your services.
- Keep track of the results of your methods.
- Utilize all sources of information, including friends, neighbors, professionals, people in businesses of all kinds, and social contacts.
- Make them all aware that you are in the real estate business and would appreciate all referrals.
- Follow up referrals by reporting back to the referrer. Also important: Use a computer contact management system to record referrals for future calls. A person giving a negative response now may still be in the market in the future.

■ FARM YOUR AREA

Farming is working or prospecting an area of interest for sellers as well as buyers. The area chosen for farming can be geographic or nongeographic (a special interest area). Your farm should be chosen based on your personal goals, interests, and your specific market area.

Geographic Farms

A **geographic farm** is a specific area with definite boundaries that is worked by an agent. Within the specific area, the agent seeks a dominant share of the marketplace.

Farming yields a crop of listings.

The best geographic farms tend to be homogeneous areas having similarly priced homes, or they share other characteristics such as age, attitude toward recreational activity, family type, and so forth. Areas of common identity such as a particular subdivision generally make good farming areas. By farming the area he or she already lives in, the agent will have existing contacts and exposure within the farm area.

In choosing a farm area, consider how you relate to the people in the area or group. If you are comfortable with and have a special interest in the area or group, you are likely to put forth the effort required for success.

If someone already is actively farming an area with great success, you might consider an area with less active competition. Although you should not mind competition, there may be equally desirable areas with little or no competition, which would mean less resistance to overcome. Just one day of knocking on doors or using the phone could reveal an area being farmed by another professional.

Some experts claim that a farm area should not exceed about 500 homes. We believe the size should be based on the size of the area, considering reasonable identifiable boundaries as well as the agent's available time and techniques used to devote to farming activities. The fact that there are no hard and fast rules governing farm size can be shown by *megafarming*. Some agents farm areas of several thousand homes. Some of these agents use salaried assistants to help them. The Internet is an easy and almost costfree method of farming and allows for larger farms. Still other agents are able to handle larger than normal farms by specializing in listing activities rather than sales.

A farm takes time to produce a crop of sellers and buyers. Like an agricultural farm, it must be constantly worked to be productive. Generally, agents working geographic farms strive for a minimum of one contact per month with every owner within their farm area. The contact might be direct mail, the Internet, a phone conversation or a face-to-face meeting. Getting to know owners and, more important, letting them get to know you places you in an excellent position to work with owners as buyers or sellers when a sale or purchase is needed or desired.

Nongeographic Farms

A **nongeographic farm** is a particular segment of the marketplace defined according to property differentiation or buyer/seller differentiation.

For example, an agent could choose to work a particular ethnic group. If an agent works a particular ethnic or nationality segment of the population, it would be a significant plus if the agent were a member of the group and had the necessary language skills of the group.

An agent might work only a type of property for small investors, such as duplexes. There are a number of agents who specialize in horse properties (properties zoned for horses).

In a nongeographic farm, door-to-door canvassing will seldom be effective. Acquiring membership lists of organizations and even religious groups as well as buying specialized mailing lists will allow you to work this type of farm by phone and direct mail.

The Internet can be a valuable source for leads when working a nongeographic farm. Using one of the search engines, you should be able to zero in on your area of specialty within your marketing area. You will find organizations, companies, or groups that can provide leads as to buyers, sellers, lessors, or lessees. You will also find organizations, companies, or groups outside your marketing area that have access to information within your marketing area.

Whatever type or area of farm you choose, keep in mind that farming must be continuous. If you slow down your efforts, you will begin to lose market share from your farm at a fairly rapid pace. Although every successful agent does not farm, either by geographic areas or by special interest, every successful agent *does* prospect for buyers and sellers.

Niche Marketing

Specializing in a narrow segment of the market is known as **niche marketing.** As you gain exposure to the many possibilities of niche marketing, you may decide to choose a niche that you feel best meets your personality, experience, and needs.

In choosing a niche that serves a particular group of buyers or sellers, you must be cognizant of both your moral and your legal responsibilities concerning discrimination. (See Chapter 2.)

Niche marketing is specialization in a narrow segment of the marketplace.

An excellent way to find a niche category of buyers is to go through your old files to see if you have been serving a certain group more than other groups. When you have identified a customer segment, draw a profile of its demographic and psychological characteristics. Prospecting and after-sale surveys are two avenues for accumulating this kind of information. When you analyze past customers, try to determine why they came to you, how effectively you helped them, and the areas in which you feel you may have been weak. This will help you put together a plan to draw more people like them to your customer segment. You also will gain more from your advertising and marketing strategies if these strategies are coordinated around those surveys. Customer segment specialization helps you build a known area of expertise that will enhance your reputation, result in referrals, and keep your customers coming to you, as opposed to going somewhere else.

■ DEVELOP A PROSPECTING PLAN

Without a definite prospecting plan, prospecting will likely be a "when you think about it" activity. The results will be far less than optimum. Figure 4.4 is a sample prospecting plan.

FIGURE 4.4

Sample Prospecting Plan

1. Each Monday morning call on the weekend FSBO ads as well as FSBO signs you have observed.

2. Contact owners within a one-block radius of every new listing taken within three days of listing.

3. Make calls Friday morning on foreclosures and evictions listed in a legal newspaper.

4. Contact at least one former buyer each week to ask about friends and/or relatives interested in your area or neighbors who might be relocating.

4. Have lunch at least once each week with a person who has provided or can provide referrals.

5. Make a minimum of 35 telephone calls each week using a reverse directory to locate a home for a prospective buyer with whom you are working.

6. For new investment property listings, contact owners of similar property within the neighborhood of the listing. (You need not be limited to your office listings.)

7. Conduct at least one open house each week.

8. Ask at least three people each week for referrals and buyer-seller leads.

9. Contact people whom you have asked for help at least once each month.

You can evaluate the effectiveness of your prospecting plan by keeping track of the sources of new prospects as well as of the results of working with the prospects. Quality of leads is really more important than quantity of leads.

By considering the time spent on your prospecting activities, you may discover that your interests would be better served by a reallocation of time and/or a change in your plan. Your initial prospecting plan should not be cast in stone. It is a guide that may change, based on your interests and effectiveness in working with different types of situations.

■ MANAGING YOUR CONTACTS

A paper note on a likely sale or listing prospect becomes a lost prospect if the note cannot be found. Forgetting to follow up on a lead creates opportunities for others. You not only want to have before you the names, addresses, telephone, cellphone, and e-mail numbers of your prospects, you want them organized by what action is required on your part and when, as well as buyer prospects categorized by interests so they can be contacted as available inventory changes. In short, you want a **contact management system.**

There are many contact management software programs available. Check what programs other successful agents are using and get their feelings as to benefits and shortcomings before you invest in contact management software.

■ SUMMARY

Prospecting is a process used to locate prospective buyers and sellers of real property. There are many methods of prospecting, including door-to-door canvassing, phone canvassing, direct-mail canvassing, expired listings, newspaper leads (For-Sale-by-Owner ads; rental ads; trades; engagement, marriage, and birth announcements; and death notices), legal notices (foreclosures, probate, evictions, building permits, code violations, bankruptcy, tax delinquency), advertising, looking for problems, the Internet, property neighbors, investors and speculators, lenders, chambers of commerce, open houses, endless chain, your sellers, your buyers, your neighbors, centers of influence, and community services.

Farming is working a particular segment of the market intensively. It can be a geographic area or a nongeographic area, which could consist of a certain type of property or an ethnic group.

A prospecting plan forces an agent to evaluate how he or she will prospect and to evaluate results. It is important to have a contact management system so that contacts don't slip away.

■ CLASS DISCUSSION TOPICS

1. Be prepared to role-play a telephone canvassing and/or a door-to-door canvassing situation with another student.
2. Identify what you feel would be logical geographic farms in your area, as well as nongeographic farming opportunities.
3. Prepare a prospecting plan for yourself. Include goals and time to be spent executing the plan.
4. List what you expect will be your five best sources of listings in order of effectiveness.
5. Identify three centers of influence that should be useful to you in prospecting.
6. Bring to class one current-events article dealing with some aspect of real estate practice for class discussion.

■ CHAPTER 4 QUIZ

1. A reverse directory provides an agent with
   a. names of former owners.
   b. names from addresses.
   c. legal descriptions from addresses.
   d. unlisted phone numbers.

2. The best prospecting approach is to ask owners if they
   a. will help you make a sale.
   b. want top dollar for their home and a quick sale.
   c. can help you find a home for a particular family.
   d. want to make a profit.

3. Direct-mail solicitation for listings is more effective if you
   a. use window envelopes.
   b. use a mailing machine and bulk rate.
   c. use mailing labels.
   d. indicate that you will be calling.

4. The most likely reason that a listing expires unsold is that the
   a. agent failed to hold an open house.
   b. property was in an undesirable area.
   c. home was not competitively priced.
   d. agent did not advertise enough.

5. Which of the following classified ad categories is likely to provide listing leads?
   a. Homes for rent
   b. Leases/options to purchase
   c. Mobile homes for rent
   d. All of the above

6. Legal notices provide good leads for listings. Which of the following is not a legal notice?
   a. Eviction
   b. Foreclosure
   c. Probate
   d. Vacancy

7. Which of the following would be an indication that an owner might be interested in selling an income property?
   a. A high vacancy rate.
   b. Tenant evictions
   c. Code violations
   d. All of the above

8. *Endless chain* refers to
   a. the long-term effects of advertising.
   b. obtaining additional prospects from every lead.
   c. the fact that your buyer will eventually become a seller.
   d. the fact that most buyers are sellers and sellers are buyers.

9. The term *farming* as used in real estate refers to
   a. determining what your market area will be.
   b. operation by season, such as a listing season, open house season, selling season and so forth.
   c. specialization in a particular field of real estate activity.
   d. working or prospecting a geographic area or special interest area for buyers and sellers.

10. An example of a nongeographic farm would be specialization in
    a. mobile homes.
    b. income property.
    c. lots.
    d. all of the above.

LISTING PRESENTATION PACKAGE

■ KEY TERMS

adjusted selling price	estimated seller's	listing presentation
competitive market	proceeds	manual
analysis	For Sale by Owner	

■ LEARNING OBJECTIVES

This chapter provides you with the basic knowledge to prepare effective tools for obtaining listings. These tools include the competitive market analysis, estimated seller's proceeds, and a listing presentation manual. (Separate manuals should be prepared for seller and buyer listings). By possessing these tools and learning how to use them, you will be able to make effective listing presentations that will result in greater success.

■ COMPETITIVE MARKET ANALYSIS

The **competitive market analysis** (CMA) is really a comparison analysis used by real estate agents to aid in determining a proper list price for a property. The CMA provides information on similar properties that have been placed in the marketplace so that they can be compared with the property that is to be evaluated to determine an offering price. (Comparables are often referred to as *comps*.)

The CMA is not a formal appraisal. It should be used for single-family residences and for multifamily residential properties of up to four units. In some cases, the CMA can be used for lots. It is, however, not an effective tool for larger residential income properties or for commercial or industrial properties.

The CMA reflects the realities of the marketplace. It should include the following three separate areas:

1. On-market-now
2. Reported-sold-prior-six-months
3. Reported-expired-prior-six-months

While compilation of the data formerly took many hours of an agent's time, today agents can download information from a multiple-listing service (MLS) in a matter of minutes. (Title and escrow companies are also sources for comparables, but compilation of data there could be time consuming.)

It is important to have information about all sales in the immediate area over approximately the past six months. If there have been relatively few sales, you might have to go back to the prior year and/or expand the analysis to include similarly desirable areas.

An agent could be liable for damages if a CMA negligently omitted recent similar sales and used comparables that resulted in the owner selling a property for less than fair market value.

If a court determines that a CMA was prepared to intentionally mislead an owner as to value, then a court might award the owner punitive damages in addition to compensatory damages.

> By using comparable properties, the competitive market analysis reflects the reality of the marketplace.

The *on-market-now* list merely indicates to an owner the prices that competitors (other owners) are asking for their products (homes). Other owners are competitors because they are seeking to attract the same buyers. The on-market-now list shows an owner what a prospective buyer will see and how the owner's pricing will compare with that of the competition. It does not indicate what an owner can expect to receive from a sale.

The *reported-sold-prior-six-months* list is more valuable than the list of current properties on the market because it shows actual sale prices. In a market undergoing change, the older the data are, the less reliable they are. Prices paid six months ago could be significantly higher than a seller might expect to receive today if the market is falling. On the other hand, prices paid six months ago could be lower than might be anticipated today if the market is rising. Therefore, strive to obtain data covering a period of about the past three months. Use older data only when more-current data are not available; even then, older data should be adjusted for market changes.

No two properties are identical. Properties differ by size, age, condition, design, area, view, orientation, as well as by amenities. Adjustments to comparable properties should be made based upon the property that is the subject of the CMA. As an example, if the comparable property had a better view than the subject property, then the sale price of the comparable would be reduced. If the comparable had two baths and the subject property had 2½ baths, the adjustment would be a higher price for the comparable. The adjusted price is known as the **adjusted selling price**.

Subject Property	Comparable Property	Adjustment to Comparable
2-car garage	3-car garage	–
2½ bath	2 baths	+
12,000 sq. ft. lot	9,000 sq. ft. lot	–
Excellent condition	Needs work	+

There may be sale prices that seem unusual. These too-high or too-low prices are often the result of market imperfections, as covered in Chapter 1. It is also possible that the price paid reflects particular problems or benefits of a property that are not evident from the listing data provided. While prices of sold comparables can be expected to vary within a 10 percent range of what you consider the value to be (mean point), a variation of 20 percent, not reflected by the property itself, is likely to be an aberration and not reflect a true market picture. Before you use figures, pull out the old listings and make certain you are not comparing apples and oranges. Information about a property that is significantly different in terms of utility and desirability will give an owner a false sense of value.

The *reported-expired-prior-six-months* group is the list of losers. These properties are losers because they failed to sell. Like properties that sold, the more current the expiration of a listing, the more valuable it is for comparison purposes. Often, a property fails to sell because it is overpriced in relation to its competition. From your data you will find that the average list price of homes that failed to sell will be higher than the average list price of homes that sold. Listing prices might be significantly higher than the actual selling prices of the homes that sold. This information can point out to an owner in a powerful manner that you will not be doing him or her a favor if you overprice the property. In fact, you could be doing the owner a disservice because the likelihood of selling the property will be decreased. Even when an owner merely hopes for a higher price but will take less, overpricing will keep buyers away. The reported-expired-prior-six-months group also should reinforce your own knowledge that an overpriced listing is not an asset. Instead, it is a liability because it will steal the time and money you spend promoting it with little likelihood of success.

Obtaining Comparables

Comparables, or comps, are easy to come by. Using a password, you can log onto the real estate board computer in the office or at home and order comps from the computer. The computer needs to know the area desired (usually by using Thomas map coordinates), the square footage, and other amenities, in order to give you a list of comparable homes that have sold recently in the area. The advantage is speed—the computer produces comps within five minutes to ten minutes. Of course, you also can obtain comparables from your title company. You can use the computer to check the current listings as well as the expired listings in the area.

Computerized CMA

A number of computer programs exist that will take your multiple-listing service information and complete a form or spreadsheet for your CMA. A number of these programs provide a price-per-square-foot comparison as well as the sale or list prices. By attaching photos to these computerized printouts, they can become a valuable tool (you may be able to print out the photos from MLS computer data).

Customized CMA

If you treat the CMA you have prepared as a valuable document, it will increase the owners' feeling of value. When you give owners a CMA, you want them to feel that you did some hard work on their behalf. A feeling of indebtedness or obligation goes a long way toward the signing of a listing agreement.

Many offices bind a CMA with a plastic ring binder and prepare a nice cover, using a laser printer. The cover indicates that the CMA was prepared for the named owners by the agent and also indicates the basis of the information enclosed.

The customized CMA starts with a sheet on the owners' property. It shows owners that you appreciate their home. Be certain that the narrative includes features that owners particularly pointed out to you when they showed you their home. Owners must feel that you have carefully evaluated the property.

Include a picture of their home as well as pictures of other comparables. You should be able to download them from MLS information on the Internet. If you don't have a good photo but the comparable has good eye appeal, take the time to get a photograph. A photograph of a house that looks as nice as or better than the home you are attempting to list for sale, coupled with a list price or sale price less than owners have indicated they desire, can go a long way toward putting owners in a realistic frame of mind. It's trite but it's true: "A picture is worth a thousand words."

If a comparable has features that the home you want to list lacks, take a yellow highlighting pen and mark those features. It emphasizes the strength of the competition.

Your CMA data always should be as accurate and as current as possible. It should lead to the last page, your estimate of the price range in which the owners' home could be sold. This estimate should consider the owners' property, comparable sales, and market changes. A range is more realistic than a single price because it allows for minor variations in the marketplace. Be scrupulous in preparing your CMA. Again, using only the comparables that support your own position is dishonest, if not actually fraudulent.

Although an owner might want to list at a price toward the top edge of the range, by using the range, you have prepared the owner to consider any offer within the range as being a reasonable reflection of value. In a sellers' market, with many buyers and few sellers, the range is likely to be far narrower than it would be in a buyers' market, with many more prospective properties available than there are buyers. So, although you show the range, you might want to recommend a listing at the midpoint or even near the low limit of the range. The reasoning for your recommendation should be made clear by the attachments to the CMA, which are explained following.

Attachments to the CMA

Consider several attachments to your CMA. Once prepared, these attachments can be used for a great many presentations. The attachments could show the effect of pricing a home at, above, or below the price indicated by the CMA on both time to sell and the likelihood of a sale within a reasonable period of time. (See Figures 5.2 and 5.3.)

To prepare these attachments, use as many listings as possible that have been sold or expired for which a CMA was prepared. A bar graph is a good visual means of showing the results. It is more readily understood than a line graph or other types of graphs.

Computer people use the term *GIGO*, which stands for *garbage in—garbage out*. If your comps were not realistic, you will have a hard time developing a trend. A sale far outside your anticipated range is an aberration, but it should be considered in determining averages. (See Figures 5.2 and 5.3.)

This material can be a help not only in listing at the price indicated by your CMA but also in listing below the price your CMA recommends as a list price when the seller is strongly motivated to sell. Often a sale at a below-market price is in an owner's best interest, when compared with the alternative of not procuring a buyer during the listing period.

CMA Software Progams

There are a number of software programs that will make CMA preparation relatively easy and provide a professional-appearing document. These programs utilize photographs and property details to help you arrive at a recommended list price. We have included CMA material from *Toolkit for Presentations*, a software program of *Realty Tools, Inc. (www.realtytools.com)* as Figure 5.1A through Figure 5.1I.

FIGURES 5.1A—5.1I

CMA Material from *Toolkit for Presentations*

A.

Determining the Value of Your Home

A Comparative Market Analysis (CMA) is essential to determine the value of residential property. Location and characteristics of the property are the key elements in determining value, therefore the basis for valuation is similar properties in your area. The market analysis takes into account the amount received from recent sales of comparable properties and the quantity and quality of comparable properties currently on the market. The desired end result is to find a price that will attract a willing and able buyer in a reasonable time.

Once the value of your home has been determined, you can decide on an offering price that will achieve your goals. Generally, the price should not exceed the value by more than 5% or potential buyers may not even make offers. Naturally, if you want to sell quickly your asking price should be very near the value.

The following are a few things to keep in mind about pricing:

♦ Realistic pricing will achieve maximum price in a reasonable time.

♦ Your cost or profit desire is irrelevant; the market determines the price.

♦ The cost of improvements are almost always more than the added value.

♦ Houses that remain on the market for a long time do not get shown.

♦ A house that is priced right from the beginning achieves the highest proceeds.

Angela McKendrick
Office: (410) 555-6500
Direct Line: (410) 555-6509
Home Office: (410) 233-5532
Cellular: (410) 554-7676
E-mail: amckendrick@demorealty.com

Your Logo

B.

The Importance of Intelligent Pricing

Determining the best asking price for a home can be one of the most challenging aspects of selling a home. It is also one of the most important. If your home is listed at a price that is above market value, you will miss out on prospective buyers who would otherwise be prime candidates to purchase your home. If you list at a price that is below market value, you will ultimately sell for a price that is not the optimum value for your home. As Figure 1 illustrates, more buyers purchase their properties at market value than above market value. The percentage increases as the price falls even further below market value. Therefore, by pricing your property at market value, you expose it to a much greater percentage of prospective buyers. Thus increasing your chances for a sale while ensuring a final sale price that properly reflects the market value of your home.

Figure 2 - Activity versus Timing

Another critical factor to keep in mind when pricing your home is timing. A property attracts the most attention, excitement and interest from the real estate community and potential buyers when it is first listed on the market (see Figure 2). Improper pricing at the initial listing misses out on this peak interest period and may result in your property languishing on the market. Eventually leading to a below market value sale price (see Figure 3), or, even worse, no sale at all. Therefore, your home has the highest chances for a fruitful sale when it is new on the market and the price is reasonably established.

We can give you up-to-date information on what is happening in the marketplace and the price, financing, terms, and condition of competing properties. These are key factors in getting your property sold at the best price, quickly and with minimum hassle.

Figure 3 - The Effect of Overpricing

Angela McKendrick
Office: (410) 555-6500
Direct Line: (410) 555-6509
Home Office: (410) 233-5532
Cellular: (410) 554-7676
E-mail: amckendrick@demorealty.com

Your Logo

C.

Subject Property Profile for

2321 Pine Tree Lane

We have identified the following features of your home to aid us in the search for properties that are comparable to yours. This will help us to determine proper pricing for your home.

City: Hunt Valley	*Neighborhood:* Ivy Hill	*Year Built:* 1996
Fin SqFt: 4325	*Lot Desc:* Level	*Lot Size:* 3.12 acres
Style: Colonial	*Levels:* 2	*Bedrooms:* 5
Bathrooms: 4	*Const:* Brick	*Roofing:* Slate
Basement: Fully Finished	*Basement:* Walk out	*Heat:* Heat Pump(s)
Fuel: Electric	*Cool:* Central A/C	*Parking:* Garage
Garage Spaces: 3	*Exter Feat:* Deck	*Water:* Well
Sewer: Septic	*# Fireplaces:* 2	*Amenities:* Built-In Bookcases
Amenities: Cathedral Ceilings	*Amenities:* Hardwood Floors	*Amenities:* 3 Sky Lights
Other Rms: Family Room	*Other Rms:* Formal Dining	*Other Rms:* Game Room

Angela McKendrick
Office: (410) 555-6500
Direct Line: (410) 555-6509
Home Office: (410) 233-5532
Cellular: (410) 554-7676
E-mail: amckendrick@demorealty.com

Your Logo

D.

Comparable Properties

Currently On The Market
5 Springhill Farm Ct
List Price: $699,500

Yr Blt: 1991	*Lot Size:* 2.430000	*Area:* Springhill
Fin Sqft: 5142	*Style:* Colonial	*Elem Sch:* Pinewood
Bedrooms: 4	*Levels:* 2	*Middle Sch:* Ridgely
Bathrooms: 4/1	*Const:* Brick	*High Sch:* Dulaney
Heating: Heat Pump(s)	*Const:*	*Amenities:* Auto Gar Dr Opn
Fuel: Electric	*Parking:* Garage	*Amenities:* Bidet
Cooling:	*Garage Spaces:* 3	*Other Rms:* Family Room
Water: Well	*Basement:* Full	*Other Rms:* Laundry-Kit Lvl

Remarks: Custom Built By Present Owner, Oversized Rooms, High Ceilings, MarbleFoyer, Designer Kitchen. First Floor Office, 3 Car Garage, Southern Exposure, All Brick Construction. First Floor Master Suite. Perfectly Maintained. ******$10,000 Bonus To Selling Realtor For Ratified Contract On Or Before October 31St!!****

Recently Sold
65 Montvieu Ct

List Price: $650,000	*Sold Price:* $590,000	*Area:* Sherwood
Yr Blt: 1989	*Lot Size:* 10.080000	*Elem Sch:*
Fin Sqft: 4937	*Style:* Colonial	*Middle Sch:*
Bedrooms: 5	*Levels:* 3	*High Sch:*
Bathrooms: 4/1	*Const:* Stucco	*Amenities:* Fp Glass Doors
Heating: Electric Air Fi	*Const:*	*Amenities:* Mbr/Sep Shwr
Fuel: Electric	*Parking:* Garage	*Other Rms:* Family Room
Cooling: Central A/C	*Garage Spaces:* 3	*Other Rms:* Florida/Sun Rm
Water: Conditioner	*Basement:* Full	

Remarks: Incredibly Built Home W/Custom Features Beyond Belief. 1St Flr 14'x10',Library/Office, Fully

Recently Sold
24 Springhill Farm Ct

List Price: $699,900	*Sold Price:* $650,000	*Area:* Springhill
Yr Blt: 1996	*Lot Size:* 2.830000	*Elem Sch:*
Fin Sqft: 4800	*Style:* Colonial	*Middle Sch:*
Bedrooms: 3/1	*Const:* Brick	*High Sch:*
Bathrooms: 3/1	*Const:* Cedar Siding	*Amenities:* Auto Gar Dr Opn
Heating: Forced Air	*Parking:* Drvwy/Off Str	*Amenities:* Built-In Bookca
Fuel: Bottled Ga	*Garage Spaces:* 3	*Other Rms:* Family Room
Cooling: Heat Pump(s)	*Basement:* Full	*Other Rms:* Laundry-Kit Lvl
Water: Multi-Tank		

Remarks: Elegant Georgian Colonial Built By Mel Berhoff. Finest ConstructionAnd Details. All Amenities. Fabulous Family Room With Fireplace. Gourmet Kitchen. Lavish Built-Ins. Master Suite With Fireplace And Double Walk-In Closets. 1St Floor Library. Private Landscaped Lot Backs To Trees.

Angela McKendrick
Office: (410) 555-6500
Direct Line: (410) 555-6509
Home Office: (410) 233-5532
Cellular: (410) 554-7676
E-mail: amckendrick@demorealty.com

 Your Logo

FIGURES 5.1A–5.1I

CMA Material from *Toolkit for Presentations* (continued)

Comparative Market Analysis Statistics

Graphic Analysis of Recently Sold Properties

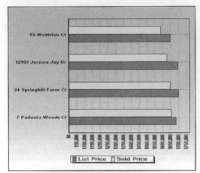

Summary Statistics of 4 Properties:

Average Price: $631,400
High Price: $655,600
Low Price: $590,000
Median Price: $650,000
Average $ per SqFt: $135.75
Average Year Built: 1992
Average Sale to List Ratio: 92.38%

Angela McKendrick
Office: (410) 555-6500
Direct Line: (410) 555-6509
Home Office: (410) 233-5532
Cellular: (410) 554-7676
E-mail: amckendrick@demorealty.com

E.

Comparative Market Analysis Summary

Currently On The Market

ADDRESS	NEIGHBHOOD	CONSTRUCT	STYLE	BDS	BTHS	LIST PRICE
1 Hillsyde Ct	Hillsyde Hu	Brick	Colonial	5	4/1	$685,000
824 Katesford Rd	Laurelford	Brick	Contempo	6	3/1	$698,000
9 Jules Brentony	Shawan At H	Brick	Colonial	5	4/1	$698,900
5 Springhill Farm	Springhill	Brick	Colonial	5	4/1	$699,500

Average of 4 Properties: $695,350   Min: $685,000   Max: $699,500   Median: $698,900

Under Contract

ADDRESS	NEIGHBHOOD	CONSTRUCT	STYLE	BDS	BTHS	LIST PRICE
17 Hillsyde Ct	Hillsyde Hu	Cedar Sidi	Colonial	4	3/1	$639,000
9 Ivy Reach Court	Ivy Reach	Brick	Colonial	4	2/1	$642,925

Average of 2 Properties: $640,962   Min: $639,000   Max: $642,925   Median: $642,925

Recently Sold

ADDRESS	NEIGHBHOOD	CONSTRUCT	STYLE	BDS	BTHS	SOLD PRICE
65 Montvieu Ct	Sherwood	Stucco	Colonial	5	4/1	$590,000
12993 Jerome Jay D	Laurelford/	Brick	Colonial	5	3/1	$630,000
24 Springhill Farm	Springhill	Brick	Colonial	4	3/1	$650,000
7 Padonia Woods Ct	Hillsyde Hu	Brick	Colonial	5	4/2	$655,600
12995 Jerome Jay D	Laurelford/	Brick	Colonial	4	4/1	$685,000

Average of 5 Properties: $642,120   Min: $590,000   Max: $685,000   Median: $650,000

Off The Market

ADDRESS	NEIGHBHOOD	CONSTRUCT	STYLE	BDS	BTHS	LIST PRICE
13213 Beaver Dam R	Ivy Hill	Cedar Sidi		4	3/2	$709,900
12218 Cleghorn Roa	Laurelford	Brick And	Victoria	4	2/2	$714,900

Average of 2 Properties: $712,400   Min: $709,900   Max: $714,900   Median: $714,900

Angela McKendrick
Office: (410) 555-6500
Direct Line: (410) 555-6509
Home Office: (410) 233-5532
Cellular: (410) 554-7676
E-mail: amckendrick@demorealty.com

F.

Comparative Market Analysis

This report utilizes the market data approach to determine value. The following properties have been selected based on recent real estate transactions for properties comparable and in close proximity to yours.

Street Address	2327 Pine Tree Lane	12308 Michaelsford Rd	Adjustments	66 Montvieu Ct	Adjustments	24 Springhill Farm Ct	Adjustments
Sold Price		$655,000	555000	$590,000	590000	$650,000	650000
Sold$ SQFT		$103.08				$162.50	
List Price		$589,000		$650,000		$609,900	
List$ SQFT		$109.40				$174.97	
Sold Date		11/21/97		9/30/97		8/12/97	
City	Hunt Valley			Cockeysville			
Neighborhood	Ivy Hill	Laurelford		Sherwood		Springhill Farm	
Fin SqFt	4325	5584		4937		4000	
Year Built	1996	1988		1989		1996	
Lot Desc	Level	Backs To Trees		Backs To Trees		Bcks-Prbnd	
Lot Size	3.12 acres	1.040000		10.080000		2.830000	
Style	Colonial	Colonial		Colonial		Colonial	
Levels	2	3		3		2	
Construction	Brick	Cedar Siding		Stucco		Brick	
Bedrooms	5	4	18000	5	18000	4	
Bathrooms	4	3	6000	4	6000	4	
Basement	Fully Finished	Fully Finished		Full Fully Finishd		Full Unfinished	12000
Heat	Heat Pump(s)	Walkout Level		Electric Air Fi		Forced Air	
Fuel	Electric	Heat Pump(s)		Electric		Bottled Gas/Pro	
		Electric					
Cool	Central A/C	Central A/C		Ceiling Fan(s)		Central A/C	
Parking	Garage	Garage		Garage		Drwy/Off Str	
Garage Sp	3	2		3		3	
Exter Feat	Deck	Deck		Deck		Deck	
Water	Well	Well		Conditioner		Multi-Tank	
Sewer	Septic	Septic		Septic		Septic	
Fireplaces	2	2		3		2	
Amenities	Built-In Bookcases	Auto Gar Dr Opn		Fp Glass Doors		Auto Gar Dr Opn	
Amenities	Cathedral Ceilings	Built-In Bookcases		Mba/Sep Shwr		Built-In Bookcases	
Amenities	Hardwood Floors	Mba/Sep Shwr		Mba/Sep Tub		Drapery Rods	
Other Rms	Family Room	Den/Stdy/Lib		Den/Stdy/Lib		Den/Stdy/Lib	
Other Rms	Formal Dining	Family Room		Family Room		Family Room	
Other Rms	Game Room	Game/Exer Rm		Florida/Sun Rm		Laundry-Kit Lvl	
Total Adj		**$618,333**		**$579,000**		**$614,000**		**$662,000**

Angela McKendrick
Office: (410) 555-6500
Direct Line: (410) 555-6509
Home Office: (410) 233-5532
Cellular: (410) 554-7676
E-mail: amckendrick@demorealty.com

G.

Pricing Strategy

General Rules...

Let's review some important considerations. There are certain factors that are beyond our control and certain factors that are within our control. Those factors outside of our control are: the location of the property, the finished square feet and types of rooms and the amenities that are in place. Those factors we can control are: the appearance of the property inside and out, how aggressively we market the property and the price, including terms. It is critical for us to accept those factors that are beyond our control and to focus on pricing and preparation.

Local Market Observations...

Our market is currently steady. Properties are not moving very fast but they are not languishing for months either. Given the current interest rate situation we should continue to experience relatively low mortgage rates and thus the market should remain steady for awhile.

Suggested Price Strategy...

My analysis of the comparable properties suggests a list price range of $599,800 to $636,900. This range should achieve your primary goal which is a reasonably quick sale.

Angela McKendrick
Office: (410) 555-6500
Direct Line: (410) 555-6509
Home Office: (410) 233-5532
Cellular: (410) 554-7676
E-mail: amckendrick@demorealty.com

H.

FIGURES 5.1A–5.1I

CMA Material from *Toolkit for Presentations* (continued)

Pricing Your Property to Sell

Pricing your property correctly is crucial. You want to sell your property in a timely manner at the highest price possible. Current market conditions determine the value.

Pricing too high or too low can cost you time and money. Realistic pricing will achieve a maximum sale price in a reasonable amount of time.

Analysis of the comparable properties suggests a list price range of:

$599,800 to $636,900

Angela McKendrick
Office: (410) 555-6800
Direct Line: (410) 555-6509
Home Office: (410) 233-8532
Cellular: (410) 554-7676
E-mail: amckendrick@demorealty.com

Your Logo

I.

■ ESTIMATED SELLER'S PROCEEDS

The *estimated seller's proceeds* should show what the seller would net, based on a particular sale price.

The **estimated seller's proceeds**, what an owner actually receives in cash and/or paper from a sale, are of vital importance to owners. Owners who receive less than what they anticipated are not happy campers. They are going to be unhappy with you and your firm. When owners are unhappy, the chances that problems will arise during escrow tend to escalate. From the standpoints of good business, agency duty, and basic fairness, you want the owners to understand what they will net from a sale if sold at list price. The owners should know what costs they will incur.

While there are computer programs that will give you printouts of seller costs based on data you supply to the computer, CAR Form ESP-11 (Figure 5.4), entitled "Estimated Seller's Proceeds" is an excellent form to use because owners can readily understand it. Because of the completeness of the form, actual figures are likely to vary only slightly from the estimate. Many agents like to estimate seller costs just a little on the high side, so any surprises are more likely to be pleasant ones.

You would prepare a new Estimated Seller's Proceeds form if the price were adjusted or if an offer were received at a price other than that set forth in the listing.

FIGURE 5.2

How Selling Price Influences Selling Time

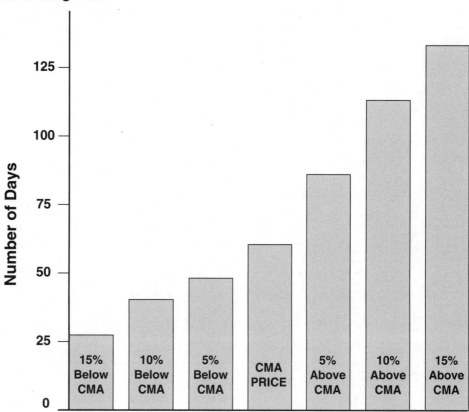

■ THE LISTING PRESENTATION MANUAL

The **listing presentation manual** is a valuable tool for obtaining listings. It is a visual tool that works hand in hand with the agent's dialogue to make a structured and effective presentation. The listing presentation manual sells the owner on benefits, the benefit of using an exclusive agent, and the benefit of your firm as that agent. It should not be used in place of the verbal presentation. Basically, as the agent turns the pages of the presentation manual, the visual message reinforces the agent's verbal message.

Separate listing presentation manuals should be prepared for sale listings and buyer listings although some of the pages will be identical.

We recommend using a three-ring binder for the presentation manual with three-hole plastic protector sheets used for each page. These are readily available at any stationery store. For a professional appearance, a laser printer coupled with one of the desktop publishing programs can result in excellent quality rather than an amateur-appearing presentation.

FIGURE 5.3

Sale Price and the Likelihood of a Sale within 90 Days

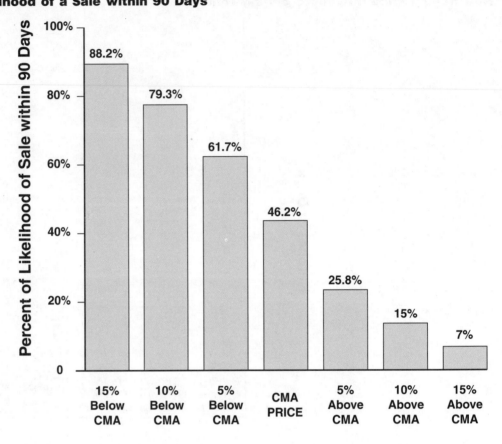

Listing presentation manuals should be divided into two areas:

1. *Why* list?
2. *Why* us?

You must convince the owner or buyer about the concept of a listing as your first step and then show that you should have the listing.

■ SALE LISTINGS

Owner's feel that a listing will cost them money. They are likely to initially view the idea of a listing as *negative* rather than look at the *benefits* you can offer. Therefore, you must overcome the negative thoughts and help owners realize the benefits offered.

Why List?

When you deal with a **For Sale by Owner** (FSBO), realize that a significant reason the owners want to sell the home themselves is to save the real estate agent's commission. They feel if they can sell their property without an agent, the agent's fee will be additional money for them. Therefore, begin your presentation with a discussion of who actually saves when an agent is not involved.

FIGURE 5.4

Estimated Seller's Proceeds

 CALIFORNIA
ASSOCIATION
OF REALTORS®

ESTIMATED SELLER'S PROCEEDS

SELLER _____ DATE _____

PROPERTY ADDRESS _____

This estimate is based on costs associated with _____ type of financing.

PROJECTED CLOSING DATE _____	ESTIMATED SELLING PRICE $ _____	
ESTIMATED COSTS:	**ENCUMBRANCES** (Approximate):	
Escrow Fee $ _____	First Trust Deed	$ _____
Drawing, Recording, Notary _____	Second Trust Deed	_____
Title Insurance Policy _____	Bonds, Liens	_____
Documentary Transfer Tax:	Other Encumbrances	_____
County _____	**TOTAL:**	$ _____
City _____	**GROSS EQUITY:**	$ _____
Transfer Tax _____	**APPROXIMATE CREDITS:**	
Prepayment Penalty _____	Prorated Taxes	$ _____
Bene/Demand Fee _____	Prorated Insurance	_____
Prorated Interest (all loans) _____	Impound Accounts	_____
Reconveyance Deed _____	Other: _____	_____
Misc. Lender Fees _____	Other: _____	_____
Appraisal Fee _____	**TOTAL:**	$ _____
VA/FHA Discount _____ Points _____	**RECAP:**	
Preparation of Documents _____	**ESTIMATED SELLING PRICE:**	$ _____
Misc. VA/FHA Fees _____	**LESS:**	
Prorated Taxes _____	Total Encumbrances	- _____
Structural Pest Control Inspection _____	Estimated Costs	- _____
Structural Pest Control Repairs _____	Sub-Total	$ _____
Other Required Repairs _____	**PLUS:**	
Natural Hazard Disclosure Report _____	Approximate Credits	+ _____
Home Protection Policy _____	**ESTIMATED SELLER'S PROCEEDS:**	$ _____
Brokerage Fee _____	**LESS:**	
Buyer's Closing Costs _____	Purchase Money Note	- _____
Security Deposits _____	(If carried by Seller)	
Prorated Rents _____	**PLUS:**	
Administrative/Transaction Fee _____	Proceeds From Sale of	
Other Fees/Costs: _____	Purchase Money Note	+ _____
_____ _____	**ESTIMATED SELLER'S CASH PROCEEDS:** $ _____	
_____ _____		
_____ _____		

ESTIMATED TOTAL COSTS: $ _____

This estimate, based upon the above projected selling price, type of financing and projected closing date, has been prepared to assist the Seller in computing his/her costs and proceeds. Lenders, title companies and escrow holders will vary in their charges. Expenses will also vary depending upon any required repairs, differences in unpaid loan balances, bond assessments, other liens, impound account, if any, and other items. Therefore, these figures cannot be guaranteed by the Broker or his/her representatives. All estimates and information are from sources believed reliable but not guaranteed.

I have read the above figures and acknowledge receipt of a copy of this form.   Real Estate Broker (Firm) _____

Presented by _____

SELLER _____ Date _____   Address _____

SELLER _____ Date _____   Phone _____

Published and Distributed by:
REAL ESTATE BUSINESS SERVICES, INC.
a subsidiary of the CALIFORNIA ASSOCIATION OF REALTORS®
525 South Virgil Avenue, Los Angeles, California 90020

Reviewed by _____

Broker or Designee _____ Date _____

EQUAL HOUSING OPPORTUNITY

REVISION DATE 10/2000   Print Date
ESP-11 (PAGE 1 OF 1)

ESTIMATED SELLER'S PROCEEDS (ESP-11 PAGE 1 OF 1)

Even when you are not dealing with an FSBO, you could be in competition with the owners as well as with other agents for a listing. While not stated or even denied, the owners could be considering selling without an agent as one of their options. Therefore, we believe that every listing presentation should begin with a discussion of false savings of FSBO offerings.

Consider starting your presentation book with the following question and answer:

> *Question:*
> Who saves when an owner sells without an agent?
> *Answer:*
> The buyer.

The primary reason owners want to sell without an agent is to avoid paying a commission.

Note: This question-and-answer technique is very effective and is easy to prepare. Put only one question and answer on a page, with all pages being read on the right side of your book. We show suggested verbal presentations within quotation marks following each question and answer. You can use appropriate ideas to tailor your own presentation book and presentation to your needs.

"I understand why you would want to sell [might consider selling] your home without an agent. You would like to save the agent's fee. Owners who do succeed in selling without an agent—and there aren't that many of them—find that they're not the ones who save. If there are any savings to be had, the buyer enjoys them.

"Buyers who approach owners who advertise their homes for sale or put signs in their front yards will want to reduce any offer they might make by at least the amount of the commission, even though the price might have been set to reflect all or part of this savings."

"Buyers will not even settle for half because they realize it is buyers, not sellers, who really pay the commission. The price the buyer pays includes a commission, and although the seller may pay it, it is paid for with dollars that come from the buyer's savings and not the seller's pockets. When an owner sells direct, losing the commission is just for starters. Buyers tend to view For Sale by Owner situations as an opportunity to make a profit for them. They believe that For Sale by Owner indicates a distress sale, and that belief explains some of the ridiculous offers owners receive."

> *Question*
> Why are most For Sale by Owner signs replaced by agent signs?
> *Answer*
> Because owners are seldom successful in selling their homes.

"Few buyers seek out For Sale by Owner ads and signs, and when they do give an offer it is usually at a price the owner will not consider."

Question
Who does this sign attract?

    Answer:
- Bargain hunters
- Lookie Lous
- Unqualified buyers

"With a For Sale by Owner sign on your front lawn you will attract bargain hunters of all types.

"Your home will be on the Sunday entertainment tour of Lookie Lous who might be interested only in how you have decorated your home or are simply using you as a way to fill an otherwise vacant day.

"Your For Sale by Owner ads and signs will attract people who might truly love your home but don't have a prayer of getting necessary financing. These people can waste a great deal of your time. Even if they give you an offer, the sale will never be closed.

"A For Sale sign says 'Come on in' to the whole world. When you show people your home and belongings, you are really allowing strangers in. You let them see into closets and places that your best friend will never see, and you have no idea why they are there. I wish it wasn't a problem, but safety *is* a problem today. People put in expensive alarm systems and then invite strangers into their homes to see who lives there and what there is. Is this wise?"

    Question:
What does this sign mean?
    Answer:
- Wasted time
- Wasted effort
- Likelihood of legal problems
- Failure

"Owners who try to sell without an agent are prisoners in their own homes, waiting for a phone call on the ad or a passerby to ring their doorbell.

"When they accept an offer, they might find that the other party views the agreement differently from what the owners thought was agreed to. The likelihood of a lawsuit is magnified many times when an agent is not part of the transaction.

"Actually, a lawsuit is seldom a problem, because most owners who try to sell without an agent never even get an offer."

    Question:
Why do most serious buyers contact real estate agents?

Answer:

Because agents have the inventory.

"[Mr. and Mrs._____], when *you* were looking for a home to purchase, I bet you visited real estate agents, am I right? The reason you went to at least one agent is because agents knew what was on the market and were able to quickly locate properties that met your needs. Without agents, buyers would have to contact dozens of individual property owners to check out property, even though inspection might reveal that the property did not come close to meeting their needs. Buyers today are no different than you were when you purchased this home. Buyers who are serious about buying contact agents. Buyers dealing with agents understand they will have to pay a price dictated by the market and that they are not going to get anything for nothing."

We suggest you take a positive approach regarding the benefits of agency representation. Owners who understand the benefits of professional representation are less likely to resist paying a reasonable fee for these services. **Note:** The word *fee* denotes a professional charge for benefits, whereas *commission* has a negative connotation to some people.

> The word *commission* has a negative connotation, but *fee* is positive in that it is a charge for benefits received.

Question:

What do you get for your fee?

Answer:

These important benefits:

- Help and advice on making your home more salable
- Promotion and advertising (paid by the agent)
- Multiple-listing benefits
- Qualifying of all prospects
- Freedom to enjoy your time
- Advice on offers and counteroffers
- Problem solving during escrow

"We work with you to make your house salable at the highest possible price. We promote your home with advertising and open houses. We prepare advertising fliers on your home for other agents, for responses to inquiries and for those visiting your home. We also feature your home on our own Web site as well as other Web sites. Of course, we bear all of these costs.

"Information on your home is made available through our multiple-listing service to [137] offices and more than [1,814] agents and through the _____ Web site that has [more than 3,000] hits per day. This is the kind of exposure that is possible for your home.

"We properly qualify anyone we bring to your home. We know who they are, where they live and work, and who can afford to buy your home before they cross your threshold.

"You receive our advice on all offers received. We will work with you and the buyer in turning an unacceptable offer into an advantageous sale.

"We work with buyers in obtaining financing to ensure that the purchase will close.

FIGURE 5.5

Services You Will Receive

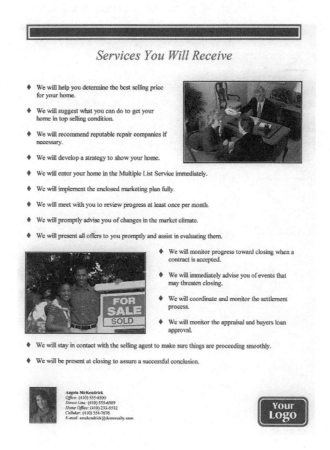

Services You Will Receive

♦ We will help you determine the best selling price for your home.

♦ We will suggest what you can do to get your home in top selling condition.

♦ We will recommend reputable repair companies if necessary.

♦ We will develop a strategy to show your home.

♦ We will enter your home in the Multiple List Service immediately.

♦ We will implement the enclosed marketing plan fully.

♦ We will meet with you to review progress at least once per month.

♦ We will promptly advise you of changes in the market climate.

♦ We will present all offers to you promptly and assist in evaluating them.

♦ We will monitor progress toward closing when a contract is accepted.

♦ We will immediately advise you of events that may threaten closing.

♦ We will coordinate and monitor the settlement process.

♦ We will monitor the appraisal and buyers loan approval.

♦ We will stay in contact with the selling agent to make sure things are proceeding smoothly.

♦ We will be present at closing to assure a successful conclusion.

Angela McKendrick
Office: (410) 555-6500
Direct Line: (410) 555-6809
Home Office: (410) 233-5532
Cellular: (410) 554-7676
E-mail: amakendrick@demorealty.com

Your Logo

"We monitor escrow to make certain there are no hang-ups. If a problem arises, we inform you and work to overcome it so the sale can progress."

This question-and-answer approach is just one of many approaches that can be used for your listing presentation material. Whatever material you use should flow toward the desired goal of overcoming any resistance by the owners to signing an agency agreement. You must be comfortable with the approach you use. If you are not comfortable with the material, chances are your effort will reflect your attitude, which will translate into few successful listings.

A number of real estate software providers have software programs available for listing presentation manuals. Figure 5.5 was provided by Realty Tools, Inc. (*www.realtytools.com*), shows the benefits of listing having agency representation.

Why Us?

To obtain a listing, you have to convince owners that you and your firm deserve their trust. This is particularly important when owners are hesitant about listing their property because of a previous unsatisfactory experience with another agent.

You must build rapport with property owners. The owners must not only want to list their property, they must want to list with you because they feel you are a capable person representing a capable firm. In addition, they must like you as a person.

Sell yourself to the owners as a caring person who understands their problems and wants to help produce solutions. If you can't do this, you could end up doing all the groundwork for an easy listing by another agent who has been able to develop greater empathy with the owners.

Listen to what the owners say during and after your presentation. And be formal. Address them by their last names (Mr. Owner, Mrs. Seller). Answer questions slowly and fully. Ask questions to determine if you are communicating fully with the owners.

> **You must sell yourself as worthy of an owner's trust.**

Don't *tell* the owners, *ask* them. Don't talk down to them or dismiss questions with flippant remarks. Don't use technical terms or acronyms. They may not understand what this girl Fannie Mae has to do with their property. In the initial phase of the presentation, keep in mind that the product you are selling is really yourself.

The *Why Us?* portion of your listing presentation book should cover you personally as well as your firm. You might want to start with a one-page résumé entitled "Want To Know About [Lester Jones]?"

Keep your résumé simple. You should have extra copies of this résumé so you can give the owners a copy. You are asking them to entrust you with the sale of their home, so they deserve to know something about you. When you give the owners your résumé, take no more than one minute to tell them about yourself. You should emphasize knowledge of the community, success in sales, special training, professional designations and so forth.

A photo of your office or, if more than one office, a collage of photos can be effective. If your office has been in business a long time, a caption such as "Servicing [Midvale] since [1953]" is appropriate. If you are with a large firm or franchise, the caption could read "[8] offices and [146] professionals ready to serve you."

If you have a large office, a group photo of your sales force with the name of your firm is effective.

Your narrative could simply be

> "We offer the advantage of [8] offices and [146] salespeople. Isn't this the kind of sales force you want for success?"

For a franchise, consider:

[Franchise Name] [Logo]
[1,823] Offices
[36,000] Salespeople

Our Name Means:
- Instant Recognition
- National Referrals

Your possible narrative:

> "The name [VIP Realty] means instant recognition even to those who are new to our community. Because we are a [VIP] office, you can benefit from our national referral system."

If your firm is small, use a photo of your office and turn your small size into a positive with a narrative such as

> "Because we·specialize in a small number of select properties, our owners receive maximum service. Your home will not be competing with 400 other office listings. We can provide the individual attention your home deserves in order to have a successful sale."

You must sell the benefits that your firm has to offer.

As an alternative, you might show your small firm as part of a large organization with a caption:

> "[Loring Realty] is part of a multiple-listing service offering you [237] offices and more than [2,000] salespeople, all working for your success."

Your narrative might be

> "With [Loring Realty] representing you, you can take advantage of this huge sales force working together for your success."

Perhaps you want a separate sheet providing information on your multiple-listing service. Your possible narrative:

> "By appointing [Loring Realty] as your agent, in less than one hour the information on your home will be available to these [237] offices and more than [2,000] salespeople. This sales force can be working for you."

An alternative narrative for a multiple-listing service would be

> "Assume every agent in our multiple-listing service is working with just two buyers for a home in your home's general price range. Now that may seem to be a very low figure. But consider that tomorrow morning your home can be exposed to those two buyers by [2,000] agents. That's [4,000] potential buyers for your home."

If you are a REALTOR®, consider a sheet with just the REALTOR® trademark. Your narrative:

"Every broker is not a REALTOR®. Only REALTORS® can use this symbol. [Loring Realty] is a member of the California Association of REALTORS® and the National Association of REALTORS®. As REALTORS® we are pledged to a Code of Professional Conduct."

If your firm is a member of the National Association of Real Estate Brokers, a similar approach could be used.

A collage of press releases about your firm on both right-hand and left-hand pages of the book is effective. Your narrative:

"The fact that [Loring Realty] has played a dominant role in [community activities] and [development] brings us instant name recognition as a professional leader."

Tell owners how your firm advertises to attract potential buyers. For a larger firm you could have a sheet stating

2003
[$1 Million] + Advertising Budget

Your narrative could be

"Our advertising budget of [$] means [$] per week spent to bring in buyers. This budget has given us name recognition and dominance in the marketplace. Our dominance is reflected in our sales record."

For a small firm, consider a collage of your ads, covering both left-hand and right-hand pages. You could say

"You can see we publicize our listings."

If your office advertises in a foreign paper or has relationships with brokerage offices in other countries, this should be emphasized. Many owners feel that foreign buyers pay top price, so that access to them is important.

The Only Office in [Sacramento]
Advertising in
Nihon Keizai Shimbun
Japan's Largest Business Daily Newspaper

"We market our properties to the largest possible market. We go to the buyers. Through international advertising, we have built up a referral network of agents who work with us to locate buyers."

If your office has a home protection plan:

[Loring Realty] Offers a
Home Protection Plan
That Makes Your Home More Desirable

"Our home protection plan protects buyers against structural problems and system breakdowns for [one] year after purchase. This protection has given us a word-of-mouth reputation to the extent that many buyers would not consider using another agent to purchase a home."

If your office belongs to a national referral network but is not a franchise office, consider a sheet that reads

Member
[Home Relocators]
A National Relocation Referral Service
[1,838] Cooperating Member Firms in 50 States

Your possible narrative:

"Would you like to take advantage of referrals from every corner of the nation? We constantly receive calls about people relocating to our area because of our [Home Relocators] membership. We want our owners to have every sales advantage possible. I'm sure that's the kind of representation you want."

Emphasize your Internet site: "I'm sure you realize that the Internet is gaining increasing importance in selling real estate. These are a few pictures of our Internet site." Show a home presentation from the site as well as your office home site. If your site features virtual reality tours, explain virtual reality tours and the benefits:

"[Loring Realty] does not take second place to anyone in using technology to market our homes."

If your firm specializes in the area where you are seeking a listing, a sheet should show this specialization:

[Palm Desert Greens]
Housing Specialists

Your narrative could be

"We specialize in [Palm Desert Greens]. We have built up a reputation of being the [Palm Desert Greens] broker. Prospective buyers come to us because we have the inventory and make the sales. When other agents get a buyer who is interested in [Palm Desert Greens], they call us. Our cooperation with others and our knowledge of the market has resulted in a record of success in [Palm Desert Greens] that is second to none."

By using computer information from your local multiple-listing service, you should be able to find statistics that show your firm is outstanding in several areas. Sheets should be prepared to showcase these distinctions. But be careful when you use statistics. If you emphasize that 50 percent of your listings are sold, it also points out a 50 percent failure rate. Approaches that are more positive would be

[Loring Realty]
[42%] Better Record of Success

"According to the records of the [Tri-County Multiple-Listing Service], listings with [Loring Realty] had a [42 percent] greater chance of success than the board average for [2003]."

[Loring Realty]
We Get More for Your Home

"According to the records of the [Tri-County Multiple-Listing Service], the average home in [2003] sold at [84 percent] of its listed price. In [2003], [Loring Realty] home sales averaged [94 percent] of list price. That's [10 percent] more money in the pockets of our sellers than our competition. Is getting the most money from your home important to you?"

Another approach could be

"For all practical purposes you get our services free. Let me tell you why. The average sale as reported by the [Tri-County Multiple-Listing Service] for [2003] was at [84 percent] of list price. In [2003], [Loring Realty] sales averaged [94 percent] of list price. Therefore, we were able to get our owners an increase over the average sale in excess of our fees received."

The percentage of your own listings that are sold by your office can be a positive statement about your firm:

[2003] Multiple-Listing Figures
Sales Made by Listing Office
Average [26%]
[Loring Realty] [51%]

"At [Loring Realty] we don't just list and hope one of the cooperating offices finds a buyer. From these figures, you can see that we feel obligated to work hard for our owners. When we represent you, you come first."

The last page of your presentation book should really be a trial closing.

"[Mr. and Mrs. Garczynski], don't you want [Loring Realty] to represent you?"

Your narrative would simply be the question asked.

By use of a laser printer, you can personalize this closing.

Figures 5.6A through 5.6E were supplied by Realty Tools, Inc. They are samples prepared from their software package.

■ BUYER LISTINGS

To obtain listings from buyers you should explain the normal agency where the agent represents the seller or has dual agency duties. An understanding of seller agency will make the need for buyer agency representation very apparent.

The owner must also understand what you will do for him or her and how you will be paid your fee. You can use a variation of the questions and answers technique with just questions where the answers are obvious.

"Who does the property listing agent represent?"

FIGURES 5.6A–5.6E

Why Us? Samples

A.

Why List With Demo Realty?

Buying or selling a home is the biggest, most important, financial transaction people experience in their lifetime. Once you decide to sell your home, choosing the right real estate company and agent to represent you during this transaction is the most important decision you will make. Consider the following reasons why you should list with Demo Realty.

♦ We are a leader in listing and selling homes in your market area.

♦ We have more top producers than any other company in the area.

♦ We have comprehensive print, TV, and direct mail advertising programs.

♦ We are members of an international relocation network.

♦ We have satisfied past customers which provide a source of potential buyers.

♦ We have full time agents who receive extensive on-going training.

♦ We have efficient, computerized accounting and property information systems.

♦ We have a computer resource department for agent training in the use of personal computers.

♦ We have a corporate commitment to excellence in all areas of the real estate business.

List with Demo Realty and we will see to it that your home is sold for the best price, in the shortest amount of time, with the least inconvenience to you.

Why Not List With The Best?

Angela McKendrick
Office: (410) 555-6500
Direct Line: (410) 555-6509
Home Office: (410) 233-5532
Cellular: (410) 554-7676
E-mail: amckendrick@demorealty.com

Your Logo

B.

Marketing Plan of Action

First Week on the Market

- Enter listing into MLS system.
- Put up "For Sale" sign.
- Install lock box.
- Schedule property photos.
- Review showing tips.
- Prepare property flyer/brochure.

Second Week on the Market

- Invite local Realtors to tour home.
- Run ad in Sunday paper.
- Mail postcard to top agents.
- Review status with sellers.

Third Week on the Market

- Hold Sunday Open House.
- Place Homes Magazine ad.
- Discuss comments from agents & prospects.

On-going

- Report weekly to sellers.
- Show property to prospects.
- Review price based on agent input & market conditions.

ASAP

Obtain an acceptable contract on your property!

Angela McKendrick
Office: (410) 555-6500
Direct Line: (410) 555-6509
Home Office: (410) 233-5532
Cellular: (410) 554-7676
E-mail: amckendrick@demorealty.com

Your Logo

C.

Customer References

Sellers...

Fred & Susan Fredericks	23 Elm Street	822-4554
Joe & Lisa Johnson	1400 N. Timonium Road	922-2222
Ron & Dawn Larkin	2311 E. Roundtop Circle	444-3948
Debra Jones	433 Forest Drive	231-6932
Don & Julia Smith	32 E. Running Road	211-4599
Len & Hanna Leonard	443 Forest Drive	343-6798

Buyers...

Mark & Joan Dawson	2300 S. Timonium Road	666-3033
Suzanne Swift	22 Forrest Avenue	667-9888
Ron & Joan Burns	55 W. Running Road	333-9843
Joe & Ann Reese	321 Pine Forest Lane	222-4563
Robert Johnson	324 82nd Terrace	342-6879
Jay & Sarah Volker	75 Winding Way	234-1098

Angela McKendrick
Office: (410) 555-6500
Direct Line: (410) 555-6509
Home Office: (410) 233-5532
Cellular: (410) 554-7676
E-mail: amckendrick@demorealty.com

Your Logo

D.

In Conclusion

You should choose Angela McKendrick because:

♦ We will provide you with excellent service and support.

♦ We have made a thorough market analysis of your home.

♦ We have developed a winning marketing plan.

♦ We will make every effort to sell your home promptly.

♦ We have the resources of Demo Realty.

*Let Us
List Your
Home Now!*

Angela McKendrick
Office: (410) 555-6500
Direct Line: (410) 555-6509
Home Office: (410) 233-5532
Cellular: (410) 554-7676
E-mail: amckendrick@demorealty.com

Your Logo

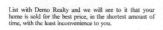

FIGURES 5.6A–5.6E

Why Us? **Samples (continued)**

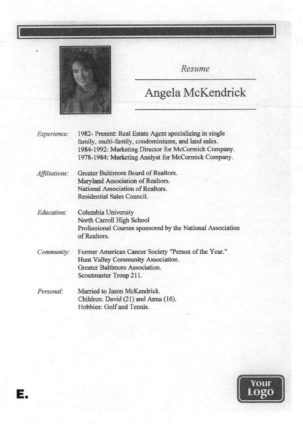

Resume

Angela McKendrick

Experience:	1982- Present: Real Estate Agent specializing in single family, multi-family, condominiums, and land sales. 1984-1992: Marketing Director for McCormick Company. 1978-1984: Marketing Analyst for McCormick Company.
Affiliations:	Greater Baltimore Board of Realtors. Maryland Association of Realtors. National Association of Realtors. Residential Sales Council.
Education:	Columbia University North Carroll High School Professional Courses sponsored by the National Association of Realtors.
Community:	Former American Cancer Society "Person of the Year." Hunt Valley Community Association. Greater Baltimore Association. Scoutmaster Troup 211.
Personal:	Married to Jason McKendrick. Children: David (21) and Anna (16). Hobbies: Golf and Tennis.

Your Logo

E.

"Will the property listing agent try to find the home that is best for your or will he or she try to sell their clients' property?"

"Will the property listing agent try to sell you the property at the lowest possible price?"

"Does the property listing agent get greater compensation when the price is greater?"

"The sellers have an agent looking out for their best interests, should you be similarly protected?"

You should explain that your services will generally be paid for by the seller because you will accept the multiple-listing service commission split as compensation, which is paid by the seller.

For your presentation, consider the following material developed by Realty Tools, Inc. (Figures 5.7A through 5.7E). In addition, some of the same material you developed for sales listings would be applicable to buyer listings.

FIGURES 5.7A–5.7E

Presentation Samples

A.

April 3, 2002

John & Susan Smith
2321 Pine Tree Lane
Hunt Valley, MD 21030

Dear John & Susan,

Thank you very much for giving me the opportunity to present the enclosed proposal for real estate services. I appreciate the time you spent with me outlining the criteria for your new home.

You will receive competent and professional service when you select me and Demo Realty to assist you in your search for a new home. We have assisted many families in this area in their search for their ideal home. I hope you will select me as your agent in this very important transaction.

This proposal includes information on me and Demo Realty that will confirm my qualifications.

Sincerely,

Angela McKendrick
REALTOR®

B.

Why Choose Demo Realty?

Buying or selling a home is the biggest, and most important, financial transaction people experience in their lifetime. And, once you decide to sell your home, choosing the right real estate company and agent to represent you during this transaction is the most important decision you will make. Consider the following reasons why you should choose Demo Realty.

- ◆ We are a leader in listing and selling homes in your market area.
- ◆ We have more top producers than any other company in the area.

- ◆ We have comprehensive print, TV, and direct mail advertising programs.
- ◆ We are members of an international relocation network.
- ◆ We have satisfied past customers which provide a source of potential buyers.
- ◆ We have full time agents who receive extensive on-going training.
- ◆ We have efficient, computerized accounting and property information systems.
- ◆ We have a computer resource department for agent training in the use of personal computers.
- ◆ We have a corporate commitment to excellence in all areas of the real estate business.

Search with Demo Realty and we will see to it that your new home is found in the shortest amount of time, with the least inconvenience to you and purchased at the best price.

Angela McKendrick
Office: (410) 555-6500
Direct Line: (410) 555-6509
Home Office: (410) 233-5532
Cellular: (410) 554-7676
E-mail: amckendrick@demorealty.com

C.

Services You Will Receive

- ◆ We will help you determine the required characteristics of your new home.
- ◆ We will identify available homes that meet your criteria whether they are listed by Demo Realty or another Realtor.
- ◆ We will provide you with information on communities, schools, churches and any other area characteristics you need.
- ◆ We will determine the maximum mortgage amount for which you are qualified.
- ◆ We will advise you of the financing options available to you.
- ◆ We will give you an estimate of the cash required for purchase.
- ◆ We will research past appreciation rates for the communities you are considering.
- ◆ We will meet with you periodically to review progress.

- ◆ We will help you inspect the property prior to settlement.
- ◆ We will advise you on the preparation of an offer.
- ◆ We will monitor progress toward closing when your contract is accepted.
- ◆ We will immediately advise you of events that may threaten closing.

- ◆ We will stay in contact with the listing agent to make sure things are proceeding smoothly.
- ◆ We will attend the settlement with you.

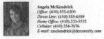
Angela McKendrick
Office: (410) 555-6500
Direct Line: (410) 555-6509
Home Office: (410) 233-5532
Cellular: (410) 554-7676
E-mail: amckendrick@demorealty.com

D.

Action Plan To Find Your Home

- ◆ Complete the ideal home survey sheet.
- ◆ Complete the financial information questionnaire.
- ◆ Indicate criteria for community selection or specify specific communities.
- ◆ I will complete a mortgage qualification report and review it with you.
- ◆ We will review the ideal home and community criteria and reconcile that with the mortgage qualification if necessary.
- ◆ I will search the MLS and other sources available to me in order to prepare a list of candidate properties.
- ◆ I will set up appointments to see the selected homes.

The remaining plan of action will depend upon our success with the initial list of candidate properties. We will either proceed to the settlement process if we find the right home during our initial search, or continue to monitor the market in the event that we were unable to find the right home from those currently available for sale.

Angela McKendrick
Office: (410) 555-6500
Direct Line: (410) 555-6509
Home Office: (410) 233-5532
Cellular: (410) 554-7676
E-mail: amckendrick@demorealty.com

FIGURES 5.7A–5.7E

Presentation Samples (continued)

Home Finders' Profile

E.

■ **SUMMARY**

The competitive market analysis is an excellent tool for arriving at a recommended list price, as well as for convincing owners that it is in their best interests to initially list their home at a realistic price. The attachments you provide clearly illustrate the effect of pricing on the time to sell as well as on the likelihood of success.

The Estimated Seller's Proceeds form is really a disclosure form to fully inform the owner of what he or she will net from a sale at list price. By disclosing this information at the time of listing, the owner is prepared for what he or she will actually receive. Unpleasant surprises can mean sales that fail to close.

The listing presentation manual is a visual tool to be used along with the agent's narrative to provide a structured, effective listing presentation.

The presentation manual is broken down into two sections. One is *Why List?* and the other is *Why Us?* The *Why List?* presentation shows the owner why it is in the owner's best interests to employ an exclusive selling agent. The *Why Us?* presentation tells the owner about you and your firm. It shows the owner the advantages your firm offers. It is a positive approach because it sells benefits and leads to a trial closing.

A separate listing presentation manual should be prepared for buyer listings.

■ CLASS DISCUSSION TOPICS

1. Competitive Market Analysis

   Prepare a competitive market analysis on a property (use real or fictitious comparables). Present the analysis to an owner (use another student) and explain how you arrived at your recommendations.

2. Estimated Seller's Proceeds

   Prepare an Estimated Seller's Proceeds form, based on costs in your area, for a home that has an $81,000 first trust deed that is to be assumed. The seller will carry back a second trust deed for $8,000, and the seller will be paying a 6 percent commission on the $100,000 sale. (Do not prorate taxes, insurance, or consider impound accounts.)

3. Listing Presentation Manual

   Prepare either the *Why List?* or *Why Us?* portion of the listing presentation manual. Be prepared to make a presentation in class on your portion of the listing presentation manual to another student as if you were addressing an owner.

4. A prospective seller will be interviewing other agents.

   Prepare, in writing, the reasons the prospective seller should choose you or your firm rather than your competitors.

5. Bring to class one current-events article dealing with some aspect of real estate practice for class discussion.

■ CHAPTER 5 QUIZ

1. A CMA is best described as
   a. a formal appraisal.
   b. the cooperative marketing approach of multiple listings.
   c. a reflection of the reality of the market-place.
   d. the comparative mortgage analysis per-formed by agents in advising buyers as to lender and loan type.

2. In making your recommendation of list price for a single-family home, the most important portion of the analysis deals with
   a. list prices of homes on the market now.
   b. list prices of homes where the listings expired.
   c. prices of comparable properties that sold.
   d. possible rental income.

3. You should realize that for data used on a CMA
   a. the older the data are, the less reliable they are.
   b. sale prices that seem unusually high or low are often the result of market imper-fections.
   c. Both a and b are true.
   d. Both a and b are false.

4. Owners must be made to realize that
   a. the higher they price their home over fair market value, the longer it will take to sell.
   b. the higher they price their home over fair market value, the lower the likelihood of a sale during the listing period.
   c. Both a and b are true.
   d. Both a and b are false.

5. A recommended list price below what the CMA indicates as the likely sale range is in an owner's best interest when
   a. a sellers' market exists.
   b. the seller must get the highest net.
   c. the seller must sell quickly.
   d. the seller is not strongly motivated to sell.

6. What a seller receives in hand from a sale is the
   a. gross sale price.
   b. net sale price.
   c. net profit.
   d. seller's proceeds.

7. The principal reason owners try to sell their homes without an agent is
   a. to have a quick sale.
   b. to save the commission.
   c. to be able to pick the buyer.
   d. none of the above.

8. Your listing presentation book should
   a. be organized to follow your listing presentation.
   b. not be used in lieu of a verbal presentation.
   c. help you sell an owner on the concept of listing in general and listing with your firm in particular.
   d. be all of the above.

9. Which of the following statements is the best approach to take when selling the benefits of listing with a small office?
   a. We try harder because of the competition.
   b. All we need to find is one buyer, and even we can do that.
   c. We need the business more than the large firms.
   d. We specialize in a small number of select properties.

10. In your listing presentation, what would be your least effective statement?
    a. Of our listings, 32 percent are sold during the listing period, compared with an average of only 21 percent from the entire board.
    b. Our average sale is at 94 percent of the list price, compared with an MLS average of only 86 percent.
    c. Listings with our office have more than a 32 percent greater chance of a sale than the average listings with an MLS.
    d. Our average sale time is 32 percent shorter than the average for an MLS.

CHAPTER SIX

LISTING PRESENTATIONS

■ KEY TERMS

bilateral agreement
clincher
exclusive-agency listing
exclusive-authorization-
and-right-to-sell listing

Exclusive Authorization
  To Acquire Property
net listing
open listing
option combined with a
  listing

safety clause
trial closing
unilateral contract

■ LEARNING OBJECTIVES

This chapter reviews the essentials of a listing agreement and types of listings. You gain an in-depth knowledge of the meaning of each paragraph of the California Association of REALTORS® right-to-sell and buyer-seller agreement forms. You learn the mechanics of the listing preparation as well as making the listing presentation.

■ THE LISTING AGREEMENT

Of all the documents used in the real estate business, none is more important than the listing agreement. This is the instrument that defines a broker's rights and duties. It is the broker's employment contract and gives him or her a right to a commission.

Definition

A *listing agreement*, when executed (signed) by the parties, becomes a legally binding contract that authorizes a broker to serve as agent for a principal in a real estate activity. Listing contracts may be entered into for the purpose of securing qualified persons to buy, sell, lease, or rent property. Generally, though, licensed agents are authorized to find a purchaser for a particular property at a specified price and terms, often within a certain time limit, or to locate a property for a prospective buyer, which is commonly known as a buyer agency listing. The agreement spells out the mutual benefits to and obligations of the broker and the seller or the broker and buyer.

The agreement is an agency contract to perform a specified action, such as finding a buyer for the principal's property, for a commission. The broker who fulfills his or her part of the contract is entitled, both legally and morally, to be paid for these efforts. Just a few years ago, buyer agency listings were practically unknown. Now they are actively sought by a great many successful agents.

Elements

Because the listing is a real estate contract, it must include all the essential elements of a *contract*, including competency of parties, lawful object, proper offer and acceptance (mutual consent), and consideration.

To be enforceable, listing contracts must be in writing [Civil Code 1624(5)]. Oral listings provide the broker with no legal protection whatsoever because without a written contract the broker cannot enforce payment of a commission if the seller refuses to pay it.

The *consideration* in a listing contract is the broker's promise to "use diligence in locating a ready, willing, and able buyer" in exchange for the seller's promise to pay a commission or the agent's promise to locate a property for a buyer with compensation paid by the buyer or the seller. The promise (seller/ buyer to pay commission) given for a promise (broker to use diligence in finding a buyer/property) makes a **bilateral agreement**. The consideration that passes between parties in a real estate contract can be anything of value.

Types of Listing Agreements

There are many variations of the basic listing agreement from various publishers, as well as computer program forms. Some are for general residential property; others are for special types of property, such as industrial, income, farm, or unimproved property. Despite the variations, there are six basic kinds of listings: open listings, exclusive-authorization-and-right-to-sell listings, exclusive-agency

FIGURE 6.1

Who May Sell a Property and Receive a Commission Under Three Types of Listing Agreements

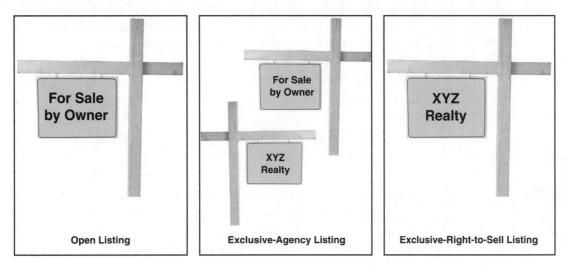

listings, net listings, option listings, and exclusive authorizations to acquire real property (a buyer's listing can also be an open listing). The purpose of a listing agreement generally is to define the relationship between the seller (or buyer, in the case of a buyer's listing) and the broker. You may find it useful to group listings into two kinds of agreements, exclusive and nonexclusive. Figure 6.1 classifies listings according to the relationship between seller and broker.

Open Listing.   An **open listing** is a written memorandum that when signed by the seller or buyer, authorizes the broker to serve as an agent for the sale or purchase of property. Under an open listing, the owner agrees to pay a commission if the broker procures a buyer or property that is purchased. Because the broker is not obligated to use diligence to locate a buyer or property, an open listing is considered to be a **unilateral contract.** It is a promise that is accepted by the agent's action in procuring a buyer or a property.

The seller or buyer may give this type of listing to as many brokers as he or she sees fit. The first agent who finds, according to the listing terms, a ready, willing, and able buyer acceptable to the seller or an acceptable property for the buyer gets the commission. This cancels all other open listings and negates the payment of any other commission. An open listing allows the owner to sell the property himself or herself or the buyer to buy him or herself without being liable to the broker(s) for a commission.

From the seller's and buyer's point of view, open listings may appear to provide a wider market than exclusive agreements. However, more-sophisticated sellers and buyers often conclude that brokers receiving this type of listing are unlikely to give them preferred attention. Sellers and buyers soon discover that "what is everybody's business is nobody's business" and that carefully selecting a single competent broker is almost always to their advantage.

Most real estate offices will not take an open sale listing because they know that the likelihood of a sale is slight and that allowing the owner to feel they are using diligence could be a disservice to the owner. Experienced agents will hold out for an exclusive-right-to-sell listing and if they are unable to obtain one, will walk away. The fact that others might agree to an open listing can actually help them. After the owner and the open listing agents have tried unsuccessfully to market the property for several months, the owner should be more receptive to a prepared marketing plan under an exclusive-right-to-sell listing.

Exclusive-Authorization-and-Right-To-Sell Listing. An **exclusive-authorization-and-right-to-sell listing** gives a broker the sole right to procure a purchaser for a property. With this type of listing the broker is the sole agent and has the right to a commission if a buyer is found for the property by anyone—even the owner—during the term of the listing. The listing broker has earned a commission when a bona fide offer at a specified or accepted price and terms is produced, whether or not escrow closes. (The listing is to produce a buyer.)

> An *exclusive-authorization-and-right-to-sell listing* entitles the listing agent to the commission no matter who sells the property.

All exclusive listings, by law, must have a definite termination date. Listings should be dated when they are taken, and the effective term should be set forth so clearly and definitely that there can be no mistake. An exclusive listing may not contain such wording as "effective until date of sale" or "until canceled in writing." California Real Estate Law Section 10176(f) states that a licensee is subject to disciplinary action for "claiming, demanding, or receiving a fee, compensation, or commission under any *exclusive* agreement authorizing or employing a licensee to sell, buy, or exchange real estate for compensation or commission where such agreement does not contain a *definite, specified date* of final and complete termination [italics added]."

The agent must give the owner a copy of any exclusive listing at the time it is signed. Because open listings are frequently just letters from an owner and need not be signed by the agent, an agent is not required to give the owner copies of these open listings, although it is strongly recommended that the owner receive copies of all listings. Figure 6.2 is a residential listing agreement, an exclusive-authorization-and-right-to-sell listing form.

Exclusive-Agency Listing. An **exclusive-agency listing** differs from the exclusive-authorization-and-right-to-sell listing in one major respect: The seller will pay a commission to the listing broker regardless of which agency makes the sale, but it does not prevent owners from selling their own property and paying no commission.

> With an *exclusive-agency listing*, the broker is not entitled to a commission if the owner sells without an agent's assistance.

Note: Because the exclusive-agency listing refers to an "agency" rather than a "right to sell," the owner, not being an agent, may personally effect the sale without incurring liability for a commission to the broker holding this type of listing.

FIGURE 6.2

Residential Listing Agreement (Exclusive Authorization and Right To Sell)

CALIFORNIA ASSOCIATION OF REALTORS®

RESIDENTIAL LISTING AGREEMENT
(Exclusive Authorization and Right to Sell)
(C.A.R. Form LA, Revised 10/02)

1. **EXCLUSIVE RIGHT TO SELL:** _____ ("Seller")
hereby employs and grants _____ ("Broker")
beginning (date) _____ and ending at 11:59 P.M. on (date) _____ ("Listing Period")
the exclusive and irrevocable right to sell or exchange the real property in the City of _____,
County of _____, California, described as: _____
_____ ("Property").

2. **ITEMS EXCLUDED AND INCLUDED:** Unless otherwise specified in a real estate purchase agreement, all fixtures and fittings that are attached to the Property are included, and personal property items are excluded, from the purchase price.
ADDITIONAL ITEMS EXCLUDED: _____.
ADDITIONAL ITEMS INCLUDED: _____.
Seller intends that the above items be excluded or included in offering the Property for sale, but understands that: **(i)** the purchase agreement supersedes any intention expressed above and will ultimately determine which items are excluded and included in the sale; and **(ii)** Broker is not responsible for and does not guarantee that the above exclusions and/or inclusions will be in the purchase agreement.

3. **LISTING PRICE AND TERMS:**
   A. The listing price shall be: _____
   _____ Dollars ($ _____).
   B. Additional Terms: _____
   _____

4. **COMPENSATION TO BROKER:**
   Notice: The amount or rate of real estate commissions is not fixed by law. They are set by each Broker individually and may be negotiable between Seller and Broker (real estate commissions include all compensation and fees to Broker).
   A. Seller agrees to pay to Broker as compensation for services irrespective of agency relationship(s), either ☐ _____ percent of the listing price (or if a purchase agreement is entered into, of the purchase price), or ☐ $ _____,
   AND _____, as follows:
   (1) If Broker, Seller, cooperating broker, or any other person procures a buyer(s) who offers to purchase the Property on the above price and terms, or on any price and terms acceptable to Seller during the Listing Period, or any extension.
   (2) If Seller, within _____ calendar days after the end of the Listing Period or any extension, enters into a contract to sell, convey, lease or otherwise transfer the Property to anyone ("Prospective Buyer") or that person's related entity: **(i)** who physically entered and was shown the Property during the Listing Period or any extension by Broker or a cooperating broker; or **(ii)** for whom Broker or any cooperating broker submitted to Seller a signed, written offer to acquire, lease, exchange or obtain an option on the Property. Seller, however, shall have no obligation to Broker under paragraph 4A(2) unless, not later than **3 calendar days** after the end of the Listing Period or any extension, Broker has given Seller a written notice of the names of such Prospective Buyers.
   (3) If, without Broker's prior written consent, the Property is withdrawn from sale, conveyed, leased, rented, otherwise transferred, or made unmarketable by a voluntary act of Seller during the Listing Period, or any extension.
   B. If completion of the sale is prevented by a party to the transaction other than Seller, then compensation due under paragraph 4A shall be payable only if and when Seller collects damages by suit, arbitration, settlement or otherwise, and then in an amount equal to the lesser of one-half of the damages recovered or the above compensation, after first deducting title and escrow expenses and the expenses of collection, if any.
   C. In addition, Seller agrees to pay Broker: _____.
   D. **(1)** Broker is authorized to cooperate with and compensate brokers participating through the multiple listing service(s) ("MLS"): **(i)** in any manner; **OR (ii)** (if checked) by offering MLS brokers: either ☐ _____ percent of the purchase price, or ☐ $ _____.
   (2) Broker is authorized to cooperate with and compensate brokers operating outside the MLS in any manner.
   E. Seller hereby irrevocably assigns to Broker the above compensation from Seller's funds and proceeds in escrow. Broker may submit this agreement, as instructions to compensate Broker pursuant to paragraph 4A, to any escrow regarding the Property involving Seller and a buyer, Prospective Buyer or other transferee.
   F. **(1)** Seller represents that Seller has not previously entered into a listing agreement with another broker regarding the Property, unless specified as follows: _____.
   (2) Seller warrants that Seller has no obligation to pay compensation to any other broker regarding the Property unless the Property is transferred to any of the following individuals or entities: _____
   _____
   (3) If the Property is sold to anyone listed above during the time Seller is obligated to compensate another broker: **(i)** Broker is not entitled to compensation under this agreement; and **(ii)** Broker is not obligated to represent Seller in such transaction.

Seller acknowledges receipt of a copy of this page.
Seller's Initials (_____)(_____)

Reviewed by _____ Date _____

EQUAL HOUSING OPPORTUNITY

LA REVISED 10/02 (PAGE 1 OF 3) Print Date

RESIDENTIAL LISTING AGREEMENT-EXCLUSIVE (LA PAGE 1 OF 3)

FIGURE 6.2

Residential Listing Agreement (Exclusive Authorization and Right To Sell) (continued)

Property Address: _____ Date: _____

5. **OWNERSHIP, TITLE AND AUTHORITY:** Seller warrants that: **(i)** Seller is the owner of the Property; **(ii)** no other persons or entities have title to the Property; and **(iii)** Seller has the authority to both execute this agreement and sell the Property. Exceptions to ownership, title and authority are as follows: _____.

6. **MULTIPLE LISTING SERVICE:** Information about this listing will (or ☐ will not) be provided to the MLS of Broker's selection. All terms of the transaction, including financing, if applicable, will be provided to the selected MLS for publication, dissemination and use by persons and entities on terms approved by the MLS. Seller authorizes Broker to comply with all applicable MLS rules. MLS rules allow MLS data to be made available by the MLS to additional Internet sites unless Broker gives the MLS instructions to the contrary.

7. **SELLER REPRESENTATIONS:** Seller represents that, unless otherwise specified in writing, Seller is unaware of: **(i)** any Notice of Default recorded against the Property; **(ii)** any delinquent amounts due under any loan secured by, or other obligation affecting, the Property; **(iii)** any bankruptcy, insolvency or similar proceeding affecting the Property; **(iv)** any litigation, arbitration, administrative action, government investigation or other pending or threatened action that affects or may affect the Property or Seller's ability to transfer it; and **(v)** any current, pending or proposed special assessments affecting the Property. Seller shall promptly notify Broker in writing if Seller becomes aware of any of these items during the Listing Period or any extension thereof.

8. **BROKER'S AND SELLER'S DUTIES:** Broker agrees to exercise reasonable effort and due diligence to achieve the purposes of this agreement. Unless Seller gives Broker written instructions to the contrary, Broker is authorized to order reports and disclosures as appropriate or necessary and advertise and market the Property by any method and in any medium selected by Broker, including MLS and the Internet, and, to the extent permitted by these media, control the dissemination of the information submitted to any medium. Seller agrees to consider offers presented by Broker, and to act in good faith to accomplish the sale of the Property by, among other things, making the Property available for showing at reasonable times and referring to Broker all inquiries of any party interested in the Property. Seller is responsible for determining at what price to list and sell the Property. **Seller further agrees to indemnify, defend and hold Broker harmless from all claims, disputes, litigation, judgments and attorney fees arising from any incorrect information supplied by Seller, or from any material facts that Seller knows but fails to disclose.**

9. **DEPOSIT:** Broker is authorized to accept and hold on Seller's behalf any deposits to be applied toward the purchase price.

10. **AGENCY RELATIONSHIPS:**
    A. **Disclosure:** If the Property includes residential property with one-to-four dwelling units, Seller shall receive a "Disclosure Regarding Agency Relationships" form prior to entering into this agreement.
    B. **Seller Representation:** Broker shall represent Seller in any resulting transaction, except as specified in paragraph 4F.
    C. **Possible Dual Agency With Buyer:** Depending upon the circumstances, it may be necessary or appropriate for Broker to act as an agent for both Seller and buyer, exchange party, or one or more additional parties ("Buyer"). Broker shall, as soon as practicable, disclose to Seller any election to act as a dual agent representing both Seller and Buyer. If a Buyer is procured directly by Broker or an associate licensee in Broker's firm, Seller hereby consents to Broker acting as a dual agent for Seller and such Buyer. In the event of an exchange, Seller hereby consents to Broker collecting compensation from additional parties for services rendered, provided there is disclosure to all parties of such agency and compensation. Seller understands and agrees that: **(i)** Broker, without the prior written consent of Seller, will not disclose to Buyer that Seller is willing to sell the Property at a price less than the listing price; **(ii)** Broker, without the prior written consent of Buyer, will not disclose to Seller that Buyer is willing to pay a price greater than the offered price; and **(iii)** except for (i) and (ii) above, a dual agent is obligated to disclose known facts materially affecting the value or desirability of the Property to both parties.
    D. **Other Sellers:** Seller understands that Broker may have or obtain listings on other properties, and that potential buyers may consider, make offers on, or purchase through Broker, property the same as or similar to Seller's Property. Seller consents to Broker's representation of sellers and buyers of other properties before, during and after the end of this agreement.
    E. **Confirmation:** If the Property includes residential property with one-to-four dwelling units, Broker shall confirm the agency relationship described above, or as modified, in writing, prior to or concurrent with Seller's execution of a purchase agreement.

11. **SECURITY AND INSURANCE:** Broker is not responsible for loss of or damage to personal or real property, or person, whether attributable to use of a keysafe/lockbox, a showing of the Property, or otherwise. Third parties, including, but not limited to, appraisers, inspectors, brokers and prospective buyers, may have access to, and take videos and photographs of, the interior of the Property. Seller agrees: **(i)** to take reasonable precautions to safeguard and protect valuables that might be accessible during showings of the Property; and **(ii)** to obtain insurance to protect against these risks. Broker does not maintain insurance to protect Seller.

12. **KEYSAFE/LOCKBOX:** A keysafe/lockbox is designed to hold a key to the Property to permit access to the Property by Broker, cooperating brokers, MLS participants, their authorized licensees and representatives, authorized inspectors, and accompanied prospective buyers. Broker, cooperating brokers, MLS and Associations/Boards of REALTORS® are **not** insurers against injury, theft, loss, vandalism or damage attributed to the use of a keysafe/lockbox. Seller does (or if checked ☐ does not) authorize Broker to install a keysafe/lockbox. If Seller does not occupy the Property, Seller shall be responsible for obtaining occupant(s)' written permission for use of a keysafe/lockbox.

13. **SIGN:** Seller does (or if checked ☐ does not) authorize Broker to install a FOR SALE/SOLD sign on the Property.

14. **EQUAL HOUSING OPPORTUNITY:** The Property is offered in compliance with federal, state and local anti-discrimination laws.

15. **ATTORNEY FEES:** In any action, proceeding or arbitration between Seller and Broker regarding the obligation to pay compensation under this agreement, the prevailing Seller or Broker shall be entitled to reasonable attorney fees and costs from the non-prevailing Seller or Broker, except as provided in paragraph 19A.

16. **ADDITIONAL TERMS:** _____
    _____
    _____

17. **MANAGEMENT APPROVAL:** If an associate licensee in Broker's office (salesperson or broker-associate) enters into this agreement on Broker's behalf, and Broker or Manager does not approve of its terms, Broker or Manager has the right to cancel this agreement, in writing, within 5 days after its execution.

18. **SUCCESSORS AND ASSIGNS:** This agreement shall be binding upon Seller and Seller's successors and assigns.

Seller acknowledges receipt of a copy of this page.
Seller's Initials (_____)(_____)

| Reviewed by _____ Date _____ |

LA REVISED 10/02 (PAGE 2 OF 3)

RESIDENTIAL LISTING AGREEMENT-EXCLUSIVE (LA PAGE 2 OF 3)

FIGURE 6.2

Residential Listing Agreement (Exclusive Authorization and Right To Sell) (continued)

Property Address: _____ Date: _____

19. **DISPUTE RESOLUTION:**

    A. **MEDIATION:** Seller and Broker agree to mediate any dispute or claim arising between them out of this agreement, or any resulting transaction, before resorting to arbitration or court action, subject to paragraph 19B(2) below. Paragraph 19B(2) below applies whether or not the arbitration provision is initialed. Mediation fees, if any, shall be divided equally among the parties involved. If, for any dispute or claim to which this paragraph applies, any party commences an action without first attempting to resolve the matter through mediation, or refuses to mediate after a request has been made, then that party shall not be entitled to recover attorney fees, even if they would otherwise be available to that party in any such action. THIS MEDIATION PROVISION APPLIES WHETHER OR NOT THE ARBITRATION PROVISION IS INITIALED.

    B. **ARBITRATION OF DISPUTES: (1)** Seller and Broker agree that any dispute or claim in Law or equity arising between them regarding the obligation to pay compensation under this agreement, which is not settled through mediation, shall be decided by neutral, binding arbitration, including and subject to paragraph 19B(2) below. The arbitrator shall be a retired judge or justice, or an attorney with at least 5 years of residential real estate law experience, unless the parties mutually agree to a different arbitrator, who shall render an award in accordance with substantive California Law. The parties shall have the right to discovery in accordance with Code of Civil Procedure §1283.05. In all other respects, the arbitration shall be conducted in accordance with Title 9 of Part III of the California Code of Civil Procedure. Judgment upon the award of the arbitrator(s) may be entered in any court having jurisdiction. Interpretation of this agreement to arbitrate shall be governed by the Federal Arbitration Act.
    (2) EXCLUSIONS FROM MEDIATION AND ARBITRATION: The following matters are excluded from mediation and arbitration hereunder: **(i)** a judicial or non-judicial foreclosure or other action or proceeding to enforce a deed of trust, mortgage, or installment land sale contract as defined in Civil Code §2985; **(ii)** an unlawful detainer action; **(iii)** the filing or enforcement of a mechanic's lien; and **(iv)** any matter that is within the jurisdiction of a probate, small claims, or bankruptcy court. The filing of a court action to enable the recording of a notice of pending action, for order of attachment, receivership, injunction, or other provisional remedies, shall not constitute a waiver of the mediation and arbitration provisions.
    "NOTICE: BY INITIALING IN THE SPACE BELOW YOU ARE AGREEING TO HAVE ANY DISPUTE ARISING OUT OF THE MATTERS INCLUDED IN THE 'ARBITRATION OF DISPUTES' PROVISION DECIDED BY NEUTRAL ARBITRATION AS PROVIDED BY CALIFORNIA LAW AND YOU ARE GIVING UP ANY RIGHTS YOU MIGHT POSSESS TO HAVE THE DISPUTE LITIGATED IN A COURT OR JURY TRIAL. BY INITIALING IN THE SPACE BELOW YOU ARE GIVING UP YOUR JUDICIAL RIGHTS TO DISCOVERY AND APPEAL, UNLESS THOSE RIGHTS ARE SPECIFICALLY INCLUDED IN THE 'ARBITRATION OF DISPUTES' PROVISION. IF YOU REFUSE TO SUBMIT TO ARBITRATION AFTER AGREEING TO THIS PROVISION, YOU MAY BE COMPELLED TO ARBITRATE UNDER THE AUTHORITY OF THE CALIFORNIA CODE OF CIVIL PROCEDURE. YOUR AGREEMENT TO THIS ARBITRATION PROVISION IS VOLUNTARY."
    "WE HAVE READ AND UNDERSTAND THE FOREGOING AND AGREE TO SUBMIT DISPUTES ARISING OUT OF THE MATTERS INCLUDED IN THE 'ARBITRATION OF DISPUTES' PROVISION TO NEUTRAL ARBITRATION."

Seller's Initials _____ / _____	Broker's Initials _____ / _____

20. **ENTIRE CONTRACT:** All prior discussions, negotiations and agreements between the parties concerning the subject matter of this agreement are superseded by this agreement, which constitutes the entire contract and a complete and exclusive expression of their agreement, and may not be contradicted by evidence of any prior agreement or contemporaneous oral agreement. If any provision of this agreement is held to be ineffective or invalid, the remaining provisions will nevertheless be given full force and effect. This agreement and any supplement, addendum or modification, including any photocopy or facsimile, may be executed in counterparts.

By signing below, Seller acknowledges that Seller has read, understands, accepts and has received a copy of this agreement.

Seller _____ Date _____
Address _____ City _____ State _____ Zip _____
Telephone _____ Fax _____ E-mail _____

Seller _____ Date _____
Address _____ City _____ State _____ Zip _____
Telephone _____ Fax _____ E-mail _____

Real Estate Broker (Firm) _____
By (Agent) _____ Date _____
Address _____ City _____ State _____ Zip _____
Telephone _____ Fax _____ E-mail _____

SURE TRAC
The System for Success™

Published by the
California Association of REALTORS®

Reviewed by _____ Date _____

EQUAL HOUSING
OPPORTUNITY

LA REVISED 10/02 (PAGE 3 OF 3)

RESIDENTIAL LISTING AGREEMENT-EXCLUSIVE (LA PAGE 3 OF 3)

Net Listing. A **net listing** is not truly a type of listing. Net listings could be open, exclusive-right-to sell, or exclusive-agency listings. "Net" refers to commission. A clause in the agreement states that the owner is asking a certain sum of money from the sale of property. All expenses, including the broker's commission, are to be covered by any sum the broker is able to obtain in excess of the selling price (net) specified by the seller.

> *Net listings* provide that the commission shall be the excess over a net sale price.

Net listings are seldom used. They make agents vulnerable to charges of fraud, misrepresentation, and other abuses against which the real estate law offers sellers protection. For example, a broker might be tempted to persuade the seller to ask for the lowest possible amount so that the broker can sell the property at a much higher price to collect a large commission. This type of action goes against the broker's duties as an agent. In fact, net listings are illegal in a number of states because of the inherent conflict of interests.

Nevertheless, if a broker takes a net listing, California law requires that the broker disclose in writing to both the seller and the buyer the selling price involved in the net listing. This declaration must be made within one month of the closing of the transaction. In practice, this information may be disclosed by the escrow holder's closing statement. **Note:** An agent's failure to disclose the selling price under a net listing is cause for revocation or suspension of his or her license.

Option Combined With a Listing. Law forbids a listing broker who has an **option combined with a listing** to *profit at the expense of the owner*. If the broker finds a buyer willing to pay more than the option price, and if the broker then exercises his or her option to buy to make a greater profit from resale of the property, the broker must make a full disclosure to the owner. California law covering this is stated as follows:

> If a broker employed to sell property is also given an option to purchase the property himself, he occupies the dual status of agent and purchaser and he is not entitled to exercise his option except by divesting himself of his obligation as agent by making a full disclosure of any information in his possession as to the prospect of making a sale to another.

Even though an option listing may be legal if the proper disclosures are made, an agent who makes an extraordinary profit might nevertheless become involved in a lawsuit. This action could negatively reflect on his or her reputation.

Exclusive Authorization To Acquire Property (Buyer-Broker Agreement). According to the National Association of REALTORS® handbook, "The cooperating broker in a cooperative real estate transaction is the subagent of the listing broker and not the agent of the buyer." This poses the problem of who represents the buyer in a transaction. In an attempt to solve this problem, the California Association of REALTORS® has developed a new contract form entitled *Exclusive Authorization To Acquire Property,* shown in Figure 6.3. Although this form is for an exclusive representation, buyer listings (like seller listings) could be exclusive-agency, under which a buyer could buy without an agent and not be obligated to pay a fee, or could even be an open listing.

The form is similar in many respects to the exclusive-authorization-and-right-to-sell listing. It gives authority to the broker to act as the agent of the buyer rather than the seller. The buyer's broker looks at the entire transaction from the buyer's standpoint, without a shared loyalty. The new contract form allows the buyer to tailor the broker's services to meet the buyer's needs and adjust the compensation accordingly.

The buyer's broker is held to the same standard of performance in serving the buyer as the listing broker owes to the seller. The commission is negotiable, and the contract must contain a definite termination date.

The buyer's broker, who is compensated by the buyer, is motivated to show the buyer all known available properties, including

- For Sale by Owner properties,
- foreclosure and probate sales,
- unlisted property,
- open listings, and
- any other available properties.

The CAR form shown in Figure 6.3 is a written contract between the broker and a buyer. Therefore, it must be filled out correctly and signed by the necessary parties. **Note:** Specific clauses and organization will vary in forms prepared by different publishers.

■ ANALYSIS OF THE EXCLUSIVE-AUTHORIZATION-AND-RIGHT-TO-SELL LISTING FORM

Because the listing agreement is a written contract between the broker and the seller, it must be filled out correctly and signed by the necessary parties. The exact wording on each listing form will vary, depending on the details of the transaction. However, certain basic provisions are part of each listing contract. Figure 6.2 is a form for an exclusive-authorization-and-right-to-sell listing. The following paragraphs analyze this sample form.

Paragraph 1:
Exclusive-Right-To-Sell

Enter here the name of the owner and the real estate office or broker receiving the listing. If a salesperson rather than a broker takes the listing, the salesperson should write his or her employing broker's name. The salesperson completing the form signs his or her name at the bottom of the form. Note that the words *exclusive and irrevocable* make this listing an exclusive authorization and right to sell.

FIGURE 6.3

Exclusive Authorization To Acquire Property

CALIFORNIA ASSOCIATION OF REALTORS®

EXCLUSIVE AUTHORIZATION TO ACQUIRE PROPERTY
BUYER BROKER COMPENSATION CONTRACT
(C.A.R. Form AAP, Revised 4/02)

1. **EXCLUSIVE RIGHT TO REPRESENT:** _____ ("Buyer")
grants _____ ("Broker")
beginning on (date) _____ and ending at **(i)** 11:59 p.m. on (date) _____ or **(ii)** completion of a resulting transaction, whichever occurs first ("Representation Period"), the exclusive and irrevocable right, on the terms specified in this Agreement, to represent Buyer in acquiring real property or a manufactured home. Broker agrees to exercise due diligence and reasonable efforts to fulfill the following authorizations and obligations. Broker will perform its obligations under this Agreement through the individual signing for Broker below, who is either Broker individually or an associate-licensee (an individual licensed as a real estate salesperson or broker who works under Broker's real estate license). Buyer agrees that Broker's duties are limited by the terms of this Agreement, including those limitations set forth in paragraphs 5 and 6.

2. **AGENCY RELATIONSHIPS:**
   A. **DISCLOSURE:** If the property described in paragraph 4 includes residential property with one-to-four dwelling units, Buyer acknowledges receipt of the "Disclosure Regarding Real Estate Agency Relationships" form prior to entering into this Agreement.
   B. **BUYER REPRESENTATION:** Broker will represent, as described in this Agreement, Buyer in any resulting transaction.
   C. **(1) POSSIBLE DUAL AGENCY WITH SELLER:** (C(1) APPLIES UNLESS C(2)(i) or (ii) is checked below.)
   Depending on the circumstances, it may be necessary or appropriate for Broker to act as an agent for both Buyer and a seller, exchange party, or one of more additional parties ("Seller"). Broker shall, as soon as practicable, disclose to Buyer any election to act as a dual agent representing both Buyer and Seller. If Buyer is shown property listed with Broker, Buyer consents to Broker becoming a dual agent representing both Buyer and Seller with respect to those properties. In event of dual agency, Buyer agrees that: **(a)** Broker, without the prior written consent of Buyer, will not disclose to Seller that the Buyer is willing to pay a price greater than the price offered; **(b)** Broker, without the prior written consent of Seller, will not disclose to Buyer that Seller is willing to sell property at a price less than the listing price; and **(c)** other than as set forth in (a) and (b) above, a dual agent is obligated to disclose known facts materially affecting the value or desirability of the Property to both parties.
   OR (2) SINGLE AGENCY ONLY: (APPLIES ONLY IF (i) or (ii) is checked below.)
   ☐ **(i) Broker's firm lists properties for sale:** Buyer understands that this election will prevent Broker from showing Buyer those properties that are listed with Broker's firm or from representing Buyer in connection with those properties. Buyer's acquisition of a property listed with Broker's firm shall not affect Broker's right to be compensated under paragraph 3. In any resulting transaction in which Seller's property is not listed with Broker's firm, Broker will be the exclusive agent of Buyer and not a dual agent also representing Seller.
   OR ☐ **(ii) Broker's firm DOES NOT list property:** Entire brokerage firm only represents buyers and does not list property. In any resulting transaction, Broker will be the exclusive agent of Buyer and not a dual agent also representing Seller.
   D. **OTHER POTENTIAL BUYERS:** Buyer understands that other potential buyers may, through Broker, consider, make offers on or acquire the same or similar properties as those Buyer is seeking to acquire. Buyer consents to Broker's representation of such other potential buyers before, during and after the Representation Period, or any extension thereof.
   E. **CONFIRMATION:** If the Property includes residential property with one-to-four dwelling units, Broker shall confirm the agency relationship described above, or as modified, in writing, prior to or coincident with Buyer's execution of a Property Contract.

3. **COMPENSATION TO BROKER:**
   NOTICE: The amount or rate of real estate commissions is not fixed by law. They are set by each Broker individually and may be negotiable between Buyer and Broker (real estate commissions include all compensation and fees to Broker).
   Buyer agrees to pay to Broker, irrespective of agency relationship(s), as follows:
   A. **AMOUNT OF COMPENSATION: (Check (1), (2) or (3). Check only one.)**
   ☐ **(1)** _____ percent of the acquisition price AND (if checked ☐) $ _____.
   OR ☐ **(2)** $_____.
   OR ☐ **(3)** Pursuant to the compensation schedule attached as an addendum _____.
   B. **BROKER RIGHT TO COMPENSATION:** Broker shall be entitled to the compensation provided for in paragraph 3A:
   (1) If Buyer enters into an agreement to acquire property described in paragraph 4, on those terms or any other terms acceptable to Buyer during the Representation Period, or any extension thereof.
   (2) If, within ___ **calendar days** after expiration of the Representation Period or any extension thereof, Buyer enters into an agreement to acquire property described in paragraph 4, which property Broker introduced to Buyer, or for which Broker acted on Buyer's behalf. The obligation to pay compensation pursuant to this paragraph shall arise only if, prior to or within 3 (or ☐ _____) **calendar days** after expiration of this Agreement or any extension thereof, Broker gives Buyer a written notice of those properties which Broker introduced to Buyer, or for which Broker acted on Buyer's behalf.

AAP-11 REVISED 4/02 (PAGE 1 OF 4) Print Date

Buyer and Broker acknowledge receipt of a copy of this page.
Buyer's Initials (_____)(_____)
Broker's Initials (_____)(_____)

EQUAL HOUSING OPPORTUNITY

Reviewed by _____
Broker or Designee _____ Date _____

EXCLUSIVE AUTHORIZATION TO ACQUIRE PROPERTY (AAP-11 PAGE 1 OF 4)

FIGURE 6.3

Exclusive Authorization To Acquire Property (continued)

Buyer: _____   Date: _____

    C. **PAYMENT OF COMPENSATION:** Compensation is payable:
        (1) Upon completion of any resulting transaction, and if an escrow is used, through escrow.
        (2) If acquisition is prevented by default of Buyer, upon Buyer's default.
        (3) If acquisition is prevented by a party to the transaction other than Buyer, when Buyer collects damages by suit, settlement or otherwise. Compensation shall equal one-half of the damages recovered, not to exceed the compensation provided for in paragraph 3A, after first deducting the unreimbursed expenses of collection, if any.
    D. **BUYER OBLIGATION TO PAY COMPENSATION:** Buyer is responsible for payment of compensation provided for in this Agreement. **However, if anyone other than Buyer compensates Broker for services covered by this Agreement, that amount shall be credited toward Buyer's obligation to pay compensation.** If the amount of compensation Broker receives from anyone other than Buyer exceeds Buyer's obligation, the excess amount shall be disclosed to Buyer and if allowed by law paid to Broker, or (if checked) ☐ credited to Buyer or ☐ other _____.
    E. Buyer hereby irrevocably assigns to Broker the compensation provided for in paragraph 3A from Buyer's funds and proceeds in escrow. Buyer agrees to submit to escrow any funds needed to compensate Broker under this Agreement. Broker may submit this Agreement, as instructions to compensate Broker, to any escrow regarding Property involving Buyer and a seller or other transferor.
    F. **"BUYER"** includes any person or entity, other than Broker, related to Buyer or who in any manner acts on Buyer's behalf to acquire property described in paragraph 4.
    G. **(1)** Buyer has not previously entered into a representation agreement with another brokerage firm regarding property described in paragraph 4, unless specified as follows (name other brokerage firm here): _____
                _____.
        (2) Buyer warrants that Buyer has no obligation to pay compensation to any other brokerage firm regarding property described in paragraph 4, unless Buyer acquires the following property(ies):_____.
        (3) If Buyer acquires a property specified in G(2) above during the time Buyer is obligated to compensate another broker, Broker is neither **(i)** entitled to compensation under this Agreement nor **(ii)** obligated to represent Buyer in such transaction.

4. **PROPERTY TO BE ACQUIRED:**
Any purchase, lease or other acquisition of any real property or manufactured home described as follows:
_____
_____
_____
Price range: $_____   to $_____

5. **BROKER AUTHORIZATIONS AND OBLIGATIONS:**
    A. Buyer authorizes Broker to: **(i)** locate and present selected properties to Buyer, present offers authorized by Buyer, and assist Buyer in negotiating for acceptance of such offers; **(ii)** assist Buyer with the financing process, including obtaining loan pre-qualification; **(iii)** upon request, provide Buyer with a list of professionals or vendors who perform the services described in the attached Buyer's Inspection Advisory; **(iv)** order reports, and schedule and attend meetings and appointments with professionals chosen by Buyer; **(v)** provide guidance to help Buyer with the acquisition of property; and **(vi)** obtain a credit report on Buyer.
    B. For property transactions of which Broker is aware and not precluded from participating in by Buyer, Broker shall provide and review forms to create a property contract ("Property Contract") for the acquisition of a specific property ("Property"). With respect to such Property, Broker shall: **(i)** if the Property contains residential property with one-to-four dwelling units, conduct a reasonably competent and diligent on-site visual inspection of the accessible areas of the Property (excluding any common areas), and disclose to Buyer all facts materially affecting the value or desirability of such Property that are revealed by this inspection; **(ii)** deliver or communicate to Buyer any disclosures, materials or information received by, in the personal possession of or personally known to the individual signing for Broker below during the Representation Period; and **(iii)** facilitate the escrow process, including assisting Buyer in negotiating with Seller. Unless otherwise specified in writing, any information provided through Broker in the course of representing Buyer has not been and will not be verified by Broker. Broker's services are performed in compliance with federal, state and local anti-discrimination laws.

6. **SCOPE OF BROKER DUTY:**
    A. While Broker will perform the duties described in paragraph 5B, Broker recommends that Buyer select other professionals, as described in the attached Buyer's Inspection Advisory, to investigate the Property through inspections, investigations, tests, surveys, reports, studies and other available information ("Inspections") during the transaction. Buyer agrees that these Inspections, to the extent they exceed the obligations described in paragraph 5B, are not within the scope of Broker's agency duties. Broker informs Buyer that it is in Buyer's best interest to obtain such Inspections.
    B. Buyer acknowledges and agrees that Broker: **(i)** does not decide what price Buyer should pay or Seller should accept; **(ii)** does not guarantee the condition of the Property; **(iii)** does not guarantee the performance, adequacy or completeness of Inspections, services, products or repairs provided or made by Seller or others to Buyer or Seller; **(iv)** shall not be responsible for identifying defects that are not known to Broker and either **(a)** are not visually observable in reasonably accessible areas of the Property or **(b)** are in common areas; **(v)** shall not be responsible for identifying the location of boundary lines or other items affecting title; **(vi)** shall not be responsible for verifying square footage, representations of others or information contained in Inspection reports; **(vii)** shall not be responsible for providing legal or tax advice regarding any aspect of a transaction entered into by Buyer in the course of this representation; and **(viii)** shall not be responsible for providing other advice or information that exceeds the knowledge, education and experience required to perform real estate licensed activities. Buyer agrees to seek legal, tax, insurance, title and other desired assistance from appropriate professionals.

AAP-11 REVISED 4/02 (PAGE 2 OF 4) Print Date

Buyer and Broker acknowledge receipt of a copy of this page.
Buyer's Initials (_____)(_____)
Broker's Initials (_____)(_____)

EQUAL HOUSING OPPORTUNITY

Reviewed by
Broker or Designee _____ Date _____

EXCLUSIVE AUTHORIZATION TO ACQUIRE PROPERTY (AAP-11 PAGE 2 OF 4)

FIGURE 6.3

Exclusive Authorization To Acquire Property (continued)

Buyer: _____ Date: _____

    C. Broker owes no duty to inspect for common environmental hazards, earthquake weaknesses, or geologic and seismic hazards. If Buyer receives the booklets titled "Environmental Hazards: A Guide for Homeowners, Buyers, Landlords and Tenants," "The Homeowner's Guide to Earthquake Safety," or "The Commercial Property Owner's Guide to Earthquake Safety," the booklets are deemed adequate to inform buyer regarding the information contained in the booklets and, other than as specified in 5B above, Broker is not required to provide Buyer with additional information about the matters described in the booklets.

7. BUYER OBLIGATIONS:

    A. Buyer agrees to timely view and consider properties selected by Broker and to negotiate in good faith to acquire a property. Buyer further agrees to act in good faith toward the completion of any Property Contract entered into in furtherance of this Agreement. Within 5 **(or** ☐ **_____) calendar days** from the execution of this Agreement, Buyer shall provide relevant personal and financial information to Broker to assure Buyer's ability to acquire property described in paragraph 4. If Buyer fails to provide such information, or if Buyer does not qualify financially to acquire property described in paragraph 4, then Broker may cancel this Agreement in writing. Buyer has an affirmative duty to take steps to protect him/herself, including discovery of the legal, practical and technical implications of discovered or disclosed facts, and investigation of information and facts which are known to Buyer or are within the diligent attention and observation of Buyer. Buyer is obligated to and agrees to read all documents provided to Buyer. Buyer agrees to seek desired assistance from appropriate professionals, selected by Buyer, such as those referenced in the attached Buyer's Inspection Advisory.

    B. Buyer shall notify Broker in writing of any material issue to Buyer, such as, but not limited to, Buyer requests for information on, or concerns regarding, any particular area of interest or importance to Buyer ("Material Consideration").

    C. Buyer agrees to (i) indemnify, defend and hold Broker harmless from all claims, disputes, litigation, judgments, costs and attorney fees arising from any incorrect information supplied by Buyer, or from any Material Consideration that Buyer fails to disclose in writing to Broker, and (ii) pay for reports, Inspections and meetings arranged by Broker on Buyer's behalf.

    D. Buyer is advised to read the attached Buyer's Inspection Advisory for a list of items and other concerns that typically warrant Inspections or investigation by Buyer or other professionals.

8. DISPUTE RESOLUTION:

    A. MEDIATION: Buyer and Broker agree to mediate any dispute or claim arising between them out of this Agreement, or any resulting transaction, before resorting to arbitration or court action, subject to paragraph 8B(2) below. Paragraph 8B(2) below applies whether or not the arbitration provision is initialed. Mediation fees, if any, shall be divided equally among the parties involved. If, for any dispute or claim to which this paragraph applies, any party commences an action without first attempting to resolve the matter through mediation, or refuses to mediate after a request has been made, then that party shall not be entitled to recover attorney fees even if they would otherwise be available to that party in any such action. THIS MEDIATION PROVISION APPLIES WHETHER OR NOT THE ARBITRATION PROVISION IS INITIALED.

    B. ARBITRATION OF DISPUTES: (1) Buyer and Broker agree that any dispute or claim in law or equity arising between them regarding the obligation to pay compensation under this Agreement, which is not settled through mediation, shall be decided by neutral, binding arbitration, including and subject to paragraph 8B(2) below. The arbitrator shall be a retired judge or justice, or an attorney with at least five years of residential real estate law experience, unless the parties mutually agree to a different arbitrator, who shall render an award in accordance with substantive California law. In all other respects, the arbitration shall be conducted in accordance with Part III, Title 9 of the California Code of Civil Procedure. Judgment upon the award of the arbitrator(s) may be entered in any court having jurisdiction. The parties shall have the right to discovery in accordance with Code of Civil Procedure §1283.05.

    (2) EXCLUSIONS FROM MEDIATION AND ARBITRATION: The following matters are excluded from mediation and arbitration hereunder: **(i)** a judicial or non-judicial foreclosure or other action or proceeding to enforce a deed of trust, mortgage, or installment land sale contract as defined in Civil Code §2985; **(ii)** an unlawful detainer action; **(iii)** the filing or enforcement of a mechanic's lien; **(iv)** any matter that is within the jurisdiction of a probate, small claims, or bankruptcy court; and **(v)** an action for bodily injury or wrongful death, or for any right of action to which Code of Civil Procedure §337.1 or §337.15 applies. The filing of a court action to enable the recording of a notice of pending action, for order of attachment, receivership, injunction, or other provisional remedies, shall not constitute a waiver of the mediation and arbitration provisions.

    "NOTICE: BY INITIALING IN THE SPACE BELOW YOU ARE AGREEING TO HAVE ANY DISPUTE ARISING OUT OF THE MATTERS INCLUDED IN THE 'ARBITRATION OF DISPUTES' PROVISION DECIDED BY NEUTRAL ARBITRATION AS PROVIDED BY CALIFORNIA LAW AND YOU ARE GIVING UP ANY RIGHTS YOU MIGHT POSSESS TO HAVE THE DISPUTE LITIGATED IN A COURT OR JURY TRIAL. BY INITIALING IN THE SPACE BELOW YOU ARE GIVING UP YOUR JUDICIAL RIGHTS TO DISCOVERY AND APPEAL, UNLESS THOSE RIGHTS ARE SPECIFICALLY INCLUDED IN THE 'ARBITRATION OF DISPUTES' PROVISION. IF YOU REFUSE TO SUBMIT TO ARBITRATION AFTER AGREEING TO THIS PROVISION, YOU MAY BE COMPELLED TO ARBITRATE UNDER THE AUTHORITY OF THE CALIFORNIA CODE OF CIVIL PROCEDURE. YOUR AGREEMENT TO THIS ARBITRATION PROVISION IS VOLUNTARY."

    "WE HAVE READ AND UNDERSTAND THE FOREGOING AND AGREE TO SUBMIT DISPUTES ARISING OUT OF THE MATTERS INCLUDED IN THE 'ARBITRATION OF DISPUTES' PROVISION TO NEUTRAL ARBITRATION."

Buyer's Initials _____/_____   Broker's Initials _____/_____

AAP-11 REVISED 4/02 (PAGE 3 OF 4) Print Date

Buyer and Broker acknowledge receipt of a copy of this page.
Buyer's Initials (_____)(_____)
Broker's Initials (_____)(_____)

EQUAL HOUSING OPPORTUNITY

Reviewed by
Broker or Designee _____ Date _____

EXCLUSIVE AUTHORIZATION TO ACQUIRE PROPERTY (AAP-11 PAGE 3 OF 4)

FIGURE 6.3

Exclusive Authorization To Acquire Property (continued)

Buyer: _____   Date: _____

9. **TIME TO BRING LEGAL ACTION:** Legal action for breach of this Agreement, or any obligation arising therefrom, shall be brought no more than two years from the expiration of the Representation Period or from the date such cause of action may arise, whichever occurs first.

10. **OTHER TERMS AND CONDITIONS,** including ATTACHED SUPPLEMENTS: ☑ Buyer's Inspection Advisory (C.A.R. Form BIA-11)
_____
_____
_____
_____
_____

11. **ATTORNEY FEES:** In any action, proceeding or arbitration between Buyer and Broker regarding the obligation to pay compensation under this Agreement, the prevailing Buyer or Broker shall be entitled to reasonable attorney fees and costs, except as provided in paragraph 8A.

12. **ENTIRE CONTRACT:** All understandings between the parties are incorporated in this Agreement. Its terms are intended by the parties as a final, complete and exclusive expression of their agreement with respect to its subject matter, and may not be contradicted by evidence of any prior agreement or contemporaneous oral agreement. This Agreement may not be extended, amended, modified, altered or changed, except in writing signed by Buyer and Broker. In the event that any provision of this Agreement is held to be ineffective or invalid, the remaining provisions will nevertheless be given full force and effect. This Agreement and any supplement, addendum or modification, including any copy, whether by copier, facsimile, NCR or electronic, may be signed in two or more counterparts, all of which shall constitute one and the same writing.

Buyer acknowledges that Buyer has read, understands, accepts and has received a copy of this Agreement.

Buyer _____ Date _____
Address _____ City _____ State ____ Zip _____
Telephone _____ Fax _____ E-mail _____

Buyer _____ Date _____
Address _____ City _____ State ____ Zip _____
Telephone _____ Fax _____ E-mail _____

Real Estate Broker (Firm) _____
By (Agent) _____ Date _____
Address _____ City _____ State ____ Zip _____
Telephone _____ Fax _____ E-mail _____

AAP-11 REVISED 4/02 (PAGE 4 OF 4) Print Date

EXCLUSIVE AUTHORIZATION TO ACQUIRE PROPERTY (AAP-11 PAGE 4 OF 4)

After the broker's name, enter the time period, including the beginning and the termination dates. Three-month to six-month periods are common; however, if the broker thinks the property will take longer to sell, he or she may ask for more time.

Next, enter the location of the property by city and county as well as by an unmistakable address within the city. Occasionally, in addition to the street address, the location by lot, block, and tract, or a metes-and-bounds legal description may be given. It may be necessary to add a legal description as a signed attachment to the listing.

Paragraph 2: Items Included and Excluded

Items of personal property that may be included in the purchase are listed, as are items of real or personal property excluded from the sale. Misunderstandings can arise as to what property the seller intends to include, and listing the items will help alleviate such a problem. Examples of personal property often sold with a residence are major appliances and drapes.

Paragraph 3: Listing Price and Terms

The terms of sale include the price at which the property is being offered. Additional space is provided for stipulating the exact terms the owner requires to sell the property. This includes financial arrangements, such as cash, second trust deeds, or loan assumptions. Unless terms are specified, the owner is not obligated to pay a commission when he or she refuses a full-price offer unless the offer is for cash.

Paragraph 4: Compensation to Broker

Bold face type points out that commission is negotiable and not set by law. This statement is required for listings of 1- to 4-unit residential properties.

Subparagraph A indicates the rate or amount of commission that will be paid if the property is sold.

Subparagraph A-1 stipulates that commission is due regardless of who actually produces a potential buyer. All that is required is that the purchase offer either meets the price and terms of the agreement (as stated in Paragraph 2) or includes a different price and terms that are acceptable to the seller. The offer also must be made during the listing period stated in Paragraph 1.

Subparagraph A-2 is the **safety clause.** It provides that the listing agent shall be entitled to a commission if the property is sold within a specified number of days after expiration of the listing to a prospective buyer whose name was furnished by the agent to the owner within *three* calendar days of expiration of the listing or was sold to a buyer who was shown and physically entered the property during the listing period.

> The *safety clause* protects you from attempts to evade paying your fee.

Subparagraph A-3 states that the seller agrees to pay a commission if the seller sells, leases, or rents the property; withdraws it from the market without the consent of the broker; or otherwise renders the property unavailable for sale before the expiration date.

Subparagraph B provides that if completion of the sale is prevented by a party other than the seller and the seller collects damages, then the total commission is to be the lesser of the commission due under paragraph 4A or one-half of the damages recovered after deducting expenses.

Subparagraph C provides for any additional seller compensation, such as MLS fees or other broker expenses.

Note: A number of large brokerage firms are now charging sellers a transaction fee or document preparation fee in the $200 range in addition to the commission. If any additional charges are to be made to the seller, they should be clearly set forth in the listing contract.

Subparagraph D provides that the broker may cooperate with other brokers and divide the commission in any manner acceptable to them or an agreed percentage.

Subparagraph E states that the seller irrevocably assigns to the broker the broker's compensation from the seller's proceeds. In the past, some sellers have notified an escrow not to pay the broker but to turn the funds over to the sellers. Because the escrow is not the agent of the broker, the escrows complied. An assignment agreement protects the broker's fee.

Subparagraph F is the owner's warranty that the owner is not obligated to pay a commission to any other broker if the property is sold during the listing period, with the exception of listed prospective buyers. If such a listed buyer purchases the property during the listing, the broker is not obligated to pay the listing broker and the listing broker is not obligated to represent the owner in the sale.

**Paragraph 5:
Ownership Title and
Authority**

This paragraph warrants that the sellers are the only persons who have title to the property unless indicated otherwise, and that the seller has the authority to execute this agreement and sell the property.

**Paragraph 6:
Multiple-Listing Service**

By checking the appropriate block, the parties state whether listing information is to be provided to a multiple-listing service (MLS). Without authorization from the owner, the agent would not have the right to cooperate with subagents or give the listing or sale information to an MLS or to third parties.

**Paragraph 7:
Seller Representations**

Seller represents that he or she is unaware a notice of default recorded against the property; delinquencies due under loans; bankruptcy, insolvency, or other proceedings affecting the property as well as any litigation pending or threatened that could affect the seller's ability to sell and any current or proposed special assessments. If the seller becomes aware of any of the above during the listing, the seller agrees to promptly notify the agent.

Paragraph 8:
Broker's and Seller's
Duties

The broker agrees to use diligence in achieving the purpose of the listing agreement. The seller agrees to consider offers received in good faith and to hold the broker harmless for claims resulting from incorrect information supplied or the failure to disclose information to the broker.

Paragraph 9:
Deposit

This section authorizes the listing agent to accept the deposit. Without this authorization, an agent taking a deposit could be doing so as the agent of the buyer.

Paragraph 10:
Agency Relationships

This paragraph explains that the broker represents the seller and will not be the agent of the buyer; however, if a buyer is procured by the listing agent, it may be necessary for the broker to act in a dual agency capacity. The seller is informed that the broker also represents other sellers. The agency is to be confirmed prior to or concurrent with the execution of a purchase agreement.

Paragraph 11:
Security and Insurance

This section explains that the broker is not responsible for loss or damage to personal property, regardless of the presence of a lockbox, and that the owner must take precautions to protect valuables and obtain insurance for risks involved.

Paragraph 12:
Key Safe/Lockbox

This provides authorization to install a lockbox. The lockbox makes the property more available for showing by other agents in the MLS. The agent is not liable to the owner for loss or damage resulting from access via the lockbox. If the seller wants the property shown by appointment only, then the listing agent may not want to use a lockbox and the seller can elect whether or not to use it.

Paragraph 13:
Sign

Putting a For Sale sign on the property makes the property more recognizable. However, the agent must obtain authorization from the seller to do so.

Paragraph 14:
Equal Housing
Opportunity

The property is offered in compliance with antidiscrimination laws. The seller cannot reject an offer on the property because of discrimination based on race, color, creed, etc.

Paragraph 15:
Attorney's Fees

If there is any disagreement between the seller and broker and they go either to court or to arbitration, the loser in either incident must pay the costs. This paragraph tends to reduce frivolous lawsuits.

Paragraph 16:
Additional Terms

Space is provided for any other owner-broker agreement or terms.

Paragraph 17:
Management Approval

If an associate licensee enters into this agreement, the broker or manager has the right to cancel this agreement within five days.

Paragraph 18:
Successors and Assigns

This agreement shall be binding upon the seller and seller's successors and assigns.

Paragraph 19:
Dispute Resolution

Subparagraph A provides that the broker and seller agree to mediate any disputes arising from this agreement prior to any other action that is available. They are not, however, required to resolve the dispute through mediation.

Subparagraph B provides that by initialing, the parties agree to neutral binding arbitration of any dispute, thus giving up rights to have the dispute litigated in the courts.

The paragraph also provides that matters excluded from mediation and arbitration include foreclosure proceedings, unlawful detainer action, mechanics' liens, matters within court jurisdiction, and tort injuries from latent or patent defects to the property.

Paragraph 20:
Entire Contact

It is agreed that this agreement is the entire agreement and may not be contradicted by prior agreements or verbal statements.

Signatures

The seller acknowledges that he or she has read, understands and accepts the agreement and has received a copy of it.

■ ANALYSIS OF THE EXCLUSIVE-AUTHORIZATION-TO-ACQUIRE-PROPERTY AGREEMENT (BUYER'S LISTING)

Compare this buyer's listing with the seller listing (exclusive-authorization-and-right-to-sell agreement) in Figure 6.2. You will notice similarities and differences.

The exclusive-authoization-to-acquire-property agrrecment sets forth the type of property that the buyer wishes to purchase, its general location, and the price range.

The specific duties and obligations of the buyer and broker are set forth. In addition, the listing clearly states matters that shall not be the responsibility of the broker. Professional assistance is recommended for buyer protection.

The agency is a buyer's agency but could possibly become a dual agency unless the parties initial that it shall be a single agency only.

While the buyer is responsible for the broker's compensation, compensation received from others shall apply to the amount owed by the buyer (cooperative sales). By checking the appropriate block, the disposition of any excess commission can be agreed to.

■ THE LISTING TRANSACTION

Real estate brokers must pay careful attention to listing details to ensure a smooth transaction.

Preparing for the Listing   An old adage about the listing process is that it is "80 percent preparation and 20 percent selling." The time spent on research before the first appointment with a prospective seller is critical in getting the listing.

Step 1:   Obtain Information about the Property. Some real estate offices today have microfiche readers with microfilm records of the county. The microfiche contains records of the tax site and plat maps. The microfiche also may provide lot size and shape, vesting, square footage of the home, and code information on the property, type of roof, and so forth. The major advantage of microfiche is the speed at which the agent can obtain the information—approximately five minutes to ten minutes, plus another five minutes for copying data if the microfiche reader has no printer. (Microfiche is rapidly being replaced by computerized data.)

A property profile can generally be obtained within an hour or less from any title company you use. Besides title and liens, you should ask for a search of federal tax liens. In addition to a computer printout, your title company also can give you comparable sales by neighborhood, or even by street, and provide copies of deeds if desired.

Step 2:   Prepare Your Competitive Market Analysis (CMA). (See Chapter 5.)

Step 3:   Drive by the Current and Expired Listings and by the Property That Has Sold. Drive by the prospective property and then by the comparables to get a feeling for the amenities of the property you are going to list as well as to compare it visually with other existing and expired listings in the marketplace. Take photos, if none are available, so the owners can see the types of property their home will be competing with for buyers.

Keep an open mind as to value until you have analyzed the available data. Just like owners, agents will sometimes have preconceived notions about value, based on a single sale or misinformation.

Check comparable properties before you go for your listing presentation. Often what appears as a comparable on your printout is not even close to being a comparable property when utility and desirability are considered. If an owner knows the property you are using as a comparable and knows of problems it has that should have excluded it as a comparable, you will have lost credibility as an expert. Your chances of obtaining a listing could be significantly reduced.

The Sales Listing Interview

With your preparation and research taken care of, you are ready to call on your listing prospect.

On the first visit, you should ascertain the owners' motivation for selling and view the property to prepare your competitive market analysis and your listing presentation. Normally, you will make your listing presentation on your second visit to the property; however, if the owners appear receptive and you have a good feel for the value, you should go into your listing presentation during your first visit to the property.

After arriving for your second visit, ask the owners if it is all right if you go through their home once again. This relieves tension and shows your interest. If you haven't yet determined the owners' reason for selling, ask them. They will generally give you an honest response.

Show your interest in the home and ask questions about it and what the owners have done to the home. Owners will be more receptive to agents who they feel appreciate their home.

An excellent place to present your material to owners or occupants is the kitchen table. It presents a nonthreatening informal setting, and you are able to sit close to the owners. (It is easier to be argumentative from a distance.) You might want to sit across from the owners or beside them. Try not to sit between spouses.

The Competitive Market Analysis (CMA).   In presenting your competitive market analysis, don't rush. You must show you appreciate their house, but present the comparables fairly to lead up to your recommendations.

Watch owners for reactions. If they show little reaction, ask questions such as "Are there any recent area sales that I missed?"

Sometimes owners have an inflated idea of what their property is worth. It may be based on a sale under different conditions or on what they heard someone say a house sold for. Often owners have a value in mind based simply on what they want. Consider the following:

> "[Mrs. Jones], buyers, not sellers or brokers, determine market value. I have shown you what homes similar to yours have sold for. Is there any information you know of that I have not considered?"

> If the owners say that another agent told them they could get more for their house, ask to see the competitive market analysis that the price was based on. Chances are there won't be one. Then consider the following rebuttal:

"I don't know how that agent was able to arrive at a value so quickly and without a detailed analysis. A value off the top of one's head is a hunch at best. If it is too high, a listing at that price simply means a lot of time wasted and no sale. I showed you the effect of overpricing a home on the likelihood of a sale. If a hunch is too low, someone will get a bargain at your expense. I won't price your home on a hunch, and I'm sure you wouldn't want me to do that."

There are many approaches, but all have the same goal: to convince the owners that your value has validity and that offering the property at that price would be in the owners' best interests.

The Listing Presentation.   After you have finished presenting your competitive market analysis, ask the owners if they can spare a few minutes for you to present some information they will want to hear. Because you have gone to a great deal of effort on behalf of the owners, you can expect a positive response.

Go through the listing presentation book, using narratives such as those developed in Chapter 5. Of course, use your narratives with your visuals as you turn the pages of your book. When you have finished the book, you should be ready for a closing.

> **Be Positive**
> Use positive terms in your presentation. An "agency representation" indicates you will be doing something for an owner whereas "listing" may have a negative connotation. In the same manner, a "fee" is something that they can understand is due a professional, but "commission" is a word to be avoided.

If the owners have been very receptive to your presentation with the competitive market analysis or if the owners contacted you to list the property, it should not be necessary for you to go through the listing presentation book. You can cut right to the listing. Start by obtaining the owners' signatures on the Estimated Seller's Proceeds form. (See Chapter 5.) Never delay when parties are receptive because delay can lead to their wanting to think it over.

Make certain the owners understand what they will actually net from an offer. Be up front with them. When you use the Estimated Seller's Proceeds form, be realistic in your figures. As previously stated, it is better to be on the low side than to estimate a net significantly higher than the owner will actually receive. Disappointed owners lead to loss of goodwill toward your firm and could result in a failure to close the sale. After the sellers sign the statement, give them a copy.

Once they have signed the Estimated Seller's Proceeds form, which obligates the sellers to nothing, it usually is a natural act to sign the listing when it is presented.

A **trial closing** tries for an agreement to sign the listing. The choice should not be to list or not to list. As an example, the question "Would you want me to serve as your marketing agent for 90 days or should we make it 120 days?" gives owners a choice between two positives, not between a positive and a negative.

If the owners respond positively to your trial closing, give each of the owners a copy of the listing. It could be prepared in advance so you need to insert only minor items. Go through the listing slowly. Answer any owner questions. When you get to items calling for initials, give each owner a pen and ask each to initial where recommended. Make certain they understand that the option is theirs.

Every presentation you give will not necessarily run smoothly. There will be objections that must be overcome in a straightforward, logical manner. You might consider starting with

"I'm glad you mentioned that because. . . "

"That's an excellent point. You're absolutely right but. . . "

Owners who hesitate to sign the agreement are signaling that they have a problem. You must find out what the problem is if you are to overcome it. Most of the objections should be readily overcome by material covered in Chapter 5 and included in your listing presentation.

A common objection is "I want to sell, in fact I need to sell. That's why I can't be tied up with a listing." Your response could be

"That's exactly why I suggest an exclusive-right-to-sell agency agreement at the price I have indicated. We know from experience that it takes longer for an owner not represented by an agent to sell a home than it takes with an agent. In addition, in working on your own, you more than double your chance of running into time-consuming and costly problems when you do find a buyer. You are not tying up your property with an exclusive-right-to-sell agency agreement; instead, you are taking the first step toward a sale."

Many objections center on paying a commission. As previously stated, you should always refer to it as a *fee*. Consider the following approaches:

| Who pays your fee? |

"Actually, it is the buyer who pays our fee. The fee is paid out of money the buyer puts up. The buyer's price includes the fee. When buyers know that an agent isn't involved, they typically reduce any offer that they're willing to make by an amount to cover the fee involved with an agent. They're usually not willing to split it because buyers feel that it comes out of their money."

If an owner asks you to reduce your fee to a lesser amount, one approach to use would be

"A reduced fee would not be fair to you. It would likely mean that you wouldn't have to pay any fee because your home would not be sold. Most sales are cooperative. There are [ ] agents in my office and [ ] agents in our multiple-listing service all trying to sell your home. If they have a chance to get a normal fee or a reduced fee, which property do you suppose will get their greatest efforts?"

If there are varying commission rates in your area, check the records of your listing service before making the listing presentation. You may discover that listings taken by firms offering a significantly lower fee have a lower sales record than listings taken by your firm at a more normal fee. If so, you could present this information visually with a bar graph and use a narrative such as

> "Based on the computer records of [Cedar Creek Brokers Association], listings taken by [Champion Realty] at a [6 percent] fee have a [46 percent] greater likelihood of being sold during the listing period than listings taken by other firms at a [4 percent] fee. This points out that you get what you pay for. A lower fee simply reduces the likelihood of a sale. A lower fee and an unsold house is no bargain."

Another objection concerns listing price. Some owners want to add your fee to what they want for the home to determine an offering price. Owners may be unrealistic for many reasons, but it isn't enough just to get a listing; you want a listing that is likely to sell. While you have a duty to an owner to get the maximum possible from a property, you also have a duty to advise the owner as to what would be in the owner's best interests.

Several approaches you can use include

> "Let's assume that we offer the property at the price you suggest [$]. Assume further that we find a buyer at that price. The sale would be unlikely to be made because lenders make loans based on appraisals of market value, not what a buyer is willing to pay. From my comparables, I have shown you data on market value. Appraisers have access to this same data. What do you suppose will happen when the buyer is notified that the loan is not approved because the property is worth considerably less than the buyer has offered?"

> "Assume you are a buyer and you are looking at homes and you see these comparable properties I have shown you at lower prices than your home is listed at. What do you suppose a buyer's reaction will be? Pricing that is not reflective of the market would not be fair to you, because you would be eliminating many potential buyers."

If the owners indicate that they want to list at their price to see what happens and that they might reduce the price later, an approach to use would be

> "When a property is realistically listed, agents are enthusiastic and will spend their best efforts on selling that property. If they regard a listing as a 'hard sell,' they will show the property only if more attractively priced properties are not available."

| Too high a list price does not help the owner. |

"When you finally reduce your price, that price adjustment is not greeted with the enthusiasm of a new listing. In addition, when buyers know a price was reduced and the property has been on the market for a long time, they will sense desperation. Any offer will then likely be significantly less than the reduced price. If you really want to sell your home at the best possible price, I suggest we list it at [$]. Doesn't this make sense?"

Sometimes it takes a **clincher**.

A clincher for an owner who has been trying to sell without an agent could be

"[Mr. and Mrs. Jones], do you realize that this house is holding you prisoner? With your sign and your ads, you are likely stuck here every weekend waiting for the telephone or doorbell to ring. Even people who say they will be here seldom show up. I'm offering you your freedom."

This is, of course, the time to hand the owner a pen. Whenever you make a closing that implies a signature, hand the owner an open pen. The owner who puts it down still has questions that must be eliminated. Don't be afraid to try again and again for a closing. A closing is not a one-time win-or-lose proposition.

Prepare yourself so answers to objections and closings come naturally. If you can't close a listing, you won't be able to close a sale. If you can't close a sale, you become an order taker who shows merchandise and waits for a buyer to decide, not a problem solver—and certainly not a professional salesperson.

Follow Through.   After you obtain the listing, thank the owners. Be certain you leave

- a copy of the signed listing with your card attached,
- a copy of your competitive market analysis,
- the Estimated Seller's Proceeds form, and
- the agency disclosure form.

Let the owners know what will be happening (your marketing plan) and when you will be contacting them again.

The Buyer Agency Presentation

It is difficult to get buyers to agree that you should be their exclusive agent to find them property to buy unless they feel that you fully understand their needs, that you are competent and able to locate a property for them, and that it would be in their best interests to have you as their exclusive agent. Similarly, you don't want to take an agency responsibility and expend your best efforts for prospective buyers until you realize they are motivated to buy, they have the resources and/or credit to consummate a purchase, and they have needs you can reasonably fulfill.

A good time to make a presentation for exclusive agency representation to buyers would be after you have interviewed them about their needs, shown them several properties, and questioned them further about property impressions. By then, you will have understood fairly well the buyers and sold yourself as a professional.

A good approach would be to tell your prospective buyer(s) that you would like to have them obtain preapproval for a loan so that they'll have the financing when they find a property. By handling an Internet loan application and printing out a loan approval, you will show your professionalism and make the prospects feel they are a step closer to a new home.

You could now conduct a presentation using a buyer-listing presentation book or you could use a narrative such as the following:

> "I would like to help you in finding the best home for you. I imagine we will spend a good deal of time together in accomplishing this goal. Do you feel comfortable working with me?"

You can, of course, expect a positive response and people are unlikely to say they would are uncomfortable working with you.

> "Most agents are really agents of the owners and have a duty to get the highest price possible for a property. However, I would like to represent you alone rather than an owner. As your agent, my duty would be to fulfill your needs with the best property for you at the lowest price. Is that what you want?"

Prospective buyers can be expected to give a positive response, as they of course want the best property at the lowest price.

> "I'll be using my best efforts on your behalf to meet your needs. However, my services will likely be paid, not by you, but by sellers who have listed properties with other agents. While I'll share in the fee paid by a seller, my sole obligation will be to you. Does that type of arrangement sound reasonable to you?"

Note: You are asking if it sounds reasonable and the response will likely be positive. It is implied that they are agreeing to an agency relationship.

> "I want you to be partners with me in meeting your needs. If you see a house that is for sale, you're interested in, or an ad that perks your interest, give me a call and I'll get more information for you. If it seems promising, I'll arrange for you to see the property."

> "I would like to go over the agency representation that I think would best meet your needs."

You can then give your prospective buyer(s) copies of the Exclusive Authorization To Acquire Property and go through the agreement with them explaining the meaning of each paragraph. By having them initial each page as you complete the agreement, signing it will be a natural act.

■ SUMMARY

A valid listing must be in writing and must meet the four requirements of any contract:

1. Competent parties
2. Lawful object

3. Proper offer and acceptance

4. Consideration

There are six basic types of listings:

1. Open listing (nonexclusive)

2. Exclusive-authorization-and-right-to-sell listing

3. Exclusive-agency listing

4. Net listing

5. Option listing

6. Buyer's listing

The real estate agent must understand every paragraph used in the listing forms to answer owners' questions and properly meet owners' needs.

The agent must prepare for the listing transaction. The first step is to obtain information about the property; the second step is to prepare the competitive market analysis; the third step is to drive by comparables to make certain that your comparables are truly comparable and that you have a good sense of value.

The listing presentation normally starts with going through the competitive market analysis. The seller should understand the validity of your information before you proceed further.

If the owners are not ready to list their property, go through your listing presentation manual, using a narrative with your visuals. This should lead you to a trial closing that is intended to gain an agreement to sign the listing. After a listing is signed, be certain to leave a copy along with copies of the Estimated Seller's Proceeds form and your competitive market analysis and agency disclosure information. Be certain the owners know when you will contact them again.

To obtain a buyer's agency agreement you must prove your competency to locate property and the buyers must feel you fully understand their needs and are willing to work for them.

■ CLASS DISCUSSION TOPICS

1. Prepare a list of ten possible objections that an owner might raise to signing a listing.

2. Be prepared to enact a classroom role-playing situation in which objections are raised by the owner. (You might be called on to take the part of either the agent or the owner.)

3. Prepare a five-minute (maximum) presentation to a prospective buyer, showing why he or she should be represented under a signed buyer-listing agreement.

4. Role-play closing a listing with your instructor as the owner. Be prepared with more than one closing.

5. Special Assignments (if indicated by instructor)

 a. Using a form supplied by your instructor or one used in your area, complete an exclusive-authorization-and-right-to-sell agreement for the following:

Property:	Single-family residence, 217 W. Clark Lane, Fillmore, Calif., Ventura County
Owners:	Sam and Loretta Smyth
Broker:	(Name Yourself)
Listing Period:	Four months commencing this date.
Price:	$248,000
Personal Property:	Refrigerator, pool equipment, and fireplace accessories go with property.
Special Conditions:	No lockbox or sign. Two-hour notice of all showings limited to 3–5 P.M. daily and 8 A.M. until noon on weekends and holidays.
Broker's Compensation:	Six percent of sale price. 90-day safety period for commissions to parties whom agent(s) negotiated with prior to expiration of listing and whose names were furnished to owner.

 b. Using a form supplied by your instructor, complete an exclusive-authorization-to-acquire-property agreement for the following:

Buyer:	Henry and Sally Corleone
Broker:	(Name Yourself)
Period of Authorization:	Three months from this date.
Property:	Single story 3–4 BR home with 2½ baths, 3-car garage, fireplace, and golf course views in gated community.
Price:	$450,000 to $550,000
General Location:	Palm Desert, Rancho Mirage or Indian Wells, California
Other:	Spanish architecture preferred
Compensation:	3½ percent of acquiring price. If compensation is paid by another party any excess shall be paid to broker. If within 60 days of termination buyer buys a property that broker introduced buyer to during life of this agreement, then buyer shall pay broker the compensation.
Agency:	This shall be a single agency only.

6. Explain either a sales listing or buyer agency form, paragraph by paragraph, as if you were explaining it to a prospective seller or buyer.

7. Bring to class one current-events article dealing with some aspect of real estate practice for class discussion.

■ CHAPTER 6 QUIZ

1. A valid exclusive listing requires
   a. a lawful purpose.
   b. mutual consent.
   c. consideration.
   d. all of the above.

2. An agent sold a property where the owner had verbally agreed to pay a commission. The agent would be legally entitled to a commission from the owner for the sale if the agent had
   a. relied on the verbal promise.
   b. made a written memorandum of the agreement signed by the agent.
   c. a valid buyer listing agreement.
   d. None of the above

3. Which listing would you be least likely to advertise?
   a. For nonresidential property
   b. An open listing
   c. An exclusive-agency listing
   d. An exclusive-right-to-sell listing

4. A listing under which the owner can sell the listed property without payment of a commission but the agent is nevertheless an exclusive agent is a(n)
   a. open listing.
   b. exclusive-right-to-sell listing.
   c. exclusive-agency listing.
   d. net listing.

5. An agency under which the seller might be competing with the agent in selling a property is a(n)
   a. exclusive-agency listing.
   b. exclusive-right-to-sell listing.
   c. both a and b.
   d. neither a nor b.

6. An exclusive-right-to-sell listing likely includes
   a. an agency relationship disclosure.
   b. an attorney fee provision.
   c. an arbitration agreement.
   d. all of the above.

7. All of the following are true regarding an exclusive-right-to-sell listing except
   a. escrow does not have to close for an agent to be entitled to a commission.
   b. it must have a termination date for the agent to be able to collect a commission.
   c. the agent must give the owner a copy of the listing when the owner signs.
   d. the agent is precluded from working with other agents to sell the property.

8. The type of listing that has the greatest likelihood of resulting in a sale, would be a(n)
   a. open listing.
   b. exclusive-agency listing.
   c. exclusive-right-to-sell listing.
   d. reduced-fee listing.

9. An owner tells you that Agent Jones told her she could get far more for her home than your CMA indicates. What is your best response?

    a. "Many unethical agents will promise the moon to get listings and then fail to perform."

    b. "I am willing to take the listing at that price, but if we don't attract buyers we will reevaluate the price."

    c. "I don't believe it. No agent who knows the market would set a price that high."

    d. "I think my competitive market analysis covers all recent comparables and clearly shows the market value. May I please look at the competitive market analysis that Agent Jones prepared for you?"

10. By taking a listing at a signficantly reduced fee, you are benefiting

    a. your office.

    b. a selling office.

    c. the owner.

    d. none of the above.

CHAPTER SEVEN

SERVICING THE LISTING

■ KEY TERMS

agent open house
agent property evaluation
caravan
communication

homeowner instructions
information boxes
neighborhood
 information request

open house
property brief
talking sign
weekly activity report

■ LEARNING OBJECTIVES

This chapter stresses the importance of honest and open communication with the owner. You will learn the what, when, and how of this communication.

This chapter shows how your various activities can be integrated into a marketing plan for a property. The marketing plan can include signs, rider strips, an information box, use of a multiple-listing service (MLS), a property brief, advertising, Web sites, office caravans, MLS caravans, canvassing for buyers by letter and phone, an agent open house, and buyer open houses.

You learn that servicing a listing is much more than trying for an extension when the listing expires. It is planning, working, and evaluating to meet the needs of an owner.

■ OWNER-AGENT COMMUNICATIONS

The reason most often cited by owners who have been unhappy with the agent who took the listing on their property is not the failure of the agent to secure a buyer; it is failure of the agent to communicate with them after the listing is signed.

It's easy for owners to feel abandoned by their agents. There is a For Sale sign on the lawn and occasionally an ad in a paper that could be for their home or one of a dozen others. Occasionally someone calls for an appointment, and people rush through their home in silence.

Owners want to know what is happening. Some agents even become hard to reach when owners want to know what is happening. The agent paved the way so smoothly in the presentation to get the listing, but now there seems to be a communication gridlock.

> Owner discontent is usually based on the agent's failure to communicate with the client.

The problem in these cases may be that the agent failed to explain what would be happening in advance and doesn't want to tell an owner that very little is happening now. Sometimes, unprofessional agents make unrealistic promises to get listings and want to avoid the unpleasant task of telling the owners that they have not located buyers for their properties. When a listing expires, some agents don't even want to face the owners again to try for an extension.

What Will Be Happening

Owner-agent **communication** should start with the listing. Agents should inform owners what will be happening in the next few days. Agents should make definite appointments to meet soon after a listing to discuss their marketing approaches.

Broker Introduction

Chances are the owners have never met your broker. Your broker should send a letter to the owners thanking them for entrusting the sale of their home to his or her firm. The letter should state that the listing agent is the owners' contact person with the firm but if any problems arise, they should feel free to contact the broker.

Postlisting Meeting

You should consider a postlisting meeting with the owners on the day after the listing was obtained. At the postlisting meeting, go through the house again and make recommendations to the owners of things they should do to help market their home. Impress on the owners that marketing is really a team effort.

Homeowner Instructions. Give the owners **homeowner instructions** to follow. (See Figure 7.1.)

> The owner's cooperation can increase the likelihood of a sale.

When you recognize that work needs to be done, advise the owners to do it or have it done. Show that it is in the owners' interest and not yours that the house appear at its best.

FIGURE 7.1

Instructions for Sellers

Homeowner Hints for a Successful Sale

I. Exterior

  A. Grass and shrubs: Keep trimmed. Consider a fast-greening fertilizer such as ammonium sulfate (inexpensive) for a deep green lawn.

  B. Pets: If you have a dog, clean up any dog dirt on a daily basis. If you have a cat, change your litter box daily. Secure pets when the house is being shown.

  C. Fences: Make any needed repairs. A neat, well-painted fence gives a positive impression.

  D. Flowers: Plant seasonal blooming flowers, especially near the front door and in any patio area. A profusion of color can have your home half-sold before the door is even opened.

  E. Bird feeders: Hummingbird feeders and birdhouses create a pleasant mood, especially when they are close to any patio area.

  F. Paint:

    1. Front door should be refinished or painted if it shows excessive wear.

    2. Check exterior paint. Often only the trim or, depending on sun exposure, only one or two sides of the house need painting. Keep in mind the fact that paint is cheap compared to the extra dollars a home with a clean fresh appearance will bring.

  G. Lawn furniture: Place lawn furniture in an attractive, leisurely manner. A badminton net or croquet set-up gives a positive image as well.

  H. Roof: If the roof needs to be repaired or replaced, it's best to have the work done. Otherwise, buyers will want to deduct the cost even if your price already reflects the required work. Delaying repairs can actually cost you twice as much.

II. Interior

  A. Housekeeping: You are competing against model homes, so your home must look as much like a model as possible. Floors, bath fixtures, and appliances must be sparkling. Make beds early in the day. Unmade beds and late sleepers create a very negative image.

  B. Odors and aromas: Avoid using vinegar or frying or cooking strong-smelling foods such as cabbage just before showing. The odors last and work against the image you are trying to create. On the other hand, some smells have a positive effect on people: Baked bread, apple pie, chocolate chip cookies, and cinnamon rolls are examples of foods that can help sell your home. Consider keeping packaged cookie or bread dough in the refrigerator. Just before a scheduled showing, the smell of these baking foods can be a great help to us.

  C. Paint: If you have leftover paint, you can accomplish a great deal by touching up paint where needed. If the paint is dark, repaint with light colors such as off-white, oyster, light beige, or pale yellow. Light colors make rooms appear fresh as well as larger.

  D. Plumbing: Repair any leaky faucets. Make certain you don't have a gurgling toilet.

  E. Shades and blinds: Replace any torn shades or broken blinds.

  F. Drapes: If drapes need cleaning, have it done. If they are old and worn, stained or dark, consider replacing them with light colors. (Large department stores or catalog houses will have products that can solve the problem.) Vertical blinds should be considered as an alternative to drapes. They are less expensive than all but the cheapest drapes and have a clean, modern appearance.

  G. Carpets: Dirty carpets should be either professionally steam cleaned (preferred), or you should rent a heavy-duty cleaner to do it yourself.

  H. Lighting: If any room appears dark, increase the wattage of your light bulbs. Before a showing, open the blinds and drapes and turn on the lights, even during the day. You want the house as light as possible. Make certain your light fixtures and windows are clean.

  I. Closets: If closets appear crowded, remove items not needed and put them in boxes. The boxes can then be stacked neatly in a corner of the basement, attic, or garage.

  J. Too much furniture: Many houses appear crowded, with too many pieces of large furniture as well as bric-a-brac. Consider putting excess furniture in storage.

FIGURE 7.1

Instructions for Sellers (continued)

K. Garage and basement: Spruce up your work area. Consider a garage sale to get rid of the excess items too good to throw away but of no use to you. Put excess items in boxes and stack them neatly in a corner. Consider using a commercial garage floor cleaner to remove excess oil and grease marks on the garage floor and driveway. You might consider a commercial steam cleaner (not carpet cleaner).

L. Temperature: On cold days, a natural fire in the fireplace will help us sell your home. Start the fire before the showing is scheduled. On hot days, consider turning the air conditioner four to five degrees cooler than normal. The contrast will seem phenomenal, giving a very positive reaction. In moderate weather, open windows for fresh air.

III. You

When your home is shown, it's best that you disappear for a while. Buyers feel restrained with an owner present. If buyers will not voice their concerns, then their questions cannot be answered and their problems cannot be solved.

If you must remain in the house, try to stay in one area. Excellent places to be are working in the garden, on the lawn, or in the workshop. These activities create a positive image. While soft music is fine, do not have a TV on.

Never, never follow the agent around the house during the showing, volunteer any information, or answer questions the buyers may have. You have engaged professional real estate salespersons. We will ask you questions if necessary.

[Clyde Realty]

[555-8200]
www.CRE.com

Besides cleaning and performing needed repairs, there could be a situation in which an improvement would increase property value in excess of the cost of the improvement. Should this be the case, inform the owners. In the event they improve the property after it is listed, an adjustment in the list price should be considered.

It is not enough that owners understand what is expected of them, they should understand *why*. Owners must understand that their house is in competition with other homes for the same buyers. Therefore, they must do everything feasible to make their home a winner.

Some owners may want to meet prospective buyers and follow you around and volunteer information; after all, it is their home. They should understand that having them there inhibits prospective buyers from voicing concerns. If a concern of a prospective buyer is not known to you, you can't overcome it. You must explain that like most people, most buyers have concerns for feelings of others and don't want to criticize because it could be taken personally. On the other hand, voicing a problem to you is really a sign of interest with a "but" attached. Getting rid of the "but" can turn that interest into a sale.

Explain to the owners that at times prospective buyers may come to their door. Owners should ask for the name of the prospect and call your office at once, so an agent will come to show them the home.

Figure 7.2 "Preparing Your Home" and Figure 7.3 "When An Appointment Is Made" are taken from Toolkit for Presentations and are reproduced with the permission of Realty Tools, Inc.

FIGURE 7.2

Preparing Your Home for Showing and Sale

Preparing Your Home

Your home has just one chance to make a great impression with each potential buyer. And it can! The following "tricks of the trade" will help you keep track of what needs to be done. The whole idea is to present a clean, spacious clutter-free home--the kind of place you'd like to buy. Accomplish a little everyday, and before long your home will be ready to make the impression that can make the sale.

Your Home's Curb Appeal
- Mow lawn
- Trim shrubs
- Edge gardens and walkways
- Weed and mulch
- Sweep walkways and driveway, remove branches, litter or toys
- Add color and fill in bare spots with plantings
- Remove mildew or moss from walls or walks with bleach and water or other cleaner
- Take stains off your driveway with cleanser or kitty litter
- Stack woodpile neatly
- Clean and repair patio and deck area
- Remove any outdoor furniture which is not in good repair
- Make sure pool or spa sparkles
- Replace old storm doors
- Check for flat-fitting roof shingles
- Repair broken windows and shutters, replace torn screens, make sure frames and seams have solid caulking
- Hose off exterior wood and trim, replace damaged bricks or wood
- Touch up exterior paint, repair gutters and eaves
- Clean and remove rust from any window air conditioning units
- Paint the front door and mailbox
- Add a new front door mat and consider a seasonal door decoration
- Shine brass hardware on front door, outside lighting fixtures, etc.
- Make sure doorbell is in good working order

General Interior Tips
- Add a fresh coat of interior paint in light, neutral colors
- Shampoo carpeting, replace if necessary
- Clean and wax hardwood floors, refinish if necessary
- Clean and wash kitchen and bathroom floors
- Wash all windows, vacuum blinds, wash window sills
- Clean the fireplace
- Clean out and organize closets, add extra space by packing clothes and items you won't need again until after you've moved

- Remove extra furniture, worn rugs, and items you don't use; keep papers, toys, etc. picked up--especially on stairways
- Repair problems such as loose door knobs, cracked molding, leaking taps and toilets, squeaky doors, closets or screen doors which are off their tracks
- Add dishes of potpourri, or drop of vanilla or bath oil on light bulbs for scent
- Secure jewelry cash and other valuables

The Living Room
- Make it cozy and inviting, discard chipped or worn furniture and frayed or worn rugs

The Dining Room
- Polish any visible silver and crystal
- Set the table for a formal dinner to help viewers imagine entertaining here

The Kitchen
- Make sure appliances are spotless inside and out (try baking soda for cleaning Formica stains)
- Make sure all appliances are in perfect working order
- Clean often forgotten spots on top of refrigerator and under sink
- Wax or sponge floor to brilliant shine, clean baseboards
- Unclutter all counter space, remove countertop appliances
- Organize items inside cabinets, pre-pack anything you won't be using before you move

The Bathrooms
- Remove all rust and mildew
- Make sure tile, fixtures, shower doors, etc. are immaculate and shining
- Make sure all fixtures are in good repair
- Replace loose caulking or grout
- Make sure lighting is bright, but soft

The Master Bedroom
- Organize furnishings to create a spacious look with well-defined sitting, sleeping, and dressing areas

The Garage
- Sell, give away, or throw out unnecessary items
- Clean oily cement floor
- Provide strong overhead light
- Tidy storage or work areas

The Basement
- Sell, give away, or throw out unnecessary items
- Organize and create more floor space by hanging tools and placing items on shelves
- Clean water heater and drain sediment
- Change furnace filter
- Make inspection access easy
- Clean and paint concrete floor and walls
- Provide strong overhead light

The Attic
- Tidy up by discarding or pre-packing
- Make sure energy-saving insulation is apparent
- Make sure air vent is in working order
- Provide strong overhead lighting

When It's Time To Show
- Make sure your property profile folder, utility bills, MLS profile, house location survey, etc. are available
- Open all draperies and shades, turn on all lights
- Pick up toys and other clutter, check to make sure beds are made and clothes are put away
- Give the carpets a quick vacuuming
- Add some strategically placed fresh flowers
- Open bathroom windows for fresh air
- Pop a spicy dessert or just a pan of cinnamon in the oven for aroma
- Turn off the television and turn on the radio music at a low volume
- Make a fire in the fireplace if appropriate
- Put pets in the backyard or arrange for a friend to keep them
- Make sure pet areas are clean and odor-free
- Make sure all trash is disposed of in neatly covered bins

Angela McKendrick
Office: (410) 555-6500
Direct Line: (410) 555-6509
Home Office: (410) 233-5532
Cellular: (410) 554-7676
E-mail: amckendrick@demorealty.com

Weekly Activity Report. Tell the owners what you have already done, what you are doing, and what you will be doing. Owners should understand that you will be sending them a **weekly activity report** and that if they have any questions at any time, they should call you. (See Figure 7.4.)

While some agents would rather make monthly reports simply because they show more activity, owners don't want to wait that long. Prepare reports on all of your listings every week so they become a part of your routine. Weekly reports also will force you to review your own sales activity and to consider what can or should be done to bring about a sale.

FIGURE 7.3

When An Appointment Is Made to See Your Home

When An Appointment Is Made

Agents from many real estate firms will want to show your home. Please allow any agent who calls to show your home at the suggested time. If you are not frequently available, it is suggested that you allow a lockbox to be installed on your door. You will increase your odds for a sale by allowing more qualified buyers to see your home. You do not want to miss an out-of-town transferee because your home was not able to be shown.

During a showing:

♦ Open all draperies and window shades during daylight hours.

♦ Turn on all lights and replace bulbs with high wattage bulbs where needed.

♦ Open windows one half hour before showing to circulate fresh air.

♦ Open all the doors between rooms to give an inviting feeling.

♦ Place fresh flowers on kitchen table and/or in the living room.

♦ If possible. bake cookies or bread to add an inviting aroma.

♦ The kitchen & bathroom should sparkle.

♦ Pets should be confined or restricted from view. Eliminate pet odors. Not everyone may share your love of animals. Some people may be allergic to them.

♦ All jewelry and small valuables should be stored in a safety deposit box or in a locked closet.

♦ Replace any items not included in the sale, or tag them appropriately with "to be replaced with…" or "not included" signs.

♦ Beds should be made & clothes picked up. Bathrooms should be clean, with towels folded and toilet lid down.

♦ When you leave the house, please leave it as if you know it is going to be shown. You never know when the right person is going to look at it!

Angela McKendrick
Office: (410) 555-6500
Direct Line: (410) 555-6509
Home Office: (410) 233-5532
Cellular: (410) 554-7676
E-mail: amckendrick@demorealty.com

Your Logo

As an attachment to weekly activity reports, you can include ads for the property, a printout of your MLS page for the property, and copies of property postings on Internet sites, and even e-mails sent promoting the property (don't include the addressee).

Showings.   Owners must understand that although agents try to give them notice well in advance of a showing, this may not always be practical. Explain that in showing another property, an agent might realize that the owners' property better fits the needs of a certain buyer than properties that originally were selected for viewing. At times, prospective buyers may ask agents about certain houses while looking at other properties. If a property fits a buyer's needs, the prospective

FIGURE 7.4

Weekly Activity Report Form

[Jones Realty]

Weekly Progress Report   Week Ending _____

Property: _____

Owners: _____

Number of Inquiries: _____

Number of Showings: _____

Advertising: _____

_____

Open House Dates(s): _____

Number of Visitors: _____

Comments of Agents and Prospective Buyers: _____

_____

_____

_____

_____

---

buyer could well turn into an actual buyer. The fact that they, not the agent, found the property can influence a sale.

Also explain that the reverse can happen; owners might be prepared for a visit by an agent who fails to show. While you generally will notify owners of canceled appointments, there will be times when such notification is difficult.

During hot weather, suggest that the owner leave soft drinks in the refrigerator for agents from your office and their prospective buyers. Explain that offering prospects a soda and getting them to sit down can help them view the home from a more relaxed point of view. If the owners agree to do this, and they generally will, make certain the agents within your office know about it. Incidentally, a good place to sit is close to a pool or garden if available. Otherwise, pick the room that has the best ambiance.

Understanding Advertising.   Help your owners fully understand your advertising policy and the media used. Explain that every home is not advertised every day because this isn't necessary to successfully market a property. Explain that buyers often buy a different house from the one in the advertisement that attracted their attention. Explain that many people who answer ads are hoping for a bargain and tend to inquire about homes priced at less than they expect to spend.

In the same vein, other homes priced in the same or even a higher or a lower price range create inquiries. When qualifying these prospective buyers, the agent may discover that the owners' house is likely to meet the buyers' needs. Thus, advertising for other houses creates prospects for their home. Explain that by endeavoring to cover a range of both price and special features, you can in effect advertise every home in your inventory each day with just a handful of ads.

Neighborhood Information Request.   Another way in which you can make the owners feel they are part of your marketing effort is to ask them to complete a **neighborhood information request** (Figure 7.5). This information can be extremely valuable, and filled-out copies should be readily available to all salespersons in your office. Agents who know what buyers want will have special ammunition to sell particular houses. Although other homes might have area activities or neighbors that would make them equally desirable, the agent who does not have the information cannot use it to make the sale. As an example:

The owner can be a source of valuable information.

> "Johnny, do you like baseball? Well, you're in luck, there is a Little League here, and they play just two blocks away at McKinley Park."

Change in Agents

If an agent who took a listing leaves the office, the broker should assign another salesperson to serve as listing agent and liaison with the owners. This agent should meet with the owners and go over their work to that point in time as well as to discuss ways the property can be made more readily salable (if applicable).

Preparing the Owners for an Offer.   Give owners a blank copy of a purchase contract and explain to them that the form is the one that will be used by a buyer. By explaining the clauses and leaving a copy with the owners, you will reduce the chance that they will get upset about any clause when they receive an offer.

Also prepare owners for quick offers. Explain that the first few weeks after a listing is taken can be very productive because other agents as well as prospective buyers tend to get excited over new listings. You can point out that when some owners get a quick offer, they feel that it indicates they set their price too low. They reject good offers, and they later regret the rejection. In pointing out this fact you reduce the likelihood of a negative reaction to a quick offer.

FIGURE 7.5

Neighborhood Information Request

Neighborhood Information Request

Having an in-depth knowledge of your neighborhood and neighbors can give us a competitive advantage over less informed sales agents who represent other properties.

We would therefore appreciate your completion of this form to the best of your ability.

1. Neighborhood features you feel a buyer would likely be most pleased with: _____

   _____

   _____

2. School districts are: _____

   _____

3. School bus stops at: _____

   _____

4. Names, ages and schools attended by neighboring children (include private schools):

   _____ ____ _____

   _____ ____ _____

   _____ ____ _____

   _____ ____ _____

   _____ ____ _____

5. Youth activities in the area (Little League, junior hockey, soccer league, etc.): _____

   _____

■ NECESSARY INFORMATION AND DISCLOSURES

You want the sellers to complete the Real Estate Transfer Disclosure Statement (see Chapter 3) as soon as possible. If the seller reveals problems that you feel should be corrected before a sale, you should advise the owners to take corrective action.

FIGURE 7.5

Neighborhood Information Request (continued)

6. Public recreational facilities in area (parks, pools, playgrounds, tennis courts, etc.): _____

_____

7. Nearest public transportation route: _____

_____

8. Nearest medical facility: _____

_____

9. Nearest community center (for children, seniors, etc): _____

_____

10. Nearest churches and synagogues (and denominations):

_____

_____

11. Nearest shopping area: _____

_____

12. People living in area that might interest a possible buyer (doctor, banker, attorney, professor or another professional):

_____

_____

Please send your completed form to my attention in the enclosed postage paid envelope.

Your help in providing this data is greatly appreciated.

Appreciatively yours,

_____

Have the owners complete the FIRPTA/California Withholding form (Chapter 14).

If the property is leased, obtain copies of lease(s). You should also obtain estoppel certificates from tenant(s) that they have no defenses or offsets against the landlord.

If the property is a common interest development, you should obtain copies of the bylaws, CC&Rs, current financial statement, minutes of meetings, and any information about changes in assessments or pending legal actions.

You should have the sellers sign the Water Heater Statement of Compliance that the water heater will be properly braced as of close of escrow, as well as the Smoke Detector Statement of Compliance that operable smoke detectors shall be in place at close of escrow as required by law.

The Lead-based Paint and Lead-based Hazards Disclosure Acknowledgement and Addendum should also be signed by owners indicating any knowledge of or no knowledge of lead-based paint.

You will want a property profile from a title company. This could reveal problems that could make a sale difficult if not corrected or even impossible.

You will want to measure the house as to approximate square footage and room sizes. You will also want to know the lot size which may be available from plat maps.

You should check to determine if the property is in an earthquake fault zone, seismic hazard zone, area of potential flooding, flood hazard area, state responsibility fire area, very high fire hazard severity zone, state fire responsibility areas, and wildland area that may contain substantial fire risks and other hazards.

■ LISTING MODIFICATION

If it becomes apparent that you made an error in your assessment of the property value, let the owners know at once. If you suggest a different price, be able to defend your position. Never suggest a price be "lowered." If you suggest lowering the price, you are, in effect, asking the owners to give up something they think they have, because that is what "lowering" implies. *Modification* does not have the immediate negative connotation of *lowering*.

Changes in the market can turn a proper original listing price into a price that is either too high or too low. After taking the listing, for example, if several comparable properties are put on the market at significantly lower prices, it will affect the ability of your pricing to attract interest.

If owners refuse to adjust their price when you feel such an action is necessary to find a buyer, consider the ultimate in persuasion: offer to return the listing. Ask the owners to sign a release relieving you of all agency obligations under the listing. Ask to be let out of your agreement to exercise diligence on their behalf. Although owners might not really be sold on your representing them, no one likes to be the one rejected. A release offer often convinces owners to adjust their price to the level recommended.

The worst-case scenario is that you will give up an overpriced listing that had less than a good chance of attracting buyers. From a rational point of view, of course, giving up a poor listing makes sense, but we are not always rational. The problem is that if you don't succeed, you will feel like a loser. However, you actually will be a winner; you will be able to devote your time to probabilities rather than remote possibilities.

Don't look at this approach as a bluff, because you shouldn't be bluffing. To be sure, it's an either/or approach, but it's unfair to the owners to continue to offer their home at a price that will fail to attract prospective buyers.

Don't change the original listing when making a listing modification. Use a modification form that will enable you to later determine what was done should a problem arise. Figure 7.6 is an example of a Modification of Terms form.

A significant downward price adjustment on a listing should be communicated to area cooperating brokers and salespersons by e-mail. It will get more attention than an MLS computer update by itself.

■ LISTING EXTENSION

Several weeks before your listing expires, schedule a meeting with the owners to go over the listing and what you have been doing on their behalf. If owners feel that you have been diligent in working for them and have kept them informed, you have an excellent chance of obtaining a listing extension. However, if you fail to keep the owners informed so they have to call you to find out what is happening, your chances of obtaining an extension to the listing are materially diminished.

If you obtain an extension, a thank-you letter from your broker is appropriate. Also, don't forget to immediately communicate the extension to your MLS.

■ YOUR MARKETING PLAN

You should have a marketing plan. By following the suggestions in this section, you will see a marketing plan develop. A copy should be provided to the owner(s) as soon as it is prepared. See Figure 5.6B on page 161 for a sample plan.

Signs

When you obtain the listing, put up a For Sale sign immediately after leaving the house. If you do not, you should tell the owner when one will be installed. If your office uses huge wooden holders for metal signs, you should have smaller lawn signs that can be used in the interim. Tell the owners when your large sign will be installed.

FIGURE 7.6

Modification of Terms Authorization and Right To Sell, Acquire, or Rent

CALIFORNIA ASSOCIATION OF REALTORS®

**MODIFICATION OF TERMS
AUTHORIZATION AND RIGHT TO SELL,
ACQUIRE OR RENT**
(C.A.R. Form MT, Revised 4/02)

The Authorization and Right To Sell (or, if checked, ☐ Authorization to Acquire, ☐ Authorization to Lease or Rent)

dated_____, between _____ ("Broker")

and _____ ("Principal"), regarding the real property or

manufactured home described as _____

_____

is modified as follows:

PRICE: The listing price, price range, lease or rental amount shall be changed to:

_____

_____ Dollars ($ _____)

EXPIRATION DATE: The expiration date is changed to: _____.

OTHER: _____

_____

_____

_____

_____

_____

_____

All other terms of the Authorization and Right to Sell, Authorization to Acquire, or Authorization to Lease or Rent, as applicable, remain in full force and effect, except as modified herein.

I acknowledge that I have read and understand this Modification Agreement and have received a copy.

Date_____   at_____, California

_____   _____
Principal   Principal

Broker _____   By _____ Date_____
          (Firm)   (Agent)

The copyright laws of the United States (Title 17 U.S. Code) forbid the unauthorized reproduction of this form, or any portion thereof, by photocopy machine or any other means, including facsimile or computerized formats. Copyright © 1991-2002 CALIFORNIA ASSOCIATION OF REALTORS®, INC. ALL RIGHTS RESERVED.
THIS FORM HAS BEEN APPROVED BY THE CALIFORNIA ASSOCIATION OF REALTORS® (C.A.R.). NO REPRESENTATION IS MADE AS TO THE LEGAL VALIDITY OR ADEQUACY OF ANY PROVISION IN ANY SPECIFIC TRANSACTION. A REAL ESTATE BROKER IS THE PERSON QUALIFIED TO ADVISE ON REAL ESTATE TRANSACTIONS. IF YOU DESIRE LEGAL OR TAX ADVICE, CONSULT AN APPROPRIATE PROFESSIONAL.
This form is available for use by the entire real estate industry. It is not intended to identify the user as a REALTOR®. REALTOR® is a registered collective membership mark which may be used only by members of the NATIONAL ASSOCIATION OF REALTORS® who subscribe to its Code of Ethics.

Published and Distributed by:
REAL ESTATE BUSINESS SERVICES, INC.
a subsidiary of the CALIFORNIA ASSOCIATION OF REALTORS®
525 South Virgil Avenue, Los Angeles, California 90020

Reviewed by _____
Broker or Designee _____ Date _____

EQUAL HOUSING OPPORTUNITY

MT-11 REVISED 4/02 (PAGE 1 OF 1) Print Date

MODIFICATION OF TERMS (MT-11 PAGE 1 OF 1)

FIGURE 7.7

Rider Strip Example

Besides the broker's name and telephone number, some brokers are including their Web site address so that prospective buyers can obtain more information.

Rider Strips.   Have a rider strip on the sign with your evening telephone or cellular phone number, as in Figure 7.7. This rider strip can lead to calls after hours and on weekends that you would not otherwise receive. You must be available when interest is high. An evening telephone or cellular phone number should be under the sign portion, but note any special feature of the house on a rider strip on top of the sign, as shown in the figure.

Talking Signs.   If you use talking signs, prepare the message as soon as possible and install the broadcasting machine at the owners' home within a day or two of taking the listing. A **talking sign** is a radio transmitter that sends out a message lasting up to about two minutes. This radio broadcast is either AM or FM. AM models have greater range (up to 250 feet). Having these signs is an excellent listing tool because the units can be readily demonstrated. Your radio message should be prepared with the same care in choice of words that you would use for an ad. Talking signs are generally the property of the listing agent, not the broker. However, representations made by the talking sign, as all representations, must be truthful and not misrepresent the property. Remember, the broker is responsible for representations of his or her salespersons.

Information Boxes

All of the real estate supply houses as well as some boards of REALTORS® stores carry *information boxes* or tubes that can be attached to your yard signs. These boxes are a low-cost, effective way to interest buyers. Inside the box, insert a supply of property briefs that describe the listed property in a manner that is likely to interest the reader and encourage the reader to contact your office. Information boxes can also include information on similar properties, the broker's Internet address where more information is available, as well as an e-mail address.

Photos

Photographs of the home should be taken as soon as possible after the listing is taken. You will want interior photos emphasizing desirable aspects of the home as well as exterior photos. You will want the photos for property magazines, property briefs, ads, mailings, and displays as well as for your office Internet site. Photos will also have to be taken for virtual tours if your Internet site includes them.

Lockbox

If possible, install a lockbox, or keybox, used by your multiple-listing service (MLS) right after taking the listing. If there is going to be a delay, inform the owners when a lockbox will be installed.

Lockboxes are simply large boxes that have a separately locked compartment to hold the house keys. They may be locked to door handles, electric meters, metal railings, etc.

The latest lockbox models are electronic marvels. Besides containing the key, they tell you by a simple phone call who has used the lockbox. This information is valuable for security reasons. It also lets you tell the owner in your weekly activity report who entered the property by using the lockbox. You can also call agents who viewed the property for their comments. This is the type of information an owner should be made aware of. Like the talking sign, these electronic lockboxes are a superb marketing tool that can be effectively used in your listing presentation.

Owners should understand that allowing other people access to their homes when they or you are not present does create a security risk. You should suggest that they make certain that their insurance will adequately cover theft or mysterious disappearances of furnishings. You might also suggest that expensive objects be locked up or removed from the premises.

The Multiple-Listing Service

To provide greater market coverage for their listings, a group of brokers often conducts a cooperative listing service or multiple-listing service (MLS). The group often consists of members of a local real estate board or association; however, membership in the board or association is not a prerequisite to membership in the service. The MLS is used most often with an exclusive-authorization-and-right-to-sell listing, but it may be used with other listings as well. A member of the group who takes any listing turns it in to a central bureau that distributes it to all participants in the service usually on the Internet or on a computer disk. All members have the right to sell the property. However, they must have the listing broker's permission to advertise or promote it. When a sale is made on an MLS listing, the listing broker and the broker who found the buyer share the commission.

FIGURE 7.8

Splitting a Commission on an MLS Listing

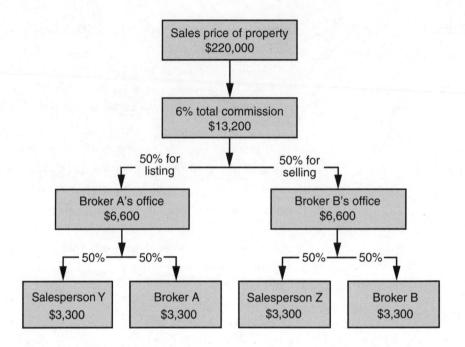

Suppose, for example, an MLS commission split was 50/50. The listing broker would get 50 percent of the commission, and the broker who found the buyer would get the other 50 percent. Within each agency the broker would, according to the contractual agreement between the broker and the salesperson, also split his or her share of the commission with the salesperson who had actual contact with the seller or buyer. (Only brokers may receive commissions, but they may share them with the salespeople who work with them.) When property is sold out of an MLS, the licensee who makes the sale is considered to be a subagent of the listing owner. Figure 7.8 illustrates a possible split of the 6 percent commission on a property that sold for $220,000.

Give information on your listing to your MLS office as soon as possible. This will add the listings to the computer system and ensure its availability to other offices as soon as possible. When you can get a computer printout of the listing, send a copy to the owners. It shows them that things are happening. Remember, owners like to see action.

It is important that owners fully understand the role of an MLS service and the agency implications.

Your Internet Site

A new listing should be placed on your office Internet site as soon as possible. A printout of the material included on the site should be provided to the owner(s). For information about what your Internet site should include, see Chapter 8.

Property Brief

A property brief is an advertising flyer about a particular property.

As soon as you have your photographs, prepare a property brief. A **property brief** is simply a one-page flier about the property pointing out attractive features. It must have a photograph or drawing of the home. If the owners purchased the property from a developer, there is a good chance they have kept the original sales material; check it over if they do have it. There could be an attractive pen-and-ink drawing of the house that would reproduce well for your property brief. If there is a floor plan, it may be possible to reproduce this on the back of the property brief along with some information on special features.

The property briefs should also include an Internet address where the prospect can obtain further information including photos on the property as well as other properties. With most computer printers and computer scanners, you can do a superb job of copying color photographs.

A professional-quality property brief can be prepared in a few minutes with a laser printer and any number of desktop publishing software programs that are available. Owners will be impressed with a quality flier featuring their home so soon after you have taken the listing. (See Figure 7.9.)

Copies of the property brief should be left at the home to be given to prospects as well as agents who will view the property. Therefore, deliver the property briefs to the home before any visits take place. They should be placed close to the front door, preferably on a table, so that a visitor will not miss them. A small "Take One" sign can be used. If the For Sale sign has an information box, a good supply should be placed inside it. Give a supply of property briefs to every agent in your office. You might also give them to agents from other offices who are particularly active in the area or in the type of property you are offering.

Property briefs also are given out at open houses. It is a good idea to have a supply of property briefs on similar homes as well as briefs on the home that is open. Briefs may also be mailed in response to mail or phone inquiries.

Other Internet Sites

The National Association of REALTORS® has a site, *www.realtor.com*, where a prospective buyer or tenant can find properties in all areas of the country. The site allows a broker to post a picture of the property as well as a great deal of information to interest prospective buyers. The viewer can obtain further information and a blowup picture of the property on request. In addition, a number of boards of REALTORS® and groups of boards have area sites.

You will be limited to what you place on sites that you don't control. You want a good exterior photo as you will likely be allowed to place only one on the Web sites. The information you provide will likely have to be in a specific format. While you should carefully choose descriptive wording on your own Web site, multiple-broker sites generally limit your descriptions.

Virtual Reality Home Tours

Technology has evolved so that it is possible to offer virtual home tours while seated before a personal computer. Providing virtual reality home tours on the Internet impresses owners of listed property and saves buyers' and agents' time. A viewer can move from side to side, backward and forward, and from room to room when viewing the site. A specially trained photographer usually takes 360° photographs of the interior, exterior, and even the neighborhood. Today, software programs are available that allow an agent to prepare a virtual reality tour using a plain digital camera and a software program that costs around $300. If you are interested in creating your own virtual reality tour, two of the sources you might wish to consider are, *www.visualtour.com* and Photo Vista Virtual Tour available through *z-lawsoftwareinfo@z-law.com*. This program can produce film or digital photographs.

Walk through homes on the Internet.

While at present, it is estimated that less than 5 percent of listings can be seen as a virtual tour, having virtual tours on your Web site is an excellent marketing tool for both selling properties and obtaining listings.

Before you prepare a virtual tour, obtain the owner's permission in writing to do so. There is a danger that the virtual tour will provide access information to persons interested in what is in the house and not the house itself. Owners should be advised to review their insurance coverage, especially if the home contains valuable art objects and/or antiques.

Brokers find that with virtual tours they can show a home when it is not available for a physical showing. It is believed by many brokers that virtual tours will replace the flat photographs currently used on most Web sites.

Many of the house-hunter sites, such as *www.listinglink.com* and *www.coldwellbanker.com*, now offer virtual tours.

Advertising

After you have given the listing to your MLS, prepared a property brief, and posted the property information and photograph on the Internet, prepare at least three classified advertisements on the property, as well as one open-house ad. Take your time because you want your ads to have maximum effectiveness. There are a number of excellent books that can help you produce superior ads. Using different approaches, your ad can be tailored to appeal to various groups of readers, based on features advertised and the form of your appeal. By preparing at least three ads, you are less likely to repeat an ad, which generally results in reduced response. You won't be caught with an ad deadline and six other tasks that need immediate attention, which usually means a mediocre ad at best.

If your firm uses one of the home magazines, prepare an ad for it as well, even though a decision may not yet have been made to advertise the listing there. By having the ad ready, the likelihood of its being advertised has measurably increased.

FIGURE 7.9

Example of a Property Brief

PAT PRESENTS

Indian Wells Country Club
45-667 Oswego Lane

** Four Suites in Main House
** Two Suites in Guest House
** Half Acre & Mountain Views
** State-of-the-Art Security System
** Sauna/Steam Shower in Master
** Indirect Lighting

** Family Room, Walk-in Bar w/Icemak
** Huge Back Yard
** 3 Fireplaces, Including one in Mastei
** 4020 Sq. Ft., Main House
** 810 Sq. Ft., Guest House
** Vaulted Ceilings

REDUCED TO $945,000

CALL PAT FLEMING

FIGURE 7.9

Example of a Property Brief (continued)

45-667 OSWEGO LANE
ADDED AMENITIES

COMPLETE BUILT-IN VACUUM SYSTEM
KITCHEN ISLAND WITH NUTONE PROCESSING CENTER,
BLENDER INCLUDED
GAS GAGINEAU RANGE WITH ELECTRIC GRILL & GRIDDLE
42"-WIDE OVERSIZED GE REFRIGERATOR
HI-TECH FAUCETS AND FIXTURES
SURROUND-SOUND STEREO IN FAMILY ROOM. TUNER RE-
MAINS WITH HOME STEREO SPEAKERS IN LIVING ROOM,
DINING, FAMILY ROOM, MASTER SUITE
INDIRECT LIGHTING AROUND FIREPLACES IN LIVING ROOM
SOFFITS
EXTENSIVE EXTERIOR LIGHTING. SOME ON SENSORS, SOME
ON SWITCHES AND CONTROLLED FROM INTERIOR
THREE LOCKED GATES, ALL LOCKS KEYED ALIKE

GAS OUTLET FOR BARBECUE NEAR SINGLE PILLAR ON
KITCHEN PATIO
TOP-OF-LINE COMTRON SECURITY SYSTEM INCLUDES MOVE-
MENT DETECTORS. SELLER WILL ACTIVATE FOR BUYER.
THREE SEPARATE WATER HEATERS
WASHROOM IN GARAGE ALSO CONTAINS VACUUM EQUIP-
MENT AND ROUGH PLUMBING FOR WATER SOFTENER
ALL WINDOWS ARE TOP-OF-LINE THERMAL, DUAL PANED,
AND TINTED
CEMENT PAD NEAR POOL COULD BE USED FOR GAZEBO
POOL HAS HIDDEN FLOAT, WHICH SERVES AS AUTOMATIC
WATER LEVEL CONTROL
SWITCH IN GUEST HOUSE ACTIVATES SPILLWATER FROM SPA
TO POOL FOR WATERFALL EFFECT
UTILITY METERS ARE OUTSIDE GATES
DRAINAGE SYSTEM MOVES EXCESS WATER FROM BACKYARD
TO STREET
THREE-CAR GARAGE HAS STALL FOR VAN
GARAGE DOOR SYSTEM IS CHILDPROOF WITH SEPARATE
SWITCH
INSULATION—R-19 FACTOR. CEILING HAS R-17 BETWEEN SUP-
PORT BEAMS & INSULATION IN POLY/FOAM CEILING IS SR-35,
FOR TOTAL OF R-52

FIGURE 7.10

Agent Property Evaluation

Agent Property Evaluation

Property Address _____

Name of Owners(s) _____

1. Features of the house that will be most appealing to buyers:

   _____

   _____

   _____

2. Features or lack of features that buyers are likely to view

   as a negative: _____

   _____

   _____

   _____

3. I feel that the price is

   ☐ Too high   ☐ Too Low   ☐ Realistic

   By how much? $ _____

   Why? _____

   _____

4. To increase salability, the owner should consider:

   _____

   _____

   _____

Be sure to send owners copies of the ads on their property when it is advertised.

Keep in mind that advertising does not sell property—salespersons sell. What advertising does is to create responses that knowledgeable agents can convert into sales.

Office Caravans

The owners should be told in advance about the office caravan and the MLS caravan. Many offices caravan their office listings. The name **caravan** comes from the long lines of cars that agents drive from home to home to view properties. Have each of the salespeople fill out an agent questionnaire after they walk through the property (Figure 7.10). The information from this **agent property evaluation** questionnaire should be supplied to the owners with your suggestions. If the agent property evaluation indicates a serious problem, meet with the owners as soon as possible to decide how to resolve it.

MLS Caravan

Large real estate MLSs have many more listings than the agents could possibly visit in one morning or even in one day. However, the listings are broken down into areas. Most agents want to see only the homes at the price and in the area where they feel they are most likely going to have prospective buyers. Again, the effective agent concentrates more on probabilities than on possibilities.

Give the owners as much advance notice as you can about the caravan. The owners should have the property "standing tall for inspection." The following are some general rules for caravans:

- Owners should not be at home. Agents tend to spend more time in a home when owners are not present.

- Offer agents hot coffee or lemonade, depending on the weather. Fill the cups or glasses about two-thirds full, so the agents can carry them while they view the home. This will tend to slow the viewing process.

- Give each agent a property brief. The agents see so many homes that most will not remember which features went with which house.

- Consider mood setting. Have the stereo playing soft music. If the weather is cold, have the fireplace going; if it is hot, set the air-conditioning between 68° and 70° so it feels like a cold blast when agents enter the house.

> Concentrate your viewing time on properties you're most likely to sell.

- Ask the owner to bake some chocolate chip cookies, cinnamon rolls, or fresh bread. The aroma will be pleasant and agents will like something free to eat.

- If possible, be at the house during the caravan.

During slow markets, some agents put out a buffet lunch for caravan members. In a large MLS, instead of having only 15 percent of the agents visit the property, you may increase it to 60 percent or more of the agents on caravan by providing them food. An expenditure such as this makes sense for a property that shows well and is priced right.

Some agents use the Internet to view property rather than go on caravans. It is likely that at some time in the future, caravans will no longer be necessary.

Area Canvass Letter

Within one week of taking a new listing, you should send a letter to residents living within about one block of the listed property. This letter informs the neighbors of the listing and asks their help in locating a buyer. The letter should indicate that you will be calling them. (See Figure 7.11.)

FIGURE 7.11

Canvas Letter

[Date]

_____

_____

_____

Dear [   ]:

Our office has recently listed the home of your neighbor [John Jones] at [322 Maple Lane] for sale. You have probably noticed our For Sale sign.

I am writing to ask for your help in locating a buyer for this fine home.

I have enclosed a descriptive sheet on the property. We think it is a lot of house for the money, and the neighborhood is great so you would be helping anyone you suggest. I'll be calling you in a few days to see if you have been able to come up with any suggestions about your friends who might also want to be your neighbors.

Sincerely,

_____

_____

[*Note:* Be certain to include a property flier and follow through.]

Check the Files

As soon as you get a new listing in an office, all salespersons in the office should go through their prospect files to try to match their current prospects with the new listing. This activity has two major advantages:

1. Prospective buyers tend to get excited over brand-new listings. They might treat property on the market for a long period of time as shopworn merchandise, but a new listing elicits interest and can also have a sense of urgency. They are seeing this property before it is being visited by perhaps hundreds of agents, all of whom have prospective buyers. Right now the property can be theirs if they wish.

   This is one of the reasons that the most productive period for sales tends to be the first 20 days after the listing is taken.

2. The second advantage of immediately calling prospects is that it creates traffic within a few days of taking the listing. The owners' impression of you as a professional and of your firm is likely to be set within the first few weeks of the agency. After that period, it will be difficult to change the owners' perception.

Some brokers make the consideration of new listings part of their weekly meetings. The broker asks agents to think about their prospects and who likely would be interested in the property. By directing thoughts toward solving a problem, agents frequently generate ideas they would not have had otherwise.

Agent Open House

Having an open house on an overpriced property will generally be a waste of both time and money. In addition, it will leave viewers with a negative feeling towards both you and your firm. Therefore, you want open houses that are priced competitively. Best results can be expected from fresh property (recently listed).

If you have an unusual property, a property that must be sold or several identical properties close to each other, consider an **agent open house.** In large associations, agents can't physically visit every new listing. They have to pick and choose. Therefore, a great many agents could miss your home on a caravan because they only visited, say, 12 of 35 new listings. Even listings that were visited were only viewed for a few minutes, and if you asked an agent a week later which home had which feature, most agents would give you a wrong answer.

> Agent open houses provide maximum exposure of new listings to agents, whereas the MLS caravan only allows quick viewing of a small portion.

Because of the longer period of time spent at a property, an agent open house impresses on agents the details of that property. The offer to stop by for food and drink can bring in many agents. It also serves a dual purpose because owners like these events; it shows extraordinary marketing.

Although you may have balloons, flags, and other accoutrements outside, you don't have to host an elaborate party to attract agents. Cheese, crackers, and nuts will do. Wine or champagne should be served in plastic glasses. One way to encourage agents to linger awhile is a drawing using agents' business cards. The prize could be anything from a book of ten free car washes to a weekend vacation package.

If you have the cards of the agents who were there, you can get them to complete a questionnaire giving their views on the property location and price, as well as letting you know whether they are working with any potential buyers.

Open House

Owners must be encouraged to have the house as presentable as possible for a standard **open house.** Treat the buyer open house as you treated homes for caravans and agent open houses. You want the home to appear light, bright, and as fresh as possible. There is one exception to having the house as close to perfect as is possible. That is an open house for a property advertised as a fixer-upper. If this is the case, the home will not need minor repairs or touch-up, although it should be clean.

You want to know who visits your open house. By asking each visitor to fill out a registration card, you can find out why they came and if they are buyers or sellers. Instead of registration cards, some agents give visitors clipboards with attached pencils, asking them to rate the house as to how it fits their needs.

> ### Draw Attention to the Property
> Besides ads, you should have signs and arrows directing traffic from major streets. Always ask other property owners if you can put a directional sign on their lawns. They will generally allow you to do so, but if you do not ask, the sign likely will be removed.
>
> Some agents tie a group of balloons to a mailbox or tree to attract attention. This is fine, as are flags, banners, helium balloons, and so forth. One Los Angeles area broker uses a machine to spew out thousands of large soap bubbles. Another agent flies a 20-foot helium-filled blimp lettered "Open House." Anything to make the house stand out can be used. You don't want to keep an open house a secret. Invite neighbors as well as prospective buyers you are working with who have not seen the house. You want to generate traffic.

Figure 7.12 is an example of such a form. Of course, the comments from visitors should be relayed to your owners in their weekly activity report.

Give every open-house visitor a copy of your property brief and your business card.

Property briefs of other homes you have in the same and lower price brackets should be available. By questioning visitors, you can find their interests and needs, and you may excite their interest in a property better suited to them.

Open houses are a time to make contacts and gather information, so ask questions. You can use general qualifying questions as well as determine specifics. If visitors seem enthusiastic, use a trial closing. Don't think the sole function of an open house is only to show; it is to sell as well. Open houses tend to please owners because they show positive action on your part. They are often a source of listings because many visitors must sell before they can buy. They are a source of prospective buyers for other properties as well as the property shown. Therefore, you should look at the whole picture. With every visitor ask yourself, "How can I fulfill this person's real estate needs?"

Open houses provide a variety of benefits.

When you have or your office has several open houses in the same general area and price range, each open house should have a property brief of the other open house(s) and maps showing how to get from one property to the other.

Some agents advertise an open-house "Lotto" where a visitor to one house gets a card and a sticker. Another sticker is given at each additional home visited. If all the homes are visited, the visitor is awarded a gift such as a baseball cap (with the firm's name).

FIGURE 7.12

Visitor Rating Form

Visitor Rating

Property _____

Your name _____ Phone _____

Address _____ e-mail _____

Date _____

I am visiting this open house because of ☐ Advertising

　　☐ Signs　　☐ Other (specify): _____

_____

Features I particularly like: _____

_____

_____

Features I do not like: _____

_____

_____

_____

I believe the price quoted is: ☐ Low ☐ About right ☐ High

My reason for visiting is: _____

_____

Do you presently own your home? _____ Is it currently for sale? _____

General comments: _____

_____

_____

☐ I would like to receive e-mails, with pictures, of new listings.

Servicing Buyer's Agency Agreements

While normally keeping in touch with buyers is not a problem, prospective buyers you were unsuccessful in helping should not be forgotten, even if you don't have an agency agreement with them.

It is a good idea to send e-mails or letters at least once a week on new listings. Provide Web site information for viewing or send property briefs. At least every two weeks you should contact the prospects by phone and ask for their comments about properties presented. If positive, set up a showing. It is not uncommon for some buyers to spend months looking for a home. While this could be the fault of the salespersons, some people are just procrastinators when it comes to a final decision. Keep working and help them decide.

■ THE OFFER AND BEYOND

Servicing the listing actually includes your communication and efforts from obtaining an offer to purchase through the close of escrow. This aspect of servicing the listing is included within Chapter 11, "From Offer to Closing."

■ SUMMARY

In this chapter you learned that honest and complete agent-owner communication, even when the communication is not good news, is better than a breakdown of communication. Owners want and deserve to know what is happening.

Owner-agent communications start with the listing. Owners should know when they will be seeing you again and why. The purpose of your next visit probably will be a postlisting meeting, when you will inform them what you will be doing, including your marketing plan, and what you expect of them.

The owners should understand the instructions given them and the reasons for those instructions. Owners who do not understand why an instruction is given and that it is given for their best interests are not likely to follow the instruction.

The owners should understand that they will be receiving weekly activity reports about what is happening. Let owners know that if they have any questions or suggestions, they can contact you.

Owners who understand the showing procedure will realize the need to be prepared for showings at short notice.

Owners should not expect to see ads on their home in the paper each day. They should realize that by advertising other houses agents are bringing in calls about a wide range of properties. After buyers are qualified, it often is determined that a house other than the one inquired about better meets the needs of prospective buyers.

Obtaining neighborhood information from the owners furnishes your office with the special ammunition necessary to give prospective buyers that last little nudge that results in a sale. Knowledge about the neighbors, similar interests, ages of children, and even employment can make a home more desirable to buyers.

Should an agent leave an office, the broker should immediately notify the owners of his or her listings and establish a new contact person to meet with the owners as soon as possible.

If a listing needs to be modified for any reason, let the owners know and meet with them. If you made a mistake in pricing, admit it and show the owners what it should be. If conditions have changed since the owners gave their listing, show them the changes along with your recommendations.

If you feel a modification is necessary in order to find buyers and the owners will not accept the modification, ask to be relieved of the listing. This powerful approach will often serve to convince owners to accept your recommendations. If you do give back the listing, chances are you got rid of a liability, not an asset.

Go to owners for an extension before a listing expires. Review what you have done for them. If you have used diligent effort on behalf of the owners and have communicated with them, you will have a good chance of obtaining an extension.

The owners should understand your marketing plan, a plan that likely begins with a For Sale sign. A rider strip showing your evening phone number can give you additional calls. A rider strip for a particularly desirable feature such as "four bedrooms" will increase the sign's effectiveness.

Talking signs are radio transmitters. The sign outside directs owners to tune to a station number. The signs, usually the property of the listing agent, are an excellent listing tool.

A number of information boxes are available that can be attached to For Sale signs. They are used to hold brochures or property briefs on the property being sold. They are an effective tool to interest prospective buyers.

The lockbox, if appropriate, should be attached as soon as possible after the listing is taken. New electronic lockboxes can provide you with information about all persons who used the lockbox.

Take photographs of the property listed as soon as the proper light is available. They will be needed for the MLS, property briefs, office display boards, window displays, and Internet presentations.

Post the property on your Internet site as well as on other sites as soon as possible. If you prepare a virtual reality tour, take proper pictures of the property.

Get the listing information to your MLS as soon as possible. Prepare a property brief within a day or two of taking a listing. Also prepare advertisements for placement.

Prepare owners for the office caravan, showing the property to agents from your office. Ask agents to complete an agent property evaluation so you can provide the owners with the reactions of other professionals. The owners should also be prepared for an MLS caravan of agents from other offices. If possible, the listing agent should be at the property during the caravan period.

Immediate interest in the listing can be obtained by direct mail or telephone calls to neighbors asking them for help in finding a buyer and by all agents going through their files for likely buyers.

An agent open house is another way to bring agents into the property. By offering food and drinks at the end of the day, many agents will come to these open houses.

Regular open houses must be prepared for in the same manner as a caravan showing. The open house can serve as a source of listings and a source of buyers for other properties as well as for the open-house property.

Servicing the listing extends all the way until close of escrow. It is a process whereby you plan, work your plan, and communicate.

■ CLASS DISCUSSION TOPICS

1. Prepare a marketing plan with dates from the listing for a single-family home. (Use the following assumptions: The owner is highly motivated to sell, and the property is listed at a price below those of most comparable properties; however, there have been few recent sales in the area.)

2. Prepare a property brief for a specific property.

3. Complete CAR Form MT-11, Modification of Terms: Authorization and Right to Sell, Acquire or Rent, showing a new sales price and an extension period.

4. Visit one open house held by another office. Discuss how it was held and what suggestions you would make for the agent (if any).

5. Discuss any property you know of that you feel is not being properly marketed. Be prepared to justify your recommendations.

6. Bring to class one current-events article dealing with some aspect of real estate practice for class discussion.

■ CHAPTER 7 QUIZ

1. The reason that an expired listing was not extended with the original listing office most likely is dissatisfaction with
   a. the commission percentage.
   b. communications.
   c. price.
   d. the length of listing.

2. Agent advice to owners on showing their home would not include
   a. instructions to be present so they can volunteer information.
   b. cleaning instructions.
   c. landscaping instructions.
   d. repair instructions.

3. When there has been little, if any, interest in a property, the listing salesperson should
   a. convey this information.
   b. tell the owner the property is priced 10 percent too high.
   c. wait until there is something good to report.
   d. tell the owner that you are expecting an offer.

4. In explaining your advertising policy you want owners to understand that
   a. you can't afford to advertise their property if the ads fail to create interest.
   b. you just have so many dollars to spend advertising a great many properties.
   c. advertising other similar properties will attract prospects for their property.
   d. the bulk of your advertising budget is for homes that have reduced prices.

5. You want owners to give you neighborhood information to
   a. keep the owners busy.
   b. give your listings a competitive advantage.
   c. use it to get more listings.
   d. None of the above

6. An owner should understand that reducing a list price to the CMA value
   a. increases the likelihood of a sale.
   b. does not mean that an owner is giving up anything.
   c. Both a and b
   d. Neither a nor b

7. If possible, you should place a rider strip on your listing signs that shows
   a. your fax number.
   b. all your professional designations.
   c. a home phone number as your evening number.
   d. all of the above.

8. A property brief should not be used as a
   a. handout at open houses.
   b. substitute for newspaper advertising.
   c. handout at caravans.
   d. mailing piece to answer inquiries.

9. An agent open house is of greatest value when the property
   a. is in a large market with many agents.
   b. has unusual features making it difficult to sell.
   c. has a very limited use.
   d. has been reduced in price.

10. Advantages of open houses include
    a. pleasing owners because they indicate activity.
    b. locating buyers for other property.
    c. obtaining leads for listings.
    d. all of the above.

CHAPTER EIGHT

ADVERTISING

■ KEY TERMS

AIDA approach
annual percentage rate
bait-and-switch
  advertising
blind ads
business card
car sign
CD business cards

classified advertising
company dollar
direct mail
display advertising
institutional advertising
media choice
name tag
newsletters

operational advertising
outdoor advertising
press releases
specialty gifts
specific advertising
Truth-in-Lending Act

■ LEARNING OBJECTIVES

In this chapter you learn the importance of advertising to the real estate industry and about the AIDA advertising approach of Attention, Interest, Desire, and Action, as well as some basic advertising guidelines. You gain insight into the use of the primary media for real estate advertising and learn about preparing classified ads for newspapers and the Internet. You are shown the importance of being able to evaluate the effectiveness of your advertising as well as the means of evaluation. You also are alerted to the legal implications of real estate advertising.

■ ADVERTISING OBJECTIVES

Advertising is the process of calling peoples' attention to something to arouse a desire to buy or to obtain more information about the product or service being promoted. The real estate industry could not exist without advertising. In addition to advertising products for lease or sale, the real estate industry also advertises for sellers and for salespeople. You will see that real estate advertising takes many forms.

Real estate advertising may be divided into two major types: institutional advertising and specific advertising. These two categories describe the two goals of real estate advertising.

Institutional advertising attempts to create a favorable image of the real estate company, the broker, and the salesperson. It keeps the company's name in the public eye and aims to inspire trust, confidence, and goodwill. Institutional advertising, often done by organized groups having similar interests, manifests pride in and respect for the real estate business. Individual brokers may be required to share some of the costs incurred in this type of advertising.

Specific advertising, also called **operational advertising,** is concerned with immediate results. It describes a particular piece of property and stimulates activity in a specific property or an entire tract of homes. In specific advertising, a broker's advertisements are in direct competition with the advertisements of other brokers.

■ THE AIDA APPROACH TO ADVERTISING

The most common, and probably most important, reason for advertising is to find ready, willing, and able buyers for your sale listings. All the listings in the world will do you no good unless someone finds a ready, willing, and able buyer and makes that elusive sale.

Why do people buy? Prospective purchasers will buy a particular piece of property for the benefits it offers. The most fundamental benefit is shelter, but the property also might provide other things that are important—security, good schools, convenience, recreation, prestige, and a lot more. The purpose of advertising is to communicate these benefits through the property's features—its price, size, location, and so on.

If an ad is to be read and thus attract buyers, it usually must be designed to grab the reader's Attention, stimulate his or her Interest, generate a Desire, and lead the reader to Action. This is commonly referred to as the **AIDA approach,** from an acronym made up of the first letter of each step involved.

- ■ Attention—The first step in any type of advertising is to gain attention. *Attention getters* include headlines that use words and word combinations as well as typefaces and layouts that attract prospective buyers and encourage them to read further. You might gain attention with color, movement, message, sound, or even something odd or out of place, such as a misspelled word or an outrageous statement. It could even be humor. Whatever is used, you cannot get a message across until you have gained the attention of the intended recipient of the message.

- Interest—The ad should arouse interest in the specific product or service offered. Probably one of the best ways to arouse interest is through curiosity. Curiosity can be stimulated by ensuring that the ad allows the reader to imagine using and enjoying the benefits of the product or service.

- Desire—Once the reader's attention is attracted and his or her interest is aroused, the ad can create desire by appealing to the senses and emotions. At this stage, language must be clear and concise and inspire the reader's confidence. Wherever possible, the advertising should try to build mental images and picture the reader as the final recipient of the product or service.

- Action—Finally, the ad should move readers to take action. The advertisement should be directed toward helping readers make a decision, to convince them that they want to know more. The action desired by a real estate advertisement is either a phone call, e-mail, or fax to you or your office or an actual visit to your office, an open house or a project, or a visit to your Web site for pictures and more information. If an ad fails to evoke action from a recipient of the message, then, to that person, the ad is really institutional in nature. It helps in name identification and general goodwill, but has failed to bring in a prospective buyer.

The **AIDA** approach: Attention, Interest, Desire, Action

■ ADVERTISING GUIDELINES

There are five basic tenets of advertising:

1. Advertise the right property.
2. Know when to advertise.
3. Choose the right market.
4. Use the proper media.
5. Use correct advertising techniques.

Obviously, a real estate office cannot advertise all its listings at the same time, so the advertising strategy has to be based on accomplishing certain objectives. For example, if you are trying to generate a great number of prospects, consider the listings that have the greatest general appeal.

We know that buyers responding to a real estate advertisement actually are likely to buy a property other than the property advertised. For this reason we strive to advertise properties in areas and/or price ranges where we also have other available properties. This tactic increases the likelihood that prospects who respond to advertisements will become buyers.

Knowing when to advertise, whom you want to reach, and the features to emphasize is extremely important. You probably would not feature a swimming pool in an advertisement for a home in northern California at the beginning of a cold winter; a fireplace would be a more appropriate feature. Likewise, you would probably avoid advertising an elegant, expensive home in a local newspaper that is distributed primarily to low-income families.

Choosing Advertising Media

In determining **media choice,** the advertiser must begin with three basic considerations:

1. The target audience to be reached
2. The message to be conveyed
3. The money available for media purchases

This means that in addition to determining what to say, the broker must evaluate which medium or combination of media will deliver the maximum number of potential customers for the expenditure the broker can afford.

Because the message cannot contribute to sales until prospective buyers are exposed to it, the message must be delivered within sight or earshot of such prospects. The various advertising media perform the delivery function.

Media choices available include the following:

- Personal advertising
- Newspapers
- General circulation daily
- General circulation weekly
- Weekly throwaway
- Foreign language and ethnic
- Special interest (such as mobile-home news)
- Magazines
- Area magazines
- Special interest publications
- Homebuyer magazines
- Radio
- Television
- Outdoor advertising
- Signs

- Direct mail
- Newsletters
- Telephone directories
- Press releases
- Specialty gifts
- Internet

When choosing the medium, keep in mind that the objective is not necessarily to reach the largest number of people but to reach the greatest number of potential prospects at the least possible cost.

In determining the media to be used, ask yourself the following two questions:

1. What are my marketing goals?
   - To get more sale listings?
   - To attract more potential buyers?
   - To increase market share?
   - To enhance recognition of name?
   - To enhance recognition of professionalism?
   - To sell listed properties?
2. Which specific media will reach my target audience

Personal Advertising

Personal advertising should start with a **name tag** identifying you as a real estate professional. The tag should be readable from at least six feet away. Preferably, it should use the same color as your office signs and business cards. If you are a REALTOR®, REALTOR® should be on your name tag. If you have achieved a significant professional designation, such as GRI, this also should be on your name tag.

> Personal advertising concentrates on you, rather than your firm.

Your personal advertising should include your **business card.** You want people to be able to identify your card among a group of cards. The easiest way to accomplish this is with your photograph on the card. As stated in Chapter 1, your card should include your e-mail address, fax number, and cellular telephone number. If you have foreign language skills and feel they are important in your work, your card should indicate those skills.

Because of the amount of information that you may require, you might consider a foldout card.

CD business cards are CD-ROM cards that can be shaped like a normal business card. A CD business card can be inserted in any CD-ROM drive. The CD business card can contain more than just normal business card information. It can feature your current inventory with pictures and descriptions, e-brochures, virtual tours, and even videos. The CD business card should include direct links to your Web site. CD business cards are easy to make and update. A number of firms sell do-it-yourself kits such as *www.impactbuilder.com.* CD business cards can also be printed. They are presented in a vinyl sleeve with a label. While they cost from 75¢ each to about $1 each in quantities of 100, many agents have found them to be effective and their use within the real estate profession has rapidly increased.

A magnetic **car sign** is a good low-cost advertising tool. Include your name, the name of your firm, REALTOR® (if applicable), and firm logo (a firm-identifying design). The logo should appear in all advertisements, signs, cards, and so forth.

Some agents have their own Internet sites that include personal information as well as information on property they are offering, frequently with links to other sites. Because salespersons in 100 percent commission offices act much like independent brokers, it makes sense for such agents to have their own Internet sites.

It is a good idea to print out copies of your resume with your photograph. You can give them to prospective buyers and sellers as well as use them as an enclosure with mailings (both snail mail and e-mail).

Newspaper Advertising

Newspapers are the oldest advertising medium in the nation and the keystone of the real estate business. Although the first advertisement appeared in the *Boston Newsletter* in 1704, newspapers were rather scarce until 1790. From that point on, growth was rapid; today in the United States more than 50 million newspapers are sold each day, and more than 9,000 different newspapers are published every week.

Newspapers have a degree of audience selectivity. Because of their wide circulation, they may be considered to have extensive coverage. They also have time-and-place flexibility and are especially important for local advertising. Because of their tremendous circulation, newspapers reach all classes of consumers and are considered by most licensees to be one of the more effective mediums. One of the drawbacks of newspaper advertising is that its effective life span is short.

Newspaper advertising is divided into classified and display advertisements. Any newspaper ad should provide a broker name, phone number, and Internet address. Advertisements that do not identify the advertiser as a broker are called **blind ads** and are illegal in California.

Classified Advertisements.   All forms of newspaper advertising are important, but the most common form used in the real estate business is still **classified advertising.**

More than half of the average broker's advertising budget is presently spent on classified ads. The reason? Classified advertising is effective. Most people who are interested in buying or leasing real estate check the classifieds.

The largest portion of a broker's advertising dollar is likely to be spent on classified ads.

Keep in mind that your classified advertisements will be in direct competition with many other ads. A mediocre ad generally means mediocre response. Strive for ads that achieve maximum effectiveness by analyzing likely buyers for a property and appealing to those buyers' needs.

Your classified ad should indicate an Internet address that offers more information and/or additional properties: "More information and properties *www.seeahome.com*" or "Property Tour, *www.seeahome.com*" are examples. People who find attractive properties on the Internet feel that they played an active role in a home search rather than a passive role where a salesperson decided which homes they were going to see. When a prospective buyer "discovers" a property, the chances of an actual offer are enhanced.

Classified ads are read by willing readers looking for property. Therefore, the best heading would be the most desirable feature of the property: "No Down Payment," "4 Bedrooms," "Beverly Hills," or even price, such as "$97,500." (However, you would not waste an ad heading such as "Beverly Hills" if the newspaper classification was for "Beverly Hills Property.")

Figure 8.1 includes examples of ads with headings that cover one or more of a home's prime attractions shown were taken from *The Big Book of Real Estate Ads–1001 Ads That Sell,* William H. Pivar and Bradley A. Pivar, Dearborn™ Real Estate Education, Chicago, 2004.

When you don't have a super feature to advertise or there are a great many competing ads, consider an attention-grabbing heading to make your ad stand out from the others. Figure 8.2 includes examples of such ads.

Advertisements normally tell us how good a product is. An ad that listed faults of a product could be expected only from an advertiser with a death wish. Real estate, however, is different. Ads for fixer-upper property often result in an exceptional response. A likely reason is that a property with problems spells opportunity to a great many buyers. The worse you make a property appear, the greater the response. Figure 8.3 includes fixer-upper type ads. Before you use ads of this type, however, obtain the owners' permission in writing. Many owners will become upset if you degrade or make fun of their home, even if it brings in a buyer.

Adjectives.   The use of adjectives to paint word pictures of features can enhance the readers' interest. It generally is false economy to write bare-bones ads in a competitive market. Often an ad that is 20 percent longer because of the use of adjectives earns a response rate that far outweighs the 20 percent higher ad cost. A response increase exceeding 100 percent is not uncommon.

Adjectives add desirability to ads.

FIGURE 8.1

Sample Ads

Westlake

You can own a like-new, 3BR, 2½-bath Tennessee Colonial with all the fine detailing and craftsmanship you thought had been forgotten. A 2½-car garage, central air, a family room and a prestigious

WESTLAKE

address are yours for just $487,500

UR
HOME REALTY
555-8200
www.ur-home.net

You can call attention to location by using a split heading, which is effective for a highly desirable area.

Spanish Omelet

Arches, tile and huge beams combine to make this 3-bedroom, 2-bath, West Side masterpiece a very tasty dish at

$579,500

Special features include family room, 3-car garage, central air, delightful fenced yard and giant Norway pine. One look and we will put up the "sold" sign.

UR
HOME REALTY
555-8200
www.ur-home.net

The split heading features architectural style and price.

Southport under $200,000

Imagine owning a 2-bedroom bungalow in the most prestigious area on a huge lot at a price within your reach. Get ready to be envied if you call today.

UR
HOME REALTY
555-8200
www.ur-home.net

It isn't necessary to give the exact price. The ad emphasizes location.

Beverly Hills Address

and a 3BR, 2-bath American Colonial with family room and double garage are available but

Without the Price.

That's right. The most impressive address imaginable at only $795,000.

UR
HOME REALTY
555-8200
www.ur-home.net

This ad sells the home's address, not the home itself. You can also use the name of a prestigious street or subdivision.

FIGURE 8.2

Sample Ads

Maxine and Marvin Slept Here

for 10 years, but Marvin was transferred to Phoenix, so they must regretfully take their bed and leave this 3BR, 2-bath, red brick Georgian Colonial in the nicest area in all of Woodland Glen. The home features a tantalizing Jacuzzi tub in the master bath, which is why the shower is practically new; walk-in closets; music room for little Ralph, who is learning to play the drums; and a kitchen any chef would fry for. Priced to get Maxine and Marvin on their way at $337,500.

UR
HOME REALTY

555-8200
www.ur-home.net

Who Used the Tub?

We suspect Mr. Buckley of our office has been bathing in the Italian marble tub in the sumptuous master bath of this 3BR, 2½-bath Italian Renaissance estate in Westhaven. Every afternoon he visits the house and takes along a towel. When he returns, he's singing Italian arias. When you see the tantalizing Roman baths, you'll want to join him. The estate has an aura of elegance that makes you want to pamper yourself. With more than 3,500 sq. ft. of sheer luxury and almost a half-acre of grounds, this is your chance to be good to yourself for $649,500. After all, who deserves it more?

UR
HOME REALTY

555-8200
www.ur-home.net

The above heading is a real attention getter.

Lady Saxophone Player

must sell her 3BR, cedarshake, Westfield Cape Cod in order to seek fame and fortune. There is a garage, several magnificent hickory trees, a family of squirrels, a somewhat neglected garden and a kitchen big enough to seat an 8-piece band. The price hits a pleasant note at $329,500.

UR
HOME REALTY

555-8200
www.ur-home.net

Before you feature an owner in your ad, obtain the owner's permission to run the ad.

FIGURE 8.2

Sample Ads (continued)

A Curious Raccoon

watched as we put up the For Sale sign on this 3BR, 2-bath sprawling brick ranch home just 20 minutes from the city. The home features big-city conveniences; large, bright rooms; central air; a quiet den; and a rose brick fireplace with the added charm of rural America. You will love the miles of trails, trees, wild animals and friendly neighbors (both 2- and 4-legged). Set on 3 acres all your own, this is the chance to make all your labors worthwhile. $287,500.

UR
HOME REALTY
555-8200
www.ur-home.net

We Lost Charlie

He went to show this older 8-room Colonial on 2 lovely wooded acres last week, and we haven't heard from his since. While the rooms are large, we should have found him by now. The office took up a collection, and we're offering a reward of $39. Oh, unless Charlie sold it, the house is still available at $289,500, but please return Charlie if you find him.

UR
HOME REALTY
555-8200
www.ur-home.net

The ad is of course a spoof to sell a large, older home at a reasonable price. It is designed to prompt readers to call for more information about the house, not Charlie.

"Love"
in the Afternoon

You have your choice of 6 courts as the owner of this 3BR, 2-bath, Southwest Contemporary, single-family home in Hidden Palms Estates. A home that has it all: family room, 3-car garage, soaring ceilings, every conceivable built-in, plus friendly neighbors in a premier gate-guarded community. It will be first come, first served at $397,500.

UR
HOME REALTY
555-8200
www.ur-home.net

Again, this ad is an attention getter.

FIGURE 8.2

Sample Ads (continued)

Ralph Washington Slept Here

It is reputed that Ralph, no relation to George, spent at least 1 night in this new, 3BR, 2-bath Colonial while it was under construction. Despite Ralph's brief occupancy, the home turned out extremely well. The wood floors and trim; used-brick fireplace with a mantle made from an ancient beam; and brick, copper, and tile family kitchen all add a feeling of gentle warmth. You'll love the bay windows and the family room that opens onto your own wooded grove. Of course, all the amenities are present, such as air-conditioning, a 2½-car garage, and a full basement awaiting your finishing touches. After Ralph, you can be the second person to sleep here for $397,500. This moment in history is brought to you by

UR
HOME REALTY
555-8200
www.ur-home.net

This ad is a takeoff on ads used by some brokers on historic homes.

The Collie Next Door

hopes the new owners of this 3BR, 1½-bath, split-level in Washington Heights have a friendly dog to share her trees with and to gossip through the back fence. By the way, besides a fully fenced yard the home offers several large trees of its own, a lovely flower garden (perfect for burying bones), a double garage, a fireplace to cuddle up by, a large room for romping and a country kitchen with the biggest refrigerator you ever saw (perfect for storing bones). The friendly owner priced it at $249,500, so pick up the phone and give a "whoof" to

UR
HOME REALTY
555-8200
www.ur-home.net

Ansel Adams

loved these majestic mountains framed through the walls of glass in this Colorado Contemporary. The view comes complete with 3 bedrooms, 2½ baths, a 30-foot family room opening onto a deck with a stone barbecue and just about every convenience known to man. The view goes on forever, but at $449,500 your opportunity is right now.

UR
HOME REALTY
555-8200
www.ur-home.net

This ad is targeted at a buyer likely to recognize the name of Ansel Adams, world-renowned photographer known for his mountain vistas.

FIGURE 8.3

Sample Fixer-Upper Ads

A Monument to Bad Taste

If you have more money than taste, you'll love this gaudy French Provincial with Italianate influence, finished to excess in a sort of baroque style. There are 11 huge rooms, all equally ugly. It does command a premier West Hills location, offering every conceivable amenity; but while you might like to visit, you wouldn't want to live here. Mr. Clements of our office, a former Edsel owner, thinks it's beautiful—just the way he imagines a movie star's home to be. It's priced far below reproduction costs at $489,000, but then who would want to reproduce it?

UR
HOME REALTY
555-8200
www.ur-home.net

As strange as it may seem, this ad will bring in calls from qualified buyers.

Decorator's Nightmare

Leprous yellow walls, jarring purple accents, and blood-red tile are just a few of the features in this 3-bedroom Dutch Colonial that prove money and good taste aren't synonymous. This appears structurally sound, and it does offer an excellent West Side location as well as an attractive exterior and landscaping. The price reflects the poor taste of the decorator—$269,500.

UR
HOME REALTY
555-8200
www.ur-home.net

This ad is a variation on the fixer-upper ad. Be certain you have the owner's permission before you comment negatively on the decorating.

It Could Be Worse

The roof doesn't appear to leak, but just about everything else in this 3BR, 2-bath, brick English Tudor in Westwood is in need of mending. While it has expansive lawns, hedges and flower beds, you'll have to imagine how it will look trimmed without the weeds and bare spots and with flowers blooming. If you love to tinker, you have enough work for a lifetime. The only redeeming feature is the price, $239,500.

UR
HOME REALTY
555-8200
www.ur-home.net

Yuk! This Place Is Unbelievable

This 3-bedroom, West Side American Traditional appears to have been neglected from the day it was built. It will take a semi to haul away the junk in the backyard. Perhaps under all that dirt you may find shining spendor, but don't count on it. But then for $89,500, what do you expect?

UR
HOME REALTY
555-8200
www.ur-home.net

This was adapted from an ad by Ian Price, Surfer's Paradise, Australia.

As an example of how descriptive words can paint an image, consider how you could describe a bathroom to paint a picture for the reader:

> Sumptuous master bath, sensuous master bath, sinfully sensuous master bath, deliciously sumptuous bath, Roman bath, Phoenician bath, Grecian bath, garden tub, antique claw-footed tub, opulent Phoenician bath, sky-lit bath, enchanting garden bath, and so forth.

You can see that adjectives can bring a desired image to the reader, so use them.

Large Circulation Papers.   The greater a paper's circulation, the higher the cost of advertising. It doesn't take many large classified ads in the *Los Angeles Times* to use up the advertising budget of many firms. You can use a relatively short ad to perk a reader's interest to check further on the Internet. Here are examples:

Lazy Owner Condo ($189,500) Not a thing to do in this like-new 2 BR unit in Westhaven. See why—check #48 at **UR** H O M E R E A L T Y **555-8200** *www.ur-home.net*	**Herman Didn't Know** that he could buy a 3 BR Home with less than $2,000 down. Full price— $174,500. See what Herman missed at #50 at **UR** H O M E R E A L T Y **555-8200** *www.ur-home.net*

Many single office real estate brokers avoid large newspapers, such as the *Los Angeles Times*, because so much of the circulation is beyond the brokers' market area. They attempt to target their areas by advertising in smaller circulation papers that are local in scope.

Display Advertisements.   **Display advertising** may be either institutional or operational in nature. It may combine the two, so that it is used primarily to build goodwill and prestige and keep the name before the public, while at the same time advertising specific property. We suggest you include in all display ads an Internet address that can offer additional information.

Because of costs, display ads are primarily used for selling developments rather than single homes. An exception would be newspapers in smaller communities offering lower advertising costs. Consider obtaining professional help for display advertisements.

General Rules for Display Advertising

- Most people read from the upper left corner to the lower right corner. Therefore, the ad should be composed with the heading on top, illustration and copy in the center, and firm name and phone number in the lower right quarter.

- One large picture is generally more effective than several small pictures.

- If reproduced well, photographs may be more effective than drawings, but most photographs require professional retouching to increase contrast, remove distracting features, and blur backgrounds.

- Include white space. White space emphasizes the message.

- Don't use more than two typefaces in an ad.

- Ads in the outside columns will generate more interest than ads in the inside columns.

- Typefaces with serifs (the fine lines at the end of letter strokes) are generally more readable than sans-serif typefaces (without the lines).

- Lowercase letters are easier to read than capital letters.

- Short sentences are more readable than long sentences.

- Short words are more readable than long words.

- If you pull the reader through the first three lines, he or she is likely to read the entire ad.

- Use words that are readily understood.

- Don't be too subtle or sophisticated.

- Always tell the reader what to do (call, come in, or check the Internet).

- Always use the same logo in your ads.

Magazine Advertising

The cost of advertising in a magazine having mass appeal generally is prohibitive. However, magazines appealing to special-interest groups could be productive for the right property. As an example, if you had 40 acres zoned for a salvage yard with railroad siding access, you might consider advertising it in a trade magazine for salvage yard operators.

Special city or area magazines are usually slick paper magazines with very limited circulation. They are likely to be most effective for very impressive homes.

Area homebuyer magazines are found in most areas of California. These magazines are particularly effective for newcomers to the area. There are variations of these magazines that cover just new home developments and rentals.

Similar to homebuyer magazines, e-brochures are for the Internet. They can be sent as e-mails or included on a CD business card. Software to prepare e-brochures can also be used to prepare printed brochures. You might want to check *www.inprev.net* for more information.

Radio and TV Advertising

Compared with print media, radio broadcasting is a relatively new advertising medium. The first paid advertisement on radio appeared in 1922. Today radio can reach, at one time or another, nearly 99 percent of the households in the United States. Customers can be reached traveling to and from work, to and from the market, at the beach, or in their own homes. It can be effective because the audience can listen to it while doing something else.

In using radio advertising, match the property with the demographics of those who listen to the station. Unless you hope to sell a multimillion-dollar estate to a rock star, don't advertise it on a hard-rock station.

Television delivers advertising messages to both the eye and the ear. What is more, it permits the use of motion and color and usually delivers the message in the home.

Television advertising, however, is expensive, and it is used sparingly for general real estate advertising. It is used most often by large real estate firms, franchisers, and developers.

Home showcase programs are becoming popular on television. These generally are used for more spectacular homes. However, there are other aspects to television advertising. There are cable stations that have 24-hour bulletin boards of things for sale. Some brokers have reported excellent responses to using these bulletin-board stations for low-cost and low-down-payment homes as well as rentals.

Outdoor Advertising

Outdoor advertising is used less frequently than other media, depending largely on the size of the town and the availability of advertising billboards. Usually, billboards are used by larger brokerage offices or chain operations. However, signs may be painted on buildings, fences, bus-stop benches, or other places by individual real estate offices as well.

Because of their cost, which can be several thousand dollars per month, depending on features and location, the real estate use of billboards has been primarily for large new developments.

For Sale Signs

The design of a licensee's For Sale signs should be unique, original, quickly informative, and as attractive as possible. The attention-getting value of the signs will be enhanced through the use of color, unique design, an identifiable logo, and type and size of print. Rather than plain paint for your For Sale signs, consider reflective paint that stands out when light hits the sign. A new twist is a glowin-the-dark paint that remains bright for several hours after dusk. (Your sign firm should be able to offer this product.)

Colors used should provide a high degree of contrast for readability (the best color contrast is yellow and black). To distinguish their signs from those of competitors, some brokers have changed the shape of their signs. A simple change is a vertical rectangle rather than a horizontal one. Others have gone to oversized signs or odd-shaped signs. Whatever their makeup, signs should be coordinated with any printed material being created for the office. Riders for special features or for listing a salesperson's name and phone number and even an Internet address should be considered. (Talking signs and sign information boxes were covered in Chapter 7.)

> Your sign should be distinguishable from that of your competition.

Direct Mail

Although **direct-mail** advertising is rather expensive per contact, it can be an effective way to reach a selected audience. It may be institutional in nature or be designed to promote a new subdivision, an area, even a specific piece of property. Various vehicles are used in this method of advertising, including pamphlets, brochures, letters, postcards, booklets, pictures, and maps. You can spread the word about new listings with regularly scheduled direct targeted mail using readily available merge software.

This medium may encourage the reader to seek more information by returning a response device that may result in additional material and inclusion in mailing lists and other sales promotions. Another effective approach is to follow up the mailing with a telephone call. Of course, every direct mail piece should reference your firm's Web site. Direct-mail approaches were more fully discussed in Chapter 4.

Direct e-mail

We have shown you one way to obtain e-mail addresses of prospects with the visitor rating form in Chapter 7 (pg 220). We will be showing you more ways to have prospects willingly provide their e-mail addresses. The beauty of a direct approach with e-mail is the fact that except for preparation time, it is a no-cost approach. Direct approach e-mails can include colored pictures, movement (motion), and even sound. You can e-mail a zip code by utilizing mailing list firms that also have e-mail addresses. Like any other advertising, you want your direct mail and e-mail ads to stand out from the commonplace.

Newsletters

Many offices, as well as individual agents, successfully use **newsletters.** They include information that would be of interest to the recipient as well as information about the firm or agent. They are particularly valuable in niche marketing. As an example, one agent who has established her niche in marketing mobile homes in a particular park has a monthly newsletter that includes personal information about residents and information on new residents and club schedules, as well as special events. Computer programs and services are available that will allow you to quickly publish a quality newsletter.

Telephone Directories

Although real estate firms have yellow-page listings, often in bold type, display ads in telephone directories are not likely to be as cost-effective as those in other advertising media. The effectiveness of your yellow-page ad can be increased significantly by use of your Internet address, for example, "View Available Homes *www.seeahome.com.*"

Press Releases

> Press releases are free advertisements.

Press releases are really free advertisements. If you look in the real estate section of any newspaper, you will find that most of the articles are taken from press releases. Your local newspaper will publish press releases that are well-written, typed double-spaced, and have a newsworthy message. Some examples of such messages are the grand opening of an office, the groundbreaking for a development, the listing of a historic building, any sale where the buyers or sellers are newsworthy, special awards or designations received by agents, and office promotions.

Whenever possible, include a glossy 5" x 7" or 8" x 10" photo. Include a caption (taped with masking tape to the bottom of the photo). If people are shown, be sure to identify them in the caption.

Specialty Gifts

Most offices include **specialty gifts,** promotional giveaway items, in their advertising budget. These may include notepads, maps, magnetic holders, calendars, pencils, directories, and pens with a salesperson's and/or firm's identification. Such items promote you or your company continually and can be dispensed through the office, at business and social gatherings, at open houses, and during door-to-door canvassing. They are excellent door openers and can be used effectively to get acquainted in a neighborhood.

The Internet

The Internet is rapidly growing in importance as a marketing tool. Just a few years ago, it was rare to have a transaction where the buyer or seller contact resulted from information contained on an Internet site. Today, some offices are reporting that about 25 percent of their contacts result from Internet postings. Surveys of property buyers reveal that in many areas over 50 percent of buyers indicated that they utilized the Internet for their property search. While there are a great many sites that you can post your listings on, it is extremely important that you have your own office site if you are going to be competitive.

Internet sites have been getting more elaborate, frequently with multiple pictures of each property sound and motion. Virtual reality tours allow a viewer to "walk through" the property; this virtual "walk through" can either half sell the property or eliminate it for a prospective buyer.

One advantage of the Internet is its relatively low cost once the site has been established. However, the Internet cannot be used effectively as a sole advertising medium because buyers and sellers need to know of the existence of the site. Be sure to include your Web address in all your advertising in other media.

Before you prepare a Web site, we recommend you view the Web sites of a number of large brokerage offices in major metropolitan areas across the country. Note the differences in quality of the sites and in site features. Make a note of the features you want in your site as well as why you feel some sites were outstanding. Now you are ready for your Web page preparation.

Features that the authors strongly recommend are the following features:

- *About Us*—The ability of a viewer to obtain information about your firm and its personnel.

- *Inventory*—This should include photos and descriptions of your listings. If there are a great many listings, the viewer should be able to enter parameters such as price, size, and location to zero in on properties. If a property is advertised by number, the viewer should be able to go directly to that property. The inventory should also include ability to increase size of photos as well as view additional photos.

- *Area Map*—This can show the locations of properties.

- *E-mail Offer*—Each page of your site should offer the viewer an opportunity to receive e-mails of new listings before they are advertised.

- *Motion and/or Sound*—These features hold the viewer's attention and will distinguish your site from other sites.

- *Loan Qualifying Opportunity*—This viewer option will provide information on the prospect and will allow further direct contact.

- *800 Telephone Number*—By providing this number, you encourage calls from outside your immediate area.

- *Back to Home Page*—This feature should be on every page of your Web site.

- *Contact Us*—This will allow the viewer to send an e-mail to you.

While agents can prepare their own Web pages using one of the inexpensive Web page programs, these are usually boilerplate sites and fail to provide maximum viewer impact. As previously stated, we strongly suggest that a professional Web page designer create the Web site. A correctly designed Web site can insure long-term use and will attract prospective buyers, sellers, lessors, and lessees.

Other Forms of Advertising

There are many other ways to advertise: movie screens, videotapes, window displays, transit ads, electric message boards, marquee ads, and so on. You will find that your advertising is limited only by the limits of your imagination and the thickness of your pocketbook.

■ ADVERTISING EFFECTIVENESS

Is your advertising program producing the results you want? There is an old saying in advertising: "Half of my advertising is worth the money. The problem is that

I don't know *which* half!" If you don't set up an evaluation system, you will never know. Identifying the part of your advertising dollar that is producing your sales can be critical to success. You must be able to determine which types of advertising are most effective for you and which produce the most income. You can do that by tracking ads and determining their cost relative to the amount of business they generate. We can carry this even farther to discover which approach and/or medium is most effective for a particular type of property.

The key to a good measurement system is *simplicity*. One method to use when you run a newspaper ad or send out a letter or direct-mail piece is to put a code on the bottom of the piece. A simple technique is to use a designated telephone number. Thus, respondents who contact you by a call to that number indicate that they are responding to a particular ad. If possible, try to identify separately for each ad the number of prospects and sales that result, so you will know the quality as well as the quantity of leads you obtain. Then determine the cost of each advertisement. Many offices require that the secretary who handles incoming calls keep telephone logs. The secretary can ascertain the type of ad seen by the caller, and the ad medium, and can enter this information into the log.

> You should evaluate ads for effectiveness.

Just because one medium is not as effective as another in terms of number of responses does not mean the medium is ineffective.

■ **EXAMPLE:** Jane Freyman placed two ads in different newspapers for the same period. The ads were identical. She knew that this was important because she wanted to test which publication worked best. If she used different-quality ads, one would naturally pull better because it was a better ad, not because the publication was better. She ran the ads at the same time for the same reason. The only difference was that the ad in Paper *A* directed people to ask for Department X, whereas the ad in Paper *B* told people to ask for Department Y.

There was a difference in the cost of running the ads. Paper *A* had a circulation of 20,000 and charged $200 for the ad. Paper *B* had a circulation of 100,000 and charged $1,000. The following are the results that Freyman tabulated:

Paper *A*	Paper *B*
15 prospects	27 prospects
5 eventual sales	9 eventual sales

Which paper is a more attractive advertising medium? Does Freyman simply want greater numbers of sales, or does she want to get more sales more cost-effectively?

Assuming that the amounts of the individual sales were comparable, *B* probably would be more attractive to Freyman if she wanted more sales. The ad in *B* generated more eventual sales. However, if Freyman was more interested in cost-effectiveness, she probably would prefer *A*. The sales numbers were smaller, but so were the costs—not only the cost of the ad but also the cost per sale:

$$\$200 \div 5 \text{ sales} = \$40 \text{ per sale}$$
$$\$1,000 \div 9 \text{ sales} = \$110 \text{ per sale}$$

■ LEGAL IMPLICATIONS OF ADVERTISING

Advertising of real property is regulated by the California Real Estate Law, the Regulations of the Real Estate Commissioner, and the Federal Consumer Protection Act (Truth-in-Lending Act).

California
Real Estate Law

Section 10139—"Penalties for Unlicensed Person." This law stipulates that any unlicensed person acting as a licensee who advertises using words indicating that he or she is a broker is subject to a fine not to exceed $1,000 and/or imprisonment in the county jail for a term not to exceed six months. If the violator is a corporation, it is subject to a fine of $10,000.

Section 10140—"False Advertising." This section states that every officer or employee who knowingly advertises a false statement concerning any land or subdivision is subject to a fine of $1,000 and/or one year's imprisonment. In addition, the licensee may have his or her license suspended or revoked.

Section 10140.5—"Disclosure of Name." Each advertisement published by a licensee that offers to assist in filing applications for the purchase or lease of government land must indicate the name of the broker and the state in which he or she is licensed.

Section 10140.6—"False Advertising." A licensee may not publish in any newspaper or periodical or by mail an ad for any activity for which a real estate license is required that does not contain a designation disclosure that he or she is performing acts for which a license is required.

Section 1023—"Misleading Advertisement." A licensee may not advertise, print, display, publish, distribute, televise, or broadcast false or misleading statements regarding rates and terms or conditions for making, purchasing, or negotiating loans or real property sales contracts, nor may a licensee permit others to do so.

Section 10236.1—"Inducements." A licensee may not advertise to offer a prospective purchaser, borrower, or lender any gift as an inducement for making a loan or purchasing a promissory note secured directly by a lien on real property or a real property sales contract.

Section 10131.7—"Mobile-Home Advertising." A licensee is prohibited from engaging in the following activities:

- Advertising a mobile home that is not in an established mobile-home park or is being sold with the land

- Failing to withdraw an advertisement of a mobile home within 48 hours of removal from the market

- Advertising or representing a used mobile home as a new one

- Making a false statement that a mobile home is capable of traveling on California highways

- Falsely advertising that no down payment is required on the sale of a mobile home when in fact one is required

Regulations of the Real Estate Commissioner

The Real Estate Commissioner can adopt regulations that have the same force and intent as law. Two of these regulations follow.

Article 9, Section 2770—"Advertising."   A salesperson may not advertise any service for which a license is required without identifying the name of his or her employing broker.

Article 9, Section 2770.1—"Advertising, License Designation."   Abbreviations such as "bro." and "agt.," referring to "broker" or "agent," are deemed sufficient identification in ads to comply with the Business and Professions Code.

(These legal references are merely condensations of the actual regulations.)

Code of Ethics of the National Association of REALTORS®

Even though the Code of Ethics of the National Association of REALTORS® is a moral code and as such is not enforceable by law, its guidelines are observed by most real estate licensees in the state. Professional courtesy and ethics should not end with those acts that have been sanctioned by law. The individual who tries only to stay on the border of the law may at some time step across that border.

Regarding advertising, Article 19 of the Code of Ethics states

The REALTORS® shall be careful at all times to present a true picture in their advertising and representations to the public.

REALTORS® shall also ensure that their professional status (e.g., broker, appraiser, property manager, etc.) or status as REALTORS® is clearly identifiable in any such advertising.

19-1 REALTORS® shall not offer for sale/lease or advertise property without authority.

19-3 REALTORS®, when advertising unlisted real property for sale/lease in which they have an ownership interest, shall disclose their status as both owners/landlords and REALTORS® or real estate licensees.

19-4 REALTORS® shall not advertise nor permit any person employed by or affiliated with them to advertise listed property without disclosing the name of the firm.

Truth-in-Lending Act

The **Truth-in-Lending Act**, or Regulation Z, a part of the federal Consumers Credit Protection Act of 1968, requires disclosure of credit costs as a percent as well as total finance charges. It is enforced by the Federal Trade Commission.

Truth-in-lending applies to credit extended with a finance charge or credit payable in more than four installments. If the amount or percentage of down payment, the number of payments or period of repayment, or the amount of payment or amount of finance charges (trigger terms) is included in any advertisement, then the ad must include three elements:

1. Amount or percentage of down payment
2. Terms of repayment
3. Annual percentage rate (APR) (the true interest rate considering points and other loan costs; the nominal rate is the rate stated on the note)

Advertising the APR alone will not trigger the above disclosures.

If creditors extend credit secured by a dwelling more than five times per year, they must furnish the purchaser a truth-in-lending disclosure showing all loan facts. However, the total amount of finance charges for the term of the loan need not be shown for first mortgages or loans used to purchase real property. (Because escrow impounds for taxes and insurance are not considered loan costs, they need not be listed.)

Truth-in-lending makes **bait-and-switch advertising** (advertising property that agents don't intend to sell or that is not available in order to attract buyers for other property) a federal offense.

Rescission Right.   If the loan is for consumer credit secured by the borrower's residence, the borrower has the right to reconsider and cancel. This right is valid until midnight on the third business day following loan completion. (Rescission right does not apply to home purchase loans.)

Exemptions.   Loans exempt from all truth-in-lending disclosure requirements are business loans, agricultural loans, construction loans, personal property loans over $25,000, and interest-free loans with four or fewer installments. Nonowner-occupied housing is considered a business and thus exempt from disclosure. Carry-back financing for most sellers (not more than five times per year) also is exempt.

CIVIL RIGHTS ACT OF 1968

The Civil Rights Act of 1968 (see Chapter 2), prohibits discriminatory advertising. Discriminatory advertising includes advertising that indicates any preference, limitation, or discrimination because of race, color, religion, sex, handicap, familial status, or national origin.

There are some discriminatory words and phrases that are not readily recognized by many as being discriminatory. In addition, some words carry different connotations among different social, ethnic, and economic groups. Words also have different meanings based upon geographic location.

A number of groups have tried to clarify what was and was not acceptable wording for advertising by publishing lists. These lists varied greatly. Some lists went so far as to indicate that advertising the "view" was discriminatory to the blind.

While the Department of Housing and Urban Development (HUD) enforces the fair housing act, they were reluctant to provide guidance.

There was a partial clarification on January 9, 1995, when HUD sent a memo to its staff as to guidelines for investigation of discrimination allegations. The memo addressed the following five points:

1. *Race, Color, National Origin.* Complaints should not be filed for use of "master bedroom," "rare find" or "desirable neighborhood." Some groups had felt that "master" indicated slavery and "rare find," and "desirable neighborhood" indicated areas without minorities.

2. *Religion.* Statements such as "apartment complex with chapel" or "services" such as "kosher meals available" do not, on their face, state a preference for persons who might use such facilities. Prior to HUD's memo, groups were advising that any reference in an ad to religion would violate the Federal Fair Housing Act.

3. *Sex.* Use of the term "master bedroom," "mother-in-law suite," and "bachelor apartment" do not violate the act because they are commonly used physical descriptions.

4. *Handicap.* Descriptions of properties such as "great view," "fourth-floor walk-up," and "walk-in closets" do not violate the Act. Services or facilities such as "jogging trails" or references to neighborhoods, such as "walk to bus stop" do not violate the Act.

   Because many handicapped individuals cannot perform these activities, it was formerly thought that references to walking, biking, jogging, and so on would violate the law. It also is acceptable to describe the conduct required of residents such as "nonsmoking" or "sober." You can't, however, say "nonsmokers" or "no alcoholics" because these describe persons, not barred activities. You can advertise accessibility features such as "wheelchair ramp."

5. *Familial Status.* While advertisements may not contain a limitation on the number or ages of children or state a preference for adults, couples or singles, you are not "facially discriminatory" by advertising the properties as "2-BR, cozy, family room," services and facilities with "no bicycles allowed," or neighborhoods with "quiet streets."

The HUD memo still leaves a great deal unanswered, however, HUD seems to indicate that the rule is one of reasonableness. If an ordinary person would feel an ad favored or disfavored a protected group, it would be discriminatory.

Organizations have come up with updated lists that tend to reflect this thinking. The Fair Housing Advertising Word and Phrase List seen in Figure 8.4 was developed by the Miami Valley Fair Housing Center, Inc., Dayton, Ohio (*www.Mvfairhousing.com*). You will note that they have divided the words into categories as *Not Acceptable*, *Caution*, and *Acceptable*.

■ ADVERTISING BUDGET

Every successful real estate office has developed a system for budgeting its expenses. One of the expenses that must be accounted for is advertising. Advertising is one of the most important steps in the marketing of real property, but it does cost money. Soon after starting in the business, the broker will learn that a certain amount of the firm's income dollar must be allocated to this item to maximize returns.

The advertising budget of an office is dictated by the advertising costs within a community as well as by market conditions. As a general rule, the time to increase advertising is when market sales are increasing.

Many offices plan their advertising budget as a percentage of their anticipated income dollar. As an example, a firm might plan to use 20 percent of the office share of commissions (the **company dollar**) for advertising. Because economic changes can be rapid, a budget should be adjusted to reflect market change.

■ SUMMARY

Advertising is the process of calling people's attention to a product or service. The real estate industry could not exist without the ability to disseminate information.

Advertising falls into two broad categories: institutional, which is basically advertising to promote the goodwill of the firm, and specific or operational advertising, to sell or lease a particular property.

The AIDA approach to advertising is basically that an effective ad should gain Attention, Interest the party intended, create Desire, and result in Action.

Advertising really begins with the salesperson's personal advertising that includes a name tag, business cards, and magnetic car signs.

While a broad array of media choices is available, the majority of a firm's advertising budget will be devoted to classified advertising. To be effective, a classified ad must have a highly desirable feature in the heading or else have an attention-getting heading. While negative ads are generally not successful, in real estate they may be very effective. Fixer-upper ads that emphasize what is wrong with a property often receive an exceptional rate of response.

FIGURE 8.4

Advertising Word List

This word and phrase list is intended as a guideline to assist in complying with state and federal fair housing laws. It is not intended as a complete list of every work or phrase that could violate any local, state, or federal statutes.

   This list is intended to educate and provide general guidance to the many businesses in the Miami Valley that create and publish real estate advertising. This is not intended to provide legal advice. By its nature, a general list cannot cover particular

persons' situations or questions. The list is intended to make you aware of and sensitive to the important legal obligations concerning discriminatory real estate advertising.

For additional information, contact the Miami Valley Fair Housing Center at (937) 223-6035. Additional notes are at the bottom of this page. There is also a PDF format version of this list.

Bold = Acceptable	*Italic* = Caution	~~Cross-Though~~ = Not acceptable

A
~~able-bodied~~
Active
~~adult community~~
~~adult living~~
~~adult park~~
~~adults only~~
~~African~~
Agile
~~AIDS, no~~
~~Alcoholics, no~~
~~Appalachian, no~~
~~American Indians~~
~~Asian~~
Assistance animal(s)
Assistance animal(s) only

B
Bachelor
~~Bachelor pad~~
~~Blacks, no~~
~~blind, no~~
board approval

C
Catholic
~~Caucasian~~
~~Chicano, no~~
~~children, no~~
~~Chinese~~
Christian
~~Churches, near~~
Close to
college students, no
~~Colored~~
~~Congregation~~
Convalescent home
Convenient to
~~Couple~~
~~couples only~~
Credit check required
~~crippled, no~~
Curfew

D
~~Deaf, no~~
Den
~~disabled, no~~
domestic quarters
Drug users, no
Drugs, no

E
~~employed, must be~~
~~empty nesters~~
~~English only~~
Equal Housing Opportunity
~~ethnic references~~
Exclusive
Executive

F
~~families, no~~
families welcome
family room
family, great for
*female roommate***
*female(s) only***
*55 and older community**
fixer-upper
gated community

G
Gays, no
Gender
~~golden-agers, only~~
golf course, near
~~group home(s)no~~
guest house

H
handicap accessible
~~handicap parking, no~~
~~Handicapped, not for healthy only~~
~~Hindu, no~~

~~Hispanic~~
~~HIV, no~~
~~housing for older persons/seniors *~~
~~Hungarian, no~~

I
Ideal for . . . (should not describe people)
~~impaired, no~~
~~Indian~~
~~Integrated~~
~~Irish, no~~
~~Italian, no~~

J
Jewish

K
kids welcome

L
Landmark reference
~~Latino~~
Lesbians, no

M
*male roommate***
~~male(s) only***~~
*man(men) only***
Mature
~~mature complex~~
~~mature couple~~
~~mature individuals~~
~~mature person(s)~~
membership available
Membership approval required
~~Mentally handicapped, no~~
~~Mentally ill, no~~
~~Mexican~~
Mexican-American

~~Migrant workers, no~~
~~Mormon Temple~~
Mosque
Mother in law apartment
Muslim

N
Nanny's room
Nationality
Near
~~Negro, no~~
Neighborhood name
~~Newlyweds~~
Nice
non smokers
# of bedrooms
~~# of children~~
# of persons
# of sleeping areas
Nursery
nursing home

O
Older person(s)
~~one child~~
~~one person~~
~~Oriental~~

P
~~Parish~~
perfect for . . . (should not describe people)
pets limited to assistance animals
pets, no
~~Philippine or Filipinos, no~~
~~physically fit~~
~~play area, no~~
~~preferred community~~
Prestigious
Privacy
Private

FIGURE 8.4

Advertising Word List (continued)

Private driveway	**S**	*single woman, man* *	**Townhouse**
Private entrance	*safe neighborhood*	~~singles only~~	~~traditional neighborhood~~
Private property	*school name or school*	*sixty-two and older*	**traditional style**
Private setting	*district*	*community* *	*tranquil setting*
Public transportation	**se habla espanol**	*Smoker(s)no*	*two people*
(near)	**seasonal rates**	**Smoking, no**	
~~Puerto Rican~~	**seasonal worker(s), no**	*Snowbirds**	**U**
	Secluded	**sober**	~~Unemployed, no~~
Q	**section 8 accepted/**	*Sophisticated*	
Quality construction	**welcome**	**Spanish speaking**	**V**
quality neighborhood	*section 8, no*	~~Spanish speaking, no~~	**Verifiable Income**
Quiet	*Secure*	**Square feet**	
Quiet neighborhood	**security provided**	*Straight only*	**W**
	senior adult community *	**student(s)**	*walking distance of, within*
R	*senior citizen(s)* *	*Students, no*	~~Wheelchairs, no~~
references required	~~senior discount~~	~~Supplemental Security~~	~~White~~
~~religious references~~	*senior housing* *	~~Income(SSI), no~~	~~White(s) only~~
Responsible	*senior(s)* *	~~Synagogue, near~~	**winter rental rates**
~~Restricted~~	*sex or gender* **		*winter/summer visitors* *
~~retarded, no~~	~~Shrine~~	**T**	*woman (women) only***
Retirees	**single family home**	~~temple, near~~	
Retirement home	~~single person~~	~~tenant (description of)~~	

* Permitted to be used only when complex or development qualifies as housing for older persons.

** Permitted to be used only when describing shared living areas or dwelling units used exclusively as dormitory
facilities by educational institutions.

All cautionary words are unacceptable if utilized in a context that states an unlawful preference or limitation. Furthermore, all cautionary words are "red flags" to fair housing enforcement agencies. Use of these words will only serve to invite further investigation and/or testing.

It is essential that a firm understand the effectiveness of its advertising. By keeping track of responses, we can learn which medium or approach is most effective for which type of property. This knowledge will allow advertising planning based on past results, not just intuition.

As a licensee you are responsible for knowing the legal implications of real estate advertising. Licensees are prohibited from false, misleading, and discriminatory advertising. Of particular interest is the Truth-in-Lending Act. Besides prohibiting bait-and-switch advertising, advertising the amount or percentage of down payment, the number of payments or the period of repayment, or the amount of payment or the amount of the finance charge will trigger the full-disclosure provision of this law. Certain words may have discriminatory connotations so care must be taken in describing properties.

■ CLASS DISCUSSION TOPICS

1. In addition to a photograph, what other ways can an agent make his or her business card stand out?

2. Prepare two classified ads, one with a feature heading and the other with an attention-getting heading, to sell the home in which you live.

3. Discuss all of the ways a typical real estate office in your area advertises (include both institutional advertising and specific advertising).

4. Check the Internet sites of local brokers. Evaluate the sites as to quality giving your reasons for your evaluation.

5. From the cautionary words shown on the Miami Valley word and phrase list, pick out a word that could be used in both a discriminatory and nondiscriminatory manner and be prepared to give examples.

6. Bring to class one current-events article dealing with some aspect of real estate practice for class discussion.

■ CHAPTER 8 QUIZ

1. The AIDA approach does *not* include
   a. attention.
   b. demand.
   c. interest.
   d. action.

2. Personal advertising includes
   a. name tags.
   b. calling cards.
   c. car signs.
   d. all of the above

3. What does the term *logo* refer to?
   a. Your firm name
   b. An identifying design or symbol
   c. Length of gross opportunity, which refers to the time span of attention generated by an ad
   d. None of the above

4. Blind ads are ads that fail to include
   a. a price.
   b. the address of property.
   c. broker identification.
   d. property specifics.

5. The most cost-effective advertising medium for selling a home likely would be
   a. television.
   b. Internet.
   c. classified newspaper ads.
   d. billboards.

6. Classified ads are different from other forms of real estate advertising because they are
   a. actually sought out by the reader.
   b. ineffective for expensive homes.
   c. less reader-selective than other printed ads.
   d. unemotional.

7. Real estate professionals know that ads that tell about the problems of a property are
   a. a waste of advertising dollars.
   b. likely to give a firm a bad name.
   c. unlikely to attract any calls.
   d. none of the above.

8. An advertiser with an extremely low advertising budget would most likely avoid
   a. press releases.
   b. For Sale signs.
   c. billboards.
   d. the Internet.

9. Which of the following is *false* about display ads?
   a. Readers' eyes tend to move from upper left to lower right.
   b. One large picture is generally more effective than several smaller ones.
   c. Short words are easier to read than long words.
   d. Capital letters are easier to read than lowercase letters.

10. In preparing display ads, a good advertiser should
    a. eliminate as much white space in the ad as possible for maximum effect.
    b. use different logos in different ads to avoid repetition.
    c. use no more than two typefaces in an ad.
    d. avoid using a serif typeface in the text.

CHAPTER NINE

THE BUYER AND THE PROPERTY SHOWING

■ KEY TERMS

back-end qualification	negative motivation	switch property
floor time	prequalify	tie-downs
front-end qualification		

■ LEARNING OBJECTIVES

This chapter takes you from preparing to meet prospective buyers through showing the property. In this chapter you learn

- ■ why a call from a prospective buyer resulting from a sign differs from an inquiry resulting from an ad or from your Web site;

- ■ how to turn inquiries into firm appointments as well as how to overcome prospects' attempts to obtain the address so they can just drive by the property;

- ■ a simple technique to keep prospects from calling other agents after they call you;

■ how to prepare for your first meeting with prospective buyers and how to qualify these prospective buyers regarding needs, motivation, and financial ability;

■ how to use qualifying information in selecting homes to view;

■ that qualifying should be an ongoing process that continues right through to the offer to purchase; and

■ how to effectively show property and set the stage for closing the sale, covered in Chapter 10.

■ THE APPOINTMENT

Your initial buyer contact from advertising generally takes the form of a telephone call. Prospective buyers generally call about ads, For Sale signs, or your Web site picture and description, rather than coming to your office for general information. Your goal regarding the call is not to sell the property—no one *buys* property over the telephone. Your goal is to turn that call into an appointment so you can be in a position in which a sale is possible.

Consider a call a valuable commodity. A telephone inquiry from which you fail to obtain an appointment or, at the very least, the caller's name and telephone number is a total loss of advertising dollars. If you were to compute all office overhead, including advertising, and divide that monthly figure by the number of telephone inquiries your office receives in the month, you would understand how much it really costs to bring in each inquiry. Wasting a telephone inquiry might well be equivalent to throwing a $50 bill into the wind. Good telephone technique reduces the percentage of wasted calls.

Many offices have designated periods of **floor time** where the agents are given inquiries in rotation. If you have floor time, be prepared to turn telephone inquiries into appointments.

Prepare to Receive Telephone Calls

If you are receiving inquiries, have copies of both your own current ads and your office ads from the prior weekend under a plastic protector on your desk. Make notations on the ads so you know what property each ad refers to. Review the listings so the information is fresh in your mind. Also jot down likely **switch property** priced up to 20 percent more or less than the advertised property. In the event you reveal some feature that "turns off" the person inquiring, you need something to switch to.

Switch properties are other properties that a caller about a particular property is likely to be interested in.

Have a map of your community readily available with numbered adhesive markers referencing all your office listings. If you have wall space near your desk, this is the appropriate place for this map. This map is essential because callers on For Sale signs often have the wrong street but usually the right general area. Consider switch property for sign inquiries. As a general rule we know that callers on For Sale signs

- like or would be satisfied with the area;
- like or would be satisfied with the appearance of a home with an exterior that appears to meet the caller's basic needs.

People calling about classified ads tend to buy property other than the property they initially inquired about. The same is true for calls prompted by For Sale signs. This is why it is important to know your inventory. You will be able to readily switch your discussion to appropriate properties as necessary.

Many people will not tell you that a price you have quoted is beyond their means. In fact, they might even ask for more information. However, you won't know this unless you mention a switch property priced significantly less than the property called about. If the caller shows interest in the switch property, the original property that they called about is likely too expensive. As to switch properties, keep in mind that while callers on For Sale signs are often looking beyond their means, callers on priced ads are often hopeful of buying a property that is less than they can afford to pay.

If a caller has viewed the property on the Internet, you know that the caller likes the appearance of the property and the description seems to "fit" his or her needs. You also know that the property is priced within the range the caller expects to pay and that the property's location and address are satisfactory. An Internet inquiry is therefore the most valuable inquiry because a caller has half sold him or herself on the property.

Handling the Inquiry

The following are some general rules about dealing with telephone inquiries from prospective buyers.

- Obtain the caller's name and telephone number.
- Get more information than you give.
- Find out what the prospective buyer is interested in and why.
- Hold the details—give a little more information than was in the ad. The less information given, the greater the chance of ending the telephone call with an appointment.
- Answer home elimination questions with a question. For example, if a caller asks, "Does that house have three bedrooms plus a den?" your answer should be "[Mrs. Jones], do you *need* three bedrooms plus a den?" If the questioning reveals complete unsuitability of the property, you should be able to switch to a similar property that has the required features.
- Close on an appointment. The choice given should be what time, not if they want to see the property.

- Set the place for the meeting. There are only two places for an initial meeting with a potential buyer:

  1. At your office (preferred)

  2. At the prospective buyers' home (only if the prospect can't possibly come to your office)

- Include mention of other property that may interest the prospects. This will help reduce the likelihood of a no show.

- Keep the call short. End the call after the appointment is set.

For an Internet inquiry, because the caller generally wants to see the property, there should be no difficulty setting up the appointment.

> Lovely 3BR, 2-bath ranch home
> in Willow Springs.
> Reduced to $189,500.
> Owner financing available.
>
>
> Oasis Realty   976-4132
>
>
> www.oasispropertytour.com

A suggested approach to calls on the ad shown would be:

"My name is Howard Young. What is your name, please?"

Note: If the ad indicated an Internet address, you want to know if the caller viewed the property on the Internet. If the caller has, treat the call like *gold* because the caller is already half sold on the property.

"Yes, that is a lovely three-bedroom home. How large is your family, [Mr./Mrs.] Jones?"

"What are the ages of your children?"

"That home is available now. When do you need a new home, [Mr./ Mrs.] Jones?"

"Where do you live now?"

"Do you own your present home?"

"Is your home currently for sale?"

"That home is in one of the nicer areas of Willow Springs. Is that the area you are interested in?"

"Are there any other areas that you are considering?"

"That home is priced at $189,500. Is that the general price range you are interested in?"

"I can arrange to show this lovely home as well as another home that I think will interest you and [Mr./Mrs.] Jones at 5 P.M. today, or would 6 P.M. be more convenient for you?"

Notice that the choice is the time, not whether they want to see the property. If your prospective caller indicates neither time is convenient, ask when it would be convenient to show the property.

If the caller indicates he or she is not free at all today, say

"Let's set it up for tomorrow at 5 P.M. I'll meet you and your spouse at my office."

If the caller doesn't object, you have a definite appointment. Whenever you have an appointment for the next day, call the prospects in the morning of that day to remind them of the appointment. When you call, be enthusiastic and tell them you have another property you feel they also will be interested in. This will reduce the "no-shows." Never indicate you have another property if you don't have one.

As you see, asking questions gives you control of the conversation. You get an appointment without giving out too much information and without undue delay.

| Get more information from the caller than you give. |

By mentioning another house to Mr. or Mrs. Jones, you probably aroused some interest and set the stage for alternative properties if necessary. Now say

"I will see you and [Mr./Mrs.] Jones at my office at 6 P.M. Do you have a pencil and paper handy? Our office is at [1911 Elm Street across from the Security Bank]. Are you familiar with the area? [If not, give specific directions.] Again, my name is Howard Young. I look forward to seeing you."

Your question is about their knowledge of your office location, not where you will meet them. You are telling, not asking for, the place of the meeting.

You can see from this sample script that the agent didn't really give information beyond what was in the ad. Instead, the agent asked for information. The call was kept very short and was ended as soon as an appointment had been set.

As we have stated, there are only two places to meet a prospective buyer for the first time. These are at the buyer's home or in the agent's office. Some agents like to visit the buyer's home to get a better insight into the buyer's lifestyle and needs, but the agent's office allows for an uninterrupted qualifying process controlled by the agent. It also means the agent has access to secretarial, internet or computer assistance, should he or she need it. If you must meet prospective buyers at their home, it is usually just to determine needs and obtain buyer qualifying information. Unless you have wireless access to your multiple listing service, a second meeting would be required to show property.

When the Caller Won't Give a Name

If your office uses a secretary to answer telephones, the secretary usually will get a caller's name for you. At times callers will, for one reason or another, resist giving their names. If this happens, don't make an issue of it because there are a number of simple techniques you can use to get the caller's name.

If the call results in an appointment, try

> "In the unlikely event I get tied up for some reason, what is your home number so I can call you to reset the appointment?" (Even though you have their number with your caller ID, you want them to *give* you their number.)

If they give you their number, they probably also will give their name if asked.

Another effective way to get a caller's name owes its effectiveness to the fact that it is nonthreatening:

> "I have a flier with a photo of that property as well as information on several other properties, one in particular that I feel you will be interested in. Would it be all right if I prepared a packet of information and put it in the mail to you?"

If you offer sincere, knowledgeable assistance, this nonthreatening approach of mailing the information will result in a positive response in 90 percent of cases in which a prospect initially refuses to give a name. The caller must now give you a name and address. After you have the caller's name and address, ask if they have a fax number so you can fax the information. Also ask if they have an e-mail address so you can alert them to new listings. Once you have a prospect's name, he or she will provide the other information you need.

If it is obvious that you will not obtain an appointment and have not been able to obtain an appointment the following approach will likely work:

> "I e-mail pictures and details of new listings to prospective buyers who request them. These are sent out before the property is advertised. Are you interested in being alerted to new listings and having first chance?"

"I Just Want the Address"

You will have callers who just want the address of the property so they can drive by for a quick look. Generally, the caller wants an exterior look to either eliminate the property from consideration or make a decision to view it. As a response to such a request, consider

> "[Mr. Jones], it wouldn't be fair to you to give you the address. Driving by would likely cause you to miss the unique advantages this home has to offer. I think this is too good an opportunity for you and that you will want to know everything about this fine home. In addition, I have another home we just listed that you should see and that I think you might like even better. It's priced at [$]."

The second home should be priced less than the home the caller inquired about and should be a relatively recent listing. Again, you must come across as a sincere and knowledgeable person who wants to help.

If the caller who asks for the address claims to have an agent and wants the information for the agent, consider a response similar to the following:

> "No problem. I'll be happy to call your agent and give [him/her] the details of this really exceptional property; or if it is more convenient for you, I can show it to you myself. I would also like to show you a brand new listing that you might like even more. By the way, it's priced at only [$ (price less than the property inquired about)]. I'm free today so I could show you these fine homes at 2 P.M. or would you prefer 3 P.M.?"

There's a good chance the agent is nonexistent. Assume this to be the case, and go for the appointment. Incidentally, never make any buyer you are working with feel that they must do your job by locating properties for you to show them.

An alternative approach is to ask the caller if he or she has an e-mail address. If so, you can offer to e-mail pictures and details from your Web site. This will give you an e-mail address, and there should be no problem then in obtaining the caller's name and telephone number. Explain that you will call back in about a half hour to discuss the property.

If you are unable to get an appointment with the caller and then he or she wants the property address, it is good policy to get the caller's name and telephone number before giving out the address. This is very important because should the prospective buyer not be particularly interested in the property from a drive-by look, he or she would be lost to you for future contact. However, if you have their name and telephone number, you can encourage the prospect to drive by the property and also note any other properties nearby with For Sale signs that appear interesting. Let the caller know you will call them back for their impressions of the property and to obtain information for them on other properties that appeared desirable.

Technology and Caller Data

Technology has gone beyond caller ID where you only have the number of a caller. It is now possible to have the name of the caller, where he or she lives, family size, and even financial data. This information is now available, not just for the calls you answer, but for calls that were unanswered because your line was busy or they called after hours and failed to leave a message. If you desire information on such services, one service provider is *www.callsource.com*.

Locking in the Caller

When callers are motivated buyer's, there is a good likelihood that they will continue looking through ads and will call other agents. You can't do anything about calls made before the prospective buyers called you, but it is relatively easy for you to keep them off the phone.

After the appointment—keep the prospect off the phone.

"[Mrs. Smith], if you have the time, I would appreciate it if you could go through the classified ads and circle any other properties that interest you. Bring the paper with you when we meet at [4 P.M. today], and I'll be able to give you information on other properties. Perhaps you might want to see one or more of them. By having you circle the ads that interest you, I can also learn a great deal about what you desire."

This keeps the possible buyer off the phone. It might possibly give you other property to show and does provide information on the buyer's desires.

Can't Get an Appointment

If you can't turn a call into an appointment, use it to set the stage for further contact.

"Would it be all right if I called you should a property be listed that [has five bedrooms and is priced under $150,000]?"

This approach will generally result in a positive response and a name and telephone number if you have otherwise been unable to obtain this information.

Similarly, you could ask

"Would it be all right if I mailed you some information on other properties that I think might interest you?"

This nonthreatening approach is likely to receive a positive response.

You might also ask the caller if he or she has access to the Internet. If yes, ask if it would be all right if you sent e-mails, including pictures, of any new listings that you feel might interest the caller. It's a nonthreatening approach, and you now have a reason to call to discuss any e-mail property you presented. Of course, you should again try to set up an appointment.

■ THE MEETING

Your Safety

Unfortunately, personal safety has become an issue in recent years. Agents have been attacked by "buyers." To reduce the likelihood of jeopardizing your personal safety, meet prospective buyers at your office whenever possible. Persons who have anything on their minds other than a purchase will not want to show themselves to other people. After they have come to your office and undergone a qualifying process, the likelihood of a safety problem will have been practically eliminated.

Prepare To Meet the Prospective Buyer

Before you meet your prospective buyers for the first time, think through the qualifying process. You also might want to make some tentative appointments to show specific properties.

Because the qualifying process often reveals that properties inquired about do not really meet the needs and/or resources of the prospective buyers, you want the

Schedule your first meeting with a prospective buyer at your office.

owners—your principals—to understand that the appointments are only tentative at this time and may need to be canceled or postponed.

Make certain you have a "qualifying room" free and clean, with fresh coffee or soft drinks available. We suggest you qualify prospective buyers in a separate office or closing room. This reduces distractions and provides a chance to learn about the prospects without interruption.

First Impressions

When you meet with prospective buyers, make a mental point of remembering their names. By repeating their last name several times to yourself and thinking of people you know with the same first names, you are less likely to have to ask the buyers their names when writing an offer to purchase.

Make certain you are pronouncing names correctly. If you are uncertain, ask. Because people like to be addressed by their names, use them frequently during the discussions.

Explain that you will be able to save the prospective buyers a great deal of time by spending just a few minutes to decide what they really need in a home.

Serve large cups of hot or iced coffee (or tea). Seat the clients close to you during your qualifying session.

Needs and Interests

Keep in mind that the primary purpose of this meeting is for you to gain information. When you are talking, it should usually involve asking a question. People like people who are interested in them, and chances are they're not really interested in you. Their interest is in what you can do for them.

Many agents use a qualification form so they won't forget the information prospective buyers give them. The use of a form also reduces the chances of forgetting to obtain some needed information. Figure 9.1 is an example of a form you might consider using. You can also put the information directly into your contact management system in your PDA.

> **Buyer Qualifying Process**
> The qualifying process is really a three-part process involving
> 1. needs and interests of the buyers;
> 2. the buyers' motivation; and
> 3. the financial resources of the buyers in regard to the
>   a. down payment,
>   b. amount that they can finance, and
>   c. payments they can make.

FIGURE 9.1

Prospective Buyer Confidential Information Sheet

Prospective Buyer Confidential Information Sheet

Name(s) _____Phone no. _____

Fax Number _____e-mail _____

Address _____

Size of family _____

Names and ages of children or other dependents living with you: _____

_____

_____

Initial contact with the firm was because of (advertisement, sign, referral, etc.) _____

Present address _____

How long at above address? _____

Do you presently own your own home? _____

If yes, must you sell before you buy? _____

If yes, is your present home currently listed for sale? _____

With _____

How long has it been on the market? _____

Your reason for seeking to buy a new home _____

What features don't you like about your present home?_____

_____

Why? _____

What feature(s) do you consider essential for your new home?_____

_____

Why?_____

_____

_____

What are your hobbies or special interests? _____

_____

_____

_____

Have you qualified for or been turned down for a home loan within the past year? _____

If you qualified for a loan, what was the name of the firm and loan amount?

_____

The form tells you the needs of buyers as well as why they are buyers. Keep in mind that qualifying buyers is a continuing process that continues right up to receiving an offer. By asking for reactions to homes shown you gain insight into what prospective buyers really want. It could be far different from what a buyer claims to want. Your contact management systems should not only include the information you obtain as to prospect needs and interests, it should also indicate the properties they have seen and their reactions to the showings.

Financial Qualifying.   You should know FHA and VA loan limits and down payment requirements (See Chapter 12) if your prospective buyers are likely to be eligible for these types of financing. You also should know down payment requirements for various types of loan.

> You should have an in-depth understanding of current qualifying ratios being used by lenders in your area. You should also understand how the FHA and VA qualify purchasers.

Lenders use the terms *front-end* and *back-end* (or bottom) *loan/qualifications*, which refer to ratios. **Front-end qualification** customarily refers to the ratio of a buyer's housing costs to income. Generally, gross income is used for front-end qualifying. If the front-end ratio is 28 percent, it means the buyers' total housing costs cannot exceed 28 percent of their gross income.

Total monthly payment ÷ Gross monthly income = 28%

Using the following chart, you can find the maximum monthly amount buyers could spend for house payments at a variety of gross annual income levels using a 28 percent ratio.

Gross Annual Income	Monthly Mortgage Payment
$20,000	$467
30,000	700
40,000	933
50,000	1,167
60,000	1,400
70,000	1,633
80,000	1,867
90,000	2,100
100,000	2,333
130,000	3,033
150,000	3,500
200,000	4,667

A **back-end qualification** ratio might be 36 percent, which means that a person's total housing expense plus long-term debt obligations cannot exceed 36 percent of gross income.

Total monthly credit obligations ÷ Gross monthly income = 36%

Qualifying ratios will be covered in more detail in Chapter 12.

The following chart illustrates the maximum monthly amount buyers could spend for total credit obligations (including housing) at a variety of income levels and still remain within a 36 percent guideline:

Gross Annual Income	Maximum Monthly Credit Obligation
$20,000	$600
30,000	700
40,000	1,200
50,000	1,500
60,000	1,800
70,000	2,100
80,000	2,400
90,000	2,700
100,000	3,000
130,000	3,900
150,000	4,600
200,000	6,000

Down payment requirements vary by the lender and type of loan. Lenders express the loan-to-value ratio by the acronym LTV. If the borrower pays for private mortgage insurance, the down payments requirement may be reduced.

Self-employed individuals frequently have difficulty qualifying for loans. Lenders often require that self-employed buyers furnish two years of tax returns with their loan applications. Although buyers may indicate to you or the lender that they make x dollars a year, the tax returns may reveal a very different financial profile. Self-employed buyers may have to consider homes for which seller financing is available or be willing to pay a higher interest rate from a subprime lender.

Figure 9.2 is a sample qualification form that will help you determine if buyers can qualify for a loan. The maximum loan for which they can qualify plus their down payment sets the maximum limit on housing that prospective buyers can purchase. Further details on financial qualification of buyers are included in Chapter 12.

We recommend that you **prequalify** buyers whenever possible before you show them property. Failure to prequalify prospective buyers could result in showing the prospects homes they cannot afford. Besides resulting in wasted effort, it becomes difficult to sell the prospects less costly housing later.

Figure 9.3 is an example of a lender's prequalification form. By completing a prequalification form and faxing it to a lender or giving the information over the telephone or the Internet, you can get a prequalification for a loan amount based on verification of given information.

You should be sending prequalification lending information to lenders by e-mail, fax, or telephone, before you leave your office to show property. If you don't get

FIGURE 9.2

Loan Qualification Worksheet

Loan Qualification Worksheet

Gross Income

1.	Client's monthly income	$_____
2.	Spouse's monthly income	$_____
3.	Total monthly gross income [1 + 2]	$_____

PITI (use PITI worksheet)

4.	PITI	$_____

Monthly Expenses

5.	Car	$_____
6.	Alimony/child support	$_____
7.	Credit cards	$_____
	(_____ × .05)	
8.	Other loan payments	$_____
9.	Total monthly expenses [5 + 6 + 7 + 8]	$_____
10.	Total PITI and monthly expenses [4 + 9]	$_____

Ratios

11.	Income ratio [4 ÷ 3]	_____ %
12.	Debt ratio [10 ÷ 3]	_____ %

> Start the lender financial qualification process before you leave to show homes to customers.

an immediate answer, this is a reason for the prospective buyers to come back to your office after the showing. Also, by prequalifying a buyer, you have changed the buyers' attitude from looking to buying. Prequalifying buyers also reduces the likelihood that they will seek out other agents. Prequalifying buyers can make them your customers.

If you handle the qualifying process in a professional manner, you will be setting the stage for the buyers to regard you as a professional and a person they can relate to. (Another advantage of financial qualifying is that you tend to eliminate "Lookie Lous.")

Preparing the Buyer

During the financial qualification process you discussed the down payment. Before you show property, you should discuss earnest money. Earnest money deposits are made with offers. Prospective buyers should understand that their check will be held uncashed until their offer is accepted. Ask a question that makes the prospective buyers visualize writing a check, such as

"If we are fortunate and find the perfect home for you today, would you be able to make a deposit of [$] with your offer?"

Give prospective buyers a copy of the purchase contract your office uses before you leave the office. Ask them to look the form over at their convenience, and explain that when you succeed in finding them a home they wish to purchase, this will be the form used. Buyers who receive the form up front are less likely to object to the form at a later time, and signing it will be an easier task.

What Happens to the Buyer's Offer?
Buyers should understand that three things can happen when they make an offer.

1. *Acceptance* means that they have purchased a home.
2. A *counteroffer* from the owners gives the buyers the opportunity to accept it and have a house, make their own counter to the counteroffer or reject it.
3. *Rejection* of the offer means the entire earnest money deposit is returned to the offerors.

If you approach the qualifying process in an organized fashion, you should be able to start looking at homes less than an hour from the time prospective buyers arrive at your office.

Be certain to explain agencies and have your prospective buyers sign the agency form. (See Chapter 3.) You should explain your disclosure obligations as well as disclosures of the owner when buyers find a home that meets their needs.

You may decide that you can best serve your prospective buyer as a buyer agent. If this is the case, you should discuss the benefits of exclusive buyer representation with your prospective buyers and obtain a buyer listing.

Planning Your Efforts

From your qualifying questions you will have determined why the prospective buyers want to buy and if they can buy now. If they must sell a home first to become buyers, discuss an offer contingent on the sale of their own home should they find a house that meets their needs. If your prospects want to *sell* before they place an offer, you should still spend some time with them to whet their appetites for a new home. One showing session plus frequent phone calls about the progress of their own home sale as well as e-mails on new listings that you feel would be of interest is an advisable approach.

If you know about a person's special interests, you can use this information in selecting homes for showing. As an example, if a prospective buyer has a strong interest in photography, showing a house with a room that was formerly used or that could be used as a darkroom would be a wise choice. This knowledge also could be used to turn a showing into a sale. For example, if an owner currently has a darkroom setup and your prospective buyer indicated an interest in a property with a darkroom, a good approach would be not to mention this fact prior to showing the property; let the buyer discover the darkroom.

FIGURE 9.3

Lender Prequalification Form

HERITAGE
FINANCIAL SERVICES

LOAN PROSPECT WORKSHEET

Borrower: _____ Date: _____

Co-Borrower: _____ Loan Consultant: _____

Mailing Address: _____ Telephone #: _____

_____ Telephone #: _____

Originating Source: [ ] Phone   [ ] RE Agent _____   [ ] Other _____

PROPERTY INFORMATION

Property Address: _____ Owner Occupied [ ]

_____ Non Owner Occupied [ ]

Property Type: [ ] Single Family Residence   [ ] 2-4 Units (# of Units _____)

[ ] PUD   [ ] Condo   # of Units in Project _____   Year Built _____

# of Units Owner Occupied _____ Conversion Y or N

PURCHASE	REFINANCE
Sales Price: $ _____	Estimated Value: $ _____
Loan Amount: $ _____	Loan Amount: $ _____
Secondary Financing: $ _____	Loan to Value: _____ %
Down Payment: $ _____	Existing Liens: $ _____ (1)
Source of Down Payment: _____	$ _____ (2)
_____	$ _____ (3)
Loan to Value: _____ % Combined LTV %: _____ %	Date Purchased: _____
Realtor: _____	Purpose of Refinance: _____
Firm: _____	_____
Telephone #: _____	_____

QUALIFYING INFORMATION

MONTHLY INCOME

	BORROWER	CO-BORROWER
Base:	$ _____	$ _____
Overtime:	_____	_____
Commission:	_____	_____
Bonus:	_____	_____
Other:	_____	_____
Other:	_____	_____
TOTAL:	$ _____	_____
TOTAL COMBINED:	(A) $ _____	

RATIOS

B÷A=Housing Ratio _____

B+C÷A=Debt Ratio _____

PROPOSED MONTHLY HOUSING DEBT

Payment (P & I):	$ _____
Est. Property Taxes:	_____
Est. Property Insur.:	_____
Homeowners Dues:	_____
Mo. PMI:	_____
Other:	_____
TOTAL:	(B) _____

MONTHLY OBLIGATIONS

Revolving Debts:	$ _____
Installment Debts:	_____
Auto Payment:	_____
Other:	_____
Other:	_____
TOTAL:	(C) $ _____

LOAN PROGRAM QUOTED

Program: _____ Term: _____ Fees: _____ % + $ _____

Initial Rate: _____ % Pay Rate: _____ % Spread: _____ % Cap: _____ %

Notes: _____

_____

_____

_____

_____

_____

_____

When one of the authors first began in real estate sales, he showed a listing sight unseen. The prospective buyers, a well-dressed couple with a young daughter, stopped in the office after seeing an ad that indicated the home was located on a large wooded lot, and that it had seven rooms and a large garage-workshop. Because it was located in an excellent area, the potential buyers wanted to know if the listed price of the property, which was low, was a mistake. Before this coauthor showed the property, one of the other agents told him, "It's a dog. You'll never sell it!"

The coauthor discovered that the home was an old farmhouse with imitation brick, roll-asphalt siding, and the garage was a large machine-shed/barn with a dirt floor.

The floors in the house were of pine covered with linoleum. There were no closets in the bedrooms, and because the house had been vacant for a long period of time, there was a very unpleasant odor throughout the place.

The coauthor asked the prospective buyers what they thought of the home. The response was, "It definitely has possibilities." Fifteen minutes later they signed an offer and within a month had moved into their new home. A disabled veteran and his wife, they wanted to move to the area because they wanted their daughter to have the advantage of the desirable school district. This was the only home that they could afford within that school district. It was the answer to their dreams, but to other agents it was a dog. There was nothing wrong with the property; it simply needed to be matched with the right buyers. This example teaches a lesson: You should not substitute what *you* want for what *others* want.

In selling, the ability to be a good listener is even more important than the ability to be a good talker. Unfortunately, most people have poor listening skills; they pretend to listen, but they do not hear. To add to the problem, the human mind can hear and process around 500 words a minute, yet we speak at a rate of only about 100 to 150 words a minute. The difference makes it easy to be distracted and allow one's mind to wander. Practice active listening so you will be sure to hear words that are relevant to the customer's needs, problems and solutions.

A good listener listens actively by reinforcing the speaker with words of understanding, repeating what was said (especially when objections arise), and nodding or making some show of approval.

Silence also is an excellent tool; when in doubt, the best solution is to keep silent. Discreet silence at the right time often shows an excellent command of the language. Also, active listeners do not interrupt or formulate a response when the speaker is talking.

> ### Remember to Listen
> Remember, you will not make sales by winning arguments. Speakers need the opportunity to make known their points and voice their feelings of doubt or displeasure. Listen with your eyes as well as with your ears. Keep a relaxed tone while speaking, and mean what you say. When you are finished, stop.

■ THE SHOWING

Preparing To Show

To show property to prospective buyers intelligently, you must make adequate preparation.

- Know all available properties in the area.
- Be able to identify school boundaries.
- Be cognizant of shopping and recreational facilities in the area.
- Be aware of public transportation routes.
- Be aware of any other information about the area that might help prospects make a favorable decision.

Select previously visited houses for viewing considering the benefits offered by particular properties to particular buyers.

In selecting property to show, avoid those that your prospective buyers cannot afford. Otherwise, you will likely spoil the buyers for what they can afford.

Don't show property just to please the owners. Some agents try to show property to impress owners with their work on the owners' behalf rather than to make a sale. This tactic often backfires because prospective buyers will realize that you really aren't listening to them. Instead, you are wasting their time. This tactic materially lessens the likelihood of having a second chance to show property to these prospects.

Some agents try to hold back what they consider to be the best property for their prospects. Instead, they show overpriced or unsuitable property first. They believe the property they hope to sell then will appear in a more favorable light. This practice could be considered unethical because the result could be to give prospective buyers a false impression of property values.

If the qualifying process indicates that the homes you initially selected for viewing are unsuitable, cancel appointments made and make new ones before leaving your office. Try to show vacant homes on lockboxes first, so that you give owners time to prepare for a showing.

Some agents like to show no more than three or four properties. How many you show should be dictated by the situation. As an example, if buyers have flown into your area to buy a home because of a job transfer, then you want to show them as many appropriate properties as possible. You can keep confusion to a minimum when you show a large number of properties by giving them information sheets with photos of each house. You can break showings into groups of three or four. Take a coffee break after showing each group and discuss the comparative values of the homes. Find out which one of the group buyers liked best. If a clear winner does not appear, consider a second showing of the best home in each group.

Some agents like the idea of showing what they consider the best as their last scheduled showing. They feel that the first homes give the buyers a basis of comparison that allows the benefits of the final home to be fully appreciated.

Showing Techniques

Sell the Neighborhood.   Plan your route to sell the neighborhood. Choose the most scenic route, one that includes schools, public parks, golf courses, and shopping areas. If possible, adapt your route to the interests of the prospective buyers, but do not plan a route to avoid what *you* regard as a negative factor in the area. If you feel there is a negative element that might influence prospective buyers, this must be revealed to them. *However, the presence of a different racial or ethnic group in the area is not considered a negative factor and should not be revealed as if it were.* In fact, if you were to reveal this type of information, it might be regarded as racial steering, that is, directing people based on race. This is a violation of the Civil Rights Act of 1968.

Because people buy a neighborhood as much as they do a specific property, selling the neighborhood cannot be emphasized enough. While driving to the property, endeavor to educate the buyers by discussing only relevant items. If necessary, prepare leading questions. Try to keep the buyers' attention focused on houses of similar price and on the quality of the neighborhood itself. Point out recent sales of comparably priced homes. This should increase the buyers' trust in you and establish a price range in their minds.

A **negative motivation** technique that entails warning buyers about any objectionable feature often works well. Buyers build these features up in their minds and are relieved when they find you have exaggerated a bit. Also, avoid overenthusiasm on specific points; it may backfire. Instead, permit the buyers' discoveries to be new and exciting experiences.

When you arrive at the property to be shown, park across the street from it if it has good curb appeal. If you pause for a moment when you get out of the car, your buyers will do the same. Ask for their opinion of the house and the area.

Create a Favorable Ambiance.   It is interesting to note that although some buyers are interested in construction and utility, most are attracted by color, glamour, texture, and style. They usually buy what they want and what they feel good with. Cater to these feelings by creating a favorable ambiance—proper mood and atmosphere. Have the owner provide fresh flowers in vases. Depending on the weather, either prepare the fireplace or have the air-conditioning operating. Encourage the buyer to relax and feel at home.

You want prospective buyers to think like owners. Use language such as "[Jeffrey's school/Longview Middle School] is only three blocks away. Would you like to look at the school after we leave?"

Involve the Whole Family.   Ask questions of all family members. If you are receiving positive vibrations from prospective buyers, consider "[Jennifer], which bedroom would be yours?"

Ask, Do Not Tell.   The following story illustrates what to do and what not to do when you show property.

> Mr. and Mrs. Doe are potential real estate buyers. They have decided to go for the traditional afternoon time killer, the Sunday drive. As they tour their town, complaining about the traffic, Mrs. Doe's face lights up when she sees a lovely home with lots of little flags flying. It is crisp, modern, and obviously open for inspection, so she decides that they should stop and look it over. They walk into the house and are greeted by a real estate salesperson, who puts down a comic book and slowly gets up. The salesperson then proceeds to give the demonstration—the Cook's tour.
>
> "This is the living room," the salesperson proclaims with a sweep of the hand. "This is the dining room; notice the roominess. . . . This is the kitchen. These are the kitchen cabinets. This is the oven; it's big and modern." The salesperson continues, "Notice how wide the hall is. Why don't you both look at this bedroom with me? Isn't your husband interested in bedrooms? This is a closet."
>
> By this time the Does have had enough. They remember how much they wanted a chocolate malt, and off they go. The salesperson returns to the comic book.

Now imagine the same scene with a different character—a professional salesperson who knows how to communicate.

> This salesperson rises but waits to let the customers look around the living room for a moment. Then he or she turns to Mrs. Doe and says, "Where in this living room would you place your sofa?" (Do not sell the space, sell the benefits of the space.)
>
> In the kitchen the salesperson opens a cabinet and says, "What would you put in here, dry groceries or your kitchen china?" Opening the oven, the salesperson says, "How big a turkey do you think this oven would take?"

True professionals never say "This is the second bedroom." They always ask, "Whose bedroom will this be?" A professional does not state obvious facts. A professional *sells* by asking who, what, where, or how for every room and every feature.

- "There's plenty of room in the bedroom for a king-size bed plus an office area. Would you put the desk in the window alcove?"
- "Mr. Thomas, how would you use this workroom?"
- "Would you use this room as a study or as a spare bedroom?"

Ask questions and listen to the answers.

■ "How do you think your dog will like having her own trees in the fenced yard?"

■ "Would you use the covered patio for summer entertaining?"

Sell Benefits, Not Just Features.   A gourmet kitchen is a place to indulge in one's culinary hobby, not to mention a pleasant atmosphere in which to work out tensions. A fireplace contributes to family togetherness and the kindling of romance. A dishwasher is not a luxury, it is a necessity, given the hectic demands on most people's time. A spa and sun deck are status symbols. Listen carefully to uncover features and benefits that are important to the buyer, as well as probing when appropriate, and then sell those features and benefits.

Because the qualifying process is a continual one, after each house shown you must ask questions, not state opinions. By asking questions about what prospective buyers liked and what they didn't like and probing for the reasons behind these feelings, you may find that your showing schedule needs modification.

Use Tie-Downs.   A good communicator uses **tie-downs.** They can be used to check out whether a benefit is important as well as to build a sense of ownership. No professional salesperson ever makes a positive statement without tying it down:

■ This is a spacious room, *isn't it?*

■ You really need four bedrooms, *don't you?*

■ Your children should be close to school, *shouldn't they?*

■ This is the sound investment you've been looking for, *isn't it?*

> A series of yes responses can lead to the big YES!

These words—*isn't it, can it, won't it, don't you, can't you,* and so on—are powerful selling tools. Little yeses easily lead to the big yes. Sell on minor points.

Invite Comparisons.   The comparison technique gets buyers involved. Ask such questions as "Did you like the vanity off the bedroom, as it was in the house you just saw, or do you prefer this style?" "Will this dining room set off your antique hutch, or can you see it better in the other house?" These questions get the buyers involved in defining what is important to them. Buyers start selling themselves and get prepared to make the big decision by making a lot of little ones.

> By use of comparisons you can discover preferences.

Additional Showing Tips.   Here are other items that may enhance your presentation:

■ Occasionally allow the buyers privacy. They may want to feel that they're alone when they discuss personal things.

■ Do not assume that just because you like a feature of the property the buyers will like it as well.

■ Do not resent the presence of a friend of the family. Use the friend as an ally.

■ Always overcome any objections on the scene. If space is an issue, use a tape measure (let the customer measure). Try to settle any questions on the spot.

■ Begin and end the tour of the home in the most beautiful and unique part of the house.

- The buyers will follow your lead. Whenever you enter a room, they will follow.

- Involve children. Wherever possible, involve them as helpers.

- Speak plainly, and avoid technical terms. When people do not understand, your point is lost.

- Call attention to outstanding features, but do not go overboard or you will close the door on the sale of another property.

- Show the rooms in the most productive order. In a home this is usually front hall, living room, dining room, kitchen, bedrooms, yard or garden, and last of all the most attractive rooms on the first floor. This procedure may be varied to suit special cases.

- If the rooms are small, do not stand in the middle of the room; stand along the side.

Rules of Professional Conduct

The following rules will help you maintain goodwill and a professional manner as you plan for and conduct showings:

- If you arrive at a property and notice that someone else is showing it, wait inconspicuously until the other salesperson and his or her clients have left.

- When showing a home, leave it as you found it. If drapes were closed, see that they're closed when you leave. If inner doors were closed, reclose them when you leave. Double-check all outside doors to see that they're locked. Be sure to replace the key in the lockbox where you found it. If dogs, cats, or other animals are confined to a given room, yard, garage, and so forth, see that they do not gain access to other rooms or to the street.

- Notify the listing office immediately if something seems to be amiss at a property you have shown. Treat all listings as you would want to have your own listing treated.

- If a listing specifies "Call first," never take a customer to the door and ask to show the home. If, while showing a property, you decide to show another and cannot reach the owner by phone, leave the client in the car while you go to the door and ask the owner for belated permission to show the property. Then abide by the owner's wishes.

- If a listing indicates that the property is to be shown only during certain hours or gives other information regarding particular conditions of showing, do not violate these requests. There must be a reason for them.

- Leave your business card at each property. It is a courtesy to the owner (whether at home or not). It also helps to advertise your own office. It is a good idea to write the date and the time on the back of the card.

- Interoffice courtesy requires that when calling another agency for information, you immediately identify yourself and your company.

- Do not enter a house with a lighted cigarette, pipe, or cigar, and do not light one while in a house.

- Avoid making uncomplimentary remarks about a house, its condition, or its furnishings while in the house. The owner may be in the next room and be embarrassed or hurt by your comments.

■ KEEP THEM YOURS

You want prospective buyers to feel an obligation to work with you.

After you have completed your first session of showing homes to prospective buyers, it is a good idea to ask them to return to the office to discuss the properties they have seen. If a closing is not going to be possible, consider a way to tie up the prospects so they regard you as their agent. Consider the following approach:

> "I prefer to work with just a few buyers. I dedicate my efforts to finding them a property that best meets their needs. Usually I'm able to meet the needs of my buyers in just a few weeks. I am willing to work for you and concentrate my efforts on your behalf if you are serious buyers. At times buyers don't really have the down payment they say they have, or for some other reason are not in a position to buy. Are you serious buyers?"

Your buyers can be expected to assure you that they are serious. Continue:

> "If you are willing to let me take over the exclusive responsibility of finding the home you want, I will use all my efforts to locate the property that meets all your needs. If you see an ad that interests you, if you drive by a home you like, or even if you see an open-house sign, call me about it. If another broker contacts you, tell that broker to call me and I will cooperate with him or her. If you are willing to work with me, I am willing to go all out for you. Does this seem fair?"

The answer will usually be positive, and many people will live up to the agreement, but it would be better to bring out a buyer-agency agreement at this time. When you find the house that meets their needs, committed buyers will often feel obligated to make an offer when they might otherwise have procrastinated.

■ SUMMARY

Advertising contacts generally begin with a phone call. Be prepared for phone inquiries by having current ads, switch property, and location of office listings readily available.

Find out the names and addresses of callers as well as their needs. Give minimum property information, but extract the maximum information on callers' needs and motivations. By giving callers just enough information to keep their interest level high, you can obtain an appointment using a choice of time, not a choice between meeting and not meeting. By asking motivated prospective buyers to mark other ads that interest them, you can lock the prospects in and keep them from calling other agents.

In preparing to meet prospective buyers you should have some tentative property showing appointments and a qualifying plan. Before you show any property, you must ascertain prospects' needs, their motivation to buy, and their financial qualifications: the down payment they can afford and the maximum loan they can carry.

The motivation of prospects will affect the level of priority and energy that should be planned for prospective buyers. Based on prospects' needs and financial abilities, your selection of property for showing might need modification. Do not show prospective buyers properties they cannot afford.

Plan your showings and ask questions. Don't give opinions during the showing process. Keep in mind that when you conduct a showing, you are selling benefits. Involve the entire family with your questions.

■ CLASS DISCUSSION TOPICS

1. Role-play an inquiry about your own home with another student. Your goal will be to obtain a name, address, basic needs, and a firm appointment.

2. Role-play a need and motivation buyer-qualification process with another student.

3. Role-play a showing of your classroom with another student cast as a prospective buyer of a classroom.

4. Bring to class one current-events article dealing with some aspect of real estate practice for class discussion.

■ CHAPTER 9 QUIZ

1. Callers from a For Sale sign are likely to be
   a. satisfied with the area.
   b. looking for a more expensive home.
   c. satisfied with the general exterior appearance.
   d. both a and c

2. If we compare callers from classified ads with those from For Sale signs, in general,
   a. callers from signs are more likely to end up buying homes that cost less than the home they called about.
   b. callers from ads are more likely to end up buying homes that cost more than the home they called about.
   c. both a and b are true
   d. both a and b are false

3. A caller about a home with a one-car garage asks, "Does the home have a double garage?" What would be the best response?
   a. "No, it does not."
   b. "I'm not sure, let's see it."
   c. "While it is a one-car garage, it is quite large."
   d. "Did you want a double garage?"

4. In handling a phone inquiry it is good policy to
   a. arrange to meet the prospects at the property.
   b. give as much information as possible so the caller will know all there is to know about the property.
   c. obtain the caller's name and phone number.
   d. avoid asking personal questions until the caller knows you better.

5. The qualifying process includes discovering
    a. the buyers' motivation.
    b. the buyers' needs and interests.
    c. a down payment they can make and the amount they can finance.
    d. all of the above.

6. The front-end loan qualifying ratio is the ratio of
    a. gross housing cost to gross income.
    b. gross income to gross housing cost.
    c. net housing cost to net income.
    d. none of the above.

7. The back-end qualifying ratio refers to the ratio of
    a. gross housing cost to gross income.
    b. total housing expense plus long-term debt to gross income.
    c. gross income to net income plus housing cost.
    d. none of the above.

8. In showing property you should
    a. never show a prospect more than three homes in one day.
    b. show prospects a really nice home they can't afford to keep up their interest.
    c. never change your showing plans once you start.
    d. do none of the above.

9. In a showing you should not
    a. begin with the nicest room.
    b. involve the prospects' children with your questions.
    c. allow the buyers to have any time to themselves.
    d. try to impress the customers with technical jargon they don't understand.

10. If another agent is showing a home when you arrive for a showing, what should you do?
    a. Bring your prospects in and let them know they are competing with other buyers for the house.
    b. Cross the house off your showing list until you are sure it has not been sold.
    c. Wait inconspicuously until the other agent completes his or her showing and leaves.
    d. Tell your clients that you are certain that the other prospects are buyers so they had better act fast.

10

OBTAINING THE OFFER AND CREATING THE SALES AGREEMENT

■ KEY TERMS

assumptive close
buying motives
buying signals
closed-end questions
estimated buyer's costs

inducement
mirroring
negative motivation
open-end questions
persuasion
positive choice

California Residential
   Purchase Agreement
   and Joint Escrow
   Instructions
short sale
trial close

■ LEARNING OBJECTIVES

This chapter teaches you the *what* and *how* of selling. You will discover that selling is persuading, communicating, discovering, knowing your customer, and knowing your product.

You learn about various types of prospects, how to deal with them, and the steps you have to take to obtain an offer. You learn about the motives that incite a buyer to act. These include survival, security, pride of ownership, love of family, health, desire for profit or gain, and desire for comfort and convenience. You also learn about the difference between reason and emotion.

You learn how to recognize buying signals and how to meet and overcome buyers' objections to sell successfully. By understanding trial closings and other closing techniques, you can translate the theory of salesmanship into its practical application.

You learn the meaning and applicability of every paragraph in the California Residential Purchase Agreement and Joint Escrow Instructions (CAR Form RPA-CA) and thus will be ready to lead buyers through to the signature stage of the sale.

■ WHAT IS SELLING?

If all you accomplished in real estate was to escort people through houses, you would be a tour guide, not a salesperson. Selling is a noble profession because it helps others fulfill their desires. As a salesperson, you influence the outcome of a showing. You influence prospective buyers to become owners by executing a real property purchase contract.

A favorite definition of salesmanship says it is "seven **P**s in a pod": **P**ersuade **P**lenty of **P**eople to **P**urchase **P**roperty **P**leasurably at a **P**rofit. *Plenty of people* indicates that nearly everyone is a customer at some time. *Purchasing property* for live-in purposes or for investment is a decision everyone faces. *Pleasurably* has two implications:

> **The 7 Ps of Selling**
> Persuade
> Plenty of
> People to
> Purchase
> Property
> Pleasurably at a
> Profit

1. If the experience is pleasurable for the buyer, he or she will be your best prospect for future sales as well as leads.
2. If the sale is a pleasurable experience for the salesperson, it will encourage increased efforts for future sales.

Profit is the key to economic life. Everyone expects businesspeople to make a profit—if they do, they will stay in business; if they do not, they may go bankrupt.

In more formal and traditional terms, *salesmanship* is the persuasive leadership that influences people to buy or sell goods under circumstances that benefit all parties to the transaction.

Selling Is Persuading

Persuasion is the central theme in many descriptions of the selling process:

- The personal or impersonal process of persuading a prospective customer to buy a commodity or service
- The art of persuading someone to accept or to follow certain ideas that lead him or her to a desired action
- Persuading people to want what you have in terms of products, services, or ideas

Unfortunately, the word *persuasion* reminds many people of someone who convinces them to buy unnecessary products. You can avoid this problem by understanding that people buy benefits that will satisfy their wants and needs, both conscious and unconscious. Your job is to address the needs and show your customers that satisfying *their* needs is most important to *you*. The good feelings that result will lead to long-term customer satisfaction and future business.

Selling Is Effective Communication

Without effective communication, there is no understanding. Know what you want to say; use listeners' language. Do not use fancy words when simple ones will do. Use the "KISS" method—**K**eep **I**t **S**imple and **S**incere.

> For effective communication, Keep It Simple and Sincere!

Idea.   The most common cause of poor communication is the communicator's own failure to understand the idea he or she wants to express. You must have something to communicate. As a rule, if you are unsure about what you really mean or are lacking essential facts, it is best not to try to communicate your thoughts to others.

Facts.   To make the sales message understood, you must provide sufficient facts. Without facts the person receiving the message cannot form valid conclusions or take effective action. This is illustrated by the story of a temporary post office employee who was told to take a truck and deliver the New York mail. Six hours later the department received a collect telephone call: "I'm out of gas on the New Jersey Turnpike, 11 miles out of New York. Can you wire me some money so I can deliver the mail?" What the boss had forgotten to tell the new employee was, "When we say deliver the New York mail, we mean to drive it two blocks to Union Station and leave it on the train platform."

Language.   A clear idea, sufficient facts, and proper media are of no avail if the communicator uses language that confuses the listener. Words should be chosen with the utmost care, organized, and delivered meaningfully.

Receiver.   Words or symbols have different meanings for different people. Assess your listener before attempting to communicate. Recognition of his or her past experience, mood and temperament, as well as knowledge of the product or service, will make or break the communication chain.

> ### Your Voice Personality
> Does your selling voice communicate well? If not, the following four guidelines will help you relate to your customer more effectively:
>
> 1. Articulate clearly.
> 2. Sound positive and friendly.
> 3. Match your customer's speech in volume, speed, and tone.
>   (This is some times referred to as **mirroring**.)
> 4. Use his or her language.

Selling Is Discovering

Help your client or customer to discover. For example, ask, "Would it be all right if I ask you a few questions?" Evaluate your inquiry style by asking the following questions:

- Do my questions tell my prospect that I understand him or her?
- Do I ask property-oriented (fact-finding) questions?
- Do I follow this with people-oriented (feeling-finding) questions?
- Do I ask open-end questions to get the other party to "open up?"

In qualifying prospective buyers, use open-end questions to gain information rather than closed-end questions. **Open-end questions** ask for reasons and feelings and aid in the communication process, whereas **closed-end questions** can be answered with a simple "yes" or "no" that does not provide any background about reasoning and motivation. A child's "Why?" is an example of an open-end question.

> Open-end questions ask for reasons and feelings.

If you start with fact-finding questions, which appeal to reason, you accomplish the following three things:

1. You relax the prospect.
2. You indicate to the prospect that you have done your homework.
3. You obtain valuable information that helps guide your sales effort.

Then revert to feeling-finding questions, which appeal to emotions.

Remember that people buy not so much because they understand the product or service but because they feel that *you understand them*.

Customers' reasons for buying traditionally have been divided into two major categories: rational and emotional. *Rational motives* are usually defined as including any considerations that have to do with long-term costs, financing, and benefits from proposed expenditures. In other words, rational motives measure all the costs against all the probable gains. There are probably as many *emotional motives* for buying as there are customers. However, a few that are most frequently seen in real estate are love, fear, convenience, prestige or social approval, and self-improvement. Selling often involves giving a prospective buyer a rational reason for fulfilling an emotional need.

Selling Is Knowing Your Customer

Customers are the heart and soul of our business. Our customers do not have to love us, but it is a good idea for us to love our customers. Always keep in mind how you can best serve them.

Customer Types.   There have been numerous attempts to "pigeon-hole" prospects and customers. This can be done if you keep in mind the temperamental fluctuations that might occur. Remember, no customer is a single type; he or she is a composite of several types. Most experienced licensees have seen an individual display more than one temperament during an interview. Some customers put the salesperson on the defensive; some buyers waver; some are irritable, cynical, or good-humored. Alert salespeople adjust their approaches to the attitudes, temperaments, and buying needs of each of their customers. Figure 10.1 shows strategies for dealing with various types of prospects.

Selling Is Knowing Your Product

If you are going to satisfy customer needs and wants, you must know what properties are available and their features. Taking a listing, preparing for a showing, going through the multiple-listing service (MLS) listings, and networking with others are all good opportunities for gathering this information. Knowledge and expertise are becoming even more important as consumers become more sophisticated. Several areas of knowledge about your product are discussed in the following paragraphs.

Features of properties include those of the community as well as those of specific houses. For example, clients may want to know the following:

- Are there good schools nearby?
- Where is the nearest racquetball court?
- What are the neighbors like?

Because it is difficult to know everything about every community, many salespeople begin by specializing in a specific geographic area. Often this market area includes the neighborhoods in which you will do the most business. It will serve you well to get involved in these communities, get to know the neighborhood, and keep up with changes.

The brokerage firm, you, and the services you provide also are part of the product. Unanswered questions and objections raised in these areas can kill a sale. Early in your relationship with your clients or prospects, present information that will establish your credibility and show them that you have the resources to work hard for them. Some agents hand out fact sheets or a résumé. An anecdote about a way in which you and the firm have benefited others may help you establish rapport and provide reassurance if the situation seems appropriate.

> "There are advantages and disadvantages to this property," said the honest and well-informed real estate agent. "To the north is the gas works, to the east the glue factory, to the south a fish and chips shop, and to the west a sewage farm. These are the disadvantages."
>
> "What are the advantages?" the customer asked.
>
> "You can always tell which way the wind is blowing" was the agent's reply.

As this anecdote humorously illustrates, you often can present disadvantages as advantages.

Because it is unlikely that a piece of property will have every feature a client wants, it makes sense to play up the significant features and downplay the ones that are lacking. However, be meticulous about disclosure issues. Do not neglect or change the presentation of negative information just because it is (or may be

FIGURE 10.1

Types of Prospects   **General Strategies to Use**

Silent Prospect—the "Clam"—Does not indicate whether he or she is agreeing or disagreeing.	=	Ask leading questions; be more personal than usual.
Procrastinator—the "Putter-Offer"—Does not know his or her own mind; has difficulty making up mind.	=	Summarize benefits that prospect will lose if he or she does not act. Be positive, self-assured, and dramatic.
Glad-Hander—Talkative or over enthusiastic.	=	Lead these prospects back into the sale after letting them talk themselves out!
Argumentative Type—Usually is insincere and tries the salesperson's patience.	=	Sincerity and respect on the sales person's part will create respect. Consider, "you're absolutely right. That's why you'll appreciate..."
Slow or Methodical Type—Appears to weigh every word of the salesperson	=	Slow down and simplify details. Adjust your tempo to your prospect's. This approach is often referred to as mirroring and can lead a sales prospect comfortably to a positive decision.
Skeptical or Suspicious Type—Convinced that every salesperson is trying to "pull the wool over his or her eyes."	=	Stay with the facts, and be conservative in statements. Allay the prospect's fears.
Overcautious or Timid Type—Acts as if he or she does not trust the salesperson.	=	Take it slow and easy. Reassure on every point. Use logic and make it simple.
Impulsive Type—Apt to interrupt presentation before you state all points.	=	Speed up presentation, concentrating only on important points. Omit details when possible.
Opinionated—Ego Type—Is overconfident, with strong opinions.	=	Give these prospects "rope" by appealing to their egos. Listen attentively and guide them, using their opinions.

perceived as) a disadvantage. Both legally and morally you owe each client a high standard of care—a quality of service that a "reasonably prudent person" would provide. Since the *Easton v. Strassburger* case (see page 75), many questions have arisen in the area of responsibilities.

There will be times when you are not the person who can best serve a particular client. Perhaps he or she is looking for a home that lies outside your market area. Or someone may want a piece of investment property that will involve intricate tax and financing complications. The worst mistake you can make is thinking that you can serve everyone. It is far better to refer people to brokers or other individuals who have the required expertise.

■ OBTAINING THE OFFER

In striving to obtain an offer to purchase, you will find that each transaction is unique and has its own approach and required motivation. However, there are some general principles to apply. Understanding why customers buy and the basic steps of transactions help you prepare for a presentation that will lead to an offer. Four basic steps are illustrated in Figure 10.2. They are discussed in the following paragraphs.

Appeal to Buying Motives

Merriam-Webster's Collegiate Dictionary defines *motive* as "something (as a need or desire) that causes a person to act." Understanding a buyer's needs and wants is absolutely essential for optimum results. Remember, you are going to be selling the benefits that match those needs and wants. After all, why should an individual buy a home and be responsible for its maintenance, taxes, and so on, rather than rent for life? Why should a family skimp and save for a down payment and make monthly payments when that family could live in a public housing unit or with relatives?

> In selling property you should be selling the benefits.

Ownership of real property satisfies several basic needs or **buying motives.**

Survival.   The most basic human need is survival. If a home has no amenities other than providing shelter, it satisfies the basic human need to survive.

Security.   The desire for security is a fundamental need that has many applications in the selling process. Every licensee should appeal to it. The home is the principal financial asset of many Americans. In times of financial stress the home is always something to fall back on. People feel secure in their own homes. They do not have to worry about landlords asking them to leave because the landlords want their own children to live there.

FIGURE 10.2

Steps in Obtaining the Offer

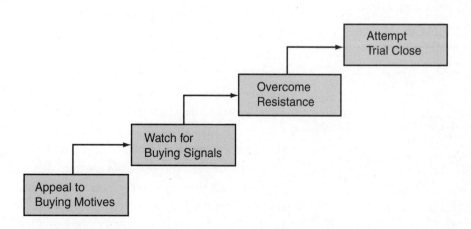

Pride of Ownership.   Once buyers obtain basic shelter, pride impels many to pay considerably more for additional benefits. What they feel their friends and/or family will think of the home influences many buyers. By a statement such as "Wouldn't you like to entertain your friends on this delightful patio?" you can create an image of pride in showing the home to others. Many salespeople use pride of ownership immediately by referring to the property being shown as if the prospective buyers were already the owners.

Love of Family.   Desirable school areas, recreational facilities, shopping conveniences, or other factors that may appeal to one or to all members of the family often induce the purchase of certain property. Many times one of the foremost factors in the buyer's mind will be how the home can help the family. Don't forget that in many families their pet is regarded as an important family member.

Health.   Motivation arising from health interests is closely allied to the survival instinct and can be a determining factor in a decision to buy. The quality of the environment—of the air and water, lower noise levels, the avoidance of urban congestion—often motivates a decision to buy.

Desire for Profit or Gain.   More people have started on the road to financial independence through home ownership than in any other way. Buying a home is an investment for the future because well-located properties usually increase in value, a process called *appreciation*. The amount of appreciation depends on numerous factors, such as the demand for housing in the area, the supply of homes, the availability of good financing, and the area's economy. Historically, property values in California have tended to increase an average of more than 3 percent a year, although there have been periods when values have declined. For the long term, home ownership is likely to be the best investment or savings program the average family will ever have.

Tax Benefits.   Home ownership as well as second-home ownership offers significant tax advantages that influence many buyers. The deductibility of property taxes as well as interest means that true costs are significantly less than they appear. The special tax exemptions available for gains on the sale of primary residences is the frosting on the cake because it makes home ownership a must for anyone concerned about income taxes. (See Chapter 14.)

Comfort and Convenience.   The human drive for comfort and convenience has less influence than the other, previously mentioned factors. When basic needs have been fulfilled, however, these may be considered as an added dimension.

Reason versus Emotion.   *Logic* makes people think, or reason. *Emotion* makes them act. Potential buyers may decide logically that a property is suited for them, but they may not act because the property does not trigger an emotional response. *In most situations buyers do not buy what they need, they buy what they want.* The successful salesperson probes to find the buyers' desires that, when satisfied, will trigger their motivation to buy. This is why communication is so important. What a buyer says he or she wants is likely to be based on reason; what the buyer really wants may be based more on emotion than on reason. If you pay attention while showing a house, you can determine the emotional needs of the buyer and select properties to show that meet those needs. You can gain an understanding of which of several properties a buyer actually wants by questions such as, "If these properties were priced identically, which property would you prefer?" Follow this up with, "Why?" By listening you can offer knowledgeable assistance based on experience of other buyers whom your buyers can relate to. It is much easier to sell buyers a property that appeals to their emotions than one that appears sensible for them.

An approach to use where a buyer can afford but needs a reason to buy a luxury home would be, "It's more than a home, it's an investment, and you don't have to wait to sell it to realize the appreciation. A great many homeowners have sent their children through college by refinancing their homes or using a home equity line of credit." Buyers are usually receptive to rational reasons to buy property that appeals to their emotions.

Sensory Appeal.   People learn about the surrounding world through their senses, which include sound, sight, smell, taste, and touch. You can enhance your presentation by employing all of the senses as well as by emphasizing the benefits that can be appreciated by various senses.

In appealing to the sense of *sight*, point out the restful and interesting views from the windows, the lush lawns, the lines of the house, the ample wall space. Be careful not to go overboard about certain colors; they may be your choice but not the buyer's.

The appeal of *sound* may be either its absence or its presence—perhaps it will be music, human-made or natural, to a buyer's ears. Where possible, call attention to the sound made by the ocean, a lake, babbling brook, or birds. Also, make buyers aware that machinery in the house, such as air conditioners, water closets, and power switches, operate quietly.

To appeal to buyers' sense of *smell*, call attention to the fresh air, flower scents or, if possible, the smell of cedar from closets or chests.

The sense of *taste* might be appealed to by testing the flavor of well water, vegetables from the garden, or fruit from the trees. An excellent technique is to cut open an orange or other fruit with a pocketknife and offer a slice to the prospective buyers.

Appeal to the sense of *touch* by touching the carpeting, knocking on the solid wood paneling, or breaking up a lump of garden soil in your hand. Get your prospects to do the same. By touching they come a little closer to ownership.

Negative Motivation. **Negative motivation** applies to knowing what someone does *not* want. There are many things we do not want: pain, hunger, fatigue, worry, strife, just to mention a few. Negative motivation can be more immediate and real to a person than positive motivation. People seem to know what they do not want better than what they do want.

To avoid a fruitless, time-wasting search, the salesperson should endeavor to learn buyers' negative motivations as well as the positive ones. Some disadvantages of home ownership are described in Figure 10.3: large initial investment, risk, increased expenses, restricted mobility, a low level of liquidity, and greater responsibility.

Watch for Buying Signals

In many situations and at various psychological moments during your presentation, prospects may signal that they are ready to buy. These **buying signals**—some action, phrase, or facial expression of buyers—are tip-offs to the salesperson. A buying signal says, "I'm ready to talk terms if you are." These signals are like green lights. After prospects have exhibited a buying signal, follow up the opportunity with a closing statement. Buying signals can be actions, words, or facial expressions.

Actions. You are making a presentation, and the prospects stay mum. They do not even grunt. You start to wonder if you are talking their language. Suddenly one of them picks up the deposit receipt and reads a clause or two. Stop your presentation and swing into your close—they are interested. Prospects also are signaling when they return to an upstairs room for a second look or to measure a room.

Words. "Don't you think the price is a little too high?" Even an objection or an expression of resistance from the prospect can spell "buying signal." The alert salesperson hears it as a signal, because it shows that the buyer actually is thinking about the purchase. Other possible signals occur if a buyer

- asks the salesperson to go over the financing details again,
- inquires about possession time,
- requests information about closing costs,
- seems reluctant to leave a property, or
- starts to whisper with the spouse.

Facial Expressions. A salesperson who is not watching customers carefully may easily miss facial-expression signals. A signal may be as subtle as a raised eyebrow or a quizzical look. To an experienced salesperson, these expressions could mean "I'll take it; just ask me."

FIGURE 10.3

Disadvantages of Home Ownership

- **Large Initial Investment:** Normally, buying a home requires a down payment of 5 percent to 20 percent of the purchase price, with the exception of DVA and some FHA loans. This means the purchase price of a $200,000 home may require a down payment of between $10,000 and $40,000. In addition, the closing costs will be from $2,000 to $5,000.
- **Risk:** Whenever customers invest money, they risk losing some or all of it. However, well-located properties kept in good condition seldom lose significant value if held for a long term.
- **Increase in Expenses:** Although mortgage payments remain constant in the case of fixed-rate loans, other costs may increase. Property taxes creep upward. Maintenance costs increase as the home ages. Adjustable-rate loans could have an increase in interest and payments. Buyers have to weigh some of these increased costs against the advantages of ownership, but they should remember that rents also increase.
- **Restricted Mobility:** To a degree people are less mobile once they have bought a home. However, houses can be sold or rented out by the owner.
- **Lack of Liquidity:** Some say they dislike home ownership because their investment is not liquid. While an investment in a home is not as liquid as having money in the bank, homeowners can use their property as a source of cash. For example, homeowners might consider borrowing on the property by taking out a home equity loan. Or they could refinance the first mortgage once sufficient equity has been developed.
- **Greater Responsibility:** An investment in real property has responsibilities. Buyers must maintain the property properly. For example, they may have to climb a ladder to paint or call a painter and pay the bill. The lawn needs to be watered and cut to protect the investment.

Overcome Resistance

To obtain the offer, be prepared to answer any objections raised by the buyer. Buyer resistance will vary with each transaction. Typical objections might include some of the following statements:

- "The price is too high."
- "The water pressure is too low."
- "The rooms are too small."
- "The taxes are too high."
- "I can't buy until I sell."
- "I can't get occupancy soon enough."
- "I'll never get my kids into that school."

Human nature being what it is, some salespeople feel they must conquer objections by crushing them decisively. It is an unfortunate truth that many salespeople feel they must treat objections as barriers raised to block them from their goal—the sale or the offer. They see an objection as being in direct conflict with their best interests, and therefore they fear it and wish to combat it quickly.

In contrast to this, you should treat an objection as a prelude to a sale, a natural part of any sales routine. Objections may occur while showing the house or in your office before signing the offer. Before proceeding to your counterattack, determine two things in your own mind:

1. Is it really an objection or just a comment?
2. Is it an objection you can and should do something about?

There are ways to handle even real objections. Five basic steps to be used in meeting objections are shown in Figure 10.4. Carefully following these steps leads to obtaining the offer and closing the sale.

> You can't overcome objections if you don't know what they are.

Welcome Objections.   Do not fear objections; welcome them. Encourage prospects to tell what is on their minds. Objections help pinpoint your talk. They may be the prospects' way of asking for more information. They may throw some light on the prospects' thinking.

Concede before Answering.   To avoid putting the buyer on the defensive, recognize legitimate concerns. You might make a comment such as "Your suggestion has much to recommend it," "I can appreciate your concerns," or "I understand how you feel."

Rephrase an Objection as a Question.   The buyer might say "I don't like tract houses," to which you could reply, "As I understand it then, Mr. and Mrs. Buyer, your question is this: 'Am I better off buying a smaller custom home in a less desirable neighborhood for the same money or would I gain greater enjoyment by owning this larger home with more amenities in a great neighborhood?'" Try to restate objections as questions. Doing so shows the buyer that you are working together, not as adversaries.

FIGURE 10.4

Meeting a Buyer's Objections

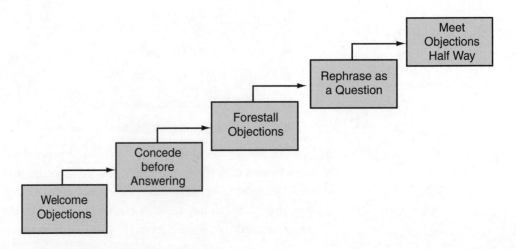

If a prospective buyer objects to a price, your first question should be "Why?" Make the prospective buyer justify a lower price and then ask, "What do you feel would be a fair price for this property?" If the buyer replies with a price, your response could be, "How did you arrive at that price?" Listen attentively. You could correct misconceptions and justify what you feel is a fair price or you could state, "While I think your price is a little low, let's try it. If the owners accept, I think you'll have made a really advantageous purchase."

Meet Objections Half Way.   A well-known technique for answering objections is the "Yes, but" technique. This technique meets objections half way. The objection may be "This is the smallest bedroom I've ever seen." The licensee could answer, "Yes, Ms. Buyer, you're right, that is a small bedroom, and I imagine it was intended for a young person. If this were your house, whose bedroom would this be?" You could then continue with "How would you furnish this room for your [son/daughter]?" If buyers can solve their own objections, you'll have gone a long way toward making a sale.

> If the buyers can solve their own objections, you are on the path to a sale.

Forestall Objections.   Your experience tells you to expect certain objections from your prospect. Bring up these potential objections before the prospect does. This is known as *forestalling* or *anticipating the objection*. Its effect is to reduce the objection's importance and to show the prospect that you do not fear it.

Answering a Question with a Question.   You must handle questions as well as objections. One way to answer a question from a buyer is to use a "hook." This is the technique of answering a question with a question. It prolongs the sales interview and keeps the buyer in the act. Three examples are:

1. *Question:* Will the sellers agree to an April 1 closing?

   Wrong Answer: I'm pretty sure they will.

   Using a Hook: Do you want an April 1 closing?

2. *Question:* Will the sellers consider a lower offer?

   Wrong Answer: Yes, they've indicated they might listen to an offer.

   Using a Hook: How much are you prepared to offer?

3. *Question:* Is the stove (refrigerator, drapes, carpeting) included?

   Wrong Answer: I'll ask the seller.

   Using a Hook: Do you want the stove (refrigerator, drapes, carpeting) included?

Attempt a Trial Close

If a salesperson successfully builds each part of the sale throughout the presentation, the close will come easily. In many cases the buyer reaction says, "I'm ready to make an offer." There is a psychological moment for a **trial close,** but it varies with each transaction. Figure 10.5 shows some signs that help licensees decide when to close.

FIGURE **10.5**

Closing Signs

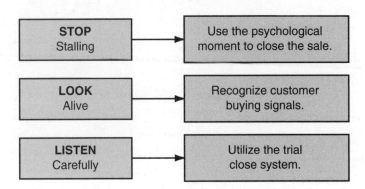

Knowing WHEN to close means—

STOP Stalling	→	Use the psychological moment to close the sale.
LOOK Alive	→	Recognize customer buying signals.
LISTEN Carefully	→	Utilize the trial close system.

> With a trial close, you get the buyers to agree to something that indicates they are willing to buy.

Attempting a trial close often is called "test and heat." To close any sale and get the buyers' signatures on the deposit receipt, do what your great-grandmother did with the old-fashioned flat-iron—test and heat. If the customer is not ready to buy, add a little "heat." This means present new evidence or reiterate key sales points and try again.

Beginning with the first interview, the salesperson must build for this moment during every phase of the sale because the buyer may make a decision at any time. Although all situations and all buyers are different, the following five basic closing principles can be set forth:

1. Throughout the sale, use "you" and "yours" or the customer(s) name.
2. Obtain agreement on a variety of things throughout the interview.
3. Tell a complete story in terms of customer(s) buying motives. Turn the features into personal benefits and hold some talking points in reserve.
4. Watch for buying signals.
5. Ask for their signature(s) if they are not volunteered.

Closing Techniques

Six basic closing techniques often are employed: the assumptive close, the positive choice, inducement, fear of loss, narrative, and asking for the deposit. Of course, there are hundreds of variations on these closing techniques.

Assumptive Close. In an **assumptive close** you assume the buyer is going to buy and you complete the deposit receipt form. This close is a natural follow-through when a buyer flashes a buying-signal question such as "Can I get possession by July 1?" Your response should be "Would you like possession by July 1?"

Other assumptive closings to consider when you are getting a positive feedback include the following:

"Does 30 days for closing meet your needs?" (If the answer is affirmative or another date is given, you should be writing this offer.)

"The property is listed at [$], but you as the buyer decide what you wish to offer. Would you want to offer [$] and be sure you have this home, or would you want to offer a different amount?"

"I think we have found your new home, let's put it on paper."

Positive Choice.   Give the buyer a **positive choice**—that is, a choice between two things rather than between something and nothing. The skillful salesperson never asks the buyer a question that can be answered with a flat no. Here are two examples of positive-choice questions:

> A *positive choice* is a choice of factors, either of which indicates a purchase.

1. "Would you prefer FHA-insured financing with a lower down payment and higher monthly payments or conventional financing with a higher down payment and lower monthly payments?"

2. "If the seller will retile the bathroom, which color tile do you prefer, white or beige?"

Inducement.   If used properly, an **inducement** can be a powerful stimulant to a close. For example:

"If you buy now, I believe we can lock in the lower interest rate. You would like the lower rate, wouldn't you?"

"I'm sure we could arrange the closing of escrow so you will not make double payments. You would like to save that money, wouldn't you?"

Be careful when you use this technique. If the outcome of the sale hinges on a lower interest rate, a change of tile, or an added refrigerator, and if you cannot deliver, you may lose the sale. Try to hedge on your commitment by saying that you will do your best to obtain the inducement. Never suggest an inducement that requires the seller to commit to something not previously agreed to, as this may be seen as unethical.

Fear of Loss.   The fear-of-loss method, often called the "standing room only" technique, is effective only if it is based on fact. Buyers have built up an immunity to such statements as "This is the last house in this plot, and the builder doesn't plan any further development." This technique works only if it is based on facts concerning a personal, immediate, and real situation.

Here is an example of a believable fear-of-loss close that is true and is based on researched facts:

"This is the last home by this builder available in this tract. All the others are sold. When the new tract is open, the price will be $5,000 higher for the same home. Wouldn't you rather buy now and save that amount?"

Narrative.   A *narrative close* involves the use of a third party as an ally. If you are able to produce third-party verification of the fact you are trying to establish, the buyer is likely to accept what you say. For example, you could show an article from the evening newspaper that states that interest rates are expected to rise. In this situation someone else is conveying the information. Or you could say, "Mr. Jones just down the street had a question similar to yours. We were able to find a solution for him. If you wish, we can call him to verify my story."

Ask for the Deposit.   Many salespeople do an excellent job of making a presentation and even covering all objections, but they are hesitant to ask for the sale. The reason is fear; they get a battlefield fear sensation. They fear a rejection, a no answer. Consequently they overlook asking or are reluctant to ask for the deposit.

> If you want a positive response, you have to ask first.

Buyers will buy if they are asked to, but many salespeople rarely ask. Practice and experiment with asking for the deposit. For example, say, "These units do offer an excellent appreciation potential if you're willing to do some fixing up. Why don't you get started on your investment program now? Will you give me your deposit check and let me get your purchase under way?"

> It's all right to ask again.

If one closing doesn't work, continue to emphasize benefits. Suggest another look at the property and try another closing. If the property fits the buyers' needs, they like the property, and they can afford it, then treat a failure as a "maybe." A little more time might be all it takes.

A coffee salesman we know once asked a close friend, the owner of a large restaurant, why he had never purchased coffee from him. The reply was, "You never asked!"

Killing a Sale

A positive sales approach is to ask leading questions, gain agreement throughout the sale, then ask for the offer. A salesperson who does not use a positive approach may be the loser. The sale also can be killed by

- talking too much and too fast,
- being overeager to sell,
- having incomplete knowledge,
- using high-pressure tactics,
- exhibiting fear,
- criticizing competitors,
- straying from the subject,
- displaying a negative selling attitude, or
- being argumentative.

Buyer Agent Closing

When you are representing the buyer under a buyer-agency agreement, you have a duty to best serve the interests of your principal. Those interests would extend from finding a house your principal wants to doing your best to obtain the property at the best price and to protect the buyer against any foreseeable problems. As a buyer's agent, you should have built a trust relationship so you can ask a simple question, "Do you like this house?" and/or "Does this house meet your needs better than anything I have found for you?" Don't ask these questions unless you know the reply will be positive. You could then continue with, "I think we should offer $ _____ because . . . And any offer should be contingent upon a professional inspection and . . . Does that make sense to you?" If the responsive is positive, and it should be, you can begin writing up the offer.

Fine-Tuning the Offer

If buyers suggest an offer at an unrealistic price and/or terms, consider writing up the offer. Before you give it to your prospective buyers, ask

"Do you like this house?"

"You say you like the house, but you want to give an offer that doesn't indicate this. If you were the sellers, what would you think about this offer?"

"If you want the property, I suggest your offer be closer to reality. Raise this offer by just [ ] percent and you'll have a chance to be an owner. Let's write it up at [$]. At that price it is still one heck of a bargain, and your offer at least will have a chance of being accepted."

Complete this offer and hand it and a pen to the prospective buyers.

■ THE CALIFORNIA RESIDENTIAL PURCHASE AGREEMENT AND JOINT ESCROW INSTRUCTIONS

"An oral contract is not worth the paper it is written on," said Samuel Goldwyn. The California Statute of Frauds stipulates that all real estate sales contracts must be in writing. An exception to that rule is a lease of real property for one year or less.

When a sale has been consummated and the offer obtained, put everything in writing to avoid costly litigation in the future. It is essential that the purchase contract include the entire agreement of the parties. Poor draftsmanship of the purchase contract is a significant factor in lawsuits between buyer, seller, and/or broker. Not only must the agreement be complete, but also the parties should fully understand the agreement before signing. Many deposit receipt forms were used in California, and the buyer's offer could be submitted on any of these. However, the number of forms caused a great deal of concern in legal circles and with the California Association of REALTORS® because brokers are seldom attorneys and may be confused by the language employed. As a result, in 1985, the California Association of REALTORS®, in cooperation with the state bar and with the approval of the Department of Real Estate, developed a model form, the Residential Purchase Agreement [and Receipt for Deposit], now the *California Residential Purchase Agreement and Joint Escrow Instructions* that in its present, updated form is widely used in California. (See Figure 10.6.)

FIGURE 10.6

California Residential Purchase Agreement and Joint Escrow Instructions

CALIFORNIA ASSOCIATION OF REALTORS®

CALIFORNIA RESIDENTIAL PURCHASE AGREEMENT AND JOINT ESCROW INSTRUCTIONS
For Use With Single Family Residential Property — Attached or Detached
(C.A.R. Form RPA-CA, Revised 10/02)

Date _____, at _____, California.

1. **OFFER:**
   A. **THIS IS AN OFFER FROM** _____ ("Buyer").
   B. **THE REAL PROPERTY TO BE ACQUIRED** is described as _____
      _____, Assessor's Parcel No. _____, situated in
      _____, County of _____, California, ("Property").
   C. **THE PURCHASE PRICE** offered is _____
      _____ Dollars $ _____.
   D. **CLOSE OF ESCROW** shall occur on _____ (date)(or ☐ _____ **Days** After Acceptance).

2. **FINANCE TERMS:** Obtaining the loans below **is a contingency** of this Agreement unless: **(i)** either 2K or 2L is checked below; or **(ii)** otherwise agreed in writing. Buyer shall act diligently and in good faith to obtain the designated loans. Obtaining deposit, down payment and closing costs **is not a contingency.** Buyer represents that funds will be good when deposited with Escrow Holder.
   A. **INITIAL DEPOSIT:** Buyer has given a deposit in the amount of . . . .$ _____
      to the agent submitting the offer (or to ☐ _____), by personal check
      (or ☐ _____), made payable to _____,
      which shall be held uncashed until Acceptance and then deposited within 3 business days after
      Acceptance (or ☐ _____), with
      Escrow Holder, (or ☐ into Broker's trust account).
   B. **INCREASED DEPOSIT:** Buyer shall deposit with Escrow Holder an increased deposit in the amount of . . .$ _____
      within _____ **Days** After Acceptance, or ☐ _____.
   C. **FIRST LOAN IN THE AMOUNT OF** . . . .$ _____
      (1) NEW First Deed of Trust in favor of lender, encumbering the Property, securing a note payable at
      maximum interest of _____% fixed rate, or _____% initial adjustable rate with a maximum
      interest rate of _____%, balance due in _____ years, amortized over _____ years. Buyer
      shall pay loan fees/points not to exceed _____. (These terms apply whether the designated loan
      is conventional, FHA or VA.)
      (2) ☐ FHA ☐ VA: (The following terms only apply to the FHA or VA loan that is checked.)
      Seller shall pay _____% discount points. Seller shall pay other fees not allowed to be paid by
      Buyer, ☐ not to exceed $_____. Seller shall pay the cost of lender required Repairs
      (including those for wood destroying pest) not otherwise provided for in this Agreement, ☐ not to
      exceed $ _____. (Actual loan amount may increase if mortgage insurance premiums,
      funding fees or closing costs are financed.)
   D. **ADDITIONAL FINANCING TERMS:** ☐ Seller financing, (C.A.R. Form SFA); ☐ secondary financing, ...$ _____
      (C.A.R. Form PAA, paragraph 4A); ☐ assumed financing (C.A.R. Form PAA, paragraph 4B)
      _____
      _____
   E. **BALANCE OF PURCHASE PRICE** (not including costs of obtaining loans and other closing costs) in the amount of . . .$ _____
      to be deposited with Escrow Holder within sufficient time to close escrow.
   F. **PURCHASE PRICE (TOTAL):** . . . .$ _____
   G. **LOAN APPLICATIONS:** Within 7 (or ☐ _____) **Days** After Acceptance, Buyer shall provide Seller a letter from lender or mortgage loan broker stating that, based on a review of Buyer's written application and credit report, Buyer is prequalified or preapproved for the NEW loan specified in 2C above.
   H. **VERIFICATION OF DOWN PAYMENT AND CLOSING COSTS:** Buyer (or Buyer's lender or loan broker pursuant to 2G) shall, within 7 (or ☐ _____) **Days** After Acceptance, provide Seller written verification of Buyer's down payment and closing costs.
   I. **LOAN CONTINGENCY REMOVAL: (i)** Within 17 (or ☐ _____) **Days** After Acceptance, Buyer shall, as specified in paragraph 14, remove the loan contingency or cancel this Agreement; **OR (ii)** (if checked) ☐ the loan contingency shall remain in effect until the designated loans are funded.
   J. **APPRAISAL CONTINGENCY AND REMOVAL:** This Agreement is (**OR,** if checked, ☐ is NOT) contingent upon the Property appraising at no less than the specified purchase price. Buyer shall, as specified in paragraph 14, remove the appraisal contingency or cancel this Agreement when the loan contingency is removed (or, if checked, ☐ within 17 (or ☐ _____) **Days** After Acceptance).
   K. ☐ **NO LOAN CONTINGENCY** (If checked): Obtaining any loan in paragraphs 2C, 2D or elsewhere in this Agreement is NOT a contingency of this Agreement. If Buyer does not obtain the loan and as a result Buyer does not purchase the Property, Seller may be entitled to Buyer's deposit or other legal remedies.
   L. ☐ **ALL CASH OFFER** (If checked): No loan is needed to purchase the Property. Buyer shall, within 7 (or ☐ _____) **Days** After Acceptance, provide Seller written verification of sufficient funds to close this transaction.

3. **CLOSING AND OCCUPANCY:**
   A. Buyer intends (or ☐ does not intend) to occupy the Property as Buyer's primary residence.
   B. **Seller-occupied or vacant property:** Occupancy shall be delivered to Buyer at _____ AM/PM, ☐ on the date of Close Of Escrow; ☐ on _____; or ☐ no later than _____ **Days** After Close Of Escrow. (C.A.R. Form PAA, paragraph 2.) If transfer of title and occupancy do not occur at the same time, Buyer and Seller are advised to: **(i)** enter into a written occupancy agreement; and **(ii)** consult with their insurance and legal advisors.

Buyer's Initials (_____)(_____)
Seller's Initials (_____)(_____)

Reviewed by _____ Date _____

EQUAL HOUSING OPPORTUNITY

CALIFORNIA RESIDENTIAL PURCHASE AGREEMENT (RPA-CA PAGE 1 OF 8)

FIGURE 10.6

California Residential Purchase Agreement and Joint Escrow Instructions (continued)

    C. Tenant-occupied property: (i) Property shall be vacant at least 5 (or ☐ _____) **Days** Prior to Close Of Escrow, unless otherwise agreed in writing. **Note to Seller: If you are unable to deliver Property vacant in accordance with rent control and other applicable Law, you may be in breach of this Agreement.**

    OR (ii) (if checked) ☐ **Tenant to remain in possession.** The attached addendum is incorporated into this Agreement (C.A.R. Form PAA, paragraph 3.);

    OR (iii) (if checked) ☐ **This Agreement is contingent** upon Buyer and Seller entering into a written agreement regarding occupancy of the Property within the time specified in paragraph 14. If no written agreement is reached within this time, either Buyer or Seller may cancel this Agreement in writing.

    D. At Close Of Escrow, Seller assigns to Buyer any assignable warranty rights for items included in the sale and shall provide any available Copies of such warranties. Brokers cannot and will not determine the assignability of any warranties.

    E. At Close Of Escrow, unless otherwise agreed in writing, Seller shall provide keys and/or means to operate all locks, mailboxes, security systems, alarms and garage door openers. If Property is a condominium or located in a common interest subdivision, Buyer may be required to pay a deposit to the Homeowners' Association ("HOA") to obtain keys to accessible HOA facilities.

4. ALLOCATION OF COSTS (If checked): Unless otherwise specified here, this paragraph only determines who is to pay for the report, inspection, test or service mentioned. If not specified here or elsewhere in this Agreement, the determination of who is to pay for any work recommended or identified by any such report, inspection, test or service shall be by the method specified in paragraph 14.

    A. WOOD DESTROYING PEST INSPECTION:

      (1) ☐ Buyer ☐ Seller shall pay for an inspection and report for wood destroying pests and organisms ("Report") which shall be prepared by _____, a registered structural pest control company. The Report shall cover the accessible areas of the main building and attached structures and, if checked: ☐ detached garages and carports, ☐ detached decks, ☐ the following other structures or areas _____. The Report shall not include roof coverings. If Property is a condominium or located in a common interest subdivision, the Report shall include only the separate interest and any exclusive-use areas being transferred and shall not include common areas, unless otherwise agreed. Water tests of shower pans on upper level units may not be performed without consent of the owners of property below the shower.

    OR (2) ☐ (If checked) The attached addendum (C.A.R. Form WPA) regarding wood destroying pest inspection and allocation of cost is incorporated into this Agreement.

    B. OTHER INSPECTIONS AND REPORTS:

      (1) ☐ Buyer ☐ Seller shall pay to have septic or private sewage disposal systems inspected _____.

      (2) ☐ Buyer ☐ Seller shall pay to have domestic wells tested for water potability and productivity _____.

      (3) ☐ Buyer ☐ Seller shall pay for a natural hazard zone disclosure report prepared by _____.

      (4) ☐ Buyer ☐ Seller shall pay for the following inspection or report _____.

      (5) ☐ Buyer ☐ Seller shall pay for the following inspection or report _____.

    C. GOVERNMENT REQUIREMENTS AND RETROFIT:

      (1) ☐ Buyer ☐ Seller shall pay for smoke detector installation and/or water heater bracing, if required by Law. Prior to Close Of Escrow, Seller shall provide Buyer a written statement of compliance in accordance with state and local Law, unless exempt.

      (2) ☐ Buyer ☐ Seller shall pay the cost of compliance with any other minimum mandatory government retrofit standards, inspections and reports if required as a condition of closing escrow under any Law. _____.

    D. ESCROW AND TITLE:

      (1) ☐ Buyer ☐ Seller shall pay escrow fee _____. Escrow Holder shall be _____.

      (2) ☐ Buyer ☐ Seller shall pay for **owner's** title insurance policy specified in paragraph 12 _____. Owner's title policy to be issued by _____. (Buyer shall pay for any title insurance policy insuring Buyer's **lender**, unless otherwise agreed in writing.)

    E. OTHER COSTS:

      (1) ☐ Buyer ☐ Seller shall pay County transfer tax or transfer fee _____.

      (2) ☐ Buyer ☐ Seller shall pay City transfer tax or transfer fee _____.

      (3) ☐ Buyer ☐ Seller shall pay HOA transfer fee _____.

      (4) ☐ Buyer ☐ Seller shall pay HOA document preparation fees _____.

      (5) ☐ Buyer ☐ Seller shall pay the cost, not to exceed $ _____, of a one-year home warranty plan, issued by _____, with the following optional coverage: _____.

      (6) ☐ Buyer ☐ Seller shall pay for _____.

      (7) ☐ Buyer ☐ Seller shall pay for _____.

5. STATUTORY DISCLOSURES (INCLUDING LEAD-BASED PAINT HAZARD DISCLOSURES) AND CANCELLATION RIGHTS:

    A. (1) Seller shall, within the time specified in paragraph 14, deliver to Buyer, if required by Law: **(i)** Federal Lead-Based Paint Disclosures and pamphlet ("Lead Disclosures"); and **(ii)** disclosures or notices required by sections 1102 et. seq. and 1103 et. seq. of the California Civil Code ("Statutory Disclosures"). Statutory Disclosures include, but are not limited to, a Real Estate Transfer Disclosure Statement ("TDS"), Natural Hazard Disclosure Statement ("NHD"), notice or actual knowledge of release of illegal controlled substance, notice of special tax and/or assessments (or, if allowed, substantially equivalent notice regarding the Mello-Roos Community Facilities Act and Improvement Bond Act of 1915) and, if Seller has actual knowledge, an industrial use and military ordnance location disclosure (C.A.R. Form SSD).

      (2) Buyer shall, within the time specified in paragraph 14, return Signed Copies of the Statutory and Lead Disclosures to Seller.

      (3) In the event Seller, prior to Close Of Escrow, becomes aware of adverse conditions materially affecting the Property, or any material inaccuracy in disclosures, information or representations previously provided to Buyer of which Buyer is otherwise unaware, Seller shall promptly provide a subsequent or amended disclosure or notice, in writing, covering those items. **However, a subsequent or amended disclosure shall not be required for conditions and material inaccuracies disclosed in reports ordered and paid for by Buyer.**

Buyer's Initials (_____)(_____)
Seller's Initials (_____)(_____)

RPA-CA REVISED 10/02 (PAGE 2 OF 8)

Reviewed by _____ Date _____

CALIFORNIA RESIDENTIAL PURCHASE AGREEMENT (RPA-CA PAGE 2 OF 8)

FIGURE 10.6

California Residential Purchase Agreement and Joint Escrow Instructions (continued)

Property Address: _____ Date: _____

      (4) If any disclosure or notice specified in 5A(1), or subsequent or amended disclosure or notice is delivered to Buyer after the offer is Signed, Buyer shall have the right to cancel this Agreement within **3 Days** After delivery in person, or **5 Days** After delivery by deposit in the mail, by giving written notice of cancellation to Seller or Seller's agent. (Lead Disclosures sent by mail must be sent certified mail or better.)

      (5) **Note to Buyer and Seller: Waiver of Statutory and Lead Disclosures is prohibited by Law.**

  B. **NATURAL AND ENVIRONMENTAL HAZARDS:** Within the time specified in paragraph 14, Seller shall, if required by Law: **(i)** deliver to Buyer earthquake guides (and questionnaire) and environmental hazards booklet; **(ii)** even if exempt from the obligation to provide a NHD, disclose if the Property is located in a Special Flood Hazard Area; Potential Flooding (Inundation) Area; Very High Fire Hazard Zone; State Fire Responsibility Area; Earthquake Fault Zone; Seismic Hazard Zone; and **(iii)** disclose any other zone as required by Law and provide any other information required for those zones.

  C. **DATA BASE DISCLOSURE:** NOTICE: The California Department of Justice, sheriff's departments, police departments serving jurisdictions of 200,000 or more and many other local law enforcement authorities maintain for public access a data base of the locations of persons required to register pursuant to paragraph (1) of subdivision (a) of Section 290.4 of the Penal Code. The data base is updated on a quarterly basis and a source of information about the presence of these individuals in any neighborhood. The Department of Justice also maintains a Sex Offender Identification Line through which inquiries about individuals may be made. This is a "900" telephone service. Callers must have specific information about individuals they are checking. Information regarding neighborhoods is not available through the "900" telephone service.

6. **CONDOMINIUM/PLANNED UNIT DEVELOPMENT DISCLOSURES:**

  A. **SELLER HAS: 7 (or ☐ _____) Days** After Acceptance to disclose to Buyer whether the Property is a condominium, or is located in a planned unit development or other common interest subdivision.

  B. If the Property is a condominium or is located in a planned unit development or other common interest subdivision, Seller has 3 (or ☐ _____) **Days** After Acceptance to request from the HOA (C.A.R. Form HOA): **(i)** Copies of any documents required by Law; **(ii)** disclosure of any pending or anticipated claim or litigation by or against the HOA; **(iii)** a statement containing the location and number of designated parking and storage spaces; **(iv)** Copies of the most recent 12 months of HOA minutes for regular and special meetings; and **(v)** the names and contact information of all HOAs governing the Property (collectively, "CI Disclosures"). Seller shall itemize and deliver to Buyer all CI Disclosures received from the HOA and any CI Disclosures in Seller's possession. Buyer's approval of CI Disclosures is a contingency of this Agreement as specified in paragraph 14.

7. **CONDITIONS AFFECTING PROPERTY:**

  A. Unless otherwise agreed: **(i) the Property is sold (a) in its PRESENT physical condition as of the date of Acceptance and (b) subject to Buyer's Investigation rights; (ii)** the Property, including pool, spa, landscaping and grounds, is to be maintained in substantially the same condition as on the date of Acceptance; and **(iii)** all debris and personal property not included in the sale shall be removed by Close Of Escrow.

  B. **SELLER SHALL**, within the time specified in paragraph 14, **DISCLOSE KNOWN MATERIAL FACTS AND DEFECTS affecting the Property, including known insurance claims within the past five years, AND MAKE OTHER DISCLOSURES REQUIRED BY LAW.**

  C. **NOTE TO BUYER:** You are strongly advised to conduct investigations of the entire Property in order to determine its present condition since Seller may not be aware of all defects affecting the Property or other factors that you consider important. Property improvements may not be built according to code, in compliance with current Law, or have had permits issued.

  D. **NOTE TO SELLER: Buyer has the right to inspect the Property and, as specified in paragraph 14, based upon information discovered in those inspections: (i) cancel this Agreement; or (ii) request that you make Repairs or take other action.**

8. **ITEMS INCLUDED AND EXCLUDED:**

  A. **NOTE TO BUYER AND SELLER:** Items listed as included or excluded in the MLS, flyers or marketing materials are **not** included in the purchase price or excluded from the sale unless specified in 8B or C.

  B. **ITEMS INCLUDED IN SALE:**

      (1) All EXISTING fixtures and fittings that are attached to the Property;

      (2) Existing electrical, mechanical, lighting, plumbing and heating fixtures, ceiling fans, fireplace inserts, gas logs and grates, solar systems, built-in appliances, window and door screens, awnings, shutters, window coverings, attached floor coverings, television antennas, satellite dishes, private integrated telephone systems, air coolers/conditioners, pool/spa equipment, garage door openers/remote controls, mailbox, in-ground landscaping, trees/shrubs, water softeners, water purifiers, security systems/alarms;

      (3) The following items: _____
      _____

      (4) Seller represents that all items included in the purchase price, unless otherwise specified, are owned by Seller.

      (5) All items included shall be transferred free of liens and without Seller warranty.

  C. **ITEMS EXCLUDED FROM SALE:** _____
    _____

9. **BUYER'S INVESTIGATION OF PROPERTY AND MATTERS AFFECTING PROPERTY:**

  A. Buyer's acceptance of the condition of, and any other matter affecting the Property, is a contingency of this Agreement as specified in this paragraph and paragraph 14. Within the time specified in paragraph 14, Buyer shall have the right, at Buyer's expense unless otherwise agreed, to conduct inspections, investigations, tests, surveys and other studies ("Buyer Investigations"), including, but not limited to, the right to: **(i)** inspect for lead-based paint and other lead-based paint hazards; **(ii)** inspect for wood destroying pests and organisms; **(iii)** review the registered sex offender database; **(iv)** confirm the insurability of Buyer and the Property; and **(v)** satisfy Buyer as to any matter specified in the attached Buyer's Inspection Advisory (C.A.R. Form BIA). Without Seller's prior written consent, Buyer shall neither make nor cause to be made: **(i)** invasive or destructive Buyer's Investigations; or **(ii)** inspections by any governmental building or zoning inspector or government employee, unless required by Law.

  B. Buyer shall complete Buyer Investigations and, as specified in paragraph 14, remove the contingency or cancel the Agreement. Buyer shall give Seller, at no cost, complete Copies of all Buyer Investigation reports obtained by Buyer. Seller shall make the Property available for all Buyer Investigations. Seller shall have water, gas, electricity and all operable pilot lights on for Buyer's Investigations and through the date possession is made available to Buyer.

Buyer's Initials (_____)(_____)
Seller's Initials (_____)(_____)

RPA-CA REVISED 10/02 (PAGE 3 OF 8)

Reviewed by _____ Date _____

EQUAL HOUSING OPPORTUNITY

CALIFORNIA RESIDENTIAL PURCHASE AGREEMENT (RPA-CA PAGE 3 OF 8)

FIGURE 10.6

California Residential Purchase Agreement and Joint Escrow Instructions (continued)

Property Address: _____   Date: _____

10. **REPAIRS:** Repairs shall be completed prior to final verification of condition unless otherwise agreed in writing. Repairs to be performed at Seller's expense may be performed by Seller or through others, provided that the work complies with applicable Law, including governmental permit, inspection and approval requirements. Repairs shall be performed in a good, skillful manner with materials of quality and appearance comparable to existing materials. It is understood that exact restoration of appearance or cosmetic items following all Repairs may not be possible. Seller shall: **(i)** obtain receipts for Repairs performed by others; **(ii)** prepare a written statement indicating the Repairs performed by Seller and the date of such Repairs; and **(iii)** provide Copies of receipts and statements to Buyer prior to final verification of condition.

11. **BUYER INDEMNITY AND SELLER PROTECTION FOR ENTRY UPON PROPERTY:** Buyer shall: **(i)** keep the Property free and clear of liens; **(ii)** Repair all damage arising from Buyer Investigations; and **(iii)** indemnify and hold Seller harmless from all resulting liability, claims, demands, damages and costs. Buyer shall carry, or Buyer shall require anyone acting on Buyer's behalf to carry, policies of liability, workers' compensation and other applicable insurance, defending and protecting Seller from liability for any injuries to persons or property occurring during any Buyer Investigations or work done on the Property at Buyer's direction prior to Close Of Escrow. Seller is advised that certain protections may be afforded Seller by recording a "Notice of Non-responsibility" (C.A.R. Form NNR) for Buyer Investigations and work done on the Property at Buyer's direction. Buyer's obligations under this paragraph shall survive the termination of this Agreement.

12. **TITLE AND VESTING:**
   A. Within the time specified in paragraph 14, Buyer shall be provided a current preliminary (title) report, which is only an offer by the title insurer to issue a policy of title insurance and may not contain every item affecting title. Buyer's review of the preliminary report and any other matters which may affect title are a contingency of this Agreement as specified in paragraph 14.
   B. Title is taken in its present condition subject to all encumbrances, easements, covenants, conditions, restrictions, rights and other matters, whether of record or not, as of the date of Acceptance except: **(i)** monetary liens of record unless Buyer is assuming those obligations or taking the Property subject to those obligations; and **(ii)** those matters which Seller has agreed to remove in writing.
   C. Within the time specified in paragraph 14, Seller has a duty to disclose to Buyer all matters known to Seller affecting title, whether of record or not.
   D. At Close Of Escrow, Buyer shall receive a grant deed conveying title (or, for stock cooperative or long-term lease, an assignment of stock certificate or of Seller's leasehold interest), including oil, mineral and water rights if currently owned by Seller. Title shall vest as designated in Buyer's supplemental escrow instructions. THE MANNER OF TAKING TITLE MAY HAVE SIGNIFICANT LEGAL AND TAX CONSEQUENCES. CONSULT AN APPROPRIATE PROFESSIONAL.
   E. Buyer shall receive a CLTA/ALTA Homeowner's Policy of Title Insurance. A title company, at Buyer's request, can provide information about the availability, desirability, coverage, and cost of various title insurance coverages and endorsements. If Buyer desires title coverage other than that required by this paragraph, Buyer shall instruct Escrow Holder in writing and pay any increase in cost.

13. **SALE OF BUYER'S PROPERTY:**
   A. This Agreement is NOT contingent upon the sale of any property owned by Buyer.
   OR B. ☐ (If checked): The attached addendum (C.A.R. Form COP) regarding the contingency for the sale of property owned by Buyer is incorporated into this Agreement.

14. **TIME PERIODS; REMOVAL OF CONTINGENCIES; CANCELLATION RIGHTS: The following time periods may only be extended, altered, modified or changed by mutual written agreement. Any removal of contingencies or cancellation under this paragraph must be in writing (C.A.R. Form RRCR).**
   A. **SELLER HAS: 7 (or ☐ _____) Days** After Acceptance to deliver to Buyer all reports, disclosures and information for which Seller is responsible under paragraphs 4, 5A and B, 6A, 7B and 12.
   B. (1) **BUYER HAS: 17 (or ☐ _____) Days** After Acceptance, unless otherwise agreed in writing, to:
      (i) complete all Buyer Investigations; approve all disclosures, reports and other applicable information, which Buyer receives from Seller; and approve all matters affecting the Property (including lead-based paint and lead-based paint hazards as well as other information specified in paragraph 5 and insurability of Buyer and the Property); and
      (ii) return to Seller Signed Copies of Statutory and Lead Disclosures delivered by Seller in accordance with paragraph 5A.
      (2) Within the time specified in 14B(1), Buyer may request that Seller make repairs or take any other action regarding the Property. Seller has no obligation to agree to or respond to Buyer's requests. (C.A.R. Form RR)
      (3) By the end of the time specified in 14B(1) (or 2I for loan contingency or 2J for appraisal contingency), Buyer shall, in writing, remove the applicable contingency (C.A.R. Form RRCR) or cancel this Agreement. However, if the following inspections, reports or disclosures are not made within the time specified in 14A, then Buyer has 5 (or ☐ _____) Days after receipt of any such items, or the time specified in 14B(1), whichever is later, to remove the applicable contingency or cancel this Agreement in writing: **(i)** government-mandated inspections or reports required as a condition of closing; or **(ii)** Common Interest Disclosures pursuant to paragraph 6B.
   C. **CONTINUATION OF CONTINGENCY OR CONTRACTUAL OBLIGATION; SELLER RIGHT TO CANCEL:**
      (1) **Seller right to Cancel; Buyer Contingencies:** Seller, after first giving Buyer a Notice to Buyer to Perform (as specified below), may cancel this Agreement in writing and authorize return of Buyer's deposit if, by the time specified in this Agreement, Buyer does not remove in writing the applicable contingency or cancel this Agreement. Once all contingencies have been removed, failure of either Buyer or Seller to close escrow on time may be a breach of this Agreement.
      (2) **Continuation of Contingency:** Even after the expiration of the time specified in 14B(1), Buyer retains the right to make requests to Seller, remove in writing the applicable contingency or cancel this Agreement until Seller cancels pursuant to 14C(1). Once Seller receives Buyer's written removal of all contingencies, Seller may not cancel this Agreement pursuant to 14C(1).
      (3) **Seller right to Cancel; Buyer Contract Obligations:** Seller, after first giving Buyer a Notice to Buyer to Perform (as specified below), may cancel this Agreement in writing and authorize return of Buyer's deposit for any of the following reasons: **(i)** if Buyer fails to deposit funds as required by 2A or 2B; **(ii)** if the funds deposited pursuant to 2A or 2B are not good when deposited; **(iii)** if Buyer fails to provide a letter as required by 2G; **(iv)** if Buyer fails to provide verification as required by 2H or 2L; **(v)** if Seller reasonably disapproves of the verification provided by 2H or 2L; **(vi)** if Buyer fails to return Statutory and Lead Disclosures as required by paragraph 5A(2); or **(vii)** if Buyer fails to sign or initial a separate liquidated damage form for an increased deposit as required by paragraph 16. **Seller is not required to give Buyer a Notice to Perform regarding Close of Escrow.**
      (4) **Notice To Buyer To Perform:** The Notice to Buyer to Perform (C.A.R. Form NBP) shall: **(i)** be in writing; **(ii)** be signed by Seller; and **(iii)** give Buyer at least 24 (or ☐ _____) hours (or until the time specified in the applicable paragraph, whichever occurs last) to take the applicable action. A Notice to Buyer to Perform may not be given any earlier than **2 Days** Prior to the expiration of the applicable time for Buyer to remove a contingency or cancel this Agreement or meet a 14C(3) obligation.

Buyer's Initials (_____)(_____)
Seller's Initials (_____)(_____)

RPA-CA REVISED 10/02 (PAGE 4 OF 8)

Reviewed by _____ Date _____

CALIFORNIA RESIDENTIAL PURCHASE AGREEMENT (RPA-CA PAGE 4 OF 8)

FIGURE 10.6

California Residential Purchase Agreement and Joint Escrow Instructions (continued)

Property Address: _____ Date: _____

D. EFFECT OF BUYER'S REMOVAL OF CONTINGENCIES : If Buyer removes, in writing, any contingency or cancellation rights, unless otherwise specified in a separate written agreement between Buyer and Seller, Buyer shall conclusively be deemed to have: **(i)** completed all Buyer Investigations, and review of reports and other applicable information and disclosures pertaining to that contingency or cancellation right; **(ii)** elected to proceed with the transaction; and **(iii)** assumed all liability, responsibility and expense for Repairs or corrections pertaining to that contingency or cancellation right, or for inability to obtain financing.

E. EFFECT OF CANCELLATION ON DEPOSITS: If Buyer or Seller gives written notice of cancellation pursuant to rights duly exercised under the terms of this Agreement, Buyer and Seller agree to Sign mutual instructions to cancel the sale and escrow and release deposits, less fees and costs, to the party entitled to the funds. Fees and costs may be payable to service providers and vendors for services and products provided during escrow. **Release of funds will require mutual Signed release instructions from Buyer and Seller, judicial decision or arbitration award. A party may be subject to a civil penalty of up to $1,000 for refusal to sign such instructions if no good faith dispute exists as to who is entitled to the deposited funds (Civil Code §1057.3).**

15. FINAL VERIFICATION OF CONDITION: Buyer shall have the right to make a final inspection of the Property within **5 (or _____) Days** Prior to Close Of Escrow, NOT AS A CONTINGENCY OF THE SALE, but solely to confirm: **(i)** the Property is maintained pursuant to paragraph 7A; **(ii)** Repairs have been completed as agreed; and **(iii)** Seller has complied with Seller's other obligations under this Agreement.

16. LIQUIDATED DAMAGES: If Buyer fails to complete this purchase because of Buyer's default, Seller shall retain, as liquidated damages, the deposit actually paid. If the Property is a dwelling with no more than four units, one of which Buyer intends to occupy, then the amount retained shall be no more than 3% of the purchase price. Any excess shall be returned to Buyer. Release of funds will require mutual, Signed release instructions from both Buyer and Seller, judicial decision or arbitration award.
BUYER AND SELLER SHALL SIGN A SEPARATE LIQUIDATED DAMAGES PROVISION FOR ANY INCREASED DEPOSIT. (C.A.R. FORM RID)

Buyer's Initials _____/_____	Seller's Initials _____/_____

17. DISPUTE RESOLUTION:

A. MEDIATION: Buyer and Seller agree to mediate any dispute or claim arising between them out of this Agreement, or any resulting transaction, before resorting to arbitration or court action. Paragraphs 17B(2) and (3) below apply whether or not the Arbitration provision is initialed. Mediation fees, if any, shall be divided equally among the parties involved. If, for any dispute or claim to which this paragraph applies, any party commences an action without first attempting to resolve the matter through mediation, or refuses to mediate after a request has been made, then that party shall not be entitled to recover attorney fees, even if they would otherwise be available to that party in any such action. THIS MEDIATION PROVISION APPLIES WHETHER OR NOT THE ARBITRATION PROVISION IS INITIALED.

B. ARBITRATION OF DISPUTES: (1) Buyer and Seller agree that any dispute or claim in Law or equity arising between them out of this Agreement or any resulting transaction, which is not settled through mediation, shall be decided by neutral, binding arbitration, including and subject to paragraphs 17B(2) and (3) below. The arbitrator shall be a retired judge or justice, or an attorney with at least 5 years of residential real estate Law experience, unless the parties mutually agree to a different arbitrator, who shall render an award in accordance with substantive California Law. The parties shall have the right to discovery in accordance with California Code of Civil Procedure §1283.05. In all other respects, the arbitration shall be conducted in accordance with Title 9 of Part III of the California Code of Civil Procedure. Judgment upon the award of the arbitrator(s) may be entered into any court having jurisdiction. Interpretation of this agreement to arbitrate shall be governed by the Federal Arbitration Act.
(2) EXCLUSIONS FROM MEDIATION AND ARBITRATION: The following matters are excluded from mediation and arbitration: **(i)** a judicial or non-judicial foreclosure or other action or proceeding to enforce a deed of trust, mortgage or installment land sale contract as defined in California Civil Code §2985; **(ii)** an unlawful detainer action; **(iii)** the filing or enforcement of a mechanic's lien; and **(iv)** any matter that is within the jurisdiction of a probate, small claims or bankruptcy court. The filing of a court action to enable the recording of a notice of pending action, for order of attachment, receivership, injunction, or other provisional remedies, shall not constitute a waiver of the mediation and arbitration provisions.
(3) BROKERS: Buyer and Seller agree to mediate and arbitrate disputes or claims involving either or both Brokers, consistent with 17 A and B, provided either or both Brokers shall have agreed to such mediation or arbitration prior to, or within a reasonable time after, the dispute or claim is presented to Brokers. Any election by either or both Brokers to participate in mediation or arbitration shall not result in Brokers being deemed parties to the Agreement.

"NOTICE: BY INITIALING IN THE SPACE BELOW YOU ARE AGREEING TO HAVE ANY DISPUTE ARISING OUT OF THE MATTERS INCLUDED IN THE 'ARBITRATION OF DISPUTES' PROVISION DECIDED BY NEUTRAL ARBITRATION AS PROVIDED BY CALIFORNIA LAW AND YOU ARE GIVING UP ANY RIGHTS YOU MIGHT POSSESS TO HAVE THE DISPUTE LITIGATED IN A COURT OR JURY TRIAL. BY INITIALING IN THE SPACE BELOW YOU ARE GIVING UP YOUR JUDICIAL RIGHTS TO DISCOVERY AND APPEAL, UNLESS THOSE RIGHTS ARE SPECIFICALLY INCLUDED IN THE 'ARBITRATION OF DISPUTES' PROVISION. IF YOU REFUSE TO SUBMIT TO ARBITRATION AFTER AGREEING TO THIS PROVISION, YOU MAY BE COMPELLED TO ARBITRATE UNDER THE AUTHORITY OF THE CALIFORNIA CODE OF CIVIL PROCEDURE. YOUR AGREEMENT TO THIS ARBITRATION PROVISION IS VOLUNTARY."

"WE HAVE READ AND UNDERSTAND THE FOREGOING AND AGREE TO SUBMIT DISPUTES ARISING OUT OF THE MATTERS INCLUDED IN THE 'ARBITRATION OF DISPUTES' PROVISION TO NEUTRAL ARBITRATION."

Buyer's Initials _____/_____	Seller's Initials _____/_____

Buyer's Initials (_____)(_____)
Seller's Initials (_____)(_____)

Reviewed by _____ Date _____

EQUAL HOUSING OPPORTUNITY

RPA-CA REVISED 10/02 (PAGE 5 OF 8)

CALIFORNIA RESIDENTIAL PURCHASE AGREEMENT (RPA-CA PAGE 5 OF 8)

FIGURE 10.6

California Residential Purchase Agreement and Joint Escrow Instructions (continued)

Property Address: _____   Date: _____

18. **PRORATIONS OF PROPERTY TAXES AND OTHER ITEMS:** Unless otherwise agreed in writing, the following items shall be PAID CURRENT and prorated between Buyer and Seller as of Close Of Escrow: real property taxes and assessments, interest, rents, HOA regular, special, and emergency dues and assessments imposed prior to Close Of Escrow, premiums on insurance assumed by Buyer, payments on bonds and assessments assumed by Buyer, and payments on Mello-Roos and other Special Assessment District bonds and assessments that are now a lien. The following items shall be assumed by Buyer WITHOUT CREDIT toward the purchase price: prorated payments on Mello-Roos and other Special Assessment District bonds and assessments and HOA special assessments that are now a lien but not yet due. Property will be reassessed upon change of ownership. Any supplemental tax bills shall be paid as follows: **(i)** for periods after Close Of Escrow, by Buyer; and **(ii)** for periods prior to Close Of Escrow, by Seller. TAX BILLS ISSUED AFTER CLOSE OF ESCROW SHALL BE HANDLED DIRECTLY BETWEEN BUYER AND SELLER. Prorations shall be made based on a 30-day month.
19. **WITHHOLDING TAXES:** Seller and Buyer agree to execute any instrument, affidavit, statement or instruction reasonably necessary to comply with federal (FIRPTA) and California withholding Law, if required (C.A.R. Forms AS and AB).
20. **MULTIPLE LISTING SERVICE ("MLS"):** Brokers are authorized to report to the MLS a pending sale and, upon Close Of Escrow, the terms of this transaction to be published and disseminated to persons and entities authorized to use the information on terms approved by the MLS.
21. **EQUAL HOUSING OPPORTUNITY:** The Property is sold in compliance with federal, state and local anti-discrimination Laws.
22. **ATTORNEY FEES:** In any action, proceeding, or arbitration between Buyer and Seller arising out of this Agreement, the prevailing Buyer or Seller shall be entitled to reasonable attorney fees and costs from the non-prevailing Buyer or Seller, except as provided in paragraph 17A.
23. **SELECTION OF SERVICE PROVIDERS:** If Brokers refer Buyer or Seller to persons, vendors, or service or product providers ("Providers"), Brokers do not guarantee the performance of any Providers. Buyer and Seller may select ANY Providers of their own choosing.
24. **TIME OF ESSENCE; ENTIRE CONTRACT; CHANGES:** Time is of the essence. All understandings between the parties are incorporated in this Agreement. Its terms are intended by the parties as a final, complete and exclusive expression of their Agreement with respect to its subject matter, and may not be contradicted by evidence of any prior agreement or contemporaneous oral agreement. If any provision of this Agreement is held to be ineffective or invalid, the remaining provisions will nevertheless be given full force and effect. **Neither this Agreement nor any provision in it may be extended, amended, modified, altered or changed, except in writing Signed by Buyer and Seller.**
25. **OTHER TERMS AND CONDITIONS,** including attached supplements:
    A. ☑ Buyer's Inspection Advisory (C.A.R. Form BIA)
    B. ☐ Purchase Agreement Addendum (C.A.R. Form PAA paragraph numbers: _____) _____
    C. _____
    _____
26. **DEFINITIONS:** As used in this Agreement:
    A. **"Acceptance"** means the time the offer or final counter offer is accepted in writing by a party and is delivered to and personally received by the other party or that party's authorized agent in accordance with the terms of this offer or a final counter offer.
    B. **"Agreement"** means the terms and conditions of this accepted California Residential Purchase Agreement and any accepted counter offers and addenda.
    C. **"C.A.R. Form"** means the specific form referenced or another comparable form agreed to by the parties.
    D. **"Close Of Escrow"** means the date the grant deed, or other evidence of transfer of title, is recorded. If the scheduled close of escrow falls on a Saturday, Sunday or legal holiday, then close of escrow shall be the next business day after the scheduled close of escrow date.
    E. **"Copy"** means copy by any means including photocopy, NCR, facsimile and electronic.
    F. **"Days"** means calendar days, unless otherwise required by Law.
    G. **"Days After"** means the specified number of calendar days after the occurrence of the event specified, not counting the calendar date on which the specified event occurs, and ending at 11:59PM on the final day.
    H. **"Days Prior"** means the specified number of calendar days before the occurrence of the event specified, not counting the calendar date on which the specified event is scheduled to occur.
    I. **"Electronic Copy"** or **"Electronic Signature"** means, as applicable, an electronic copy or signature complying with California Law. Buyer and Seller agree that electronic means will not be used by either party to modify or alter the content or integrity of this Agreement without the knowledge and consent of the other.
    J. **"Law"** means any law, code, statute, ordinance, regulation, rule or order, which is adopted by a controlling city, county, state or federal legislative, judicial or executive body or agency.
    K. **"Notice to Buyer to Perform"** means a document (C.A.R. Form NBP), which shall be in writing and Signed by Seller and shall give Buyer at least 24 hours **(or as otherwise specified in paragraph 14C(4))** to remove a contingency or perform as applicable.
    L. **"Repairs"** means any repairs (including pest control), alterations, replacements, modifications or retrofitting of the Property provided for under this Agreement.
    M. **"Signed"** means either a handwritten or electronic signature on an original document, Copy or any counterpart.
    N. **Singular and Plural** terms each include the other, when appropriate.

Buyer's Initials (_____)(_____)
Seller's Initials (_____)(_____)

RPA-CA REVISED 10/02 (PAGE 6 OF 8)

Reviewed by _____ Date _____

EQUAL HOUSING OPPORTUNITY

CALIFORNIA RESIDENTIAL PURCHASE AGREEMENT (RPA-CA PAGE 6 OF 8)

FIGURE 10.6

California Residential Purchase Agreement and Joint Escrow Instructions (continued)

Property Address: _____   Date: _____

27. **AGENCY:**
    A. **DISCLOSURE:** Buyer and Seller each acknowledge prior receipt of C.A.R. Form AD "Disclosure Regarding Real Estate Agency Relationships."
    B. **POTENTIALLY COMPETING BUYERS AND SELLERS:** Buyer and Seller each acknowledge receipt of a disclosure of the possibility of multiple representation by the Broker representing that principal. This disclosure may be part of a listing agreement, buyer-broker agreement or separate document (C.A.R. Form DA). Buyer understands that Broker representing Buyer may also represent other potential buyers, who may consider, make offers on or ultimately acquire the Property. Seller understands that Broker representing Seller may also represent other sellers with competing properties of interest to this Buyer.
    C. **CONFIRMATION:** The following agency relationships are hereby confirmed for this transaction:
    Listing Agent _____ (Print Firm Name) is the agent
    of (check one): ☐ the Seller exclusively; or ☐ both the Buyer and Seller.
    Selling Agent _____ (Print Firm Name) (if not same
    as Listing Agent) is the agent of (check one): ☐ the Buyer exclusively; or ☐ the Seller exclusively; or ☐ both the Buyer and Seller. Real Estate Brokers are not parties to the Agreement between Buyer and Seller.

28. **JOINT ESCROW INSTRUCTIONS TO ESCROW HOLDER:**
    A. **The following paragraphs, or applicable portions thereof, of this Agreement constitute the joint escrow instructions of Buyer and Seller to Escrow Holder,** which Escrow Holder is to use along with any related counter offers and addenda, and any additional mutual instructions to close the escrow: 1, 2, 4, 12, 13B, 14E, 18, 19, 24, 25B and C, 26, 28, 29, 32A, 33 and paragraph D of the section titled Real Estate Brokers on page 8. If a Copy of the separate compensation agreement(s) provided for in paragraph 29 or 32A, or paragraph D of the section titled Real Estate Brokers on page 8 is deposited with Escrow Holder by Broker, Escrow Holder shall accept such agreement(s) and pay out from Buyer's or Seller's funds, or both, as applicable, the Broker's compensation provided for in such agreement(s). The terms and conditions of this Agreement not set forth in the specified paragraphs are additional matters for the information of Escrow Holder, but about which Escrow Holder need not be concerned. Buyer and Seller will receive Escrow Holder's general provisions directly from Escrow Holder and will execute such provisions upon Escrow Holder's request. To the extent the general provisions are inconsistent or conflict with this Agreement, the general provisions will control as to the duties and obligations of Escrow Holder only. Buyer and Seller will execute additional instructions, documents and forms provided by Escrow Holder that are reasonably necessary to close escrow.
    B. A Copy of this Agreement shall be delivered to Escrow Holder within **3** business days after Acceptance (or ☐ _____). Buyer and Seller authorize Escrow Holder to accept and rely on Copies and Signatures as defined in this Agreement as originals, to open escrow and for other purposes of escrow. The validity of this Agreement as between Buyer and Seller is not affected by whether or when Escrow Holder Signs this Agreement.
    C. Brokers are a party to the escrow for the sole purpose of compensation pursuant to paragraphs 29, 32A and paragraph D of the section titled Real Estate Brokers on page 8. Buyer and Seller irrevocably assign to Brokers compensation specified in paragraphs 29 and 32A, respectively, and irrevocably instruct Escrow Holder to disburse those funds to Brokers at Close Of Escrow or pursuant to any other mutually executed cancellation agreement. Compensation instructions can be amended or revoked only with the written consent of Brokers. Escrow Holder shall immediately notify Brokers: **(i)** if Buyer's initial or any additional deposit is not made pursuant to this Agreement, or is not good at time of deposit with Escrow Holder; or **(ii)** if Buyer and Seller instruct Escrow Holder to cancel escrow.
    D. A Copy of any amendment that affects any paragraph of this Agreement for which Escrow Holder is responsible shall be delivered to Escrow Holder within **2** business days after mutual execution of the amendment.

29. **BROKER COMPENSATION FROM BUYER:** If applicable, upon Close Of Escrow, **Buyer** agrees to pay compensation to Broker as specified in a separate written agreement between Buyer and Broker.

30. **TERMS AND CONDITIONS OF OFFER:**
    This is an offer to purchase the Property on the above terms and conditions. All paragraphs with spaces for initials by Buyer and Seller are incorporated in this Agreement only if initialed by all parties. If at least one but not all parties initial, a counter offer is required until agreement is reached. Seller has the right to continue to offer the Property for sale and to accept any other offer at any time prior to notification of Acceptance. Buyer has read and acknowledges receipt of a Copy of the offer and agrees to the above confirmation of agency relationships. If this offer is accepted and Buyer subsequently defaults, Buyer may be responsible for payment of Brokers' compensation. This Agreement and any supplement, addendum or modification, including any Copy, may be Signed in two or more counterparts, all of which shall constitute one and the same writing.

Buyer's Initials (_____)(_____)
Seller's Initials (_____)(_____)

RPA-CA REVISED 10/02 (PAGE 7 OF 8)

Reviewed by _____ Date _____

FIGURE 10.6

California Residential Purchase Agreement and Joint Escrow Instructions (continued)

Property Address: _____   Date: _____

31. EXPIRATION OF OFFER: This offer shall be deemed revoked and the deposit shall be returned unless the offer is Signed by Seller and a Copy of the Signed offer is personally received by Buyer, or by _____, who is authorized to receive it by 5:00 PM on the third calendar day after this offer is signed by Buyer (or, if checked) ☐ by _____ (date), at _____ AM/PM).

Date _____   Date _____

BUYER _____   BUYER _____

(Print name) _____   (Print name) _____

(Address) _____

32. BROKER COMPENSATION FROM SELLER:
   A. Upon Close Of Escrow, **Seller** agrees to pay compensation to Broker as specified in a separate written agreement between Seller and Broker.
   B. If escrow does not close, compensation is payable as specified in that separate written agreement.
33. ACCEPTANCE OF OFFER: Seller warrants that Seller is the owner of the Property, or has the authority to execute this Agreement. Seller accepts the above offer, agrees to sell the Property on the above terms and conditions, and agrees to the above confirmation of agency relationships. Seller has read and acknowledges receipt of a Copy of this Agreement, and authorizes Broker to deliver a Signed Copy to Buyer.
   ☐ (If checked) **SUBJECT TO ATTACHED COUNTER OFFER, DATED** _____.

Date _____   Date _____

SELLER _____   SELLER _____

(Print name) _____   (Print name) _____

(Address) _____

(____/____)   **CONFIRMATION OF ACCEPTANCE:** A Copy of Signed Acceptance was personally received by Buyer or Buyer's authorized
(Initials)   agent on (date) _____ at _____ AM/PM. **A binding Agreement is created when a Copy of Signed Acceptance is personally received by Buyer or Buyer's authorized agent whether or not confirmed in this document. Completion of this confirmation is not legally required in order to create a binding Agreement; it is solely intended to evidence the date that Confirmation of Acceptance has occurred.**

REAL ESTATE BROKERS:
A. Real Estate Brokers are not parties to the Agreement between Buyer and Seller.
B. Agency relationships are confirmed as stated in paragraph 2A.
C. If specified in paragraph 2A, Agent who submitted the offer for Buyer acknowledges receipt of deposit.
D. **COOPERATING BROKER COMPENSATION:** Listing Broker agrees to pay Cooperating Broker (**Selling Firm**) and Cooperating Broker agrees to accept, out of Listing Broker's proceeds in escrow: **(i)** the amount specified in the MLS, provided Cooperating Broker is a Participant of the MLS in which the Property is offered for sale or a reciprocal MLS; or **(ii)** ☐ (if checked) the amount specified in a separate written agreement (C.A.R. Form CBC) between Listing Broker and Cooperating Broker.
Real Estate Broker (Selling Firm) _____
By _____   Date _____
Address _____ City _____ State _____ Zip _____
Telephone _____ Fax _____ E-mail _____

Real Estate Broker (Listing Firm) _____
By _____   Date _____
Address _____ City _____ State _____ Zip _____
Telephone _____ Fax _____ E-mail _____

ESCROW HOLDER ACKNOWLEDGMENT:
Escrow Holder acknowledges receipt of a Copy of this Agreement, (if checked, ☐ a deposit in the amount of $ _____),
counter offer numbers _____ and _____
_____, and agrees to act as Escrow Holder subject to paragraph 28 of this Agreement, any supplemental escrow instructions and the terms of Escrow Holder's general provisions.

Escrow Holder is advised that the date of Confirmation of Acceptance of the Agreement as between Buyer and Seller is _____

Escrow Holder _____   Escrow # _____
By _____   Date _____
Address _____
Phone/Fax/E-mail _____
Escrow Holder is licensed by the California Department of ☐ Corporations, ☐ Insurance, ☐ Real Estate. License # _____

SURE TRAC
The System for Success™
Published by the
California Association of REALTORS®

RPA-CA REVISED 10/02 (PAGE 8 OF 8)   Reviewed by _____ Date _____   EQUAL HOUSING OPPORTUNITY

CALIFORNIA RESIDENTIAL PURCHASE AGREEMENT (RPA-CA PAGE 8 OF 8)

Content of the Form

Essentially, the form acts as a checklist to ensure a contract that is complete in all respects. The responsible parties must comply with the requirements stipulated to help both parties avoid entangling legal complications. Any changes should be dated and initialed by the principals to the transaction.

Understanding the Purchase Agreement Form

Introductory Information.   Fill out this section as follows:

- In inserting the date, avoid abbreviations.
- Insert the name of the place (city, town, etc.) where the buyer actually signs the offer to purchase.

Paragraph 1: Basic Offer.   1A shows the buyer or buyers; 1B describes the property by address, legal descriptions, and/or assessor's parcel number and further indicates the city or county where the property is located; 1C sets forth the purchase price, and 1D sets the time for close of escrow to complete the transaction.

Paragraph 2: Finance Terms.   The buyer's obtaining financing is a contingency of this agreement.

Subparagraphs A through L under Financing are explained below.

A. This provides for the initial earnest money deposit, its form, and if it is to be deposited (escrow or trust account) or held uncashed.

B. Provision is made for increasing the earnest money (used in cases of low initial deposits).

C. Paragraph (1) states the requirements of the new first loan on which this offer is contingent. If the buyer cannot obtain the loan, the buyer is relieved of any purchase obligation. For this paragraph, consider setting the interest rate and points above current market interest, so that a minor fluctuation will not relieve the buyer from the purchase obligation. Paragraph (2) applies to terms if FHA or VA financing is sought.

D. This provides for additional financing terms such as seller financing, loan assumptions, balloon payments, etc.

E. Provision is made for the balance of the purchase price to be deposited in escrow prior to closing.

F. This paragraph shows the total purchase price. (**Note:** The down payment and loans assumed and/or new loans by lenders or seller should equal the purchase price.)

G. This paragraph requires the buyer to provide the seller a loan prequalification letter within a stated time after the offer is accepted.

H. This paragraph requires the buyer to verify that he or she has the down payment and closing costs.

I. This paragraph (by checking) either requires removal of the loan contingency or specifies that the loan contingency shall remain in effect until the loan is funded.

J.   This paragraph provides, by checking, if or if not the agreement is to be contingent upon an appraisal equal or greater than the purchase price.

K.   This paragraph, if checked, indicates that the offer is not contingent upon obtaining financing.

L.   By checking this paragraph, the buyer indicates that it will be an all cash purchase with no loan.

Paragraph 3: Closing and Occupancy.

A.   This paragraph states whether the buyer intends to occupy the premises as a principal residence. If the buyer intends the property to be a principal residence, then liquidated damages resulting from buyer default cannot exceed 3 percent of the purchase price. (See paragraph 16.)

B.   This paragraph provides the date on which property shall be turned over to the buyer. If the seller does not get occupancy until after close of escrow, a written occupancy agreement should be entered into and the parties should consult with their insurance carriers.

C.   This paragraph provides that tenant occupied property shall be vacant prior to close of escrow unless agreed otherwise.

D.   This paragraph provides that the seller shall assign to the buyer any assignable warranty rights.

E.   This paragraph provides that keys, openers, etc., shall be given to the buyer.

Paragraph 4: Allocation of Costs.   Checking the appropriate box determines who is to pay which costs.

Paragraph 5: Statutory Disclosures.   This paragraph provides that the seller shall provide the buyer with required disclosures including the Transfer Disclosure Statement, Lead-Based Paint Disclosure, Natural and Environmental Hazards Disclosures as well as database disclosures of registered sex offenders (Megan's Law).

Paragraph 6: Condominium/Planned Unit Development Disclosures.
Provides for disclosure of the number and location of parking spaces, storage areas, etc., pending claims or litigation involving the Homeowner Association (HOA), HOA minutes for preceding 12 months, contact persons for the HOA as well as other documents required by law such as associations' bylaws and financial statements.

Paragraph 7: Conditions Affecting Property.

A.   This paragraph provides that property is sold in its present condition subject to the buyer's investigation rights and that debris and personal property will be removed.

B. This paragraph requires seller disclosure of known material facts and defects as well as other disclosures required by law.

C. This paragraph provides advice to the buyer to investigate the entire property.

D. This paragraph informs the buyer of the right to cancel the agreement based upon discovery or to request repairs or other action.

Paragraph 8: Items Included and Excluded. This paragraph makes it clear that designated fixtures remain with the property, but it also provides for inclusion of other items in the sale as well as exclusion of designated items from the sale.

Paragraph 9: Buyer's Investigation of Property and Matters Affecting Property. This paragraph provides for the buyer's rights to inspection and provides for either the removal of the inspection contingency or cancellation of the agreement. Utilities shall be on for buyer's inspection.

Paragraph 10: Repairs. This paragraph requires that the repairs by the seller be done in a proper manner and show that they have been paid for.

Paragraph 11: Buyer Indemnity and Seller Protection for Entry upon Property. This paragraph states that the buyer agrees to keep property free from liens (pay for investigative work), repair any damage and costs associated with inspection, and protect the owner from any liability because of such investigations and inspections.

Paragraph 12: Title and Vesting.

A. This paragraph provides that the buyer shall receive a preliminary title report.

B. This paragraph indicates that title shall be subject to stated nonmonetary encumbrances.

C. This paragraph sets forth the seller's duty to disclose all matters known to the seller affecting title.

D. This paragraph provides that title will be transferred by a grant deed, and the buyer is notified to obtain professional advice as to the manner of taking title.

E. This paragraphs provides that the buyer shall receive a homeowner policy of title insurance.

Paragraph 13: Sale of Buyer's Property. If checked, the sale is contingent upon the sale of buyer's property.

Paragraph 14: Time Periods; Removal of Contingencies; Cancellation Rights. This paragraph sets forth all time periods for compliance and disclosures. Modification of time periods must be in writing. If the seller removes contingencies, this shall be conclusive evidence of the buyer's election to proceed with the transaction. If the buyer and seller agree to cancellation of the agreement, release of the funds will require mutual signed agreement (civil penalty up to $1,000 for refusal to sign the agreement if no good faith dispute exists).

Paragraph 15: Final Verification of Condition.   This paragraph provides buyer the right to conduct final inspection prior to close of escrow to confirm that the property has been properly maintained, repairs have been made, and the seller has complied with other contractual obligations.

Paragraph 16: Liquidated Damages.   If property is a one- to four-unit residential property and buyer intends to occupy it as a principal residence, liquidated damages in event of buyer default cannot exceed 3 percent of the purchase price. Any excess deposit must be returned to buyer. (See Paragraph 3.)

Paragraph 17: Dispute Resolution.   The parties agree to try to settle any dispute by mediation. By initialing, the parties agree to binding arbitration of any dispute not settled by mediation. (If it is not initialed, parties could settle disputes through the courts.)

Disputes with brokers are subject to mediation and arbitration only if the brokers agree to such resolution.

Paragraph 18: Prorations of Property Taxes and Other Items.   This paragraph provides for portions of taxes and other items. Bonds shall be assumed without buyer credit if not yet due.

Paragraph 19: Withholding Taxes.   The buyer and seller agree to comply with state and federal regulations regarding the Foreign Investment in Real Property Tax Act (FIRPTA) and California withholding.

Paragraph 20: Multiple-Listing Service.   This paragraph gives the broker the right to report the sale terms to an MLS service to be published. Without this authorization, release of information by an agent could breach the duty of confidentiality.

Paragraph 21: Equal Housing Opportunity.   States that the sale is being made in compliance with antidiscrimination laws.

Paragraph 22: Attorney's Fees.   In the event of a legal proceeding or arbitration, the prevailing party shall be entitled to reasonable attorney's fees.

Paragraph 23: Selection of Service Providers.   Broker does not guarantee performance of any service provider he or she may have referred to the buyer and/or seller.

Paragraph 24: Time of Essence; Entire Contract; Changes.   This is the complete agreement and may not be contradicted by prior agreements or contemporaneous oral agreements. It cannot be extended, modified, or changed except in writing signed by both buyer and seller.

Paragraph 25: Other Terms and Conditions.   This paragraph allows other terms and conditions to be incorporated into the agreement.

Paragraph 26: Definitions.   This paragraph provides definitions of terms used.

Paragraph 27: Agency.   This paragraph references agency disclosure, explains the broker's role, and confirms the agency elected for both listing agent and selling agent.

Paragraph 28: Joint Escrow Instructions to Escrow Holder.   This paragraph provides that designated paragraphs of the agreement are joint escrow instructions and that the agreement shall be delivered to the escrow within a designated period. It makes clear that the broker is a party to the escrow only so far as those commission rights are concerned that have been irrevocably assigned to the broker.

Paragraph 29: Broker Compensation from Buyer.   The buyer can agree to pay a commission under a separate written agreement (Buyer's Brokerage).

Paragraph 30: Terms and Conditions of Offer.   This paragraph makes it clear it is an offer that includes initialed paragraphs and provides that should the buyer default after acceptance, the buyer may be responsible for the broker's commission.

Paragraph 31: Expiration of Offer.   This paragraph provides a definite termination time and date for the offer if it is not accepted by that time and date. The buyer's signature as to the offer is included in this paragraph.

Paragraph 32: Broker Compensation from Seller.   This paragraph provides for payment of the commission as specified in the listing agreement, on close of escrow. If escrow does not close, payment shall be in accordance with listing agreement.

Paragraph 33: Acceptance of Offer.   Seller warrants ownership and accepts the offer on terms indicated, or by checking the appropriate block indicates acceptance subject to attached counter offer.

The buyer initials confirmation of receipt of acceptance.

There is a block for the broker to sign in which the broker agrees to Cooperating Broker Compensation.

Another block is signed by the escrow holder acknowledging receipt of copy of the agreement.

■ ESTIMATED BUYER'S COSTS

When formulating the purchase offer, provide the buyer with the **estimated buyer's costs**—an estimate of the total cash requirements, as well as estimated monthly payments based on the offer. Although costs will vary between lenders and escrow companies, you must nevertheless strive to be realistic. Be honest and full in your disclosures. It is best for any error to be on the high side. (Keep in mind that real estate surprises make people unhappy.)

■ SUMMARY

Selling is helping others meet their needs. Selling can give buyers the security of home ownership.

Selling involves elements such as persuasion, communication, discovery, and knowledge of the customer and knowledge of the product. Your strategy should be based on the type of prospect and the prospect's attitude toward purchasing in general and purchasing a special property in particular.

To close a sale you must appeal to buying motives, watch for buying signals, overcome any resistance that is raised, and attempt a trial close. Buying motives include survival, security, pride of ownership, love of family, health, desire for profit or gain, and desire for comfort and convenience.

If you understand buying signals, you know when to close. Timing can be essential. Treat objections as a natural part of a sale. Welcome the objection, concede before answering, rephrase the objection as a question, and meet the objection. You can forestall an obvious objection by bringing it up yourself and covering it.

You have a choice of six basic techniques with untold variations for closing:

1. an assumptive close asks a question that assumes the prospect will buy;
2. the positive choice gives the prospect a choice between positive actions;
3. the inducement technique contains a benefit for buying now;
4. the fear of loss or approval is based on a "last chance";
5. the narrative close uses third-party verification; and
6. the ask-for-a-deposit close, which gets right to the heart of the matter.

Sales can be lost for many reasons. Generally, salespersons lose sales by talking when they should be listening and not knowing when they should be silent. Over-eagerness, incomplete knowledge, too much pressure, appearing frightened, criticizing competitors, wandering from your purpose, displaying a negative attitude, and being argumentative or negative are all reasons why salespeople fail.

The eight-page California Residential Purchase Agreement and Joint Escrow Instructions form is a complete agreement that you must fully understand before attempting to sell a property. The form is designed to aid you in explaining the agreement and in meeting your obligations.

■ CLASS DISCUSSION TOPICS

1. How would you overcome the following buyer objections?
    a. I wanted a house with a [pool] and this house doesn't have a [pool].
    b. I didn't want an older house.
    c. I don't like the location.
    d. The price is too high.
    e. The monthly assessments are way too high.
    f. The interest rate is too high; I better wait.
    g. The mortgage payments are more than my rent.
    h. The financing is too complicated.
    i. I'm worried about [my job/the economy].
    j. I want to sell my present home first.
    k. We want to think it over.
    l. I'd like to discuss it with [my accountant/lawyer/son-in-law/etc.].

2. Using another student to represent a buyer, demonstrate a closing (no more than three minutes).

3. Complete a Residential Purchase Agreement for the residential property in Chapter 6 in the Class Discussion Topic number 5 according to the following:

    Buyers: Orem and Melody Rosatta

    Deposit: Personal check for $5,000.

    Purchase Price: $230,000.

    Financing Contingency: Contingent on obtaining a new 90 percent fixed rate loan at no more than 6¾ percent interest and no more than $5,000 in loan fees and discount points. Buyers shall provide evidence that they are prequalified for a loan meeting above terms within 5 days of acceptance.

    Appraisal Contingency: Offer contingent on property appraisal for no less than purchase price (there are no other contingencies).

    Closing: Within 60 days of acceptance. Possession at closing.

    Occupancy: Buyers intend property as their permanent residence.

    Fees and Costs: Seller shall pay transfer fees and title insurance. Escrow fees shall be split equally. Apex Escrow shall be the escrow for the transaction. Sewer and well costs are not applicable. Seller shall pay for smoke detector and water heater bracing as required. All other costs are to be borne by seller.

    Seller shall pay for a one-year home warranty as well as a pest control inspection, and seller shall pay for any corrective work indicated.

Condition: Seller shall pay for inspections (1) and (2) set forth in paragraph 4B of the purchase contract.

Personal Property Included: Refrigerator, pool equipment, fireplace accessories, window coverings, portable steel garden building, and riding lawn mower.

Time periods specified in paragraph 14 are adequate.

4.   Bring to class one current-events article dealing with some aspect of real estate practice for class discussion.

■ CHAPTER 10 QUIZ

1.   A good salesperson
   a.   uses technical terms whenever possible to impress buyers.
   b.   speaks fast so he or she can reach the closing.
   c.   approaches every customer in the same way.
   d.   does none of the above.

2.   A salesperson appeals to buying motives. Which of the following is a buying motive?
   a.   Love of family
   b.   Comfort and convenience
   c.   Security
   d.   All of the above

3.   Disadvantages of home ownership include
   a.   increase in expenses.
   b.   risk.
   c.   lack of liquidity.
   d.   all of the above.

4.   Buying signals might include a buyer's
   a.   whispering with a spouse.
   b.   pacing off a room.
   c.   seeming reluctant to leave a property.
   d.   behavior in all of the above.

5.   A prospective buyer says, "The price is too high." The best response is
   a.   "I think the price is fair."
   b.   "Why don't you offer less?"
   c.   "The comparable sales don't bear that out."
   d.   "What do you think would be a fair price for this home?"

6.   A professional salesperson knows that
   a.   telling is more effective than asking.
   b.   appealing to emotions should be avoided.
   c.   in dealing with a cautious buyer one should be assertive and push for a decision.
   d.   none of the above is true.

7.   When you ask a prospective buyer if he or she would prefer June 1 or August 1 for possession, what type of closing technique are you using?
   a.   Inducement
   b.   Positive choice
   c.   Fear of loss
   d.   Narrative close

8. The paragraph in the purchase contract in which the buyer indicates an intention to occupy the property (applies to one- to four-unit residential properties) is important because it relates to
   a. liquidated damages.
   b. vesting of title.
   c. smoke detectors.
   d. home protection plans.

9. Who can modify an accepted offer to purchase?
   a. The selling broker
   b. The listing broker
   c. The listing broker and the seller
   d. The buyer and seller by mutual agreement

10. In making a property inspection, the inspector hired by the buyer negligently damaged the air-conditioning unit. Who is responsible for the damage based on the California Residential Purchase Agreement and Joint Escrow Instructions?
    a. The seller
    b. The buyer
    c. The buyer's agent
    d. The seller's agent

CHAPTER ELEVEN

11

FROM OFFER TO CLOSING

■ KEY TERMS

acceptance	history of the sale	rent skimming
buyers' remorse	multiple offers	seller objections
"cash-out" scheme	price	subordination clause
closing	rejection	terms
counteroffer	release of contract	

■ LEARNING OBJECTIVES

In this chapter, you learn what preparation is required before you submit an offer to purchase to the owners and how to present the offer. You discover the importance of reviewing the history of the listing as well as of telling the owners about the buyers. You learn why you should strive for an acceptance rather than a counteroffer when the offer is within reasonable limits and when to recommend that an offer be rejected or that a counteroffer be given. This chapter alerts you to the need to protect owners from unscrupulous buyers. You learn how to handle multiple offers and the practical aspects of getting the acceptance or counteroffer and, finally, what you should be doing between acceptance of the offer and closing.

■ THE OFFER TO PURCHASE

The offer to purchase is really the California Residential Purchase Agreement and Joint Escrow Instructions that was covered in Chapter 10. When signed by the buyers, we customarily refer to it as an *offer to purchase*. Keep in mind that selling real estate really involves the following three separate sales:

1. Selling the owner on a listing or the buyer on agency representation
2. Selling the buyer on an offer
3. Selling the seller on an acceptance

While two out of three might be a tremendous average in baseball, you have totally failed if the third sale is not completed.

> The third sale—acceptance of the offer—is the one that means success.

A seller's agent must continue sales efforts until an offer has been accepted. To cease working to sell a property merely because an offer was received is not in the owners' best interest. It could be regarded as unethical conduct.

Preparing To Submit the Offer

After you receive an offer to purchase, preparation is normally necessary for your presentation of the offer to the owners.

The Appointment. If you are the listing agent, it is your responsibility to make an appointment with the owners to present the offer to them. It also might be your responsibility to make the presentation. If another agent has prepared the offer to purchase, that agent might accompany you. Some listing brokers feel it is their obligation to present offers alone to avoid any undue pressure a selling agent might exert.

If you are the selling agent and not the listing agent, then the positions become reversed. You might accompany the listing agent to the presentation in order to provide backup information on your buyers and the offer. Listing agents might delegate the actual presentation of the offer to the selling agent, who is familiar with the buyers and better understands the reasons for the offer being written as it is.

If the listing agent does not have much experience, his or her broker may want to be present. However, three real estate agents can appear intimidating, so you might suggest to the listing agent's broker that you make the presentation of the offer with the listing agent serving in a backup role.

If you are the selling agent, contact the listing agent to set up the presentation appointment. Don't give the listing agent any details of your offer. Too often, if information gets back to sellers, they build a psychological wall that can be impenetrable. You want to meet sellers who have open minds.

For your own listings, consider having a secretary or another agent call the owners with a simple request that they meet you at a specific time to discuss their property. Do not give the person who is calling for you any information. In this way, that person can truthfully answer owners' questions without telling them that there is an offer.

There is a reason why you should not tell the owners about an offer in advance. They immediately will want to know how much it is. If you don't tell them, they will assume the worst and take a defensive posture when you try to present the offer. You need to present the entire offer, not just the price. Revealing only one aspect of an offer, when not presented as part of the total package, could result in antagonistic owners' rejecting an offer, an action that could be to their detriment.

When viewed as a whole, the offer might appear much more acceptable, or it could be the starting point for an acceptable counteroffer.

You want to be able to present the offer to all of the owners at once. Whenever possible schedule the presentation after small children, if present, have gone to bed because interruptions can make your job extremely difficult.

Should the owners contact you before you present the offer and ask you if you have an offer, the only answer to give is "yes." If the owners want you to tell them over the telephone what the offer is, we suggest this answer:

> "It wouldn't be fair to you or the buyers to condense the offer into a minute or two. This offer deserves careful consideration as well as explanation. You will want to see this offer."

If the owner persists, ask, "Can you and [spouse or co-owner, if applicable] meet with me right now?"

Generally, you should not present an offer over the telephone. The sellers can't accept over the phone, but they can say no. A phone presentation also gives owners time to talk to others about the offer before your presentation to them. Unfortunately, friends tend to give uninformed advice they think the owners will want to hear, for example, "Oh! Your home is worth more than that!"

Estimated Sellers' Proceeds.   For an offer less than list price, prepare an Estimated Sellers' Proceeds form, based on the offer received. Show the owners what they will net from the offer. Use of this form shows the owners that you are being straightforward in your dealings with them. Your recommendations will bear more weight when it is clear to the owners that you are being totally aboveboard in your dealings.

Competitive Market Analysis.   If market values have been falling and the property has been on the market for several months, update the competitive market analysis (CMA) that you prepared when you took the listing. If a comparable used has been sold, you want to be able to present the sale information.

Avoid giving any details about an offer to an owner until you can present the offer in its entirety.

Owners can't accept offers over the phone so don't present them over the phone.

Make certain the sellers know what they will receive.

Anticipate Problems. Role-playing exercises such as those discussed in Chapter 1 can be an important part of your preparation. From analysis of the offer, you can anticipate the objections you will receive. Decide how you are going to help the owners overcome problem areas (if you believe it is in their best interests to accept the offer).

Some agents lose sight of their agency duties and substitute their own interests for those of their principals. This is unethical conduct and cannot be tolerated. It might mean a commission now, but in the long run, it will have far greater negative impact on your reputation and future business.

Presenting the Offer. Immediately before you present the offer to purchase, meet with any other agent who may be involved, so it will be clear what your roles will be in the presentation. This could be important in a case where you have never worked with a particular agent before. Local custom and office policy can vary as to who actually presents the offer to the owner.

Multiple Offers. When more than one offer has been received on a property, you must present the **multiple offers** together. If you know of another offer that has not yet been received, you have a duty to inform the owners of it. You even have a duty to inform owners of verbal offers, although they're not binding nor can they be accepted.

| Present multiple offers in an impartial manner. |

Keep in mind that your first duty is to your principal, not to your firm or for your personal gain. Offers should be presented in a nonprejudicial manner so that owners can compare the offers and make their decision. With multiple offers, you might want to suggest obtaining loan prequalifications on the prospective purchasers. The owners might otherwise accept an offer from a buyer who is unable to obtain financing and reject the offer from a prospective buyer who would have no difficulty obtaining the necessary loan.

Setting the Mood. If possible, present the offer at the kitchen table (likely in the same location where you took the listing). This is a nonthreatening environment, and you can physically be quite close to your sellers. If you present it in any other room, use a table such as a cocktail table, and you need to be sitting close together.

To set a positive mood, mention some feature that played a part in the sale and that the owners are proud of. For example:

> "Frankly, I think the reason I have an offer on the house is because of your delightful garden. The buyers fell in love with your rose bushes."

or

> "While [Mrs. Wilson] loves your light and bright decorating, [Mr. Wilson] was sold on your house because of the workroom in the garage. It's something he has always wanted."

This is also the time to confirm agency election and obtain the seller's signature on the confirmation unless it is part of the purchase contract.

Stages of the Presentation.   Professional presentations are well organized. One organization plan is a three-stage presentation, including

1. A history of the property sales effort and any problems with the property.
2. Information about the buyers. Make the buyers appear to be people whom the sellers would like. The buyers should not be portrayed as trying to take advantage of the sellers.
3. The offer itself.

As in a sale, the agent should use a closing if he or she is recommending an acceptance.

History of the Sale.   If the property has been on the market for several months or longer, go over the **history of the sale.**

Cover

- the length of period on the market (in days);
- previous listings or sale efforts (For Sale by Owner);
- advertising (all types);
- the role of the multiple-listing service;
- Internet postings;
- agent caravans;
- open houses;
- showings;
- responses to showings—reasons why other buyers rejected the home (negative features or lack of features); and
- any other offer(s) received.

If the property was recently listed and you already have received an offer, it is possible that the owners may feel that they must have set their sale price too low. These owners can become adamant about not giving one inch. Consider the following approach.

"[Mr. and Mrs. Finch], when you listed the property with me, I explained that offers are very often received within a few days of the property being placed on the market. When this happens you are fortunate, and you're fortunate today. Real estate agents as well as buyers get excited over new listings, because they feel they're getting first chance at a home rather than it being shopworn merchandise that hundreds of buyers have rejected. In fact, the most active sale period for a listing is the first 20 days it is on the market.

When it's on the market longer than that, it often becomes much harder work to locate a buyer.

"Often owners reject offers that they receive within days of the listing and then go for many months without another offer. Do you know what happens then? In most cases when they do get an offer, it is for less than they received earlier. I'm telling you this so you don't respond emotionally to this offer but rather receive it with reason."

About the Buyers. Paint a verbal picture of the buyers that will make the sellers feel they are likable people who will appreciate the home. For example:

"The buyers are the [Henleys], the young family who came here last Thursday and then again yesterday. [Tom Henley] is [chief of security] at the [Nesco Corporation] and [Mary Henley] is an [associate editor] for the [Daily News].

"Their daughter [Tricia] [age nine] goes to [Sunnyvale School]. One of the reasons they like your home is that the children would not have to change schools. Their son [Jeffrey] is just four years old and is in preschool."

Keep in mind that a home sale is emotional; although owners may have reasons to sell, there is often reluctance at the same time.

In addition to reassuring sellers that the prospective buyers are nice people, you also want their offer to appear reasonable. If the buyers also are interested in another property, and most buyers are, point this out. When they receive an offer, owners tend to forget that they're competing with many other sellers.

> Cover all three steps:
> 1. History
> 2. Buyers
> 3. Offer

"The [Henleys] were undecided between your house and a three-bedroom, two-and-one-half-bath Spanish-style home off [Wedgewood Way]. That house has two and a half baths, versus your home with two baths, and had concrete block walls, but I was able to convince the [Henleys] that your house met their total needs better because it doesn't require [Tricia] to change schools, and the workroom in the garage was just what [Tom] wanted for his woodworking. He carves duck decoys."

With the above kind of comparison, you have shown the owners to be winners over the competition (the house off Wedgewood Way). The owners will feel their house is appreciated and that you have been working for them.

Never use an imaginary competitive house. Remember, be honest. All you need to do is to tell the owners why they are winners.

The Offer

We recommend that you gain agreement on the little things before you hand the offer to the sellers. As an example, get agreement about

- the occupancy date,

- what stays with the house or goes,

- seller preparing a transfer disclosure statement,

- name of escrow and if costs are to be split,
- prorating of taxes,
- keys to be turned over, and
- other pertinent terms.

Then hand copies of the offer to each owner.

Some agents like to use a silent approach and wait for owners to react. If the offer is substantially in accordance with the listing, you could simply state the folowing:

> "[Mr. & Mrs. Finch], I have sold your home. As we go through the offer I have here, you will see that I have been able to obtain for you what I said I would."

Now go through the offer paragraph by paragraph with the owners. Answer any questions they may have. When you are finished, ask them to initial clauses where appropriate and to approve the agreement (that is, sign) where you have indicated.

Justify the Offer

> You don't want the buyer to appear arbitrary as to price.

When an offer is less than the list price, you must be able to justify the offer, or you are in danger that the sellers will regard the buyers as arbitrary. Explain how or why the buyer decided on the offering price. When sellers and buyers have a high regard for each other, there is less likelihood of a sale's failing during escrow. An example of such an explanation is

> "While the offer I have is less than we had hoped, I nevertheless believe it is a fair offer. While I convinced the [Henleys] that your home met their needs better than [the house off Wedgewood Way], they didn't feel they should pay more for it than what they would have paid for the [Wedgewood Way] house."

Not only does the above statement justify the price, it again emphasizes that the sellers are in competition with other sellers. In cases in which an offer is reasonable, acceptance rather than a counteroffer should be sought. By accepting, your sellers will be the winners over the owners of the competing house. Always be completely honest in justifying acceptance of an offer.

Agent Recommendations— Accept, Reject, or Counteroffer

It is unethical for a seller's agent to recommend to owners that an offer be accepted if the agent does not feel that the offer is in the best interests of the owners, considering the market, the property, and their needs. If an offer is clearly not in the owners' best interests, tell them. This is part of your fiduciary duty. The less sophisticated the owners, the greater is your duty to advise them. The name of the game is not "a commission by any means."

> **Owners' Responses to Offers**
> Keep in mind that owners have three choices when an offer is received.
> 1. Acceptance
> 2. Rejection
> 3. Counteroffer

It would be unusual if you were to recommend outright **rejection**. This recommendation likely would be made only in cases of clearly frivolous offers or offers in which the buyers are attempting to take unconscionable advantage of the sellers.

If an offer is fair, work for its acceptance rather than for a counteroffer. Many agents are too quick to suggest a counteroffer when it isn't necessarily in the owners' best interests. Some agents like to push for a counteroffer because it is relatively easy and avoids further confrontation with the owners. If you truly represent the owners, you have a duty to try to make them understand that a counteroffer rejects the offer and gives the buyers an out. Once an offer is rejected, the owners have lost their right to accept and form a contract. The offer is dead.

> Until accepted an offer can be withdrawn.

Explain **buyers' remorse**. Buyers' remorse is like a virus. Most buyers get it—some worse than others. They question their wisdom in having made the offer at the price they did and wonder whether it should have been made at all. They wonder if they should have spent more time looking. To some, a counteroffer is like a heaven-sent escape.

Even buyers who intend to accept a counteroffer frequently decide to spend one more day looking before they sign. All too often, they find something they like. A great many owners have lost advantageous deals because they tried to squeeze just a little more out of buyers. A counteroffer gives up the "bird in the hand."

It is not unethical conduct to use your persuasive skills to persuade an owner to accept an offer you believe is reasonable. In fact, it is the only truly ethical way to deal with the situation.

When the Seller Is Not Represented By an Agent

If an agent does not represent the seller, then you, as a buyer's agent have a duty to try to get your client's offer accepted. However, you must be absolutely honest about any facts you present to influence the seller. You must never aid the buyer in fraud. You also must fully explain the offer to the seller, especially any provision that is unusual or provides the buyer with a right to cancel the agreement.

It is important that the seller understand that you represent the buyer as a buyer's agent.

Protecting the Seller

As the sellers' agent, you have a duty to protect them from fraudulent or "sharp" practices. There are offers that on careful reading do not actually state what you expect them to.

If you are unsure of the meaning of an offer that has come through another agent, suggest the owners obtain legal help or reword the offer in a counteroffer. Be especially wary of any offer received on an offer form you are not familiar with. Some sharp operators use their own forms prepared with a laser printer. They may even label the form with a designation number so it will look like a standard form. By submitting forms that contain what appear to be standard or "boilerplate" clauses, they could, for example, require that the sellers pay all of the buyers' loan costs as well as all closing costs.

Be particularly alert for any purchase in which it appears the buyer could be promoting a **"cash-out" scheme.** While there are a number of ways this can be done, the most popular is by use of a **subordination clause.** Where the property is owned free and clear or the sellers have substantial equity, the buyer offers a large cash amount and asks the sellers to carry the balance with a trust deed. The catch is that the trust deed is a "subordinate" trust deed.

■   **EXAMPLE:**   Ina Cent owns her home free and clear. She wants to sell it for $400,000. After the home has been on the market for several months, Cent receives an offer from Joe Sharp. Sharp offers her full price for the home with $100,000 down. He asks that she carry a subordinate trust deed for the $300,000 balance at 10 percent interest, all due and payable in one year. This offer looks terrific to Ina Cent, so she accepts the offer. Sharp arranges for a first trust deed at $250,000 (remember, the $300,000 trust deed is subordinate). He uses $100,000 for his down payment and has $150,000 left. He is a cash-out buyer.

The normal scenario is that Sharp would make no payments on the $250,000 first trust deed or the $300,000 subordinate (second) trust deed. The first trust deed would either foreclose and wipe out Ina Cent's equity or she would have to cure the first trust deed and foreclose on her second trust deed, leaving her in possession of her house but with a $250,000 trust deed against it. Joe Sharp, in the meantime, is spending his money.

Other buyers to be on the alert for are those who enter into a purchase with no investment. While many no-down-payment sales are legitimate, there have been horror cases. No-down buyers have rented the property, collecting rent without making payments. This is called **rent skimming.** The definition of rent skimming has been expanded to cover collecting rents and deposits on property not owned or controlled by the renter. Other no-down buyers have harvested trees and sold personal property that was included in the sale but was not separately secured by a lien.

At the very least, you have a duty to warn the owners of negative possibilities. You also might suggest that a check be made of court dockets to determine if such potential buyers have been defendants in lawsuits.

Be wary of offers in which buyers want to exchange personal property or real property. Again, many exchanges are valid transactions, but there also have been many sharp deals. Make certain the value of the property being received has been properly verified. Don't accept at face value appraisals provided by the buyers. Be particularly careful if a property profile indicates that buyers have only recently acquired the property. If a trust deed is being traded for property, be on guard if it is a new trust deed. Also, determine the value of the property. Some buyers have created trust deeds on nearly worthless property to use as trading material for valuable property.

A few years ago sharp buyers were using uncut diamonds and colored gemstones as trading material. They also were including appraisals. Sellers who accepted the stones often found they had sold their properties for less than ten cents on the dollar.

Because real estate involves large amounts of money, it can attract some very unscrupulous people. Many of these people are very intelligent and will devise elaborate schemes to get something for as close to nothing as possible. Many seminars have promoted these unethical and often illegal schemes to attendees as a get-rich-quick answer to all their dreams. It is your duty as a real estate professional to look carefully at any deal that looks too good to be true. You have a fiduciary duty to protect your principal against the devious schemes of others. Of course, this points out why sellers should be represented by agents. (Even if you are a buyer's agent, you don't want to be an accomplice in an unethical and/or fraudulent scheme.)

Gaining an Acceptance

Many sellers will accept your recommendations for acceptance when those recommendations are logical and you have built up a relationship of trust with the owners. However, a home sale is not all logic. Emotions play a significant role in acceptance or rejection of a purchase offer. The primary **seller objections** concern price and terms.

Price. The most common objection to an offer is about **price.** The sellers might have counted on obtaining a specified price, and they feel that accepting less is a price cut. You can answer this objection by minimizing the difference. The goal of minimizing the difference is to make the difference—the unattained portion—appear small in relation to the whole.

> "Buyers, not sellers, determine price. A price set by sellers is merely a wish unless they have a buyer. Right now, we have a buyer. While the offer is less than we had hoped, it is within [7 percent] of the competitive market analysis, which places the offer in the realm of reasonableness. You are being offered [93 percent] of what you hoped for. You are only a signature away from a sale."

An excellent approach when sellers are adamant on a price is

"[Mr. and Mrs. Jones], if you did not own this house and you were given the opportunity to buy it right now, would you buy the house if it could be yours for [the price of the offer]?"

The answer to such a question probably will be "No, we don't need the house; that's why we are selling it!" You should now continue with the very logical

"Then why are you bidding on it? When you turn down an offer for [$289,000], you're really saying that the house is worth more to you than has been offered. You're an active bidder competing against this buyer. If you wouldn't pay [$289,000] for this house today, then you should be accepting an offer to sell it at [$289,000]."

If the owners indicate an offer is ridiculous, point out the following:

"Right now I have a check for [$10,000]; now that's not ridiculous. I also have an offer for [$289,000]. It may be less than you had hoped for, but it is only [7 percent] less than the value established by our competitive market analysis. That to me is not ridiculous. It is a serious offer deserving serious consideration."

You will likely hear the "friend said . . ." response. Basically, it is that someone they know, who is "very knowledgeable" about real estate, who told them, "Don't take a dollar less than [$300,000] for your home." The way to deal with this invisible friend is

"[Mr. and Mrs. Jones], let us assume that you reject this offer, and that, despite my best efforts, months pass without another offer on your house. Let us also assume we finally obtain another offer at far less than the present offer. Now assume you accept this offer. Will your friend make up your loss?"

This shows that the owners alone bear the results of the decision and that it should not be made by anyone else. You can point out actual case histories that sellers can relate to. Chances are your broker can tell you many stories that follow this identical scenario.

Put the difference in perspective; show it as a percentage.

The sellers are thinking in terms of thousands of dollars less than they had hoped for; however, you must present the positive side of a reasonable offer. You can do this by showing the difference not in dollars but in a percentage, for example:

"Right now we have an offer giving you 93 percent of what you wanted to receive for your home. I think that's a pretty good offer."

The following "gambler" argument is also an excellent approach that uses percentages:

"[Mr. and Mrs. Jones], you certainly are gamblers. By accepting the offer before us, you can tie the buyers to this agreement. You are proposing a counteroffer that will give you [7 percent] more than this offer. You are wagering [93 percent] against [7 percent]. To me those seem like pretty long odds. I know I wouldn't gamble [93 cents] to make [7 cents] and I don't think you should either."

Terms.   At times, **terms** are stumbling blocks. For example, if there is seller carryback financing, the sellers may object to the size of the down payment. If the sellers have owned the property for a number of years, consider

"[Mr. and Mrs. Henderson], when you purchased this home, how much of a down payment did you make?"

Chances are it was relatively small. If so, continue:

"Young families are not much different today than they were when you purchased this home. If you couldn't have purchased it with a low down payment, chances are you would never have become an owner. The fact that our buyers, the [Cliffords], have [$] to put down is a positive reason to approve this agreement."

If sellers complain about the interest rate on sellers' financing, consider

"[Mr. and Mrs. Smith], do you know the rates banks pay on Certificates of Deposits today?"

More than likely, the rate is less than the seller-financing rate. This leads into

"The rate is [4 percent]. Now the buyers are proposing to pay you [7½ percent]. That's [3½ percent] higher than what you could obtain from the bank if the buyers had paid cash. I think this is an advantageous offer."

If the owners have the offers before them while you are making any of the above presentations, and they should, a simple closing technique is to hand a pen to each owner.

■ THE COUNTEROFFER

A little more work on the offer might eliminate the need for a counteroffer.

If agents worked harder with buyers in formulating offers, the need for **counteroffers** would be diminished. Unfortunately, some agents accept unreasonable offers from potential purchasers without expending much effort to improve the offer. This allows prospective buyers to believe that a terrific bargain is possible. What the agent is hoping for isn't acceptance but a counteroffer that might be accepted. Unfortunately, it can be difficult to get a reasonable counteroffer accepted, once prospective buyers have been given these false hopes. Nevertheless, an unreasonable offer should be countered rather than rejected, because there is still the chance of a sale. Try to structure the counteroffer in such a manner that it will be met with acceptance.

What is a Reasonable Offer?

What is an unreasonable offer will vary, depending on the market. In a sellers' market with many buyers and relatively few sellers, an offer of 10 percent below the CMA might be viewed as unreasonable. However, in a buyers' market with many sellers, such an offer might be regarded as reasonable. As a rule of thumb, a reasonable and acceptable offer falls within 10 percent of the value established by the CMA, but this varies with the market.

If the seller's agent does not feel acceptance of an offer is in the principal's best interest, the agent should advise against acceptance and make suggestions for a counteroffer that will serve his or her principal's interests. However, when an agent feels that the principal's best interests would be served by acceptance of an offer, the agent should strongly recommend acceptance and explain his or her reasons for the recommendation.

Licensees may be plagued with some of the following counteroffer problems:

- Proposed wording that is unacceptable to the seller
- Changes in the amount or terms of loans
- Changes in date of possession
- Limitations on the liability for termite damage, repairs, and so forth
- Exclusions of personal property items to be included in the package
- Limitation of time required for the buyer to obtain financing

When all other efforts have failed to obtain acceptance of the offer in its present form, persuade the seller to make a counteroffer or a new offer in response to a potential buyer's offer. Any alteration to an offer, even a change in date or time of close, is considered a counteroffer.

The following are the most common conditions desired by the seller when making a counteroffer:

- Safeguard provisions for the seller when the buyer's offer is conditional on sale of other property
- Increase in purchase price and/or cash deposit
- Limitations on the seller's warranties or demands that the buyer accept property as is
- Change of amount, terms, and conditions relating to loans to be carried
- Limitations on time allowed to obtain financing and the right of the seller to assist in locating a lender
- Limitation on the liability for termite work, repairs, and the like

- Change in date of possession and demand for free occupancy
- The seller's right to accept other offers until the counteroffer is accepted

The following dos and don'ts will assist you to prepare and present a legitimate counteroffer:

- *Do* start by amending the acceptance clause to incorporate reference to the counteroffer.
- *Do* have the seller sign the printed acceptance clause as amended if a separate acceptance clause is not inserted in the provisions of the counteroffer.
- *Don't* make changes in the contract simply for the sake of change.
- *Don't* pressure your principal to agree when the other party wishes to have some particular right or remedy inserted.
- *Do* make sure that the addendum is dated and proper reference is made to the contract of which it is a part.
- *Don't* make piecemeal changes in important terms. Instead, rewrite the whole paragraph in which the terms occur for better clarity.
- *Do* number the items of the counteroffer and refer to the contract paragraph where possible.
- *Don't* let disagreement concerning language terminate the sale.
- *Do* use a simple checklist for all points to be included in the counteroffer when drafting it.
- *Do* be sure that all changes are initialed or signed properly and that all parties receive copies of the final contract executed by both sides.

> Use a separate form for a counteroffer. Do not make changes on the purchase contract.

If you recommend a counteroffer, we suggest using the CAR Form CO (Figure 11.1). Do not make changes on the purchase contract. If you change the purchase contract and the buyers counter the counteroffer and the sellers then counter the counter-counteroffer, you have a form that becomes difficult to understand. Tracing the chronological order of the sale also becomes difficult. If you use separate forms, what was agreed to and when will be clear. The CAR Form provides for numbering of each counter offer so that it is clear what the final agreement is.

A counteroffer at full asking price isn't much of a counteroffer, even if the original price was fair or below market value. You must allow the buyers to receive some advantage from the negotiations. Many sales are lost because of hardheaded buyers and sellers. Sellers refuse to give an inch, and buyers want to "save face" by gaining some concession. Many buyers will walk away from an advantageous purchase rather than paying the full price.

Unless care is exercised in negotiations, a psychological wall may be built between the buyer and the seller. Figure 11.2 shows the bricks of a psychological wall between two principals.

FIGURE 11.1

Counteroffer

CALIFORNIA
ASSOCIATION
OF REALTORS®

COUNTER OFFER No. _____

For use by Seller or Buyer. May be used for Multiple Counter Offer.
(C.A.R. Form CO, Revised 10/02)

Date _____, at _____, California.
This is a counter offer to the: ☐ California Residential Purchase Agreement, ☐ Counter Offer, or ☐ Other _____ ("Offer"),
dated _____, on property known as _____ ("Property"),
between _____ ("Buyer") and _____ ("Seller").
1. **TERMS:** The terms and conditions of the above referenced document are **accepted subject to the following:**
    A. **Paragraphs in the Offer that require initials by all parties, but are not initialed by all parties, are excluded from the final agreement unless specifically referenced for inclusion in paragraph 1C of this or another Counter Offer.**
    B. **Unless otherwise agreed in writing, down payment and loan amount(s) will be adjusted in the same proportion as in the original Offer.**
    C. _____
        _____
        _____
        _____
        _____
        _____
        _____
        _____
        _____
        _____
    D. **The following attached supplements are incorporated in this Counter Offer:** ☐ Addendum No. _____
        ☐   ☐
2. **RIGHT TO ACCEPT OTHER OFFERS:** Seller has the right to continue to offer the Property for sale or for other transaction, and to accept any other offer at any time prior to notification of acceptance, as described in paragraph 3. If this is a Seller Counter Offer, Seller's acceptance of another offer prior to Buyer's acceptance and communication of notification of this Counter Offer, shall revoke this Counter Offer.
3. **EXPIRATION:** This Counter Offer shall be deemed revoked and the deposits, if any, shall be returned unless this Counter Offer is Signed by the Buyer or Seller to whom it is sent and a Copy of the Signed Counter Offer is personally received by the person making this Counter Offer or _____
    who is authorized to receive it, by 5:00 PM on the third Day After this Counter Offer is made or, (if checked)
    by ☐ _____ (date), at _____ AM/PM. This Counter Offer may be executed in counterparts.
4. ☐ **(If checked:) MULTIPLE COUNTER OFFER:** Seller is making a Counter Offer(s) to another prospective buyer(s) on terms that may or may not be the same as in this Counter Offer. Acceptance of this Counter Offer by Buyer shall **not** be binding unless and until it is subsequently re-Signed by Seller in paragraph 7 below and a Copy of the Counter Offer Signed in paragraph 7 is personally received by Buyer or by _____, who is authorized to receive it. Prior to the completion of all of these events, Buyer and Seller shall have no duties or obligations for the purchase or sale of the Property.
5. **OFFER: BUYER OR SELLER MAKES THIS COUNTER OFFER ON THE TERMS ABOVE AND ACKNOWLEDGES RECEIPT OF A COPY.**
    _____ Date _____
    _____ Date _____
6. **ACCEPTANCE: I/WE** accept the above Counter Offer (**If checked** ☐ **SUBJECT TO THE ATTACHED COUNTER OFFER)** and acknowledge receipt of a Copy.
    _____ Date _____ Time _____ AM/PM
    _____ Date _____ Time _____ AM/PM
7. **MULTIPLE COUNTER OFFER SIGNATURE LINE: By signing below, Seller accepts this Multiple Counter Offer.**
    NOTE TO SELLER: Do NOT sign in this box until after Buyer signs in paragraph 6. (Paragraph 7 applies only if paragraph 4 is checked.)
    _____ Date _____ Time _____ AM/PM
    _____ Date _____ Time _____ AM/PM
8. (____/____) (Initials) **Confirmation of Acceptance:** A Copy of Signed Acceptance was personally received by the maker of the Counter Offer, or that person's authorized agent as specified in paragraph 3 (or, if this is a Multiple Counter Offer, the Buyer or Buyer's authorized agent as specified in paragraph 4) on (date) _____, at _____ AM/PM. A binding Agreement is created when a Copy of Signed Acceptance is personally received by the the maker of the Counter Offer, or that person's authorized agent (or, if this is a Multiple Counter Offer, the Buyer or Buyer's authorized agent) whether or not confirmed in this document. Completion of this confirmation is not legally required in order to create a binding Agreement; it is solely intended to evidence the date that Confirmation of Acceptance has occurred.

SURE TRAC
The System for Success™

Published by the
California Association of REALTORS®

EQUAL HOUSING
OPPORTUNITY

CO REVISED 10/02 (PAGE 1 OF 1) Print Date

Reviewed by _____ Date _____

COUNTER OFFER (CO PAGE 1 OF 1)

FIGURE 11.2

Building a Psychological Wall between Principals

Hurting seller's pride
You have unintentionally belittled the property.

Putting seller down
You have belittled the seller and made him or her feel foolish or inadequate.

Using inadequate words
You have made it difficult for the seller to understand.

Inadequate explanation
You have not made the conditions and terms perfectly clear.

Not listening
Your preoccupation with other things closes your ears.

Lack of empathy
You have failed to show your concern for the seller's needs.

Failure to heed signals
You have failed to watch for closing signals, verbal and nonverbal.

A good approach to use when sellers do not want to give buyers a concession on a counteroffer is

> "Why not split the difference? The offer is for [$260,000] and you want [$290,000]. Why not counter at [$275,000]?"

In presenting the counteroffer to the buyers, you can make the sellers appear reasonable, because "splitting the difference" is often considered fair. Although there is no rational justification for splitting the difference, very often it is accepted.

There are often counters to counteroffers and counters to the counters to the counteroffers. You can feel like a messenger. Much of the running could ordinarily have been avoided by pressing to improve the offer when originally prepared.

■ THE ACCEPTANCE

| Acceptance must be unqualified or it becomes a counteroffer. |

Acceptance of an offer must be unqualified; a *qualified acceptance* must be considered as a new offer or a counteroffer. The legal effect of any changes is to reject the original offer and bar its later acceptance.

Keep in mind that acceptance does not take place until the person making the offer is notified of the acceptance. Until that time the offeror is free to revoke his or her offer. Notification of acceptance is the delivery of a signed copy of the acceptance to the offeror. Placing the acceptance in the mail constitutes notification.

We recommend that you deliver the acceptance to the buyers immediately on receiving it.

Leave a completed offer form with the buyers, and let them know the procedure to be followed as well as when you will contact them again. Be certain to give the buyers assurances of value and that they have purchased a fine house. People need to know that they have done the right thing.

If buyers enjoy a home, they will not feel that they have overpaid, no matter what the price. On the other hand, if buyers are not happy in their home, even though they thought the home was a bargain—they overpaid. What really counts in the long run are the benefits, not the price tag.

FAX and E-mail Acceptance

There will be circumstances where you will be unable to present offers in person. In California, a FAX can be used. When you present an offer by FAX, you should put your recommendations and your reasoning in a cover letter. If accepted by FAX or a counteroffer is made, the seller should generate a transmission report reflecting the accurate transmission of the document.

Since e-mail is considered an increasingly common means of modern communication, e-mail acceptances of offers are considered to be possible although court case decisions are not clear in this area. Because acceptance requires a signature, the seller would have to obtain a pad that allows signatures to be electronically attached to a document. A problem with these pads is the quality of the signature, allowing signatures to be easily forged. Therefore, we recommend FAX or overnight delivery services as an alternative to e-mail acceptance of offers.

■ CHECKLIST FOR CLOSING

Your job isn't finished with the accepted offer. Because you don't receive compensation until the escrow closes, you must make certain the **closing** actually takes place. There are many things you must do to be sure no delays occur during closing. When there are delays, the likelihood of something happening to "kill" the sale tends to increase.

Because the individuals involved in the closing of a transaction may miss certain details and errors may creep in, it is your job to check frequently to uncover small problems before they become big ones. Check frequently to see if everything is moving according to schedule. Keep all parties fully informed of all events and conclusions. Remember, referrals depend on good follow-through.

Some agents tend to lose a great many deals during escrow. They like to blame it on bad luck, but they would be surprised how much luckier they could have been if they had worked just a little harder during escrow. There are a number of low-cost computer programs available to aid you in tracking the progress of escrows.

Closing Checklist

The following checklist contains some of the things you should be doing:

■ Provide information to escrow so the escrow holder can prepare escrow instructions.

■ Make certain all applicable disclosures discussed in Chapter 3 or stated in the purchase contract are made.

■ If the offer calls for a structural pest control inspection and/or home inspection, make certain that it is ordered as soon as possible.

■ If the offer provides for a professional home inspection, make certain arrangements are made.

■ Make certain that parties sign the escrow instructions as soon as they are available (if they are not part of the purchase contract) as well as the necessary transfer documentation.

■ Provide the purchasers with loan information and either make an appointment with a loan officer for your buyers or help them make a loan application on the Internet. Make certain that the purchasers complete their loan application along with any required supporting documentation.

■ Communicate with both buyer and seller at least once each week. Let both know what is happening and what you are doing for them. If there are any problems, disclose them and work with both parties toward a solution.

■ If there is a walk-through final inspection, you should be there. You don't want a nervous buyer and seller getting together without you.

■ Make certain the seller has labeled all keys and left behind any applicable appliance manuals, warranties, matching paint, garage-door openers, etc. Also, be sure the property is in clean condition. If necessary, suggest that the seller have the carpet cleaned as soon as the house is vacated.

■ Communicate with the escrow on a weekly basis. You want to know if a party has not done something or if there is a problem.

■ Contact the lending officer on a regular basis to make certain things are running smoothly.

■ After closing, thank both buyer and seller for their faith in you.

Should the buyer and/or seller be unable or unwilling to complete the purchase, you will want the buyer and seller to agree, as soon as possible, as to the disposition of the deposit. By immediately addressing the problem, you will reduce the likelihood of legal action. A lawsuit means time spent testifying as a witness or, possibly, a defendant. Figure 11.3 is a simple CAR **release-of-contract** form that can be signed by the agent as well as by the buyer and seller.

FIGURE 11.3

Release of Contract

CALIFORNIA
ASSOCIATION
OF REALTORS®

RELEASE OF CONTRACT

The undersigned Buyer and Seller (or exchange party(ies), if applicable), are parties to that certain:
(Check all that apply):

☐ Residential Purchase Agreement and Receipt for Deposit

☐ Manufactured Home Purchase Agreement and Receipt for Deposit

☐ Residential Income Property Purchase Agreement

☐ Commercial Property Purchase Agreement

☐ Other _____ ,

dated _____ , including all amendments and related documents, covering the property described as:

_____

_____

and ☐ (if applicable), escrow #_____ with _____ , Escrow Holder
(collectively "Agreement").

Buyer and Seller mutually release each other from all obligation to buy, sell, or exchange under the Agreement and from all claims, actions, and demands which each may have against the other(s) by reason of the Agreement. Buyer and Seller intend that all rights and obligations arising out of the Agreement are null and void.

_____ is hereby instructed to cancel Escrow Number _____ .
(Name of Escrow Holder)

_____ , holder of the deposit under the terms of the Agreement, is
(Name of Broker or Escrow Holder)
hereby instructed to disburse the deposit as follows:

$ _____   To _____

$ _____   To _____

$ _____   To _____

$ _____   To _____

Date _____   Date _____

Buyer _____   Seller _____

Buyer _____   Seller _____

R I E B S   Published and Distributed by:
REAL ESTATE BUSINESS SERVICES, INC.
a subsidiary of the CALIFORNIA ASSOCIATION OF REALTORS®
525 South Virgil Avenue, Los Angeles, California 90020

PRINT DATE

REVISED 10/99

┌─ OFFICE USE ONLY ─┐
Reviewed by Broker
or Designee _____
Date _____

EQUAL HOUSING
OPPORTUNITY

FORM RC-11

■ SUMMARY

It is important that the owners not know the details of any offer you have until you present it, so they can see the entire offer. Otherwise, they may build psychological walls that will make communication difficult. Before meeting with the owners, you should prepare a new estimated sellers' proceeds form, and you might want to update the competitive market analysis.

Before you present the offer, set the mood by discussing what sold the buyers on the house. You also want the owners to sign the agency confirmation. The presentation process itself involves three stages:

1. The history of the sale
2. About the buyers
3. The offer itself

By covering the history of the sale, you will bring out the problems, if any, with the property that led other prospective buyers to reject the property. This helps deflate unrealistic expectations.

When you tell the owners about the buyers, make the buyers appear as nice people that the sellers would like in their home. The buyers cannot appear to be arbitrary.

After covering the minor points, explain how the offer was arrived at. Recommend acceptance of a reasonable offer rather than advising a counteroffer. If the offer is not in the owners' best interests, however, recommend rejection or a counteroffer. If multiple offers are obtained, they should be presented in a nonprejudicial manner. Consider prequalifying buyers when multiple offers are received.

You must protect owners against fraud and sharp operators. Be on the alert for buyers who use their own forms, who want the sellers to carry a subordinate note or who could otherwise be cash-out buyers. Also, be concerned if buyers are to obtain possession without any cash investment or if buyers want to exchange real or personal property for the owners' property. Don't place any value on appraisals provided by the buyers—verify everything. Be on the alert for buyers who recently acquired trust deeds or property and want to use them as trade property.

The most common objection raised by sellers to buyers' offers is price. It is in the owners' best interests to accept a reasonable offer rather than make a counteroffer that frees the buyers from the agreement. Counteroffers should consider benefits to both buyers and sellers and should be written on a separate form rather than modifying the purchase contract. In this way it will be easier to determine what exactly was agreed on and when.

Buyers can withdraw an offer any time before acceptance. Acceptance does not take place until the accepted offer is mailed or delivered to the buyers.

Monitor the sale closely from acceptance to close of escrow while communicating with the buyers, sellers, escrow officer and loan officer on a regular basis. You must help the parties and make certain everything gets done; remember, a commission is not received until the closing.

■ CLASS DISCUSSION TOPICS

1. Present a completed offer to an owner (another student). Your presentation shall be either
    a. the history of the sale,
    b. information about the buyer, or
    c. the offer itself.

2. How would you handle the following objections of the seller to an offer?
    a. "That's $20,000 less than I paid."
    b. "Last year the house across the street from me sold for $10,000 more than this offer, and my house is nicer than their house."
    c. "If I have to cut my price, then you have to cut your commission or I won't accept the offer."
    d. "We would like to think it over."
    e. "The house is paid for. We can wait until we receive our price."

3. Bring to class one current-events article dealing with some aspect of real estate practice for class discussion.

■ CHAPTER 11 QUIZ

1. Selling real estate involves three separate sales. Which of the following is *not* one of them?
    a. Obtaining the listing
    b. Advertising for buyers
    c. Obtaining the offer
    d. Gaining acceptance of the offer

2. You receive two offers on a property you have listed. One is from your own firm and the other, which was received an hour earlier, is from another firm. You should
    a. present the offers in the order received.
    b. present the highest price offer first and, if not accepted, present the next offer.
    c. present the offers at the same time.
    d. always present your firm's offer before offers from other firms.

3. It would be most difficult to persuade an owner to accept a reasonable offer received
    a. 3 days after listing the property.
    b. 30 days after listing the property.
    c. 90 days after listing the property.
    d. 180 days after listing the property.

4. When presenting an offer on your listing for less than list price, it is good policy to
    a. immediately tell the seller what the offer is.
    b. not recommend acceptance or rejection.
    c. recommend that sellers counter or reject offers when acceptance is not in their best interest.
    d. have a number of your office staff present to intimidate the sellers.

5. Many buyers have second thoughts after placing an offer. This buyer apprehension is commonly known as
   a. feedback.
   b. the gambler syndrome.
   c. buyers' remorse.
   d. negative motivation.

6. Which of the following is *false* about counteroffers?
   a. A counteroffer serves as a rejection of an offer.
   b. If the counteroffer is not accepted, the owner has the option of accepting the original offer.
   c. A counteroffer turns the original offeree (the owner) into an offeror.
   d. All of the above are false.

7. You should be particularly wary if an offer is received on your listing that contains the word(s)
   a. "subordination."
   b. "transfer disclosure."
   c. "time is of the essence."
   d. "liquidated damages."

8. Rent skimming is
   a. charging minorities an exorbitant rent.
   b. a property manager's failure to disclose all rents received.
   c. a buyer's failure to apply rents to loans that were assumed.
   d. a tenant making monthly rent payments every 40 days.

9. You receive an offer on one of your listings. Although for less than the listing amount, the offer is certainly reasonable, based on the CMA. You should recommend to the owners that
   a. they counteroffer at a price halfway between list price and the offer to split the difference.
   b. the offer be rejected so that the offeror will raise the offer to the list price.
   c. they let the offer period expire without taking any action to make the offeror anxious.
   d. they accept the offer.

10. After an offer is accepted, the listing agent should
   a. keep track of escrow progress.
   b. make certain all papers are signed by the parties.
   c. make certain that conditions are being met.
   d. do all of the above.

CHAPTER TWELVE

12

REAL ESTATE FINANCING

■ KEY TERMS

adjustable-rate mortgage
adjustment period
annual percentage rate
back-end ratio
blanket trust deed
Cal Vet loan certificate of
   reasonable value
closing the loan
combination fixed-
   adjustable-loan
commercial banks
computerized loan
   origination
conforming loans
controlled business
   arrangement
conventional loans
convertible ARM
cosigner
credit union
direct endorsement

DVA-guaranteed loan
due-on-sale clause
Fair Credit Reporting
   Act
Fannie Mae
Farmer Mac
FHA-insured loan
fixed-rate loan
Freddie Mac
front-end ratio
Ginnie Mae
hard money makers and
   arrangers
index
institutional lenders
jumbo loans
life insurance company
margin
mortgage banker
mortgage companies

mortgage loan disclosure
   statement
mortgage loan broker
nonconforming loans
noninstitutional lenders
open-end trust deed
participation loan
payment shock
pension fund
portfolio loans
predatory lending
primary mortgage market
private mortgage
   insurance
qualfying borrowers
real estate investment
   trust
Real Estate Settlement
   Procedures Act
release clause

■ KEY TERMS (CONTINUED)

renegotiable-rate mortgages	secondary mortgage market	third-party originator
reverse mortgage	seller carryback financing	verification of employment
savings associations	subprime lender	wraparound trust deed
secondary financing	take-out loan	

■ LEARNING OBJECTIVES

In this chapter, you learn the practical application of real estate financing to real estate brokerage activities. You learn the difference between primary and secondary financing as well as that between primary and secondary mortgage markets and about the function of the secondary mortgage market, its purpose, and the agencies involved. You discover the sources of real estate financing funds and the roles played by various types of lenders. You learn about government participation loans and conventional loans as well as criteria to be used in choosing specific loan types. From this chapter you should gain an understanding of lenders' needs, of the financing process, and of how lenders qualify buyers.

■ INTEREST RATES AND THE REAL ESTATE MARKET

The health of the real estate industry is directly related to the cost of money or interest rates. Lower interest rates mean lower payments, which in turn means that more people become qualified for loans. With more buyers, we tend to have a seller's market and see real estate prices increase.

The real estate marketplace has been the one bright spot in the U.S. economy since 1990. Despite recessionary trends, real estate sales have been strong because of affordability brought about by low interest rates. Strong real estate sales have also aided construction-related industries, as well as sales of furniture, appliances, and textile for households. Without the counter economic effect of the strength in the real estate marketplace, the recent recession would have been far worse.

One negative effect of high housing affordability has been on the rental market. As prime renters have been able to become homeowners, the vacancy rates across the nation have generally increased and, in many areas of the country, per unit rents have decreased.

When interest rates increase, real estate sales tend to decrease. (Sales are related inversely to interest rates.) With a slow market, sellers can often be encouraged to help finance buyers and creative financing arrangements become common-place. Higher housing costs associated with higher interest rates tend to increase the number of foreclosures.

■ SOURCES OF FUNDS

Almost everyone is at some time a user, a buyer, or a seller of real estate. On the average, in this country a person spends more than 20 percent of his or her lifetime income on some form of real estate, either for rental or for purchase as an investment or as a residence. Because real estate is the largest purchase most people make in their lifetimes, few are prepared to pay cash. Thus, the completion of most real estate sales will depend on funds available in the money market at the time of the transaction.

Because most buyers are unable or unwilling to pay cash for real property, long-term financing in the form of a mortgage (or trust deed) loan is necessary. Understanding the use of real estate mortgage money requires an understanding of the sources of these funds. Money to finance real estate purchases is available through two primary money market areas: *directly* from someone or some institution that has accumulated this money, or *indirectly*, from a lending institution that loans money deposited in customers' accounts. You should be constantly aware of the status of the money market in your area, including policies of lenders, interest rates, and points and lending costs.

Different lenders offer variations in products (loans) and have different under-writing standards for different types of properties. An experienced agent will help clients select a lender whose standards meet the property being purchased as well as the specific client needs.

■ PRIMARY AND SECONDARY FINANCING

Primary financing refers to first trust deeds. Because interest rates are related to risk, primary financing generally has lower interest rates than other loans in which the security interest is secondary.

> Primary financing refers to first trust deeds, secondary financing to second trust deeds.

Any junior trust deed is **secondary financing.** Holders of a second trust deed bear a greater risk than holders of a first trust deed; therefore, second trust deeds customarily bear a higher rate of interest. In the event of default of the first trust deed, the holders of the second have to either cure the default and foreclose on the second trust deed or wait until the foreclosure and bid cash. If holders of the second trust deed fail to do either, they may lose their security.

While primary financing refers to first trust deeds, the **primary mortgage market** refers to loans being made directly to borrowers, either first or second trust deeds. The **secondary mortgage market** refers to the resale of existing mortgages and trust deeds.

Three agencies—Fannie Mae (FNMA), Ginnie Mae (GNMA), and Freddie Mac (FHLMC)—are responsible for creating and establishing a viable secondary mortgage market. Their operations have created a national securities market for the sale of real estate debt instruments by the originators to second buyers. Selling the loans frees capital to create more real estate mortgages. The secondary market also minimizes the effects of regional cycles and redistributes the funds from cash-rich areas to cash-poor ones.

Fannie Mae

Fannie Mae, formerly the Federal National Mortgage Association (FNMA), was established to stimulate the secondary mortgage market by buying FHA-insured and DVA-guaranteed mortgages made by private lenders. Fannie Mae has evolved into a private, profit-oriented corporation that markets its own securities and handles a variety of real estate loans. These loans are purchased (sometimes at a discount) and can be resold to other lenders or investors. Stabilizing the market gives lenders a sense of security and encourages them to make more loans.

Ginnie Mae

Ginnie Mae, once the Government National Mortgage Association (GNMA), is presently a wholly government-owned agency, but privatization is being considered. Higher-risk—but important—programs, such as urban renewal, low-income housing, and other special-purpose government-backed programs, are financed through this agency. Ginnie Mae participates in the secondary mortgage market through its mortgage-backed securities programs. Qualified mortgage lenders and approved dealers can obtain additional capital for mortgages by pooling a group of homogeneous existing loans and pledging them as collateral. Ginnie Mae guarantees that holders of these securities will receive timely principal and interest payments.

Freddie Mac

Freddie Mac, formerly the Federal Home Loan Mortgage Corporation (FHLMC), was founded with money provided by the 12 Federal Home Loan Banks when new mortgage loans could not be made because money was flowing out of the savings and loan associations (S&Ls). Freddie Mac created needed funds by floating its own securities, backed by its pool of mortgages and guaranteed by Ginnie Mae. This gave S&Ls a secondary market for selling their conventional mortgages. Freddie Mac buys loans that have been closed within one year at specified discount rates. Freddie Mac, like Fannie Mae, is now a profit-oriented corporation.

Federal Agricultural Mortgage Corporation

Farmer Mac, the Federal Agricultural Mortgage Corporation, is a government-chartered, but now private, corporation that provides a secondary mortgage market for farm and rural housing.

■ CONFORMING LOANS

A lender that makes a loan either keeps the loan in its portfolio or sells the loan in the secondary mortgage market. Loans that the lender keeps (does not sell) are called **portfolio loans.** Loans that the lender sells are called *nonportfolio loans.* **Conforming loans** are conventional loans that meet the underwriting standards

FIGURE 12.1

Institutional Lenders

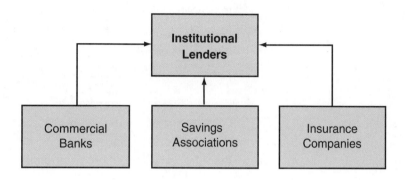

Conforming loans meet
Fannie Mae and Freddie
Mac purchase criteria.

for purchase by Fannie Mae or Freddie Mac. These loans are written for 15-year or 30-year terms and are not assumable. They have strict guidelines regarding down payments and maximum amounts. At the time of this writing, a single-family loan has a limit to $322,700 if it is to be eligible for purchase by Fannie Mae or Freddie Mac. (This limit is subject to annual change.) Because of the ready market for these loans, lenders are willing to make them and to purchase them on the secondary mortgage market. Because of their strict underwriting requirements, the interest rates for conforming loans are generally less than rates charged for **nonconforming loans.**

Loans for amounts of $322,700 and more are customarily referred to as **jumbo loans.** Interest rates on jumbo loans are higher than rates for conforming loans.

◼ LENDERS

Lenders generally can be divided into two groups: institutional lenders and non-institutional lenders.

Institutional Lenders

There are three major types of **institutional lenders:** commercial banks, savings associations, and life insurance companies. (See Figure 12.1.)

Commercial Banks.   **Commercial banks** are familiarly known as the "department stores" of financial institutions because of the variety of operations in which they engage. A principal activity of commercial banks is lending money. Commercial banks prefer to make loans to their customers because this preference helps to create depositors.

Banks often charge lower loan fees than other institutional lenders. They are quite versatile in the type of loans they may consider, but they seldom allow secondary financing at the time of providing a purchase-money loan.

Banks have been expanding their home equity loans (second trust deeds). Some offer an open-end line of credit secured by borrowers' home equity.

> ### Banks in California
>
> In California, banks are either federally chartered or state chartered and are regulated by federal and state laws, respectively. They tend to favor short-term loans and follow relatively conservative appraisal and lending practices. Their real estate loans generally are 80 percent or less of the appraised value of the property. Borrowers who are unable to put at least 20 percent down will likely be required to buy **private mortgage insurance** (PMI). A homeowner can cancel the mortgage insurance when the balance of the loan is less than 75 percent of the price paid, payments are current, and there has not been more than one late payment in the prior year.

Banks have also gone into the mortgage banking business in that they make loans, which they then sell to other lenders or investors such as pension plans. They may continue to service loans that they sell.

Savings Associations.   **Savings associations,** also known as "thrifts," and once known as savings and loan associations (S&Ls), formerly accounted for more home loans than any other source. After deregulation in the 1980s, they branched into other higher-yielding but higher-risk loans, which led to a great many S&L failures. Today, like banks, savings associations are state or federally chartered. They are allowed to loan up to 95 percent of the property's appraised value, although an 80 percent loan-to-value ratio (LTV) is most usual. The distinction between banks and savings associations has almost disappeared since the S&L failures, and most California S&Ls have become banks.

Life Insurance Companies.   The lending policies of **life insurance companies** are governed by the laws of the state in which the company is chartered, the laws of the state in which the loan originates, the policies of management, and the availability of loan funds.

Insurance companies supply many of the loans on properties for which huge loans are required (commercial properties, shopping centers, industrial properties, hotels). In California, they make loans for up to 75 percent of the property's market value. Their commercial loans are commonly for 25 years to 30 years. Insurance companies' interest rates often are lower than those of banks or savings associations. These loans seldom have due-on-sale clauses.

Insurance companies frequently demand an equity position as a limited partner as a condition of making a loan (**participation loan**). Many insurance companies were motivated by the added benefit of an equity position to make large commercial loans. Insurance company lending in the mid-1980s contributed to the overbuilding of shopping centers and office structures in many areas of the country.

FIGURE 12.2

Noninstitutional Lenders

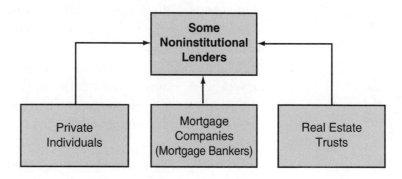

Noninstitutional Lenders

Noninstitutional lenders that make real estate loans include pension funds, credit unions, private individuals, and real estate investment trusts. (See Figure 12.2.)

Mortgage Companies or Mortgage Bankers

Mortgage companies are also known as mortgage bankers. They can be licensed in California by either the Department of Real Estate or the Department of Corporations.

Mortgage bankers or **mortgage companies** make loans using their own capital. They usually resell the loans to institutional lenders on the secondary mortgage market. They usually have a close working relationship with one or more lenders and receive daily rate sheets. Mortgage bankers are currently the largest single source of residential mortgage loan origination in California. You will see that the lender Internet sites listed in the Appendix are primarily mortgage bankers.

Mortgage bankers make money on origination fees as well as loan servicing fees. Though they generally resell the loans that they originate, mortgage bankers often continue to service these loans.

Mortgage bankers might hold off selling mortgages that they originated if they believe that mortgage interest rates would drop. If they are right, mortgages made at higher rates could be sold at a premium above face value.

Mortgage bankers are careful in qualifying borrowers because loans that fail to conform to Fannie Mae and Freddie Mac purchase requirements are difficult to sell on the secondary mortgage market. Mortgage bankers will generally only make loans when they have a buyer for them.

Mortgage bankers are able to make many difficult loans that most banks would decline such as loans for mixed-use properties or a loan where the buyer has had credit problems. They might place such loans with **subprime lenders** who will make difficult loans at a higher rate of interest.

Real Estate Investment Trusts

The **real estate investment trust** (REIT) was created in 1960 to encourage small investors to pool their resources with others to raise venture capital for real estate transactions. To qualify as a REIT, the trust must have at least 100 investors, and 90 percent of the trust's income must be distributed annually to its investors.

While a number of equity trusts invest solely in ownership of real property, there are many mortgage trusts that invest their money in mortgages, either directly or through a mortgage company. There also are hybrid trusts that invest in both equity ownership and mortgages.

Pension Funds. At one time, **pension funds** invested primarily in stocks. However, they now are becoming a more important factor in the mortgage market. They prefer to lend on large projects but will buy home loans. Pension funds generally buy loans originated by mortgage companies or loan direct, working with a third-party loan originator.

Credit Unions. At one time, **credit unions** offered mostly low-dollar loans for consumer purchases. Credit unions have evolved to become major lenders. While they limit loans to members, they have expanded their loan activity. Unlike profit-oriented lenders, their loans are more community based. Besides home equity loans and home purchase loans, credit unions have expanded their community lender role to include construction and development loans. Credit unions in many ways now resemble commercial banks.

Seller Carryback Financing

When conventional financing is not available to a buyer in the amount required or is too costly, a seller often can be persuaded to carry back a first or second mortgage on property to facilitate a sale. If a seller does not need the cash and the purchaser will pay a rate of interest higher than that provided by a certificate of deposit, the seller is a likely candidate for carryback financing.

Generally, **seller carryback financing** is customized to the needs of the parties. Such loans are generally fixed-rate loans with payments based on a 30-year amortization but due and payable in from five years to seven years. Most sellers are not interested in having their money tied up for longer periods of time.

Because most loans now have due-on-sale clauses, seller carryback financing is limited to situations where the property is owned by the seller free of loans, where the lender will agree to a loan assumption, where the existing loan does not have a due-on-sale clause, or where the seller will hold a secondary loan after the buyer obtains primary financing.

Real Estate Brokers

According to the *California Mortgage Loan Brokerage Law*, a **mortgage loan broker** is a person who acts for compensation in negotiating a new loan and is required to be licensed as a real estate broker or salesperson. Real estate brokers who negotiate mortgage loans under the Mortgage Loan Brokerage Law are limited in the amount that they may charge as a commission for arranging the loan and for costs and expenses of making the loan. Loans on first trust deeds of $30,000 or more or on second trust deeds of $20,000 or more do not come within the purview of the law, but commissions and expenses are negotiable between the broker and the buyer.

Commission maximums under the law are as follows:

- First trust deeds (less than $30,000)—5 percent of the principal if less than three years; 10 percent if three years or more
- Second trust deeds (less than $20,000)—5 percent of the principal if less than two years; 10 percent if at least two years but less than three years; 15 percent if three years or more

If the loan comes under the purview of the law, the expenses of making the loan charged to the borrower, that is, appraisal fees, escrow fees, title charges, notary fees, recording fees, and credit investigation fees, cannot exceed 5 percent of the principal amount of the loan. However, if 5 percent of the loan is less than $390, the broker may charge up to that amount. Regardless of the size of the loan, the buyer (borrower) cannot be charged more than $750 for costs and expenses. In no event may the maximum be charged if it exceeds the actual costs and expenses incurred.

Borrowers usually go to mortgage loan brokers when they are unable to obtain a loan through other sources. Mortgage loan brokers generally have relatively high loan costs; fees and interest rates are generally high. Mortgage loan brokers are required to provide a **mortgage loan disclosure** statement to borrowers. (See Figure 12.3.)

Because most loans arranged by mortgage loan brokers are first trust deeds of $30,000 or more or second trust deeds of $20,000 or more, these limitations on loan cost and commissions seldom become an issue. The lender can charge whatever the market will bear for loans above the amounts stated.

Mortgage loan brokers arrange a wide variety of loans. Because the mortgage loan broker is a middleman, the security for the loan must satisfy the *lender's criteria* for the loan. Mortgage loan brokers generally do not service the loans they arrange.

Scope of Lending Activity—Real Estate Brokers.   There are three distinct areas of lending activity that a real estate broker can engage in.

1. **Hard moneymakers and arrangers**—A *hard money loan* is a cash loan rather than an extension such as seller financing. Articles V and VII of the real estate law primarily deal with hard money loans where the mortgage broker acts as an intermediary, bringing together lenders and borrowers. This activity is commonly known as *mortgage brokerage*, and the real estate licensee is acting as a *mortgage broker*.

   The loans are not made in the broker's name. They are made in the name of the lender. Most of the hard money loans are equity loans rather than purchase loans. Lenders are often private individuals.

FIGURE 12.3

Mortgage Loan Disclosure Statement

CALIFORNIA ASSOCIATION OF REALTORS®

MORTGAGE LOAN DISCLOSURE STATEMENT (BORROWER)
(As required by the Business and Professions Code §10241 and Title 10, California Administrative Code, §2840)

_____
(Name of Broker/Arranger of Credit)

_____
(Business Address of Broker)

I. SUMMARY OF LOAN TERMS

A. PRINCIPAL AMOUNT . . . . $ _____

B. ESTIMATED DEDUCTIONS FROM PRINCIPAL AMOUNT

  1. Costs and Expenses (See Paragraph III-A). . . . . $ _____

  *2. Broker Commission/Organization Fee (See Paragraph III-B). . . . . $ _____

  3. Lender Origination Fee/Discounts (See Paragraph III-B) . . . . $ _____

  4. Additional compensation will/may be received from lender not deducted from loan proceeds.
    ☐ YES $ _____ (if known) or ☐ NO

  5. Amount to be Paid on Authorization of Borrower (See Paragraph III). . . . . $ _____

C. ESTIMATED CASH PAYABLE TO BORROWER (A less B) . . . . $ _____

II. GENERAL INFORMATION ABOUT LOAN

A. If this loan is made, Borrower will be required to pay the principal and interest at _____% per year, payable as follows: _____ _____ payments of $ _____
(number of payments)   (monthly/quarterly/annually)
and a **FINAL/BALLOON** payment of $ _____ to pay off the loan in full.

NOTICE TO BORROWER: IF YOU DO NOT HAVE THE FUNDS TO PAY THE BALLOON PAYMENT WHEN IT COMES DUE, YOU MAY HAVE TO OBTAIN A NEW LOAN AGAINST YOUR PROPERTY TO MAKE THE BALLOON PAYMENT. IN THAT CASE, YOU MAY AGAIN HAVE TO PAY COMMISSIONS, FEES AND EXPENSES FOR THE ARRANGING OF THE NEW LOAN. IN ADDITION, IF YOU ARE UNABLE TO MAKE THE MONTHLY PAYMENTS OR THE BALLOON PAYMENT, YOU MAY LOSE THE PROPERTY AND ALL OF YOUR EQUITY THROUGH FORECLOSURE. KEEP THIS IN MIND IN DECIDING UPON THE AMOUNT AND TERMS OF THIS LOAN.

B. This loan will be evidenced by a promissory note and secured by a deed of trust on property identified as (street address or legal description):
_____
_____

C. 1. Liens presently against this property (do not include loan being applied for):

Nature of Lien	Priority	Lienholder's Name	Amount Owing
_____	_____	_____	_____
_____	_____	_____	_____
_____	_____	_____	_____

  2. Liens that will remain against this property after the loan being applied for is made or arranged (include loan being applied for):

Nature of Lien	Priority	Lienholder's Name	Amount Owing
_____	_____	_____	_____
_____	_____	_____	_____
_____	_____	_____	_____

NOTICE TO BORROWER: Be sure that you state the amount of all liens as accurately as possible. If you contract with the broker to arrange this loan, but it cannot be arranged because you did not state these liens correctly, you may be liable to pay commissions, fees and expenses even though you do not obtain the loan.

REVISION DATE 10/2000   Print Date
MS-11 (PAGE 1 OF 3)

Borrower acknowledges receipt of copy of this page.
Borrower's Initials (_____)(_____)

EQUAL HOUSING OPPORTUNITY

Reviewed by
Broker or Designee _____ Date _____

MORTGAGE LOAN DISCLOSURE STATEMENT (MS-11 PAGE 1 OF 3)

FIGURE 12.3

Mortgage Loan Disclosure Statement (continued)

Property Address: _____   Date: _____

D. If Borrower pays all or part of the loan principal before it is due, a PREPAYMENT PENALTY computed as follows may be charged:

_____
_____

E. Late Charges: ☐ YES, see loan documents   or   ☐ NO
F. The purchase of credit life or credit disability insurance by a borrower is not required as a condition of making this loan.
G. Is the real property which will secure the requested loan an "owner-occupied dwelling?" ☐ YES_____ or ☐ NO_____
   (Borrower initial opposite YES or NO)
   An "owner-occupied dwelling" means a single dwelling unit in a condominium or cooperative or residential building of four or fewer separate dwelling units, one of which will be owned and occupied by a signatory to the mortgage or deed of trust for this loan within 90 days of the signing of the mortgage or deed of trust.

III. DEDUCTIONS FROM LOAN PROCEEDS
A. Estimated Maximum Costs and Expenses of Arranging the Loan to be Paid Out of Loan Principal:

	PAYABLE TO	
	Broker	Others
1. Appraisal fee	_____	_____
2. Escrow fee	_____	_____
3. Title insurance policy	_____	_____
4. Notary fees	_____	_____
5. Recording fees	_____	_____
6. Credit investigation fees	_____	_____
7. Other costs and expenses:		
_____	_____	_____
_____	_____	_____
Total Costs and Expenses	$ _____	

*B. Compensation . . . . $ _____
   1. Brokerage Commission/Origination Fee . . . . . . $ _____
   2. Lender Origination Fee/Discounts . . . . $ _____
C. Estimated Payment to be Made out of Loan Principal on Authorization of Borrower

	PAYABLE TO	
	Broker	Others
1. Fire or other hazard insurance premiums	_____	_____
2. Credit life or disability insurance premiums (see Paragraph II-F)	_____	_____
3. Beneficiary statement fees	_____	_____
4. Reconveyance and similar fees	_____	_____
5. Discharge of existing liens against property:		
_____	_____	_____
_____	_____	_____
6. Other:		
_____	_____	_____
_____	_____	_____
Total to be Paid on Authorization of Borrower	$ _____	

If this loan is secured by a first deed of trust on dwellings in a principal amount of less than $30,000 or secured by a junior lien on dwellings in a principal amount of less than $20,000, the undersigned licensee certifies that the loan will be made in compliance with Article 7 of Chapter 3 of the Real Estate Law.

*This loan **may / will / will not** (delete two) be made wholly or in part from broker-controlled funds as defined in Section 10241(j) of the Business and Professions Code.

REVISION DATE 10/2000   Print Date
MS-11 (PAGE 2 OF 3)

Borrower acknowledges receipt of copy of this page.
Borrower's Initials (_____)(_____)

EQUAL HOUSING OPPORTUNITY

Reviewed by
Broker or Designee _____ Date _____

MORTGAGE LOAN DISCLOSURE STATEMENT (MS-11 PAGE 2 OF 3)

FIGURE 12.3

Mortgage Loan Disclosure Statement (continued)

Property Address: _____ Date: _____

*NOTICE TO BORROWER: This disclosure statement may be used if the Broker is acting as an agent in arranging the loan by a third person or if the loan will be made with funds owned or controlled by the broker. If the Broker indicates in the above statement that the loan "may" be made out of Broker-controlled funds, the Broker must notify the borrower prior to the close of escrow if the funds to be received by the Borrower are in fact Broker-controlled funds.

_____   _____
Name of Broker   Broker Representative

_____   _____
License Number   License Number

_____ OR _____
Signature of Broker   Signature

The Department of Real Estate License Information phone number is _____.

NOTICE TO BORROWER:

DO NOT SIGN THIS STATEMENT UNTIL YOU HAVE READ AND UNDERSTAND ALL OF THE INFORMATION IN IT. ALL PARTS OF THE FORM MUST BE COMPLETED BEFORE YOU SIGN.

Borrower hereby acknowledges the receipt of a copy of this statement.

DATED _____   _____
                                                               (Borrower)

                                                               _____
                                                               (Borrower)

Broker Review: Signature of Real Estate Broker after review of this statement.

DATED _____   _____
                                                               Real Estate Broker or Assistant Pursuant to Section 2725

Published and Distributed by:
REAL ESTATE BUSINESS SERVICES, INC.
a subsidiary of the CALIFORNIA ASSOCIATION OF REALTORS®
525 South Virgil Avenue, Los Angeles, California 90020

Reviewed by _____
Broker or Designee _____ Date _____

EQUAL HOUSING OPPORTUNITY

The mortgage broker brings together individual lenders and borrowers.

2. **Third-party originators**—Third-party originators prepare loan applications for borrowers, which they submit to lenders. They may be agents of the borrower or the lender or dual agents of both borrower and lender. Out-of-state lenders who wish to invest directly in California mortgages frequently use third-party originators, as do pension plans and trusts. Thus, lenders who are not prepared to take loan applications in California can be direct lenders rather than having to purchase loans that were originated by others in the secondary mortgage market. They primarily deal in purchase money loans.

Mortgage bankers are regulated by either the Department of Real Estate or the Department of Corporations.

3. **Mortgage bankers**—Not all mortgage bankers are real estate brokers. Some mortgage bankers are licensed under the *California Residential Mortgage Lending Act* that is administered by the Department of Corporations. A mortgage banker must elect which license to operate under. Thus we have two state agencies, the Department of Real Estate and the Department of Corporations, regulating the same type of activity, based on which license the mortgage banker is operating under. (The broker makes loans while operating as a mortgage banker; however, the broker only *arranges loans as a third party* when operating as a mortgage broker.)

■ TYPES OF LOANS

Real estate financing has become quite confusing in light of the economic environment of the past few years. While the majority of one- to four-unit dwellings still are financed by conventional loans, the choice of a loan is no longer a foregone conclusion. Both buyers and sellers need to know what is currently available, which loan best suits their requirements, and even where to go for financing. With real estate firms allying themselves with financial institutions, even the players are changing every day.

■ CONVENTIONAL LOANS

Conventional loans have no government insurance or guarantee.

A **conventional loan** is any loan that is not backed by the government. The advantages of conventional over government-backed loans are that conventional loans involve less red tape and shorter processing time. Government loans do not have equivalent flexibility. Buyers can obtain a larger loan amount, and because there are more sources for conventional loans, borrowers have the option of choosing a variety of fixed or adjustable rate loans.

Disadvantages of conventional loans in comparison with government-backed loans can include higher down payments and prepayment penalties. Furthermore, PMI will be required if a purchaser has less than a 20 percent down payment.

How to Compare Lenders
Borrowers should compare lenders on the basis of

- LTV (the percentage of the appraised value that the lender will lend this determines down payment requirements),
- interest rate and if it can be changed,
- loan costs and fees required,
- prepayment penalties,
- length of loan (longer-term loans result in lower monthly payments), and
- initial rate, adjustment period, caps, index, and margin of adjustable rate loans.

Government Participation Loans

There are three types of government-backed loans: **FHA-insured loans, DVA-guaranteed loans,** and **Cal Vet loans.** These types of loans are compared in Figure 12.4.

Federal Housing Administration. The purposes of the Federal Housing Administration (FHA) are stated in its preamble: to "encourage improvement in housing standards and conditions, to provide a system of mutual mortgage insurance, and for other purposes."

There are two divisions under which this protection is granted: Title I and Title II. In general, the following types of loans are available:

- Title I—loans for modernization, repairs, or alterations on existing homes
- Title II—loans for purchase or construction of residential structures

Section 203(b) of Title II accounts for most loans for one- to four-unit residences.

FHA loans provide high LTVs based on appraisal.

The maximum FHA loan varies by region, but the purchaser generally must have a minimum down payment of 3 percent.

The mortgage insurance premium (MIP) must be paid at the time of loan origination. Based on the down payment, a MIP is also added to payments.

Lenders may be authorized to make the underwriting decision that a loan qualifies for FHA insurance. This is known as **direct endorsement,** and it serves to speed up the loan processing time.

Department of Veterans' Affairs (DVA)

The *Servicemen's Readjustment Act of 1944* (GI Bill) was intended to assist veterans to make the necessary readjustments to civilian life, particularly to assist them in the acquisition of homes. The DVA does not make loans, but it guarantees a portion of the loan. Figure 12.5 explains the DVA guaranteed loan.

FIGURE 12.4

Government Home Loan Programs

	FHA-Insured	DVA-Guaranteed (GI)	Cal Vet
Who is eligible?	Anyone who qualifies	U.S. veterans	California residents who have met the veteran requirements
Who makes the loans?	Approved lending institutions	Approved lending institutions	Calif. Dept. of Veterans' Affairs (mortgage brokers can originate loans)
Type of loan	Insure (up-front insurance premium may be financed)	Guaranteed (see Figure 12.5)	Land contract
Points and fees	Loan fee 1%	Negotiable loan fees plus a funding fee from 1% to 2% (in addition to origination fee)	1.25% to 3% (may be financed)
Interest rates	May be negotiated	May be negotiated	Flexible rate based on cost of bonds
What is the maximum you can pay for a home?	No limit	Loan cannot exceed appraisal	Cannot exceed the Cal Vet appraisal (certificate of reasonable value [CRV])
Maximum loan allowed	1 unit, $160,950 (for high-cost counties)	No money down, to $240,000; loan can't exceed the certificate of reasonable value [CRV]	$322,700 (same as Fannie Mae)
Term	Usually 30 years	Maximum 30 years	40 years but usually 30 years
Down payment	Approximately 3%	None required	2% to 3%
Secondary financing	Not allowed at time of sale, but can be placed later	Generally not allowed at time of sale, but can be placed later	Yes but the 1st and 2nd cannot exceed 90% of the Cal Vet appraisal
Prepayment penalty	None	None	6 months' interest on original loan amount if paid during first 5 years
Assumability	Loans prior to Dec. 15, 1989, are assumable; subsequent loans assumable with FHA approval	Loans before Mar. 1, 1988, are assumable; subsequent loans require buyer to quality	Assumable with prior Cal Vet approval

FIGURE 12.5

DVA Guaranteed Loan (GI)

Loans	Guarantee
Up to 45,000	40% of loan
$45,000 to $144,000	Minimum guarantee of $22,500 Maximum guarantee is 40% of loan up to $36,000
More than $144,000	25% of loan up to a maximum of $60,000

The largest DVA loan on which no down payment is required is $240,000. DVA loans can be used

■ to buy or build a home or business property;

■ to purchase a farm or farm equipment;

■ to alter, repair, or improve real estate;

■ to purchase a mobile home; and

■ to refinance existing mortgage loans for dwellings owned and occupied by veterans.

To qualify for a DVA-guaranteed loan, an individual must have had 181 days of active service. An appraiser approved by the DVA checks the property.

The amount of the loan is not regulated. However, the loan cannot exceed the appraisal known as the **certificate of reasonable value** (CRV). (The loan amount is not regulated, but the guarantee is.)

Cal Vet Loans.   Under the Cal Vet loan program (the California Farm and Home Purchase Program), California veterans can acquire suitable farm or a single-family residence at a low financing cost. The State of California actually takes title to the property and sells it to the veteran under a land contract. Following are some features of the Cal Vet loan:

> With a *Cal Vet loan*, the veteran is buying under a land contract.

■ Cal Vet loans can now be arranged through lenders approved to make Cal Vet loans.

■ Cal Vet loans are now processed with DVA guidelines. The loans are now available to peacetime as well as wartime veterans and active duty military. The maximum loan amount is the same as for Fannie Mae (currently $322,700).

■ Cal Vet loans require 2 percent to 3 percent down payments and currently are pegged at 6.95 percent interest for a home loan (1 percent higher for mobile homes in rental parks).

■ Cal Vet loans require that the veteran carry insurance for flood, earthquake, fire, life, and disability. (Earthquake coverage is provided by the state at a relatively low cost.)

■ Cal Vet loans have changeable rates but have a cap of 7.5 percent.

■ Mortgage brokers who originate and process Cal Vet loans receive a $350 processing fee plus a 1 percent origination fee.

■ The state raises the funds for Cal Vet loans by issuing tax-exempt bonds.

For more information on Cal Vet loans, call 1 (800) 952-5626 or check the Web site at *www.cdva.ca.gov/calvet.*

Other Types of Mortgages and Trust Deeds

Open-End Trust Deed.   An **open-end trust deed** allows the borrower to receive additional loan money up to an agreed amount, using the same trust deed or mortgage as security.

Blanket Trust Deed.   With a **blanket trust deed** the borrower uses more than one parcel of property as security. This type of document should contain a **release clause** that allows the reconveyance of part of the property on repayment of a portion of the loan.

Wraparound Trust Deed.   A **wraparound trust deed** also is called an *all-inclusive trust deed.* There are times when it is almost impossible for borrowers to refinance an existing loan on investment real estate to raise additional capital. With a wraparound mortgage the existing loan is not disturbed. The seller continues the payments on the existing mortgage or trust deed while giving the borrower a new, increased loan, usually at a higher interest rate. The new loan is for the amount due on the existing loan plus the amount of the seller's equity being financed.

Assume a property is being sold for $200,000 with $20,000 down. Also assume that there is a $90,000 trust deed against the property at 7 percent interest. If the buyer was willing to pay 9 percent interest, the seller could take advantage of this interest difference with a wraparound loan.

$90,000 loan	7%	
		$180,000 wraparound loan at 9%
$90,000 seller's equity	9%	

In the above case the seller receives 9 percent on his or her equity plus a 2 percent differential on the 7 percent being paid on the existing loan. This really gives the seller 11 percent interest on his or her equity. In addition, because the seller continues to make the payments on the $90,000 loan, the seller knows that the payments are being made. If the seller had allowed the buyer to assume the existing loan, then the buyer, not the seller, would have taken advantage of the low financing.

To use a wraparound loan, the underlying loan must not have a **due-on-sale clause.** (A due-on-sale clause accelerates loan payments making the entire loan amount due upon a sale. These clauses are enforceable by lenders. While a number of ways have been devised to get around the clauses, the methods basically are based on deception. Advocating use of such methods could subject you to liability, disciplinary action, as well as result in a buyer losing a home because of inability to obtain a new loan.)

Gap Loan.   These loans are usually short-term loans such as loans between construction loans and the **take-out loan** (permanent financing) or by buyers who have found a new home but have not yet sold their prior residence. They are also referred to as *swing loans* or *bridge loans*. They generally bear a relatively high rate of interest.

Fixed-Rate Loans.   Lenders will make fixed-rate long-term amortized loans when they must do so, but they actually prefer adjustable-rate or shorter-term loans. The reason is that they were hurt in the past by long-term **fixed-rate loans.**

In the late 1970s and early 1980s, many lenders, particularly S&Ls, had a great deal of their capital invested in long-term fixed-rate loans. During this period the United States had great inflation, and interest rates increased dramatically. Lenders had to pay higher interest rates on accounts to attract funds. In many cases, the average yield from their portfolios of loans was less than the average rate they were paying depositors for funds. While relatively short-lived, lenders had been burned and still worry that history could repeat itself.

To encourage borrowers to use other types of loans, lenders offer lower loan costs than for fixed-rate loans and even lower interest rates.

15-Year versus 30-Year Fixed-Rate Loans.   If a buyer is able to pay the additional monthly payment on a 15-year loan, significant savings are possible compared with a 30-year loan.

As an example, at 7½ percent interest the monthly payment on a $100,000 loan for 15 years comes to $927.02. For a 30-year loan having the same rate of interest, the monthly payment is $699.22. For the 30-year loan, total payments equal

$$12 \text{ (months)} \times 30 \text{ (years)} \times \$699.22 = \$251,719.20$$

or interest of $151,719.20. For a 15-year loan the total payments are

$$12 \text{ (months)} \times 15 \text{ (years)} \times \$927.02 = \$166,863.60$$

or interest payments of $66,863.60. The interest paid on the 30-year loan is more than twice the interest of the 15-year loan, and the payments are only $227.80 higher than the 30-year loan payments.

The savings are likely to be significantly greater than those shown in the above example because 15-year loans usually have an interest rate from .375 percent to .75 percent lower than a similar 30-year loan. Lower interest rates are used because shorter-term loans are considered by lenders to present less risk.

Renegotiable-Rate Mortgages.   **Renegotiable-rate mortgages,** also known as *rollover loans*, usually have payments based on a 30-year amortization. However, they are only partially amortized. Generally they are due in full in five or seven years. The lender will rewrite the loan at this time at the current interest rate, or the borrower can refinance with another lender.

Because the lender is not locked into the interest rate for a long period, lenders offer these loans for a lower interest rate than the 30-year rate. Frequently, the rate is around 1 percent less than fixed-rate loans. Lenders also might offer lower loan origination fees and costs.

Combination Fixed-Adjustable-Rate Loans.   Lenders will offer **combination fixed-adjustable-rate loans** such as a 5–30 where the first 5 years are at a fixed rate and the balance of the loan (25 years) is at an adjustable rate. In order to sell borrowers on the loan, the fixed-rate portion of the loan has an interest rate less than for a 30-year fixed-rate loan. This allows borrowers to qualify for the loan that might not qualify for a 30-year fixed-rate loan.

Reverse Mortgage (Reverse Annuity Mortgage).   This unusual loan is not for home purchases. A **reverse mortgage** is a loan whereby the lender annuitizes the value of the borrowers' home and makes monthly payments to the borrowers based on the value of the property and the age of the borrowers. The loan is not repaid until the borrowers die or the property is sold.

A normal loan charges simple interest, that is, the interest for the previous month is paid with each payment and is charged on the principal balance only. A reverse mortgage, however, has compound interest (interest is charged on interest). Each month the interest is greater than the previous month because more principal has been advanced; therefore, the principal *balance* has increased, and accrued interest also has been added to the principal and has increased the balance due.

Reverse mortgages have higher interest rates and higher loan fees than most other loans. Several lenders have agreed to make settlements because of alleged unconscionable loan costs and fees for their reverse mortgages.

Piggyback Loan.   This is a loan shared by two lenders, where one takes the bottom portion (greater security) and the second lender takes the greater risk with the top portion. It is really a first and second trust deed in one instrument.

Adjustable-Rate Mortgage (ARM).   In contrast to a fixed-rate loan, the interest rate in an **adjustable-rate mortgage** (ARM) changes periodically, usually in relation to an index, with payments going up or down accordingly. Lenders usually charge lower initial interest rates for ARMs than for fixed-rate loans, which makes the ARM easier on the borrower's pocketbook than a fixed-rate loan for the same amount and also makes it easier for the borrower to qualify for the loan. In addition, it could mean that the borrower could qualify for a larger loan, because lenders sometimes qualify buyers on the basis of current income and the first year's payment. This means the buyer (borrower) could maintain a better lifestyle with an ARM. Moreover, an ARM might be less expensive over a long period than a fixed-rate loan. For example, interest rates may remain steady or drop.

Another advantage of an ARM is that they generally do not have prepayment penalties. Therefore, if the borrower expects to be reselling within a relatively short period, the absence of this penalty could give the ARM a significant advantage over loans requiring prepayment penalties.

To induce borrowers to choose an ARM, lenders usually have lower loan origination costs for ARMs than for fixed rate loans.

Against these advantages the buyer must weigh the risk that an increase in interest rates will lead to higher monthly payments in the future. The trade-off with an ARM is that the borrower obtains a lower rate in exchange for assuming more risk. The borrower considering an ARM should consider a worst-case scenario with interest increasing to the set limit to fully understand the degree of risk involved.

Many types of ARMs (around 150 varieties at last count) are being offered by financial institutions today. It is important for both the borrower and his or her agent to learn to ask questions so that they may compare loans adequately. Here are four basic questions the buyer needs to consider:

1. Is my income likely to rise enough to cover higher mortgage payments if interest rates go up, or can I afford the higher payment?

2. Will I be taking on other sizable debts, such as a loan for a car or school tuition, in the near future?

3. How long do I plan to own this home? If I plan to sell soon, rising interest rates may not pose the problem they will if I plan to own the home for a long time.

4. Can my payments increase even if interest rates in general do not increase?

If the buyer can answer these questions satisfactorily, an ARM might be the loan of choice. However, the borrower still has to decide which ARM to take out, which entails obtaining the answers to many more questions.

The real estate agent needs to understand and be able to explain certain terms that do not apply to fixed-rate loans when discussing an ARM with a borrower. These include *adjustment period, index, margin, interest rate cap, overall cap, payment cap, negative amortization,* and *conversion clause*. The remainder of this section defines these terms and explains the calculations that will enable a borrower to choose the proper ARM for his or her circumstances.

Adjustment Period. The **adjustment period** of an ARM is the period of time between one interest rate and monthly payment change and the next. (Some ARMs have two adjustments: one for rate, the other for payment.) This period is different for each ARM; it may occur once a month, every six months, once a year, or every three years. A loan with an adjustment period of one year is called a *one-year* ARM, and the interest rate can change once each year. Lenders often have a longer adjustment period for the first adjustment. Different lenders use different adjustment periods. Because a single lender might offer four different types of ARMs, each with a different adjustment period, it is important for the borrower to read the loan documents and understand the adjustment period before the loan documents are cut or signed.

Index and Margin.   Most lenders tie ARM interest rate changes to changes of an **index** rate. The only requirements a lender must meet in selecting an interest index are

- the index control cannot be the lender and
- the index must be readily available to and verifiable by the public.

These indexes usually go up and down with the general movement of interest rates. If the index moves up, so does the interest rate on the loan, meaning the borrower will probably have to make higher monthly payments. If, on the other hand, the index rate goes down, interest rate and monthly payments may go down.

Lenders base ARM rates on a variety of indexes; in fact the index can be almost any interest rate the lender selects. Also, different lenders may offer a variety of ARMs, and each may have a different index and margin. Among the most common indexes are six-month, three-year, or five-year Treasury securities (T-bills); national or regional cost of funds to savings associations (11th district cost of funds of the Federal Home Loan Bank Board [FHLBB]); and the London Inter-Bank Offering Rate (LIBOR). Borrowers and their agents should ask what index will be used and how often it changes. Also, find out how the index has behaved in the past and where it is published so the borrower can trace it in the future.

> The index rate plus the margin equals the interest rate.

To determine the interest rate on an ARM, lenders add to the index rate a few percentage points (two to three), called the **margin** (also *differential* or *spread*).

$$\text{ARM Rate} = \text{Index rate} + \text{Margin}$$

The amount of the margin can differ from one lender to another, but it is always constant over the life of the loan. Loans that have lower loan-origination costs tend to have higher margins. Upward adjustments of the ARM interest rate are made at the lender's option, but downward adjustments are mandatory. Actual adjustments to the borrowers' mortgage interest rate can occur only on a predetermined time schedule (the adjustment period, as described above). On each loan the borrowers' terms, including initial rate, caps, index, margin, interest rate change frequency, and payment change frequency, are stated in the note that accompanies the deed of trust. Terms will vary from lender to lender.

In comparing ARMs, look at both the index and the margin for each plan. Some indexes have higher average values, but they are usually used with lower margins. Be sure to discuss the margin with the lender.

In calculating an ARM payment, the first period is calculated in exactly the same way as a fixed-rate loan payment. After the first-period adjustment, it is as if the borrower were starting a new loan: Calculations must be made to figure the loan balance and the number of payments left, and the new interest rate must be taken into account. Of course, because no one can anticipate accurately whether interest rates will increase or decrease, in analyzing various ARMs a borrower is considering, the agent can accurately calculate the loan payment for only the first period.

ARM Discounts. Some lenders offer initial ARM rates that are lower than the sum of the index and the margin. Such rates, called *discounted rates*, *introductory rates*, *tickler rates*, or *teaser rates*, are usually combined with loan fees (points) and with higher interest rates after the discount expires. Many lenders currently offer introductory rates that are significantly below market interest rates. The discount rates may expire after the first adjustment period (for example, after one month, six months, or one year). At the end of the introductory discount rate period, the ARM interest rate automatically increases to the contract interest rate (index plus margin). This can mean a substantial increase in the borrower's interest rate and monthly payment. If the index rate has moved upward, the interest rate and payment adjustment can be even higher. Even if the index rate has decreased, the borrower's interest rate and monthly payment will likely be adjusted *upward* at the end of the introductory period.

Many lenders use the first year's payment as the basis for qualifying a borrower for a loan. So even if a lender approves the loan, based on the low introductory rate, it is the borrower's responsibility to determine whether he or she will be able to afford payments in later years, when the discount expires and the rate is adjusted. With a discounted ARM any savings made during the discounted period may be offset during the life of the loan or be included in the price of the home. In fact, this kind of loan subjects the borrower to greater risk, including that of **payment shock,** which may occur when the mortgage payment rises at the first adjustment.

Whenever the lender's advertised qualifying interest rate is lower than the lender's current ARM index rate plus margin, a below-market rate is being offered. Assume the current index rate is 5 percent and the margin 2 percent. That makes the ARM rate 7 percent. If the advertised qualifying introductory rate is 5 percent, the introductory rate is 2 percent below the market rate, a discounted rate. Any qualifying rate below 7 percent in this case is called an *introductory rate* or a *below-market rate*.

Many lenders describe the introductory rate in their documentation as follows: "There is no rate change in the first six months. Thereafter, the interest rate is established by adding a rate differential (margin) to the index provided in the note."

The **annual percentage rate** (APR) gives a more accurate picture of the cost of a loan and must be disclosed by law. The APR represents a rate based on a buyer's net loan proceeds, the loan amount less the cost of credit. This is outlined in the

RESPA letter sent within three days of application for a loan. When calculating the APR, lenders who offer below-market rates must account for the higher index rate that will be charged in the future.

A borrower who chooses an ARM impulsively because of a low initial rate could end up in difficult straits. Agents can help borrowers protect themselves from large increases by looking at a mortgage with certain features that are explained in the next sections. Remember that all loans are different and that many different types of ARMs exist. Agents must help borrowers shop around until they find the loan that will meet their needs with minimal risk.

> Caps can limit payment increases and loan interest.

Caps on an ARM.   Most ARMs have caps that protect borrowers from increases in interest rates or monthly payments beyond an amount specified in the note. If loans have no interest rate or payment caps, borrowers might be exposed to unlimited upward adjustments in monthly payments, should interest rates rise. Some lenders also allow borrowers to convert an ARM to a fixed-rate loan.

Caps vary from lender to lender. The borrower needs to check with the lender to determine the cap rates in the loan under consideration. Two types of interest rate caps are used.

1. A *periodic cap* limits the interest rate increase or decrease from one adjustment period to the next. These caps are usually 1 percentage point to 2 percentage points or sometimes 7.5 percent of the previous period's payment amount.

2. A *lifetime cap* or *overall cap* limits the interest rate increase over the life of the loan. Assume the introductory rate is 6 percent, below the market rate, and at the first adjustment the rate becomes 8 percent. The overall cap will be attached to the 8 percent; thus, a 5 percent cap could mean an interest rate as high as 13 percent.

An ARM usually has both a periodic and an overall interest rate cap. A drop in the index does not always lead to an immediate drop in monthly payments. In fact, with some ARMs that have interest rate caps, the monthly payment may increase, even though the index rate has stayed the same or declined. This may happen after an interest rate cap has been holding the interest rate below the sum of the index plus margin. When the next adjustment period comes along and the interest rate stays the same or declines, previous obligations are in arrears and must be paid; thus, the monthly payment will increase.

The rate on a loan can go up at any scheduled adjustment when the index plus margin is higher than the rate before the adjustment. As stated earlier, an ARM usually has an overall interest rate cap. Some ARMs have a stated cap, such as 15 percent; others specify a percentage *over* the initial rate, such as an overall interest rate cap of 5 percent. Again, caps vary from lender to lender and sometimes from loan to loan offered by the same lender. It is important for the borrower to know what caps are available and what the borrower is obtaining with a loan.

As previously stated, some ARMs include a payment cap that limits the monthly payment increase at the time of each adjustment, usually to a percentage of the previous payment. In other words, if the payment cap is 7.5 percent, a payment of $1,000 could not increase or decrease by more than $75 in the next adjustment period.

Because payment caps limit only the amount of payment increases and not interest rate increases, payments sometimes do not cover all of the interest due on a loan. Sometimes called negative amortization, this means the mortgage balance is increasing. The interest shortage in the payment is automatically added to the loan, and interest may be charged on that amount. The borrower therefore might owe the lender more later in the loan term than at the start. However, an increase in the value of the home might make up for the increase in the amount owed because of *negative amortization*. The agent should be sure the borrower understands the provisions for this "deferred interest" in any ARM that contains a payment cap. Some loans allow negative amortization but have a cap on the rate of negative amortization possible. Most loans prohibit negative amortization. In these cases, if a payment is not sufficient to pay the interest, the unpaid interest is forgiven and not added to the loan amount.

Convertible ARMs. A borrower whose financial circumstances may change at some time during the term of the loan may decide that he or she does not want to risk any further changes in the interest rate and payment amount; or interest rates may drop, and the borrower might want to lock in the lower rate. In such cases a *conversion clause* becomes important. A **convertible ARM** clause is one that allows the borrower to convert the ARM to a fixed-rate loan at designated times. When the borrower converts, the new rate is generally set at the current market rate for fixed-rate loans plus at least .375 of 1 percent as a servicing premium.

Assumable ARMs. Although the majority of ARMs are assumable, lenders normally place conditions on the assumption of the loan. The lender may require that the new borrower supply credit information, complete a credit application, and meet the customary credit standards applied by the lender. In some cases, the lender may charge points or other fees when a loan is assumed.

Some lenders allow only one assumption. Other lenders allow assumption but adjust the overall cap or the margin to the rate in effect at the time of assumption. Some lenders allow assumptions with the original lifetime cap already in effect. Because conditions of assumption vary greatly among lenders, the documentation should be checked for this information.

Figure 12.6 contains a list of questions that a borrower should ask and the agent or lender should be able to answer when the borrower is looking for an ARM.

FIGURE 12.6

ARM Checklist

❏ What is the initial (or qualifying) interest rate on the ARM?

❏ How long is this initial rate in effect? When is the first rate and/or payment adjustment?

❏ To what index is the ARM's interest rate tied?

❏ What is the current level of the index?

❏ What margin above the index is used to calculate the actual ARM rate?

❏ How can the index and margin be used to calculate the mortgage rate initially and at the first adjustment?

❏ What will happen to the interest rate at the first adjustment, assuming the index rate stays the same?

❏ What is the annual percentage rate (APR) of the loan? How does this compare with the APR on other ARMs and that on a fixed-rate loan?

❏ How often is the interest rate on the mortgage adjusted? How often does the monthly payment change?

❏ Does the ARM have a periodic interest rate cap? If so, what is the limit on the increase in the ARM rate at each adjustment? If the index rate increases more than this limit, can the unused change in the index be carried over to the next adjustment period? Does the periodic interest rate cap apply to the first adjustment? Does the periodic rate cap apply to the rate decreases as well as to any increases?

❏ If negative amortization is possible for this ARM, how often is the loan recast to pay off the increase in principal balance? When the loan is recast, is there any limit on how much the payment can increase?

❏ Does the ARM have an overall cap rate? If so, what are the maximum and minimum rates?

❏ Does the ARM have a payment cap? If so, what is the maximum that the monthly payment can increase at each adjustment? Does the payment cap apply to the first payment adjustment?

❏ Does negative amortization result if the interest rate increase requires a higher payment than the payment cap allows? Does the payment cap apply to any increases in payments that result from a recasting of the loan due to negative amortization?

❏ Can the borrower convert this ARM to a fixed-rate loan at any time? Does this ARM have an open-end credit feature? What other features does this ARM have?

❏ Is this ARM assumable? Is this assumption feature limited to one time only? What are the qualification features? Will the original caps still be in effect? If not, what are the new caps?

❏ Does the ARM have a loan-to-value ratio greater than 80 percent? If so, is private mortgage insurance required on the loan?

Loan Costs

In comparing loans, you must also compare loan costs. Lenders break down loan costs so that consumers will understand exactly what they are paying for. No matter what the cost or fee is called the bottom line is the total of all loan costs. For many loans, these costs can be added to the amount of the loan.

Calculating Loan Costs

- an initial application fee;
- a flat fee in addition to loan points;
- loan points;
- loan escrow costs (if not a purchase-money loan);
- title insurance (if not a purchase-money loan);
- document fees;
- private mortgage insurance; and
- a number of charges developed by different lenders, such as *processing fees,* which are generally fees for miscellaneous lender services. (These fees are often referred to as "garbage fees.")

■ CHOOSING AMONG LOAN CATEGORIES

Lenders offer a number of different basic loan classifications, with different lenders offering different variations. Because of differing loan provisions, interest rates, and loan costs, it becomes difficult for borrowers to decide which loan type and lender best meet their particular needs.

Borrowers will find that they must shop for loans the same way they shop for any other large purchase. There are significant variations in costs among lenders. In some cases loan costs can be negotiated.

Borrowers who believe they will remain in a property for many years likely will want an overall lower interest rate and will be willing to pay higher loan-origination costs to obtain that rate.

Borrowers who expect to remain in a property for only a few years likely will want a loan that can be prepaid without a penalty and that has low loan-origination costs. Such borrowers likely will be willing to pay a higher interest rate to obtain the lower origination costs. Generally, lower loan-origination fees mean a higher interest rate.

Borrowers who believe interest rates are about as low as they will go are likely to want a long-term fixed-rate mortgage. Borrowers who believe interest rates are likely to drop probably will want a loan without a prepayment penalty, a short-term loan that can be rewritten at a future interest rate, or an adjustable-rate loan that can be converted to a fixed-rate loan.

Borrowers who have very low down payments would be interested in loans having a high LTV, such as FHA-insured loans, DVA-guaranteed loans, and loans with PMI. And if borrowers have a low income for loan qualifying purposes, they likely will want an ARM with low initial payments.

For many buyers the deciding factor will be the additional improvement in lifestyle afforded by using an ARM. Usually an ARM allows borrowers to buy more home for their money than would be possible with a fixed-rate loan. Assume fixed-rate loans are at 8 percent, and ARMs have a lower interest rate. If the agent knows how much the buyer can afford for a monthly payment, the agent can calculate the loan amount for which the borrower can qualify. The easiest way to do this is simply to use an amortization table and check the qualifying rate to determine how large a loan that payment will support.

The real estate agent needs to understand the lending business and be willing to communicate with the lender when the agent does not know why a certain interest rate, point, loan fee, or PMI is required or does not understand other conditions of the loan.

One of the fundamental misunderstandings about financing arises because real estate buyers and sellers do not realize that money is a commodity. Money is like a loaf of bread, a car, a home, or any other commodity, and it is bought and sold. When it is bought and sold, the lender expects to make a profit on the sale. Some like to compare loaning money to renting. The payment of interest is the cost of renting the money, and points are like first and last months' rent or the security deposit. Every lender needs to make a profit on the rental of money to stay in business.

The lender is in business to make a profit. If the lender reduces one cost to a borrower in one area, the lender generally will raise it in another area to compensate for the loss. As an example, a lender offering a lower interest rate may charge higher loan costs, as well as a larger prepayment penalty, than a lender offering the higher interest rate. Help your borrower choose the loan that offers the combination of features that best meets that borrower's specific needs.

Computerized Loan Origination

Computerized loan origination (CLO) is now possible on the Internet. Various Web sites provide interest rates, points, and APRs for various types of loans. Agents can print out and/or complete a loan application on the Internet and in many cases have loan approval, subject to verifications, before the client leaves your office.

There are also several large multilender shopping sites for loans that allow a borrower to view loan offerings from a great many lenders on a competitive basis. These sites are updated daily.

A borrower can evaluate loan types, points, costs, and rates to make an informed decision and then be qualified by the selected lender as well as complete the loan application, all on the Internet. The result of competition is often lower loan costs for the borrower. Because of this advantage, many buyer's agents use these shopping sites.

The Web sites also avoid the possibility that the borrower is being charged an overage. An *overage* is a charge, typically points, by a mortgage banker that exceeds what a lender would charge.

Currently, the four major shopping Web sites are

1. *www.eloan.com*
2. *www.homeadvisor.com*
3. *www.quickenmortgage.com*
4. *www.homeshark.com*

The authors suggest that you gain familiarity with these Web sites as well as with the process of qualification and loan application. You should also be familiar with the other sites, including local market lenders that are used by your office.

When a fee is charged to a borrower for CLO, a disclosure must be provided to the borrower in a format specified by RESPA. The disclosure must inform the borrower that the fee can be avoided by approaching lenders directly.

■ THE FINANCING PROCESS

The basic steps for obtaining real estate financing are much the same with any type of lender. Figure 12.7 illustrates the following five-step financing process:

1. Qualifying the borrower
2. Qualifying the property
3. Approving and processing the loan
4. Closing the loan
5. Servicing the loan

Qualifying the Borrower

In understanding lender requirements for **qualifying borrowers,** you should realize that lender requirements often are dictated by the secondary mortgage market. Unless a lender expects to hold on to a loan for the life of the loan, the lender wants the loan to meet the requirements of a holder in the secondary market, such as Fannie Mae (FNMA).

Chapter 9 introduced you to lender qualifying requirements in prequalifying prospective purchasers. Lenders first ask prospective borrowers to complete an application form. Most applications are similar to the one in Figure 12.8, which asks for the borrower's employment record, credit references, and a financial statement of assets and liabilities. To verify the accuracy of the information, the loan officer checks with past employers, requests verification of deposits from the bank(s), and contacts references. The loan officer also may obtain a Dun & Bradstreet report (in case of commercial loans) and a credit report by an outside agency, so there is no question of the borrower's ability to repay the loan.

FIGURE 12.7

The Financing Process

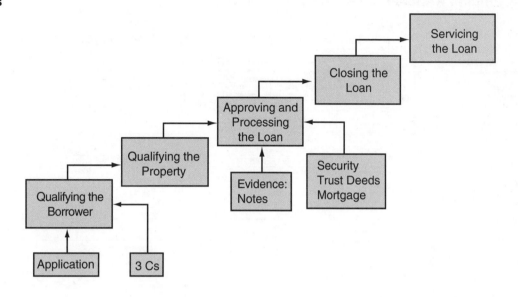

In addition, most lenders use the "three Cs"—*character, capacity,* and *collateral*—as a screening device to determine if the borrower meets the qualifications set by the lender.

Character.   With regard to prospective borrowers' *character,* lenders consider their attitude toward financial obligations as evidenced by their track record of borrowing and repaying loans evidenced by credit reports. Lenders also try to ascertain whether borrowers are honest in their dealings.

The desire to pay is very difficult to measure. There are methods used by a lender to determine the borrower's desire to make timely payments such as FICO Score. Fair Issac Corporation developed this scoring system used by most lenders. Scores of 660 or more are very desirable although scores of 620 to 660 are acceptable. Scores below 620 generally mean institutional lenders will not make the loan. The applicants' credit report will show if the borrowers have any late payments. If the borrower has a number of late payments, this usually means the borrower does not have a desire or cannot afford to make timely payments.

Capacity.   In considering borrowers' *capacity,* lenders want to know their ability to repay the debt. Capacity is strengthened by an occupation that ensures a steady income. The level of present debts and obligations also is a factor; too much debt may prevent a borrower from discharging a new obligation.

FIGURE 12.8

Uniform Residential Loan Application Form

Uniform Residential Loan Application

This application is designed to be completed by the applicant(s) with the lender's assistance. Applicants should complete this form as "Borrower" or "Co-Borrower", as applicable. Co-Borrower information must also be provided (and the appropriate box checked) when ☐ the income or assets of a person other than the "Borrower" (including the Borrower's spouse) will be used as a basis for loan qualification or ☐ the income or assets of the Borrower's spouse will not be used as a basis for loan qualification, but his or her liabilities must be considered because the Borrower resides in a community property state, the security property is located in a community property state, or the Borrower is relying on other property located in a community property state as a basis for repayment of the loan.

I. TYPE OF MORTGAGE AND TERMS OF LOAN

Mortgage Applied for:	☐ VA ☐ Conventional ☐ Other: ☐ FHA ☐ FmHA		Agency Case Number	Lender Case Number
Amount $	Interest Rate %	No. of Months	Amortization Type: ☐ Fixed Rate ☐ GPM	☐ Other (explain): ☐ ARM (type):

II. PROPERTY INFORMATION AND PURPOSE OF LOAN

Subject Property Address (street, city, state & zip code)	County	No. of Units
Legal Description of Subject Property (attach description if necessary)		Year Built

Purpose of Loan ☐ Purchase ☐ Construction ☐ Other (explain): ☐ Refinance ☐ Construction-Permanent	Property will be: ☐ Primary Residence ☐ Secondary Residence ☐ Investment

Complete this line if construction or construction-permanent loan.

Year Lot Acquired	Original Cost $	Amount Existing Liens $	(a) Present Value of Lot $	(b) Cost of Improvements $	Total (a+b) $

Complete this line if this is a refinance loan.

Year Acquired	Original Cost $	Amount Existing Liens $	Purpose of Refinance	Describe Improvements ☐ made ☐ to be made
				Cost: $

Title will be held in what Name(s)	Manner in which Title will be held	Estate will be held in: ☐ Fee Simple ☐ Leasehold (show expiration date)

Source of Down Payment, Settlement Charges and/or Subordinate Financing (explain)

III. BORROWER INFORMATION

Borrower	Co-Borrower
Borrower's Name (include Jr. or Sr. if applicable)	Co-Borrower's Name (include Jr. or Sr. if applicable)
Social Security Number / Home Phone (incl. area code) / Age / Yrs. School	Social Security Number / Home Phone (incl. area code) / Age / Yrs. School
☐ Married ☐ Unmarried (include single, divorced, widowed) ☐ Separated / Dependents (not listed by Co-Borrower) no. / ages	☐ Married ☐ Unmarried (include single, divorced, widowed) ☐ Separated / Dependents (not listed by Borrower) no. / ages
Present Address (street, city, state, zip code) ☐ Own ☐ Rent ___ No. Yrs.	Present Address (street, city, state, zip code) ☐ Own ☐ Rent ___ No. Yrs.

If residing at present address for less than two years, complete the following:

Former Address (street, city, state, zip code) ☐ Own ☐ Rent ___ No. Yrs.	Former Address (street, city, state, zip code) ☐ Own ☐ Rent ___ No. Yrs.
Former Address (street, city, state, zip code) ☐ Own ☐ Rent ___ No. Yrs.	Former Address (street, city, state, zip code) ☐ Own ☐ Rent ___ No. Yrs.

IV. EMPLOYMENT INFORMATION

Borrower	Co-Borrower
Name & Address of Employer ☐ Self Employed / Yrs. on this job / Yrs. employed in this line of work/profession	Name & Address of Employer ☐ Self Employed / Yrs. on this job / Yrs. employed in this line of work/profession
Position/Title/Type of Business / Business Phone (incl. area code)	Position/Title/Type of Business / Business Phone (incl. area code)

If employed in current position for less than two years or if currently employed in more than one position, complete the following:

Name & Address of Employer ☐ Self Employed / Dates (from - to) / Monthly Income $	Name & Address of Employer ☐ Self Employed / Dates (from - to) / Monthly Income $
Position/Title/Type of Business / Business Phone (incl. area code)	Position/Title/Type of Business / Business Phone (incl. area code)
Name & Address of Employer ☐ Self Employed / Dates (from - to) / Monthly Income $	Name & Address of Employer ☐ Self Employed / Dates (from - to) / Monthly Income $
Position/Title/Type of Business / Business Phone (incl. area code)	Position/Title/Type of Business / Business Phone (incl. area code)

Freddie Mac Form 65/Rev. 10/92   Page 1 of 4   Fannie Mae Form 1003/Rev. 10/92

Borrower's Initials   Co-Borrower's Initials

FIGURE 12.8

Uniform Residential Loan Application Form (continued)

V.   MONTHLY INCOME AND COMBINED HOUSING EXPENSE INFORMATION

Gross Monthly Income	Borrower	Co-Borrower	Total	Combined Monthly Housing Expense	Present	Proposed
Base Empl. Income*	$	$	$	Rent	$	
Overtime				First Mortgage (P&I)		$
Bonuses				Other Financing (P&I)		
Commissions				Hazard Insurance		
Dividends/Interest				Real Estate Taxes		
Net Rental Income				Mortgage Insurance		
Other (before completing, see the notice in 'describe other income' below)				Homeowner Assn. Dues		
				Other:		
Total	$	$	$	**Total**	$	$

* Self Employed Borrower(s) may be required to provide additional documentation such as tax returns and financial statements.

B/C	Describe Other Income Notice: Alimony, child support, or separate maintenance income need not be revealed if the Borrower (B) or Co-borrower (C) does not choose to have it considered for repaying this loan.	Monthly Amount
		$

VI.   ASSETS AND LIABILITIES

This Statement and any applicable supporting schedules may be completed jointly by both married and unmarried Co-Borrowers if their assets and liabilities are sufficiently joined so that the Statement can be meaningfully and fairly presented on a combined basis; otherwise separate Statements and Schedules are required. If the Co-Borrower section was completed about a spouse, this Statement and supporting schedules must be completed about that spouse also.   Completed [ ] Jointly [ ] Not Jointly

ASSETS Description	Cash or Market Value	Liabilities and Pledged Assets. List the creditor's name, address and account number for all outstanding debts, including automobile loans, revolving charge accounts, real estate loans, alimony, child support, stock pledges, etc. Use continuation sheet, if necessary. Indicate by (*) those liabilities which will be satisfied upon sale of real estate owned or upon refinancing of the subject property.	Monthly Payt. & Mos. Left to Pay	Unpaid Balance
Cash deposit toward purchase held by:	$	**LIABILITIES**		
		Name and address of Company	$ Payt./Mos.	$
List checking and saving accounts below				
Name and address of Bank, S&L, or Credit Union				
		Acct. no.		
		Name and address of Company	$ Payt./Mos.	$
Acct. no.	$			
Name and address of Bank, S&L, or Credit Union				
		Acct. no.		
		Name and address of Company	$ Payt./Mos.	$
Acct. no.	$			
Name and address of Bank, S&L, or Credit Union				
		Acct. no.		
		Name and address of Company	$ Payt./Mos.	$
Acct. no.	$			
Name and address of Bank, S&L, or Credit Union				
		Acct. no.		
		Name and address of Company	$ Payt./Mos.	$
Acct. no.	$			
Stock & Bonds (Company name/number & description)	$			
		Acct. no.		
		Name and address of Company	$ Payt./Mos.	$
Life insurance net cash value	$			
Face amount: $				
Subtotal Liquid Assets	$			
Real estate owned (enter market value from schedule of real estate owned)	$	Acct. no.		
Vested interest in retirement fund	$	Name and address of Company	$ Payt./Mos.	$
Net worth of business(es) owned (attach financial statement)	$			
Automobiles owned (make and year)	$			
		Acct. no.		
		Alimony/Child Support/Separate Maintenance Payments Owed to:	$	
Other Assets (itemize)	$	Job Related Expense (child care, union dues, etc.)	$	
		Total Monthly Payments	$	
Total Assets a.	$	**Net Worth (a minus b)** $	**Total Liabilities b.**	$

FIGURE 12.8

Uniform Residential Loan Application Form (continued)

VI. ASSETS AND LIABILITIES (cont.)

Schedule of Real Estate Owned (If additional properties are owned, use continuation sheet.)

Property Address (enter S if sold, PS if pending sale or R if rental being held for income)	Type of Property	Present Market Value	Amount of Mortgages & Liens	Gross Rental Income	Mortgage Payments	Insurance, Maintenance, Taxes & Misc.	Net Rental Income
		$	$	$	$	$	$
Totals		$	$	$	$	$	$

List any additional names under which credit has previously been received and indicate appropriate creditor name(s) and account number(s):

Alternate Name	Creditor Name	Account Number

VII. DETAILS OF TRANSACTION

a. Purchase price	$
b. Alterations, improvements, repairs	
c. Land (if acquired separately)	
d. Refinance (incl. debts to be paid off)	
e. Estimated prepaid items	
f. Estimated closing costs	
g. PMI, MIP, Funding Fee	
h. Discount (if Borrower will pay)	
i. Total costs (add items a through h)	
j. Subordinate financing	
k. Borrower's closing costs paid by Seller	
l. Other Credits (explain)	
m. Loan amount (exclude PMI, MIP, Funding Fee financed)	
n. PMI, MIP, Funding Fee financed	
o. Loan amount (add m & n)	
p. Cash Borrower (subtract j, k, l & o from i)	

VIII. DECLARATIONS

If you answer "yes" to any questions a through i, please use continuation sheet for explanation.

Borrower: Yes / No   Co-Borrower: Yes / No

a. Are there any outstanding judgments against you?

b. Have you been declared bankrupt within the past 7 years?

c. Have you had property foreclosed upon or given title or deed in lieu thereof in the last 7 years?

d. Are you a party to a lawsuit?

e. Have you directly or indirectly been obligated on any loan which resulted in foreclosure, transfer of title in lieu of foreclosure, or judgment? (This would include such loans as home mortgage loans, SBA loans, home improvement loans, educational loans, manufactured (mobile) home loans, any mortgage, financial obligation, bond, or loan guarantee. If "Yes," provide details, including date, name and address of Lender, FHA or VA case number, if any, and reasons for the action.)

f. Are you presently delinquent or in default on any Federal debt or any other loan, mortgage, financial obligation, bond, or loan guarantee? If "Yes," give details as described in the preceding question.

g. Are you obligated to pay alimony, child support, or separate maintenance?

h. Is any part of the down payment borrowed?

i. Are you a co-maker or endorser on a note?

j. Are you a U.S. citizen?

k. Are you a permanent resident alien?

l. Do you intend to occupy the property as your primary residence? If "Yes," complete question m below.

m. Have you had an ownership interest in a property in the last three years?

(1) What type of property did you own - principal residence (PR), second home (SH), or investment property (IP)?

(2) How did you hold title to the home - solely by yourself (S), jointly with your spouse (SP), or jointly with another person (O)?

IX. ACKNOWLEDGMENT AND AGREEMENT

The undersigned specifically acknowledge(s) and agree(s) that: (1) the loan requested by this application will be secured by a first mortgage or deed of trust on the property described herein; (2) the property will not be used for any illegal or prohibited purpose or use; (3) all statements made in this application are made for the purpose of obtaining the loan indicated herein; (4) occupation of the property will be as indicated above; (5) verification or reverification of any information contained in the application may be made at any time by the Lender, its agents, successors and assigns, either directly or through a credit reporting agency, from any source named in this application, and the original copy of this application will be retained by the Lender, even if the loan is not approved; (6) the Lender, its agents, successors and assigns will rely on the information contained in the application and I/we have a continuing obligation to amend and/or supplement the information provided in this application if any of the material facts which I/we have represented herein should change prior to closing; (7) in the event my/our payments on the loan indicated in this application become delinquent, the Lender, its agents, successors and assigns, may, in addition to all their other rights and remedies, report my/our name(s) and account information to a credit reporting agency; (8) ownership of the loan may be transferred to successor or assign of the Lender without notice to me and/or the administration of the loan account may be transferred to an agent, successor or assign of the Lender with prior notice to me; (9) the Lender, its agents, successors and assigns make no representation or warranties, express or implied, to the Borrower(s) regarding the property, the condition of the property, or the value of the property.

Right to Receive Copy of Appraisal. I/We have the right to a copy of the appraisal report used in connection with this application for credit. To obtain a copy, I/we must send Lender a written request at the mailing address Lender has provided. Lender must hear from me/us no later than 90 days after Lender notifies me/us about the action taken on this application, or I/we withdraw this application.

Certification: I/We certify that the information provided in this application is true and correct as of the date set forth opposite my/our signature(s) on this application and acknowledge my/our understanding that any intentional or negligent misrepresentation(s) of the information contained in this application may result in civil liability and/or criminal penalties including, but not limited to, fine or imprisonment or both under the provisions of Title 18, United States Code, Section 1001, et seq. and liability for monetary damages to the Lender, its agents, successors and assigns, insurers and any other person who may suffer any loss due to reliance upon any misrepresentation which I/we have made on this application.

Borrower's Signature	Date	Co-Borrower's Signature	Date
X		X	

X. INFORMATION FOR GOVERNMENT MONITORING PURPOSES

The following information is requested by the Federal Government for certain types of loans related to a dwelling, in order to monitor the Lender's compliance with equal credit opportunity, fair housing and home mortgage disclosure laws. You are not required to furnish this information, but are encouraged to do so. The law provides that a Lender may neither discriminate on the basis of this information, nor on whether you choose to furnish it. However, if you choose not to furnish it, under Federal regulations this Lender is required to note race and sex on the basis of visual observation or surname. If you do not wish to furnish the above information, please check the box below. (Lender must review the above material to assure that the disclosures satisfy all requirements to which the Lender is subject under applicable state law for the particular type of loan applied for.)

BORROWER

☐ I do not wish to furnish this information

Race/National Origin: ☐ American Indian or Alaskan Native ☐ Asian or Pacific Islander ☐ Black, not of Hispanic origin ☐ Hispanic ☐ White, not of Hispanic origin ☐ Other (specify) _____

Sex: ☐ Female ☐ Male

CO-BORROWER

☐ I do not wish to furnish this information

Race/National Origin: ☐ American Indian or Alaskan Native ☐ Asian or Pacific Islander ☐ Black, not of Hispanic origin ☐ Hispanic ☐ White, not of Hispanic origin ☐ Other (specify) _____

Sex: ☐ Female ☐ Male

To be Completed by Interviewer	Interviewer's Name (print or type)	Name and Address of Interviewer's Employer
This application was taken by: ☐ face-to-face interview ☐ by mail ☐ by telephone	Interviewer's Signature Date	
	Interviewer's Phone Number (incl. area code)	

FIGURE 12.8

Uniform Residential Loan Application Form (continued)

Continuation Sheet/Residential Loan Application

Use this continuation sheet if you need more space to complete the Residentail Loan Application. Mark **B** for Borrower or **C** for Co-Borrower.	Borrower:	Agency Case Number:
	Co-Borrower:	Lender Case Number:

I/We fully understand that it is a Federal crime punishable by fine or imprisonment, or both, to knowingly make any false statements concerning any of the above facts as applicable under the provisions of Title 18, United States Code, Section 1001, et seq.

Borrower's Signature	Date	Co-Borrower's Signature	Date
X		X	

Freddie Mac Form 65/Rev. 10/92 Page 4 of 4 Fannie Mae Form 1003/Rev. 10/92

Lenders will consider second job income if the applicant has a history of second job income.

Lending institutions sometimes take overtime wages into consideration. Other lenders will consider both spouses' wages in computing the gross income of the borrower, even if only one spouse is applying for the loan. Occasionally, a lender will request a **cosigner**—a person with additional capital who agrees to share liability for the loan—to strengthen the borrower's application. Lenders also might reduce down payment requirements with a cosigner.

When a lender qualifies a borrower, the lender is attempting to answer two questions:

1. Can the borrower afford the payments?
2. Will the borrower make the payments on time? (This question refers to character.)
3. Can the borrower afford the payments?

To determine whether the borrower has the capacity to make the monthly payments, the lender needs to answer these questions:

- Does the borrower earn enough to make the payments?
- Will the income be a steady source of income?
- Does the borrower have the down payment?
- Can the borrower make the payments on time?

The lender is going to verify the applicant's ability to make timely monthly payments and his or her employment history (steady stream of income). The lender will want to know the down payment on the property before determining the loan amount. This information is usually confirmed by the lender through the use of verifications of deposits and employment.

Once the lender knows the loan amount, he or she can calculate the principal, interest, taxes, and insurance (PITI) on it. This is the first step in the qualification process. To show how a lender qualifies a borrower for a loan, we will use a worksheet (Figure 12.9) that is designed to qualify a borrower. These are also qualifying programs available for your PDA or computer.

To qualify the borrower, we examine two ratios (percentages). The **front-end ratio,** also called *top ratio* (mortgage payment ratio), is the mortgage payment (PITI) divided by the borrower's gross income. Conforming loans require that the front-end ratio be approximately 28 percent or less. The reason it is called the *top ratio* is because it is at the top of the form (above the bottom ratio). The other ratio is the **back-end ratio,** or *bottom ratio* (total obligation ratio). This ratio should be approximately 36 percent or less to qualify for a conforming loan. Nonconforming loans may have different values for these ratios. The preceding ratios (28 percent and 36 percent) are for loans that do not require PMI. For

FIGURE 12.9

Loan Qualifying Worksheet—Fixed at 10%, 30 years

LOAN QUALIFYING WORKSHEET

Name: Ben & Betty Bior

Residence: _____

Property: _____

Fixed Rate Loan

Bus. Phone: _____

Res. Phone: _____

Owner Occupied: Yes: _X_   No: _____

Property Type: _Single Family Residence_

MONTHLY INCOME

Borrower: $ 5,500

Co-borrower: $ _____

[A] Gross Income: $ 5,500

PAYMENTS

SP/Value $ 200,000

LTV/Down Payment $ 40,000

Loan Amount $ 160,000

REFI: CURRENT LOANS & CASH OUT

1st T.D.	$ _____	@	_____ %
2nd T.D.	$ _____	@	_____ %
3rd T.D.	$ _____	@	_____ %
Total Loans	$ _____		
Plus Cash Out	$ _____		
Plus Costs	$ _____		
Proposed Loan	$ _____		

	FIXED	ARM
Rate:	10 %	_____ %
P & I 1st:	$ 1,404	$ _____
P.M.I.	$ _____	$ _____
Taxes:	$ 208	$ _____
Insurance/HOA:	$ 40	$ _____
	$ _____	$ _____
[B] PITI =	$ 1,652	$ _____

	FIXED	ARM
[B] = $ 1,652		
—	TOP: 30 %	_____ %
[A] = $ 5,500		
[C] = $ 2,192		
—	BOT: 40 %	_____ %
[A] = $ 5,500		

BILLS

		Balanced	Payments
Car #1 :		$ 10,000	$ 500
Car _____ :		$ _____	$ _____
CC Visa :		$ 800	
CC _____ :		$ _____	
CC _____ :		$ _____	
CC _____ :		$ _____	
CC _____ :		$ _____	
Total CC		$ 800	
Total CC × .05			$ 40

TOTAL OBLIGATIONS (PITI + Bills):

	FIXED	ARM
[C] =	$ 2,192	$ _____

SELLING AGENT:

Bus. Phone: _____

Res. Phone: _____

LISTING AGENT:

Bus. Phone: _____

Res. Phone: _____

TO CLOSE APPROXIMATELY:

THIS ESCROW:

Bus. Phone: _____

Officer: _____

Escrow #: _____

HOME SALE ESCROW:

Bus. Phone: _____

Officer: _____

Escrow #: _____

Permission to reproduce this form from Dr. Gregg Figgins, Real Estate Instructor at Riverside Community College, Glendale College, Palomar College, and Rancho Santiago College.

> 28 percent and 36 percent are the important qualifying ratios.

loans with PMI the ratios might be top = 33 percent and bottom = 38 percent. For our discussion we will use a loan with no PMI, in which the top = 28 percent and the bottom = 36 percent.

From the **verification of employment** and other financial information, the lender determines the borrower's gross income. Lenders require a signed statement from the borrower to permit a check with the borrower's employer to verify wages and length of employment. *Gross income* is defined as the income made by the borrower before taxes and deductions. For a husband and wife the gross income for a loan is generally the total gross income of the husband plus the total gross income of the wife. Employment usually must be verified for two years.

The lender also needs to determine the monthly long-term rotating credit bills owed by the borrower. These include car payments, credit cards, furniture payments, student loans, and other bank or credit union loans, including mortgage loans. If a credit bill will be paid in less than ten months, it is not included.

The following example shows how a lender will qualify the borrower:

■ **EXAMPLE:** Ben and Betty Bior want to buy a home for $200,000. They have $40,000 for the down payment. They also have enough in the bank for closing costs. This would leave them a loan amount of $160,000. Assume the interest rate on a fully amortized loan over 30 years is 10 percent. There will be no PMI on this loan because it has an LTV of 80 percent. Ben Bior is an engineer and makes $3,500 per month. Betty is a teacher making $2,000 per month. Their total monthly income is $5,500. Their expenses are as follows:

Expense	Balance	Monthly Payment
Car	$10,000	$500
Credit Card	$800	$40

According to the completed loan qualifying worksheet in Figure 12.9, their top ratio is 30 percent, which would not qualify. The bottom ratio is 40 percent, which also would not qualify.

What if they decided to get an ARM at 8 percent amortized over 30 years? (See Figure 12.10 for the completed form.) They would qualify for the ARM. What would you suggest that they do?

Qualifying the Property

Collateral. After the loan is granted, the lender has to rely for a long time on the value of the security for the loan for the safety of the investment, should the borrower default. For this reason, lenders consider it important to qualify the property as well as the borrower.

> Collateral refers to the value of the security for the loan.

Because the underlying security for almost every property loan is the property itself, lenders require a careful valuation of the property, the *collateral*. The value depends on the property's location, age, architecture, physical condition, zoning,

FIGURE 12.10

Loan Qualifying Worksheet—ARM at 8%, 30 years

LOAN QUALIFYING WORKSHEET

Name: Ben & Betty Bior	Bus. Phone: _____
Residence: _____	Res. Phone: _____
Property: _____	Owner Occupied: Yes: X No: _____
ARM	Property Type: Single Family Residence

MONTHLY INCOME

Borrower:	$ 5,500
Co-borrower:	$ _____
[A] Gross Income:	$ 5,500

PAYMENTS

SP/Value	$ 200,000
LTV/Down Payment	$ 40,000
Loan Amount	$ 160,000

REFI: CURRENT LOANS & CASH OUT

1st T.D.	$ _____	@ _____ %
2nd T.D.	$ _____	@ _____ %
3rd T.D.	$ _____	@ _____ %
Total Loans	$ _____	
Plus Cash Out	$ _____	
Plus Costs	$ _____	
Proposed Loan	$ _____	

	FIXED	ARM
Rate:	_____ %	8 %
P & I 1st:	$ _____	$ 1,174
P.M.I.	$ _____	$ _____
Taxes:	$ _____	$ 208
Insurance/HOA:	$ _____	$ 40
	$ _____	$ _____
[B] PITI =	$ _____	$ 1,422

	FIXED	ARM
[B] = $ 1,422		
—	TOP: _____ %	26 %
[A] = $ 5,500		
[C] = $ 1,962		
—	BOT: _____ %	36 %
[A] = $ 5,500		

BILLS

		Balanced	Payments
Car #1 :	$	10,000	$ 500
Car _____ :	$	_____	$ _____
CC Visa :	$	800	
CC _____ :	$	_____	
CC _____ :	$	_____	
CC _____ :	$	_____	
CC _____ :	$	_____	
Total CC	$	800	
Total CC × .05			$ 40

SELLING AGENT:

Bus. Phone: _____

Res. Phone: _____

TOTAL OBLIGATIONS (PITI + Bills):

	FIXED	ARM
[C] =	$ _____	$ 1,962

LISTING AGENT:

Bus. Phone: _____

Res. Phone: _____

TO CLOSE APPROXIMATELY:

THIS ESCROW:

Bus. Phone: _____

Officer: _____

Escrow #: _____

HOME SALE ESCROW:

Bus. Phone: _____

Officer: _____

Escrow #: _____

floor plan, and general appearance. The lender will have an appraisal done by the financial institution's appraiser or by an outside fee appraiser. Brokers who are familiar with lending policies of loan companies are in a good position to make accurate and helpful estimates.

After the Savings and Loans were deregulated in the 1980s, allowing them to make commercial loans, many S&L's made high-value loans at significantly higher interest than was possible for residential loans. Competition for many of these loans was intense and S&L's did not want to lose choice loan opportunities because of conservative appraisals. They encouraged more liberal appraisals, but appraisers who failed to cooperate found themselves shut out from lucrative business. In the mid-1980s, there was a collapse in the S&L industry with over 500 S&L bankruptcies and a government bail out. Instead of placing the blame on greed of the S&L's, the blame was placed largely on the appraisers. In 1989, the federal government passed the Financial Institutions Reform, Recovery, and Enforcement Act (FIRREA). Part of the law created an Appraisal Foundation and required state-certified and state-license appraisers.

Even though we now have certification and licensing of appraisers, the basic problem of lenders encouraging over-generous appraisals has not gone away.

When an appraisal is less than the purchase price, it requires the seller to lower the price or the buyer to come up with a larger down payment as the amount of a loan will be reduced. The purchaser often does not have the resources for the large down payment. In addition, many offers include a contingency that the appraisal will be at least the amount of the purchase price. This provides an avenue of escape for the buyers.

A great many mortgage loan officers are paid by commission. They don't get paid when a loan cannot be funded. Many real estate professionals are presently concerned that appraisals seldom come in at less than the purchase price. They believe that some appraisals are being inflated by appraisers in order to gain referrals. This could result in lenders having insufficient security in case of buyer default.

Approving and Processing the Loan

Processing involves drawing up loan papers, preparing disclosure forms regarding loan fees, and issuing instructions for the escrow and title companies. Loan papers include the *promissory note* (the evidence of the debt) and the security instruments (the *trust deed* or mortgage).

Closing the Loan

Closing the loan involves signing all the loan papers and preparing the closing statements. First-time buyers, especially, are often confused by the various fees involved. Real estate licensees play a vital role in making this transition period smooth.

Servicing the Loan

After the title has been transferred and the escrow closed, the loan-servicing portion of the transaction begins. This refers to the record-keeping process once the loan has been placed. Many lenders do their own servicing, whereas others use outside sources. The goal of loan servicing is to see that the borrower makes timely payments so that the lender makes the expected yield on the loan, which keeps the cost of the entire package at a minimum.

■ REGULATION OF REAL ESTATE FINANCING

Because this is a real estate practices text, all references to the regulations governing real estate financing will, of necessity, be brief. For further information relating to this subject, consult a real estate finance book.

Truth-in-Lending Act

The *Truth-in-Lending Act* (Regulation Z) is a key portion of the federal *Consumer Credit Protection Act* passed in 1969. The Truth-in-Lending Act applies to banks, savings associations, credit unions, consumer finance companies, and residential mortgage brokers. This disclosure act requires that lenders reveal to customers how much they're being charged for credit in terms of an annual percentage rate. Customers can then make credit cost comparisons among various credit sources.

The act gives individuals seeking credit a right of rescission of the contract. This means that under certain circumstances a customer has the right to cancel a credit transaction up until midnight of the third day after signing. This right of rescission applies to loans that place a lien on the borrower's residence. The rescission rights do not apply to primary financing (first trust deed) to finance the purchase of the borrower's residence (purchase-money loan).

Real Estate Settlement Procedures Act

The regulations contained in the **Real Estate Settlement Procedures Act** (RESPA) apply only to first loans on one- to four-unit residential properties. This is another disclosure act. Within three days of the date of the loan application a lender must furnish the buyer with an itemized list of all closing costs that will be encountered in escrow. This must be a good-faith estimate provided to every person requesting credit. Each charge for each settlement service the buyer is likely to incur must be expressed as a dollar amount or range. The lender also must furnish a copy of a special information booklet prepared by the secretary of the Department of Housing and Urban Development (HUD). It must be delivered or placed in the mail to the applicant no later than three business days after the application is received.

A **controlled business arrangement** (CBA) is a situation where a broker offers "one-stop shopping" for a number of broker-controlled services, such as financing arrangements, home inspection, title insurance, property insurance, escrow, etc. RESPA permits such controlled business arrangements as long as the consumer is clearly informed of the relationship between the broker and the service providers and other providers are available. Fees may not be exchanged between the companies simply for referrals. A broker-controlled mortgage company must have its own employees and cannot contract out its services or it would violate RESPA provisions that prohibit kickbacks for referral services.

It's the position of the attorney general of California that a broker may not pay referral fees to a real estate salesperson for referral to broker-affiliated services.

Fair Credit Reporting Act

The **Fair Credit Reporting Act** affects credit reporting agencies and users of credit information. If a loan is rejected because of information disclosed in a credit report, the borrower must be notified and is entitled to know all the information the agency has in its file on the buyer, as well as the sources and the names of all creditors who received reports within the past six months.

Predatory Lending

California law prohibits predatory lending. Loans made to homeowners by finance companies, real estate brokers, and residential mortgage lenders without considering the borrowers' ability to repay would be considered **predatory lending.** Violation would subject the lender to civil penalties. This law was enacted because some loans were made where the lenders actually wanted the borrowers to default in order to foreclose on the properties securing the loans.

■ SUMMARY

Whereas primary financing refers to first trust deeds and secondary financing refers to junior liens, the primary and the secondary mortgage markets are far different. The primary mortgage market refers to lenders making loans direct to borrowers; the secondary mortgage market refers to the sale of existing loans.

Fannie Mae (The Federal National Mortgage Association) and Freddie Mac (the Federal Home Loan Mortgage Corporation) create a secondary mortgage market by buying FHA, DVA, and conforming conventional loans. Conforming loans are loans that meet the standards established by Fannie Mae.

Institutional lenders such as banks, savings associations, and life insurance companies are major sources of primary real estate financing. Noninstitutional lenders include mortgage companies, which originate most real estate loans today. Mortgage companies (mortgage bankers) generally sell loans in the secondary market or act as loan correspondents for other lenders.

Mortgage loan brokers are real estate brokers who serve as middlemen for loans. These loans generally have a high loan cost and bear a higher rate of interest than do loans from institutional lenders. Other noninstitutional lenders include real estate investment trusts, pension funds and credit unions.

Seller carryback financing is also a source of funding for real estate purchases.

Conventional loans are loans made without any government participation, guarantee, or insurance.

Government participation loans provide for lower down payment requirements and include FHA, DVA, and Cal Vet loans.

Today borrowers have a wide choice of types of loans and loan variations, including fixed-rate loans, renegotiable-rate mortgages, reverse mortgages, and adjustable-rate mortgages. The special features of the loans vary by lender. A buyer must analyze his or her needs and the important factors of down payment, loan costs, interest, assumability, convertibility, loan term, qualifying rate of interest, and so forth, as they pertain to those needs.

The Internet provides a convenient and efficient way to shop for loans as well as to complete and submit loan applications.

The financing process involves qualifying the buyer, using front-end and back-end ratios and FICO scores, qualifying the property, approving and processing the loan, closing the loan, and servicing the loan.

■ CLASS DISCUSSION TOPICS

1. Using a front-end (top) ratio of 33 percent and a back-end (bottom) ratio of 38 percent, qualify a buyer earning $100,000 per year for a 30-year loan of $400,000 with an 8 percent interest rate. Assume taxes at $5,000 per year and insurance at $1,000 per year. Assume the buyer is making payments on loans of $43,000 and his or her monthly payments are $2,080.

2. Obtain the ARM terms from three different lenders. Lay them out on paper, showing the differences. Which loan would be best suited for a person having what needs?

3. Discuss prequalification practices of local lenders.

4. Complete a loan application for a fictitious borrower, using realistic income, expense, debt, and savings figures. How large a conforming loan will this fictitious applicant qualify for?

5. Bring to class one current-events article dealing with some aspect of real estate practice.

■ CHAPTER 12 QUIZ

1. A loan covering more than one property would be a
   a. compound loan.
   b. blanket encumbrance.
   c. subordinated loan.
   d. reverse mortgage.

2. What type of mortgage has compound interest?
   a. Reverse mortgage
   b. Renegotiable-rate mortgage
   c. Adjustable-rate mortgage
   d. Straight mortgage

3. The difference between the interest rate of an index and the rate charged by a lender under an adjustable-rate mortgage is known as the
   a. discount.   c. margin.
   b. gap.   d. cap.

4. A lender who believes interest rates will be rising significantly will be least interested in a(n)
   a. renegotiable-rate mortgage.
   b. 30-year fixed-rate mortgage.
   c. 15-year fixed-rate mortgage.
   d. adjustable-rate mortgage.

5. A danger that an adjustable-rate mortgage poses to a buyer is
   a. higher payments if interest rates increase.
   b. a longer payment period if interest rates increase.
   c. that the margin will increase.
   d. none of the above.

6. An adjustable-rate loan index is 6 percent at the time a loan is made. The margin for the loan is 2.5 percent. With a 5 percent lifetime cap, the highest the interest rate could go is
   a. 6 percent.   c. 11 percent.
   b. 8.5 percent.   d. 13.5 percent.

7. A convertible ARM is a loan that can be changed to
   a. a shorter-term loan.
   b. a fixed-rate loan.
   c. another property.
   d. another borrower.

8. A buyer intends to sell a house within two years. The buyer would prefer
   a. a loan with no prepayment penalty.
   b. a loan with low initial loan costs.
   c. an assumable loan.
   d. all of the above.

9. Which loan type is most likely to meet all the criteria of question 8?
   a. Renegotiable-rate mortgage
   b. Adjustable-rate mortgage
   c. Fixed-rate mortgage
   d. Reverse mortgage

10. The underlying security for a loan is the
    a. borrower's character.
    b. borrower's capital.
    c. borrower's capacity.
    d. property

13

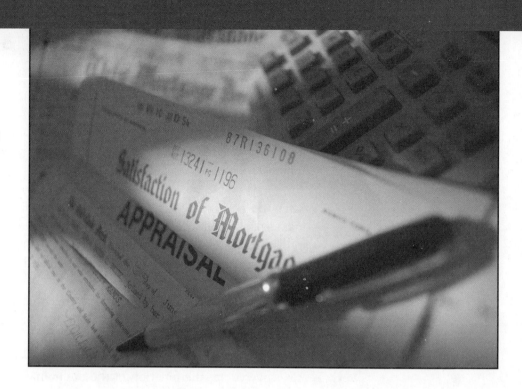

ESCROW AND TITLE INSURANCE

■ KEY TERMS

abstract	debits	preliminary title report
ALTA policy	deed of reconveyance	proration
amend the escrow	escrow	rebate law
instructions	escrow instructions	recurring costs
beneficiary statement	extended policy	special title insurance
closing costs	good funds	policies
CLTA policy	impound account	standard policy
credits	marketable title	title insurance

■ LEARNING OBJECTIVES

In this chapter, you learn about what an escrow is, escrow requirements and responsibilities, parties to the escrow, and who can be an escrow. You also learn what the responsibilities of a broker are when he or she acts as an escrow.

This chapter explains escrow procedures, how an escrow is opened, what materials are needed for the escrow instructions, and the purpose of the escrow instructions. You learn about escrow licensing and the broker-exemption to the licensing requirements.

After you have read this chapter, you will understand how an escrow may be amended, and you will have gained an understanding of the closing costs, credits, and debits of an escrow statement. You will understand the broker's duty of explaining the escrow function to the buyer and seller.

You learn why we use title insurance rather than abstracts of title in California and about the coverage as well as the exclusions of both the standard and extended coverage policies of title insurance.

Also covered are the function of the preliminary title report, special policies of title insurance, and the rebate law.

■ ESCROW

The word **escrow** is derived from the French word *escroue*, meaning scroll or roll of writing. An owner of real property executed an instrument in the form of a deed, conveying land to another party on the fulfillment of certain conditions. This instrument, the *escroue*, was given to a third person with instructions that it would take effect as a deed on the performance of an act or the occurrence of an event, such as payment of a designated sum of money. The term was taken in English as escrow, meaning "a deed, a bond, money, or a piece of property held in trust by a third party, to be turned over to the grantee only on fulfillment of a condition."

Escrow is the last step in a property transaction. The California Financial Code defines escrow as follows:

> Escrow means any transaction wherein one person for the purpose of effecting the sale, transfer, encumbering, or leasing of real or personal property to another person, delivers any written instrument, money, evidence of title to real or personal property or other things of value to a third person to be held by such third person until the happening of a specified event. The performance is then to be delivered by such third person to a grantee, grantor, promisee, promisor, obligee, obligor, bailee, or bailor, or any agent or employee or any of the latter.

The escrow is an impartial "stakeholder."

This definition has been changed somewhat, and the activities of an escrow agent have been expanded considerably. In brief, an escrow agent is an impartial third party or "stakeholder who receives and disburses documents, money, and papers from every party involved in a transaction, such as a sale of real estate." The escrow operates in an agency capacity.

Escrow Requirements

When the buyer offers a sum of money to the seller and the seller's acceptance is transmitted to the buyer, a binding contract is formed. Generally, this is the first requirement for a sales escrow. Escrow is created on the conditional delivery of transfer instruments and monies to a third party.

Although escrows are not generally required by law in California, they have become an almost indispensable mechanism in this state to protect the parties involved in exchanges, leases, and sales of securities, loans, mobile-home sales, and primarily real property sales.

In some states, the listing real estate office handles escrow functions. In other states, attorneys are used for real estate closings. In some communities, the local lender handles the closing functions. However, closings are primarily handled by third-party escrows in California.

Escrow Responsibility

The escrow agent holds all money and documents during the transaction. When conditions agreed upon by the buyer and seller are met, the deed and the monies involved are disbursed concurrently to the appropriate parties. (See Figure 13.1.) Funds must be **good funds** before they can be disbursed. Good funds include cash, cashier's checks, and personal checks that have cleared.

Broker Responsibility

Once the escrow instructions have been signed, the escrow acts in a dual-agency capacity to carry out the instructions of the buyer and seller. However, the broker still has agency duties.

The broker should track the escrow to make certain that the escrow is receiving what it requires, when it is required. If there are problems concerning the escrow, the broker should notify the parties and attempt to resolve these problems.

The broker also should monitor the loan application and keep in contact with the lender to avoid or resolve any problems or delays.

Parties to an Escrow

Buyers.   When buyers have performed in full (paid the purchase price), they are entitled to a deed transferring title, subject only to encumbrances agreed on by both parties. Buyers do not want to pay sellers until the buyers know they are certain of obtaining title to the property as agreed. While the title search is being conducted, the buyers' deposits are held in escrow.

Sellers.   Although sellers may have made a firm contract to sell their real property, they do not want to give up their title until they are certain of receiving their money. They therefore retain legal title to the property as security until they have the money in hand. The sellers' legal title usually is transferred by deed. The title is placed in escrow until buyers have produced the full purchase price for the property. If a seller dies before a transaction has been completed, that seller's right to the unpaid part of the purchase price may pass to his or her heirs.

FIGURE 13.1

Escrow Responsibility

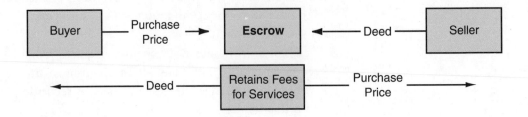

If a buyer dies, the heirs may be required to continue with the purchase. However, the loan may be affected owing to qualification.

Lenders.   In lending money to buyers to complete a purchase, lenders, like buyers, do not want to commit their funds without assurance that titles to the properties in question are free and clear. Therefore, impartial third parties (escrow agents) hold money, deeds, and other documents until liens have been paid off and clear titles have been confirmed. Thereafter it is the escrow agent's responsibility to see that the proper disbursements are made.

Brokers.   Real estate agents, unless principals to the transaction, are not parties to the escrow. While the agent is not a party to the escrow, agents should understand escrow procedure so that they can both monitor the escrow to avoid delays and other problems and explain the escrow procedures to their clients and help them comply with escrow requirements. Once the escrow has been opened, the escrow may not make any changes to the escrow instructions based on orders of a real estate agent unless authorized to do so by the principals. However, the escrow instructions might provide for the payment of the commission out of escrow, and that the brokers commission rights cannot be canceled. On a case-by-case basis, the broker can authorize that a commission be paid directly to a salesperson out of broker-entitled funds upon a closing.

> The broker is not a party to an escrow.

Escrow Agents

In California, all escrow companies must be corporations and, as such, must be licensed by the California Commissioner of Corporations. Individuals cannot be licensed under the escrow law, but certain organizations and individuals are permitted to act as escrow agents without licensure. These include

> Escrows are corporations under the jurisdiction of the Commissioner of Corporations.

- banks,
- attorneys (to act as an escrow, an attorney must have had a prior client relationship with a party to the escrow),
- brokers,
- title and trust companies, and
- savings associations.

In some northern California areas, escrow transactions are handled by title insurance companies; they usually process the escrow and issue the title insurance policy together. In southern California, escrow companies handle the majority of escrow transactions with a title company issuing the title insurance separately. There are other regional deviations in the way escrows operate.

Broker as Escrow

A broker can act as an unlicensed escrow only if the broker is a principal or represents the buyer or seller.

The real estate broker-exemption from licensing as an escrow is applicable only when the broker represents the buyer or the seller or is a principal in the transaction. The broker may charge for his or her services. Many larger offices have escrow services as a separate profit center for their operations. A number of computer escrow programs are available to aid in this function.

While a broker is exempt from the licensing requirements for his or her own transactions, this exemption applies only to the broker. The broker cannot delegate the escrow duties to others. The exemption is not available to any association of brokers for the purpose of conducting escrows for the group.

A real estate broker cannot advertise that he or she conducts escrow business unless the broker specifies that such services are only in connection with the real estate brokerage business. The broker also is prohibited from using a fictitious or corporate name that contains the word *escrow*. While acting as an escrow, a broker must put aside agency relationships as well as any special interests and adopt the position of a neutral depository, the same as any other escrow.

Escrow funds held by a broker must be placed in a special trust account, subject to periodic inspection by the Commissioner of Corporations and, at the broker's own expense, subject to an independent annual audit.

A broker can be licensed separately as an escrow and operate the escrow business in a controlled business arrangement (Chapter 12).

Requirements for Escrow Licensure

Any corporation applying for an escrow license under the Escrow Act must

- be financially solvent;
- furnish a surety bond for $10,000;
- arrange for the bonding of responsible employees;
- set up a trust fund for all monies deposited in escrow;
- keep accurate records, subject to audit at any time by the Commissioner of Corporations and the Department of Real Estate; and
- submit to an independent audit annually at its own expense.

FIGURE 13.2

Legal Requirements for Escrow Officers

Officers Must	**Officers May Not**
act according to issued written instructions.	make a transaction for another officer.
act as a neutral party at all times.	negotiate with the parties separately.
hold monies deposited by parties until disbursed.	suggest that terms or provisions be inserted in the escrow.
follow escrow instructions in every detail unless instructions are in violation of the law.	act as collection agencies to persuade a client to furnish funds.
give to parties only that information that concerns them.	notify parties that they have not ordered a certain document that may be necessary to close an escrow.
make sure that escrow does not close with an unverified check.	

Laws Governing Escrow

No escrow licensee may

- disseminate misleading or deceptive statements referring to its supervision by the State of California;

- describe either orally or in writing any transaction that is not included under the definition of escrow in the California Financial Code;

- pay referral fees to anyone except a regular employee of its own escrow company;

- solicit or accept escrow instructions or amended or supplemental instructions containing any blanks to be filled in after the instructions are signed; or

- permit any person to make additions to, deletions from, or alterations of an escrow instruction unless it is signed or initialed by all signers of the original instructions.

Figure 13.2 summarizes legal requirements pertaining to the actions of escrow officers.

> Before closing, the escrow is a dual agent. After closing, the escrow has separate agency duties.

Escrow is a limited agency relationship governed by the content of the escrow instructions, and the escrow holder acts only on specific written instructions of the principals as agent for both parties. When the escrow is closed, the escrow holder becomes agent for each principal with respect to those things in escrow to which the respective parties have become completely entitled. Oral instructions should not be accepted or acted on.

Escrow Procedures

Certain procedures must be followed to fulfill the legal requirements for escrow procedures. The broker needs to provide certain information to the escrow agent. Buyers and sellers must be aware of the responsibilities each must assume in the escrow procedure.

Escrow is a many-faceted procedure, as illustrated in Figure 13.3.

Advantages of an Escrow

If you decide to buy a television set, you make your purchase from an appliance store. You pay for it by giving cash or adding it to your credit account. You likely would not give a second thought to whether the store has a right to sell the set to you. You probably give no thought at all to whether you need written evidence of your right to own the appliance. It is a simple sales transaction. With the sale of real property, the procedure is much more complicated. The seller could sign a simple deed of conveyance and deliver it to the buyer in exchange for the purchase price. However, neither the buyer nor the seller should agree to such an arrangement, for these reasons:

- Title to the property may be encumbered. The buyer needs someone to make a title search for the purpose of issuing a title insurance policy.
- An accurate description of the property is necessary for legal purposes.
- The seller and the buyer need an experienced person to prepare the instrument of conveyance for their signatures.
- The buyer and the seller need assurance that their instructions have been carried out and that the deeds will be delivered and any monies transferred only when all terms of the contract have been met.

There are distinct advantages to escrow and the use of a neutral third party in the transaction:

- Escrow provides a custodian of papers, instructions, funds, and documents until the transaction is closed.
- It makes possible the handling of accounting details in a professional manner.
- It assures the validity of a binding contract between participating parties.
- It is of value to the buyers, assuring them that their monies will not be transferred until the title is conditioned to the specifications of their contract or agreement.
- It is of value to the sellers, assuring them that the monies have been paid and all other terms and conditions have been met.

Escrow Instructions.   **Escrow instructions** are the written directions from the principals to the impartial third party, the escrow agent, to do all the necessary acts to carry out the escrow agreement of the principals. All principals in the escrow agreement (buyers, sellers, lenders, borrowers) sign identical or conforming instructions that fully set out the understanding of the parties to the transactions. They deliver the signed instructions to the escrow agent.

Figure 10.6 on page 294 contains CAR Form RPA-CA entitled California Residential Purchase Agreement and Joint Escrow Instructions. The form provides that when the purchase offer is accepted, portions of the purchase agreement become the escrow instructions. The wide use of this form has significantly

FIGURE 13.3

Procedures of an Escrow

Life of an Escrow

Prepare Escrow Instructions
and Pertinent Documents

Obtain Signatures

Order Preliminary
Title Report

Forward required
Documents to Lender

Receive and Review
Preliminary Report

Request
Beneficiary Statement

Verify Lender has
Necessary Documentation
for Submission of Loan

Request Demands (if any),
Request Clarification of
Other Leins (if any) and
Review Taxes on Report

Request Beneficiary Statement and Enter
into File ... Review Terms of Transfer
and Current Payment Status
(Is Prior Approval Necessary to Record?)

Obtain Loan Approval
and Determine that
Terms are Correct

Receive Demands and
Enter into File

Request Loan
Documents

Review File to Determine that All Conditions Have Been Met and that all
Documents are Accurate and Available for Signature. (Termite Inspection,
Contingencies Released, Fire Insurance Ordered, Additional
Documents...Grant Deed, Deeds of Trust, etc... have been prepared.)

Figure File and Request Signatures
on All Remaining Documents

Forward Documents
to Title Company

Obtain Funds from Buyer
(cashier check)

Return Loan Documents
to Lender

Request Loan Funds

Receive Lenders Loan Funds and Order Recording

Close File: Prepare Closing Statements and Disburse Funds

Complete Closing. Forward Final Documents to All Interested Parties...
Buyer, Seller, Lender

reduced the necessity of escrow instructions being prepared by the escrow holder or agent.

Communities vary in their escrow procedures. However, a title or escrow company would likely use preprinted forms for instructions, whereas a bank or other authorized agent may issue instructions by letter.

When both parties have signed the instructions, the parties are contractually bound to their agreement. If signed separate escrow instructions vary from the purchase agreement, the escrow instructions generally prevail because they most likely were the last agreement signed. In the absence of a purchase contract, the signed escrow instructions become the purchase contract.

Amending the Escrow Instructions.   Once both buyer and seller have signed the escrow instructions, the escrow is bound to carry out their agreement. If any changes are necessary, both buyer and seller must agree to **amend the escrow instructions.** Neither buyer nor seller can unilaterally modify the escrow agreement once it is signed.

> Amendments to the escrow instructions must be signed by all parties to the escrow.

Closing the Escrow.   When the escrow agent has fulfilled all instructions from the buyer, seller, and lender; when the remainder of the purchase price has been produced; and when a deed has been signed, the escrow arrangements are complete. The basic steps in closing escrow are as follows:

1. A statement showing the condition of the indebtedness and the unpaid balance of the current loan is requested from the beneficiary, the lender. By law the beneficiary must respond within 21 days of receipt of the request.

2. When the escrow agent has received all funds, documents, and instructions necessary to close the escrow, he or she makes any necessary adjustments and prorations on a settlement sheet.

3. All instruments pertinent to the transaction are then sent to the title insurance company for recording. At this point, time becomes important.

4. The title search runs right up to the last minute of the escrow recording to ensure that nothing has been inserted in the record. If no changes have occurred, the deed and other instruments are recorded on the following morning. Thus, a title policy can be issued with the assurance that no intervening matters of record against the real property have occurred since the last search.

5. On the day the deed is recorded, the escrow agent disburses funds to the parties, according to their signed instructions. These include

   ■ seller's lender—amount of loan(s) remaining at date of recording;

   ■ listing and selling brokers' sales commissions;

■ contractors—termite work, roof repairs, plumbing and/or electrical repairs, and so forth; and

■ other liens against the property.

6. After recording, the escrow agent presents closing statements to the parties who should receive them.

7. The title insurance company endeavors to issue a policy of title insurance on the day of recordation.

8. Shortly thereafter the recorded deed is sent from the county recorder to the customer.

Failed Escrow.   If an escrow cannot be completed, the parties must agree to the release of funds (less costs and fees). If a party refuses to agree to the release of funds when there is not a good-faith dispute as to who is entitled to the funds, that party can be liable for treble damages but not less than $100 or more than $1,000 (CC1057.3(b)).

Terms Used in Escrow Transactions

Recurring Costs.   Impound account costs for taxes and insurance are referred to as **recurring costs.**

Impound Account.   When a real estate loan is made, monthly payments for taxes and fire insurance often are required. The lender estimates the funds needed for taxes and insurance, which vary from year to year. These funds are placed in a special trust fund called an **impound account.** When the sale of the property is final and the loan is paid off, the seller is entitled to the unused portion of the impound account.

Beneficiary Statement.   If an existing loan is to be paid or assumed by the buyer, the escrow agent will obtain a **beneficiary statement** showing the exact balance due from the one holding the deed of trust so that the buyer can receive the proper amount of credit.

Reconveyance.   If the seller has a loan that is not being assumed by the buyer, the loan must be paid off to clear the title. The seller instructs the escrow agent to pay off the loan, for which the seller receives a **deed of reconveyance.** A *reconveyance fee* is charged the seller for this service. The sum due the lender is entered in the seller's escrow instructions as an estimate. The total figure will not be known until the final computations are made by the escrow officer at the time of closing.

Closing Costs.   The sum that the seller and buyer have to pay beyond the purchase price is called the **closing costs.** Closing costs consist of fees charged for the mortgage loan, title insurance, escrow services, reconveyances, recording of documents, and transfer tax, among others. Amounts vary, depending on the particular locale involved and the price of the property. Figure 13.4 shows a sample of the customary seller's closing costs, but these costs vary regionally. Costs also vary, not only from area to area but also from institution to institution within an

FIGURE 13.4

Closing Costs Customarily Paid by the Seller

Legal Closing

1. Owner's title policy
2. Escrow services
3. Drawing deed
4. Obtaining reconveyance deed
5. Notary fees
6. Recording reconveyance
7. Documentary transfer tax (provided county and/or city has adopted this tax), $.55 for each $500 or fractional part thereof (Check your local area for differences in rates and requirements for transfer taxes.)
8. Other agreed-on charges

Financial Closing

1. Mortgage discounts (points)
2. Appraisal charge for advance commitment
3. Structural pest control report or structural repair (if any needed). Typically, inspections are paid for by buyer and clearance is provided by seller.
4. Interest on existing loan from last monthly payment to closing date.
5. Beneficiary statement (balance on existing loan)
6. Loan payoff (first trust deed and/or any junior trust deed)
7. Prepayment penalty
8. Other agreed-on charges

Adjustments Between Seller and Buyer (depend on closing or other date agreed on)

1. Pay any tax arrears in full
2. Pay any improvement assessment arrears (assessment may have to be paid in full)
3. Pay any other liens or judgments necessary to pass clear title
4. Pay broker's commission
5. Reimburse buyer for prepaid rents and deposits and adjust taxes, insurance, and interest as required
6. Occupancy adjustments

Source: California Department of Real Estate Reference Book, 1989–1990 Edition.

area. Some costs change with fluctuations in the economy. Figure 13.5 lists those items for which the buyer is responsible.

As indicated in these lists, certain costs are customarily charged to the buyer and others to the seller. However, the two parties may agree to share some costs. Adapt this division of charges to your area. For actual fees, obtain copies of fee schedules from an escrow or title company in your area.

Prorations

The adjustment and distribution of costs to be shared by buyer and seller is called **proration.** Costs typically prorated include interest, taxes, insurance, and, in the event income property is involved, prepaid rents. Costs are prorated in escrow as of the closing of escrow or an agreed-on date. Who is responsible for the day of

FIGURE 13.5

Closing Costs Customarily Paid by the Buyer

Legal Closing

1. Standard or owner's policy in some areas (usually a negotiable charge)
2. ALTA policy and inspection fee, if ordered
3. Escrow services
4. Drawing second mortgage (if used)
5. Notary fee
6. Recording deed
7. Other agreed-on charges

Financial Closing

1. Loan origination fee
2. Appraisal fee
3. Credit report
4. Drawing up note(s) and trust deeds(s)
5. Notary fees
6. Recording trust deed
7. Tax agency fee
8. Termite inspection fee (if agreed on)
9. Interest on new loan (from date of closing until first monthly payment due)
10. Assumption fee
11. Other agreed-on charges
12. New fire insurance premium one year prepaid, if applicable
13. For new FHA-insured loan, mortgage insurance premium

Adjustments Between Seller and Buyer (depend on closing or other date agreed on)

1. Reimburse seller for prepaid taxes
2. Reimburse seller for prepaid insurance
3. Reimburse seller for prepaid improvement assessment
4. Reimburse seller for prepaid impounds (in case buyer is assuming an existing loan)
5. Other occupancy adjustments

Reserves (impounds) Limitations by Real Estate Settlement Procedures Act (RESPA)—Variations

1. Any variation from custom in closing a transaction should be agreed on in advance. Some times through sheer bargaining power one party can demand relief from and be relieved of all or some of the customary charges and offsets generally assessed. The financial aspects of each transaction differ and should always be negotiated by the parties.
2. Accruals: Unless agreed on in advance, interest-bearing debts are accrued up to date of settlement and constitute a charge against the seller.

Source: California Department of Real Estate Reference Book, 1989–1990 Edition.

closing tends to vary by local custom, although this can be changed by agreement. Proration in California is generally based on a 30-day month and a 360-day year.

Property Taxes.   Property taxes are levied annually (July 1 to June 30 is the tax year) and are paid in two installments. Taxes usually require proration. If, for example, the seller had paid the first installment of a given year's taxes but completed the sale before that tax period was over, he or she would receive a credit for the remainder of that period's taxes. If, on the other hand, the seller retained the property through part of the second tax period but had not yet paid taxes for that period, the amount due would be prorated between seller and buyer, with the seller having to pay for the portion of the tax period during which he or she still owned the property.

Insurance. Fire insurance is normally paid for one year in advance. If the buyer assumes a fire insurance policy that has not yet expired, the seller is entitled to a prorated refund of the unused premium.

Interest. If a loan of record is being taken over by the buyer, interest will be prorated between buyer and seller. Because interest is normally paid in arrears, if a closing is set for the 15th of the month and the buyer assumes a loan with payments due on the 1st of the month, the seller owes the buyer for one-half-month's interest.

Rents. Prepaid rents will be prorated in cases involving income-producing properties.

Closing Statements

Procedure for Closing Statements. Closing statements do not follow usual bookkeeping formulas. In a normal accounting situation, such as balancing a checkbook, all the credits (deposits to the account) are added. Then all the debits (checks written) are totaled and deducted from the credits, and the remainder is the balance.

At a closing, separate statements are issued for the buyer and the seller. Each settlement sheet includes **debits** (amounts owed) and **credits** (amounts entitled to receive). In contrast to usual accounting procedures, on the seller's settlement sheet all the credits to the seller are added (selling price of the property, prorations, etc.). Any debits owed by the seller are then totaled and deducted from the credits. The difference is entered as a cash credit (usually) to the seller, and the escrow agent forwards a check for this amount at the close of escrow.

On the buyer's settlement sheet the buyer is charged (debited) with the purchase price of the property. The loans the buyer has obtained are credited to him or her. Cash is credited, prorations may be debited or credited (as the case warrants) and escrow fees and closing costs are debited. The difference between the total debits and credits usually is required in cash by the escrow agent. The cash payment into escrow becomes an additional credit and forces the account to balance. Because of the forced balances, the totals on the buyers' and sellers' statements will be different from each other and from the purchase price. Figure 13.6 will help you understand the debits and credits of closing statements.

FIGURE 13.6

The Closing Statement

Mr. and Mrs. Allen are purchasing a single-family residence from Mr. and Mrs. Baxter. The property is located in Block 15 Tract 6 in the Via Santos Estates in Blythe Beach, California. The purchase price is $150,000. Terms are cash to a $120,000 assumable loan. The close of escrow is October 1, 2003. The purchaser is to assume the first trust deed having interest at 9.5 percent. The seller has paid the interest up to September 1, 2003. Taxes for the year were $1,200 and have not been paid.

The purchaser is to assume a one-year fire insurance policy with a prepaid premium of $360 and a beginning date of June 1, 2003. The parties agreed that escrow expenses of $410 would be divided equally and the standard title insurance policy of $350 would be paid by the sellers. The sellers also are to pay the broker's commission of 5 percent of the sales price.

The closing statements for this transaction follows:

Seller's Statement

Debit		Credit	
First trust deed	$120,000	Selling price	$150,000
Commission	7,500	Prepaid insurance	120
Property taxes	300		
Title insurance	350		
Escrow	205		
Interest	950		
Subtotal	$129,305		
Cash to seller	20,815		
Total	$150,120	Total	$150,120

Buyer's Statement

Debit		Credit	
Purchase price	$150,000	First trust deed assumed	$120,000
Escrow	205	Prepaid interest	950
Prepaid insurance	120	Property taxes	300
		Subtotal	$121,250
		Final payment	29,075
Total	$150,325	Total	$150,325

Not shown in the above statements:

Cost to draft instruments	—	generally a debit to the person who prepared the document
Notary fees	—	generally a debit to the person who executed the document
Recording fees	—	the person receiving an instrument pays to record it
Documentary transfer tax	—	can be paid by either buyer or seller
Reconveyance deed	—	a debit to seller
Beneficiary statement costs	—	a debit to seller
Impound account	—	a credit to seller and a debit to buyer (impound accounts are owned by the borrower but taxes and insurance are prorated)

Broker's Added Responsibility

Despite the care taken in escrow, mistakes can be made. The real estate broker's final duties are to meet with the buyers or sellers and explain the closing statement, to help them understand all charges and credits on the statement and to verify that they have received the correct amount from escrow or paid the correct amount into escrow.

> **When is Escrow Complete?**
> Escrow is complete when the following actions have been taken:
> ■ The escrow officer sends the deed and deeds of trust to the recorder's office to be recorded. This offers protection of the title to the buyer and of the lien to the lender. The broker's responsibility is to confirm the recordation and inform the clients.
> ■ The escrow agent sends to the seller and buyer the closing statements showing the disbursement of funds.
> ■ The escrow agent forwards the title policy assuring the buyer of marketable title, except for certain items; the agent sends the original copy to the buyer.

Liability of an Escrow

Escrow could be held liable for its negligence or breach of duty. However, escrow companies do not have any duty to warn a party of possible fraud or point out any detrimental fact or risk of a transaction. If, however, the escrow was a broker, the broker would have these disclosure obligations.

■ TITLE INSURANCE

In a number of states, **marketable title** is shown by an **abstract.** An *abstract of title* is a recorded history of a property. It includes a summary of every recorded document concerning the property. An attorney reads the abstract and gives an opinion of title based on what the abstract reveals. A problem with using abstracts to verify title is that the records of recordation do not reveal title defects such as a forged instrument in the chain of title, unknown spousal interests, incapacity of a grantor, an illegal contract or failure of delivery. These risks and more are covered by title insurance, which explains why the use of title insurance has been expanding.

Title insurance insures the ownership of real property (land, buildings, and minerals below the surface) against any encumbrances and other items that may cloud the title. These are primarily claims that might be made by a third party against the property. Buyers are assured that a thorough search has been made of all public records affecting the property being purchased and that they have a marketable title.

Title insurance is paid for once, at the time title passes from one owner to another, and it remains in effect until the property is sold again, at which time title passes to the new owner. If a property owner dies, title insurance continues to protect the owner's heirs.

If a buyer does not elect to buy title insurance protection, that buyer is not protected, even though a prior owner had title insurance.

Both the lender and the buyer should have title insurance, the buyer to ensure clear title and thus protect his or her investment and the lender to protect his or her interest in the property.

The two basic types of policies are the California Land Title Association (CLTA) policy and the American Land Title Association (ALTA) policy. In 1987 the title insurance industry issued a new set of policies, with new coverages and exclusions.

Standard Policy

The policy usually used by the buyer is the **CLTA policy.** This policy is called a **standard policy.** The standard policy of title insurance covers matters of record, if not specifically excluded from coverage, as well as specified risks not of record, such as

> A standard CLTA policy protects the buyer as to matters of record and specified risks.

- forgery;
- lack of capacity of a grantor;
- undisclosed spousal interests (a grantor who claimed to be single had a spouse with community property interests);
- failure of delivery of a prior deed;
- federal estate tax liens;
- deeds of a corporation whose charter has expired; and
- deeds of an agent whose capacity has terminated;

Excluded from coverage by a standard policy of title insurance are

- defects known by the insured and not disclosed to the title insurer;
- zoning (although a special endorsement is possible that a current use is authorized by current zoning);
- mining claims (filed in mining districts; legal descriptions are not required);
- taxes and assessments that are not yet liens;
- easements and liens not a matter of record (such as prescriptive easements and rights to a mechanic's lien);
- rights of parties in possession (unrecorded deeds, leases, options, etc.);
- matters not a matter of record that would be disclosed by checking the property (such as encroachment);

- matters that would be revealed by a correct survey;
- water rights; and
- reservations in government patents.

Generally, in southern California the seller pays for the standard policy of title insurance. In some northern California communities the buyer pays for this coverage. Any agreement of the parties as to who pays takes precedence over local custom.

ALTA Policy

An **ALTA policy,** also called an **extended policy,** is generally purchased for the benefit of the lender. The buyer pays for this lender protection. It insures that the lender has a valid and enforceable lien, subject to only the exclusions from coverage noted in the exception schedule of the policy. It insures the lender for the amount of the loan, not the purchase price of the property. There are three basic ALTA policies: One deals with homes described by lot, block, and tract; one deals with homes described by either the metes-and-bounds or government-survey system; and one deals with construction loans.

> An ALTA lender policy provides extended coverage to the lender, not the buyer.

The extended coverage lender policy protects the lender only, not the purchaser, from the risks covered. Buyers who desire extended protection must pay for that protection. An owner's policy is available that offers this extended protection. (Both CLTA and ALTA issue homeowner extended coverage policies.)

In addition to the coverage offered by the standard policy, the extended coverage policy of title insurance includes

- unrecorded liens;
- off-record easements;
- rights of parties in physical possession, including tenants and buyers under unrecorded instruments;
- rights and claims that a correct survey or physical inspection would disclose;
- mining claims;
- water rights; and
- lack of access.

Insurers generally require a survey before they issue an extended coverage policy of title insurance. The extended coverage policy does not cover

- matters known by the insured but not conveyed to the insurer;
- government regulations such as zoning;
- liens placed by the insured;
- eminent domain; and
- violations of the map act.

FIGURE 13.7

Owner's Title Insurance Policy

Standard Coverage	Extended Coverage	Not Covered by Either Policy
1. Defects found in public records 2. Forged documents 3. Incompetent grantors 4. Incorrect marital statements 5. Improperly delivered deeds	Standard Coverage plus defects discoverable through: 1. Property inspection, including unrecorded rights of persons in possession 2. Examination of survey 3. Unrecorded liens not known of by policyholder	1. Defects and liens listed in policy 2. Defects known to buyer 3. Changes in land use brought about by zoning ordinances

SOURCE: *Modern Real Estate Practice,* Galaty, Allaway, and Kyle, 15th Edition, Dearborn™ Real Estate Education, Chicago, 2000.

The coverage of standard and extended coverage policies can be seen in Figure 13.7.

Preliminary Title Report

Prior to the issuance of a policy of title insurance, the issuer issues a **preliminary title report.** This report is designed to provide an interim response to an application for title insurance. It is also intended to facilitate the issuance of a particular type of policy. The preliminary report identifies the title to the estate or interest in the prescribed land. It also contains a list of the defects, liens, encumbrances, and restrictions that would be excluded from coverage if the requested policy were to be issued as of the date of the report.

> The preliminary title report does not provide any insurance.

A licensee often will obtain a copy of the preliminary report in order to discuss the matters set forth in it with his or her clients. Thus, a preliminary report provides the opportunity to seek the removal of items referenced in the report that are unacceptable to the prospective insured. Such arrangements can be made with the assistance of the escrow office.

With respect to preliminary reports, the title industry has been making a concerted effort to improve communications with agents representing sellers and buyers.

The latest forms are distinguished from early versions in that the printed encumbrances and exclusions are set forth verbatim and not incorporated by reference. Consequently, the preliminary report now constitutes a more complete communication of the offer to issue a title insurance policy.

In fact, preliminary reports are just one of the steps in the risk elimination process. Risk elimination includes the maintenance and collection of title records (known as the title plant), the searching and examination of the records, and the underwriting standards of each title insurance company.

Despite this focus on risk elimination, the California title insurance industry has paid out close to $200 million in loss expenses since January 1980. (This amount is just a small fraction of the premiums paid.)

The preliminary report does not necessarily show the condition of the title; it merely reports the current vesting of title and the items the title company will exclude from coverage if the policy should be issued later. The elements of this definition are threefold:

1. A preliminary report is an offer.
2. It is *not* an abstract of title reporting a complete chain of title.
3. It is a statement of the terms and conditions of the offer to issue a title policy.

The title insurer customarily makes a last-minute check to ensure there are no new recordings concerning a property's title before issuing its policy of insurance.

Special Policies

There are a number of **special title insurance policies,** such as construction lender policies and policies for vendees (purchasers under real property sales contracts), policies insuring leasehold interest, even policies for oil and gas interests. There also are special coverage policy amendments that can be purchased.

Policy Interpretation

Title insurance policies are interpreted in accordance with the reasonable expectations of the insured. In the event of ambiguities, they normally would be resolved against the insurer.

Rebate Law

Title insurance companies are precluded by law from providing rebates to brokers for referral of business. They must charge brokers the same as other customers and make a sincere effort to collect any premiums due. The **rebate law** extends to escrows as well as to title insurers. Besides being grounds for disciplinary action, receiving a rebate from a title insurer is considered commercial bribery and could subject a licensee to up to one year in jail and a $10,000 fine for each transaction.

■ SUMMARY

An escrow is a third-party "stakeholder" who receives and disburses documents and funds in a real property transaction. The escrow cannot be completed until all conditions are met. The escrow basically has agency duties to both buyer and seller. There may be duties to a lender as well. The broker is not a party to the escrow, and the escrow agent has no duty to obey instructions of the broker after the escrow instructions have been signed.

A broker can act as an escrow without a license if the broker was a principal to the transaction or represented either the buyer or the seller. Aside from the broker, lender, and attorney exemptions, an escrow must be a corporation and must meet strict licensing requirements.

An escrow is opened with the parties signing escrow instructions. A valid escrow consists of a signed agreement and conditional delivery of transfer documents to the escrow. The delivery is conditioned on the buyer's fully meeting his or her obligations. The broker may supply the information needed by the escrow to prepare instructions by telephone. Once escrow instructions have been signed by both buyer and seller, any change to the instructions requires the signatures of both buyer and seller.

When the escrow disburses funds and records the deed, the escrow is considered to be closed. A closing statement is issued by the escrow showing the debits and credits of the transaction. Rents, taxes, interest, and insurance are likely to be prorated by the escrow. Proration is based on a 30-day month and a 360-day year. After escrow closes, the broker should make certain his or her client fully understands the closing statement.

Escrow companies are liable for their negligence, but they are not liable for failure to warn a party of possible fraud or to point out a detrimental fact or risk of a transaction.

An abstract shows only the recorded history of a property. A title opinion based on an abstract does not reveal defects such as forgery, lack of capacity, unknown spousal interests, and so forth. These and other risks are covered by a standard policy of title insurance, which covers risks of record. Greater coverage for lenders can be obtained with an ALTA extended coverage policy. If buyers want this protection for themselves, they have to buy an extended coverage owners' policy.

The preliminary title report is an offer to insure and does not give the buyer any protection unless a policy of title insurance is purchased. There are special title insurance policies for specific needs.

The rebate law prohibits title insurance carriers and escrows from rebating fees for referrals or otherwise providing special advantages or deals to brokers.

■ CLASS DISCUSSION TOPICS

1. Which offices and developments in your area handle their own escrows? Why?

2. In your area, are escrow instructions separate for buyer and seller or are the instructions a single agreement?

3. What are typical escrow costs for the sale of a $300,000 residence in your area?

4. What does it cost for a standard policy of title insurance for a $300,000 home in your area?

5. What does it cost for a $300,000 extended coverage policy of title insurance for lender protection?

6. What does it cost for a preliminary title report on a $300,000 home sale?

7. How does a preliminary title report differ from a property profile provided by a title insurer?

8. Bring to class one current-events article dealing with some aspect of real estate practice for class discussion.

■ CHAPTER 13 QUIZ

1. A broker can act as an escrow when the broker
   a. represents the buyer in the transaction.
   b. represents the seller in the transaction.
   c. is a principal in the transaction.
   d. is any of the above.

2. An escrow is prohibited from
   a. paying referral fees to anyone other than an employee of the escrow company.
   b. bonding employees.
   c. doing both a and b.
   d. doing neither a nor b.

3. To determine the balance due on a loan, escrow requests a(n)
   a. closing statement.
   b. beneficiary statement.
   c. reconveyance.
   d. impound statement.

4. Which of the following is a debit to the seller on a seller's closing statement?
   a. Selling price
   b. Prepaid insurance
   c. First trust deed to be assumed by buyer
   d. All of the above

5. Which of the following is a credit to the buyer on the buyer's closing statement?
   a. Purchase price
   b. Escrow costs
   c. Title insurance
   d. First trust deed assumed

6. An escrow company has a duty to
   a. warn parties if the escrow knows of possible fraud.
   b. suggest changes when one party is not being adequately protected.
   c. do both a and b.
   d. do neither a nor b.

7. A standard policy of title insurance is used to show that
   a. there are no encumbrances against a property.
   b. the seller has a marketable title.
   c. both a and b are true.
   d. both a and b are false.

8. Which of the following is covered by the CLTA standard policy of title insurance?
   a. Easements not a matter of public record
   b. Rights of a party in possession
   c. Unknown spousal interests
   d. Encroachment

9. Which of the following is *not* covered by an ALTA extended coverage policy of title insurance?
   a. Mining claims
   b. Liens placed by the insured
   c. Water rights
   d. Off-record easements

10. Title insurance companies may
    a. give rebates to brokers for referrals.
    b. give brokers preferential rates on their own purchases.
    c. charge brokers the same as others but make no effort to collect.
    d. do none of the above.

CHAPTER FOURTEEN

14

TAXATION

■ KEY TERMS

acquisition indebtedness
adjusted basis
ad valorem taxes
basis
boot
deferred gain
depreciable basis
depreciation
entity rule
equity indebtedness
excluded gain
Foreign Investment in
  Real Property Tax Act

home improvements
homeowner's exemption
installment sale
investment property rule
like-kind rule
no-choice rule
no-loss rule
original basis
primary personal
  residence
Proposition 13
Proposition 58

Proposition 60
Proposition 90
realized gain
recognized gain
reverse exchange
sale-leaseback
special assessments
supplemental tax bill
tax-deferred exchange
1031 exchange
veteran's exemption

■ LEARNING OBJECTIVES

In this chapter, you learn the basis of real property tax assessments and how real property is assessed, reassessed, and billed. You also learn about available exemptions from taxation and reassessment.

You learn the role depreciation plays in income taxation and how depreciation is calculated; how taxes can be deferred through 1031 exchanges; that exchanges can be delayed transactions; and when a transfer qualifies for a tax-deferred exchange. You learn the benefits of installment sales, as well as sale-leasebacks.

When you have finished this chapter, you will understand the meaning and tax implications of both primary and secondary personal residences and how the cost basis is determined for various forms of acquisition. You will have learned about the tax benefits of home ownership as well as the benefits given by the Taxpayer Relief Act of 1997, a law that lowered capital gains rates and excludes up to $500,000 profit from the sale of a residence from taxation ($250,000 for a single person) if ownership and occupancy requirements are met. You will also learn about the 2003 Tax Relief Act. You will understand buyer responsibility when dealing with a foreign seller regarding both federal and California tax withholding, and you will understand California withholding for California sellers.

■ REAL PROPERTY TAXES

Real property taxes are based on value.

Real property taxes are **ad valorem taxes.** *Ad valorem* is a Latin expression that means "according to value." Real estate tax rates are a percentage of the property's "full cash value." The concept is not new; throughout history, people's wealth has been determined largely by the amount of real property they own. Landowners almost always have been taxed on the basis of their property holdings. Governments favor real estate taxation because it is the one form of taxation that cannot be evaded. If a taxpayer fails to pay taxes, the levying body can foreclose on its tax lien to satisfy the taxpayer's obligations. In the United States, property taxes are deductible on a homeowner's income tax return. However, special assessments for improvements are not a tax-deductible expense.

The levying of real property taxes profoundly affects the real estate market. If taxes are high, potential customers may hesitate to involve themselves with such an expense by purchasing property. On the positive side, revenues from property taxes are a vital source of government income on the local level, enabling local government to provide for the health, education, safety, and welfare of the citizenry.

Real Property Tax Calendar

A basic understanding of real property taxes in California begins with knowing the chronological order for processing real property taxes. This is illustrated in the real property tax calendar in Figure 14.1.

Billing

If taxes are to be paid through a lending agency, the county sends a tax bill to that agency and a copy of it to the owner. The owner's copy states that it is for information only. If the owner is to pay the taxes, the original bill is sent directly to the owner for payment. The tax bill includes special assessments. Unpaid taxes become delinquent, and a penalty is charged even if the taxpayer never received

FIGURE 14.1

Real Property Tax Calendar

January	February	March
Jan. 1: Taxes for the next year become a lien on property.	*Feb. 1:* Second installment of taxes due.	

April	May	June
April 10: Second installment of taxes becomes delinquent at 5:00 P.M. *April 15:* Homeowner's exemption must be filed.		*June 8:* Delinquency list is published. *June 30:* "Book sale" is held. *June 30:* Tax year ends

July	August	September
July 1: Tax year begins.		*Sept. 1:* Tax rates are determined.

October	November	December
	Nov. 1: First installment of taxes due	*Dec. 10:* First installment of taxes becomes delinquent at 5:00 P.M.

Note: If taxes become due on a holiday or weekend, the due date is extended to the next business day.

a notice of taxes due. It is the taxpayer's responsibility to make sure that tax payment deadlines are met.

Figure 14.2 shows a sample tax bill.

Typical California Tax Bill

The contents of a typical California tax bill include

- an identifying parcel number, with reference to the map page and property number or other description;
- a breakdown between land assessments and improvement assessments;
- the full cash value as of March 1, 1975, for property purchased prior to this date or as of the date of a subsequent reassessment event;
- a breakdown of the bonded indebtedness or special assessments; the full amount of the tax; and
- itemized or perhaps separate payment cards with the full tax equally divided into first and second installments.

Supplemental Tax Bill.   A recent homebuyer may come into an agent's office and say, "I paid my property tax, and a month later I received a new assessment for almost the same amount. How much are my taxes on this property?" Before the property is purchased, the agent should explain to buyers that in the first year of ownership, they will receive two or three tax bills: the regular tax bill and one or two **supplemental tax bills.**

The supplemental tax bill covers the difference between the seller's assessed valuation and the new valuation based on the sale price.

Property taxes are billed and paid for the fiscal year of July 1 through June 30. When a buyer purchases a new home, it takes time to notify the tax collector's office of the sale of property and for the tax collector's office to issue the new property tax bill based on the new assessed value. The county assessor is directed to put new values on a supplemental assessment roll from the completion date of construction or the change of ownership date (for example, a sale). If the new value is higher than the current assessed value, a supplemental tax bill is sent to the property owner that reflects the higher valuation for the remainder of the tax year.

■ **EXAMPLE:**   Mr. and Mrs. Newly Boute purchased a home on January 2 of this year for $300,000. Assume no bond issues or assessment other than the basic levy of 1 percent. The new property tax will be $3,000 (1 percent of $300,000). The old assessment on the home was $100,000. Therefore, the property tax on the home was $1,000 for the fiscal year from July 1 of last year to June 30 of this year. So, when the Boutes purchased their home, their tax bill for the second installment of the fiscal year would be $500 (half of $1,000) due February and delinquent April 10, which is the old bill. The Boutes should be paying $1,500 on the new tax bill (half of $3,000). Because they paid $500 on the old bill, they will have to pay a supplemental tax bill of $1,000 ($1,500 – $500). See the chart below.

	FISCAL YEAR	
	July 1 Last Year Jan. 1	This Year June 30
Old Assessed Value $100,000 × .01 = $1,000 Property Tax	$500	$500
New Assessed Value $300,000 × .01 × 5 = $3,000 Property Tax (for only half a year)		$1,500
Difference Assessed Value $200,000 Property Tax		$1,000

FIGURE 14.2

Sample Tax Bill

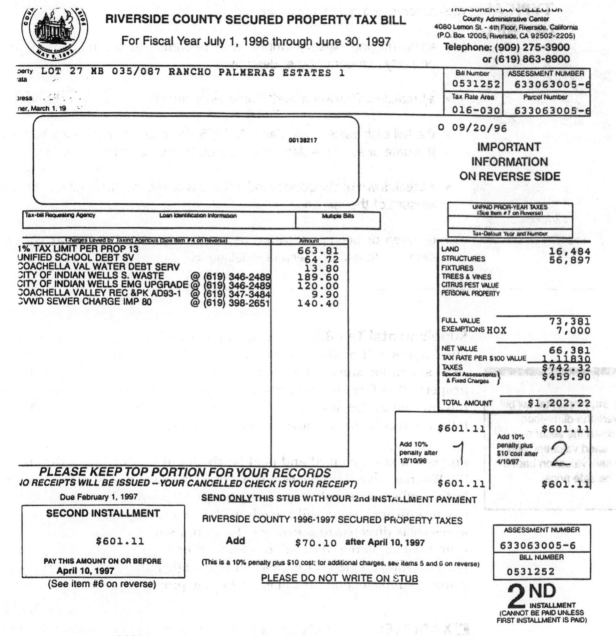

RIVERSIDE COUNTY SECURED PROPERTY TAX BILL

For Fiscal Year July 1, 1996 through June 30, 1997

TREASURER-TAX COLLECTOR
County Administrative Center
4080 Lemon St. - 4th Floor, Riverside, California
(P.O. Box 12005, Riverside, CA 92502-2205)
Telephone: (909) 275-3900
or (619) 863-8900

Property Data   LOT 27 MB 035/087 RANCHO PALMERAS ESTATES 1

Bill Number	ASSESSMENT NUMBER
0531252	633063005-6

Tax Rate Area	Parcel Number
016-030	633063005-6

Owner, March 1, 19

O 09/20/96

IMPORTANT
INFORMATION
ON REVERSE SIDE

00138217

Tax-bill Requesting Agency	Loan Identification Information	Multiple Bills

UNPAID PRIOR-YEAR TAXES
(See Item #7 on Reverse)

Tax-Default Year and Number

(Charges Levied by Taxing Agencies (See Item #4 on Reverse)		Amount
1% TAX LIMIT PER PROP 13		663.81
UNIFIED SCHOOL DEBT SV		64.72
COACHELLA VAL WATER DEBT SERV		13.80
CITY OF INDIAN WELLS S. WASTE	@ (619) 346-2489	189.60
CITY OF INDIAN WELLS EMG UPGRADE	@ (619) 346-2489	120.00
COACHELLA VALLEY REC &PK AD93-1	@ (619) 347-3484	9.90
CVWD SEWER CHARGE IMP 80	@ (619) 398-2651	140.40

LAND	16,484
STRUCTURES	56,897
FIXTURES	
TREES & VINES	
CITRUS PEST VALUE	
PERSONAL PROPERTY	
FULL VALUE	73,381
EXEMPTIONS HOX	7,000
NET VALUE	66,381
TAX RATE PER $100 VALUE	1.11830
TAXES	$742.32
Special Assessments & Fixed Charges	$459.90
TOTAL AMOUNT	$1,202.22

$601.11	$601.11
Add 10% penalty after 12/10/96 1	Add 10% penalty plus $10 cost after 4/10/97 2
$601.11	$601.11

PLEASE KEEP TOP PORTION FOR YOUR RECORDS
(NO RECEIPTS WILL BE ISSUED -- YOUR CANCELLED CHECK IS YOUR RECEIPT)

Due February 1, 1997

SECOND INSTALLMENT

$601.11

PAY THIS AMOUNT ON OR BEFORE
April 10, 1997

(See item #6 on reverse)

SEND **ONLY** THIS STUB WITH YOUR 2nd INSTALLMENT PAYMENT

RIVERSIDE COUNTY 1996-1997 SECURED PROPERTY TAXES

Add   **$70.10** after April 10, 1997

(This is a 10% penalty plus $10 cost; for additional charges, see items 5 and 6 on reverse)

PLEASE DO NOT WRITE ON STUB

ASSESSMENT NUMBER
633063005-6
BILL NUMBER
0531252

2ND
INSTALLMENT
(CANNOT BE PAID UNLESS
FIRST INSTALLMENT IS PAID)

00000060111   0296 0531252 01

0219960531252000000601110410199700000067121240

Due November 1, 1996

SEND **ONLY** THIS STUB WITH YOUR 1st INSTALLMENT PAYMENT

FIRST INSTALLMENT

RIVERSIDE COUNTY 1996-1997 SECURED PROPERTY TAXES

Special Assessments

Cities, counties, and special districts may, by a two-thirds vote of the electors of the district, impose special taxes on such districts. These **special assessments** are levied for specified local improvements such as streets, sewers, irrigation, drainage, flood control, and special lighting. This voter-approved bonded indebtedness varies from county to county and within each county.

Proposition 13

Proposition 13 was enacted in 1978. It states basically that newly acquired real estate or new construction will be assessed according to the fair market value (FMV) and taxed at a maximum tax rate of 1 percent (called the *basic levy*). In addition, the assessed values of properties acquired before 1978 will be reduced to the amount shown on the 1975 tax roll. Because different areas of a county have different bond issues or special assessments for that particular area, additional monies up to 1 percent are added to the basic levy (Proposition 13), causing the tax rate for these areas to range from 1 percent to 2 percent.

■ **EXAMPLE:** Your client, Mr. Bior, purchased a home this year for $300,000. Because of Proposition 13, the property taxes will be $3,000 ($300,000 x .01). Mr. Bior'

s area could have an additional assessment of .5 percent. Therefore, for his particular area, his property taxes could be $4,500 ($300,000 x .015).

Proposition 13 limits annual increases in assessed valuation to 2 percent.

One additional aspect of Proposition 13 is that the tax rate may be increased by up to 2 percent each year, as long as the Consumer Price Index (CPI) is not exceeded. This 2 percent increase in the assessed value represents the maximum amount the county assessor may increase the property's value each fiscal year.

■ **EXAMPLE:** Mr. Bior purchased a home for $300,000 and paid $4,500 ($300,000 x .015) in property taxes the first year. For the second year, the assessed value of the property will be $306,000 ($300,000 x 1.02). Presumably, the tax rate of 1.5 percent remains the same. Thus, Mr. Bior's property tax bill will be $4,590 ($306,000 x .015) for the second year. The property tax bill can be calculated in the same manner for each subsequent year of ownership.

One of the objectives of Proposition 13 is to keep property taxes as low as possible. According to Proposition 13, certain transfers of title (such as a sale) will cause a reassessment of the property, which will increase the property taxes. Transfers between married couples (changing from joint tenancy to community property), creation of revocable living trusts, and cosigners for loan qualification are exempt from reassessment. Thus, these will not increase property taxes.

Proposition 58

Proposition 58 allows transfers without reassessment to a spouse or children.

Proposition 58 provides that transfers of real property between spouses and transfers of the principal residence and the first $1,000,000 of other real property between parent and child are exempt from reassessment. The code defines a *child* as a natural child (any child born of the parents), any stepchild or spouse of that stepchild when the relationship of stepparent and stepchild exists, a son-in-law or daughter-in-law of the parent(s), or a child who was adopted by the age of 18.

(Note that Proposition 193 subsequently extended the exemption from reassessment to persons who inherit property from a grandparent. The grandchild can therefore keep his or her grandparent's assessment for property taxes.)

To receive this exclusion, a claim must be filed with the county assessor. The claim must contain a written certification by the transferee made under penalty of perjury that the transferee is a parent or child of the transferor. This statement must also state whether the property is the transferor's principal residence. If the property is not the transferor's principal residence and the full cash value of the real property transferred (the taxable value on the roll just prior to the date of transfer) exceeds the allowable exclusion ($1,000,000), the eligible transferee must specify the amount and allocation of the exclusion on the claim.

Proposition 60

Proposition 60 allows homeowners over 55 years of age to transfer their assessed valuation to a new residence in the same county.

Proposition 60 provides that qualified homeowners aged 55 or over, as well as taxpayers who are severely and permanently disabled, may transfer the current base-year value of their present principal residence to a replacement (that is, sell their old home and buy a new home), with the following conditions:

■ Both properties must be in the same county.

■ The transferor must be at least 55 years old as of the date of transfer (sale). (If married, only one spouse needs to be at least 55 but must reside in the residence; if co-owners, only one co-owner needs to be at least 55 and must reside in the residence.)

■ The original residence must be eligible for a homeowner's exemption at the time of sale (transfer). However, if the replacement dwelling is acquired first, then the original resident of the replacement dwelling must be qualified for a homeowner's exemption as of the date of the sale. Also, the replacement dwelling must be eligible for the homeowner's exemption after purchase as a result of the claimant's occupancy as his or her principal residence.

■ The replacement property must be purchased or newly constructed on or after November 6, 1986, and within two years of the sale of the original property. This two-year period may be either prior to or after the sale of the old residence.

■ If the replacement dwelling is purchased prior to the sale of the original property, the sales price of the replacement residence must be equal to or less than the value of the original property. If the replacement residence is purchased within the first year after the sale of the original residence, the value of the replacement residence may be 105 percent of that of the original residence. If the replacement residence is purchased within the second year, the replacement sales price may be 110 percent of the original residence's sales price.

■ **EXAMPLE:** The preceding rule can be divided into two cases. In Case I the homeowner buys the new home first, then sells the old home. In Case II the homeowner sells the old home first, then buys the new one.

Case I	Buy new home at price equal to or less than that of old home	Sell old home within 2-year period	

Case II	*After Sale*	*Year 1*	*Year 2*
	On the sale of old home, the 2-year period starts	During year 1 the purchase price can be 1.05 x sales price of old home	During year 2 the purchase price can be 1.10 x sales price of old home

■ **EXAMPLE:** Mr. and Mrs. Oldie purchased their home ten years ago for $50,000; therefore, their base-year assessment is $50,000. He is 58 years old and she is 54 at the time of sale. This year they sold their home for $300,000 and purchased, in the same year (within the first year) and in the same county, a new home for $304,000. The assessment on the new home is based on the old $50,000 assessment, not the new FMV of $304,000.

Proposition 90

Proposition 90 extends Proposition 60 to participating counties.

Proposition 90 is an extension of Proposition 60. Proposition 60 limits the purchase of the new home to the same county. Proposition 90 allows the purchase of the new home in a different county in California. However, the county the homeowner is planning to move into may reject Proposition 90. The only counties that have accepted Proposition 90 are Alameda, Kern, Los Angeles, Modoc, Orange, Santa Clara, San Diego, San Mateo, and Ventura. To qualify, a homeowner must meet all the requirements for Proposition 60.

Change-in-Ownership Statement

Any person acquiring an interest in property subject to local taxation must notify the county recorder or assessor by filing a *change-in-ownership statement* within 45 days of the date of recording or, if the transfer is not recorded, within 45 days of the date of transfer. Failure to do so will result in a penalty.

Exemptions

Some of the numerous properties that are assessed are partially or wholly tax-exempt. For example, many nonprofit charitable organizations, many churches, all government, and several nonprofit educational institutions are entirely exempt. Other relief is available in various forms for homeowners, veterans, senior citizens, and renters.

Homeowner's Exemption. Each residential property that is owner-occupied on the lien date of March 1 receives an annual tax **homeowner's exemption** of $7,000 from the "full cash value." The homeowner needs to apply only once for this homeowner's exemption if from year to year there is no change in the ownership of and residency on the property. A homeowner must have been the

Homeowner exemption is $7,000 in valuation.

FIGURE 14.3

Proposition 60 Examples

	Date of Sale	Market Value	Equal or Lessor Value Factor	Allowable Replacement Dwelling Value
Situation #1 (Replacement acquired after sale)				
Original Property	1/17/92	$100,000	x 1.05 within 1st year	= $105,000
Replacement Property	6/10/92	$106,000		NOT QUALIFIED
Situation #2 (Replacement acquired after sale)				
Original Property	1/17/92	$100,000	x 1.10 within 2nd year	= $110,000
Replacement Property	2/21/93	$106,000		QUALIFIED
Situation #3 (Replacement acquired before sale)				
Original Property	1/17/92	$100,000	x 1.00 prior to	= $100,000
Replacement Property	12/10/91	$106,000		NOT QUALIFIED
Situation #4 (Replacement acquired before sale)				
Original Property	1/17/92	$100,000	x 1.00 prior to	= $100,000
Replacement Property	12/15/91	$98,500		QUALIFIED

owner of record on or before March 1 and actually have occupied the property to claim this exemption for the upcoming tax year beginning July 1. A homeowner is allowed only one exemption at a time. Once this exemption has been filed, it remains in effect until terminated. The assessor must be notified of a termination, or an assessment plus 25 percent penalty may be made.

Veteran's Exemption.   California's war veterans may receive a $4,000 **veteran's exemption** on the full cash value of their homes. Because a person cannot take both the homeowner's and the veteran's exemptions, a person would not apply for the basic veteran's exemption if he or she were eligible for the higher homeowner's exemption. A totally disabled veteran may be eligible for an exemption of the first $100,000 of the value of his or her residence.

Senior Citizen's Property Tax Postponement.   Another form of relief is *senior citizen's property tax postponement.* A homeowner who is at least 62 years old as of January 1 may be eligible to have the State of California pay all or part of the real property tax on his or her home. Persons of any age who are blind or totally disabled and meet the income requirement are also eligible. The taxes are postponed and are not repaid until the property is sold or the claimant no longer occupies the property.

■ INCOME TAXES

Today, income taxes play an important role in real estate owners' decisions, from buying or selling their personal residences to decisions involving the most exotic real investment properties. Because the tax laws are always changing, it is important for the real estate agent to stay abreast of them. Some basic tax definitions and calculations stay the same from law change to law change. We will discuss income taxes as they relate to business and investment property as well as to a personal residence.

Capital Gains

Before the 1997 Tax Act, capital gains were taxed at a 28 percent maximum tax rate if the capital assets were held more than one year. The 1997 Tax Act reduced the rate to 20% for long term capital gains.

The 2003 Tax Relief Act has cut the long-term capital gains to a maximum of 15 percent for gains from the sale of assets held for more than 12 months. (Gains from the sale of assets held for one year or less are taxed as regular income.)

For taxpayers in the 10 percent and 15 percent tax brackets, the long-term gain was cut to 5 percent. In 2008, the long-term capital gains tax for these lower income brackets will be zero.

Business and Investment Property

Property held for business and investment has some distinct differences in federal income tax treatment from property used as a personal residence. We will begin with the concept of depreciation.

Depreciation

The two most obvious and important characteristics of real estate investments are income and expenses. Real estate is one of those assets that benefit from a special accounting device for a special kind of expense called **depreciation.**

Depreciation is a method of accounting for the wear that results from the use of a capital good. A capital good, such as a piece of equipment or a building, does not last forever. As it is used, it wears out or becomes obsolete; at some point, the owner must replace it or substantially repair it. Depreciation is used to reflect this replacement cost. The main reasons depreciation is allowed are to encourage investment in real estate and to reflect, in accounting terms, the real costs of property ownership. Only investment or income property may benefit from depreciation. (Today we use a *recovery system* instead of *depreciation*, but the word depreciation has been around for so long that it is still used.)

For depreciation purposes real estate can be divided into two categories:

1. Residential property
2. Nonresidential property

Residential property is where people live—for example, single-family residences, duplexes, triplexes, fourplexes, and multiunit apartments. Nonresidential property is property that is not residential in nature—for example, industrial, commercial, office buildings, and other similar types of properties. Since January 1, 1987, all real property must use the straight-line method of depreciation where the value of the property is depreciated in equal annual amounts over the depreciable life of the property.

Generally, residential rental property must use a useful life of 27.5 years and nonresidential property must use a useful life of 39 years. Either residential or nonresidential property may elect to use 40 years.

> The depreciation period is 27.5 years for residential property and 39 years for nonresidential property.

Basis

To explore the tax implications of investment properties, the agent must understand the concept of **basis** and know how to compute the original basis, depreciable basis, and adjusted basis correctly. The *original basis* (OB) is used to determine the depreciable basis and adjusted basis. The *depreciable basis* (DB) is used to determine the amount of allowable depreciation. The *adjusted basis* (AB), which changes as time progresses, is required to calculate the gain on the disposition of a property.

Original Basis.   The **original basis** of a property is the sum of its purchase price and the buying expenses on acquisition. When a client purchases a property, the escrow statement includes the sale price and a listing of other costs and expenses. These amounts can be classified into four basic groups:

1. Purchase price (PP)
2. Operating expenses (OE)
3. Buying expenses (BE) (nonrecurring closing costs)
4. Nondeductible items (ND) such as impound accounts

The Purchase Price.   The *purchase price* (PP) is the amount the buyer is willing to pay and the seller is willing to accept in payment for the property. On the escrow statement, the PP usually is on the top line and is called *total consideration*. Generally, the PP is financed in some manner. These loans do not affect the basis. Furthermore, if the buyer takes out a new loan, refinances, or takes out a second mortgage, these loans also do not increase the basis.

Operating Expenses. *Operating expenses* (usually recurring costs such as interest, insurance, and taxes) are written off against the income produced by the property. *Points* (loan origination fees) are nonrecurring interest costs that are amortized over the life of the loan; they are not operating expenses.

> Original basis is purchase price plus buying expenses.

Buying Expenses. *Buying expenses* are defined as *nonrecurring escrow costs* (excluding points to obtain a loan). The buying expenses are added to the purchase price, making up the original basis. Points are never added to the basis.

Original basis = Purchase price + Buying expenses

Depreciable Basis. The **depreciable basis** is defined as the original basis multiplied by the percentage of improvements to land.

Depreciable basis = Original basis × Percentage of improvements to land

An alternative formula is

Depreciable basis = Original basis − Land value

Investment real estate is composed of two items, the land and the structure; only the structure can be depreciated. Because land is not depreciable, its value must be subtracted from the total original basis to arrive at the depreciable basis, the improvements. Three methods for determining the percentage of improvements are the assessed value method, the appraisal method and the contract method.

Assessed Value Method. The county assessor's property tax statement now lists the full cash value of the land and the improvements. The value of the improvements for depreciation purposes is thus the assessor's determination of the part of the purchase price that represents the value of the improvements.

■ **EXAMPLE:** Lilli Depre purchased a property for $100,000 and received the following tax bill from the county assessor's office:

Assessed Value:	
Land	$30,000
Improvements	$70,000
Total	$100,000

The improvements give Depre a depreciable basis of 70 percent of her purchase price plus buying expenses.

Appraisal Method. The property owner may secure the services of a professional appraiser to appraise the building and land. The appraisal method may give either a more or a less favorable ratio than the assessed value method. The taxpayer should compare the ratios from the two methods to verify which is more advantageous.

Contract Method. One other method of determining the percentage of improvements is the contract method. With this method the buyer and the seller determine the relative values of the improvements and land and designate these values in the contract, deposit receipt or escrow instructions. Note that the determination must be at arm's length and reasonable. Before using this method, we strongly suggest that the agent obtain professional help.

Adjusted Basis.   The **adjusted basis** of a property is the amount that the client has invested in the property for tax purposes. In other words, the adjusted basis is equal to original basis, plus improvements made, less all depreciation taken.

Adjusted basis = Original basis + Improvements – Depreciation

It is extremely important that the homeowner or investor understand the relationship between the basis and the final sales price of the property, because basis is the beginning point for calculating the amount of gain or loss on the sale. Calculation of the basis is affected by how the property originally was acquired.

- *Basis by purchase* is the price paid for the property, as described above.

- *Basis by gift* is the donor's (gift giver's) adjusted basis plus the gift tax paid, not to exceed the fair market value at the time of the gift.

- *Basis by inheritance* generally is the fair market value at the time of the owner's death.

Computing Gain.   The basis is the beginning point for computing the gain or loss on the sale, but numerous adjustments to the basis always are made during the ownership period. Some of the costs that increase the basis are title insurance, appraisal fees, legal fees, cost of capital improvements, and sales costs on disposition. Accrued (past) depreciation is deducted from the basis. The result is the adjusted basis.

The gain (or loss) is the difference between the adjusted basis and the sales price. An example may clarify this.

$80,000	Purchase Price
+ 800	Buying expenses
+ 3,000	Capital improvements
$83,800	
– 12,500	Accumulated depreciation
$71,300	Adjusted cost basis
$100,000	Sales price
– 4,000	Sales cost
– 71,300	Adjusted cost basis
$24,700	Total gain

Computing Depreciation

To compute the depreciation, follow these six steps:

1. Compute the original basis.

2. Determine allocation between land and building.

3. Compute the depreciable basis.

4. Determine whether the property is residential or nonresidential. If residential, you must use the 27.5-year table for residential property. If nonresidential, you must use the 39-year table.

5. Find the month the property was placed into service, go to the year you want to depreciate, and find the appropriate percentage.

6. Compute the depreciation by multiplying the depreciable basis by the appropriate percentage. (See Figure 14.4.)

■ **EXAMPLE:** Mr. Gratia purchased a ten-unit apartment building on July 8 this year. He paid $800,000 plus nonrecurring closing costs of $10,000. The land is valued at $300,000. He would like to know his depreciation this year.

1. Compute the original basis.
   Purchase price + costs (nonrecurring)
   Original basis = $800,000 + $10,000 = $810,000
2. Determine allocation between land and building.
   Land value is given at $300,000.
3. Compute the depreciable basis.
   Depreciable basis = Original basis less land value
   Depreciable basis = $810,000 – $300,000 = $510,000
4. Determine the type of property.
   Apartments are residential, so use the 27.5-year table to determine the appropriate percentage.
5. Find the month the property was put into service.
   This property was put into service in July. Go to column 7 and the first year (row 1) to find the percentage figure of 1.67 percent (0.0167).
6. Multiply the percentage found in step 5 by the depreciable basis found in step 3.
   Depreciation = depreciable basis × %.
   Depreciation = $510,000 × 0.0167 = $8,517.

Capital Gains Due to Depreciation

The capital gains tax rate for gains attributable to depreciation is 25 percent. As an example:

Property cost	$300,000
Depreciation taken	– 100,000
Adjusted Cost basis	$200,000

If the property were sold at $500,000, there would be a $300,000 gain. $200,000 of the gain would be taxed at the 15 percent rate but the $100,000 of the gain that is attributable to the depreciation that was taken would be taxed at the 25 percent rate.

FIGURE 14.4

Depreciation of Real Property

—General Depreciation System					Method: Straight Line				Recovery period: 27.5 years		
The month in the 1st recovery year the property is placed in service:											
Year	1	2	3	4	5	6	7	8	9	10	11	12
1	3.485%	3.182%	2.879%	2.576%	2.273%	1.970%	1.667%	1.364%	1.061%	0.758%	0.455%	0.152%
2–8	3.636%	3.636%	3.636%	3.636%	3.636%	3.636%	3.636%	3.636%	3.636%	3.636%	3.636%	3.636%

—General Depreciation System					Method: Straight Line				Recovery period: 39 years		
The month in the 1st recovery year the property is placed in service:											
1	2.461%	2.247%	2.033%	1.819%	1.605%	1.391%	1.177%	0.963%	0.749%	0.535%	0.321%	0.107%
2–39	2.564%	2.564%	2.564%	2.564%	2.564%	2.564%	2.564%	2.564%	2.564%	2.564%	2.564%	2.564%

1031 Exchanges

The **1031 exchange** is part of federal tax law—Internal Revenue Code Section 1031 (the State of California has a similar code section). Section 1031 allows for exchange of personal property as well. Many of the concepts for 1031 tax-deferred exchanges come from court cases and IRS regulations and revenue rulings as well as from Section 1031.

With the appreciation of property, many property owners do not want to sell and be required to pay the high taxes. An exchange allows the owner to save on taxes and thus have more money to invest in a new property. Because of refinancing, many owners are in a position where their equity is not sufficient to cover their tax liability. An exchange allows them to defer tax liability.

■ **EXAMPLE:** Ms. Overtaxed owns a ten-unit apartment house she wants to dispose of and plans to buy a 20-unit apartment building. Overtaxed ten-unit would sell for $600,000, with selling costs of $25,000 and an adjusted basis of $275,000. Her taxable gain would be

Sales price	$600,000
Selling costs	– 25,000
Net sales price	$575,000
Adjusted basis	– 275,000
Taxable gain	$300,000

If she sells the property, she will have to pay federal and state taxes on the gain. She would be taxed at the 15 percent capital gains rate as well as having California state tax liability on the gain. These taxes will have to be paid out of the proceeds from the sale. If she exchanged rather than sold, she would have her entire equity to invest in the new property and could defer any tax liability.

When a client becomes involved in a 1031 exchange, two questions must be answered:

1. Does the transaction qualify for a 1031 exchange?
2. What are the mathematics of the exchange?

- How are equities balanced?
- Who is giving or receiving boot?
- Is the exchange partially or totally tax-deferred, and what is the basis in the new property?

This section discusses the transactions that qualify for a 1031 **tax-deferred exchange.**

Who Prepares an Exchange?   Most agents think of *A* exchanging with *B*. While this is essentially what happens, more often three parties are involved. The most widely used exchange is the *buy-sell exchange*, sometimes called a *three-corner exchange* or *three-legged exchange*. The three people involved are the exchanger (person wanting to exchange), the seller (a person who wants to sell property and doesn't want to retain any property), and the buyer (a person who wants property of the exchanger).

The exchange may be structured in two different ways. The buyer offers to buy the exchanger's property, but the buyer does not have any property to exchange. So the exchanger needs to find another property ("up-leg"), the property he or she wants to acquire. When the exchanger finds the up-leg, the buyer buys this property from the seller. Now the buyer has a property to exchange with the exchanger. Note that if the exchanger sold his or her property to the buyer and then bought the seller's property, this transaction would be a purchase and a sale. To satisfy the IRS, the buyer will buy the seller's property and exchange with the exchanger, and this is all done in escrow in a matter of minutes. A general rule of exchanging is that any person can be the center (hub) of the exchange *except* the person wanting the exchange. Sometimes this procedure is called the *flashing of mirrors*.

■ **EXAMPLE:**   Here is an example of improper escrow instructions. *E* wants to complete a 1031 tax-deferred exchange, and *S* and *B* agree to cooperate in completing the exchange. *E* will transfer his property to *B*, and *S* will transfer his property to *E* to complete the exchange. Here is the diagram for this transaction.

$$S \quad \rightarrow \quad E \quad \rightarrow \quad B$$

E is the hub of the exchange; hence, the exchange is invalid. If the *escrow instructions* were to read "*S* will transfer his property to *B*, *B* will transfer *S*'s property to *E*, and *E* will transfer his property to *B*," then the following diagram would apply:

$$E \quad \overset{\leftarrow}{\underset{\rightarrow}{}} \quad B \quad \leftarrow \quad S$$

The latter would be a valid exchange.

When a client wants a 1031 tax-deferred listing, a statement that the client wants to make a 1031 tax-deferred exchange should be on the listing and in the multiple-listing service. This statement helps convince the IRS that the client intends to make a 1031 exchange from the beginning of the transaction.

The Buy-Up Rule.   With the *buy-up rule*, to qualify for a totally tax-deferred exchange, the exchanger needs to trade up in value and put all of his or her equity dollars into the new property(ies).

Trade up means the new property must be equal to or greater in value than the old property. If the exchanger withdraws any cash, the cash withdrawn will be taxable. Withdrawing cash will not disallow the exchange—an exchange may be partial—but the client will not have a totally tax-deferred exchange.

■   **EXAMPLE:**   *E* wants to complete a 1031 tax-deferred exchange. The FMV of his property is $350,000; therefore, the property he is trading for must be valued at $350,000 or more. If *E* nets $150,000 and pulls out $50,000, he will pay taxes on $50,000; only the $100,000 he put into the new property will be deferred.

The Entity Rule.   Three basic entities can hold property: individuals, partnerships, and corporations. The **entity rule** can be stated as follows: The way the exchanger holds property going into an exchange is the way the exchanger must hold the property coming out of the exchange.

Although Section 1031 does not address the entity rule, the courts have addressed it. The question that is raised is whether the exchange is a "step transaction."

■   **EXAMPLE:**   Partnership *XY* owns a building. Partner *X* is not getting along with partner *Y*, so they decide to dissolve the partnership. They exchange the building in the partnership for two other buildings, which they take in their own names as individuals. The question that will be asked is: "Would they exchange the building for the two smaller buildings if they weren't going to dissolve the partnership?" The answer is no. Thus a step transaction has taken place. *X* and *Y* would not have made the exchange without the step of dissolving the partnership. In this example the partnership did not end up with the two buildings; each partner ended up with a separate building. So this transaction went from a partnership to two individuals. Therefore the entity rule was violated. The exchanging of one building by the partnership for two buildings is a valid exchange as long as it is not a step transaction.

The Investment Property Rule.   The **investment property rule** comes from Internal Revenue Code (IRC) Section 1031(a)(1):

> In General—no gain or loss shall be recognized on the exchange of property held for productive use in a trade or business or for investment if such property is exchanged solely for property of like kind which is to be held either for productive use in a trade or business or for investment.

Note: A personal residence is not held for productive use in a trade or business or for investment. Therefore, a person cannot have a tax-deferred exchange of his or her personal residence for business or investment property. (Like-kind property is discussed later in the chapter.)

There are exceptions to the above rule, listed in IRC Section 1031(a)(2):

Exception—This subsection shall not apply to any exchange of—

(A) stock in trade or other property held primarily for sale,

(B) stocks, bonds, or notes,

(C) other securities or evidences of indebtedness or interest,

(D) interests in a partnership,

(E) certificates of trust or beneficial interests, or

(F) contractual rights.

It is clear from subsection A that inventory (stock in trade or property held for sale) cannot be exchanged. Therefore, the questions are: "What is inventory, and what is investment?" These questions are a constant bone of contention between taxpayers and the IRS. Taxpayers would like to call all of their property *investments*. The IRS has a vested interest in classifying property as *inventory*. In some cases, there is no clear-cut answer. If a person makes a considerable portion of his or her income from buying and selling property, the IRS could likely consider that person a dealer and property exchanged as being inventory.

The answer to what is investment and what is inventory is determined by the taxpayer's *intent and actions*. For example, collecting rents and taking depreciation on a property over two years to three years show the intent and actions of investing. On the other hand, if a taxpayer built a fourplex and the day after it was finished he exchanged the fourplex, the IRS and the courts would consider it inventory. An asset built is considered inventory when it has not been held for two years to three years to show the intent of investing. The following example is another illustration.

■   **EXAMPLE:**   Ms. Able and Mr. Flake have buildings that are held for investment. Mr. Flake knows that Mr. Bucks would like to acquire Ms. Able's property. So, Mr. Flake and Ms. Able exchange, and Mr. Flake then sells Ms. Able's property to Mr. Bucks. The results: Ms. Able's exchange is valid; Mr. Flake's exchange does not qualify, because his intent and actions clearly show that the property was not an investment but was purchased for resale (inventory).

Definitive cases: *Regals Realty Co. v. Comm.* 127 F.2d 931 (1942) and *Griffen v. Comm.* 49 T.C. 253 (1967).

Note: In the example above one person in a transaction can have a qualified exchange and the other person be disallowed the exchange.

Like-Kind Rule.   Exchanges of property must observe the **like-kind rule.** In exchanging, property is categorized as either *personal* or *real* property. Personal property and real property are not like kind.

For personal property, like-kind property must be exactly the same in character or have the same nature, and this sometimes is very difficult to determine.

> No gain or loss is recognized if (1) a taxpayer exchanges property held for productive use in his trade or business, together with cash, for other property of like kind for the same use, such as an automobile to be used for a like purpose. [Reg. 1.1031(1)-1(c)-(1).]

For real property, like-kind property is simply any piece of real property exchanged for any other piece of real property.

> As used in section 1032(a), the words "like kind" have reference to the nature or character of the property and not to its grade or quality. One kind or class of property may not, under that section, be exchanged for property of a different kind or class. The fact that any real estate involved is improved or unimproved is not material, for that fact related only to the grade or quality of the property and not its kind or class. Unproductive real estate held by one other than a dealer for future use or future realization of the increment in value is held for investment and not primarily for sale. [Reg. 1.1031(1)-1(b).]

> . . . [A] taxpayer, who is not a dealer in real estate, exchanges city real estate for a ranch or farm, or exchanges a leasehold fee with 30 years or more to run for real estate, or exchanges improved real estate for unimproved real estate; or (3) a taxpayer exchanges investment property and cash for investment property of a like kind. [Reg. 1.1031(a)-1(c)-(2), (3).]

What is Real Property?

Real property includes

- vacant land (unimproved real estate);
- improved real estate, such as farms, buildings, orchards, and so on;
- leases that have a remaining term at the time of the exchange of 30 years or more (the 30 years may include all options); and
- mineral and water rights (if they are considered real property by the state, they are included): *Critchton* 122 F.2d 181 (1941), Rules, 55-749 and 68-3331.

Therefore, the general rule for real property is that any piece of real property may be exchanged for any other piece of real property, *except* for inventory and personal residences.

The No-Choice Rule.   If an exchange qualifies as an exchange, it must be treated as an exchange. If the real estate transaction was structured as an exchange, the gain must be deferred (postponed). The **no-choice rule** can be stated simply: An exchanger who qualifies for a 1031 tax-deferred exchange has no choice; the exchanger *cannot* recognize the gain or loss.

The No-Loss Rule.   In conjunction with the no-choice rule is a rule called the no-loss rule. If a real estate transaction qualifies as an exchange, a loss cannot be recognized. Losses must be deferred along with gains. The no-loss rule comes from IRC Section 1031(a)(1):

> In general—no gain or loss shall be recognized on the exchange of property held for productive use in a trade or business or for investment if such property is exchanged solely for property of like kind which is to be held either for productive use in a trade or business or for investment. No loss can be recognized if the transaction is a tax-deferred exchange.

Money Control.   At no time can the exchanger have control of the buyer's money. This point was emphasized by the *June P. Carlton* case. Carlton owned ranch land and wished to structure a 1031 exchange. The agreement was to sell property to General Development Corporation (GDC) if a suitable replacement property (up-leg) could be found. Two suitable parcels of land were found by Carlton: those of Lyons and Fernandez (sellers). Carlton gave an option to GDC, and GDC advanced $50,000 to Carlton. Carlton thought that this would be a 1031 exchange.

> To be a valid 1031 exchange, the exchanger cannot have control of the buyer's money.

The IRS argued, and the court agreed, that Carlton had sold the ranch land to General Development Corporation. Because Carlton had received $50,000 in her hands, the $50,000 did not go directly to the sellers, Lyons and Fernandez. One of the essences of an exchange is the transferring of property, and the mark of a sale is the receipt of cash. This case points out the extreme importance of proper procedure: The exchanger can never receive cash or even the right to cash. *June P. Carlton v. Comm.* 385 F.2d 238 (5th Cir., 1967).

Delayed Exchange.   IRC Section 1031(a)(3) allows a delayed exchange with the following characteristics:

> REQUIREMENT THAT PROPERTY BE IDENTIFIED WITHIN 45 DAYS AND THAT EXCHANGE BE COMPLETED NOT MORE THAN 180 DAYS AFTER TRANSFER OF EXCHANGED PROPERTY—For purposes of this subsection, any property received by the taxpayer shall be treated as property which is not like-kind property if—
> (A) such property is not identified as property to be received in the exchange on or before the day which is 45 days after the date on which the taxpayer transfers the property relinquished in the exchange, or
> (B) such property is received after the earlier of—
> (i) the day which is 180 days after the date on which the taxpayer transfers the property relinquished in the exchange, or
> (ii) the due date (determined with regard to extension) for the transferor's return of the tax imposed by this chapter for the taxable year in which the transfer of the relinquished property occurs.

> For a deferred exchange, the property must be identified within 45 days and the exchange completed within 180 days of transfer of the exchanged property.

The ramifications of the exchange rule can be illustrated with the following diagram:

45 days to designate   →   180 days to close   →   April 15–August 15
potential property   escrow on new   File an extension
                              property

Reverse Exchange. In a **reverse exchange** the replacement property is acquired prior to the property owner giving up his or her property. An exchange accommodation titleholder takes title to the property the exchanger wishes to acquire and holds the title until the sale of the exchange property can be arranged. This type of exchange removes the problem of acquiring property within a pre-scribed time period of the delayed exchange. However, the sale must be within 180 days.

For information on reverse exchange as well as other forms of exchanges, you may want to contact the Federation of Exchange Accommodators at fea1031@earthlink.net. Their Web site is *www.1031.org*.

Exchange Analysis. To analyze an exchange, the following computations need to be made:

1. Compute the realized (indicated) gain. This is the potential tax gain. It is found by subtracting the exchanging costs and adjusted basis from the FMV.
2. Balance the equities. This is found by subtracting the loan amount from the FMV for each property and then determining who will pay whom boot (cash boot).
3. Determine the recognized gain. This is the gain that will be taxed.
4. Determine the new depreciable basis. This is the amount less the land value and the amount that will be depreciated.

Boot. Property that is not like kind and does not qualify for an exchange is called **boot.** In many exchanges some property will be given in an exchange that is boot. Boot is taxable to the person receiving it. It is important to understand that the property needs to qualify as like kind only to the person seeking the tax-deferred exchange.

| Boot is cash received, unlike property or debt relief. | Boot may be classified as cash boot or mortgage boot. *Cash boot* is a result of the balancing of equities, which must be done in every exchange. It is defined as all other unlike properties: cash, paper (trust deeds or notes), and personal properties (cars, boats, planes, paintings, jewels, etc.). *Mortgage boot* is the difference between the loans on the conveyed property and the loans on the acquired property. This is also called *debt relief*. If the client assumes a mortgage larger than the one that he or she conveys, then he or she has *paid* mortgage boot. However, if he or she assumes a mortgage that is less than the one that he or she conveys, then he or she has *received* mortgage boot (debt relief). |

■ **EXAMPLE:**   Ms. Trade wants an exchange. Mr. Bior wants to buy Ms. Trade's property, and Ms. Sailor wants to sell her own property. Ms. Trade provides the following information:

Mr. Trade's property:

FMV	$500,000
Adjusted basis	250,000
Total loans	350,000
Exchanging costs	50,000
Has enough cash to balance equities.	

Mr. Sailor's property:

FMV	800,000
Total loans	$550,000

Mr. Bior:

   Has enough cash for the down payment.

Balance equities:

	Mr. Trade's Property	Mr. Sailor's Property
FMV	$500,000	$800,000
Loans	– 350,000	– 550,000
Equity	$150,000	$250,000

To balance the equities in this transaction, Mr. Trade is going to have to pay Mr. Sailor $100,000 ($250,000 – $150,000).

Installment Sales

Because of the inflationary appreciation of real property, owners who purchased property in past years may hesitate to sell now because the increased value of their property makes them subject to significant taxes. If they paid their income tax on the full gain on the sale in one year, their tax could be so large that it could discourage investments in real estate.

By using an **installment sale,** the investor can spread the tax gain over two or more years. The following guidelines concern the use of the installment method of reporting deferred-payment sales:

> In an installment sale the gain is taxed in the year it is received.

- The total tax to be paid in any one year may be reduced by spreading the payment amount, and thus the gain, over two or more tax years.

- The seller pays tax in future years with cheaper, inflated dollars.

- The seller does not pay the entire tax until after receiving the entire amount of the purchase price. A provision of the prior law stating that no more than 30 percent of the sales could be received in the taxable year of the sale to qualify for installment sales treatment has been eliminated.

- The installment sales method is automatic unless the taxpayer elects not to have the installment sale treatment apply.

- Mortgage over basis will be considered a payment in the year of sale.

- Because higher income is taxed at higher rates (progressive tax), spreading the gain over a number of years could mean that the gain would be taxed at a lower rate.

Sale-Leaseback

Buyers and sellers can derive tax advantages through an arrangement in which property is sold with provisions for the seller to continue occupancy as a lessee. This form of transaction is called a **sale-leaseback,** *purchase-lease, sale-lease, lease-purchase, or leaseback*.

> In a sale-leaseback the seller benefits from capital being freed and rent that is a fully tax-deductible expense.

With a sale-leaseback, seller/lessees gain the advantages of getting property exactly suited to their needs without tying up working capital in fixed assets. Often more capital can be raised than by borrowing. In addition, because leases are not considered long-term liabilities, rent is totally tax-deductible. Frequently, writing off total lease payments is better than depreciation, for the land portion of property cannot be depreciated. If a property has a significant mortgage, a sale-leaseback would remove debt from a balance sheet, which would give a positive impression on lenders and purchasers of the corporate stock.

Often only the land is sold and leased back because rent on land is a deductible expense, and improvements can be written off with depreciation deductions.

For companies working under government contracts that pay cost plus a fixed fee, rent is an allowable expense item, but mortgage interest is not. This is why many aircraft, electronics, and other defense plants are leased rather than owned.

Buyer/lessors gain the advantage of obtaining a long-term carefree investment and appreciation in the value of the property. Usually the yield on a sale-leaseback is higher than on a mortgage.

The lease payments will pay off the original investment, and the lessor still will have title to the property. The investment will not be paid off prematurely (as mortgages often are through refinancing), so the investor will not have to go out seeking another good investment to replace the one prematurely paid off. In addition, the lease terms often give the lessor a claim against other assets of the lease in the event of a default, which is better security protection than a trust deed affords. Finally, a transaction usually involves a large amount of money. It costs the investor no more to service one large loan than it costs to service small mortgages.

Principal Residence

Real estate that constitutes a homeowner's *personal residence* receives special tax treatment. The term *personal residence* is generally understood to refer to the taxpayer's **primary personal residence,** the dwelling in which a taxpayer lives and which the taxpayer occupies most of the time. A taxpayer may have only one principal residence at a time, and it may be a

- single-family house,
- houseboat,
- mobile home,
- motor home,
- trailer,

- condominium, or

- cooperative housing.

If you live in one unit of a multiple dwelling, that unit will be considered your principal residence.

Primary or Secondary Residence.   The taxpayer's primary residence is the place occupied more often than any other. All other residences are termed *secondary residences*. One secondary residence will receive favorable income tax treatment, but unlike a primary residence, a secondary residence does not qualify for universal exclusion treatment.

Land.   The term *residence* includes not only the improvements but also the land [Rev. Rul. 56 420, 1956 2 (CD 519)]. However, vacant land cannot be considered a personal residence. When a principal residence is located on a large tract of land, the question arises as to just how much of the land is included with the principal residence. There is no clear-cut answer to this question, but the courts have made the determination based on the use and the intent of the taxpayer rather than on the amount of land involved.

Universal Exclusion for Gain on Sale of Principal Residence.   A seller of any age who has owned and used the home as a principal residence for at least two years of the five years before the sale can exclude from income up to $250,000 of gain ($500,000 for joint filers meeting conditions). In general, the exclusion can only be used once every two years. More specifically, the exclusion does not apply to a home sale if, within the two-year period ending on the sale date, there was another home sale by the taxpayer to which the exclusion applied.

> The universal exclusion requires two years' occupancy and can be taken every two years.

Married couples filing jointly in the year of sale may exclude up to $500,000 of home-sale gain if either spouse owned the home for at least two of the five years before the sale. Both spouses must have used the home as a principal residence for at least two of the five years before the sale.

One spouse's inability to use the exclusion because of the once-every-two-years rule won't disqualify the other spouse from claiming the exclusion. However, the other spouse's exclusion cannot exceed $250,000.

- **EXAMPLE:**   I. M. Rich sells her principal residence in December 1999 at a $100,000 gain. She is single at that time, and qualifies for and claims the home sale exclusion. She marries Able in May 2000 and moves into the home that has been his principal residence for the 20 years of his bachelorhood. If Able sells the home the following July, up to $250,000 of his profit is tax-free.

The two-year occupancy need not be continuous. For example, a person could have occupied the property as a principal residence for 6 months and then rented it for a year but later moved back for an 18-month occupancy. If the total occupancy is 24 months during a five-year period, then the occupancy requirement will have been fully met.

California has adopted the federal universal exclusion of $250,000/$500,000. If a sale gain meets the federal criteria for exclusion, it would also be excluded from California income taxation.

Acquiring a Home

A taxpayer may acquire a home by purchasing one from the current owner, by building his or her own home, by inheriting a home, or by receiving one as a gift. Each of these has its own tax implications.

Buying.   Usually the purchaser of a home will pay from 1 percent to 2 percent of the purchase price of the home in buying costs. These costs are found on the escrow closing settlement statement (Figure 14.5) and may be classified as

- write-off itemized deductions,
- buying expenses added to basis, or
- nondeductible expenses.

Itemized deductions include real property taxes, mortgage interest, and points (loan origination fees) in the year paid. These are written off on the taxpayer's Schedule A.

Buying expenses are usually the nonrecurring closing costs. Some examples are appraisal fees, credit report, escrow fees, termite inspection, notary fees, recording fees, and title insurance.

Nondeductible items are the closing costs that are neither a write-off nor a buying expense. These include impound accounts, homeowner's insurance, and certain origination fees paid to obtain FHA or VA loans. Loan-origination fees on FHA or VA loans do not qualify as interest; they are considered to be a form of service charge (Rev. Rul. 67297; Rev. Rul. 6865).

Original Basis.   Of particular interest to the buyer of a home is the original basis (OB)—purchase price plus allowable costs—of the residence. Someday the homeowner will want to dispose of the home, and the higher the basis, the lower the gain, resulting in lower taxes. As previously mentioned, the OB is equal to the purchase price (PP) plus the buying expenses (BE):

$$OB = PP + BE$$
Original basis = Purchase price + Buying expenses

Building.   For taxpayers who build their own home, basis would be the total cost of building the home. This would include cost of the land, legal fees, permits, architectural fees, materials, and so forth. The taxpayer would not include the value of his or her own labor if no compensation were actually paid for the labor.

- **EXAMPLE:** Five years ago Ms. Doit decided to build her own personal residence, and she purchased the land for $20,000. This year she paid $3,000 for permits and plans. Materials cost her $77,000. Doit's basis in her new home is the total of these expenses, or $100,000.

FIGURE 14.5

Escrow Closing Settlement Statement

Escrow Item	Amount
Deductions:	
Taxes	$100
Interest	250
Points, conventional loan	620
Total Deductions	**$970**
Buying Expenses:	
Recording of trust deed	$3
Appraisal fee	75
Escrow fee	197
Handling of beneficiary papers	50
Total Buying Expenses	**$325**
Calculation of Original Basis:	
Purchase price	$85,000
Buying expenses	325
Total	**$85,325**

Inheriting.   For the taxpayer who inherits a home, the basis would be the FMV at the time of the decedent's death. This is called the *stepped-up basis*. An alternative valuation date also can be used; it is beyond the scope of this text, but the agent should be aware that the method exists.

■ **EXAMPLE:**   Mr. Passaway died and left his home to his son. His basis in the home was $10,000, but at the time of death it had a fair market value of $150,000. The son's basis in the home is $150,000.

Tax Benefits

Taxpayers are eligible for certain income tax write-offs while they own their homes. The general rule for income tax purposes is that ownership transfers when the title is transferred (a deed given) or when the buyer is given the rights of possession (the benefits and burdens of ownership), whichever occurs first. To be eligible for these tax deductions, a taxpayer must be the legal owner or equitable owner of the home.

Note: When the property is purchased on a land contract, the owner has equitable title. According to tax law, a buyer who has possession of the property (equity) owns the property and receives all the tax deductions of the property.

During ownership, owners may write off real estate taxes and mortgage interest in the year they are paid. Note that paying monies into an impound account is not the same as paying them to the agency to which they are owed. Monies paid into an impound account are not deductible. Only the money paid from the impound account to the proper authority can be deducted.

Home Interest.   As of January 1, 1987, new tax laws placed certain limitations on interest. If the loan is secured by a home (principal personal residence) or a second home, the interest is treated as home interest. A taxpayer needs to understand that the loan must be secured by his or her home. The examples in this chapter always will consider the loan to be secured by the home unless stated otherwise.

Interest on a primary residence and second home will be treated as home mortgage interest, whereas interest on additional secondary homes will be treated as personal interest.

For homes that qualify as either a primary home or a second home, the interest is called *home mortgage interest* or *qualified residence interest*. There are two types of home interest: acquisition indebtedness and home equity indebtedness (or equity indebtedness).

Acquisition Indebtedness.   The term **acquisition indebtedness** (AI) is defined as any indebtedness incurred in acquiring, constructing, or substantially improving any qualified residence (primary principal or second residence) and secured by such residence. The starting point for the deductibility of residential interest is the acquisition indebtedness (loan balance of the acquisition loan). The agent must be able to determine the present acquisition indebtedness for a client because the acquisition loan balance is crucial in determining the qualified residence interest and its deductibility.

The tax deductibility of interest for acquisition indebtedness is limited to $1,000,000 on both the principal and the second residences.

■   **EXAMPLE:**   Ms. T. W. O. Holmes purchased two homes this year, a personal residence with a first trust deed (loan) of $850,000 and a second residence with a first trust deed of $450,000. The two loans amount to $1,300,000 ($850,000 + $450,000). Only the interest on the first $1,000,000 will be allowed as acquisition indebtedness.

When a taxpayer takes out a loan to purchase the residence, the loan amount is called the *acquisition indebtedness* and is usually reduced by each payment of principal. The acquisition indebtedness is constantly changing and is found by looking at the loan balance on the initial acquisition indebtedness (initial or original loan).

■   **EXAMPLE:**   Mr. I. M. Byor purchased a home for $200,000 five years ago with a loan of $160,000. This loan of $160,000 is the acquisition indebtedness. Today Byor's loan balance is $150,000, so this amount is now the acquisition indebtedness. Five years from now, when the loan balance is $130,000, that amount will be the acquisition indebtedness. Acquisition indebtedness decreases with time.

There is a way to increase the acquisition indebtedness. It can be increased by substantial improvements that are financed. Notice in the following example that loans (indebtedness) increase the acquisition indebtedness and not the basis.

■ **EXAMPLE:** Ms. Remodel purchased a personal residence for $250,000 with a first trust deed of $200,000. Five years later the first trust deed has a balance of $180,000. The same year she adds a room that costs $75,000, financing $50,000 and paying $25,000 in cash. Her adjusted basis at this time is $325,000 ($250,000 + $75,000); her acquisition indebtedness is $230,000 ($180,000 + $50,000).

The acquisition indebtedness may be refinanced to take advantage of lower interest rates or other more favorable financing conditions. However, the acquisition indebtedness is limited to the amount of the original loan.

■ **EXAMPLE:** Wana Lora Interest's loan balance (acquisition indebtedness) is $150,000 at 9 percent. She can now get a $150,000 loan at 7 percent. Because there will be no increase in the indebtedness, the refinancing of acquisition indebtedness will not change the acquisition indebtedness or the deductibility of the interest.

A taxpayer who decides to build his or her own home may treat the residence under construction as a home for up to 24 months, but only if that residence becomes the taxpayer's home at the time the residence is ready for occupancy. In other words, the taxpayer must move into and occupy the new home.

■ **EXAMPLE:** Mr. I. Hope bought a lot on January 1 three years ago for $100,000 and financed the total amount. A year later he started construction of his home and borrowed $250,000. In the year of purchase he deducted the interest paid on the loan. In the second year he deducted the interest on $350,000 ($100,000 + $250,000). He completed the construction on December 31 of the third year. Because he did not complete the home in 24 months, he may deduct the interest for only the last two years (years two and three). He will have to go back and amend his tax return for year one to take off the interest deduction and pay the additional taxes and interest he owes.

Equity Indebtedness. Home equity indebtedness refers to loans made, using the home for security, for purposes other than purchase, or home improvement. **Equity indebtedness** (EI) means any indebtedness (other than acquisition indebtedness) secured by a qualified residence (home) to the extent that the aggregate amount of such indebtedness does not exceed the FMV of such qualified residence minus the acquisition indebtedness with respect to such residence. The aggregate amount treated as home equity indebtedness for any period cannot exceed $100,000 for the interest to qualify as a deductible expense. To rephrase this definition, the equity indebtedness is limited to the lesser of $100,000 (whether there is one loan or multiple loans) or the FMV less the acquisition indebtedness.

■ **EXAMPLE:** Mr. G. I. Joe owns a home with a fair market value of $125,000. The acquisition indebtedness is $75,000. He can obtain a 100 percent loan on the FMV. The amount of home equity indebtedness would be $50,000 (FMV of $125,000 less the acquisition indebtedness of $75,000). If he could obtain a loan greater than $50,000, that prorated amount of interest would be personal interest, because the loan would be greater than the FMV. Even if a loan could be obtained above the FMV, the IRS will not allow the additional interest as a deduction.

Points

Points on the refinancing of a home must be amortized over the life of the loan for the purpose of deduction. There is one exception: If the loan is used to make home improvements, the points may be written off in the year they are paid.

Determining Gain

The seller's escrow statement lists a number of expenses. The expenses are write-offs (deductions), selling expenses, or nondeductible expenses. The mortgage interest and real estate taxes are deductions. Selling expenses, however, are not deductions; they are used to reduce the gain. When sellers pay points for a buyer's loan, the points are not considered to be interest paid by the buyer. For the seller they are a sales expense that will reduce any gain.

■ **EXAMPLE:**   Ms. Sails shows you her escrow statement (Figure 14.6). She has the following selling expenses:

Policy of Title Insurance	$400
Recording Reconveyance	3
Documentary Stamps	165
Tax Service	25
Commission	7,500
Termite Report	25
Loan Company Service Charge	25
Escrow Fee	300
Preparing Deed	15
Handling Beneficiary Papers	25
Total Selling Expenses	$8,483

The gain on the sale of a residence is a capital gain. To calculate this gain, taxpayers need three pieces of information:

1. The sales price
2. The adjusted basis
3. The selling expenses

The buyer, seller, and market conditions determine the sales price.

The information in Figure 14.6 is used to compute gain, using this equation:

$$G = SP - SE - AB$$
Gain = Selling price – Selling expenses – Adjusted basis

G is the gain (**realized gain**), SP is the sales price, SE is the selling expenses, and AB is the adjusted basis.

FIGURE 14.6

Seller's Escrow Statement

Escrow Statement

NAME: Sails

ITEMS	DEBIT	CREDIT
Total Consideratoin		$150,000
First Trust Deed in Favor of GotU Mortgage		
Second Trust Deed in Favor of:		
Deposit		
Paid Outside of Escrow		
ADJUSTMENTS		
Taxes $ 400 for 6 mos. from 7/1 to 9/30	$200	
Interest on $ at % from to		
Interest on $ at % from to		
Insurance Prem. $ from to		
Rents		
DISBURSEMENTS		
Policy of Title Insurance	400	
ALTA Loan Title Insurance		
Title Company's		
Subescrow Fee		
Recording Deed		
Recording Trust Deed		
Recording Reconveyance	3	
Documentary Transfer Stamps	165	
Tax Service	25	
Termite Report	25	
Commission	7,500	
Principal of Loan Paid to: The Money Mart	50,000	
Interest on $50,000 at 12% from 9/1 to 9/30	500	
Loan Prepayment Charges		
Loan Company Service Charge	25	
Principal of Loan Paid to:		
Interest on at % from to		
Loan Prepayment Charges		
New Loan Origination or Discount Fee at % Paid to:		
Credit Report		
Appraisal Fee		
Impound Account:		
Interest on at % from to		
ESCROW CHARGES		
Escrow Fee	300	
Loan Escrow Fee	15	
Preparing Deed		
Preparing Trust Deed		
Handling Beneficiary Papers	25	
Balance due you, for which our check is endorsed	90,817	
Totals	150,000	150,000

(Please Retain This Statement for Income Tax Purposes)

Type of Gain. The gain on the sale of a capital asset—including a residence—may be placed in one of the following categories:

- *Realized gain* (loss)—When a home is sold, a gain or loss is generally realized; in other words, there usually is a potential taxable event.

- *Recognized gain*—The part of the realized gain for which income tax must be paid is called **recognized gain.** Losses on a personal residence cannot be recognized; that is, they may not be written off.

- *Deferred gain*—The part of the realized gain that may be postponed from recognition is **deferred gain;** the taxpayer may postpone paying it.

- *Excluded gain*—The part of the realized gain for which there is no tax obligation is the **excluded gain.** Excluded gain can be used with a personal residence up to $500,000 for married filing joint and $250,000 for single taxpayer.

In other words a realized gain includes the other three categories:

Realized gain = Recognized gain + Deferred gain + Excluded gain

When a gain is realized, a part may be recognized or either all of the gain or a part may be excluded. The important point is that *taxes are paid on only the recognized gain.* In the sale of a home, nonexcluded realized gain must be recognized (the taxpayer must pay taxes on all the gain). If the seller meets the two-out-of-five-year occupancy requirement, then the gain will likely be excluded from taxation in its entirety. If the occupancy requirement for exclusion is not met or the profit exceeds the exclusion, then the gain or a portion thereof exceeding the exclusion or a portion thereof exceeding the exclusion will be subject to taxation.

Examples of how to determine gain follow.

- **EXAMPLE:**   Ms. Sailor, a single person, sold her home for $750,000. It cost her $60,000 in selling costs, and at the time of sale her adjusted basis was $140,000. Her realized gain is determined with these calculations:

Sales price	$750,000	Net sales price	$690,000
Selling costs	− 60,000	Adjusted basis	−140,000
Net sales price	$690,000	Realized gain	$550,000

Realized gain	=	Recognized gain	+	Excluded gain
$550,000	=	$300,000	+	$250,000

- **EXAMPLE:**   Mr. & Mrs. O'Dam sold their home for $750,000; at the time of sale the adjusted basis of the home was $140,000. Their selling expenses were $60,000. Their realized gain is $550,000:

Sales price	$750,000	Net sales price	$690,000
Selling costs	− 60,000	Adjusted basis	−140,000
Net sales price	$690,000	Realized gain	$550,000

Realized gain	=	Recognized gain	+	Excluded gain
$550,000	=	$50,000	+	$500,000

Because all homes are considered capital assets, any gain on a home will be taxed at the applicable capital gains tax rates.

■ **EXAMPLE:**   Ms. Holmes sells the home she has owned for six years and has a $50,000 recognized gain. Holmes is in the 28 percent federal tax bracket, so she will pay $7,500 ($50,000 x .15) on the gain in addition to state taxes. (15 percent is the capital gains rate for assets held more than 12 months.)

Home Improvements   Systematically recording amounts spent for home improvements and retaining any and all receipts are of great importance to the homeowner. Unfortunately, they are often neglected. Many homeowners are completely unaware of the ultimate tax implications of the home improvements or capital improvements that are added to their properties through the years. These improvements may be added to the homeowner's basis, making the adjusted basis greater and reducing the gain at the time of sale. The adjusted basis (AB) is equal to the original basis (OB) plus home improvements (HI):

$$AB = OB + HI$$
Adjusted basis = Original basis + Home improvements

There is a great deal of misunderstanding about what items are classified as home improvements. The IRS defines improvements differently for homes than it does for rental property. Some examples of **home improvements** are

- electrical wiring (new, replacement, rearrangement),
- floors,
- heating units,
- partitions (including removal),
- pipes and drainage (including replacement),
- roof (new or reshingling over old shingles),
- walls (plastering, strengthening),
- room additions,
- patios,
- pools,
- fencing,
- landscaping (trees, shrubbery, grass seed, etc.), and
- sprinkler systems.

Maintenance items are not home improvements. Some examples are

- painting,
- papering,
- carpeting,

- drapes,

- furniture, and

- replacement of built-in appliances (stoves, ovens, dishwashers, etc.).

- **EXAMPLE:**   Mr. Overbuild purchased a home for $125,000 with buying expenses of $2,000. He has owned it for five years. During that time he has put in drapes ($1,400), a patio ($5,000), a fence ($2,000), and new plumbing ($1,000). The original basis is $127,000 ($125,000 + $2,000). Total home improvements are $8,000 ($5,000 + $2,000 + $1,000). The drapes are not a home improvement. The adjusted basis is $135,000 ($127,000 original basis + $8,000 home improvements).

Relief for "Forced" Sales.   A relief provision may apply to some taxpayers who sell their principal residence but fail to meet the once-every-two-years rule for use of the exclusion. If the taxpayer's failure to meet the rule occurs because the home must be sold due to a change in the place of employment, health status, or—to the extent provided by regulations—other unforeseen circumstances, then the taxpayer may be entitled to a partial exclusion. Under these circumstances, the excludable portion of the gain that would have been tax-free had the requirements been met is based on the relationship that the (a) aggregate periods of ownership and use of the home by the taxpayer as a principal residence during the five years ending on the sale date or (b) the period of time after the last sale to which the exclusion applied and before the date of the current sale, whichever is shorter, bears to (c) two years.

The law does not specify whether the computation should use days or months.

- **EXAMPLE:**   Ms. Travels sells her principal residence because she has a new job in another city. On the date of the sale, she has used and owned her principal residence for the past 18 months. Ms. Travels has never excluded gain from another home sale. If she had used her principal residence for two years, the entire amount of the gain ($250,000) would be excluded. Although Ms. Travels fails to meet the use and ownership requirements for the full exclusion, because the sale is forced by employment, she is entitled to a partial exclusion. The amount of gain excluded by Ms. Travel cannot exceed the amount determined by the following computation (computed using months; see the observation above): Ms. Travels occupied her home for 18 of the 24 months required for the full exclusion. Therefore, she is entitled to a 75 percent exclusion from her gain (18/24 = .75) As a result, Ms. Travels may exclude $187,500 (250,000 x .75 = $187,500) of her gain on the sale of her principal residence.

■ FIRPTA

Before 1985 a foreigner (a person who is neither a U.S. citizen nor a U.S. resident alien) could purchase property in this country and later sell it, then move back to his or her homeland and not pay income taxes on the sale of the property. Because it is very difficult if not impossible to collect delinquent taxes from such an individual, the U.S. Congress passed the **Foreign Investment in Real Property**

Tax Act (FIRPTA). It became law in January 1985. The State of California passed a similar law. To distinguish between federal and California law, the federal law will be called *FED-FIRPTA* and the state law *CAL-FIRPTA*.

Federal Withholding

FED-FIRPTA generally requires that a buyer withhold estimated taxes equal to 10 percent of the sale price in transactions involving real property in the United States sold or exchanged by a foreign person. In addition, CAL-FIRPTA requires that a buyer withhold estimated taxes equal to one-third of the amount required to be withheld under FED-FIRPTA (3⅓ percent of the sales price). The 10 percent estimated withholding must be reported and paid to the Internal Revenue Service within ten days after the close of escrow. If the buyer fails to withhold the estimated taxes and the seller fails to pay taxes on the sale, the buyer is subject to a penalty equal to 10 percent of the purchase price or the seller's actual tax liability plus interest and penalties, whichever is less.

For personal residences, FIRPTA applies only to sales prices of $300,000 or more. When a buyer signs an affidavit (Figure 14.7) stating that he or she plans to use the property as a personal residence and the purchase price is less than $300,000, the buyer is relieved of withholding estimated taxes.

All other property—investment, rental, commercial, land, and so forth—requires withholding when a foreign person sells the property. If a foreign person owns a 20-unit apartment building and sells it for $600,000, $60,000 will have to be withheld for the federal government and $20,000 for the State of California.

If more than one person owns the property and some are U.S. citizens and some are foreign, the amount of withholding must be prorated on the basis of the capital invested. If a husband and wife own property and one spouse is a citizen and the other is not, withholding will be prorated 50/50.

> Withholding under section 1.1445(a) may be reduced or eliminated pursuant to a withholding certificate issued by the Internal Revenue Service in accordance with the rules of this section. (It usually takes about six to eight weeks to receive the certificate from the IRS.)

■ **EXAMPLE:** Ms. Auslander (a foreign person) is selling her personal residence to buy a new home of more value. Considering that this transaction is not taxable, does the buyer of the old property need to withhold?

Yes. If Auslander does not want the buyer to withhold, Auslander will have to file for a withholding certificate from the IRS.

How is the buyer to know if the seller is a foreign person? The burden falls on the buyer, and there are only a few measures that will relieve the buyer of the obligation to withhold. In one such case the seller must provide the buyer with an affidavit of nonforeign status. The seller also must provide a U.S. taxpayer identification number and state, under penalty of perjury, that he or she is not a foreign person. (See Figure 14.8 for CAR form AS-14, which may be used to assert nonforeign status.)

FIGURE 14.7

Buyer's Affidavit

CALIFORNIA
ASSOCIATION
OF REALTORS®

BUYER'S AFFIDAVIT
That Buyer is acquiring property for use as a residence
and that sales price does not exceed $300,000.
(FOREIGN INVESTMENT IN REAL PROPERTY TAX ACT)

1. I am the transferee (buyer) of real property located at _____
_____.

2. The sales price (total of all consideration in the sale) does not exceed $300,000.

3. I am acquiring the real property for use as a residence. I have definite plans that I or a member of my family will reside in it for at least 50 percent of the number of days it will be in use during each of the first two 12 month periods following the transfer of the property to me. I understand that the members of my family that are included in the last sentence are my brothers, sisters, ancestors, descendents, or spouse.

4. I am making this affidavit in order to establish an exemption from withholding a portion of the sales price of the property under Internal Revenue Code §1445.

5. I understand that if the information in this affidavit is not correct, I may be liable to the Internal Revenue Service for up to 10 percent of the sales price of the property, plus interest and penalties.

Under penalties of perjury, I declare that the statements above are true, correct and complete.

Date _____   Signature _____

Typed or Printed Name _____

Date _____   Signature _____

Typed or Printed Name _____

IMPORTANT NOTICE: An affidavit should be signed by each individual transferee to whom it applies. Before you sign, any questions relating to the legal sufficiency of this form, or to whether it applies to a particular transaction, or to the definition of any of the terms used, should be referred to an attorney, certified public accountant, other professional tax advisor, or the Internal Revenue Service.

R E B S
I N C

Published and Distributed by:
REAL ESTATE BUSINESS SERVICES, INC.
a subsidiary of the CALIFORNIA ASSOCIATION OF REALTORS®
525 South Virgil Avenue, Los Angeles, California 90020

PRINT DATE

OFFICE USE ONLY
Reviewed by Broker
or Designee _____
Date _____

EQUAL HOUSING
OPPORTUNITY

FORM AB-11   REVISED 2/91

Reprinted with permission, California Associatioin of REALTORS®. Endorsement not implied.

FIGURE 14.8

Seller's Affidavit of Nonforeign Status

CALIFORNIA ASSOCIATION OF REALTORS®

SELLER'S AFFIDAVIT OF NONFOREIGN STATUS AND/OR CALIFORNIA WITHHOLDING EXEMPTION
FOREIGN INVESTMENT IN REAL PROPERTY TAX ACT (FIRPTA) AND CALIFORNIA WITHHOLDING LAW
(Use a separate form for each Transferor)
(C.A.R. Form AS, Revised 1/03)

USE ONLY FOR ESCROWS CLOSING ON OR AFTER JANUARY 1, 2003

Internal Revenue Code ("IRC") Section 1445 provides that a transferee of a U.S. real property interest must withhold tax if the transferor is a "foreign person." California Revenue and Taxation Code Section 18662 provides that a transferee of a California real property interest must withhold tax if the transferor: (i) is an individual (unless certain exemptions apply); or (ii) is any entity other than an individual ("Entity") if the transferor's proceeds will be disbursed to a financial intermediary of the transferor, or to the transferor with a last known street address outside of California. California Revenue and Taxation Code Section 18662 includes additional provisions for corporations.

I understand that this affidavit may be disclosed to the Internal Revenue Service and to the California Franchise Tax Board by the transferee, and that any false statement I have made herein (if an Entity Transferor, on behalf of the Transferor) may result in a fine, imprisonment or both.

1. **PROPERTY ADDRESS** (the address of the property being transferred): _____
_____

2. **TRANSFEROR'S INFORMATION:**
Full Name _____
Telephone No. _____
Address _____
(Use HOME address for individual transferors. Use OFFICE address for Entities: corporations, partnerships, limited liability companies, trusts and estates.)
Social Security No., Federal Employer Identification No., or California Corporation No. _____

3. **AUTHORITY TO SIGN:** If this document is signed on behalf of an Entity Transferor, THE UNDERSIGNED INDIVIDUAL DECLARES THAT HE/SHE HAS AUTHORITY TO SIGN THIS DOCUMENT ON BEHALF OF THE TRANSFEROR.

4. **FEDERAL LAW:** I, the undersigned individual, declare under penalty of perjury that, for the reason checked below, if any, I am exempt (or if signed on behalf of an Entity Transferor, the Entity is exempt) from the federal withholding law (FIRPTA):
☐ (For individual Transferors) I am not a nonresident alien for purposes of U.S. income taxation.
☐ (For corporation, partnership, limited liability company, trust and estate Transferors) The Transferor is not a foreign corporation, foreign partnership, foreign limited liability company, foreign trust, or foreign estate, as those term are defined in the Internal Revenue Code and Income Tax Regulations.

5. **CALIFORNIA LAW:** I, the undersigned individual, declare under penalty of perjury that, for the reason checked below, if any, I am exempt (or if signed on behalf of an Entity Transferor, the Entity is exempt) from the California withholding law:
☐ The total sale price for the property is $100,000 or less.
For Individual or revocable/grantor trust Transferors only:
☐ The property being transferred is in California and was my principal residence within the meaning of IRC Section 121.
☐ The property is being, or will be, exchanged for property of like kind within the meaning of IRC Section 1031.
☐ The property has been compulsorily or involuntarily converted (within the meaning of IRC 1033) and I intend to acquire property similar or related in service or use to be eligible for non-recognition of gain for California income tax purposes under IRC Section 1033.
☐ The transaction will result in a loss for California income tax purposes.
For Entity Transferors only:
☐ (For corporation Transferors) The Transferor is a corporation qualified to do business in California, or has a permanent place of business in California at the address shown in paragraph 2 ("Transferor's Information").
☐ (For limited liability company ("LLC") or partnership Transferors) The Transferor is an LLC or partnership and recorded title to the property being transferred is in the name of the LLC or partnership and the LLC or partnership will file a California tax return to report the sale and withhold on foreign and domestic nonresident partners as required.
☐ (For irrevocable trust Transferors) The Transferor is an irrevocable trust with at least one trustee who is a California resident and the trust will file a California tax return to report the sale and withhold when distributing California source taxable income to nonresident beneficiaries as required.
☐ (For estate Transferors) The Transferor is an estate of a decedent who was a California resident at the time of his/her death and the estate will file a California tax return to report the sale and withhold when distributing California source taxable income to nonresident beneficiaries as required.
☐ (For tax-exempt Entity and nonprofit organization Transferors) The Transferor is exempt from tax under California or federal law.

By_____ Date _____
(Transferor's Signature) (Indicate if you are signing as the grantor of a revocable/grantor trust.)

_____   _____
Typed or printed name   Title (If signed on behalf of entity Transferor)

SURE TRAC The System for Success™

Published by the California Association of REALTORS®

EQUAL HOUSING OPPORTUNITY

AS REVISED 1/03 (PAGE 1 OF 1) Print Date   Reviewed by _____ Date _____

SELLER'S AFFIDAVIT OF NONFOREIGN STATUS AND/OR CALIFORNIA WITHHOLDING EXEMPTION (AS PAGE 1 OF 1)

California Withholding

As previously stated, California has adopted its own law covering real property sales by foreign persons who are neither U.S. citizens nor U.S. resident aliens (CAL-FIRPTA). Starting January 1, 1991, when California real property is sold, if the seller's (other than a partnership) last known street address is located outside California, the buyer must withhold 3⅓ percent of the selling price if certain conditions are not met. Withholding is not required if any of the following conditions are present:

- The seller receives a homeowner's property tax exemption in the taxable year in which the transfer of title occurs.
- The sales price of the California property is $100,000 or less.
- The buyer has not been provided with written instructions from the real estate person.
- The seller is a bank acting as a trustee of a deed of trust.
- The property is being acquired in foreclosure by a corporation.
- The seller is a partnership.

Both the buyer who fails to withhold and the escrow agent who fails to provide written notice of the withholding requirements are subject to penalties of

- $500 or
- 10 percent of the amount required to be withheld, whichever is greater.

Although the buyer is the one required to withhold, the seller can request a waiver from withholding or a reduced amount of withholding by submitting a written request on California Form 597-A, the Application for Withholding Certificate for Disposition by Nonresidents of California Real Property Interests, to the Franchise Tax Board (FTB). The waiver request should include the seller's name, Social Security number (or California corporation number) and all pertinent facts to support no withholding or withholding at a rate less than 3⅓ percent. The FTB generally will authorize a reduced amount only if there is little or no gain on the transaction.

On a tax-deferred exchange of California real property by a nonresident, withholding is required unless a waiver is granted. The FTB is considering development of a statement to be signed by the seller that contains an affidavit that the seller will file a tax return at the end of the year to report the transaction. At this time, however, there is no such document.

If boot is given to the seller in a deferred exchange, withholding is required at the rate of 7 percent.

On an installment sale of California real property by a nonresident, the FTB normally will allow periodic payments of withholding in accordance with the installment agreement. However, the buyer and seller should request special arrangements by requesting a waiver on Form 597-A.

California Tax Withholding Extended

As of 2003, buyers of property, other than the seller's personal residence, must withhold 3.3 percent of the net proceeds of the sale and remit them to the Franchise Tax Board at close of escrow. Besides the seller's personal residence, the following are other exclusions:

- Property sold for less than $100,000
- Property sold at a loss
- Property involved in a tax deferred exchange
- Involuntary conversion (foreclosure sale)

■ TAX SHELTER

Because depreciation is shown as an expense for income tax purposes, it can reduce the tax liability of a real estate investor and could result in a paper loss even though cash receipts exceed cash expenses.

Taxpayers can use real estate operating losses (passive losses) to offset real estate income without limit. Real estate losses also can be used, with limitations, to offset active income such as wages.

> Taxpayers with adjusted gross income less than $100,000 can shelter up to $25,000 of active income with passive losses.

Taxpayers with an adjusted gross income of less than $100,000 can use real estate losses (which are considered passive losses) to shelter up to $25,000 of their active income. Taxpayers whose adjusted gross income is between $100,000 and $150,000, lose $1 of this $25,000 maximum for each $2 that their adjusted gross income exceeds $100,000.

If investors do not actively manage their property (active management includes hiring a property manager), however, then the taxpayer is precluded from sheltering active income. Because investors have no management responsibilities in investments such as limited partnerships, the investor cannot use such losses to shelter active income.

Real estate professionals can use passive losses from investment property to offset other income without any limitations if they meet specific criteria, which include devoting at least 750 hours during the tax year to property management activities.

■ SUMMARY

Real estate taxes are ad valorem taxes. Property is reassessed when sold, and property is taxed for the basic levy at a maximum rate of 1 percent of the fair market value. The tax rate cannot increase more than 2 percent per year. Additional special assessments can be added, up to 1 percent of the fair market value. The homeowner's exemption is $7,000 from the assessed valuation. There is also a veteran's exemption of the first $100,000 for totally disabled veterans.

Tax transfers between family members may be exempt from reassessment. For taxpayers over 55 years of age, a sale and repurchase of a principal residence within the same county may allow the taxpayer to keep his or her old assessed valuation if the new purchase is at the same price as or less than the sale price of the old residence. For residents over 55 years of age, the transfer of assessed value can extend to other counties if the other county has agreed to it (Proposition 90).

For some senior citizens (low income or disabled) a postponement of taxes is possible until the claimant no longer occupies the property.

Depreciation is a noncash expense for tax purposes that applies to improvements to income, business and investment property. It is a return of the investment. Any gain on sale is taxed from the basis adjusted by adding buying expenses and capital improvements to the purchase price, then deducting the accumulated depreciation (adjusted cost basis). For residential property, a 27.5-year life is used for depreciation purposes. For nonresidential property, a 39-year life is used.

A taxpayer can defer gains on the sale of business or investment property by use of a 1031 exchange. The property must be like-for-like (real property for real property), and the taxpayer would be taxed only on boot received. Boot is unlike property received as well as debt relief. A delayed tax-deferred exchange is possible if the taxpayer identifies the property within 45 days of a transfer and closes escrow within 180 days of the transfer.

Installment sales allow a taxpayer to spread a gain over the years in which the gain is received. This could mean a lower tax rate.

A sale-leaseback allows a seller to gain operating capital, reduced debt, and have the 100 percent tax deduction of business rent.

Residential property owners have a tax advantage of $1,000,000 in acquisition indebtedness (for primary and secondary residences), as well as up to $100,000 in equity indebtedness (interest deduction).

A homeowner's gain on the sale of his or her residence is determined by deducting the adjusted cost basis (cost plus improvements) and the selling expenses from the selling price. The Taxpayer Relief Act of 1997 made some significant changes to our tax law regarding gains on the sale of real estate. These changes include a once-every-two-year exclusion from taxation for gains on the sale of a principal residence that has been occupied by the sellers for at least two years during the prior five-year period. This exclusion from taxation is

■ Married couples $500,000, and
■ Single persons $250,000.

Capital gains have a tax rate of 15 percent for assets held more than 12 months. (Property held for one year or less would have gains taxed as regular income.)

When a property is sold by a foreign national, it is the buyer's responsibility to withhold 10 percent of the price for federal income taxes and 3⅓ percent for state income taxes unless the transaction is exempt from such withholding.

California has extended the 3⅓ percent withholding to sales from all sellers but excludes sales of a seller's personal residence and sales under $100,000.

■ CLASS DISCUSSION TOPICS

1. A buyer of an apartment building has $60,000 annual rent, total cash expenses of $52,000 and depreciation of $9,000. What are the investor's benefits, if any?

2. A person renting a home pays $1,200 per month in rent. The owner offers it for sale to the tenant at a price of $240,000. The tenant is offered a $200,000, 7 percent, 30-year loan; PITI payments will come to $1,650 per month.

   Although the tenant has $40,000 for the down payment, she concludes that she cannot afford the house and will continue to rent it. Discuss the wisdom of her decision. What assumptions would be necessary to arrive at any conclusion?

3. Diagram a three-party exchange. Now diagram a fourth party to the exchange.

4. Compute the adjusted basis when the original basis was $137,500, improvements to the property totaled $31,650, and depreciation taken was $11,436.

5. Bring to class one current-events article dealing with some aspect of real estate practice for class discussion.

■ CHAPTER 14 QUIZ

1. The most difficult tax to avoid is the
   a. sales tax.
   b. real property tax.
   c. income tax.
   d. estate tax.

2. The months of November, December, February, and April relate to
   a. real property taxes.
   b. income taxes.
   c. estate taxes.
   d. sales taxes.

3. What did Proposition 13 provide for?
   a. It set a maximum tax rate.
   b. It set assessments for property acquired before 1978 back to the value shown on the 1975 tax roll.
   c. The tax can be increased 2 percent per year.
   d. All of the above.

4. The proposition that allows a tax assessment for certain homeowners to be transferred from one county to another is Proposition
    a. 13.
    b. 58.
    c. 60.
    d. 90.

5. The homeowner's property tax exemption is
    a. $50,000 for a single person.
    b. $4,000 from assessed valuation.
    c. $7,000 from assessed valuation.
    d. the first $100,000 of assessed valuation.

6. Depreciation for a residential property uses
    a. the straight-line method.
    b. a 27.5-year table.
    c. a 39-year table.
    d. both a and b.

7. To have a tax-deferred delayed exchange, which of the following is required?
    a. The exchange property must be identified within 45 days after the taxpayer relinquishes his or her property.
    b. The sale must be completed within 180 days after the taxpayer relinquishes his or her property.
    c. Both a and b are required.
    d. Neither a nor b is required.

8. To have a 1031 tax-deferred exchange, you need all of the following *except*
    a. like-for-like properties.
    b. to receive boot rather than pay it.
    c. a trade of investment real property for investment real property.
    d. to hold property after the exchange in the same manner as you held property going into the exchange.

9. Albert wants to exchange property with Baker. Which of the following would be "boot" to Albert in the exchange?
    a. Cash given by Albert to balance equities
    b. Cash received by Albert to balance equities
    c. Acceptance of a greater debt by Albert
    d. Both a and c would be considered boot.

10. A homeowner can receive preferential tax treatment by
    a. an interest deduction.
    b. use of the universal exclusion.
    c. a property tax deduction.
    d. all of the above.

CHAPTER FIFTEEN

PROPERTY MANAGEMENT AND LEASING

■ **KEY TERMS**

Accredited Management
  Organization
Accredited Resident
  Manager
assignment
Certified Property
  Manager
condominium association
  management
estate at sufferance
estate at will

estate for years
exculpatory clause
gross lease
holdover clause
Institute of Real Estate
  Management
late charge
management agreement
net lease
percentage lease
periodic tenancy

recapture clause
rent schedule
resident manager
security deposit
step-up lease
sublease
thirty-day notice
three-day notice
trust ledger
unlawful detainer

■ **LEARNING OBJECTIVES**

This chapter provides an introductory overview of the broad field of property management and leasing. You learn about the growth of professionalism within the field and the types of property managers. You also gain insight into the diversity of property subject to management.

You learn the importance of a property management agreement and the meaning of its provisions and gain understanding of property management paperwork and how the computer can provide instant access to data to aid the property manager.

You learn about leasehold estates and the types of leases possible. The chapter explains the importance of specific lease clauses and shows how a lease may be terminated as well as the procedure for evicting a tenant.

■ THE PROPERTY MANAGEMENT FIELD

Property management is not a new field of specialization. In biblical days, owners employed "overseers" who supervised the running of estates. In colonial America, English companies that had land charters, such as the Virginia Company, employed managers to run their operations.

Most properties were, however, managed by owners. The growth of the modern property management profession was facilitated by two factors:

1. The invention of the electric elevator and the use of structural steel, which allowed for high-rise construction, starting in the late 1800s. These huge structures generally were owned by large companies or groups of investors, who had to hire managers for their operations.

2. The Great Depression of the 1930s, which resulted in lenders accumulating vast inventories of property because of foreclosures. To maximize the income and protect the property, these lenders required property managers.

Professionalism

The number of people involved in property management increased rapidly. However, because many of these managers lacked reasonable qualifications due to limited knowledge and abilities, there were many failures within the property management field.

In 1933, to slow down this failure trend and to improve the professional standing of this management group, approximately 100 companies met and formed the **Institute of Real Estate Management** (IREM), a subdivision of the National Association of REALTORS® (NAR). These companies certified that they would

■ refrain from commingling their clients' funds with personal funds;

■ bond all employees handling client funds; and

■ disclose all fees, commissions, or other payments received as a result of activity relating to the client's property.

This move improved the situation, but after several years it became apparent that the companies were not meeting the standards set, mainly because of constant personnel changes.

In 1938 the IREM changed its policy and developed the designation **Certified Property Manager** (CPM) to certify individual managers rather than the companies that employed them. The concept has been successful. IREM's certification requirements are designed to ensure that managers have the general business and industry-specific experience necessary to maintain high standards within the profession. To earn the CPM designation, an individual must

- actively support the institute's rules and regulations;

- demonstrate honesty, integrity, and the ability to manage real estate, including at least three years' experience in a responsible real estate management position; and

- be a member of a local real estate board and a member of the National Association of REALTORS®.

IREM also has the designation **Accredited Resident Manager** (ARM) for residential managers. **Accredited Management Organization** (AMO) is a designation given by IREM to a company. To receive this designation, a company must

- have at least one CPM in charge,

- have property management as a primary activity,

- follow minimum standards and the rules of IREM, and

- renew its accreditation yearly.

There are several other professional property management organizations. They include the Real Estate Management Broker's Institute of the National Association of Real Estate Brokers, the Apartment Owners and Managers Association of America, the Building Owners and Managers Association International (BOMA), and the National Society of Professional Resident Managers. These organizations produce publications, conduct seminars, and award professional designations.

Kinds of Property Managers

There are three basic kinds of managers: licensee/property managers, individual property managers, and resident managers.

Licensee/Property Manager. A licensee/property manager is a licensee of a real estate office or agency that manages a number of properties for various owners. Such a manager may be a member of the firm who spends full time in management, may be self-employed as a managing agent, or may be one of several managers in the management department of a large real estate company. Persons working under the direct supervision of a licensed property manager need not be licensed.

> A person working under direct supervision of a licensed property manager need not be licensed.

Individual Property Manager. An *individual property manager* manages a single property for the owner and may or may not possess a real estate license. He or she usually is employed on a straight salary basis.

Resident Manager.   A **residential manager** as the title implies, lives on the property and may be employed by the owner or by a managing agent. He or she usually is qualified for this assignment by previous management experience or by special training. Personality is critical to success; specifically, the manager should exhibit

- the merchandising ability to contact, show, and close the rental of a unit;

- a high degree of self-confidence and willingness to take charge;

- accuracy in handling money, checks, bank deposits, and other bookkeeping duties;

- awareness of and sensitivity to the events occurring on and around the property;

- orderliness and legibility in keeping records and meticulousness in filing, cataloging, and making reports;

- computer skills such as the ability to access and interpret data;

- the ability to select residents on the basis of economic capability and credit references; and

- the diligence to maintain the property. (The amount of maintenance will vary with the size of the property and the policies of management.)

State law requires a resident manager for property containing 16 or more units and specifies that the resident manager must be a "responsible person." Mobile-home parks having more than 50 units must have a resident manager.

Functions of a Property Manager

The author of the following statement is unknown, but the words give a splendid overview of the making of a property manager:

> The past is his experience, and with its valuable ramifications, he is helped immeasurably to mold the plans for his future. During his years of experience, he has built and sold houses, appraised property, dealt in long-term commercial and industrial leases, made many complicated and intricate transactions, bought and sold hotels—in short, has had a long experience with the public, including businessmen, husbands and wives, doctors and lawyers, engineers and financiers, yes, with gamblers, beggars, and thieves, mothers-in-law, fanatics, the feebleminded, strong and weak characters of every type and description, politicians too, and with this experience has automatically been turned out a well-rounded, socially conscious, alert, and aggressive person—in short, a skillful businessman, and when he has reached this point, he has automatically qualified for the job of property management.

Depending on the complexity of the property, the property manager's duties and responsibilities are many and varied. Inherent in these duties is the dual role of an administrator for the owner and an advocate for the resident.

The property manager's responsibility is to understand and communicate with both parties. The astute property manager is in an ideal position both to represent the owner and to work with the residents with procedures that are fair and equitable. He or she should recognize that the owner wants a fair return on investment and that the resident wants decent housing or space that is properly maintained.

Administrator for the Owner. As the administrator for the owner the property manager must recognize that the owner is interested primarily in

- the highest return from the property, realizing its highest and best use, and
- the enhancement or preservation of the physical value of the property.

Specific Duties of a Property Manager. Under the property management system the owner is relieved of all executive functions as well as of all details connected with the operation or physical upkeep of the property.

A conscientious manager realizes the following:

- Renters need to know what is expected of them and what they can expect from the owner. (This should be stated in writing.)
- Residents' questions should be handled properly and promptly.
- If any request is denied, the manager should state why and avoid pointless arguing.
- The owner, manager, and employees should guard against the attitude that all tenants are unreasonable. However, it would be disastrous to adopt the principle that the customer is always right. The resident is, of course, always entitled to fair and sympathetic treatment.
- The property manager must make certain that tenants' and prospective tenants' legal rights are protected.

As an agent the property manager must show good faith and loyalty to his or her principal (the owner); perform his or her duties with skill, care, and due diligence; fully disclose all pertinent facts; avoid commingling funds; and refrain from personal profits without the principal's full knowledge and consent.

State-Defined Responsibilities. In addition to the general responsibilities described above, the California Department of Real Estate has prepared a list of specific duties:

- Establish the rental schedule that will bring the highest yield consistent with good economics.
- Merchandise the space and collect the rents.
- Create and supervise maintenance schedules and repairs.
- Supervise all purchasing.

- Develop a policy for tenant-resident relations.
- Develop employee policies and supervise employees' operations.
- Maintain proper records and make regular reports to the owner.
- Qualify and investigate prospective tenants' credit.
- Prepare and execute leases.
- Prepare decorating specifications and secure estimates.
- Hire, instruct, and maintain satisfactory personnel to staff the building(s).
- Audit and pay bills.
- Advertise and publicize vacancies through selected media and broker lists.
- Plan alterations and modernizing programs.
- Inspect vacant space frequently.
- Keep abreast of economic conditions and posted competitive market conditions.
- Pay insurance premiums and taxes and recommend tax appeals when warranted.

Basic Responsibilities

The principal functions of a property manager can be summarized as seven basic responsibilities:

1. Marketing space by advertising and securing desirable tenants
2. Collecting rents
3. Handling tenant complaints and physically caring for the premises
4. Purchasing supplies and equipment and paying for repairs
5. Hiring needed employees and maintaining good public relations
6. Keeping proper records and preparing required reports
7. Making recommendations to the owner on matters of improvements, change in use and insurance coverage, as well as on operational changes requiring owner approval

Establishing Rent Schedules.   Rent levels usually are determined on the premise of scarcity and comparability of values in the area. To set up proper **rent schedules,** the manager must make a skilled and thorough analysis of the neighborhood. This analysis will include but not be limited to

- the character of the immediate neighborhood;
- the economic level and size of families;
- trends in population growth and occupants per unit;
- directional growth of the community and expansion and growth of local industries;

- availability of transportation, recreation, shopping, churches, and schools;

- the condition of the housing market versus population growth trends; and

- current area vacancy factors.

The objective of the analysis is to set up a rental schedule commensurate with the findings.

The objective of good property management is to achieve that combination of rent and vacancy that provides the owner with the greatest net. Conducting surveys and establishing rental schedules are very important. Statistics show that uncollected rent is worse than a vacancy, because the property suffers wear and tear from the occupant and the opportunity to place a desirable tenant in the unit is lost. In establishing rent levels the property manager should realize that a vacant unit is not in competition with units already rented. Its only competition is other vacant units.

■ TYPES OF PROPERTY MANAGED

The most common types of properties requiring management are office buildings, apartment buildings and other residential properties, commercial structures, shopping centers, public buildings, recreation centers, hotels, motels, specialized factories, restaurants, and theaters. Recently other properties have joined the list and are rapidly gaining in importance and popularity. These include

- industrial parks,

- mobile-home parks,

- miniwarehouses,

- marinas, and

- airports.

A few of these are described in more detail in this section.

Professional Qualifications of a Property Manager

What kind of person is qualified to be not only a human relations specialist but a detail manager as well? Such a person must be able to play the following roles:

- *Merchandising specialist.* The property manager must be able to advertise and to sell prospective tenants on the merits of a building.
- *Leasing expert.* Being well informed on all types of leases assists a manager to determine the most beneficial lease for a particular client.
- *Accounting specialist.* The law requires that certain records be kept and reports made.

- *Maintenance supervisor.* Preventive and corrective maintenance will prevent expensive repairs at some future date.
- *Purchasing supervisor.* The manager must keep up with all current technological advances in building so he or she can recommend needed replacements for obsolete installations.
- *Credit specialist.* Credit ratings are extremely important. Knowing whether a tenant can live up to the terms of a lease is vital.
- *Insurance adviser.* Understanding the various types of policies available and the extent of coverage can save both the owner and the tenant time and money.
- *Tax interpreter.* A manager must be well versed in property taxes and their effect on the property being managed. He or she should be cognizant of the relationship of depreciation to the income and profit of the property.
- *Psychology expert.* This capacity is crucial to day-to-day communication.
- *Budget manager.* A property manager must be able to maintain and operate within the budget established for the property.

Residential Properties

Residential properties are by far the most numerous of the properties subject to professional management. There are more than 70 million permanent housing units in the United States.

The housing market is stratified. There may be a high vacancy rate at one rental range and a severe housing shortage at another range. Nevertheless, a general nationwide housing shortage has existed for many years. Three million new housing starts each year would be required merely to replace end-of-the-line units that should be demolished.

Residential property managers should be familiar with local rent control ordinances to make certain that rents and/or rent increases charged are not in violation of the law. Rent control restrictions vary significantly by community. In some cities, a vacancy allows a landlord to set a new base rent without limitations. While in other communities the landlord cannot increase the base rent between tenants. Allowable rental increases are also subject to different restrictions.

Residential managers also must fully understand their obligations under state and federal fair housing legislation as well as under the Real Estate Commissioner's Regulations dealing with fair housing. (See Chapter 2 for specific requirements.)

Residential managers of lower-priced units should be familiar with Section 8 housing. This is a rental program under which all or part of a low-income tenant's rent is paid through the county. County administrators must inspect the property for eligibility, and tenants must meet stated criteria and be approved by the county.

Condominiums. Individual ownership of condominiums nearly always involves property management. Condominiums and cooperatives are similar from the standpoint of management duties.

A growing segment in the property management field is **condominium association management.** This type of management is often heavy on the accounting aspects. The duties of the condominium association manager likely would include

- collecting fees from members;

- issuing financial statements to the association;

- contracting for or hiring all maintenance and repairs;

- enforcing covenants, conditions, and restrictions (CC&Rs);

- handling tenant interpersonal disputes and/or complaints;

- filing tax returns (if applicable), as well as handling workers' compensation, unemployment compensation, insurance, and so forth;

- seeing that the property is insured as to damage as well as to owner liability;

- making suggestions to the board of directors; and

- attending directors' meetings.

In a condominium association the property manager doesn't make policy; he or she merely carries out policy as directed by the board of directors. A condominium association manager must understand that different board members have different personal agendas. As an example, some members may be primarily focused on security while others are interested in keeping assessments to a minimum. A property manager must avoid becoming involved in the politics of the homeowners association and must focus on the instructions of the board. However, the manager does have a duty to make informed recommendations to the board.

A number of computer programs designed for condominium association management provide financial records, spreadsheets, work orders and even much of the routine correspondence of the association.

Mobile-Home Parks. Management of a mobile-home park is a specialty field involving

- park development,

- public amenities,

- enforcement of park rules, and

- approval of lease assignments on sale of units.

In parks where the individual lots are owned by the mobile-unit owners, the mobile-home park management duties become almost identical to the duties of a condominium association manager. However, the park manager should be aware that the laws governing evictions are much more restrictive for park owners than for other residential landlords. The park manager must give tenants a 12-month lease on request at current rent and must furnish tenants with an annual copy of the current California Civil Code covering mobile-home parks so that tenants understand their rights and responsibilities.

> The tenant in a mobile-home park is entitled to a 12-month lease on request.

Multifamily Units.   Residential property bought for investment is the most common professionally managed property. Statistics indicate that multiple-family units account for approximately 30 percent of residential housing in the United States.

The more problems a property has, the more it needs professional management. Because properties that have had a troubled history can take a great deal of a property manager's time, the manager's fee scale is generally higher for such properties.

Public Housing.   Ownership of public housing is becoming increasingly important to property management. The largest single landlord in the United States is the collective 3,500 public housing authorities. More than 1.5 million units are controlled by public housing authorities. A great many property managers are employed by federal, state, and local housing authorities.

Single-family Homes.   Besides homes purchased for rental, there are many instances requiring single-family home managements. In resort areas, many owners use property management to care for their properties and, in some cases, to handle short-term rentals. Property management might also be required for property in probate as well as for lenders who have foreclosed. Generally, because single-family units require more management time per unit than multifamily units, management charges tend to reflect this greater effort.

Office Buildings

Office buildings are the major commercial property. Office space requirements will continue to grow owing to the increase in the number of people working in offices or similar commercial structures. The larger users of office space, such as banks, savings associations, and insurance companies, often build for their own use but also provide a large amount of excess of space for leasing purposes.

Overbuilding of office structures intensified the need for professional management because owners didn't want to give any advantage to other owners: Competition for lessees can be heated.

Some areas of California have a glut of office space. In such areas concessions are necessary to attract tenants. In some instances property managers agree to assume a tenant's current lease to encourage the tenant to take a larger space under a long-term lease. The agent then has the job of marketing the "trade-in" space.

Specialized offices, such as medical or legal offices, have special problems.

Merchandising Office Space.   Rental or lease of office space can be tied to the following criteria:

- Appearance of surroundings
- Transportation facilities
- Prestige and image of area
- Proximity to clients
- Building appearance
- Lobby appearance
- Elevator appearance and condition
- Corridor appearance
- Office interiors
- Tenant services offered
- Management
- Other tenants

Advertising is an essential part of conducting an aggressive leasing campaign for office space. Such publicity ideas as the following can be most helpful:

- Groundbreaking ceremonies
- Brochures
- Newspaper ads
- Internet site (referenced in ads and brochures)
- Mailing lists of professional groups, including attorneys, doctors, and CPAs
- Personal solicitation
- Use of a model office
- Making technical data readily available, including floor plans, available space, and space arrangements

Maintenance.   The manager of an office building must handle maintenance or service problems unique to this type of operation. This job includes such activities as

- servicing all operating equipment and public facilities, such as lobbies, lights, and washrooms;
- maintaining elevators, which are indispensable in a high-rise (usually involves an elevator maintenance contract);
- cleaning, usually done at night;

- other routine maintenance, including window cleaning, waste removal, light bulb replacement, heating, ventilation, and air-conditioning; and

- preparing and updating a maintenance operations manual that shows a list of all equipment with the vital information concerning each piece of equipment.

Protection.   Protection of the premises is a management function. It includes such vital items as

- key control,

- guard employment, and

- fire-prevention techniques.

Retail Space.   Management of retail space requires many of the same skills and concerns as office management. In multiunit commercial properties the manager should consider the effect a prospective tenant will have on the business of other tenants. Managers will often seek out particular tenants or businesses in order to contribute to the overall operation of the property.

Industrial Management

Industrial management is rather specialized because of the skills required. Industrial managers must have knowledge in many areas, including

- fire-suppression systems (sprinklers) and water capacity and pressure for various uses;

- floor and ceiling load capacities;

- hazardous and toxic substances (use and storage), as well as underground tanks;

- air and water quality control;

- loading dock requirements;

- electrical capacity and three-phase wiring;

- reading blueprints for modification;

- specific zoning regarding uses allowed;

- special insurance requirements;

- security and security systems; and

- large cooling, heating, and ventilation systems.

Industrial managers might manage specific property or an entire industrial park. The industrial property manager's duties primarily relate to renting, but they also involve protecting the property and the owners from liability.

■ SECURITY

Security is of prime importance to lessors and lessees for all types of property. It applies to personal security of tenants, employees, and guests as well as security for the lessee's property.

Because no property can be absolutely safe, a property manager should never indicate to tenants that a property is safe or secure. This could be seen by the court as a warranty as to safety. Nevertheless, your best efforts should be used to make the premises as safe as is reasonably possible.

A property manager should consider, as applicable to a property, the following:

- *Emergency evacuation plan*—In light of 9/11, such a plan is extremely important for large structures.

- *Properly marked exits*—This may require going beyond bare legal requirements.

- *Appropriate landscaping*—Remove any trees or shrubbery around entrances and walkways that could conceal a person.

- *Exterior lighting*—Take special care in entryways, walkways, and parking areas. Perimeter areas could be lighted by motion sensor lighting.

- *Interior lighting*—Light all hallways and public areas (use fluorescent bulbs that are unlikely to be removed). Battery operated emergency lighting that is kept charged by the electrical service, but goes on when service is cut should be considered.

- *Circuit breaker box*—This should be locked or in a locked room.

- *Exterior and unit doors*—All should be solid core rather than hollow core. Steel doors should be considered. Apartment doors should have peepholes and a security chain with screws at least one inch long.

- *Door Locks*—Do not use key-in-knob locks. They are easy to pry off. Do not use mortised locks as they create a very weak spot in the door. Use a dead bolt and a strike plate held in place by screws of 3 inches or longer. The more tumblers a lock has, the harder it is to pick.

- *Window locks*—Use security latches on windows.

These are just a few of the security measures you should consider. Hiring security consultants who can analyze your property could be dollars well spent.

■ MANAGEMENT AGREEMENT

It makes no difference whether the property involved is an office building, a residential property, or a shopping center; the responsibilities assumed by the manager are so important that they warrant a written agreement. The **management agreement** formalizes the relationship between the owner and the manager and points out the rights and duties of each party. The forms used for this purpose may vary, but regardless of the property involved, certain basic points must be included:

- Identification of the parties

- Sufficient identification of the property

- The contract period, including the beginning and the termination dates

- Management's and owner's responsibilities

- Management fees—the amount, when it is to be paid, and the manner of payment

- Provision for management accounting, including records to be kept and reports to be made

Management fees can cover one or a combination of the following:

- Flat fees

- Minimum fee

- Minimum plus percentage of the gross (very common compensation)

- Leasing fee (flat fee or a percentage of the lease rental; generally a higher percentage for the first year and a lower percentage for subsequent years)

- Additional fees or percentages for special services such as drafting leases; supervising repairs; or remodeling; handling evictions; overseeing contracts; and collecting delinquent accounts of former tenants

Management fees are usually a percentage of the gross, not the net.

In addition, management contracts provide for reimbursement of costs, which may or may not include such items as advertising.

Generally, the more management problems a property has, the higher the management fee percentage. Larger properties tend to be managed at lower percentages.

Figure 15.1 is the California Association of REALTORS® Property Management Agreement Form PMA-11. This excellent form is self-explanatory.

■ ACCOUNTING RECORDS

Although the number of bookkeeping records needed depends on the type of property managed and the volume of business involved, the selection and maintenance of an adequate trust fund accounting system is essential in property management because of the fiduciary nature of the business. The responsibility for trust fund records is placed on the property management broker. It is recommended that an outside accountant be employed to review and audit the accounting system.

FIGURE 15.1

Property Management Agreement

CALIFORNIA
ASSOCIATION
OF REALTORS®

PROPERTY MANAGEMENT AGREEMENT

_____ ("Owner"), and
_____ ("Broker"), agree as follows:

1. **APPOINTMENT OF BROKER:** Owner hereby appoints and grants Broker the exclusive right to rent, lease, operate, and manage the property (ies)
   known as _____
   _____, and any additional property which may later be added to this Agreement, ("Property"),
   upon the terms below, for the period beginning on (date) _____ and ending on (date) _____, at 11:59 p.m.
   (If checked:) ☐ Either party may terminate this Agreement on at least 30 days written notice _____months after the original commencement date
   of this Agreement. After the exclusive term expires, this Agreement shall continue as a Non-Exclusive Agreement which either party may terminate
   by giving at least 30 days written notice to the other.

2. **BROKER ACCEPTANCE:** Broker accepts the appointment and grant, and agrees to:
   A. Use due diligence in the performance of this Agreement.
   B. Furnish the services of its organization for the rental, leasing, operating, and management of the Property.

3. **AUTHORITY AND POWERS:** Owner grants Broker the authority and power, at Owner's expense, to:
   A. **ADVERTISING:** Display FOR RENT, FOR LEASE, and similar signs on the Property; advertise the availability for rental or lease of the Property, or
      any part of it.
   B. **RENTAL/LEASING:** Initiate, sign, renew, or cancel rental agreements and leases for the Property, or any part of it; collect and give receipts for
      rents, other charges, and security deposits. Any lease executed by Broker for Owner shall not exceed _____ year(s). Unless Owner
      authorizes a lower amount, rent shall: ☐ be a minimum of $ _____ per _____; OR ☐ see attachment.
   C. **TENANCY TERMINATION:** Sign and serve in Owner's name notices which are required or appropriate; commence and prosecute actions to
      evict tenants; recover possession of the Property in Owner's name; recover rents and other sums due; and when expedient, settle, compromise,
      and release claims, actions and suits, and/or reinstate tenancies.
   D. **REPAIR/MAINTENANCE:** Make, cause to be made, and/or supervise repairs, improvements, alterations, and decorations to the Property;
      purchase and pay bills for services and supplies. Broker shall obtain prior approval of Owner on all expenditures over $ _____ for
      any one item. Prior approval shall not be required for monthly or recurring operating charges, or, if in Broker's opinion, emergency expenditures
      over the maximum are needed to protect the Property or other property(ies) from damage, prevent injury to persons, avoid suspension of
      necessary services, avoid penalties or fines, or suspension of services to tenants required by a lease or rental agreement or by law. Broker shall
      not advance Broker's own funds in connection with the Property or this Agreement.
   E. **CONTRACTS/SERVICES:** Contract, hire, supervise and/or discharge firms and persons, including utilities, required for the operation and
      maintenance of the Property. Broker may perform any of Broker's duties through attorneys, agents, employees, or independent contractors, and,
      except for persons working in Broker's firm, shall not be responsible for their acts, omissions, defaults, negligence, and/or costs of same.
   F. **EXPENSE PAYMENTS:** Pay expenses and costs for the Property from Owner's funds held by Broker, unless otherwise directed by Owner.
      Expenses and costs may include, but are not limited to, property management fees and charges, expenses for goods and services, property
      taxes and other taxes, Owner's Association dues, assessments, loan payments, and insurance premiums.
   G. **SECURITY DEPOSITS:** Receive security deposits from tenants, which deposits shall be ☐ given to Owner, or ☐ placed in Broker's trust
      account. Owner shall be responsible to tenants for return of security deposits held by Owner.
   H. **TRUST FUNDS:** Deposit all receipts collected for Owner, less any sums properly deducted or disbursed, in a financial institution whose deposits
      are insured by an agency of the United States government. The funds shall be held in a trust account separate from Broker's personal accounts.
      Broker shall not be liable in event of bankruptcy or failure of a financial institution.
   I. **RESERVES:** Maintain a reserve in Broker's trust account of: $_____
   J. **DISBURSEMENTS:** Disburse Owner's funds, held in Broker's trust account, in the following order:
      1. Compensation due Broker under paragraph 6.
      2. All other operating expenses, costs, and disbursements payable from Owner's funds held by Broker.
      3. Reserves and security deposits held by Broker.
      4. Balance to Owner.
   K. **OWNER DISTRIBUTION:** Remit funds monthly, (or ☐ _____), to Owner.
   L. **OWNER STATEMENTS:** Render monthly, (or ☐ _____), statements of receipts, expenses and charges for each
      Property.

Owner and Broker acknowledge receipt of copy of this page, which constitutes Page 1 of _____ Pages.

Owner's Initials (_____) (_____)   Broker's Initials (_____) (_____)

Published and Distributed by:
REAL ESTATE BUSINESS SERVICES, INC.
a subsidiary of the CALIFORNIA ASSOCIATION OF REALTORS®
525 South Virgil Avenue, Los Angeles, California 90020

REVISED 4/98

PRINT DATE

┌─ OFFICE USE ONLY ─┐
Reviewed by Broker
or Designee _____
Date _____

EQUAL HOUSING
OPPORTUNITY

PROPERTY MANAGEMENT AGREEMENT (PMA-11 PAGE 1 OF 3)

FIGURE 15.1

Property Management Agreement (continued)

Owner Name: _____ Date _____

4. **OWNER RESPONSIBILITIES:** Owner shall:
   A. Provide all documentation and records required by Broker to manage and operate the Property.
   B. Indemnify, defend and hold harmless Broker, and all persons in Broker's firm, regardless of responsibility, from all costs, expenses, suits, liabilities, damages, attorney's fees, and claims of every type, including but not limited to those arising out of injury or death of any person, or damage to any real or personal property of any person, including Owner, in any way relating to the management, rental, security deposits, or operation of the Property by Broker, or any person in Broker's firm, or the performance or exercise of any of the duties, powers, or authorities granted to Broker.
   C. Carry and pay for: (i) public and premises liability insurance in an amount of no less than $1,000,000; and (ii) property damage and worker's compensation insurance adequate to protect the interests of Owner and Broker. Broker shall be named as an additional insured party on Owner's policies.
   D. Pay any late charges, penalties, and/or interest imposed by lenders or other parties for failure to make payment to those parties, if the failure is due to the fact that there are insufficient funds in Broker's trust account available for such payment.

5. **LEAD-BASED PAINT DISCLOSURE:**
   A. ☐ The Property was constructed on or after January 1, 1978.
   OR B. ☐ The Property was constructed prior to 1978.
      (1) Owner has no knowledge of lead-based paint or lead-based paint hazards in the housing except: _____
      _____
      (2) Owner has no reports or records pertaining to lead-based paint or lead-based paint hazards in the housing, except the following, which Owner shall provide to Broker:_____

6. **COMPENSATION:**
   A. Owner agrees to pay Broker fees in the amounts indicated below for:
      (1) Management: _____.
      (2) Renting or Leasing: _____.
      (3) Evictions: _____.
      (4) Preparing Property for rental, lease, or sale: _____.
      (5) Managing Property during extended periods of vacancy: _____.
      (6) An overhead and service fee added to the cost of all work performed by, or at the direction of, Broker: _____.
      (7) Other: _____
      _____
   B. This Property Management Agreement ("Agreement") does not include providing on-site management services, property sales, re-financing, preparing Property for sale or re-financing, modernization, fire or major damage restoration, rehabilitation, obtaining income tax, accounting, or legal advice, representation before public agencies, advising on proposed new construction, debt collection, counseling, attending Owner's Association meetings, or_____.
      If Owner requests Broker to perform services not included in this Agreement, a fee shall be agreed upon before these services are performed.
   C. Broker may divide compensation, fees and charges due under this Agreement in any manner acceptable to Broker.
   D. Owner further agrees that:
      (1) Broker may receive fees and charges from tenants for (i) requesting an assignment of lease or sublease of the Property, (ii) processing credit applications, and (iii) any returned checks, and (iv) any other services that are not in conflict with this Agreement.
      (2) Broker may perform any of Broker's duties, and obtain necessary products and services, through affiliated companies or organizations in which Broker may own an interest. Broker may receive fees, commissions, and/or profits from these affiliated companies or organizations. Broker has an ownership interest in the following affiliated companies or organizations: _____
      _____
      Broker shall disclose to Owner any other such relationships as they occur. Broker shall not receive any fees, commissions, or profits from unaffiliated companies in the performance of this Agreement, without prior disclosure to Owner.
      (3) Other: _____

7. **AGENCY RELATIONSHIPS:** Broker shall act as the agent for Owner in any resulting transaction. Depending upon the circumstances, it may be necessary or appropriate for Broker to act as agent for both Owner and tenant. Broker shall, as soon as practical, disclose to Owner any election to act as a dual agent representing both Owner and tenant. If tenant is procured directly by Broker or an associate licensee in Broker's firm, Owner hereby consents to Broker acting as dual agent for Owner and such tenant. Owner understands that Broker may have or obtain property management agreements on other property, and that potential tenants may consider, make offers on, or lease through Broker, property the same as or similar to Owner's Property. Owner consents to Broker's representation of other owners' properties before, during, and after the expiration of this Agreement.

8. **NOTICES:** Any written notice to Owner or Broker required under this Agreement shall be served by sending such notice by first class mail to that party at the address below, or at any different address which the parties may later designate for this purpose. Notice shall be deemed received three calendar days after deposit into the United States mail.

Owner and Broker acknowledge receipt of copy of this page, which constitutes Page 2 of _____ Pages.
Owner's Initials (_____) (_____)   Broker's Initials (_____) (_____)

OFFICE USE ONLY
Reviewed by Broker or Designee _____
Date _____

REVISED 4/98

PROPERTY MANAGEMENT AGREEMENT (PMA-11 PAGE 2 OF 3)

FIGURE 15.1

Property Management Agreement (continued)

Owner Name: _____ Date _____

9. **DISPUTE RESOLUTION**

   A. **MEDIATION:** Owner and Broker agree to mediate any dispute or claim arising between them out of this Agreement, or any resulting transaction before resorting to arbitration or court action, subject to paragraph 9C below. Mediation fees, if any, shall be divided equally among the parties involved. If any party commences an action based on a dispute or claim to which this paragraph applies, without first attempting to resolve the matter through mediation, then that party shall not be entitled to recover attorney's fees, even if they would otherwise be available to that party in any such action. THIS MEDIATION PROVISION APPLIES WHETHER OR NOT THE ARBITRATION PROVISION IS INITIALED.

   B. **ARBITRATION OF DISPUTES:** Owner and Broker agree that any dispute or claim arising between them out of the obligation to pay compensation under this Agreement, which is not settled through mediation, shall be decided by neutral, binding arbitration, subject to paragraph 9C below. The arbitrator shall be a retired judge or justice, or an attorney with at least five years of residential income real estate transactional law experience, unless the parties mutually agree to a different arbitrator, who shall render an award in accordance with substantive California Law. In all other respects, the arbitration shall be conducted in accordance with Part III, Title 9 of the California Code of Civil Procedure. Judgment upon the award of the arbitrator(s) may be entered in any court having jurisdiction. The parties shall have the right to discovery in accordance with Code of Civil Procedure §1283.05.
   "NOTICE: BY INITIALING IN THE SPACE BELOW YOU ARE AGREEING TO HAVE ANY DISPUTE ARISING OUT OF THE MATTERS INCLUDED IN THE 'ARBITRATION OF DISPUTES' PROVISION DECIDED BY NEUTRAL ARBITRATION AS PROVIDED BY CALIFORNIA LAW AND YOU ARE GIVING UP ANY RIGHTS YOU MIGHT POSSESS TO HAVE THE DISPUTE LITIGATED IN A COURT OR JURY TRIAL. BY INITIALING IN THE SPACE BELOW YOU ARE GIVING UP YOUR JUDICIAL RIGHTS TO DISCOVERY AND APPEAL, UNLESS THOSE RIGHTS ARE SPECIFICALLY INCLUDED IN THE 'ARBITRATION OF DISPUTES' PROVISION. IF YOU REFUSE TO SUBMIT TO ARBITRATION AFTER AGREEING TO THIS PROVISION, YOU MAY BE COMPELLED TO ARBITRATE UNDER THE AUTHORITY OF THE CALIFORNIA CODE OF CIVIL PROCEDURE. YOUR AGREEMENT TO THIS ARBITRATION PROVISION IS VOLUNTARY."
   "WE HAVE READ AND UNDERSTAND THE FOREGOING AND AGREE TO SUBMIT DISPUTES ARISING OUT OF THE MATTERS INCLUDED IN THE 'ARBITRATION OF DISPUTES' PROVISION TO NEUTRAL ARBITRATION."   Owner's Initials _____/_____   Broker's Initials _____/_____

   C. **EXCLUSIONS FROM MEDIATION AND ARBITRATION:** The following matters are excluded from Mediation and Arbitration hereunder: (a) A judicial or non-judicial foreclosure or other action or proceeding to enforce a deed of trust, mortgage, or installment land sale contract as defined in Civil Code §2985; (b) An unlawful detainer action; (c) The filing or enforcement of a mechanic's lien; (d) Any matter which is within the jurisdiction of a probate, small claims, or bankruptcy court; and (e) An action for bodily injury or wrongful death, or for latent or patent defects to which Code of Civil Procedure §337.1 or §337.15 applies. The filing of a court action to enable the recording of a notice of pending action, for order of attachment, receivership, injunction, or other provisional remedies, shall not constitute a violation of the mediation and arbitration provisions.

10. **EQUAL HOUSING OPPORTUNITY:** The Property is offered in compliance with federal, state, and local anti-discrimination laws.

11. **ATTORNEY'S FEES:** In any action, proceeding, or arbitration between Owner and Broker regarding the obligation to pay compensation under this Agreement, the prevailing Owner or Broker shall be entitled to reasonable attorney's fees and costs, except as provided in paragraph 9A.

12. **ADDITIONAL TERMS:** _____
    _____
    _____
    _____

13. **ENTIRE CONTRACT:** All prior discussions, negotiations, and agreements between the parties concerning the subject matter of this Agreement are superseded by this Agreement, which constitutes the entire contract and a complete and exclusive expression of their agreement, and may not be contradicted by evidence of any prior agreement or contemporaneous oral agreement. This Agreement and any supplement, addendum, or modification, including any photocopy or facsimile, may be executed in counterparts.

Owner warrants that Owner is the owner of the Property or has the authority to execute this contract. Owner acknowledges that Owner has read and understands this Agreement, and has received a copy.

Owner _____ Date _____   Owner _____ Date _____

Owner (Print Name) _____   Owner (Print Name) _____

Address _____   Address _____

City _____ State _____ Zip _____   City _____ State _____ Zip _____

| Phone | Fax | E-mail | | Phone | Fax | E-mail |

social security/tax ID # (for tax reporting purposes)   social security/tax ID # (for tax reporting purposes)

Real Estate Broker _____   Address _____

By _____   _____

Phone _____   Fax _____

REVISED 4/98

Page 3 of _____ Pages.

OFFICE USE ONLY
Reviewed by Broker
or Designee _____
Date _____

EQUAL HOUSING OPPORTUNITY

PROPERTY MANAGEMENT AGREEMENT (PMA-11 PAGE 3 OF 3)

Reasons for Accounting Records

There are a number of basic reasons for keeping orderly records in property management:

- The law states that a separate record must be kept for each managed property.

- The fiduciary relationship between the owner and the manager dictates a full disclosure.

- Contractual relationships call for an accounting of all funds.

- Records are needed for income tax purposes.

- It may be necessary to satisfy third parties who have an interest in the property.

- Accurate records serve as controls in evaluating income and expenses, analyzing costs, and preparing budgets.

- Records provide the broker with a source of information when inquiries are made or problems arise.

In the days before computers, property managers relied on file systems for each property, with file cards for each tenant. The only time the manager really understood the operating conditions of a property was when the monthly account was tabulated to show income received and disbursements. Computer programs now provide property managers with instant access to property data on one property, on a group of properties, or even on one tenant. These programs have reduced the paperwork of property management.

Computer programs for property management range in cost from only a few hundred dollars to around $10,000. Most computer companies offer free demonstration disks so you can see what a program can do. The following are just a few of the firms offering programs that are likely to meet your property management needs:

Real Estate Software Company, Inc.
10622 Montgomery Drive, Suite D
El Paso, TX 79935
(800) 327-9776

Real Data
78 North Main Street
South Norwalk, CT 06854
(203) 838-2670

Yardi Systems
819 Reddick Street
Santa Barbara, CA 93103
(805) 966-3666

Today, to operate a property management firm without computer assistance would be like running a brokerage office without a telephone. It is possible, but it is not very efficient.

Some Property Management Tasks That Can Be Performed By Computer

- Trust journals
- Security deposit registries
- Monthly, quarterly, semiannual, and annual financial reports
- Accounts-payable ledger
- Accounts-receivable ledger
- Operating account deposits
- Tenant registries
- Vacancies
- Rental analysis
- Rental summary
- Rent increase calendar
- Automatic billing
- Late charges
- Late-charge reports
- Late letters
- Notices and unlawful detainer
- Market rent variances
- Rent receipts
- Property fees
- Payment histories
- Owner's checks and/or billing
- Owner's ledger
- Owner's income/loss

- Bad-check report
- Tenant data
- Check registry
- Check writing
- Insurance register
- Lease expiration register
- Mortgage check register
- Comparative lease analysis
- Inactive property files
- Repair orders
- Lease abstracts
- Vendor lists
- Vendor history (by vendor)
- Insurance expiration data
- Tickler files (scheduling payments)
- Association fees
- Owner's 1099s
- Hold-back (reserves) registering
- Checkbook reconciliation
- Budgets (monthly and annual)
- Maintenance history
- Repetitive correspondence

Trust Ledger

Section 2830 of the commissioner's regulations requires that a **trust ledger** for property management accounts be established. As rents come in, they are posted to the owner's account. Also recorded in the trust ledger is the money paid out on behalf of the owner. This includes any repair costs, payments of encumbrances, and payments for utilities or commissions. These expenses are charged against the income of the property, and the manager sends a statement to the owner at the end of each month. Again, trust records today generally are kept using computer software.

■ LEASEHOLD ESTATES

One of the responsibilities of a property manager involves leasing the property or acting as a consultant when drawing up the terms of the lease.

A leasehold estate arises when an owner or a property manager acting as the owner's agent grants a tenant the right to occupy the owner's property for a specified period of time for a consideration. The owner is the *lessor,* and the tenant is the *lessee.*

Basic Types of Leasehold Estates

There are four basic types of leasehold estates, based on the length and nature of their duration: the estate for years, the estate from period to period, the estate at sufferance, and the estate at will.

> An estate for years has a definite termination date.

Estate for Years.   An estate that continues for a definite fixed period of time is an **estate for years.** The lease may be for any specified length of time, even for less than a year, measured in days, weeks, or months. Professional property managers will generally insist on an estate for years.

Estate from Period to Period.   An estate from period to period is commonly called a **periodic tenancy.** The lease continues from period to period (either year to year, month to month, or week to week), as designated. The most common periodic tenancy is month to month.

A periodic tenancy can be ended by a notice for the length of the rent-paying period but for no more than 30 days. However, if a residential tenant has lived on the premises for at least 12 months, a landlord must provide a 60-day notice to terminate the tenancy.

Estate at Sufferance.   An **estate at sufferance** is created when a tenant obtains possession of property legally but then remains on the property without the owner's consent after the expiration of the leasehold interest. A tenant at sufferance can be ejected like a trespasser unless rent is paid. The estate then becomes a periodic tenancy based on the rent-paying period.

Estate at Will.   An **estate at will** has no specified time limit. Possession is given with permission, but no agreement is made as to rent. As an example, possession is given to a prospective tenant before the lease terms are agreed to. In California such an estate requires a **30-day notice** to terminate.

Types of Leases

The three basic lease forms the property manager will be expected to work with are the gross lease, net lease, and percentage lease.

Gross Lease.   Under a **gross lease** the tenant pays a fixed rental and the owner pays all other expenses for the property. Most residential leases and small commercial leases are gross leases. As an example, the typical month-to-month lease is for a gross amount.

To keep a tenant on a gross lease from holding over at the end of the term, the lease might include a **holdover clause,** which materially raises the rent when the lease period expires. This encourages the tenant to either sign a new lease or vacate the premises.

> Net lease means the owner gets a net amount and property expenses are paid by the tenant.

Net Lease.   Under the terms of a **net lease** (or triple net lease) the tenant must pay utilities, real estate taxes, maintenance, repairs, and other special assessments, in addition to the stated rent.

Net leases are generally long-term leases and often are found in sale-leasebacks and where buildings are constructed for a particular tenant. The buyer (investor) wants a stated return. To keep the same relative purchasing power, the lessor on a net lease generally wants the net amount tied to an inflationary index, such as the Consumer Price Index.

Percentage Lease.   A **percentage lease** generally provides for a stated percentage of the gross receipts of a business to be paid as rent. Generally, the percentage lease is tied in with a minimum rent and a covenant to remain in business. The percentage lease also might include hours of operation and a prohibition against the lessee's conducting off-site "warehouse" sales.

Percentage leases are typically used in shopping centers, where each business aids other businesses. Shopping-center leases may have a requirement that a separate percentage of the gross be used for cooperative advertising in newspaper supplements or on radio or TV.

In addition, a percentage lease may include a **recapture clause,** which provides that should a tenant not obtain a desired gross, then the lessor has the right to terminate the lease.

Leases may combine features, for example, a basic gross lease plus a percentage of the gross. What can be done with leases is limited only by the imagination of the parties.

Figure 15.2 shows typical percentages charged for different businesses having percentage leases. In determining the percentage of gross sales that must be paid by the lessee, the greater the tenant's markup, and the higher the percentage on the lease (example: 50 percent on a parking lot rental and 2 percent on a supermarket rental).

Various professional associations publish average percentages currently being charged for different types of businesses. Lessors, of course, want the maximum percentage possible that will still allow the business to remain a viable entity.

Step-up Lease.   A **step-up lease** has a fixed rent like a gross lease, but it provides for increases at set periods. Increases may be predetermined or according to a definite formula.

Chapter 15 Property Management and Leasing **459**

FIGURE 15.2

Typical Lease Percentages Charged in 2002

Type of Business	Percent of Gross Sales
Grocery or supermarket	1–2
Discount store	1½–3
Laundromat	12–15
Shoe-repair shop	10–15
Parking lot	40–50
Parking garage	40–50

Requirements of a Valid Lease
To be valid, a lease must

- contain the names of lessor and lessee and be signed by the lessor,
- be in writing if for longer than one year (statute of frauds),
- contain an adequate description of the property,
- show the amount of rent and the manner of payment,
- be between parties who are capable of contracting,
- state the duration of time the lease is to be in force, and
- put any automatic renewal provisions in boldface type.

Note: A lease for one year or less is not required by law to be in writing to be valid.

■ RESIDENTIAL LEASING

Most rentals are residential, and most property managers are primarily involved in residential leases. The property manager has a duty to the owner to use care in the selection of tenants. A tenant who has no desire to pay rent and/or is destructive is worse than having no tenant at all. As protection, property managers should not allow occupancy to a prospective tenant until that person is cleared as being a desirable tenant for the property and deposit and rent checks have cleared.

Rental Application

Figure 15.3 is the Application to Rent Receipt for Deposit/Screening Fee form prepared by the California Association of REALTORS®. You can see that the application requires a great deal of financial data as well as employment information.

Many lessors also require a copy of the prospective lessee's last pay stub, which serves to verify income. As a minimum, the lessor should verify the present

460   California Real Estate Practice

FIGURE 15.3

Application for Rent Receipt for Deposit/Screening Fee

CALIFORNIA ASSOCIATION OF REALTORS®

APPLICATION TO RENT RECEIPT FOR DEPOSIT/SCREENING FEE
(C.A.R. Form LRA, Revised 4/01)

I. APPLICATION TO RENT

THIS SECTION TO BE COMPLETED BY APPLICANT. A SEPARATE APPLICATION TO RENT IS REQUIRED FOR EACH OCCUPANT 18 YEARS OF AGE OR OVER.

Application to rent property at _____ ("Premises").
FULL NAME OF APPLICANT _____ Date of birth _____
Soc. Sec. No._____ Driver's license no. _____ State _____ Expires _____
Phone Number: Home _____ Work _____ Other _____ Email _____
Current address_____   Previous address _____
City/State/Zip_____   City/State/Zip _____
Name of landlord/manager_____   Name of landlord/manager _____
Landlord/manager's phone_____   Landlord/manager's phone _____
How long at current address?_____   How long at this address?_____
Reason for leaving current address_____   Reason for leaving this address _____
Name(s) of all other proposed occupant(s) and relationship to applicant _____

Proposed pet(s) (number and type) _____
Current employer _____ Supervisor _____ Length of employment _____
Employer's address _____ Phone _____
Position or title _____ Gross income $ _____ per _____
Previous employer_____ Supervisor _____ Length of employment _____
Employer's address _____ Phone _____
Position or title _____ Gross income $ _____ per _____

Other income $ _____ per _____ Source _____
Auto make _____ Model _____ Year _____ License no. _____ State _____ Color _____
In case of emergency, person to notify _____ Relationship_____
Address _____ Phone _____
Does applicant plan to use liquid filled furniture? ☐ No ☐ Yes Type _____
Has applicant been a party to an unlawful detainer action or filed bankruptcy within the last seven years? ☐ No ☐ Yes
If yes, explain _____
Has applicant or any proposed occupant ever been convicted of or pleaded no contest to a felony? ☐ No ☐ Yes
If yes, explain _____

Name of creditor	Account number	Monthly payment	Balance due

Name of bank	Account Number	Address/branch	Type of account

Applicant represents the above information to be true and complete, and hereby authorizes Landlord or manager to (i) verify the information provided and (ii) obtain credit report on applicant.

Date _____ Time _____
Applicant _____

The copyright laws of the United States (Title 17 U.S. Code) forbid the unauthorized reproduction of this form, or any portion thereof, by photocopy machine or any other means, including facsimile or computerized formats. Copyright © 1993-2001, CALIFORNIA ASSOCIATION OF REALTORS®, INC. ALL RIGHTS RESERVED.

Applicant and Landlord/Manager acknowledge receipt of a copy of this page.
Applicant's Initials (_____)(_____)
Landlord/Manager's Initials (_____)(_____)

EQUAL HOUSING OPPORTUNITY

LRA-11 (PAGE 1 OF 2) Print Date

Reviewed by
Broker or Designee _____ Date _____

APPLICATION TO RENT RECEIPT FOR DEPOSIT/SCREENING FEE (LRA-11 PAGE 1 OF 2)

FIGURE 15.3

Application for Rent Receipt for Deposit/Screening Fee (continued)

THIS SECTION TO BE COMPLETED BY AGENT, LANDLORD OR MANAGER.

Applicant has deposited the sum of $_____ as a deposit on the Premises. The deposit is evidenced by:

☐ Cashier's Check, ☐ Personal Check, or ☐ other _____,
payable to _____, to be held uncashed until approval of the Application To Rent. If deposit is in cash, deposit shall be ☐ held in Broker's Trust Account or ☐ given to Owner. The executed lease or rental agreement may require additional sums to be paid, as a security deposit, or for other purposes. If the Application to Rent is approved, the deposited sum shall be applied to total sums due upon execution of a lease or rental agreement. If the Application to Rent is not approved within _____ days, the deposit shall be returned to Applicant.

III. SCREENING FEE

THIS SECTION TO BE COMPLETED BY AGENT, LANDLORD OR MANAGER.

In addition to the deposit, Applicant has paid a nonrefundable screening fee of $_____, applied as follows: (The screening fee may not exceed $30.00 (adjusted annually from 1-1-98 commensurate with the increase in the Consumer Price Index.))

$_____ for credit reports;

$_____ for _____ (other out-of-pocket expenses); and

$_____ for processing.

The undersigned has read the foregoing and acknowledges receipt of a copy.

_____ Date
Applicant Signature
The undersigned has received the deposit and screening fee indicated above.

_____ Date
Landlord or Manager or Agent Signature

R E B S I N C
Published and Distributed by:
REAL ESTATE BUSINESS SERVICES, INC.
a subsidiary of the CALIFORNIA ASSOCIATION OF REALTORS®
525 South Virgil Avenue, Los Angeles, California 90020

| Reviewed by |
| Broker or Designee _____ Date _____ |

EQUAL HOUSING OPPORTUNITY

LRA-11 (PAGE 2 OF 2)

APPLICATION TO RENT RECEIPT FOR DEPOSIT/SCREENING FEE (LRA-11 PAGE 2 OF 2)

employment and length of employment with the present employer as well as check with present or prior landlords regarding any problems they may have had. Keep in mind that checking of tenants must be the case *for all tenants*, or you could be in violation of one or more of the fair housing laws.

It is also a good practice to see and make a copy of the prospective tenant's driver's license. This will show you that the applicant is who he or she claims to be as well as provide you with a previous address.

Although the civil rights law prohibits discrimination for reasons of race, sex, age, national origin, and so forth (Chapter 2), there are valid reasons for discrimination. You can discriminate against a tenant who has had problems with other tenants at a prior rental, was late in making payments, broke rules, damaged the property, left owing rent, or generally has had a poor work or credit history. You don't have to accept a problem tenant. It is a lot easier to refuse a rental than it is to rectify a mistake once it is made.

> A landlord may charge a nonrefundable $30 screening fee.

You are allowed to charge a nonrefundable screening fee of up to $30 per applicant. This fee is to cover the costs of obtaining and gathering information to make an acceptance or rejection decision regarding a tenant. The application to rent in Figure 15.3 includes a receipt for a screening fee on the second page.

Lease Provisions

Even though you are renting on a month-to-month basis, you should nevertheless use a written lease because a lease clearly sets forth lessor and lessee duties and obligations. If you have apartment rules or regulations, they should be attached to the lease and signed by the tenant.

Don't try to draft a lease or use sections from a number of leases for a "cut and paste" lease. You could be personally liable for errors or omissions, and it also could be considered the unauthorized practice of law. If a simple form lease, such as the Residential Lease or Month-To-Month Rental Agreement prepared by the California Association of REALTORS® (Figure 15.4), is not appropriate, see an attorney.

Name of Parties.   Any lease should include the full names of all parties. If any person is under the age of 18, you ordinarily would need a cosigner unless the underage party qualifies as an emancipated minor by reason of marriage or has been declared emancipated by a court. In signing the lease the parties should sign "jointly and severally," so it is clear that each signer is liable for the entire rent and you can go to one or to all tenants for the rent.

Description of Premises.   The premises should be described in such a manner that there is no ambiguity. If a parking space or garage is included, it should be specified.

FIGURE 15.4

Residential Lease or Month-to-Month Rental Agreement

CALIFORNIA ASSOCIATION OF REALTORS®

RESIDENTIAL LEASE OR MONTH-TO-MONTH RENTAL AGREEMENT
(C.A.R. Form LR, Revised 1/03)

_____ ("Landlord") and
_____ ("Tenant") agree as follows:

1. **PROPERTY:**
   A. Landlord rents to Tenant and Tenant rents from Landlord, the real property and improvements described as: _____
   _____ ("Premises").
   B. The following personal property is included: _____
2. **TERM:** The term begins on (date) _____ ("Commencement Date"), **(Check A or B):**
   ☐ A. **Month-to-month:** and continues as a month-to-month tenancy. Tenant may terminate the tenancy by giving written notice
        at least 30 days prior to the intended termination date. Landlord may terminate the tenancy by giving written notice as
        provided by law. Such notice may be given on any date.
   ☐ B. **Lease:** and shall terminate on (date) _____ at
        _____ AM/PM. Any holding over after the term of this Agreement expires, with Landlord's consent, shall create a
        month-to-month tenancy which either party may terminate as specified in paragraph 2A. Rent shall be at a rate equal to the
        rent for the immediately preceding month, unless otherwise notified by Landlord, payable in advance. All other terms and
        conditions of this Agreement shall remain in full force and effect.
3. **RENT:** "Rent" shall mean all monetary obligations of tenant to landlord under the terms of this agreement, except security deposit.
   A. Tenant agrees to pay $ _____ per month for the term of the Agreement.
   B. Rent is payable in advance on the **1st** (or ☐ _____) **day** of each calendar month, and is delinquent on the next day.
   C. If Commencement Date falls on any day other than the first day of the month, Rent shall be prorated based on a 30-day period.
        If Tenant has paid one full month's Rent in advance of Commencement Date, Rent for the second calendar month shall be prorated
        based on a 30-day period.
   D. **PAYMENT:** The Rent shall be paid by ☐ cash, ☐ personal check, ☐ money order, ☐ cashier check, ☐ other _____,
        to (name) _____ (phone) _____
        at (address) _____
        (or at any other location specified by Landlord in writing to Tenant) between the hours of _____ and _____
        on the following days _____.
4. **SECURITY DEPOSIT:**
   A. Tenant agrees to pay $ _____ as a security deposit. Security deposit will be ☐ transferred to and
        held by the Owner of the Premises; or ☐ held in Owner's Broker's trust account.
   B. All or any portion of the security deposit may be used, as reasonably necessary, to: (1) cure Tenant's default in payment of
        Rent, (which includes Late Charges, non-sufficient funds ("NSF") fees, or other sums due); (2) repair damage, excluding
        ordinary wear and tear, caused by Tenant or by a guest or licensee of Tenant; (3) clean Premises, if necessary, upon termination
        of tenancy; and (4) replace or return personal property or appurtenances. **SECURITY DEPOSIT SHALL NOT BE USED BY
        TENANT IN LIEU OF PAYMENT OF LAST MONTH'S RENT.** If all or any portion of the security deposit is used during tenancy,
        Tenant agrees to reinstate the total security deposit within five days after written notice is delivered to Tenant. Within three
        weeks after Tenant vacates the Premises, Landlord shall: (1) furnish Tenant an itemized statement indicating the amount of any
        security deposit received and the basis for its disposition; and (2) return any remaining portion of security deposit to Tenant.
   C. No interest will be paid on security deposit unless required by local ordinance.
   D. If security deposit is held by Owner, Tenant agrees not to hold Broker responsible for its return. If security deposit is held in
        Owner's Broker's trust account, **and** Broker's authority is terminated before expiration of this Agreement, **and** security deposits
        are released to someone other than Tenant, **then** Broker shall notify Tenant, in writing, where and to whom security deposit has
        been released. Once Tenant has been provided such notice, Tenant agrees not to hold Broker responsible for security deposit.
5. **MOVE-IN COSTS RECEIVED/DUE:**

Category	Total Due	Payment Received	Balance Due	Date Due
Rent from _____ to _____ (date)				
*Security Deposit				
Other _____				
Other _____				
Total				

   *The maximum amount that Landlord may receive as security deposit, however designated, cannot exceed two month's Rent for an
   unfurnished Premises, or three month's Rent for a furnished premises.
6. **PARKING: (Check A or B)**
   ☐ A. Parking is permitted as follows: _____
        The right to parking ☐ is, ☐ is not, included in the Rent charged pursuant to paragraph 3. If not included in the Rent, the
        parking rental fee shall be an additional $ _____ per month. Parking space(s) are to be used for
        parking operable motor vehicles, except for trailers, boats, campers, buses or trucks (other than pick-up trucks). Tenant shall
        park in assigned space(s) only. Parking space(s) are to be kept clean. Vehicles leaking oil, gas or other motor vehicle fluids
        shall not be parked on the Premises. Mechanical work or storage of inoperable vehicles is not allowed in parking space(s)
        or elsewhere on the Premises.
   OR ☐ B. Parking is not permitted on the Premises.

LR REVISED 1/03 (PAGE 1 OF 4) Print Date

Landlord's Initials (_____)(_____)
Tenant's Initials   (_____)(_____)

Reviewed by _____ Date _____

EQUAL HOUSING OPPORTUNITY

RESIDENTIAL LEASE OR MONTH-TO-MONTH RENTAL AGREEMENT (LR PAGE 1 OF 4)

FIGURE 15.4

Residential Lease or Month-to-Month Rental Agreement (continued)

Premises: _____ Date: _____

7. **STORAGE: (Check A or B)**
   ☐ **A.** Storage is permitted as follows:_____
      The right to storage space ☐ is, ☐ is not, included in the Rent charged pursuant to paragraph 3. If not included in Rent, storage space shall be an additional $ _____ per month. Tenant shall store only personal property that Tenant owns, and shall not store property that is claimed by another or in which another has any right, title, or interest. Tenant shall not store any improperly packaged food or perishable goods, flammable materials, explosives, or other inherently dangerous material.
   OR ☐ **B.** Storage is not permitted on the Premises.
8. **LATE CHARGE/NSF CHECKS:** Tenant acknowledges that either late payment of Rent or issuance of a NSF check may cause Landlord to incur costs and expenses, the exact amount of which are extremely difficult and impractical to determine. These costs may include, but are not limited to, processing, enforcement and accounting expenses, and late charges imposed on Landlord. If any installment of Rent due from Tenant is not received by Landlord within **5 (or ☐ _____) calendar days** after date due, or if a check is returned NSF, Tenant shall pay to Landlord, respectively, an additional sum of $ _____ as Late Charge and $25.00 as a NSF fee, either or both of which shall be deemed additional Rent. Landlord and Tenant agree that these charges represent a fair and reasonable estimate of the costs Landlord may incur by reason of Tenant's late or NSF payment. Any Late Charge or NSF fee due shall be paid with the current installment of Rent. Landlord's acceptance of any Late Charge or NSF fee shall not constitute a waiver as to any default of Tenant. Landlord's right to collect a Late Charge or NSF fee shall not be deemed an extension of the date Rent is due under paragraph 3, or prevent Landlord from exercising any other rights and remedies under this Agreement, and as provided by law.
9. **CONDITION OF PREMISES:** Tenant has examined Premises, all furniture, furnishings, appliances, landscaping, if any, and fixtures, including smoke detector(s).
   (Check one:)
   ☐ **A.** Tenant acknowledges that these items are clean and in operative condition, with the following exceptions _____
   _____
   OR ☐ **B.** Tenant's acknowledgment of the condition of these items is contained in an attached statement of condition (C.A.R. Form MIMO).
   OR ☐ **C.** Tenant will provide Landlord a list of items that are damaged or not in operable condition within **3 (or ☐ _____) days** after Commencement Date, not as a contingency of this Agreement but rather as an acknowledgment of the condition of the Premises.
   OR ☐ **D.** Other:_____
10. **NEIGHBORHOOD CONDITIONS:** Tenant is advised to satisfy him or herself as to neighborhood or area conditions, including schools, proximity and adequacy of law enforcement, crime statistics, registered felons or offenders, fire protection, other governmental services, proximity to commercial, industrial or agricultural activities, existing and proposed transportation, construction and development that may affect noise, view, or traffic, airport noise, noise or odor from any source, wild and domestic animals, other nuisances, hazards, or circumstances, facilities and condition of common areas, conditions and influences of significance to certain cultures and/or religions, and personal needs, requirements and preferences of Tenant.
11. **UTILITIES:** Tenant agrees to pay for all utilities and services, and the following charges: _____ except _____, which shall be paid for by Landlord. If any utilities are not separately metered, Tenant shall pay Tenant's proportional share, as reasonably determined by Landlord.
12. **OCCUPANTS:** The Premises are for the sole use as a personal residence by the following named persons **only:** _____
    _____
13. **PETS:** No animal or pet shall be kept on or about the Premises without Landlord's prior written consent, except _____
14. **RULES/REGULATIONS:** Tenant agrees to comply with all rules and regulations of Landlord, which are at any time posted on the Premises or delivered to Tenant. Tenant shall not, and shall ensure that guests and licensees of Tenant shall not, disturb, annoy, endanger, or interfere with other tenants of the building or neighbors, or use the Premises for any unlawful purposes, including, but not limited to, using, manufacturing, selling, storing, or transporting illicit drugs or other contraband, or violate any law or ordinance, or commit a waste or nuisance on or about the Premises.
15. **CONDOMINIUM/PLANNED UNIT DEVELOPMENT** ☐ (If checked) The Premises is a unit in a condominium, planned unit, or other development governed by a homeowners' association ("HOA"). The name of the HOA is _____. Tenant agrees to comply with all covenants, conditions and restrictions, bylaws, rules and regulations and decisions of HOA. Landlord shall provide Tenant copies of rules and regulations, if any. Tenant shall reimburse Landlord for any fines or charges imposed by HOA or other authorities, due to any violation by Tenant, or the guests or licensees of Tenant.
16. **MAINTENANCE:**
    A. Tenant shall properly use, operate and safeguard Premises, including if applicable, any landscaping, furniture, furnishings, and appliances, and all mechanical, electrical, gas and plumbing fixtures, and keep them clean and sanitary. Tenant shall immediately notify Landlord, in writing, of any problem, malfunction or damage. Tenant shall pay for all repairs or replacements caused by Tenant, or guests of Tenant, excluding ordinary wear and tear. Tenant shall pay for all damage to Premises as a result of failure to report a problem in a timely manner. Tenant shall pay for repair of drain blockages or stoppages, unless caused by defective plumbing parts or tree roots invading sewer lines.
    B. ☐ Landlord ☐ Tenant shall water the garden, landscaping, trees and shrubs, except _____
    _____
    C. ☐ Landlord ☐ Tenant shall maintain the garden, landscaping, trees and shrubs, except _____
    _____
17. **ALTERATIONS:** Tenant shall not make any alterations in or about the Premises without Landlord's prior written consent, including: painting, wallpapering, adding or changing locks, installing antenna or satellite dish(es), placing signs, displays or exhibits, or using screws, fastening devices, large nails or adhesive materials.
18. **KEYS/LOCKS:**
    A. Tenant acknowledges receipt of (or Tenant will receive ☐ prior to the Commencement Date, or ☐ _____):
      ☐ _____ key(s) to Premises,   ☐ _____ remote control device(s) for garage door/gate opener(s),
      ☐ _____ key(s) to mailbox,   ☐ _____
      ☐ _____ key(s) to common area(s),   ☐ _____
    B. Tenant acknowledges that locks to the Premises ☐ have, ☐ have not, been rekeyed.
    C. If Tenant rekeys existing locks or opening devices, Tenant shall immediately deliver copies of all keys to Landlord. Tenant shall pay all costs and charges related to loss of any keys or opening devices. Tenant may not remove locks, even if installed by Tenant.

Landlord's Initials (_____)(_____)
Tenant's Initials (_____)(_____)

LR REVISED 1/03 (PAGE 2 OF 4)

Reviewed by _____ Date _____

EQUAL HOUSING OPPORTUNITY

FIGURE 15.4

Residential Lease or Month-to-Month Rental Agreement (continued)

Premises: _____ Date: _____

19. **ENTRY:** Tenant shall make Premises available to Landlord or representative for the purpose of entering to make necessary or agreed repairs, decorations, alterations, or improvements, or to supply necessary or agreed services, or to show Premises to prospective or actual purchasers, tenants, mortgagees, lenders, appraisers, or contractors. Landlord and Tenant agree that twenty-four (24) hours written notice shall be reasonable and sufficient notice. In an emergency, Landlord or representative may enter Premises at any time without prior notice.

20. **SIGNS:** Tenant authorizes Landlord to place For Sale/Lease signs on the Premises.

21. **ASSIGNMENT/SUBLETTING:** Tenant shall not sublet all or any part of Premises, or assign or transfer this Agreement or any interest in it, without prior written consent of Landlord. Unless such consent is obtained, any assignment, transfer or subletting of Premises or this Agreement or tenancy, by voluntary act of Tenant, operation of law, or otherwise, shall be null and void, and at the option of Landlord, terminate this Agreement. Any proposed assignee, transferee or sublessee shall submit to Landlord an application and credit information for Landlord's approval, and if approved, sign a separate written agreement with Landlord and Tenant. Landlord's consent to any one assignment, transfer or sublease, shall not be construed as consent to any subsequent assignment, transfer or sublease and does not release Tenant of Tenant's obligation under this Agreement.

22. ☐ **LEAD PAINT (CHECK IF APPLICABLE):** Premises was constructed prior to 1978. In accordance with federal law, Landlord gives and Tenant acknowledges receipt of the disclosures on the attached form (C.A.R. Form FLD) and a federally approved lead pamphlet.

23. **POSSESSION:** If Landlord is unable to deliver possession of Premises on Commencement Date, such Date shall be extended to date on which possession is made available to Tenant. If Landlord is unable to deliver possession within **5 (or ☐ _____) calendar days** after agreed Commencement Date, Tenant may terminate this Agreement by giving written notice to Landlord, and shall be refunded all Rent and security deposit paid.

24. **TENANT'S OBLIGATIONS UPON VACATING PREMISES:** Upon termination of Agreement, Tenant shall: **(a)** give Landlord all copies of all keys or opening devices to Premises, including any common areas; **(b)** vacate Premises and surrender it to Landlord empty of all persons; **(c)** vacate any/all parking and/or storage space; **(d)** deliver Premises to Landlord in the same condition as referenced in paragraph 9; **(e)** clean the Premises; **(f)** give written notice to Landlord of Tenant's forwarding address; and **(g)** _____
_____.
All improvements installed by Tenant, with or without Landlord's consent, become the property of Landlord upon termination.

25. **BREACH OF CONTRACT/EARLY TERMINATION:** In addition to any obligations established by paragraph 24, in event of termination by Tenant prior to completion of the original term of Agreement, Tenant shall also be responsible for lost Rent, rental commissions, advertising expenses and painting costs necessary to ready Premises for re-rental.

26. **TEMPORARY RELOCATION:** Tenant agrees, upon demand of Landlord, to temporarily vacate Premises for a reasonable period, to allow for fumigation, or other methods, to control wood destroying pests or organisms, or other repairs to Premises. Tenant agrees to comply with all instructions and requirements necessary to prepare Premises to accommodate pest control, fumigation or other work, including bagging or storage of food and medicine, and removal of perishables and valuables. Tenant shall only be entitled to a credit of Rent equal to the per diem Rent for the period of time Tenant is required to vacate Premises.

27. **DAMAGE TO PREMISES:** If, by no fault of Tenant, Premises are totally or partially damaged or destroyed by fire, earthquake, accident or other casualty, which render Premises uninhabitable, either Landlord or Tenant may terminate Agreement by giving the other written notice. Rent shall be abated as of date of damage. The abated amount shall be the current monthly Rent prorated on a 30-day basis. If Agreement is not terminated, Landlord shall promptly repair the damage, and Rent shall be reduced based on the extent to which the damage interferes with Tenant's reasonable use of Premises. If damage occurs as a result of an act of Tenant or Tenant's guests, only Landlord shall have the right of termination, and no reduction in Rent shall be made.

28. **INSURANCE:** Tenant's or guest's personal property and vehicles are not insured by Landlord or, if applicable, HOA, against loss or damage due to fire, theft, vandalism, rain, water, criminal or negligent acts of others, or any other cause. Tenant is to carry Tenant's own insurance (renter's insurance) to protect Tenant from any such loss.

29. **WATERBEDS:** Tenant shall not use or have waterbeds on the Premises unless: **(a)** Tenant obtains a valid waterbed insurance policy; **(b)** Tenant increases the security deposit in an amount equal to one-half of one month's Rent; and **(c)** the bed conforms to the floor load capacity of Premises.

30. **WAIVER:** The waiver of any breach shall not be construed as a continuing waiver of the same or any subsequent breach.

31. **NOTICE:** Notices may be served at the following address, or at any other location subsequently designated:
Landlord: _____   Tenant: _____
_____   _____

32. **TENANT ESTOPPEL CERTIFICATE:** Tenant shall execute and return a tenant estoppel certificate delivered to Tenant by Landlord or Landlord's agent within 3 days after its receipt. The tenant estoppel certificate acknowledges that this Agreement is unmodified and in full force, or in full force as modified, and states the modifications. Failure to comply with this requirement shall be deemed Tenant's acknowledgment that the tenant estoppel certificate is true and correct, and may be relied upon by a lender or purchaser.

33. **JOINT AND INDIVIDUAL OBLIGATIONS:** If there is more than one Tenant, each one shall be individually and completely responsible for the performance of all obligations of Tenant under this Agreement, jointly with every other Tenant, and individually, whether or not in possession.

34. ☐ **MILITARY ORDNANCE DISCLOSURE:** (If applicable and known to Landlord) Premises is located within one mile of an area once used for military training, and may contain potentially explosive munitions.

35. **TENANT REPRESENTATIONS; CREDIT:** Tenant warrants that all statements in Tenant's rental application are accurate. Tenant authorizes Landlord and Broker(s) to obtain Tenant's credit report at time of application and periodically during tenancy in connection with approval, modification, or enforcement of this Agreement. Landlord may cancel this Agreement: **(a)** before occupancy begins; **(b)** upon disapproval of the credit report(s); or **(c)** at any time, upon discovering that information in Tenant's application is false. A negative credit report reflecting on Tenant's record may be submitted to a credit reporting agency if Tenant fails to fulfill the terms of payment and other obligations under this Agreement.

36. **PERIODIC PEST CONTROL:** If Landlord has entered into a contract for periodic pest control treatment of the Premises, Landlord shall give tenant a copy of the notice originally given to Landlord by the pest control company.

Landlord's Initials (_____)(_____)
Tenant's Initials (_____)(_____)

LR REVISED 1/03 (PAGE 3 OF 4)

Reviewed by _____ Date _____

EQUAL HOUSING OPPORTUNITY

RESIDENTIAL LEASE OR MONTH-TO-MONTH RENTAL AGREEMENT (LR PAGE 3 OF 4)

FIGURE 15.4

Residential Lease or Month-to-Month Rental Agreement (continued)

Premises: _____   Date: _____

37. **DATA BASE DISCLOSURE:** NOTICE: The California Department of Justice, sheriff's departments, police departments serving jurisdictions of 200,000 or more, and many other local law enforcement authorities maintain for public access a data base of the locations of persons required to register pursuant to paragraph (1) of subdivision (a) of Section 290.4 of the Penal Code. The data base is updated on a quarterly basis and a source of information about the presence of these individuals in any neighborhood. The Department of Justice also maintains a Sex Offender Identification Line through which inquiries about individuals may be made. This is a "900" telephone service. Callers must have specific information about individuals they are checking. Information regarding neighborhoods is not available through the "900" telephone service.

38. **OTHER TERMS AND CONDITIONS/SUPPLEMENTS:** _____
_____
The following ATTACHED supplements are incorporated in this Agreement: _____
_____

39. **ATTORNEY FEES:** In any action or proceeding arising out of this Agreement, the prevailing party between Landlord and Tenant shall be entitled to reasonable attorney fees and costs.

40. **ENTIRE CONTRACT:** Time is of the essence. All prior agreements between Landlord and Tenant are incorporated in this Agreement, which constitutes the entire contract. It is intended as a final expression of the parties' agreement, and may not be contradicted by evidence of any prior agreement or contemporaneous oral agreement. The parties further intend that this Agreement constitutes the complete and exclusive statement of its terms, and that no extrinsic evidence whatsoever may be introduced in any judicial or other proceeding, if any, involving this Agreement. Any provision of this Agreement that is held to be invalid shall not affect the validity or enforceability of any other provision in this Agreement.

41. **AGENCY:**
   A. **Confirmation:** The following agency relationship(s) are hereby confirmed for this transaction:
   Listing Agent: (Print firm name) _____ is the agent of (check one): ☐ the Landlord exclusively; or ☐ both the Landlord and Tenant.
   Leasing Agent: (Print firm name) _____ (if not same as Listing Agent) is the agent of (check one): ☐ the Tenant exclusively; or ☐ the Landlord exclusively; or ☐ both the Tenant and Landlord.
   B. **Disclosure:** ☐ (If checked): The term of this lease exceeds one year. A disclosure regarding real estate agency relationships (such as C.A.R. Form AD), has been provided to Landlord and Tenant, who each acknowledge its receipt.

42. ☐ **INTERPRETER/TRANSLATOR:** The terms of this Agreement have been interpreted/translated for Tenant into the following language: _____. Interpretation/translation service has been provided by (print name) _____, who has the following Driver's License or other identification number: _____. Tenant has been advised to rely on, and has in fact solely relied on the interpretation/translation services of the above-named individual, and not on the Landlord or other person involved in negotiating the Agreement. If the Agreement has been negotiated primarily in Spanish, Tenant has been provided a Spanish language translation of this Agreement pursuant to the California Civil Code. (C.A.R. Form LR-S fulfills this requirement.)

Signature of interpreter/translator _____   Date _____

Landlord and Tenant acknowledge and agree that Brokers: **(a)** do not guarantee the condition of the Premises; **(b)** cannot verify representations made by others; **(c)** cannot provide legal or tax advice; **(d)** will not provide other advice or information that exceeds the knowledge, education or experience required to obtain a real estate license. Furthermore, if Brokers are not also acting as Landlord in this Agreement, Brokers; **(e)** do not decide what rental rate a Tenant should pay or Landlord should accept; and **(f)** do not decide upon the length or other terms of tenancy. Landlord and Tenant agree that they will seek legal, tax, insurance and other desired assistance from appropriate professionals.

Tenant _____   Date _____
Tenant _____   Date _____
Landlord _____   Date _____
(Owner or Agent with authority to enter into this lease)

Landlord _____   Date _____
(Owner or Agent with authority to enter into this lease)

Landlord Address _____ City _____ State _____ Zip _____
Telephone _____ Fax _____

Agency relationships are confirmed as above. Real estate brokers who are not also Landlord in this Agreement are not a party to the Agreement between Landlord and Tenant.

Real Estate Broker (Leasing Firm) _____
By (Agent) _____   Date _____
Address _____ City _____ State _____ Zip _____
Telephone _____ Fax _____

Real Estate Broker (Listing Firm) _____
By (Agent) _____   Date _____
Address _____ City _____ State _____ Zip _____
Telephone _____ Fax _____

THIS FORM HAS BEEN APPROVED BY THE CALIFORNIA ASSOCIATION OF REALTORS® (C.A.R.). NO REPRESENTATION IS MADE AS TO THE LEGAL VALIDITY OR ADEQUACY OF ANY PROVISION IN ANY SPECIFIC TRANSACTION. A REAL ESTATE BROKER IS THE PERSON QUALIFIED TO ADVISE ON REAL ESTATE TRANSACTIONS. IF YOU DESIRE LEGAL OR TAX ADVICE, CONSULT AN APPROPRIATE PROFESSIONAL.

This form is available for use by the entire real estate industry. It is not intended to identify the user as a REALTOR®. REALTOR® is a registered collective membership mark which may be used only by members of the NATIONAL ASSOCIATION OF REALTORS® who subscribe to its Code of Ethics.

SURE TRAC The System for Success™
Published by the
California Association of REALTORS®

LR REVISED 1/03 (PAGE 4 OF 4)

Reviewed by _____ Date _____

EQUAL HOUSING OPPORTUNITY

RESIDENTIAL LEASE OR MONTH-TO-MONTH RENTAL AGREEMENT (LR PAGE 4 OF 4)

Dates.   The lease should have a beginning and an ending date.

Rent and Late Charge.   The rent amount or rental formula should be clearly stated as well as where and when the rent is due. Consider **late charges** for late payments. Keep in mind that if the late charge is too high, a court could determine it to be a penalty and declare it unenforceable.

Pets.   Pet agreements are common in residential leases. Lessors may require an additional deposit or limit the size and type of pet allowed.

Waterbeds.   Common waterbed agreements require the tenant to have a liner on any waterbed as well as pay for a policy of waterbed insurance, should the waterbed cause damage to the premises.

Inspection.   Some leases provide for pretenancy and end-of-tenancy walk-through inspections. Deficiencies should be noted on a form provided for this purpose, which should be signed by tenant and landlord. (See Figure 15.5.)

Cleaning and Security Deposits.   A controversial item in leases and rental agreements is the **security deposit.** The security deposit functions as a form of insurance for the landlord in case the rental premises are left damaged or dirty or rent is owed. According to the law, the amount of the security deposit that may be demanded or received is limited to an amount equal to two months' rent in the case of unfurnished residential property and to three months' rent for furnished residential property. Nonrefundable deposits, such as *cleaning deposits*, are not allowed.

> Nonrefundable tenant deposits are forbidden.

At the termination of the tenancy the landlord is permitted to retain only that portion of the security deposit reasonably necessary to remedy tenant defaults. If the landlord must return any portion of the deposit to the tenant, it must be returned within three weeks after tenancy is terminated. If the landlord defaults on this obligation, the tenant may initiate legal action through an attorney or small-claims court or file a complaint with the Consumer Protection Bureau.

Lease-Option Arrangement.   With a lease-option, usually used when loans are not easily available or the lessor lacks the required downpayment, the purchaser leases the property desired with an option to purchase at a later date. A portion of the amount paid as rent usually will be applied against the purchase price. (Options also can be for lease extensions.)

Exculpatory Clause (Hold-Harmless Clause).   Leases frequently contain an **exculpatory clause,** whereby the tenant agrees to relieve the landlord from all liability for injury or property damage resulting from the condition of the property or the negligence of the owner. Many residential leases contain these clauses, but the clauses are invalid for residential leases. Even though the tenant has agreed, the tenant has not given up his or her rights under the law.

> Exculpatory clauses are invalid for residential leases.

FIGURE 15.5

Statment of Condition

CALIFORNIA
ASSOCIATION
OF REALTORS®

STATEMENT OF CONDITION
(MOVE IN / MOVE OUT)

Premises Address _____ Unit No. _____

Occupant(s) _____ **MOVE-IN** Date _____

When completing this form, check the Premises carefully, and be specific in all items noted. Use additional paper, if necessary.

SMOKE DETECTOR(S) has (have) been tested on MOVE-IN, and found to be operative, except: _____
_____

LIVING ROOM AND DINING ROOM ITEMS: doors, locks, carpeting, floors, baseboards, walls, ceiling, electrical fixtures, electrical switches and outlets, windows coverings, windows, screens, and other items: _____
_____

MOVE-IN CONDITION	MOVE-OUT CONDITION

KITCHEN ITEMS: floors, baseboards, walls, ceiling, electrical fixtures, electrical switches and outlets, cooktop, oven, hood and fan, refrigerator, plumbing fixtures, sink, disposal, cabinets, counters, window coverings, windows, screens, and other items: _____
_____

MOVE-IN CONDITION	MOVE-OUT CONDITION

Occupant acknowledges receipt of copy of this page, which constitutes Page _____ of _____ Pages.
Occupant's Initials (_____) (_____)

R E B S   I N C
Published and Distributed by:
REAL ESTATE BUSINESS SERVICES, INC.
a subsidiary of the CALIFORNIA ASSOCIATION OF REALTORS®
525 South Virgil Avenue, Los Angeles, California 90020

OFFICE USE ONLY
Reviewed by Broker
or Designee _____
Date _____

EQUAL HOUSING
OPPORTUNITY

PRINT DATE
R APR 98

STATEMENT OF CONDITION (MIMO-11 PAGE 1 OF 3) REVISED 4/98

FIGURE 15.5

Statment of Condition (continued)

Premises Address _____   Unit No. _____

BEDROOM ITEMS: doors, lock, carpeting, floors, baseboards, walls, ceiling, electrical fixtures, electrical switches and outlets, window coverings, windows, screens, closet, closet doors and tracks, and other items:_____
_____

BEDROOM 1 MOVE-IN CONDITION	BEDROOM 1 **MOVE-OUT** CONDITION

BEDROOM 2 MOVE-IN CONDITION	BEDROOM 2 **MOVE-OUT** CONDITION

BEDROOM 3 MOVE-IN CONDITION	BEDROOM 3 **MOVE-OUT** CONDITION

OTHER ITEMS/AREAS: (If applicable) Entry door and window locks, heating and air conditioning, equipment, patio or balcony, yard areas, fencing, garage or carport, and _____
_____

MOVE-IN CONDITION	MOVE-OUT CONDITION

Occupant acknowledges receipt of copy of this page, which constitutes Page ____ of ____ Pages.
Occupant's Initials (_____) (_____)

OFFICE USE ONLY
Reviewed by Broker
or Designee _____
Date _____

PRINT DATE
R APR 98

STATEMENT OF CONDITION (MIMO-11 PAGE 2 OF 3) REVISED 4/98

FIGURE 15.5

Statment of Condition (continued)

Premises Address _____   Unit No. _____

BATHROOM ITEMS: doors, locks, carpeting or flooring, baseboards, walls, ceiling, electrical fixtures, electrical switches and outlets, window coverings, windows, screens, tub or shower, shower door or curtain, toilet, sink, medicine cabinet, counter, towel racks, fan, and other items:_____
_____.

BATHROOM 1 **MOVE-IN** CONDITION	BATHROOM 1 **MOVE-OUT** CONDITION

BATHROOM 2 **MOVE-IN** CONDITION	BATHROOM 2 **MOVE-OUT** CONDITION

THIS SECTION TO BE COMPLETED AT MOVE-IN:

The **Move-In** Inspection of the Premises was performed on (date)_____ Receipt of a copy of the Statement of Condition is acknowledged by:

Occupant _____   Date _____

Occupant _____   Date _____

Landlord or Agent_____   Date _____

THIS SECTION TO BE COMPLETED AT MOVE-OUT: The **MOVE-OUT** Inspection of the Premises was perfomed on (date)_____. Receipt of a copy of the Statement of Condition is acknowledged by:

Occupant _____   Date _____

Occupant _____   Date _____

Landlord or Agent _____   Date _____

Page _____ of _____ Pages.

OFFICE USE ONLY
Reviewed by Broker
or Designee _____
Date _____

STATEMENT OF CONDITION (MIMO-11 PAGE 3 OF 3) REVISED 4/98

Right of Entry. A lease may provide the landlord the right to check the property for specific purposes. In the absence of any agreement the landlord can enter only when

- an emergency requires entry;

- the tenant consents to an entry;

- the entry is during normal business hours after a reasonable notice (24 hours is considered reasonable) to make necessary or agreed repairs, alterations, or improvements, or to show the property to prospective or actual purchasers, mortgagees, tenants, workers, or contractors;

- the tenant has abandoned or surrendered the premises; or

- the landlord has obtained a court order to enter.

Landlord's Responsibilities

A residential lease has an implied warranty of habitability. This duty does not extend to cases in which the problem is one of tenant cleanliness. The landlord must assume at least that

- plumbing is in proper working order;

- the heat, lights, and wiring work and are safe;

- the floors, stairways, and railings are in good condition;

- when rented the premises are clean and free of pests;

- areas under lessor control are maintained; and

- the roof does not leak and no doors or windows are broken.

If a landlord demands or collects rent for an untenable dwelling, the lessor is liable for actual damages sustained by the tenant and special damages of not less than $100 or more than $1,000. The tenant can also raise the defense of habitability against any eviction action.

If a landlord fails to take corrective action when a repair is the landlord's responsibility, the tenant has the following three options:

1. The tenant may abandon the property and not be held liable for back rents or an unfulfilled lease.

2. The tenant may refer the problem to a mediator, an arbitrator, or in serious circumstances the small-claims court.

3. The tenant may notify the owner in writing of an emergency situation that must be taken care of. If the owner does not respond, the tenant may call in his or her own mechanics and offset the cost of repair with up to one month's rent on the next rent check. However, tenants may do this only twice in each year of tenancy.

Note: The tenant cannot be prohibited from installing a satellite dish within the area under tenant control.

Tenant's Responsibilities   The California Civil Code states that the tenant is obligated to

- keep the living unit clean and sanitary;

- dispose of garbage and other waste sanitarily;

- use all utility fixtures properly, keeping them clean and sanitary;

- avoid defacing or damaging property;

- use property only for its intended lawful purpose;

- pay rent on time;

- abide by rules and regulations;

- give a 30-day notice when vacating (month-to-month lease);

- return door and mailbox keys when vacating; and

- leave the unit in a clean condition when vacating.

Assignment versus Sublease

Provided that the terms of the lease do not prohibit such activity, a tenant has the right to assign or sublet his or her interest in the property.

In an *assignment*, the assignee is a tenant of the landlord. In a *sublease*, the sublessee is the tenant of the sublessor.

Assignment transfers the entire leasehold rights to a third party. The third party, the assignee, pays his or her rent directly to the original lessor, thus legally eliminating the original lessee.

A **sublease** of property transfers only a part of the tenant's interest. The sublessee pays his or her rent to the original lessee, who in turn is responsible to the lessor. The original lessee is said to have a "sandwich lease."

The lease should clearly indicate if it may be assigned or subleased. Lessors frequently provide that assignment or subleasing shall be allowed only with the approval of the lessor; however, this approval must not be unreasonably withheld.

Some leases provide that if the premises are sublet at a rent higher than the lessee is paying the lessor, the higher portion shall be split between the lessor and lessee. This encourages tenants to try to sublet for a maximum amount and also allows the lessor to share in the increased rent. (See Figure 15.6 for the difference between assignments and subleases.)

■ TERMINATION OF LEASE

A tenancy for a specified period, as in an estate for years, requires no notice for termination because the date has already been specified. Other than by expiration of the lease term, termination may be made

- by the tenant for violation of the landlord's duty to place the tenant in quiet possession,

FIGURE 15.6

Assignment Versus Subletting

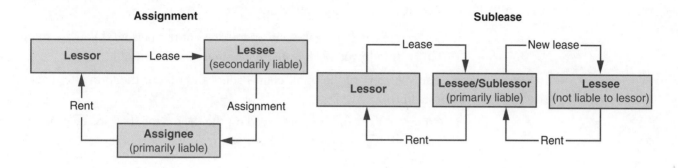

- by the tenant for the landlord's failure to repair,
- by the tenant on eviction by the landlord,
- by either party on destruction of the premises,
- by the landlord on use of the premises for unauthorized purposes or on abandonment of the premises by the tenant,
- by either party on breach of a condition of the lease, or
- by the tenant for the landlord's breach of the implied warranty of habitability.

Evictions and Unlawful Detainer

A landlord may evict a tenant and bring an **unlawful detainer** action against him or her for failure to pay rent when due, violation of provisions contained in the lease or rental agreement, or failure to vacate the premises after termination of 30 days or 60 days written notice. The process of removing a tenant for being behind in rent follows:

1. The landlord serves the tenant with a **three-day notice** to quit the premises or pay rent.

2. If the tenant fails to heed the notice, the landlord files an unlawful detainer action in municipal court.

3. If the landlord wins, the court awards the landlord a judgment. The landlord then asks for a writ of possession authorizing the sheriff to evict the tenant.

4. The sheriff sends the tenant an eviction notice. If the tenant fails to leave, the sheriff then physically removes the tenant.

Because of drug-related crime, the legislature has authorized several city attorney and prosecutor offices to bring unlawful detainer actions to abate drug-related nuisances (the landlord will be charged fees and costs).

Property managers frequently bring action against tenants and former tenants in small-claims courts for back rent or for damages to the premises. Attorneys are not allowed in small-claims courts. The maximum amount of the suit is $5,000. The procedure is simple and informal.

1. Determine the full legal name and address of the person(s) you are suing. This will help you decide where you must file your claim.

2. Visit the clerk of the small-claims court and fill out the form after paying a small fee.

3. Arrange for the order to be served on the defendant (but not by yourself). The clerk will mail it for a fee, or you may authorize someone to serve it personally.

4. While waiting for the trial, gather all important documents and have them ready. Contact all potential witnesses and arrange for them to come with you to the trial, or obtain a subpoena from the clerk for any witness who will not come voluntarily. If you need an interpreter, find out if one is available at small-claims court; otherwise, bring your own.

5. Come to the court building early and ask the clerk where your case is being heard. When you reach the courtroom, check the calendar to see that your case is listed.

6. When your case is called, give your testimony, presenting only the facts. Be brief. Submit all papers and documents you think will help your case.

7. If you win, ask the defendant for the money awarded you in the judgment.

8. If you have difficulties in collecting your money, ask the clerk to assist you.

9. As plaintiff you are not allowed to appeal if you lose (unless you must pay as the result of a counterclaim).

Retaliatory Eviction

A landlord cannot decrease services, increase rent, or evict a tenant within 180 days after the tenant exercises a right protected under the law, including

- complaining to the landlord about the habitability of the premises,
- complaining to a public agency about defects, and
- lawfully organizing a tenant association.

A tenant cannot waive his or her rights against retaliatory eviction.

Prohibition of retaliatory eviction is a defense against eviction. If a landlord has been shown to have acted maliciously, the tenant will be entitled to from $100 to $1,000 in punitive damages.

■ SUMMARY

Property management, an ancient field of real estate specialization, is on the cutting edge of technology today. Property management has made rapid strides in professionalism, and besides the Institute of Real Estate Management (IREM), there are a number of other professional organizations.

Real estate managers fall into the following three general categories:

1. Licensee/property manager, who generally works out of a property management office handling numerous properties
2. Individual property manager, who handles just one property and who usually is an employee of an owner
3. Resident property managers

Property managers' duties vary with the type of property, but basically the manager has two main duties:

1. Strive for that rent/vacancy combination that will maximize the net earnings
2. Protect the property

To accomplish these duties, a property manager needs expertise in a variety of fields, from marketing to maintenance. The property manager, as a professional, has a duty to advise the owner in the operation of the property.

While most property management is residential, residential is broken down into specialized areas such as mobile-home parks and condominiums. Property management also can involve commercial and industrial property and even public buildings, marinas, and so forth.

Commercial and industrial property management requires special lease knowledge as well as technical knowledge of buildings and tenant requirements.

The property manager has a management contract similar to a sale listing that provides for a management fee and a leasing fee. Fees are based on complexity of the management and the rent received. The manager is responsible for trust records and owner accounting. Many other accounting records can aid a property manager as well. Computer software is available to fulfill almost all needs of the property manager.

Leases are gross, net, percentage, or a combination of all three. Generally net and percentage leases are found in connection with commercial rentals. To protect the owner, in residential leasing a rental application allows an owner to check out a tenant before committing to the tenant. Leases should be used for all tenancies, even month-to-month agreements, because they spell out rights and obligations of the parties.

In a lease assignment all of the tenants' interests are transferred. In a sublease the sublessor remains on the lease and the sublessee is his or her tenant.

Leases may be terminated for a number of reasons. If a tenant has breached a lease, the owner can sue for damages. The owner also may evict a tenant for breach of a material provision of the lease or if the tenant fails to leave after proper notice.

A landlord may not evict a tenant (retaliatory eviction) because the tenant complained to the landlord or a public agency about the condition of the premises or because the tenant lawfully organized a tenant group.

■ CLASS DISCUSSION TOPICS

1. A particular percentage lease provides that after a tenant reaches a specific gross annual amount, the percentage decreases. Why was this written into the lease?

2. Identify property in your geographic area that you feel is in need of professional property management. Why?

3. Which offices in your area have separate property management departments?

4. Which properties in your area do you think would require the greatest management effort? Why?

5. Identify a nonresidential property in your community that has been vacant for a long period of time. What type of tenant would the property be suited for and how would you market the property?

6. Do you know of any property where you feel the security is inadequate? If so, why? What could be done to provide better security?

7. Bring to class one current-events article dealing with some aspect of real estate practice for class discussion.

■ CHAPTER 15 QUIZ

1. The term CPM refers to
   a. California Property Manager.
   b. Certified Property Manager.
   c. Certified Professional Manager.
   d. none of the above.

2. Which of the following is a correct statement concerning a property manager's compensation?
   a. Compensation is generally a percentage of the gross.
   b. As the income of properties managed increases, the percentage fee charged tends to increase.
   c. Both a and b are correct.
   d. Neither a nor b is correct.

3. A property manager can be protected against receiving no fees when managing a vacant property he or she is unable to rent by a
   a. holdover clause.
   b. recapture clause.
   c. minimum fee.
   d. separate leasing fee.

4. A lease for 30 months would be described as a(n)
   a. estate at sufferance.
   b. estate at will.
   c. estate for years.
   d. periodic tenancy.

5. A lease under which the tenant is to pay $500 per month for three years is a
   a. gross lease.
   b. net lease.
   c. percentage lease.
   d. month-to-month lease.

6. A lease that contains a minimum rent and a covenant to remain in business is
   a. a percentage lease.
   b. a net lease.
   c. a gross lease.
   d. none of the above

7. Which of the following businesses would likely pay the highest percentage on a percentage lease?
   a. Parking lot
   b. Supermarket
   c. Clothing store
   d. Restaurant

8. Which of the following businesses is likely to pay the lowest percentage on a percentage lease?
   a. Sporting goods store
   b. Music shop
   c. Supermarket
   d. Clothing store

9. A valid two-year lease need not
   a. have parties capable of contracting.
   b. contain a legal description of the property.
   c. contain the amount of rent and manner of payment.
   d. be a written agreement.

10. Which of the following is a true statement concerning security deposits?
    a. Nonrefundable cleaning deposits are not allowed.
    b. Deposits for furnished rentals can't exceed three months' rent.
    c. Security deposits for unfurnished rentals can't exceed two months' rent.
    d. All of the above are true statements.

INTERNET SITES FOR REAL ESTATE PROFESSIONALS

The following is a partial listing of thousands of real estate-related sites. (For a directory of more than 25,000 real estate Web sites check *www.ired.com*.)

■ LISTINGS OF PROPERTY FOR SALE

> *www.realtor.com*
> *www.forsalebyowner.com*
> *www.fsbo-ca.net*
> *www.listinglink.com*
> *www.homeseekers.com*
> *www.newhomenetwork.com*
> *www.homeadvisor.com*
> *www.homebuilder.com*
> *www.homes.com*
> *www.coldwellbanker.com*
> *www.century21.com*
> *www.realtyexecutives.com*
> *www.remax.com*
> *www.owners.com*
> *www.era.com*
> *www.househunt.com*
> *www.californiarealestate.com*
> *www.ca-homes.com*

Note: Most of the above sites also provide for loan prequalification and application.

■ APARTMENTS FOR RENT

www.allapartments.com
www.homes.com (plus mortgage center)
www.rent.com
www.springstreet.com/apartments/
www.apartmentlinks.net/

■ LOANS

www.bankrate.com
www.eloan.com
www.homeshark.com
www.lendingtree.com
www.quickenmortgage.com
www.homeadvisor.com
www.internet-is.com/homeowners/inyahoo.html
www.mortgageloan.com
www.countrywide.com
www.loantek.com
www.homeowners.com
www.mtgtech.com

■ MORTGAGE CALCULATIONS

www.homefair.com
www.interest.com
www.lendingtree.com

■ HOME PRICES

www.domania.com (Recent home prices by area)

■ VIRTUAL HOME TOURS

www.ipix.com
www.jutvision.com
www.behere.com
www.bamboo.com
www.virtual.home.tours.net/

■ GOVERNMENT-RELATED SITES

California Department of Real Estate
www.dre.ca.gov

California Office of Real Estate Appraisal
www.orea.gov

Consumer Price Index
www.stats.bls.gov/cpihome.htm

Department of Housing and Urban Development (HUD)
www.hud.gov

Department of Veterans Affairs
www.va.gov

Environmental Protection Agency
www.epa.gov

Fair Housing Commission
www.fairhousing.com

Fair Housing Information Clearinghouse (HUD)
www.circsol.com/fairhousing

Fannie Mae
www.fanniemae.com

Farmer Mac
www.farmermac.com

Federal Reserve Bank (San Francisco)
www.frbsf.org

FEMA-Flood Insurance
www.fema.gov

FHA Mortgage Letters (Changes in FHA)
www.hud.gov/fha/mletters/mltrmenu.html

Freddie Mac
www.freddiemac.com

Ginnie Mae
www.ginniemae.gov

Government Web sites (Search Engine)
www.iperess.com/writer/gov.html

HUD
www.hud.gov

National Safety Council (Environmental Hazards)
www.nsc.org

■ ASSOCIATIONS

California Association of REALTORS®
www.car.org

Federation of Exchange Accomodators
www.1031.org

National Association of Real Estate Brokers
www.nareb@aol.org

National Association of REALTORS®
www.realtor.com

NAR Code of Ethics
www.dabr.com/ethics.htm

Institute of Real Estate Management
www.irem.org

Association of Real Estate License Law Officers
www.arello.org

Real Estate Educators Association
www.reea.org

■ CHOOSING A BROKER

www.homegain.com
(homeowners post their property and desired form of representation and brokers
send their proposals)
www.californiarealestate.com

■ ENVIRONMENTAL LAW

www.ceres.ca.gov
(an information site developed by the California Resource Agency that includes
a database containing California environmental law with links to federal law)

■ ENVIRONMENTAL PROTECTION AGENCY SITE

www.epa.gov

■ REAL ESTATE ATTORNEYS

www.lawforum.net
www.martindale.com

■ PROFESSIONAL INFORMATION

Inman News Features
www.inman.com

International Real Estate Digest
www.ired.com

NAR/Real Select
www.realtimes.com

National Relocation and Real Estate Magazine
www.rismedia.com

Commercial Real Estate News and Proposed California Statutes
www.reprofile.com

Real Estate Intelligence Report
www.reintel.com

The Real Estate Professional Magazine
www.therealestatepro.com

Real Net Direct
www.realtynow.com

Federation of Exchange Accomodators
www.1031.org

Wine Country Weekly Real Estate Reader
www.rereader.com

Forms, Articles, Legal Journals
www.relibrary.com

Note: We would like to hear from you about Internet sites that you feel should be included in our next edition: *pivarfish@webtv.net*

GLOSSARY

abstract of title. A summary or digest of all recorded transfers, conveyances, legal proceedings and any other facts relied on as evidence of title to show continuity of ownership and indicate any possible impairments to title.

acceleration clause. A provision in a real estate financing instrument that allows the lender to declare the remaining indebtedness due and payable on the happening of certain conditions, such as the sale of the property or the borrower's default in payment.

acceptance. Indication by the person to whom an offer is made (the offeree) of agreement to the terms of the offer. If the offer requires a writing, the acceptance also must be in writing.

accession. The process of manufactured or natural improvement or addition to property.

accretion. Accession by natural forces, such as alluvion.

acknowledgment. A formal declaration made before an authorized person by a person who has executed a written instrument, stating that the execution of the instrument is the person's own act.

acquisition cost. For FHA-insured loans, the price to procure property, including purchase price and all nonrecurring closing costs, including discount points, FHA application fee, service charge and credit report, FHA appraisal, escrow, document preparation, title insurance, termite inspection, reconveyance, and recording fees.

acre. A measure of land equaling 160 square rods, 4,840 square yards or 43,560 square feet, or a tract about 208.71 feet square.

action for declaratory relief. Legal proceeding that is brought to determine the respective rights of the parties before a controversy arises.

action to quiet title. A court proceeding brought to establish title to real property.

actual age. The number of years since completion of a building; also called *historical* or *chronological age*.

actual authority. The authority an agent has because it is specified in the agency agreement or that the agent believes he or she has because of an unintentional or a careless act of the principal.

administrator/administratrix. Personal representative of the estate of a decedent, appointed by the probate court. *See also* **executor/executrix.**

ad valorem. A Latin phrase meaning "according to value," used to describe a tax-charged in relation to the value of the property taxed.

adverse possession. A method of acquiring title to real property by occupying the property against the interests of the true owner and fulfilling other statutory requirements.

after-acquired title. If title is acquired by a grantor only after a conveyance to a grantee, the deed to the grantee becomes effective at the time the grantor actually receives title.

agency. The relationship between a principal and the agent of the principal that arises out of a contract, whether express or implied, written, or oral, by which the agent is employed by the principal to do certain acts dealing with a third party.

agent. One who acts for and with authority from another person, called the principal; a special agent is appointed to carry out a particular act or transaction, and any other agent is a general agent.

air rights. The real property right to the reasonable use of the airspace above the surface of the land.

alienation. The transferring of property to another.

all-inclusive trust deed. *See* **wraparound mortgage or trust deed.**

alluvion. Alluvium; the increase of soil along the bank of a body of water by natural forces.

Americans with Disabilities Act. Federal law providing access for handicapped in places of public accommodation.

amortization. The payment of a financial obligation in installments; recovery over a period of time of cost or value. An amortized loan includes both principal and interest in approximately equal payments, usually due monthly, resulting in complete payment of the amount borrowed, with interest, by the end of the loan term. A loan has negative amortization when the loan payments do not cover all of the interest due, which then is added to the remaining loan balance.

annual percentage rate (APR). The relative cost of credit as determined in accordance with Regulation Z of the Board of Governors of the Federal Reserve System for implementing the federal Truth-in-Lending Act.

anticipation, principle of. Expectation that property will offer future benefits, which tends to increase present value.

apparent authority. Authority to act as an agent that someone appears to have but does not actually have, which will place no obligation on the party the agent claims to represent if that party is in no way responsible for the representation.

appraisal. An estimate of a property's monetary value on the open market; an estimate of a property's type and condition, its utility for a given purpose, or its highest and best use.

appropriation, right of. *See* **right of appropriation.**

appurtenance. Anything affixed (attached) to or used with land for its benefit that is transferred with the land.

APR. *See* **annual percentage rate.**

area. Measure of the floor or ground space with-in the perimeter of a building or land parcel.

arm's-length transaction. A transaction in which neither party acts under duress and both have full knowledge of the property's assets and defects, the property involved has been on the market a reasonable length of time, there are no unusual circumstances and the price represents the normal consideration for the property sold, without extraordinary financing.

assessed valuation. A valuation placed on a piece of property by a public authority as a basis for levying taxes on that property.

assessor. The official responsible for determining assessed values.

assumption. An undertaking or adoption of a debt or an obligation resting primarily on another person.

attachment. The process by which real or personal property of a party to a lawsuit is seized and retained in the custody of the court; intended to compel an appearance before the court or to furnish security for a debt or costs arising out of the litigation.

attorney-in-fact. An agent who has been granted a power of attorney by a principal.

avulsion. The tearing or washing away of land along the bank of a body of water by natural forces.

balance, principle of. The combination of land uses that results in the highest property values overall.

balloon payment. An installment payment on a promissory note—usually the final payment—that is significantly larger than the other installment payments.

bankruptcy. A federal court proceeding in which the court takes possession of the assets of an insolvent debtor and sells the nonexempt assets to pay off creditors on a pro rata basis; title to the debtor's assets is held by a trustee in bankruptcy.

base lines. Imaginary lines that run east-west and intersect meridians that run north-south to form the starting point for land measurement using the rectangular survey system of land description.

basis. Cost basis is the dollar amount assigned to property at the time of acquisition under provisions of the Internal Revenue Code for the purpose of determining gain, loss and depreciation in calculating the income tax to be paid on the sale or exchange of the property; adjusted cost basis is derived after the application of certain additions, such as for improvements, and deductions, such as for depreciation.

beneficiary. One on whose behalf a trustee holds property conveyed by a trustor; the lender under a deed of trust.

bequest. Transfer of property, particularly personal property, called a *legacy*, by will. *See also* **devise.**

bill of sale. Written instrument that conveys title to personal property.

blanket mortgage. A loan covering more than one property.

blind ad. An ad that fails to indicate that the advertiser is an agent.

blockbusting. The practice on the part of unscrupulous speculators or real estate agents of inducing panic selling of homes at prices below market value, especially by exploiting the prejudices of property owners in neighborhoods in which the racial makeup is changing or appears to be on the verge of changing.

bond. An obligation; a real estate bond is a written obligation issued on security of a mortgage or trust deed.

book value. The current value for accounting purposes of an asset expressed as original cost plus capital additions minus accumulated depreciation.

breach. The failure of a duty imposed by law or by contract, either by omission or commission.

building code. Standards for building, planning, and construction established by state law and local ordinance.

bundle of rights. The legal rights of ownership of real property, including the rights of possession, use, disposition, and exclusion of others from the property.

business opportunity. The assets of an existing business enterprise, including its goodwill.

Cal Vet loan. Home or farm loan procured through the California Veterans Farm and Home Purchase Program.

capital assets. Assets of a permanent nature used in the production of income, such as land, buildings, machinery, and equipment; usually distinguishable under income tax law from "inventory," assets held for sale to customers in the ordinary course of the taxpayer's trade or business.

capital gain. The amount by which the net resale proceeds of a capital item exceed the adjusted cost basis of the item.

capitalization rate. The rate of interest that is considered a reasonable return on an investment, used in the process of determining value based on net operating income; the yield necessary to attract investment.

capitalization recapture. The return of an investment; an amortization rate based on the right of the investor to get back the purchase price at the end of the term of ownership or over the productive life of the improvements; computed by straight-line depreciation, by using Inwood tables or Hoskold tables. (Students should refer to a real estate appraisal text for further explanation.)

cash flow. The net income generated by a property before depreciation and other noncash expenses.

CC&Rs. Covenants, conditions, and restrictions; limitations on land use imposed by deed, usually when land is subdivided, as a means of regulating building construction, density, and use for the benefit of other property owners; may be referred to simply as *restrictions*.

certificate of reasonable value.   Property appraisal required for a VA-guaranteed loan.

certificate of redemption.   Issued by the county tax collector when all past due amounts have been paid.

certificate of sale.   Document received by the buyer at an execution or a judicial foreclosure sale; replaced by a sheriff's deed if the debtor fails to redeem the property during the statutory redemption period.

certificate of title.   Statement of a property's owner of record as well as any existing encumbrances.

chain of title.   The history of the conveyances and encumbrances affecting the present owner's title to property, as far back as records are available.

change, principle of.   Effect on property value of constantly varying physical, economic, social, and political forces.

chattel mortgage.   Use of personal property to secure or guarantee a promissory note.

chattel real.   An estate related to real estate, such as a lease of real property.

chattels.   Personal property; any property that is not real property.

Civil Rights Act of 1866.   The first U.S. Civil Rights Act. It applied to race only and had no exceptions.

Civil Rights Act of 1968.   This comprehensive act is known as the *Fair Housing Act*.

closing.   The completion of a real estate transaction, at which point required documents are transmitted and funds are transferred.

cloud on the title.   Any claim, condition, or encumbrance that impairs title to real property.

coastal zone.   An area of about 1,800 square miles that runs the length of the state from the sea inland about 1,000 yards, with wider spots in coastal estuarine, habitat, and recreational areas; any development or improvement of land within the coastal zone must meet local requirements for coastal conservation and preservation of resources, as authorized by the Coastal Zone Conservation Act.

codicil.   Written amendment to a will, made with the same legal formalities.

color of title.   A claim of possession to real property based on a document erroneously appearing to convey title to the claimant.

commingling.   Mixing broker and principal funds.

commission.   An agent's compensation for performing the duties of the agency; in real estate practice, typically a percentage of the selling price of property, rentals, or other property value.

common law.   The body of law from England based on custom, usage, and court decisions.

community apartment project.   A form of subdivision in which the owner has an individual interest in the land and exclusive right of occupancy of an apartment on the land.

community property.   All property acquired by husband and wife during marriage except that qualifying as separate property.

community redevelopment agency (CRA).   An agency authorized by state law but formed by a local governing body to provide low- and moderate-income housing and employ low-income persons by rehabilitating existing structures and/or bringing new development.

competition, principle of.   Business profits encourage competition, which ultimately may reduce profits for any one business.

competitive market analysis.   Informal estimate of market value performed by a real estate agent for either seller or buyer, utilizing the sales history of nearby properties; usually expressed as a range of values that includes the probable market value of the subject property.

compound interest.   Interest paid on original principal and also on the accrued and unpaid interest that has accumulated as the debt matures.

concurrent ownership. Ownership of property by more than one person, not necessarily in equal shares.

condemnation. *See* **eminent domain.**

condition. A qualification of an estate granted that can be imposed only in a conveyance; it can be a condition precedent or a condition subsequent. *See also* **CC&Rs.**

condition precedent. A qualification of a contract or transfer of property providing that unless and until the performance of a certain act, the contract or transfer will not take effect.

condition subsequent. A stipulation in a contract or transfer of property that already has taken effect that will extinguish the contract or defeat the property transfer.

condominium. A subdivision providing an exclusive ownership (fee) interest in the airspace of a particular portion of real property, as well as an interest in common in a portion of that property.

conforming loan. Loan that meets Fannie Mae and Freddie Mac purchase criteria.

conformity, principle of. Holds that property values are maximized when buildings are similar in design, construction, and age, particularly in residential neighborhoods.

consideration. Anything of value given or promised by a party to induce another to enter into a contract; may be a benefit conferred on one party or a detriment suffered by the other.

constructive eviction. Interference by the landlord in a tenant's legitimate use of leased property, such as by making unwarranted alterations to the property.

contract. A written or an oral agreement to do or not to do certain things. There may be an *express* agreement of the parties, or a contract may be *implied* by their conduct. A *unilateral* contract imposes an obligation on only one of the parties, whereas both parties to a *bilateral* contract have an obligation to perform. A contract is *executory* when a contract obligation is to be performed in the future, and *executed* when all obligations have been performed and the contract transaction has been completed. A real estate contract must be a signed writing made by competent parties, for valuable consideration, with an offer by one party that is accepted by the other.

contribution, principle of. A component part of a property is valued in proportion to its contribution to the value of the entire property, regardless of its separate actual cost.

conventional loan. A loan secured by a mortgage or trust deed that is made without governmental underwriting (FHA-insured or DVA-guaranteed).

cooperative apartment. See stock cooperative.

corporation. A legal entity that acts through its board of directors and officers, generally without liability on the part of the person or persons owning it. A domestic corporation is one chartered in California—any other corporation is a foreign corporation in California.

correction lines. Guide meridians running every 24 miles east and west of a meridian, and standard parallels running every 24 miles north and south of a base line, used to correct inaccuracies in the rectangular survey system of land description caused by the earth's curvature.

cost approach. Appraisal method in which site value is added to the present reproduction or replacement cost of all property improvements, less depreciation, to determine market value.

covenant. An agreement or a promise to do or not to do a particular act, usually imposed by deed. *See also* **CC&Rs.**

covenant of quiet enjoyment. Promise of a landlord, implied by law, not to interfere in the possession or use of leased property by the tenant.

covenant to repair. Express or legally implied obligation of the landlord to make necessary repairs to leased premises.

declaration of homestead. *See* **homestead.**

dedication. The giving of land by its owner for a public use, and the acceptance of the land for such use by the appropriate government officials.

deed. Written instrument that, when properly executed and delivered, conveys title to real property from a grantor to a grantee.

deed in lieu of foreclosure. A deed to real property accepted by a lender from a defaulting borrower to avoid the necessity of foreclosure proceedings by the lender.

deed of trust. *See* **trust deed.**

defendant. A person against whom legal action is initiated for the purpose of obtaining criminal sanctions (in a case involving violation of a penal statute) or damages or other appropriate judicial relief (in a civil case).

deficiency judgment. A judgment given by a court when the value of security pledged for a loan is insufficient to pay off the debt of the defaulting borrower.

Department of Real Estate. California agency that administers the Real Estate Law, including the licensing of real estate brokers and salespeople; headed by the Real Estate Commissioner, who is appointed by the Governor and presides over the Real Estate Advisory Commission (whose ten members are appointed by and serve at the commissioner's discretion).

depreciation. Decrease in value of an asset that is allowed in computing property value for tax purposes; in appraising, a loss in the value of a property improvement from any cause; depreciation is *curable* when it can be remedied by a repair or an addition to the property, and it is *incurable* when there is no easy or economic way to cure the loss. *See also* **physical deterioration, functional obsolescence,** and **external obsolescence.**

devise. Transfer of title to property by will. *See also* **bequest.**

devisee. Person receiving title to property by will. *See also* **legatee.**

devisor. One who wills property to another.

direct endorsement. A lender who is authorized to determine if a loan qualifies for FHA insurance.

discount points. *See* **points.**

discount rate. Interest rate charged member banks by Federal Reserve Banks.

documentary transfer tax. A tax applied on all transfers of real property located in a county that the county is authorized by the state to collect; notice of payment is entered on the face of the deed or on a separate paper filed with the deed.

dominant tenement. *See* **easement.**

donee. One who receives a gift.

donor. One who makes a gift.

dual agency. An agency relationship in which the agent represents two principals in their dealings with each other.

due-on-sale clause. An acceleration clause in a real estate financing instrument granting the lender the right to demand full payment of the remaining indebtedness on a sale of the property.

easement. The right to a specific use of or the right to travel over the land of another. The land being used or traveled over is the *servient tenement*; the land that is benefited by the use is the *dominant tenement*. An *easement appurtenant* is a property interest that belongs to the owner of the dominant tenement and is transferred with the land; an *easement in gross* is a personal right that usually is not transferable by its owner.

easement by prescription. Acquiring a specific use of or the right to travel over the land of another by statutory requirements similar to those for adverse possession.

economic life. The period of time over which an improved property will yield a return on investment over and above the return attributable solely to the land.

economic obsolescence. *See* **external obsolescence.**

economic rent. The reasonable rental expectancy if the property were available for renting at the time of its valuation.

effective gross income. Property income from all sources, less allowance for vacancy and collection losses.

elder abuse law. Requirement that realty agents and others report elder financial abuse, fraud, or undue influence.

emblements. Crops produced annually by labor and industry, as distinguished from crops that grow naturally on the land.

eminent domain. The right of the government to acquire title to property for public use by condemnation; the property owner receives compensation—generally fair market value. *See also* **inverse condemnation.**

encroachment. The unlawful intrusion of a property improvement onto adjacent property.

encumbrance. Anything that affects or limits the fee simple title to or affects the condition or use of real estate.

environmental impact report (EIR). Evaluation of effects on the environment of a proposed development; may be required by local government.

environmental obsolescence. *See* **external obsolescence.**

equity of redemption. The right to redeem property during the foreclosure period, or during a statutorily prescribed time following a foreclosure sale.

escalator clause. Provision in a lease agreement for an increase in payments based on an increase in an index such as the consumer price index.

escheat. The reverting of property to the state when there are no heirs capable of inheriting.

escrow. The deposit of instruments and/or funds (with instructions) with a neutral third party to carry out the provisions of an agreement or a contract.

escrow agent. Escrow holder; the neutral third party holding funds or something of value in trust for another or others.

estate. The interest held by the owner of property.

estate at sufferance. The occupancy of a tenant after the lease term expires.

estate at will. A tenancy in which the tenant's time of possession is indefinite.

estate for years. A tenancy for a fixed term.

estate from period to period. Periodic tenancy; a tenancy for a fixed term, automatically renewed for the same term unless owner or tenant gives the other written notice of intention to terminate the tenancy.

eviction. Dispossession by process of law.

exchange. A means of trading equities in two or more real properties, treated as a single transaction through a single escrow.

exclusive-agency listing. A listing agreement employing a broker as sole agent for a seller of real property under the terms of which the broker is entitled to compensation if the property is sold through any other broker, but not if a sale is negotiated by the owner without the services of an agent.

exclusive authorization and right-to-sell listing. A listing agreement employing a broker as agent for a seller of real property under the terms of which the broker is entitled to compensation if the listed property is sold during the duration of the listing, whether by the listing agent, another agent, or the owner acting without the services of an agent.

executor/executrix. Personal representative of the estate of a decedent, named in the decedent's will. *See also* **administrator/administratrix.**

express agreement. An agreement established by a deliberate act of the parties that both parties acknowledge as their intention.

external obsolescence. Economic or environmental obsolescence; loss in value due to outside causes, such as changes in nearby land use.

Fair Employment and Housing Act. *See* **Rumford Act.**

Fannie Mae (Federal National Mortgage Association). Now a private corporation dealing in the secondary mortgage market.

Farmer Mac (Federal Agricultural Mortgage Corporation). Now a private corporation providing a secondary mortgage market for farms and rural housing.

fee simple absolute. A fee simple estate with no restrictions on its use.

fee simple defeasible. An interest in land, such as a fee simple conditional or fee simple with special limitation, that may result in the estate of ownership being defeated.

fee simple estate. The greatest interest in real property one can own, including the right to use the property at present and for an indeterminate period of time in the future.

fee simple qualified. A fee simple estate with some restrictions on the right of possession.

fiduciary. A person in a position of trust and confidence who owes a certain loyalty to another, such as an agent to a principal.

final subdivision map. *See* **tentative subdivision map.**

fiscal year. A business or an accounting year as distinguished from a calendar year.

fixture. Anything permanently attached to land or improvements so as to become real property.

foreclosure. Sale of real property by mortgagee, trustee, or other lienholder on default by the borrower. *See also* **judicial foreclosure action.**

form appraisal report. A short report, typically two pages plus addenda, using a preprinted form to summarize the data contributing to an appraiser's conclusion of value.

fraud. The intentional and successful use of any cunning, deception, collusion, or artifice to circumvent, cheat, or deceive another person, so that the other person acts on it to the loss of property and legal injury; *actual fraud* is a deliberate misrepresentation or a representation made in reckless disregard of its truth or falsity, the suppression of truth, a promise made without the intention to perform it or any other act intended to deceive; *constructive fraud* is any misrepresentation made without fraudulent intent (the deliberate intent to deceive). Fraud is *affirmative* when it is a deliberate statement of a material fact that the speaker knows to be false and on which the speaker intends another person to rely, to his or her detriment. Fraud is *negative* when it is a deliberate concealment of something that should be revealed.

Freddie Mac (Federal Home Loan Mortgage Corporation). Now a private secondary mortgage corporation.

freehold estate. An estate in land in which ownership is for an indeterminate length of time, as in a fee simple or life estate.

front foot. Property measured by the front linear foot on its street line, each front foot extending the depth of the lot.

functional obsolescence. Loss in value due to adverse factors within a structure that affect its marketability, such as its design, layout, or utility.

general partnership. An association of two or more persons to carry on a business as co-owners for profit.

general plan. Master plan; includes a statement of policy of the development and land uses within a city or county and a program to implement that policy.

gift deed. A deed for which the only consideration is "love and affection."

Ginnie Mae (Government National Mortgage Association). A government corporation that provides assistance to Federally related housing projects. Funds are raised by selling securities backed by pools of mortgages.

goodwill. An intangible but a salable asset of a business derived from the expectation of continued public patronage.

grant deed. A limited warranty deed using a granting clause—the word "grant" or words to that effect—assuring the grantee that the estate being conveyed is free from encumbrances placed on the property by the present owner (the grantor), and that the grantor has not previously conveyed the property to anyone else.

grantee. A person to whom property is transferred by grant.

grantor. A person conveying property to another by grant.

gross income. Total property income from all sources before any expenses are deducted.

gross income multiplier. Gross rent multiplier; a number derived by dividing the sales price of a comparable property by the income it produces, which then is multiplied by the gross income produced by the subject property to derive an estimate of value.

gross lease. Provides for the tenant to pay a fixed rental over the lease term, with the landlord paying all expenses of ownership, such as taxes, assessments, and insurance.

ground lease. An agreement for the use of land only, sometimes secured by improvements placed on the land by the user.

ground rent. Earnings of improved property credited to earnings of the ground itself after allowance is made for earnings of improvements.

guarantee of title. Guarantee of title as determined from examination of the public records and described in the guarantee document.

guide meridians. *See* **correction lines.**

hard money loans. Cash loans made by individual investors.

highest and best use. In appraising real estate, the most profitable, physically possible, and legally permissible use for the property under consideration.

holder in due course. Someone who takes a negotiable instrument for value, in good faith and without notice of any defense against its enforcement that might be made by any person.

holdover tenancy. Possession of property by a tenant who remains in possession after the expiration or termination of the lease term.

holographic will. A will written entirely in the testator's handwriting, signed and dated by the testator.

homestead. A statutory exemption of real property used as a home from the claims of certain creditors and judgments up to a specified amount; requires a declaration of homestead to be completed and filed in the county recorder's office.

implied warranties. Warranties by grantor to grantee that will be implied by law, even if not mentioned in the deed; the grantor warrants that he or she has not already conveyed the property, and that there are no encumbrances on the property brought about by the grantor or any person who might claim title from the grantor.

income capitalization approach. Appraisal method in which the actual or likely net operating income of property is divided by its expected rate of return (capitalization rate) to arrive at an estimate of market value. *See also* **capitalization rate.**

independent contractor. A person employed by another who has almost complete freedom to accomplish the purposes of the employment.

index method. Way of estimating building reproduction cost by multiplying the original cost of the subject building by a factor that represents the percentage change in construction costs, generally from the time of construction to the time of valuation.

inherent authority. The authority of an agent to perform activities that are not specifically mentioned in the agency agreement but are necessary or customary to carry out an authorized act.

injunction.   A writ or an order issued by a court to restrain one or more parties to a suit or proceeding from doing an act deemed to be inequitable or unjust in regard to the rights of some other party or parties in the suit or proceeding.

installment sales contract.   *See* **sales contract.**

institutional lenders.   A financial intermediary or depository, such as a savings association, commercial bank, or life insurance company, that pools the money of its depositors and then invests funds in various ways, including trust deeds and mortgage loans.

interest.   A portion, share, or right in something; partial ownership; the charge in dollars for the use of money for a period of time.

interest rate.   The percentage of a sum of money borrowed that is charged for its use.

interim loan.   A short-term temporary loan used until permanent financing is available, typically during building construction.

interpleader.   A court proceeding that may be brought by someone, such as an escrow agent, who holds property for another, for the purpose of deciding who among the claimants is legally entitled to the property.

intestate succession.   Statutory method of distribution of property that belonged to someone who died intestate (without having made a valid will).

inverse condemnation.   A legal action brought by the owner of land when government puts nearby land to a use that diminishes the value of the owner's property.

joint tenancy.   Ownership of property by two or more co-owners, each of whom has an equal share and the right of survivorship.

joint venture.   Two or more individuals or firms joining together on a single project as partners, typically with a lender contributing the necessary funds and the other partner(s) contributing his or her expertise.

judgment.   The final determination of a court of competent jurisdiction of a matter presented to it; may include an award of money damages.

judicial foreclosure action.   Proceeding in which a mortgagee, a trustee, or another lienholder on property requests a court-supervised sale of the property to cover the unpaid balance of a delinquent debt.

land.   The earth's surface, including substances beneath the surface extending downward to the center of the earth and the airspace above the surface for an indefinite distance upward.

land contract.   *See* **sales contract.**

landlord.   Lessor; one who leases his or her property to another.

lateral support.   The support that the soil of an adjoining owner gives to a neighbor's land.

lease.   A contract between a property owner, called *lessor* or *landlord*, and another, called *lessee* or *tenant*, conveying and setting forth the conditions of occupancy and use of the property by the tenant.

leaseback.   *See* **sale-leaseback.**

leasehold estate.   A tenant's right to occupy real estate during the term of the lease; a personal property interest.

legacy.   Property, usually personal property, transferred by will.

legal description.   A land description used to define a parcel of land to the exclusion of all others that is acceptable by a court of law.

legatee.   Person who receives property, called a *legacy*, by bequest. *See also* **devisee.**

letter of opinion.   A letter from appraiser to client presenting only the appraiser's conclusion of value, with no supporting data.

leverage.   Use of debt financing to purchase an investment, thus maximizing the return per dollar of equity invested; enables a purchaser to obtain possession for little or no initial cash outlay and relatively small periodic payments on the debt incurred.

lien. An encumbrance that makes property security for the payment of a debt or discharge of an obligation; a *voluntary lien* is one agreed to by the property owner, such as a deed of trust; an *involuntary lien* exists by operation of law to create a burden on property for certain unpaid debts, such as a tax lien.

life estate. An interest in real property conveying the right to possession and use for a term measured by the life or lives of one or more persons, most often the holder of the life estate.

limited equity housing cooperative. A stock cooperative financed by the California Housing Finance Agency.

limited partnership. Partnership of one or more general partners, who run the business and are liable as partners, and limited partners, investors who do not run the business and are liable only up to the amount invested.

liquidated damages. An amount agreed on by the parties to be full damages if a certain event occurs.

listing agreement. Authorization by the owner of property, acting as principal, for a real estate broker to act as the agent of the principal in finding a person to buy, lease, or rent property; may be used to employ a real estate broker to act as agent for a person seeking property to buy, lease or rent.

lot and block system. Subdivision system; method of legal description of land using parcel maps identified by tract, block, and lot numbers.

marker. *See* **metes and bounds.**

marketable title. Title that a reasonably prudent purchaser, acting with full knowledge of the facts and their legal significance, would be willing and ought to accept.

market comparison approach. *See* **sales comparison approach.**

market data approach. *See* **sales comparison approach.**

market value. The most probable price property would bring in an arm's-length transaction under normal conditions on the open market. *See also* **arm's-length transaction.**

material fact. A fact that would be likely to affect the judgment of a person to whom it is known, such as information concerning the poor physical condition of a building that is for sale.

mechanic's lien. A statutory lien against real property in favor of persons who have performed work or furnished materials for the improvement of the property.

Mello-Roos bonds. Improvement bonds that place off-site improvement costs on the home purchaser rather than the developer.

meridians. Imaginary lines that run north to south and intersect base lines that run east to west to form the starting point for land measurement using the rectangular survey system of land description.

metes and bounds. Method of legal description of land using distances (called *metes*) measured from a point of beginning and using natural or artificial boundaries (called *bounds*) as well as single objects (called *monuments* or *markers*) as points of reference.

minor. A person younger than 18 years of age.

mobile home. A structure transportable in one or more sections, designed and equipped to contain not more than two dwelling units, to be used with or without a foundation system; does not include a recreational vehicle.

mobile-home park. Any area or tract of land where two or more mobile-home lots are rented, leased, or held out for rent or lease.

monument. *See* **metes and bounds.**

mortgage. A legal instrument by which property is pledged by a borrower, the *mortgagor,* as security for the payment of a debt or an obligation owed to a lender, the *mortgagee.*

Mortgage Loan Disclosure Statement. The statement on a form approved by the Real Estate Commissioner that is required by law to be furnished by a mortgage loan broker to the prospective borrower of a loan of a statutorily prescribed amount before the borrower becomes obligated to complete the loan.

multiple-listing clause. Clause in a listing agreement, usually part of an exclusive authorization and right-to-sell listing, taken by a member of a multiple-listing service, providing that members of the multiple-listing service will have the opportunity to find a ready, willing, and able buyer for the listed property.

multiple-listing service (MLS). An organization of real estate agents providing for a pooling of listings and the sharing of commissions on transactions involving more than one agent.

narrative appraisal report. The longest and most thorough appraisal report, containing a summary of all factual materials, techniques, and appraisal methods used in setting forth the appraiser's conclusion of value.

negotiable instrument. An instrument, such as a promissory note, that is capable of being assigned or transferred in the ordinary course of business.

net listing. A listing agreement providing that the agent may retain as compensation for his or her services all sums received over and above a net price to the owner.

net, net, net lease. *See* **triple net lease.**

net operating income. Profit; the money remaining after expenses are deducted from income.

niche marketing. Specialization in an area, type of property, and/or category of buyer.

nonexclusive listing. *See* **open listing.**

notice. Knowledge of a fact; *actual notice* is express or implied knowledge of a fact; *constructive notice* is knowledge of a fact that is imputed to a person by law because of the person's actual notice of circumstances and the inquiry that a prudent person would have been expected to make; *legal notice* is information required to be given by law.

novation. The substitution or exchange of a new obligation or contract for an old one by mutual agreement of the parties.

null and void. Of no legal validity or effect.

observed condition method. Breakdown method; depreciation computed by estimating the loss in value caused by every item of depreciation, whether curable or incurable.

one hundred percent commission. An office where salespersons pay broker fees but keep commissions earned.

open listing. Nonexclusive listing; the nonexclusive right to secure a purchaser, given by a property owner to a real estate agent; more than one agent may be given such authorization, and only the first to procure a ready, willing, and able buyer—or an offer acceptable to the seller—will be entitled to compensation.

opinion of title. An attorney's written evaluation of the condition of the title to a parcel of land after examination of the abstract of title.

option. A right given for a consideration to purchase or lease property on specified terms within a specified time, with no obligation on the part of the person receiving the right to exercise it.

overriding trust deed. *See* **wraparound mortgage or trust deed.**

ownership in severalty. Separate ownership; ownership of property by one person only.

participation loan. A loan where the lender takes an equity postiion in the property as well as interest for the loan.

partition action. Court proceeding by which co-owners may force a division of the property or its sale, with co-owners reimbursed for their individual shares.

partnership. *See* **general partnership.**

percentage lease. Provides for rent as a percentage of the tenant's gross income, usually with a minimum base amount; the percentage may decrease as the tenant's income increases.

personal property. All property that is not real property.

physical deterioration. Loss in value brought about by wear and tear, disintegration, use and action of the elements.

plaintiff. The person who sues in a court action.

planned unit development (PUD). A land-use design that provides intensive utilization of the land through a combination of private and common areas with prearranged sharing of responsibilities for the common areas; individual lots are owned in fee with joint ownership of open areas; primarily residential but may include commercial and/or industrial uses.

planning commission. An agency of local government charged with planning the development, redevelopment, or preservation of an area.

plottage. Assemblage; an appraisal term for the increased value of two or more adjoining lots when they are placed under single ownership and available for use as a larger single lot.

points. One point represents one percentage point of a loan amount; may be charged by lenders at the time of loan funding to increase the loan's effective interest rate.

police power. The right of government to enact laws and enforce them to benefit the public health, safety, and general welfare.

power of attorney. A written instrument authorizing an agent to act in the capacity of the principal; a *general power of attorney* provides authority to carry out all of the business dealings of the principal; a *special power of attorney* provides authority to carry out a specific act or acts.

power of sale. The power that may be given by a promissory note to a trustee, a mortgagee, or another lienholder to sell secured property without judicial proceedings if the borrower defaults.

predatory lending. Making loans without regard to payment ability of borrower in order to obtain the security by foreclosure.

primary mortgage market. Composed of lenders that deal directly with borrowers. *See also* **secondary mortgage market.**

prime rate. Interest rate banks charge their most favorably rated commercial borrowers.

principal. The employer of an agent; one of the parties to a transaction; the amount of money borrowed.

private mortgage insurance (PMI). Mortgage guaranty insurance available to conventional lenders on the high-risk portion of a loan, with payment included in the borrower's loan installments.

probate. Court proceeding by which the property of a decedent is distributed according to the decedent's will or, if the decedent died intestate (without a will), according to the state law of intestate succession.

procuring cause. The cause originating a series of events that lead directly to the intended objective; in a real estate transaction the procuring cause is the real estate agent who first procures a ready, willing, and able buyer.

progression, principle of. The worth of a less-valuable building tends to be enhanced by proximity to buildings of greater value.

promissory note. A written promise to repay a loan under stipulated terms; establishes personal liability for payment by the person making the note.

property management. A branch of the real estate business involving the marketing, operation, maintenance, and other day-to-day requirements of rental properties by an individual or a firm acting as agent of the owner.

proration. Adjustment of interest, taxes, insurance, and other costs of property ownership on a pro rata basis as of the closing or agreed-on date; usually apportions those costs based on seller's and buyer's respective periods of ownership.

puffing. Exaggerating the attributes or benefits of property as an inducement to purchase.

purchase-money mortgage or trust deed. Trust deed or mortgage given as part or all of the purchase consideration for real property.

quantity survey method. Way of estimating building reproduction cost by making a thorough itemization of all construction costs, both direct (material and labor) and indirect (permits, overhead, profit), then totaling those costs.

quiet title. *See* **action to quiet title.**

quitclaim deed. A deed that conveys any interest the grantor may have in the property at the time of the execution of the deed, without any warranty of title or interest.

ranges. In the rectangular survey system of land description, townships running east and west of a meridian.

ratification. The adoption or approval of an act by the person on whose behalf it was performed, as when a principal ratifies conduct of an agent that was not previously authorized.

ready, willing, and able buyer. A buyer who wants and is prepared to purchase property, including being able to finance the purchase, at the agreed-on price and terms.

real estate. Real property; land; includes the surface of the earth, the substances beneath the surface, the airspace above the surface, fixtures, and anything incidental or appurtenant to the land.

real estate board. A local organization whose members consist primarily of real estate brokers and salespeople.

real estate broker. A person employed for a fee by another to carry on any of the activities listed in the Real Estate Law definition of a broker.

Real Estate Education and Research Fund. California fund financed by a fixed portion of real estate license fees, designed to encourage research in land use and real estate development.

real estate investment trust (REIT). Way for investors to pool funds for investments in real estate and mortgages, with profits taxed to individual investors rather than to the corporation.

real estate salesperson. A person licensed under the provisions of the Real Estate Law to act under the control and supervision of a real estate broker in carrying on any of the activities listed in the license law.

real estate syndicate. An organization of real estate investors, typically in the form of a limited partnership.

real property. *See* **real estate.**

reconciliation. In appraising, the final step, in which the estimates of value reached by each of the three appraisal approaches (sales comparison, cost, and income capitalization) are weighed in light of the type of property being appraised, the purpose of the appraisal, and other factors, to arrive at a final conclusion of value.

reconveyance deed. Instrument by which the trustee returns title to the trustor after the debt underlying a deed of trust is paid.

recovery account. State fund financed by real estate license fees and intended to help compensate victims of real estate licensee fraud, misrepresentation, deceit, or conversion of trust funds, when a court-ordered judgment cannot be collected.

rectangular survey system. Section and township system; U.S. government survey system; method of legal description of land using areas called *townships* measured from meridians and base lines.

recurring costs. Impound costs for taxes and insurance.

red flag. A physical indication of a possible problem with a property.

redlining. An illegal lending policy of denying real estate loans on properties in older, changing urban areas (usually with large minority populations) because of alleged higher lending risks, without due consideration of the individual loan applicant.

reformation. An action to correct a mistake in a contract, a deed, or another document.

regression, principle of. A building's value will decline if the buildings around it have a lower value.

release. Removal of part of a contract obligation, for consideration, by the party to whom the obligation is owed; removal of part of a property from a lien on payment of part of the debt owed.

reliction. The increase of a landowner's property by the receding of an adjacent body of water.

remainder. The right of future possession and use that will go to someone other than the grantor upon termination of a life estate.

rent. The consideration paid for possession and use of leased property.

rent control. A regulation imposed by a local governing body as a means of protecting tenants from relatively high rent increases over the occupancy period of a lease; if a law provides for vacancy decontrol, when a unit becomes vacant, there is no restriction on the rent set for a new tenant.

repair and deduct. Tenant's remedy when landlord is on notice of and fails to make necessary repairs to leased premises; a tenant may spend up to one month's rent on repairs, but no more than twice in any 12-month period.

replacement cost. The cost of a new building using modern construction techniques, design, and materials but having the same utility as the subject property.

reproduction cost. The cost of a new building of exactly the same design and materials as the subject property.

rescission. The cancellation of a contract and restoration of the parties to the same position they held before the contract was formed.

restraint on alienation. An illegal condition that would prohibit a property owner from transferring title to real estate.

restriction. A limitation on the use of real property; public restrictions imposed by government include zoning ordinances; private restrictions imposed by deed may require the grantee to do or refrain from doing something. *See also* **CC&Rs.**

reverse exchange. Delayed exchange where the property desired is acquired prior to sale of exchanger's property.

reverse mortgage. Mortgage where the borrower receives payments and does not repay loan until the property is sold or the borrower dies.

reversion. The right of future possession and use retained by the grantor of a life estate.

right of appropriation. Right of government to take, impound, or divert water flowing on the public domain from its natural course for some beneficial purpose.

right of entry. The right of the landlord to enter leased premises in certain circumstances.

right of survivorship. The right of surviving cotenants to share equally in the interest of a deceased cotenant; the last surviving cotenant is sole owner of the property.

riparian rights. The right of a landowner whose property borders a lake, river, or stream to the use and enjoyment of the water adjacent to or flowing over the property, provided the use does not injure other riparian landowners.

Rumford Act. California's fair housing law. Also called the Fair Employment and Housing Act.

safety clause. A clause that protects the broker's commission when a sale is consummated after a listing expires to a buyer procured by the broker.

sale-leaseback. A transaction in which at the time of sale the seller retains occupancy by concurrently agreeing to lease the property from the purchaser.

sales comparison approach. Market comparison approach; market data approach; appraisal method in which the sales prices of properties that are comparable in construction and location to the subject property are analyzed and adjusted to reflect differences between the comparables and the subject.

sales contract. Land contract; installment sales contract; a contract used in a sale of real property whereby the seller retains title to the property until all or a prescribed part of the purchase price has been paid, but no earlier than one year from the date of possession.

salvage value. In computing depreciation for tax purposes under all but the declining balance method, the reasonably anticipated fair market value of the property at the end of its useful life.

sandwich lease. A leasehold interest between the primary lease and the operating lease.

satisfaction. Discharge of an obligation before the end of its term by payment of the total debt owed.

secondary financing. A loan secured by a second (or subsequent) mortgage or trust deed on real property.

secondary mortgage market. Investment opportunities involving real property securities, other than direct loans from lender to borrower; loans may be bought, sold, or pooled to form the basis for mortgage-backed securities.

section. A standard land area of one mile square, containing 640 acres, used in the rectangular survey system of land description.

section and township system. *See* **rectangular survey system.**

security deposit. An amount paid at the start of a lease term and retained by the landlord until the tenant vacates the premises, all or part of which may be kept by the landlord at that time to cover costs of any default in rent payments or reasonable costs of repairs or cleaning necessitated by the tenant's use of the premises.

security instrument. A written document executed by a debtor that pledges the described property as the lender's assurance that the underlying debt will be repaid.

separate property. Property owned by a married person other than community property, including property owned before marriage, property acquired by gift or inheritance, income from separate property and property acquired with the proceeds of separate property.

servient tenement. *See* **easement.**

set-back ordinance. An ordinance requiring improvements built on property to be a specified distance from the property line, street or curb.

severalty, ownership in. *See* **ownership in severalty.**

sheriff's deed. Deed given to the purchaser at a court-ordered sale to satisfy a judgment, without warranties.

short sale. A sale for less than is owed on a loan where the lender agrees to accept sale proceeds to extinguish the debt.

sick building syndrome. Illness attributed to a sealed structure believed related to ventilation.

simple interest. Interest computed on the principal amount of a loan only. *See* **compound interest.**

sinking fund. Fund set aside from the income from property that, with accrued interest, eventually will pay for replacement of the improvements.

sole proprietor. Only owner of a business.

special limitation. A limiting condition specified in a transfer of fee simple ownership that, if not complied with, will immediately and automatically extinguish the estate and return title to the grantor.

special studies zone. One of the areas, typically within a quarter-mile or more of an active earthquake fault, requiring a geologic report for any new project involving improvements or structures initiated after May 4, 1975; the report may be waived by city or county if the state geologist approves.

special warranty deed. A deed in which the grantor warrants or guarantees the title only against defects arising during the grantor's ownership of the property and not against defects existing before the time of the grantor's ownership.

specific performance. Action to compel a breaching party to adhere to a contract obligation, such as an action to compel the sale of land as an alternative to money damages.

specific plan. Formulated after adoption of a general plan by a city or county to give further details of community development, including projected population density and building construction requirements.

square-foot method. Way of finding reproduction cost by multiplying the current cost per square foot of a comparable building by the number of square feet in the subject building.

standard parallels. *See* **correction lines.**

Statute of Frauds. A state law requiring that certain contracts be in writing and signed before they will be enforceable, such as a contract for the sale of real estate.

Statute of Limitations. Law that stipulates the specific time period during which a legal action must be brought following the act that gives rise to it.

statutory warranty deed. A short-term warranty deed that warrants by inference that the seller is the undisputed owner, has the right to convey the property, and will defend the title if necessary; if the seller does not do so, the new owner can defend against said claims and sue the former owner.

steering. The illegal act of directing prospective homebuyers to or from a particular residential area on the basis of the homebuyer's race or national origin.

step-up lease. Lease with set rent that provides for periodic rent increases.

stock cooperative. A form of subdivision, typically of an apartment building, in which each owner in the stock cooperative is a shareholder in a corporation that holds title to the property, each shareholder being entitled to use, rent, or sell a specific apartment unit. *See also* **limited equity housing cooperative.**

straight-line method. Depreciation computed at a constant rate over the estimated useful life of the improvement.

straight note. A note in which a borrower repays the principal in a lump sum at maturity, with interest due in installments or at maturity.

subdivision. The division of real property into separate parcels or lots for the purpose of sale, lease, or financing.

subdivision public report. Issued by the Real Estate Commissioner after a subdivision developer has met the requirements of the Subdivided Lands Law; provides details of the project and financing, and a copy must be given to all prospective purchasers; sales may begin on the basis of an approved preliminary public report, but no sales can be closed or transactions completed until the final public report is received.

subject to. When a grantee takes title to real property "subject to" a mortgage or trust deed, the grantee is not responsible to the holder of the promissory note for the payment of any portion of the amount due, and the original maker of the note retains primary responsibility for the underlying debt or obligation.

sublease. A lease given by a lessee (tenant).

subordination agreement.   An agreement by the holder of an encumbrance against real property to permit that claim to take an inferior position to other encumbrances against the property.

subprime lender.   A lender who will take loans that are considered too risky by other lenders. Subprime loans bear a higher rate of interest.

substitution, principle of.   Market value tends to be set by the present or recent cost of acquiring an equally desirable and valuable property, comparable in construction and/or utility.

supply and demand, principle of.   Takes into account the effect on market value of the relationship between the number of properties on the market at a given time and the number of potential buyers.

survey.   The process by which a parcel of land is measured and its area ascertained.

syndicate, real estate.   *See* **real estate syndicate.**

take-out loan.   The loan arranged by the owner or builder developer for a buyer; the permanent financing that pays off and replaces the interim loan used during construction.

tax deed.   Deed issued by the county tax collector when property is sold at public auction because of nonpayment of taxes.

tenancy in common.   Co-ownership of property in equal or unequal shares by two or more persons, each holding an undivided interest without right of survivorship.

tenancy in partnership.   The ownership by two or more persons, acting as partners, of property held for partnership purposes.

tenant.   Lessee under a lease; one who has the legal right to possession and use of property belonging to another.

tentative subdivision map.   The initial or tentative map required of subdividers by the Subdivision Map Act, submitted to the local planning commission, which notes its approval or disapproval; a final map embodying any changes requested by the planning commission also must be submitted.

testator.   A person who makes a will.

third-party originator.   A party that prepares loan applications for borrowers and submits the loan package to lenders.

tiers.   In the rectangular survey system of land description, townships running north and south of a base line.

time-share estate.   A right of occupancy in a time-share project (subdivision) coupled with an estate in the real property.

time-share project.   A form of subdivision of real property into rights to the recurrent, exclusive use or occupancy of a lot, parcel, unit or segment of the property on an annual or other periodic basis, for a specified period of time.

time-share use.   A license or contractual or membership right of occupancy in a time-share project that is not coupled with an estate in the real property.

title insurance.   Insurance to protect a real property owner or lender up to a specified amount against certain types of loss affecting title or marketability.

tort.   Any wrongful act, other than a breach of contract, for which a civil action may be brought by the person wronged.

township.   A standard land area of six miles square, divided into 36 sections of one mile square each, used in the rectangular survey system of land description.

toxic mold.   Usually a greenish black mold that causes respiratory problems. It usually grows on material with a high cellulose content.

trade fixtures.   Articles of personal property that are annexed by a business tenant to real property that are necessary to the carrying on of a trade and are removable by the tenant.

triple net lease.   Guarantees a specified net income to the landlord, with the tenant paying that amount plus all operating and other property expenses, such as taxes, assessments, and insurance.

trust account. An account separate from a broker's own funds (business and personal) in which the broker is required by law to deposit all funds collected for clients before disbursement.

trust deed. A deed issued by a borrower of funds (the *trustor*) conveying title to a *trustee* on behalf of a lender, the *beneficiary* of the trust; the trust deed authorizes the trustee to sell the property to pay the remaining indebtedness to the beneficiary if the trustor defaults on the underlying obligation.

trustee. One who holds property conveyed by a trustor on behalf of (in trust for) the beneficiary, to secure the performance of an obligation.

trustee in bankruptcy. *See* **bankruptcy.**

trustee's deed. Deed given to the purchaser at a foreclosure sale by the trustee acting under a deed of trust.

trustor. One who conveys property to a trustee to hold on behalf of (in trust for) a beneficiary to secure the performance of an obligation; borrower under a deed of trust.

Truth-in-Lending. Federal act requiring loan term disclosures as well as advertising disclosures.

undue influence. Use of a fiduciary or confidential relationship to obtain a fraudulent or an unfair advantage over another person because of his or her weakness of mind, distress, or necessity.

Uniform Commercial Code. Establishes a unified and comprehensive method for regulation of security transactions in personal property, superseding the existing statutes on chattel mortgages, conditional sales, trust receipts, assignments of accounts receivable, and others in this field.

unit-in-place method. Way of estimating building reproduction cost by adding the construction cost per unit of measure of each of the component parts of the subject property; each unit cost

includes material, labor, overhead, and builder's profit.

unlawful detainer. The legal action that may be brought to evict a tenant who is in unlawful possession of leased premises.

Unruh Act. California's antidiscrimination act that applies to businesses.

useful life. The period of years in which a property improvement may be used for its originally intended purpose.

U.S. government survey system. *See* **rectangular survey system.**

usury. The charging of a rate of interest on a loan that is greater than the rate permitted by law.

vacancy decontrol. *See* **rent control.**

vacancy factor. The percentage of a building's space that is unrented over a given period.

value in use. The subjective value of property to its present owner, as opposed to market value, which should be objective.

void. To have no force or effect; that which is unenforceable.

voidable. That which can be adjudged void but is not void unless action is taken to make it so.

waiver. The giving up of a right or privilege voluntarily.

warranties, implied. *See* **implied warranties.**

warranty deed. A deed that expressly warrants that the grantor has good title; the grantor thus agrees to defend the premises against the lawful claims of third persons.

warranty of habitability. Legally implied obligation of a landlord to meet minimal housing and building standards.

will. A written, legal declaration of a person called a *testator*, expressing the testator's desires for the disposition of his or her property after death.

wraparound mortgage or trust deed. Overriding or all-inclusive trust deed; a financing device in which a lender assumes payments on an existing mortgage or trust deed and takes from the borrower a junior mortgage or trust deed with a face value in an amount equal to the amount outstanding on the old instrument and the additional amount of money borrowed.

writ of execution. Court order directing the sheriff or another officer to satisfy a money judgment out of the debtor's property, including real estate not exempt from execution.

writ of possession. Order issued by the court directing the sheriff or marshal to take all legal steps necessary to remove the occupant(s) from the specified premises.

yield. Profit; return; the interest earned by an investor on an investment or by a bank on the money it has loaned.

zoning. An act of city or county government specifying the possible uses of property in a particular area.

INDEX